P9-CDE-519

DISCARD

282.092   Kertzer, David I.
KER
          The pope who would be
          king

MAY 0 1 2018

BY DAVID I. KERTZER

THE POPE WHO WOULD BE KING: THE EXILE OF PIUS IX AND
THE EMERGENCE OF MODERN EUROPE

THE POPE AND MUSSOLINI: THE SECRET HISTORY OF PIUS XI
AND THE RISE OF FASCISM IN EUROPE

AMALIA'S TALE: A POOR PEASANT, AN AMBITIOUS
ATTORNEY, AND A FIGHT FOR JUSTICE

PRISONER OF THE VATICAN: THE POPES' SECRET PLOT TO
CAPTURE ROME FROM THE NEW ITALIAN STATE

THE POPES AGAINST THE JEWS: THE VATICAN'S ROLE IN
THE RISE OF MODERN ANTI-SEMITISM

THE KIDNAPPING OF EDGARDO MORTARA

POLITICS AND SYMBOLS: THE ITALIAN COMMUNIST PARTY
AND THE FALL OF COMMUNISM

SACRIFICED FOR HONOR: ITALIAN INFANT ABANDONMENT
AND THE POLITICS OF REPRODUCTIVE CONTROL

RITUAL, POLITICS, AND POWER

FAMILY, POLITICAL ECONOMY, AND DEMOGRAPHIC CHANGE
(WITH DENNIS HOGAN)

FAMILY LIFE IN CENTRAL ITALY, 1880–1910

COMRADES AND CHRISTIANS: RELIGION AND POLITICAL
STRUGGLE IN COMMUNIST ITALY

THE
POPE WHO WOULD
BE KING

MAY 0 1 2018
479

THE
POPE WHO
WOULD BE
KING

THE EXILE OF PIUS IX
AND THE EMERGENCE OF
MODERN EUROPE

DAVID I. KERTZER

RANDOM HOUSE

NEW YORK

FAIRPORT PUBLIC LIBRARY
1 FAIRPORT VILLAGE LANDING
FAIRPORT NY 14450

Copyright © 2018 by David I. Kertzer

Maps copyright © 2018 by Laura Hartman Maestro

All rights reserved.

Published in the United States by Random House,
an imprint and division of
Penguin Random House LLC, New York.

RANDOM HOUSE and the HOUSE colophon are registered
trademarks of Penguin Random House LLC.

LIBRARY OF CONGRESS CATALOGING-IN-PUBLICATION DATA
NAMES: Kertzer, David I., author.
TITLE: The pope who would be king : the exile of Pius IX and the
emergence of modern Europe / David I. Kertzer.
DESCRIPTION: New York : Random House, 2018. | Includes
bibliographical references and index.
IDENTIFIERS: LCCN 2017038825 | ISBN 9780812989915 |
ISBN 9780812989922 (ebook)
SUBJECTS: LCSH: Pius IX, Pope, 1792–1878. | Europe—Church history—
19th century. | Europe—Politics and government—1848–1871.
CLASSIFICATION: LCC BX1373 .K47 2018 | DDC 282.092—dc23
LC record available at https://lccn.loc.gov/2017038825

Printed in the United States of America on acid-free paper

randomhousebooks.com

2 4 6 8 9 7 5 3 1

First Edition

Book design by Barbara M. Bachman

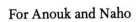

For Anouk and Naho

Let lips of iron and tongues of slaves

Fit welcome give thee; for her part,

Rome, frowning o'er her new-made graves,

Shall curse thee from her heart!

——EXCERPTED FROM
JOHN GREENLEAF WHITTIER,
"TO PIUS IX," 1849

CONTENTS

———

List of Illustrations   *xiii*

Maps   *xv*

Cast of Characters   *xix*

Prologue   *xxvii*

PART ONE: THE BELOVED

1.	THE CONCLAVE	*3*
2.	THE FOX AND THE CROW	*21*
3.	AN IMPOSSIBLE DILEMMA	*37*
4.	PAPAL MAGIC	*55*
5.	THE TIDE TURNS	*72*
6.	FENDING OFF DISASTER	*87*
7.	THE ASSASSINATION	*102*
8.	THE ESCAPE	*113*

PART TWO: THE REVILED

9.	THE REACTIONARY TURN	*125*
10.	REVOLUTION	*142*
11.	PRESSURING THE POPE	*158*
12.	THE FRIENDLY ARMY	*178*
13.	THE FRENCH ATTACK	*190*
14.	NEGOTIATING IN BAD FAITH	*207*

15. BATTLING FOR ROME   *223*

16. THE CONQUEST   *241*

17. THE OCCUPATION   *257*

PART THREE: THE FEARED

18. APPLYING THE BRAKES   *273*

19. LOUIS NAPOLEON AND THE POPE   *287*

20. THE UNPOPULAR POPE   *295*

21. "THOSE WICKED ENEMIES OF GOD"   *309*

22. RETURNING TO ROME   *322*

     EPILOGUE   *337*

     Acknowledgments   349

     Abbreviations Used in Notes   353

     Notes   355

     References   429

     Illustration Credits   445

     Index   447

LIST OF
ILLUSTRATIONS

———

1. Prince Klemens von Metternich 11
2. Pope Pius IX 19
3. Pellegrino Rossi 25
4. Giuseppe Mazzini 26
5. The popular hero Ciceruacchio 40
6. Charles Bonaparte 45
7. Giacomo Antonelli 50
8. Margaret Fuller 53
9. Pius IX 61
10. King Charles Albert of Sardinia 68
11. Terenzio Mamiani 88
12. Antonio Rosmini 95
13. The death of Pellegrino Rossi 104
14. Gaeta 116
15. Ferdinand II, King of the Two Sicilies 120
16. Louis Napoleon Bonaparte 129
17. Pietro Sterbini 134
18. Ciceruacchio speaks to the people 137
19. Felix Schwarzenberg 146
20. Moritz Esterházy 151
21. The abdication of King Charles Albert 164
22. Triumvirate of the Roman Republic: Carlo Armellini, Giuseppe Mazzini, and Aurelio Saffi 165

23. Édouard Drouyn de Lhuys, French foreign minister   176

24. Giuseppe Garibaldi   182

25. Garibaldi and his comrade-in-arms, Andrea Aguyar   184

26. General Charles Oudinot   186

27. Ferdinand de Lesseps   203

28. Pius IX blesses Spanish troops at Gaeta,
    May 26, 1849   217

29. Alexis de Tocqueville   224

30. The bombardment of Rome   232

31. French troops fire on Rome's wall, June 20, 1849   239

32. French soldiers   253

33. Garibaldi with his dying wife, Anita   279

34. The arrest of the monk Ugo Bassi   279

35. General Achille Baraguey d'Hilliers   308

36. The patriot princess Cristina Belgiojoso   313

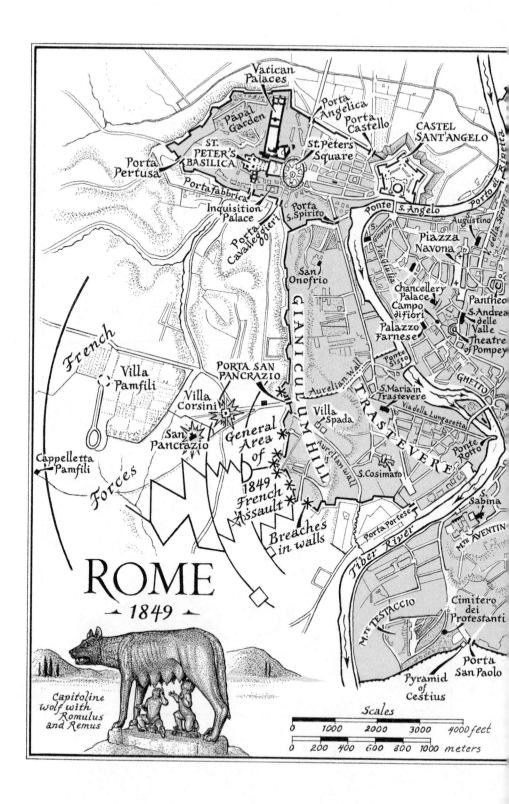

Vatican
Palaces

Porta
Angelica

Porta
Castello

CASTEL
SANT'ANGELO

Papal
Garden

ST.
PETER'S
BASILICA

St.Peters
Square

Porto di Ripetta

Porta
Pertusa

Porta fabbrica

Ponte S. Angelo

S. Augustino

Inquisition
Palace

Porta
S. Spirito

Via della Scrofa

Porta
Cavalleggieri

Giovanni

PIAZZA
NAVONA

Via Giulia

San
Onofrio

Chancellery
Palace

Pantheo

S.Andrea
delle
Valle

Campo
di fiori

GIANICULUM HILL

Palazzo
Farnese

Ponte
Sisto

Theatre
of Pompey

French

PORTA SAN
PANCRAZIO

GHETTO

Villa
Pamfili

S.Maria in
Trastevere

Villa
Corsini

Aurelian wall

TRASTEVERE

Via della Lungaretta

Villa
Spada

Ponte
Rotto

San
Pancrazio

General
Area
of

Aurelian wall

S.Cosimato

Forces

Cappelletta
Pamfili

1849
French
Assault

S.
Sabina

Porta Portese

Breaches
in walls

Tiber River

M.te AVENTIN

ROME

~ 1849 ~

M.te TESTACCIO

Cimitero
dei
Protestanti

Porta
San Paolo

Capitoline
Wolf with
Romulus
and Remus

Pyramid
of
Cestius

Scales

| 0 | 1000 | 2000 | 3000 | 4000 feet |

| 0 | 200 | 400 | 600 | 800 | 1000 meters |

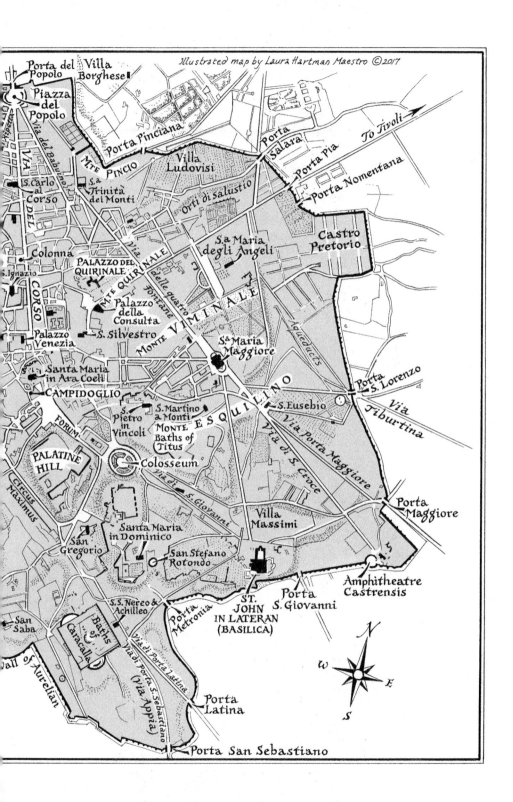

Illustrated map by Laura Hartman Maestro ©2017

Porta del Popolo
Villa Borghese
Piazza del Popolo
Porta Pinciana
Porta Salara
Porta Pia
Porta Nomentana
To Tivoli
Via del Babuino
Via del Corso
Mte PINCIO
Villa Ludovisi
S. Carlo al Corso
S.a Trinità dei Monti
Orti di Salustio
Via
CORSO
Colonna
PALAZZO DEL QUIRINALE
S.a Maria degli Angeli
Castro Pretorio
S. Ignazio
Mte QUIRINALE
Via Venti Settembre
Palazzo della Consulta
Fontane delle quatro
Palazzo Venezia
S. Silvestro
MONTE VIMINALE
Aqueducts
Santa Maria in Ara Coeli
S.a Maria Maggiore
Porta S. Lorenzo
CAMPIDOGLIO
S. Pietro in Vincoli
S. Martino a Monti
MONTE Baths of Titus
ESQUILINO
S. Eusebio
Via Tiburtina
FORUM
Via Porta Maggiore
PALATINE HILL
Colosséum
Via di S. Croce
CIRCUS MAXIMUS
Via di S. Giovanni
Villa Massimi
Porta Maggiore
San Gregorio
Santa Maria in Dominico
San Stefano Rotondo
Amphitheatre Castrensis
S.S. Nereo & Achilleo
Porta Metronia
ST. JOHN IN LATERAN (BASILICA)
Porta S. Giovanni
San Saba
Baths of Caracalla
Wall of Aurelian
Via di Porta Latina
Via di Porta S. Sebastiano (Via Appia)
Porta Latina
N
W   E
S
Porta San Sebastiano

CAST OF
CHARACTERS

The Pope and the Church

ANTONELLI, GIACOMO (CARDINAL) Born in 1806 in Sonnino, in the southern part of the Papal States, he came from a family of peasant origins, his father having become a wealthy country merchant. Antonelli entered the prelature, but he was never ordained and could not say mass. As a young man, his administrative abilities and elegant manner brought him to the attention of higher prelates as he was called on to perform ever more responsible positions in the government of the Papal States. *Pius IX*, who made him a cardinal in 1847, at age forty-one, increasingly came to rely on Antonelli, his opposite in so many ways, and it would be Antonelli, as his secretary of state, who would mastermind the pope's turn to Austria and reaction.

DELLA GENGA, GABRIELE (CARDINAL) Born in Assisi in 1801, nephew of Pope Leo XII, made cardinal at age thirty-four, Della Genga was one of the leaders of the reactionaries of the Sacred College and widely despised by the people of Rome. On the retaking of the city, in July 1849, *Pius IX* named Della Genga one of the three members of the governing commission to rule Rome until the pope's return. His strong personality ensured that he would be its driving force.

LAMBRUSCHINI, LUIGI (CARDINAL) Born in 1776, he was a Barnabite monk who became archbishop of Genoa and then nuncio to Paris. Lambruschini was closely identified with Pope Gregory XVI, serving as his secretary of state from 1836 until the pope's death a decade later. Reviled by the Romans, he ended up hiding under a pile of hay in a horse stall before fleeing the city in November 1848. A man of the old school, an inflexible champion of theocracy, despotic by nature, he nursed a deep hatred for modern ideas of freedom.

PIUS IX (GIOVANNI MASTAI FERRETTI) Born in 1792 to local nobility in Senigallia, in the middle of the Papal States, Giovanni Maria Mastai Ferretti suffered from epilepsy as a youth and had a limited seminary education before being ordained a priest in 1819. Eight years later he was made archbishop of Spoleto and then Imola, both in the Papal States. In 1840 he became a cardinal, and in June 1846, on the death of Gregory XVI, he was elected to the papacy, taking the name Pius IX. Initially feeding popular hopes that he would not only be the champion of reform and modernization in the Papal States but also help lead the battle for Italian independence, he would soon find himself in an impossible position, caught between his desire to be loved by his subjects and his fears that he was betraying the trust placed in him by the cardinals and by God.

ROSMINI, ANTONIO (ABBOT) Born in 1797 to a noble family in Rovereto, then part of Austrian-ruled northeastern Italy, Rosmini studied law and theology at the University of Padua and was ordained a priest in 1821. A prolific author and well-regarded philosopher and theologian, Rosmini urged the church to adapt to modern times and called on the pope to embrace the cause of Italian independence. *Pius IX* thought highly of Rosmini and initially valued his advice. Serving briefly as *King Charles Albert's* envoy to the pope in the summer of 1848, Rosmini later joined the pontiff in exile. He had a formidable adversary in *Cardinal Antonelli*.

The Romans and the Roman Republic

BELGIOJOSO, CRISTINA (PRINCESS) Born in 1808 as Cristina Trivulzio to one of Milan's wealthiest families, she married Prince Emilio Barbiano di Belgiojoso at age sixteen. They separated four years later. A great patron of the Italian national cause, she hurried to Rome with the proclamation of the Roman Republic and was placed in charge of the medical services for the injured. She would not take well to being called a "prostitute" by the pope.

BONAPARTE, CHARLES (PRINCE) Born in Paris in 1803, the son of Lucien, Napoleon Bonaparte's younger brother, Charles grew up on his father's feudal holding north of Rome, developing an interest in the natural sciences. Said to resemble his famous uncle, he combined his devotion to science with a strong interest in politics. He first urged greater reforms on *Pius IX*, and then championed the Roman Republic, serving as vice president of its Constituent Assembly. He would be accused of masterminding the assassination of *Pellegrino Rossi*.

CICERUACCHIO (ANGELO BRUNETTI) Born to a poor Roman family in 1800, Angelo Brunetti had an easy eloquence and a personality that inspired confidence and led him to success both in his business carting wine and produce from the neighboring hills into the city and as a leader of Rome's *popolani*, the little people of Rome. Initially *Pius IX*'s most enthusiastic champion, Ciceruacchio used his extraordinary influence with the Romans to pressure the pope to enact greater reforms. He and his two sons would meet a tragic end.

GARIBALDI, GIUSEPPE Born in 1807 in Nice, then part of the Savoyard kingdom, Garibaldi began adult life as a mariner. A follower of *Mazzini*'s Young Italy movement, he took part in the Italian revolts in 1831, leading to a long period (1835–48) of exile in South America, where he joined a series of rebellions. Returning to Italy following the upheavals of 1848, initially taking part in the battle against the Austrians in Lombardy, he was elected to the Constituent Assembly of the Roman Republic and became the most important military leader in its defense. On his majestic white horse, with his long brown hair and full beard, wearing his distinctive South American poncho, leading his army of wild-looking legionnaires who had followed him across the ocean, he became the icon of Italian independence.

MAZZINI, GIUSEPPE Born in 1805 in Genoa, his father a professor of pathology, Mazzini got a degree in law while becoming a leader of the conspiratorial groups seeking to overthrow the homegrown autocracies and foreign-ruled regimes in Italy. He would spend most of his adult life in exile, in good part in London. Through his prodigious correspondence and organizational skills, he became the prophet of Italian independence and republican rule. He arrived in Rome in March 1849 to take his seat in the Constituent Assembly of the Roman Republic. Elected to the triumvirate to lead the republic, he became its guiding light as it faced what seemed certain destruction.

The Italian Kings

CHARLES ALBERT, KING OF SAVOY Born in 1798, he became monarch of the Kingdom of Sardinia, which encompassed northwestern Italy and the island of Sardinia, in 1831. In March 1848, casting himself as the champion of a greater Italy, he responded to the popular revolt in Austrian-controlled northeastern Italy—Lombardy and Veneto—by ordering his army into battle against the Austrians. His efforts to get *Pius IX* to join with him placed the pope in a terrible bind.

FERDINAND II, KING OF NAPLES Born in 1810 while the Bourbon royal family was in exile in Sicily, Ferdinand became king on his father's death in 1830. Suspicious, superstitious, a faithful Catholic, reviled by his subjects, Ferdinand faced widespread revolt in his kingdom in 1848, quickly losing control of Sicily. The pope's unexpected appearance in his kingdom later that year proved a godsend, allowing him to pose as the great defender of Christendom. He would not be eager to see the pope return to Rome.

The Austrians

ESTERHÁZY, MORITZ (COUNT) Born in Vienna in 1807, Austrian ambassador at The Hague from 1845 to 1848, Esterházy was named Austria's ambassador to the Holy See in January 1849, following months in which Vienna had withdrawn its ambassador from Rome in protest of anti-Austrian activities. A tenacious conservative and fierce opponent of any compromise with the Roman Republic, Esterházy would come to have great influence with *Cardinal Antonelli* and the pope himself.

METTERNICH, KLEMENS VON (PRINCE) At his birth in 1773, Metternich's family estate in the Rhineland encompassed seventy-five square miles of land. Made foreign minister by the Austrian emperor in 1809, he chaired the Congress of Vienna in 1815, and became chancellor of the Austrian Empire in 1821, a position he held until a revolt in Vienna sent him into exile in March 1848. Dismissing Italy as merely a "geographic expression," Metternich sought to preserve stable conservative rule on the continent. He viewed *Pius IX*'s initial eagerness to win popular approval as a grave danger. A liberal pope, Metternich remarked, was an impossibility.

SCHWARZENBERG, FELIX (PRINCE) Born in 1800, the second son of an Austrian nobleman, he combined an early career in the military with a diplomatic career in several of Europe's major cities, before serving in the Austrian army in northern Italy during the fighting in 1848. Appointed Austrian prime minister in November 1848, he oversaw the repression of the revolts that had broken out in various parts of the Austrian Empire. He would direct Austria's efforts to retake the Papal States for the pope and to discourage any inclination *Pius IX* had to return to his reforming path.

The French

BARAGUEY D'HILLIERS, ACHILLE (GENERAL) In November 1849, eager to have all French affairs in Rome in the hands of a general, *Louis Napoleon* named the fifty-four-year-old Baraguey both ambassador to the Holy See and head of the French army in Rome. A veteran of the colonial war in Algeria, with little sympathy for republican principles, he was outraged by the pope's treatment of France. He would remain in Rome until May 1850.

BONAPARTE, LOUIS NAPOLEON Born in 1808, he was the son of Louis Bonaparte, brother of Napoleon Bonaparte, and king of Holland. From the time of his youth, he spent winter and spring each year in Rome. He joined in the rebellion against the pope in 1831 before going into exile in Switzerland. Imprisoned from 1840 to 1846 in a French fortress following an abortive attempt at organizing a revolt, he escaped to London. Two years later, in 1848, following the revolution in Paris, Louis Napoleon was elected to the French Constituent Assembly. In December of that year he was elected president of France. Proud of his name—and without much else seemingly going for him—he was eager to portray himself as restoring France's lost glory. Ironically, the former rebel against the Papal States had to decide whether to become the pope's savior.

CORCELLE, FRANCISQUE DE Born in 1802, married to a granddaughter of General Lafayette, Corcelle was elected as a liberal deputy under the July Monarchy in France, serving from 1839 to the revolution in 1848. He served in the subsequent Constituent Assembly of the new French Republic. Initially sent by the government to Rome in November 1848 to rescue the pope and take him to France, he returned to Rome as the emissary of his good friend *Alexis de Tocqueville* to serve as special French envoy to the Holy See from June to November 1849. A committed Catholic, Corcelle grew increasingly angry with Tocqueville, convinced that he was overly critical of the pope.

DROUYN DE LHUYS, ÉDOUARD Born of a wealthy and aristocratic family in 1805, he served first as envoy to The Hague and then to Madrid. In December 1848, shortly after his election as president, *Louis Napoleon* named Drouyn, then a deputy in the Constituent Assembly, foreign minister. Although opposed to French military intervention in Rome, he was eventually overruled. He urged his envoys to persuade the pope to continue on his earlier reforming path, but his efforts would be in vain. *Alexis de Tocqueville* replaced him as foreign minister in early June 1849.

FALLOUX, ALFRED DE (COUNT) Born in 1811, Falloux began his career as a conservative Catholic journalist and was elected a deputy to the Constituent Assembly following the French Revolution of 1848. In December of that year, *Louis Napoleon*, seeking support from conservative Catholics, named him minister of public instruction and religion. Falloux did not let a session of the cabinet go by without pressing for French military intervention to restore the pope to power in Rome. In *Tocqueville*'s memoirs, he characterized Falloux in the cabinet as representing no one other than the church.

HARCOURT, FRANÇOIS (DUKE) Born of a prominent aristocratic family in 1786, serving as a military officer until 1820, he became French ambassador to Madrid in 1831 and then to Constantinople. With the advent of the French Republic, he was named ambassador to the Holy See, arriving in Rome in June 1848. Deceived into thinking that the pope intended to take refuge in France, Harcourt played a role in the pontiff's escape in November of that year. Growing ever more critical of the pope's embrace of Austria and reaction, Harcourt found himself increasingly isolated. He would be recalled from Rome in July 1849.

LESSEPS, FERDINAND DE Born in Versailles in 1805, he served in a variety of diplomatic posts, before being called upon by the French government in May 1849 to serve as special envoy to Rome, charged with negotiating an end to the conflict. Thanks to the duplicity of his own government, Lesseps found his efforts to reach a peaceful agreement with the leaders of the Roman Republic undermined.

OUDINOT, CHARLES (GENERAL) Born in 1791, Oudinot was the son of the highest-ranking general in Napoleon Bonaparte's army. A career officer, he began his career fighting in some of Napoleon's last campaigns. In April 1849 Louis Napoleon sent him to command France's expeditionary army, charged with taking Rome. After a humiliating first attempt at the end of the month, he was eager to redeem his honor. Belittled by both *Tocqueville*, the foreign minister, and *Corcelle*, the French envoy in Rome, Oudinot was relieved of his command in Rome in August 1849.

RAYNEVAL, ALPHONSE DE Born in 1813, Rayneval became a career diplomat, beginning in 1833 as a French attaché in Madrid. He served as first secretary to the French embassy in Rome from 1839 to 1844, then spent the next four years at the French embassy in St. Petersburg. Named ambassador to the Kingdom of Naples in June 1848, Rayneval found himself dealing with the crisis created by the pope's surprising move to the kingdom five months later. Tirelessly trying to persuade the pope to reach out to his people with promises of reform, Rayneval faced the ire of the cardinals and the opposition of his fellow ambassadors. In May 1850, he replaced General *Baraguey* as the French ambassador to Rome, a position he remained in until 1857.

ROSSI, PELLEGRINO Born in Carrara, in 1787, he was the son of a modest merchant. First a lawyer and a professor of law at the University of Bologna, he then spent thirteen years in Switzerland, writing books on political economy and serving in the Swiss legislature before moving to Paris to accept a professorship at the Sorbonne. In 1845 he came to Rome as French envoy to the Holy See, although he was known for his indifference to religious questions. In March 1848, following the French Revolution, he was dismissed from his ambassadorship, but six months later, in a move that shocked the French government and greatly displeased the Austrians, *Pius IX* appointed Rossi to head his own government. Rossi would soon meet a violent end.

ROSTOLAN, LOUIS DE (GENERAL) Born in 1791, a veteran of the French war in Algeria, Rostolan served under General *Oudinot* in the assault on Rome in 1849 and then in August was named to replace Oudinot as commander of the French army there. Rostolan soon found himself at odds with the hard line that the French president wanted to take with the pope.

TOCQUEVILLE, ALEXIS DE Born to a French aristocratic family in 1805, Tocqueville acquired international fame with his *Democracy in America,* based on the nine months he spent touring the United States in 1830–31. First elected to the French Chamber of Deputies in 1839, he helped write the constitution of the French Republic created in the wake of the revolution of 1848. Appointed foreign minister by *Louis Napoleon* in early June 1849, just as French troops were poised to attack Rome, he found himself in the exceedingly uncomfortable position of overseeing the destruction of constitutional rule and the restoration of the papal theocracy.

PROLOGUE

―――

IN HIS APARTMENT HIGH UP IN ROME'S MASSIVE QUIRINAL PALACE, Pius IX worried that his plan to escape might end in disaster. Little more than a week earlier, thousands of Romans had besieged the Quirinal, calling for a government of their choosing and an end to priestly rule. Men had wheeled a cannon into the piazza and aimed it at the palace entrance. The pope's Noble Guardsmen, Roman aristocrats normally eager to don their medieval uniforms and hobnob with the pope, had deserted him, fearing for their lives. The cardinals, too, fled the city, blaming the pope for their misfortune. When protesters that day set fire to a Quirinal gate, a small band of Swiss Guardsmen did their best to shield the papal attendants who battled the flames. Clutching their rifles, members of the Civic Guard—composed of Romans of the better classes—climbed onto the roofs of neighboring buildings and began shooting at the palace. As the pope's scholarly secretary of Latin Letters, Monsignor Palma, looked out his window at the chaos below, a bullet punctured his chest, and he fell dead onto the marble floor. Rome had been under the pope's control for well over a thousand years. Now, as a revolutionary spirit gripped much of Europe, time seemed to have run out on the pope's kingdom on earth.[1]

The pontiff's fall had been swift. Elected in 1846, Pius IX had initially been hailed as a popular hero in the Papal States, the swath of the Italian Peninsula under his control. In March 1848 he had given his subjects a constitution, offering them rights unimaginable under his predecessors.

A huge crowd bellowing *Viva il Papa!* had poured into Quirinal Square. Unable to resist his flock's pleas, the pope had stepped out onto his loggia to bask in the warmth of the people's affection. As he raised his arms in blessing, the tens of thousands gathered below fell to their knees. That evening oil lanterns cast a holiday glow over the people who paraded through Rome's cobblestone streets. Every piazza, it seemed, boasted a band, and thousands of Romans joined in hymns of praise to their beloved pontiff.[2]

Much had happened in the months since then, and now, at five p.m., on Friday, November 24, 1848, it was time for the pope to escape. Outside the Quirinal Palace, Duke Harcourt, the diminutive French ambassador to the Holy See, stepped out of his luxurious horse-drawn carriage and entered the Quirinal gate, ready to play his part.

"The pope's authority," the ambassador had observed a week earlier, "exists in name only." Pius was, in effect, a prisoner, his palace surrounded by hostile Civic Guardsmen. Should the pope succeed in his escape, the ambassador had told Paris, he would very likely head for Marseilles, and so the French government should lose no time making arrangements for a suitable welcome.[3]

The door closed behind the ambassador as he entered the study where Pius was waiting for him. The pope was known for his good humor and easy charm, but now he was tense. He had not left the Quirinal Palace since rebels had slit his prime minister's throat nine days earlier. From a separate door, the papal steward, Count Benedetto Filippani, entered. Together the pope and the count hastened into the pope's adjacent bedroom. There, with the nobleman's help, Pius lifted his white robe over his head and pulled off his red shoes. Although Filippani urged him to change quickly, the pope lowered himself to his knees to say a final prayer, facing the crucifix on his table. "Have mercy on me, God, in your kindness. . . . In your compassion blot out my offense." To the steward's pleas that there was no time to lose, the pontiff replied with a bit of Scripture: *Spiritus quidem promptus est, caro autem infirma,* "The spirit is indeed willing, but the flesh is weak."[4]

He dressed in the clothes laid on his bed: a black clerical gown, black socks, and black shoes. Before donning the floppy black cleric's hat, he rubbed white powder in his hair. Finally he placed thick dark glasses on the bridge of his nose. "I look like a country priest," he remarked when he saw himself in a mirror.

Sitting alone in the pope's receiving room, the French ambassador kept up a one-sided conversation, eager to leave the impression to anyone listening outside that the pope was still with him. Meanwhile Pius IX and Filippani carried a candle to light their way as they passed out a side door and through the papal throne room. At the other end of the hall, they expected to meet a servant with a key to a secret passage out of the building. The man was not there. "My God," muttered the pope, "this begins badly." Filippani ran off to find the key. As the pope stood in the dark, his lips moved in prayer.

Filippani returned, key in hand, and the two men passed through the door and down the corridor, which ended in a stairway. As they descended, they faced a new obstacle. The keys to the exterior doors of the Quirinal were all held by the Civic Guardsmen, but they had earlier discovered that this particular door had a faulty lock and could be opened if two people, standing on either side, lifted it together. One of the pope's servants was waiting for them at the bottom of the stairway, while another stood outside the door. They knocked to alert the man outside. A response of three knocks meant the coast was clear, but only two knocks came in reply. Members of the Civic Guard were passing by. After a nervous wait, the pope was relieved to hear the three knocks. The two servants lifted the door as Filippani pushed. When it opened, the servants sank to their knees to receive the pope's blessing.

In the courtyard, Filippani helped the pope into his carriage. In a loud voice, he instructed the coachman, "To my house!" As the covered coach approached the guards at the gate, the steward leaned out the window to greet them, making it difficult for them to see who was with him. "Good night, Filippani," they called, waving him on. As a further precaution, the pope held a large handkerchief to his face, as if he were preparing to blow his nose.

When they were a safe distance from the Quirinal, they turned away from the road to Filippani's home and instead headed for a church on the other side of the city. There, waiting for them in a small carriage, was the Bavarian ambassador to the Holy See, nervously fingering the pistol in his pocket.

The pope climbed into the Bavarian's carriage, which then rumbled through the cobblestone streets, headed for the city gate.

Devout and good-hearted, the pope had never been comfortable with the world of politics. Now, as he contemplated what lay ahead, he could not imagine how he would ever be able to return to Rome. Where he was going, few people knew. The French ambassador was convinced the pope was on his way to France. The Spanish ambassador had been told that he was going to Spain. But their Bavarian colleague, who now had Pius in his carriage, had a very different destination in mind.[5]

PART ONE

—

THE
BELOVED

CHAPTER I

THE CONCLAVE

I T WOULD HAVE BEEN A GREAT SURPRISE TO THE CARDINALS WHO elected the rather unassuming Giovanni Mastai Ferretti to be pope in 1846 to learn that he would become the most important pontiff of modern times. In the revolutionary fervor that swept mid-nineteenth-century Europe, he was first hailed in Italy as a national hero, a savior, praised in thousands of hymns and poems. But with sickening speed, the cries of joy turned into shouts of "traitor" and even calls for the pope's death. These were times of transformation in Europe, the old order unhinged by industrialization, revolutionary advances in transportation, and increasing doubts about the divinely ordained social order. Pius IX would face these dizzying changes with a sense of alarm and, increasingly, with a frightening feeling of losing control. He was a man with benevolent instincts and deep faith but woefully limited ability to understand the larger forces that were transforming the world. Out of Pio Nono's* desperation, the modern Roman Catholic Church was formed.

He would be the last of the pope-kings, a dual role central to church doctrine and a pillar of Europe's political order for a thousand years. The demise of the pope's kingdom on earth would mark a pivotal moment in the transformation of Europe, a revolution begun more than a century earlier with the spread of radical notions of consent of the gov-

---

* *Pio Nono* is the Italian for "Pius the Ninth" and so was the way Italians referred to him.

erned and separation of church and state. Such a fateful change would not come easily, nor without the shedding of much blood.

The revolutions that swept Europe in 1848 marked the beginning of the end for the aristocratic regimes that had ruled much of the continent for centuries. While many would survive the year, and their rattled rulers would be able to return to their capitals, they would never be the same. The days of divine rule and imperial dynasty were numbered, for the people from Palermo to Venice, from Paris to Vienna, had briefly, intoxicatingly, glimpsed a very different kind of life—the life not of subjects but of empowered citizens.

Nowhere were these epochal changes more dramatic than in Rome, the Eternal City, capital of the Papal States. Nowhere was the divine right to rule more firmly established. And nowhere did local events have greater international resonance, as millions of Catholics on both sides of the Atlantic anxiously followed reports of the fall of the pope and his flight to precarious exile. Not a few predicted that the end of the papacy was near.

PIUS IX's PREDECESSOR, GREGORY XVI, had not been an attractive man. An ascetic monk, born to a family of local nobility in Lombardy, in northern Italy, he had a colossal nose, and his mouth turned downward in a permanent frown. The removal of a malignant tumor from his face had made things worse, leaving an ugly scar. Gregory had a well-earned reputation as a foe of all that was new. Opposed to allowing railroads in his kingdom, he had also forbidden his subjects from taking part in the scientific congresses that were multiplying throughout Europe at the time. Ruling as he saw fit over the corrupt and ill-governed Papal States, the pope did not seem unduly bothered by the hostility of his three million subjects.[1]

Poverty engulfed the countryside, but the sumptuous sixteenth- and seventeenth-century palaces of aristocrats and cardinals provided work for many of the people of Rome. Romans made little distinction between the two, for cardinals were typically younger sons of the nobility, the older inheriting the father's title and property. For centuries, the popes themselves had often been drawn from these same families.

Despite the wealth of its aristocrats, the splendor of their frescoed palaces, and the magnificence of many of the city's churches, the capital of Christendom was a rather shabby sight. Nearly half the land inside the city's wall consisted of abandoned fields. Scattered amid the occasional cluster of umbrella pine trees and modest vineyards lay the sun-bleached ruins of ancient thermal baths, aqueducts, and churches. Snaking through the city, the Tiber River divided the smaller right side—consisting of the Vatican's palaces to the north and Trastevere's humble dwellings to the south—from the larger left side, site of the city's major monuments and ancient ruins. Along the riverbanks, green-cloaked shepherds looked on as their goats chewed the grass and drank from the river's fetid yellow waters. When it rained, mud oozed over the city's broken cobblestone streets and made walking, and even travel in carriages, hazardous. "You have to get used to Rome," observed the visiting Russian writer and social reformer Alexander Herzen, adding, "its good sides are not obvious. There is something senile, obsolete, deserted and dilapidated in the city's exterior; its melancholy streets, its gloomy palaces."[2]

The cramped, dank apartments of the poor had no stoves, so people made their cooking fires outside, sending the pungent odor of boiled broccoli wafting through the streets. "The cat is here esteemed a delicacy among the lower classes," recalled the American sculptor William Wetmore Story, "and if you happen to own a particularly large and fat one, you must keep a sharp look out, or you will lose it."[3]

An open-air meat market radiated from the ancient Pantheon through a tangle of winding narrow streets that bustled with activity. Wires hung down from the buildings, allowing women to lift buckets of fresh water from the street up into their apartments. Meats hung from the awnings of the butchers' booths, and a hodgepodge of goods was displayed atop their counters. Detracting from what might otherwise have been an appetizing scene was the stench from the refuse, dust, feathers, and foul waters that covered the ground. Forcing their way through the crowded streets, butchers in blood-spattered smocks drove carts weighed down by cattle slaughtered at the city's edge. The butchers dispatched the smaller animals—goats, sheep, and pigs—outside their shops. Chickens, turkeys, ducks, and geese cackled in their pens, while men and women sat nearby, plucking the fowl and cramming their feathers into large baskets. As they finished each bird, they blew into its beak, inflating the creature's body to grotesque size before hanging it on a hook for sale.

On Wednesdays and Saturdays, the huge, oblong Piazza Navona hosted Rome's main fruit and vegetable market, where customers elbowed their way through the crowds, inspecting whatever was in season. Mushrooms received special attention, for over the years poisonous varieties had caused the death of more than one cardinal, along with many lesser Romans. Now, before any bag of mushrooms could be sold, a Roman official had to give it his stamp of approval.

Barbers, too, were found everywhere in Rome, plying their trade in the open air. When a customer sat down for a shave, the barber sharpened his blade with a great flourish, using the leather strap that hung from the back of the chair, and then accomplished his task with surprising speed. The next customer, suffering from a toothache, might have her tooth pulled or, if feeling unwell, be bled.[4]

But what most struck the visitor to the Eternal City was neither the markets nor the swarms of beggars—both common enough in other cities of Europe—but the omnipresence of churches and priests. Rome, a city of 170,000, had almost four hundred churches, most richly adorned. It could claim thirty-five hundred priests and monks, along with fifteen hundred mostly cloistered nuns. The clergy could not have been a more varied lot. Many members of the mendicant religious orders were almost indistinguishable from the other foul-smelling, poorly clad men who accosted passersby for handouts. By contrast, the upper clergy were the princes of the church. Living in splendor, they held all the highest government positions and controlled the best farmland, producing half of all the agricultural wealth of the Papal States, yet paying no taxes. The prelates administered the public treasury, which they regarded as the property not of the public but of the church. They were also in charge of all the schools, the courts, and the police. "A cardinal," observed the French ambassador, "is a prince in Rome, and a lord in the provinces."

The lower clergy—priests, monks, friars, and nuns—were another matter. For the most part, they were from humble families, were poorly educated, and—especially in rural areas—lived in poverty themselves. The parish priests in the capital were an exception, for they enjoyed some of the power that came from the marriage of religious and civil authority. When they encountered a parish priest in the streets of Rome, men doffed their hats, women and children kissed his hand. These priests felt free to enter any home in their parish at any hour to see if church precepts were being obeyed. They employed spies and ordered police to search homes, make arrests, and haul offenders to the city's dungeons. When those jailed were brought to court, often after some months, they came before judges who themselves were priests. There the parish priest's testimony was treated as gospel. Romans could be charged with having adulterous relations or practicing sodomy, or for swearing, or for failing to observe the ban on eating meat during Lent. All this, of course, did not endear the clergy to the people nor make them eager to support the continuation of what they called "priestly rule."[5]

The parish priests cut a distinctive figure on the streets of Rome, with their fuzzy black three-corner hats, the brim folded up on the sides to form a kind of heavy umbrella atop the cleric's head. They wore black shoes with prominent buckles, short black pants that left their calves bare, and a black gown that extended to their knees and buttoned down to their stomach. For additional effect, many carried a walking stick, capped by a shiny metal knob. But these priests were the elite of the lower clergy. The others—simple priests and monks—viewed the upper clergy with envy. They were the clergy's proletariat, as resentful of the wealth and power of the church elite as were the laypeople of the Papal States.[6]

As cardinals rode in carriages of unmatched luxury through the streets, they passed beggars who seemed to be everywhere: at every corner, every piazza, every monument, at the entrance of the churches, and pleading for handouts in the cafés. "Nothing," observed a French visitor, "equals the cynicism and the audacity of the Roman beggar. It is not a favor that he asks, it is a right that he exercises and, as he always asks in the name of the Madonna, or for the most sacred sacrament, or for the souls in purgatory, while he kisses the image of the Virgin that adorns the collection box that he holds in his hand, he offers you the chance to do a pious deed, and so considers you to be indebted to him."[7]

Yet while the people of Rome resented the power of their parish priest and the cardinals' ostentatious wealth, they were certainly religious in their own way. Every home and every shop had an image of the Madonna, beneath which at least one lamp always burned. Each family had a particular saint to whom it was devoted, and each household head belonged to a religious confraternity. "The Romans," wrote a French observer of the time, "follow the practices of devotion from habit, from fear of hell, and from fear of their parish priest." They will cheat a foreigner without scruple, he added, or knife a neighbor in a moment of anger, "but to miss Sunday mass, to fail to do the least thing due on the saint's day, or to eat meat on Friday, never."[8]

WHILE POPES HAD RULED the Papal States for over a thousand years, the extent of their territories had ebbed and flowed, as they engaged in both military campaigns and diplomatic maneuvering to enlarge their realm. In Gregory's day it extended from Ferrara and Bologna in the north, running southeast around the Grand Duchy of Tuscany to encompass a long stretch of the Adriatic coast including the port of Ancona. From the Tyrrhenian Sea on Italy's western coast, south of Tuscany, the pope's lands reached down past Rome to encompass a series of smaller towns. To the north, the Papal States bordered the Austrian kingdom of Lombardy-Veneto, to the south the Kingdom of Naples.* In all, the Papal States encompassed only 14 percent of the land of what is Italy today, but it lay right in the center of the peninsula. Most of its three million largely illiterate inhabitants were peasants, eking out a living from the land.

The technical innovations that were transforming life farther north in Europe had made little headway in the Papal States. There were few factories and no trains. But this backwardness was deceptive. The old verities on which the pope's rule rested had been under attack for several decades. In the wake of the French Revolution and the subsequent spread of its doctrines by Napoleon and the French army, people began to question the notion that God had ordained the social hierarchy to be as it was. Increasingly they resented the prerogatives of both clergy and aris-

---

* I here use the simplified name of the kingdom, whose formal name at the time was the Kingdom of the Two Sicilies.

tocracy. According to the ideology of divine right, kings were chosen not by men but by God, and so any attempt to overthrow the monarch was a sacrilege, an offense against the Almighty. But a new, subversive theory of government was spreading. Sovereignty, in this way of thinking, lay not with the ruler but with the people. A pope-king, wielding an army and a police force, increasingly came to be viewed as a vestige of the Middle Ages. While the pontiff was properly the Holy Father of the Catholic faithful worldwide, he seemed to many to have no business also serving as a king. Nor, they thought, did priests have any business running the police and the courts.

Sweeping through Europe together with these Enlightenment-fueled ideas was another powerful new doctrine, nationalism. The Italian Peninsula at the time was divided into a multitude of different states, a patchwork of kingdoms, imperial outposts, and duchies. Many were ruled directly or indirectly by the Austrian Empire. As the growing number of nationalists saw it, all of Italy should be united. Foreign armies and foreign rulers had no place there.

ALTHOUGH POPE GREGORY WAS far from a young man, his death came as something of a surprise, for he had not been ill. In late May 1846, what first appeared to be simply an irritating inflammation and swelling of his left leg quickly turned into something worse. He died on the morning of June 1.[9]

For centuries the death of a pope had triggered not only frenetic jockeying for influence among the elite but often violent popular unrest as well. Gregory XVI himself had been elected fifteen years earlier amid signs of imminent revolt in his realm. News of an uprising in Bologna, the second city of the Papal States, reached Rome in the middle of Gregory's coronation ceremonies. Soon the whole northern region of the Papal States was in flames as one city after another declared the end of papal rule. It was only thanks to the swift arrival of Austrian troops that the old order was restored. Now, a decade and a half later, the theocracy seemed no more stable. Cardinals still headed the government's major departments, and under them a network of bishops, priests, and monks still held all the most influential governmental positions, monopolized education, and sat as judges in courts that made little distinction between religious and civil matters. Gregory's successor, the London *Times* predicted, would not survive six months on his throne without requiring help from the Austrian army.[10]

Given Gregory's reputation as a bitter opponent of all that was modern, not long after his death jokes at his expense began making the rounds in Rome. As he approached Saint Peter at heaven's gate, according to one of them, Gregory was so tired that he could barely move.

"How much further is there to go?" asked the exhausted pope.

"Well," replied Saint Peter, "if you had only allowed the railroad, you would already be there!"[11]

MONARCHS RULED EUROPE'S MAJOR STATES—kings in France and Prussia, a queen in Spain, the emperor in Austria, and the czar in Russia. The smaller states, too, were ruled by royal families or families tied to royalty: Portugal, Naples, Sweden, Belgium, Denmark, the Grand Duchy of Tuscany.

While Gregory's funeral rites were under way in Rome, the courts of these rulers debated the qualities needed in a new pope. For the sovereigns of the three Catholic powers—Austria, France, and Spain—these were not simply idle conversations, for each had the centuries-old right to veto papal candidates they deemed unacceptable. Among their leaders, one stood out: Prince Klemens von Metternich, the Austrian chancellor, had, over the past quarter century, dispatched his army to prop up papal rule every time the people of the Papal States had risen up against it. He was not lacking in self-confidence. "I cannot help telling myself twenty times a day," recalled Metternich in his memoirs, "'O Lord! How right I am and how wrong they are!'" The tall, blue-eyed prince, with curly, light-colored, receding hair, was also something of a dandy. But if these traits were the subject of snide remarks elsewhere, they were forgiven by the members of the papal court, who held him in high regard. "He is not only the greatest statesman of the century," enthused the papal nuncio in Vienna, "but the best Catholic."[12]

It was Metternich who, as a young Austrian diplomat, had chaired the Congress of Vienna in 1815. There, in the wake of Napoleon's defeat,

Prince Klemens von Metternich

the victorious powers had carved out a new map of Europe. Austria's rule over Lombardy was restored, and the thousand-year reign of the Republic of Venice came to an end, as Veneto, too, was gobbled up by the Austrian Empire. Further solidifying Austrian influence over Italy, the Grand Duchy of Tuscany, as well as the smaller central Italian duchies of Modena and Parma, would be ruled by members of the Austrian imperial family, and Austrian troops would ensure the pope's continued hold over his realm. Only the Kingdom of Sardinia, consisting of the northwestern part of the peninsula and the island that gave it its name, could claim full independence from Austrian influence.

For the Austrian chancellor, as for the other pillars of the old order in Europe, the papacy was a touchstone of stability, a powerful justification for the inequalities that left the masses under the thumb of the wealthy few. Writing in 1836 to the king of Belgium, Metternich reminded him that the Catholic Church provided Europe's monarchs their most valuable support. "What the Church preaches," he wrote, "is the performance of the reciprocal duties between the people and their rulers. . . . It considers authority as emanating from God. . . . Attach yourself firmly to the Head of the Church, Sire, and it will lend you a helping hand."

But Metternich was no fool. The times were changing and, he realized, rulers who failed to adapt—albeit prudently—risked disaster. The fact that the Papal States bordered both the restive Austrian-held regions of Lombardy and Veneto and the Austrian-controlled Grand Duchy of Tuscany meant that any instability in the papal kingdom posed a direct danger to the Austrian Empire. The chancellor sought a pope who would defend the papal theocracy but who also recognized the need for some reforms. The clergy's stranglehold on government had to be eased and talented laymen brought into government.[13]

France was Europe's other great continental power, Spain having long been in decline. For three centuries, with the brief exception of the Napoleonic years, France had battled unsuccessfully with Austria for influence in Italy. Like his Austrian counterpart, the French king, Louis Philippe, wanted a pope who could preserve public order in the Papal States. But he, too, thought a reformer was needed to keep the ill-governed Papal States from collapsing. The new pope, as the French foreign minister put it, should be "enlightened, prudent, moderate . . . and not especially tied to any of [Europe's] Powers." The three French cardinals were instructed to use their king's veto against any candidate who lacked those qualities.[14]

Bordering the Papal States to the south lay the Kingdom of Naples, which encompassed all of southern Italy and the island of Sicily. Its monarch, the Bourbon king Ferdinand II, ruled over a notoriously backward and rebellious land. He felt anything but secure, as the decapitation of his French Bourbon cousin Louis XVI, half a century earlier, offered a lesson too graphic to forget. Made uneasy by the vacuum produced to his north by Pope Gregory's death, Ferdinand was eager to see a successor elected quickly. What was needed most in the new pope, the king's foreign minister advised, was someone with "much experience in political affairs and great firmness of character." As it would turn out, Gregory's successor would have neither.[15]

Throughout Europe, those in power deemed the notion that the people should choose their own governments to be pernicious and utopian. But the growing numbers of republicans, socialists, and liberals were of a very different view. There were those who thought, or at least hoped, that the next pope—the embodiment of a medieval vision of society— would also be the last.

SECOND IN AUTHORITY ONLY to the pontiff, the cardinals of the church constituted the Sacred College, responsible both for the church's gover- nance and for electing a successor on the pope's death. Some cardinals had been appointed as young men as a tribute to their noble origins; some presided over small, remote Italian dioceses. As a group they were known neither for their intelligence nor for their understanding of the changing world. "It pains me to have to observe that in the discussions that have taken place thus far," observed the Neapolitan ambassador in Rome, reporting on the cardinals gathered for the conclave to choose the new pope, "discord prevails among them together with an atmosphere of personal interests such that there is reason to fear many intrigues." Metternich was getting similar reports from Rome. The cardinals, he was told, were a mediocre lot, concerned above all with protecting their own privileges. Making matters worse, Pope Gregory had left the trea- sury bare, the government peopled with incompetents, and the army in tatters. The conclave threatened to be long and difficult.[16]

It began when the customary ten days of mourning for the pope ended. Fifty-four of the cardinals were Italian, only eight from any- where else. Of the eight, all were Europeans; only France, with three, and Austria, with two, had more than a single member of the Sacred Col- lege. Given the time it had taken to get word of the pope's death to them, and then the time it would take for them to travel to Rome, none of the non-Italian cardinals arrived on time, not even the archbishop of Milan, an Austrian cardinal who carried Metternich's veto.

It was Pope Gregory's secretary of state, seventy-year-old Luigi Lambruschini, from a noble Genoan family, who cast the largest shadow at the conclave. Like Gregory, a monk known for his austere habits, he was a man of aristocratic bearing, cold and haughty. After serving as archbishop of Genoa, he had been sent to Paris in 1827 as papal nuncio, the pope's ambassador to France. There he opposed any move by King Charles X to institute reforms or freedoms, arguing that listening to popular demands would undermine the social order that God intended. He especially warned the king against loosening censorship of the press, certain that it would spread seditious doctrines of individual rights. When, following a popular uprising in 1830, the more liberal-minded Louis Philippe replaced Charles X, the new king demanded that Lambruschini be replaced.

It was then that Lambruschini gained his cardinal's hat, and during the popular uprisings a year later, he became one of the more strident voices calling on the Austrian army to restore order in the Papal States. Most of the cardinals shared his worldview. God had destined the great mass of humanity to do their humble work and not to bother themselves with matters of government. God had entrusted the public's welfare to indulgent but firm fathers: the king in France, the emperor in Austria, and the pope in the Papal States. The notion that governments should represent the people they ruled could not have been more foreign to Lambruschini. He urged the pope to minimize the number of universities, deeming them seedbeds of dangerous modern ideas. Inflexible, despotic, and dedicated to a return of the glory days of medieval Christianity, he led the reactionary faction of the cardinals—the *zelanti*, the zealots.[17]

At six p.m. on Sunday, June 14, 1846, a long line of magnificent carriages pulled up to San Silvestro Church in the center of Rome. A cardinal stepped out of each, there to attend a special mass. Following the service, the fifty red-robed cardinals emerged into a day darkened by cloudy skies and walked the few blocks to the Quirinal Palace, flanked by two rows of papal soldiers. Each cardinal was given two rooms, the larger one for himself, the smaller for his attendants: a secretary, a waiter, and a servant. The windows were shuttered to prevent any outside communication.

Each of the cardinals then received visits from the foreign ambassadors and members of Rome's nobility, eager to curry favor and perhaps to have influence. At eleven p.m., the ritual cry of *Extra omnes!*— "Everyone out!"—was repeated three times. The doors were closed, locking the cardinals and their attendants in. Fearing violence, a staple of Rome's streets in times when there was no pope, Swiss Guardsmen dispersed the crowd of onlookers who had gathered in the piazza facing the Quirinal and built barricades to block off the nearby streets.[18]

Voting began the next morning in the Paolina Chapel. Resembling the Vatican's better-known Sistine Chapel, its walls were entirely frescoed, its vaulted ceiling towering twenty meters above. A row of small canopy-topped thrones ran along each wall, one for each cardinal, each with a little table furnished with goose quill pen, inkwell, and paper. At one end of the chapel, atop the raised candlelit altar, was a table covered with a richly decorated tapestry. There sat the three cardinals who, chosen by lot at each ballot, opened and read the votes aloud.[19]

Election required a two-thirds majority, and no one had any idea how long it would take to reach that daunting threshold. Although there was no requirement that the new pope come from among the cardinals, no one other than a cardinal had been elected since the fourteenth century. All eyes, then, were fixed on the men who gathered in conclave. Two factions prepared to do battle. For the *zelanti,* the conservatives, the choice was clear: they could count on Lambruschini to continue the policies that he had shaped in his past ten years as secretary of state. Less clear was who would be the choice of the moderates, those who believed that the church had to adjust, in some ways, to modern times.

Surprisingly, the conclave reached its conclusion in remarkably short order. As it became clear by the second ballot that Lambruschini would never reach the two-thirds vote needed, one of the lesser-known members of the Sacred College, Giovanni Mastai Ferretti, saw his fortunes unexpectedly rise.

Mastai Ferretti was born in 1792 to a family of minor nobility in Senigallia, a central Italian town in the Papal States. His mother's ambition that he become a priest was threatened when as a child he began to suffer epileptic seizures, and he would need special dispensation to be ordained. As Napoleon's forces swept through the Papal States and laid waste to papal government, two popes were, one after the other, removed by force from Rome and driven into exile by French troops. Pius VI, exiled from Rome in 1798, died the next year in Valence, France. The conclave to elect his successor, Pius VII, was held not in Rome, where the end of papal rule had been proclaimed, but in Venice. Although Pius VII was briefly allowed back to Rome, in 1809 he, too, was seized by French troops and taken to France.

Giovanni Mastai's seminary in Rome was then closed, and he had to go home. Only Napoleon's defeat in 1814 allowed Pius VII to return to the Eternal City and Mastai to resume his clerical studies. One result of these disruptions—reinforced by his own limited interest in intellectual pursuits—was that Mastai never felt fully versed in theological and cultural matters. In 1818 the newly restored Pius VII accepted him for the priesthood on the condition that, given uncertainties about his epilepsy, he celebrate mass only when assisted by another cleric.[20]

In 1827, aged thirty-five and recently returned from accompanying a church delegation to Chile, Mastai was named the archbishop of Spoleto, a town midway between his hometown and Rome. "God really is having some fun on earth," he wrote to a friend, "for he has wished to promote a miserable insect to such an honor."

When revolts against the papal government erupted in 1831, the young archbishop did not initially realize how great a threat they were. "All of the [revolutionary] forces of Perugia, Foligno, Spoleto, and Terni together barely amount to five hundred men," he informed the secretary of state in Rome. "Lacking uniforms, without leadership, far from courageous, they are incapable of intimidating anyone. . . . Either the pontifical troops are ready to fight and victory is assured, or the papal troops are entirely corrupt, and then I leave our cause in the Lord's hands and say nothing."

But papal troops did indeed prove unequal to the task, and when the town's Civic Guard joined in the uprising, Mastai was forced to flee. He took refuge in the Kingdom of Naples, where, nearly two decades later, he would again seek exile. This first stay was brief, for Austrian troops quickly regained control. On his return, Mastai, filled with self-doubt, asked the pope to relieve him of his post, citing his "inexperience in the sacred sciences," his "deficiency" in the charisma that the Apostles demand of a bishop, and in a reference to his episodic epilepsy, "the shaky health which has afflicted me for many years."[21]

Gregory XVI rejected Mastai's request and the next year transferred him to Imola, a more prestigious posting, twenty miles southeast of Bologna. Over the next decade, he would acquire a reputation there as fair-minded, principled, and good-natured, although he could be stern when necessary. He found the poor quality of the local priests especially upsetting. "Far from . . . pastors of their flocks," he complained, "they are more like the wolves, a scandal and the ruin of their flocks." He forbade priests to appear in public without their clerical garb, forbade them to carry weapons, and required all parish priests to live in their church residence.

Prince Metternich first heard of Mastai, who had only recently been made a cardinal, in an 1842 letter from his ambassador in Rome discussing possible successors to Pope Gregory. "He enjoys the esteem of all, both clergy and lay," concluded the ambassador. "The faction that wants neither a foreigner [someone from outside the Papal States] nor a monk [as were both Pope Gregory and Cardinal Lambruschini] would certainly put him forth in the next Conclave."[22]

Bishop of a minor town and lacking any experience in the intrigues of the Roman Curia—the central administration of the Holy See—Mastai was in some ways an odd choice to be pope. But he was respected for his good humor, his lack of pretension, and his success in winning popular favor in a diocese in a portion of the Papal States known for its hostility to priestly rule.[23]

For the conservatives, it was his very weakness that made him so appealing. Given his inexperience in the world of Roman politics, they thought, he might, with proper care, be led along the right path.

The fourth ballot, on June 16, proved decisive. Mastai happened to have been selected by lot as one of the three cardinals charged with reading out the results of the voting. As he called out his own name on one ballot after another, his voice began to fail him. He asked to be excused, and another cardinal took his place. When Mastai reached the two-thirds vote, the cardinal in charge rang a bell and formally asked him if he was willing to accept his election. Overwhelmed with emotion, Mastai walked to the altar and sank to his knees. His lips moved in prayer. He stood and then turned to the expectant cardinals: *"Accepto,"* he replied in Latin. The cardinals' little canopies were then taken down, all except his own. Asked what name he would take, Mastai responded that he wanted to be known as Pius IX, after Pius VII, who, like him, had served as bishop of Imola when elected to the papacy almost half a century earlier.[24]

EARLY ON JUNE 17, the day following the election, the new pontiff returned to the Paolina Chapel to receive Rome's noblemen and allow them to kiss his foot. Eleven blasts from the cannon at Castel Sant'Angelo alerted the people that a new pope was about to be announced, and thousands rushed to the Quirinal Palace. Above the front entrance of the massive building—well over a million square feet in size—the door to the loggia overlooking the piazza had been bricked up when the cardinals went into conclave. Now workers broke through. When the passage was cleared, a procession of cardinals emerged, clothed in their red silk robes. Appearing last, the cardinal deacon strode to the front to announce the name of the new pontiff. Since word of the election had begun to spread the previous evening, there had been much uncertainty about who this could be. Few in the huge crowd could make out the cardinal's words. Of those who could, few knew who Mastai was. Scattered shouts of *Evviva!* rose from the piazza, and a few hats were thrown into the air, but most, confused or disappointed, remained silent.

Then the unfamiliar white-robed figure—his relative youth and benevolent smile contrasting so sharply with his unloved predecessor—strode onto the balcony. The new pope was a good-looking man of medium height, with a broad chest and blond hair. He projected a sense of goodness and simplicity that would quickly win him sympathy. "If someone were to cut Giovanni into a million pieces," his older brother liked to say, "from each piece—as from an octopus—a priest would be born." Pius raised his arms and in a strong, clear voice blessed the crowd. Those close enough saw tears trickling onto his cheeks. The cannons of the massive, ancient Castel Sant'Angelo sounded again, and throughout the city church bells rang.[25]

That evening all of Rome's foreign missions lit up the facades of their palaces. The French ambassador, fifty-nine-year-old Pellegrino Rossi, stayed up late to send the news to Paris, eager to report that he had played no small role in the surprisingly swift election of the new pope. In

Pope Pius IX

the days leading up to the conclave, he had spoken with as many cardinals as he could, stressing the importance of acting quickly to calm the people of the Papal States and to elect someone able to meet the challenges of modern times. Although he had not specifically lobbied for the bishop of Imola, he thought that Cardinal Mastai was the kind of man the church needed.

Rossi went to the Quirinal that morning to greet the new pontiff. His eyes again tearing up with emotion, Pius took Rossi's hands in his. As the ambassador later made his way out of the crowded hall, he spoke with several cardinals. They predicted that the new pope would soon

FAIRPORT PUBLIC LIBRARY
1 FAIRPORT VILLAGE LANDING
FAIRPORT NY 14450

proclaim an amnesty for all those jailed for political crimes and also announce plans to bring railroads to the Papal States. "If that should come to pass," observed Rossi, "I see the tranquility of the land as assured."[26]

Rudolf von Lützow, the Austrian ambassador, offered a similarly enthusiastic report to Metternich in Vienna. In Spoleto and Imola, the Austrian recalled, Mastai had known how to win "the affection of his flock by his works of charity and by the paternal kindness with which he governed his diocese during such challenging times." Lützow also thought they could count on the new pope to consult closely with Austria as he considered reforms.[27] On receiving the news, Metternich expressed his pleasure both at the speed with which the cardinals had acted and at the result. Pius's election, he told his ambassador, would "console all those friends of religion and order, while spreading confusion among those so quick to denigrate the Catholic Church and brand its temporal rule as anachronistic and out of step with the needs of modern civilization." The difficulties that the new pope now faced, the Austrian chancellor acknowledged, were great, but, he added, "Every time that Pius IX will be called upon to defend the great conservative verities that the papacy has the sublime mission of preserving . . . he will find us at his side."[28]

The pope was crowned in St. Peter's Basilica. There the heads of the religious orders, the bishops, the cardinals, and hundreds of other church dignitaries marched in procession. At the back of the seemingly endless line came Pio Nono, carried aloft by twelve footmen as he sat in his *sedia gestatoria,** surrounded by Noble Guardsmen, Swiss Guardsmen, and the generals of the papal army.

While the French and Austrian governments were pleased with the new pope, the people of Rome remained uncertain. To them, he was a stranger. The crowd gathered in the basilica for his coronation greeted Pius, in the words of the Tuscan envoy, "with absolute coldness, without giving, either by voice or with their hands the least sign of happiness." The new pope was eager to find a way to win their hearts. This would turn out to be the easy part. It was keeping their love without destroying the church that would prove to be so difficult.[29]

---

* The richly adorned, silk-covered throne on which popes were carried on various ceremonial occasions.

CHAPTER 2

THE FOX AND
THE CROW

THE HUNDREDS OF MEN WHO LANGUISHED IN THE PAPAL STATES' prisons for political crimes, and the hundreds more who had gone into exile to avoid a similar fate, weighed heavily on the minds of the more enlightened men and women of the pope's dominion. Many had been in the pope's dark prisons since the last major uprising against church rule fifteen years earlier. Practically every layperson with whom the pope met in the first days of his papacy told him that there would be no better way to win people's hearts than to grant an amnesty to free the imprisoned and allow the exiles to return.

On July 1, 1846, the new pope summoned six prominent cardinals to ask their opinion before making his decision. The archconservative Lambruschini argued against such a move, but others thought it would be a good thing. On July 17, a month after the new pope's election, the decree appeared on Rome's walls, then in towns throughout the Papal States:

> Pius the Ninth to his faithful subjects. . . .
>   We commute the sentence of all of our subjects who are currently in prison as punishment for political crime.

The offenders had only to give their word of honor that they would never again rebel against the government of the Papal States. All political exiles were likewise to be allowed to return, and all those currently being tried for political crimes were to be pardoned.[1]

The next day, a Saturday, Romans flooded the streets in celebration. In each of the city's neighborhoods men and women formed processions and headed toward the papal palace, singing the new pontiff's praises. At seven p.m., as hundreds shouted *Viva Pio Nono!* in the piazza below his window, the smiling pope walked onto his loggia to thank and bless them. As more celebrants arrived, he emerged two hours later to repeat the scene. But people kept coming, twenty thousand in all, carrying long sticks topped with fluttering handkerchiefs and numerous hand-stitched banners bearing the papal crest or simply the words *Viva Pio Nono!* Their torches lit up the piazza. A band played, and shouts of praise to the new pontiff filled the air. No pope was supposed to appear in public at night, but at 10:45 p.m. Pio Nono, in his white robe and short red cape, came onto his balcony once again to bless the crowd. His subjects then streamed into the nearby streets, filling the brightly lit Corso and waving their papal banners.

Sunday morning the festivities continued. The streets were clogged, as flowers rained down from the windows amid cries of praise for the new pope. Surrounded by his joyful subjects as his carriage returned from the Roman church where he had celebrated mass, Pius slowly made his way back into the palace. When the crowd showed no sign of leaving without getting to see him, he again came out to his balcony to offer his blessing. Surveying the multitudes, many with tears of emotion in their eyes, he struggled to contain his own. Making the sign of the cross, he offered his blessing.[2]

"The amnesty is not everything," observed Pellegrino Rossi, the French ambassador, "but it is a big step." More cautiously, he added, "I hope that the new path is now open and that the Holy Father will know how to continue in it, despite all the obstacles that will certainly stand in his way." In Paris, the French foreign minister was encouraged. The new pope, he thought, might well prove the salvation of the tottering Papal States.[3]

While the French were pleased, the Austrians were not. The pope, they thought, should have given not a blanket amnesty but a limited "pardon" to individuals who expressed remorse for the crimes they had committed. This was what Cardinal Lambruschini had recommended. Austria's ambassador in Rome, Count Rudolf von Lützow, stung by the fact that the pope had neither consulted him in advance nor informed him before the announcement, let the cardinals know of his unhappiness. Several shared his alarm, fearing that the naïve pontiff was recklessly planting the seeds of revolt.[4]

As the days and weeks passed, Pius found himself in an increasingly uncomfortable spot. Crowds began gathering regularly in Rome's piazzas, as men and women shouted slogans and carried signs urging him to grant other long-sought reforms. They wanted the mercenary militias disbanded and replaced with citizen militias. They asked that the most reviled priestly functionaries be removed, they wanted laymen to replace the prelates who dominated public administration, and they urged freedom of the press. They also wanted to see a united Italy, one free of foreign armies. Many hoped that Pio Nono himself might lead this movement for national independence. But while the pope was a proud Italian, he had no interest in leading a war against Austria, a disinclination reinforced by the cardinals who saw the Austrians as their best guarantee of continued rule. As for the people's other demands for change, the thousand-year-old Papal States were not like any other states. As the cardinals kept reminding the pontiff, the laws of the papal reign were given not by man but by God.[5]

IN EARLY AUGUST, Pius named fifty-eight-year-old Cardinal Pasquale Gizzi to be his secretary of state. After the reactionary Lambruschini, the pope was looking for a man with diplomatic experience who had a more moderate outlook. Gizzi seemed a good choice, having served as papal representative to Lucerne, Turin, and Brussels, in addition to a successful term as papal legate to Forlì, in the north of the Papal States. Pius himself had voted for Gizzi at the conclave and, in a sign of affection, referred to him as *il mio papa,* "my pope."

Romans were pleased by the appointment, believing—wrongly, it turned out—that the cardinal was on the side of major reform. If the pope had hesitated several weeks before appointing him, it may have been because Gizzi was hobbled by poor health, which showed in his sallow complexion and the gout that frequently confined him to bed. His tenure as secretary of state was destined to be neither smooth nor long, as the charmless, strong-minded Gizzi increasingly found himself at odds with the pope.[6]

In trying to do something to improve the Papal States' poor economic situation, Pius turned for advice to Pellegrino Rossi, the French ambassador. Rossi had an unusual background. Born to a modest family in Carrara, in central Italy, he became a lawyer and, still in his twenties, was appointed professor of law at the University of Bologna. A few years later he moved to Geneva, where he spent the next decade writing books on political economy and serving as a member of the Swiss legislature. He then left Switzerland, taking up a professorship in Paris, a post he held until 1845, when King Louis Philippe named him French envoy to the Holy See. A short, slight man of dignified bearing, he possessed a penetrating intellect, combined with enormous self-confidence and drive. He was said to resemble the profile portraits of Dante, and some went so far as to claim that, conscious of this resemblance, he periodically struck a pose to maximize that effect.

Pius coupled his request for advice with a note of caution. "A Pope," he told Rossi, "must not plunge into utopian schemes." People had crazy ideas. There were even those, he marveled, who "speak of an Italian league to be headed by the Pope. As if such a thing were possible! As if the great powers would ever permit it!"

Rossi expressed his sympathy for the pope's plight and offered his encouragement. "You have already traced the route that you should follow," Rossi told him, one "that will bring the best results: putting an end to the abuses that, I fear, are numerous, and introducing everywhere good government. I think that is what the Holy Father has in mind."

"You are right," replied the pope. "That is my firm resolution. One must, before anything else, put our finances in order, but I need a little time."[7]

While the French ambassador was urging Pius to act quickly, others were trying to slow him down. Along with the Austrian court, the Bourbon king of Naples—not among Europe's more enlightened monarchs—had been dismayed at the pope's broad amnesty and at his unseemly eagerness to please his restive subjects. Pius's uncertain first moves, reported the king's ambassador in Rome, were allowing the *esaltati,* the fanatics, people who would have been happy to see all of

Pellegrino
Rossi

Europe's monarchs fall, to claim that the pope was on their side. Some reforms were no doubt to be desired, the Neapolitan ambassador told the pontiff when they met in the fall, but firmness was also needed. Otherwise, he warned, "pernicious influences" would grow unchecked.[8]

Alarm was spreading among the cardinals as well. "My friend," wrote Cardinal De Angelis, archbishop of Fermo, to the archbishop of Bologna, "let's not fool ourselves. This general enthusiasm for reforms . . . cannot have a natural end." Cardinal Gizzi, the secretary of state, watched uneasily as the inexperienced, impressionable pontiff was, as he saw it, manipulated by radicals through their skillful use of the crowds. In an effort to regain control, in early October Gizzi ordered an end to all popular demonstrations in the Papal States.[9]

If Gizzi suspected a plot behind the unending popular tributes to the kindly pope, he was not entirely wrong. Giuseppe Mazzini—the great champion of Italian unification and popular sovereignty, and a sworn enemy of priestly rule—was sending instructions from London to his supporters in Italy. Mazzini had been a headache for the popes—and

Italy's other rulers—for many years. Exiled from his native Genoa after the failure of the revolts of 1831, he had helped found Young Italy, a clandestine organization dedicated to unifying Italy under a republican government. After being expelled from Switzerland, he began what would be a long exile in London, scraping by while plotting insurrection and maintaining a huge international correspondence. Excited by the ferment in Rome, Mazzini urged his followers to take advantage of even the most minor concession by the pontiff to organize "festivals, songs, demonstrations, all of which give people a sense of the power that they have." The watchwords, wrote Mazzini, should be "freedom, the rights of man, progress, equality, fraternity." People would understand more easily, he added, if they contrasted these with their opposite: "despotism, privilege, slavery, monopoly."[10]

Pius IX sought his subjects' love, but he was a reluctant reformer, torn between those seeking change and those arguing that the pope's first duty was to defend the powers of the church. In October the pope met again with the French ambassador, who urged him to end the priestly

Giuseppe
Mazzini

monopoly on high government positions and to remove the prelates who were most despised by the people. Pius met with distinguished laymen from all parts of the Papal States who had come to plead the same cause. But still he hesitated.[11]

The pope soon learned a lesson in the people's displeasure. On November 4, the day honoring Saint Carlo Borromeo, sixteenth-century hero of the Counter-Reformation, he made his way in elaborate procession through the center of Rome to the saint's church. Festive tapestries hung from the windows. Forty thousand people crowded the streets to watch him pass, but—disappointed that months had gone by since the amnesty, yet priests still held the most important government positions— they stood mute. When the pope returned to the Quirinal Palace, the crowd dispersed without waiting for his blessing.[12]

The following day the pope wrote to his brother, Gabriele, "I am always hoping that my own good will for the good of the people whom God has entrusted to me is about to be reciprocated. My hope is all the more secure inasmuch as I place my great faith in the Lord, without neglecting to do all that I can." He asked Gabriele to distribute a ten-pound bag of salt to every family in their hometown. Two days later he approved the construction of five train lines in the Papal States.[13]

Perhaps it was the announcement of the first rail lines, or the excitement of the ancient ceremony, but on November 8, when the pope took possession of his seat as bishop of Rome in the magnificent Basilica of St. John Lateran, there was no doubting the people's enthusiasm. At the sound of a cannon blast from Castel Sant'Angelo just after noon, the papal procession set out from the Quirinal Palace. A long line of cavalry led the way, followed by numerous papal attendants, some in red uniforms and others with black velvet capes and white collars, swords dangling from their belts. The commander of the Swiss Guard rode a magnificent mount, his steel armor and helmet sparkling in the sun. Behind him walked a prelate bearing the papal crucifix, followed by the head of the ecclesiastical court riding incongruously atop a white mule. Only then did the pope appear, in his ornate, horse-drawn carriage, waving his arm in benediction.

As Pius rode slowly by, women ran up to hand him their bouquets. By the end of his trip, he could hardly move amid all the flowers in his

carriage. A hundred and forty thousand people, according to one chronicler, crowded the streets, waving their hats and their handkerchiefs.
Many of them had traveled from the provinces to witness the spectacle.
Behind the pontiff's coach, six carriages, each pulled by six horses, carried dignitaries of the papal court, with numerous Noble Guardsmen,
resplendent in their medieval uniforms, drawing up the rear. People
lined the streets and leaned out of their decorated windows, applauding
and shouting *Viva il Papa!*[14]

The latest outpouring of popular support for the pope only added to
the nervousness of the ambassador of Naples in Rome. "The situation in
which His Holiness finds himself is certainly thorny and full of difficulties," he observed, "but it will make it even thornier and more difficult if,
due to his sweet disposition, his mercy, his strong desire to make his
subjects happy and content, His Holiness does not show his indifference
to popular approval." The reactionaries shared with the more perceptive
moderates the belief that the pope was headed for disaster. It was not
clear that papal rule—based on divine right—was in any way compatible with the democratic principles embraced on Rome's streets. "If the
Roman court concedes all that is necessary," observed one of the democrats, "it must abdicate. If it concedes only a part, it only provokes
greater conflict. If it concedes nothing, things will be even worse."[15]

The reactionaries did have some reason to think that Pius might yet
be brought around to their view. His first encyclical, released on November 9, 1846, made clear, to those who would listen, that he would not
stray far from orthodoxy. Pius began *Qui pluribus,* addressed to all the
world's patriarchs and bishops, by praising his predecessor, Pope Gregory XVI, and confessing his own sense of unworthiness for the task that
had been entrusted in him. He warned of the great perils the church
faced:

> Each of you has noticed, venerable brothers, that a very bitter and
> fearsome war against the whole Catholic commonwealth is being
> stirred up by men bound together in a lawless alliance. . . . These
> men use these means to spread their hatred for truth and light.
> They are experienced and skillful in deceit, which they use to set
> in motion their plans to quench people's zeal for piety, justice and

virtue, to corrupt morals, to cast all divine and human laws into confusion, and to weaken and even possibly overthrow the Catholic religion and civil society. For you know, venerable brothers, that these bitter enemies of the Christian name, are carried wretchedly along by some blind momentum of their mad impiety. . . . It is with no less deceit . . . that other enemies of divine revelation, with reckless and sacrilegious effrontery, want to import the doctrine of human progress into the Catholic religion.[16]

The encyclical could hardly have expressed a more conservative message, pitting the word of God against the forces of evil, the timeless truths of the church against the new blasphemies spread by the heretical champions of "progress."

Undaunted, the liberals kept trying to convince the pope of the need for change. A week after Pius pronounced *Qui pluribus,* a young man from Bologna, second city of the Papal States, came to see him. Full of enthusiasm for the liberal, patriotic cause, twenty-eight-year-old Marco Minghetti, who had already acquired a reputation among Bologna's elite for his erudition, would one day become Italy's prime minister. Rather than raise the uncomfortable subject of the encyclical, Minghetti began the audience by thanking the pope for the changes he had already made. The pontiff expressed his appreciation for the young man's kind words but complained that people had unrealistic expectations of him.

Reasonable men, replied Minghetti, realized that reforms would not be easy but were confident that they could be reconciled with church principles.

"Yes," said the pope, "but first there must be enough time and enough calm." When his visitor urged him to dismiss those clerics in government who opposed any change, Pio Nono grew silent. He stood up, lifted his arms to bless his visitor, and sent him off.[17]

IN EARLY DECEMBER, AMID torrential rains, the swollen Tiber River flooded its banks. By the morning of the tenth, a third of the city lay underwater. The Corso had become a canal, and boats outfitted by philanthropic princes glided through the city streets, bringing food to the stranded. Worst hit were Rome's four thousand Jews, confined since the sixteenth century to a walled ghetto on the banks of the Tiber. With mud-saturated water rising several meters, the Jews could escape only through their second-floor windows. As the waters receded the next day, people learned that the pope had ordered food and clothes to be sent to those who had suffered, triggering a new surge in the pope's popularity. The Jews, too, were thankful, for in the wake of the flood's devastation, Pius IX granted their request that some of their number be allowed to settle outside the overcrowded, and now waterlogged, ghetto.[18]

Despite the order forbidding further public demonstrations, more than a thousand people marched to the pope's palace on December 26, the eve of the festival of the pope's namesake, Saint John. Shouting *Viva il Papa!* they played music and raised banners and torches. Unable to resist their pleas, the pope strode out onto his balcony to bless them.

Cardinal Gizzi, the pope's secretary of state, was not pleased. "I gave orders that the popular demonstrations for the Pope not be repeated," he told the Austrian ambassador, "but then my orders were not followed." He had been in office less than half a year but was already at wit's end. "If I am not going to be listened to," he vowed, "nothing remains but for me to resign."[19]

IN CONTRAST TO THE CARDINALS, the pope lived simply. He woke up at six or six-thirty in the morning, shaved himself, then went to his private chapel for an hour of prayer, meditating as he recited the rosary. He celebrated a mass with his attendants before eating his modest breakfast, dipping biscuits into a cup of coffee mixed with chocolate. After he gave his *maggiordomo* and other members of his entourage instructions for the day, he hosted an endless stream of visitors in his study, as cardinals, ministers of his government, heads of various ecclesiastical courts and congregations, diplomats, and assorted visitors and supplicants came to see him.

Before lunch Pius returned to his chapel for a half hour of prayer. He ate at three p.m. at a table covered in red velvet, in a vast, empty hall. Following long-established custom, the pope ate alone, his simple meal lasting no more than twenty minutes. His diet consisted largely of vegetables, favoring beans and fennel flavored with a little salt, as well as asparagus and artichokes in season. He liked his fruit green and drank a small glass of wine. He was especially partial to strong coffee, which he drank all day.

Following lunch, Pius went out with a small retinue of attendants for his daily excursion. Romans became accustomed to seeing him on the streets or in one of Rome's many churches. These afternoon outings sometimes took him beyond the city walls to visit famous ruins and reliquaries of the martyrs or simply to enjoy a walk in the country. After the dour Pope Gregory, Pio Nono was the pope who smiled. Stories circulated of his acts of charity, coming to the aid of a crying boy whose father was in debtor's prison, or taking the hand of a widow and offering help. Then by six p.m. he was back in his palace for more meetings, ending the workday only at ten-thirty at night.[20]

Forty-eight-year-old Massimo d'Azeglio, from a noble Piedmontese family in northwestern Italy, described his audience with the pope in these early months. A partisan of Italian unification but far from a radical, d'Azeglio would soon become prime minister of the Kingdom of Sardinia. After an hour in the waiting room, d'Azeglio was ushered in. Pius sat on a red leather chair, under a canopy, the desk in front of him covered by papers, a crucifix, a pair of reading glasses, two candles, and an oil lamp with a transparent lampshade. D'Azeglio kissed his foot, and Pius stretched out his hand so that d'Azeglio could kiss his ring before the pope raised his arm to invite his visitor to stand. Pius, d'Azeglio thought, was an attractive man. He spoke without a trace of affectation and had a talent for putting his visitors at ease. "I have never seen," reported d'Azeglio, "a man who was more pleasing than this." Pio Nono projected such sincerity both in his words and in his facial expression, thought d'Azeglio, that it seemed impossible to doubt him.[21]

Sharing this benevolent view of the pope, Romans had come to blame the failures of his government on his advisers, the cardinals first among them. Cardinal Gizzi found himself a particular target of the people's ire. By early 1847, the crowds' cries of *Viva Pio Nono!* were increasingly mixed with shouts of "Down with Gizzi! Down with the secretary of state!"[22]

Recent advances in typography had made cheap mass production of printed materials possible, opening the floodgates for newspapers and journals of all kinds. In mid-March 1847, Secretary of State Gizzi reaffirmed an 1825 decree that required all printed materials dealing with matters of morality, religion, or science to be subject to church censorship. In a mild bow toward popular demands for a free press, the updated edict placed laymen on a new board of censorship to review all political writings. Its job was to ensure that nothing be allowed to appear that "directly or indirectly tends to turn people against the acts and men of the government."[23]

If the pope hoped that Gizzi's measures would help him tamp down the political pressure, he was quickly disappointed. New publications proliferated, and Romans kept flouting the ban on popular demonstrations. "Cardinal Gizzi's position is becoming more difficult by the day," observed the Sardinian ambassador, reporting back to Turin. Like many others, the ambassador thought that Gizzi was acting against the pope's more liberal inclinations. "One cannot deny anymore that there is a certain friction between the Pope and the Secretary of State," the Sardinian envoy observed. "Gizzi uses a language that seems to indicate his firm intention of ending the people's demonstrations, but the facts demonstrate the opposite, and the liberal party is continually gaining in importance."[24]

On Easter Sunday the frustrated Gizzi went to see the pope to submit his resignation. Alerted to the cardinal's intentions, Pio Nono took Gizzi into his arms in a warm embrace as he entered his study and begged him to stay. The pope admitted that his tendency to follow his heart rather than his head sometimes created problems, but this, he said, was exactly why he needed a man like Gizzi at his side. Did that mean, asked Gizzi, that the pope would finally begin to heed his advice? Pius assured him he would.[25]

IN THE WAKE OF THE 1831 revolts that briefly drove the cardinal legates from Bologna and other parts of the Papal States, the French had summoned a conference of foreign powers to discuss what was to be done about the tottering papal regime. The Austrians and others all agreed with the French that for the pope to continue to exercise temporal power, he would have to make major reforms. Most important, priests would need to be replaced by laymen as heads of the various government offices. Gregory XVI had done his best to ignore the recommendations, but Europe's diplomats had not forgotten them. With belief in the separation of church and state continuing to spread through the continent, government by priests was becoming an ever more glaring anomaly.[26]

Responding to this pressure, in April 1847, Pius announced the creation of a new body, a Consultative Council. In each province of the Papal States, the prelate in charge would nominate three distinguished residents, from whom the pope would choose one for the council. The council's job would be to advise the pope on matters of public administration and good governance. Romans greeted the announcement with joy, and thousands marched through the streets celebrating the news. The torches they held aloft formed a blazing ring around the fountain in the enormous, circular Piazza del Popolo, where they gathered before streaming down the Corso and on to the pope's palace. Three rockets screamed into the air and exploded, bathing the pope's piazza in their red and white light. Men and women shouted their *vivas*, begging the pope to come out to bless them. The door to the Quirinal balcony finally opened, and the pope appeared. As he raised his arms, silence spread and the people dropped to their knees.

Witnessing these displays of affection, the American journalist Margaret Fuller, then living in Rome, expressed sympathy for the pope's plight. "He is a man of noble and good aspect," she wrote, "who, it is easy to see, has set his heart upon doing something solid for the benefit of man." His task was not an easy one, she pointed out, something Romans did not seem to appreciate. "The Italians," Fuller observed, "deliver themselves, with all the vivacity of their temperament, to perpetual hurras, vivas, rockets, and torchlight processions. I often think how grave and sad must the Pope feel, as he sits alone and hears all this noise of expectation."[27]

The momentum the pope created with these limited reforms proved hard to stop. Once it was admitted, if only tacitly, that the governing arrangements in the Papal States were not fixed by divine will, the whole rationale for ecclesiastical rule risked collapse. The Dutch ambassador observed that the new Consultative Council would only embolden those demanding a popularly elected legislative body of a kind found farther north in Europe. "Italy," he reported, "is undergoing a true moral crisis," as two ideas were taking hold: the right to constitutional guarantees, and the need to drive foreign troops back across the Alps. The pope might attempt halfway measures, concluded the ambassador, but in the end he might find himself fighting a losing battle.[28]

The aristocratic assistant to the French ambassador in Rome offered a similar opinion: "The Pope is very pleased at having had such success, not seeing that the public is craftier than he is and extracts one concession from him after another by their compliments, exactly as in the fable about the fox and the crow." When the crow took a piece of cheese up to a tree branch to eat, the fox, flattering the bird on its beautiful singing voice, got it to open its mouth in song. As the cheese fell from the crow's mouth, the fox eagerly devoured it.[29]

The Papal States, observed Metternich, who had similarly come to doubt that the pope was up to the challenges he faced, were unique, a theocracy. But, he mused, "the world rises up against the very idea of such a government. The Catholic world is based on the principle of authority, while the world does not want such an authority. Religion dictates the equality of men before God and their submission to the authorities, because this is ordained by God. The world wants civil equality and authority based on the will of the people."

Although Metternich was well aware that the long-held justifications for rule by the few were under attack, nothing would deter him from his path. His goal, which he shared with leaders of Europe's other monarchies—from the Russian czar to the king of Naples—was to stop the ever-growing drive for self-government. Protecting the pope's right to rule was crucial to his effort. How could rulers justify their own regimes as divinely ordained if the pope's heavenly mandate were cast in doubt? "The Papal States exist," Metternich told his ambassador, "and their existence is both a social and political necessity." The new pope's goodness had become a potent weapon exploited by those who sought to end the papal theocracy. The political prisoners and exiles whom the pope had freed were now returning to their homeland, intent on overthrowing the old order. The public demonstrations, the newspapers, and the new associations that were sprouting up around the Papal States were their tools. Rather than placating the people, it was becoming ever clearer that each reform the pope granted was simply increasing the popular appetite for more.[30]

IN YET ANOTHER ATTEMPT to put an end to the popular demonstrations, on June 22, 1847, Cardinal Gizzi issued a new edict. While Pius was "firmly resolved to continue on the road of improvement in all those branches of the public administration which may have need of it," the secretary of state announced, the pope was "equally decided on doing so only in a wise and well-considered course, and within the limits marked out by the very nature of the sovereignty and of the temporal government of the head of the Catholic Church." God, in his infinite wisdom, proclaimed Gizzi, had willed the pontiff to exercise temporal power, and so it was his sacred duty "to preserve intact the trust that was placed in him." The pope, he reported, was horrified to see people "taking advantage of the present state of things to put forth and enforce doctrines and thoughts totally opposed to his maxims." While Pius appreciated all the signs of his people's devotion, he now asked "for proof of these praiseworthy sentiments, and such proof should consist," explained Gizzi, "in putting an end to all unusual popular meetings, and to extraordinary popular demonstrations."[31]

Shortly after issuing his new edict, Gizzi met with the ambassador from Turin. The situation, the cardinal told him, was spiraling out of control. Although he would rather cut off his hand, he said, than sign a request to the Austrian emperor to send his army to restore order, he would nonetheless do so if, as he feared, it should prove necessary. Calling on Austrian troops to quell rebellions in the papal lands would, he knew, cause a huge wave of popular anger, but, said the cardinal, he saw no alternative.

The ambassador was taken aback. Such an act, he warned, might well engulf all Italy in a "general conflagration."

"And so," asked the secretary of state, "whom would you have me turn to? Would your king agree to send an armed force to intervene here if it was requested?"

The ambassador had no answer, but he knew the cardinal had no intention of calling on the Sardinian army. It was to Austria that he would turn.[32]

Pius felt trapped. He had reveled in his subjects' love and adulation. He thought of himself as a father to the people and took seriously his role as Christ's vicar on earth. But now it seemed that he could not carry out the responsibility that God entrusted in him as Supreme Pontiff—to protect the special divine nature of government in the Papal States—and at the same time satisfy his subjects' ever-escalating demands for change.

Seeing the pope at a church ceremony on June 30, the Austrian ambassador reported that Pius had the look "of a man who was suffering. People who have not seen him for some time find him looking ten years older. . . . His hair is now covered with gray." There were reports, too, that the stress had triggered new epileptic seizures. Pius was, it seemed, now pondering the unthinkable, wondering whether it would not be better for him to renounce St. Peter's throne and retire in prayer to a monastery.[33]

CHAPTER 3

AN IMPOSSIBLE
DILEMMA

A S THE SUMMER OF 1847 WORE ON, A HELPLESS, AND HAPLESS, Cardinal Gizzi watched while, notwithstanding all his attempts to stop them, demonstrators continued to parade through Rome's streets. Their shouts were taking on an ever more threatening tone. Pio Nono wanted to push forward with his reforms, many Romans believed, but the reactionaries, traitors, and friends of the Austrians who surrounded him were doing all they could to thwart him. Calls of "Death to the pope's evil advisers!" and "Death to Cardinal Lambruschini"—identified in the popular imagination as the ringleader of the conspiracy—were becoming ever more common, unsettling not only the cardinals but the aristocracy and other men of property.

"The law is respected," reported Rossi in early summer, "but the blood is beginning to circulate rapidly in this body that, only a year ago, was as calm and cold as a cadaver." The people and their leaders, he added, "have the ability and the know-how that the government lacks." They could, it seemed, mobilize a crowd on a moment's notice.[1]

In the view of his long-suffering secretary of state, Pius was deceiving himself if he thought he could ever satisfy those demanding change in the Papal States. The liberal party would keep pushing for the removal of priests from power, for a representative system of government, and for freedom of speech. None of these, in the view of Gizzi and his fellow cardinals, was compatible with the divinely ordained governance of the Papal States. "The time might well come," he told the Austrian ambassador in an early July meeting, "when the Pope finds himself re-duced to the painful necessity of calling for Austria's intervention." Lest the ambassador miss his meaning, Gizzi ended their conversation by tell-ing him to be sure to send Metternich "advance notice of the possibility of the request in question."[2]

Around the same time, a delegation of the more enlightened Roman aristocrats met with the pope to offer their advice. Fearful that the dem-onstrations might turn violent, they urged him to create a powerful Civic Guard, composed of the better classes of citizens. The move would have the additional benefit of satisfying one of the liberals' long-standing demands, that the pope replace the foreign mercenary security forces. Pius promised to do so without delay.[3]

Gizzi was horrified. If the pope armed the people, he told Pius, he would regret it. The day would come when he would tire of the people's never-ending demands. When it did, and he belatedly tried to resist, pre-dicted Gizzi, "you will be chased out of Rome with those same rifles that you are now giving them for your defense."

"Signor Cardinal," replied the pope, taken aback, "I have no fear of my people!"

"Don't rely too much on the goodness of your heart!" advised the cardinal. "The people are too fickle." With this last warning, Gizzi re-signed, this time for good.[4]

Feeling ever more isolated, and exhausted from his months of argu-ing with his secretary of state, Pius yearned to have a man at his side he could count on. He scribbled a short note to his cousin Cardinal Gabriele Ferretti:

> Cardinal Gizzi's state of health has led him for a second time to ask to be relieved of his duties. His Successor is Cardinal Ferretti. Come, begin, and doubt nothing, for God is with Us. I bless you.[5]

Ferretti was surely surprised by the news, but he sympathized with the pope's desire to bring the Papal States into the modern era. "He is no great intellect," observed Rossi, in reporting the new appointment to Paris, but, he added, Ferretti was not lacking in courage and was un-questionably devoted to the pope.[6]

When the new secretary of state arrived at the city gate at Piazza del Popolo late on the evening of July 15, a celebratory crowd surrounded his carriage. The despised Cardinal Gizzi was gone, and his replacement, many Romans believed, was a man much more sympathetic to their cause. As the new secretary of state made his way down the narrow Corso, residents emerged from the buildings carrying lanterns to light the way. "Long live Ferretti!" they shouted. "Justice! Throw the bastards out!"[7]

FOREIGN OBSERVERS DIFFERED IN their view of what was happening in Rome, but they all agreed on one point. Amid the mass of the *popolani*—the little people of Rome—who crowded the city streets and took part in demonstrations of affection for the pope, one man stood out. Angelo Brunetti, known by his childhood nickname, Ciceruacchio,* was forty-five years old when Pius IX became pope. He was born in one of the city's poorer neighborhoods, his father a blacksmith. Illiterate, he went to work at an early age as a carter, bringing wine from the surrounding hills down into Rome. Bright and ambitious and with an outsize personality, he soon saved up enough money to buy his own horse and wagon and began carrying hay, grains, and other goods into the city. Before long he had several horses and many wagons.

Each of Rome's fourteen neighborhoods—called *rioni*—had its own *capopopolo,* the leader determined not by any formal process but by popular designation rooted in the nightly discussions in local taverns where men gathered. The most valued traits were generosity, good judgment, and the ability to mediate local disputes. Ciceruacchio had all these qualities and more, so that he became, in effect, the *capopopolo* of all Rome. Of average height, he had broad shoulders, a powerful chest, a large neck, and thick, muscular legs. He was always the first to pitch in when heavy lifting was needed. His bright blue eyes sparkled with life, and he had a large nose, long curly brown hair that gathered above his ears, a bushy moustache, and a goatee. He spoke not Italian but the Roman dialect, *romanesco,* as did all the long-established families of the city's poorer

---

* Pronounced CHEE-chay-roo-AH-kee-oh.

classes. Good-humored and compassionate, he was quick to anger but just as quick to forgive and forget. After his rise to prominence, he dressed with a certain elegance. He was known for his courage, yet he was not immune to the sense of inferiority that plagued Rome's little people. In the presence of members of the educated elite, the larger-than-life Ciceruacchio seemed to shrink a little. Of the wider world he knew very little.

The man, it seemed, was everywhere. In December 1846, when the

The popular
hero
Ciceruacchio

streets of the city were flooded, he was on a boat handing out food to the hungry, and then in May he organized a huge popular celebration of the pope's birthday, arranging with all of Rome's flower vendors to reduce the price of bouquets so that, on the pope's appearance at his Quirinal balcony, a blizzard of flowers would swirl through the air. The next month, for the first anniversary of Pius's election as pope, Ciceruacchio masterminded yet another outpouring of popular affection, before defusing a dangerous conflict between Rome's carters and the men from the hills who drove their own carts into the city.

On a visit to Rome, Massimo d'Azeglio, the Piedmontese nobleman and fervent Italian patriot, was among those struck by Rome's man of the people. "These days," he wrote, Ciceruacchio "is Rome's first citizen. He exhorts, pontificates, he keeps the peace." In the unrest that surrounded Cardinal Gizzi's last days as secretary of state, Turin's ambassador in Rome chronicled the key role played by the *capopopolo:* "It was he, one must confess, who contributed more than anyone in damping down the threats of death that were being shouted by the crowd, and likewise it was he who must be credited for maintaining public order."[8]

A visiting Britisher, the twenty-seven-year-old Florence Nightingale, later to achieve fame as the founder of modern nursing, was also impressed by the ubiquitous *capopopolo*. "I dare say you know who Ciceruacchio is," she wrote her family. "He can hardly read or write, sells wood to all the English, has not genius, but a commonsense almost amounting to genius, and can turn the whole Roman people round his fingers. He is a sincere, good man, and means well both by the people and the pope." She was impressed as well by his modesty: "The princes send for him, court him and invite him, but he will not go."[9]

IN THE SUMMER OF 1847, just a few months before Nightingale's visit, Ciceruacchio was responsible for an unprecedented sight in Rome involving the city's Jews. Rome's Jews had long been packed into narrow, dark, and unhealthy streets, the eight gates of their ghetto locked each night by a Christian guard whose salary they were required to pay. Prohibited from owning land or exercising professions, excluded from the city's schools and hospitals, they practiced the most modest occupations. Few sights were more common in Rome than the shabbily dressed, long-bearded Jew, carrying a gray sack over his shoulder, shuffling along the road, looking up at the windows of the buildings as he passed, calling out *Roba vecchia?* "Old clothes for sale?"[10]

When, in the wake of the December flood, the pope first allowed a limited number of Jews to move out of the ghetto, tensions with Christian neighbors grew. For centuries the church had vilified the Jews as Christ-killers who should not be allowed to have contact with Christians. The sudden appearance of Jewish-owned stores and homes outside the ghetto provoked insults and threats of violence, not least from the Christian merchants who resented the new competition.

In early July, eager to keep the peace and inspired by the talk of fraternity and equality, Ciceruacchio organized a picnic on a large field. Two thousand people streamed in to share the food and wine. Speakers told of the dawn of a new era, ushered in by the goodly Pius IX, who wanted all Romans to live in harmony. The time for the old superstitions had passed, announced one speaker. Jesus on the cross had urged forgiveness, so even the Jews should be forgiven their sins.

The next day five men from Trastevere, the neighborhood just across the river from the ghetto, made their way into the Jewish quarter. They invited the men they met there to join them at a tavern outside the ghetto walls. Some of the more intrepid Jews went along and shared in the wine. The following day several Roman tanners, in festive mood, ventured into the ghetto. Worried about their intentions, the Jews asked them what they wanted. To this their leader replied, "We've come to show you that we are friends . . . and pay no heed to those who want to harm you!" The scene of the previous night was repeated, the more adventurous young men of the ghetto joining their fellow Romans in a tavern, then walking together along the Tiber back toward the ghetto, singing praises to Pius IX. It seemed as if a new era had indeed arrived.[11]

Prince Metternich had no objection to the liberation of the Jews from Rome's ghetto, but he was increasingly alarmed by the pope's loosening grip over his kingdom. It would be foolhardy, he decided, to wait until revolution exploded in the Papal States before sending troops. It was time, he thought, for a show of force.[12]

In the early morning hours of July 17, 1847, a contingent of the Austrian imperial army, consisting of eight hundred Croatian infantrymen and sixty Hungarian cavalrymen, crossed the Po River at the northeastern border of the Papal States and marched into the old walled city of Ferrara. In full battle gear, with flags flying and bayonets affixed to their rifles, they paraded through the streets to the beat of their drummer. While an Austrian garrison had been located in Ferrara since 1815, the unexpected and belligerent arrival of the reinforcements led some to speculate that this was Austria's first step in a planned military sweep through the Papal States. The fact that the Austrians had arrived on the very day people were planning to celebrate the first anniversary of Pio Nono's amnesty reinforced the darkest views of a reactionary plot against the pope. Anti-Austrian slogans began to cover the walls of the Papal States. Clandestinely published pamphlets linked the Austrians to the Jesuits in seeking to bring back the old order. There was, in fact, no conspiracy, but the people were right in one respect. Worried that the feckless pope was playing with fire, Metternich had put Austrian forces in a position to quell what increasingly looked like a revolutionary movement throughout the papal kingdom.[13]

Pius was not pleased. The Austrians had not bothered to warn him of their plans to march into Ferrara. Already under pressure to support Italian independence and to denounce the Austrians' military presence in Italy, he found himself in an increasingly uncomfortable spot.

Count Lützow, Austria's ambassador in Rome, was himself growing ever more alarmed. The local press, he reported to Metternich later in July, was filled with anti-Austrian screeds, and the pope seemed helpless as his authority slowly slipped away. Although Pius had announced that he would not make any further concessions to popular demands, he kept giving ground. The Vicar of Christ, the Austrian charged, displayed "an apathy, an indefensible blindness, pushing away his selfless friends and abandoning himself to the treacherous insinuations of those who . . . seek the loss of his Government, the destitution from Rome of the See of Our Most Holy Religion."[14]

Throughout the Papal States, seditious pamphlets were multiplying, while the shouts in the streets and the slogans scrawled on the walls mixed *Viva il Papa!* with "Death to Austria!" and *Viva l'Italia!* Of these, the last was the most significant. For decades the movement to drive foreigners out of Italy and unify all Italians—the Risorgimento—had been gaining force, fueled by the writings of intellectuals and the meetings of small bands of would-be conspirators, joined in an international network that stretched from Sicily to London. Metternich was unsympathetic. "Italy," he declared, "is a geographic expression . . . devoid of any political meaning." The pope risked becoming the rebels' dupe.

"The Revolution," the Austrian chancellor observed in August, "has taken hold of the person of Pius IX like a flag."[15]

AMONG THE BEST-KNOWN—and most colorful—figures seen on Rome's streets in these days was Charles Bonaparte, the forty-four-year-old nephew of Napoleon Bonaparte. His father, Lucien, younger brother of the French emperor, had combined a love of luxury with fierce adherence to the principles of the French Revolution. Notwithstanding his revolutionary proclivities, Lucien had had a good relationship with Pope Pius VII, who conferred on him an estate at Canino, north of Rome. Pope Leo XII later awarded him the title of prince. Both estate and title would pass down to his son Charles. Raised in Italy, Charles was bilingual in French and Italian, conversant in English, and able to read and write Latin. At age nineteen he married a first cousin, daughter of another of Napoleon Bonaparte's brothers, herself endowed with a sizable fortune. He then moved to the United States to continue his scientific studies, as he was becoming an internationally known naturalist. Back in Italy during the 1831 revolt in the Papal States, he remained loyal to the papacy, judging the then new pope Gregory XVI to be "a good man, with good intentions."

Charles shared with many of Napoleon's heirs an outsize personality, a tendency to violence, and a hankering for the limelight. A year after Pius IX's election, he could be seen proudly walking down the Corso in a Civic Guardsman uniform, short and rotund, with a thick neck and ruddy face. He had joined the Civic Guard shortly after the pope instituted it in July 1847. The tunic, modeled on that of ancient Rome, came down to his knees. Not a few thought his face bore a remarkable similarity to that of his famous uncle, although it was partially hidden under his huge guardsman helmet.

In early September, speaking to the excited crowd gathered at the Caffè delle Belle Arti—meeting place of the most fervent Italian patriots, a colored map of Italy on its wall topped by the motto "Long Live Italy!" and a portrait of Pius IX—Bonaparte gave a short speech hailing both the pope and the cause of a united Italy. He then led a group to Piazza del Popolo, where a large crowd had already gathered to protest

Charles
Bonaparte

Austria's occupation of Ferrara. "Long Live Pius IX!" "Death to the Jesuits!" "Death to the Obscurantists!" the people shouted as the prince egged them on.[16]

Within days of the Austrian troops' arrival in Ferrara, the pope's denunciation of the move appeared on walls throughout the Papal States. Again patriots sang his praises, hailing him as their champion in the battle for Italian independence.[17]

Pius could not help but be pleased by all this praise, yet his pleasure was marred by a nagging doubt. "We know where these people want to lead us," he confided to a Jesuit visitor. "We will satisfy them as far as conscience allows, but if things reach beyond that point as we already predict they will, they can cut me up into tiny pieces, but, with God's aid, we will go not one step further." For Pius there could be no doubt, his first duty was to the church. He must do nothing to weaken it.[18]

Although he sensed the danger of giving in to the crowds' pleas, he seemed unable to stop himself. In early October, little more than a year since his election to the papacy, he announced the creation of a city council for Rome. It would be composed of a hundred members, the majority drawn from the upper classes, but with merchants and men of science represented as well. While the pope would appoint the first members, subsequent selections would be made by the councilors themselves. Metternich greeted news of the pope's latest move with dismay. "Pius," he snapped, "shows himself deprived of any practical mind." The Austrian chancellor attributed the pope's shortcomings to the fact that he had been raised by a family infected by the liberal ideas that Napoleon had brought to the Italian Peninsula. The pope, he thought, had a warm heart but no understanding of what it meant to govern. "If things follow their natural course," Metternich predicted, "he will get himself chased out of Rome," adding a question that before long would be asked throughout Europe: "What will happen then?"[19]

PATRIOTS FROM THROUGHOUT THE peninsula flooded into Rome to see the reform-minded pope everyone was talking about. Among them, in late October 1847, was a thirty-four-year-old law professor from Pisa, then part of the Grand Duchy of Tuscany. Giuseppe Montanelli was already making a name for himself as a champion of a federation of Italian states. He was as enthusiastic as anyone about the pope and eager, as he put it, "to hear the voice of the man whose magic name had so often caused the crowds to tremble and be overcome with emotion."

To catch his first glimpse of the pontiff, Montanelli arrived outside the Quirinal Palace at the hour when Pius came out for his afternoon excursions. "How my heart beat!" he recalled. "Briskly, smiling, [the pope] came down the stairway, and with youthful ease climbed into the carriage. In the way he walked there was somehow something of a warrior, although his face was angelic." Montanelli watched from a crowd of a few dozen people, most, like him, from out of town. When the pope's carriage neared them, they sank to their knees. As he passed, Pius graced them with an affectionate look and raised his hand in blessing.

A few days later, eager to see the pope again, Montanelli attended a mass celebrated by the pontiff in the Quirinal chapel. His description offers some insight into why, among the chants that were now heard in Rome, one of the most frequent was *Pio Nono solo!*—"Pius IX alone!"

All the cardinals were there. I took a good look at them, one by one. I search in vain in those faces for a ray of intelligence, of love. Faces of either imbeciles or of the unhappy. What a face of a hyena Cardinal Lambruschini has! What a sinister figure Cardinal Marini cuts! What a sly fellow Antonelli.

"It was beyond me," concluded Montanelli, "to think Pius IX could have come out of this College of Cardinals!"[20]

A few days later Montanelli was granted a private audience with the pope. The young Tuscan, full of enthusiasm for the Italian cause, told the pontiff that it was not religious devotion that was leading people to shout *Viva Pio Nono!* They were applauding, he said, because of their hopes that he would bring independence, unity, and freedom to Italy.

"This is true," replied the pope. "Indeed, let me tell you that nothing pleases me more than when I hear people in Rome shouting not *'Viva Pio Nono'* but *'Viva il Santo Padre'* [Long live the Holy Father]. Because while the one is a political cry, the other is a religious one. They say *'Viva Pio Nono'* to me. *'Viva il Santo Padre'* they say to Saint Peter's successor."

What was important, responded the young Tuscan, was for the people to see the pope act justly, for in loving Pius IX, they would come to love the church that inspired him.

"This too is true," said the pope, but then he added a discordant note. "Can you imagine that in one Calabrian city," at the southern tip of the Italian boot, "they broke thieves out of jail to shouts of *'Viva Pio Nono.'* Does that not seem," he asked, "a little duplicitous to you?"

"It was this mixture of good humor with a touch of mischievousness, of grace and irony, that made Pius IX so seductive," observed the pope's visitor. He was not alone in falling under the pope's spell. In contrast to the previous pope—an austere, elderly monk who never smiled—here was a warm human being, a vigorous pope who delighted in embracing old friends, a man aware of his own limitations.[21]

AMONG THE GOVERNMENTS PLEASED by the pope's attempts to bring the Papal States into the modern world, few were as enthusiastic as Brit-

ain's. In early November, in an effort to encourage the pope on his reform path, the British government sent a special emissary, Lord Minto,
the sixty-five-year-old father-in-law of Britain's prime minister.[22]

As his British guest entered, on November 8, the pope stood up and
met him in the middle of the room before inviting him to sit down at his
table to talk. It would be the first of several conversations. "The Pope's
manner is most agreeable," wrote Minto in his diary, "his conversation
easy and unrestrained, sometimes almost playful." Minto was impressed:
"I never talked with any one who more completely invited familiar and
unreserved communication, and inspired confidence and esteem."

As the British lord got to know Pius better and spent more time in
Rome, he held to his belief in the pope's goodness, but he also began to
appreciate the difficult position in which he found himself. Neither Pius
nor his secretary of state, noted Minto, was well versed in public affairs.
"The ignorance of every thing beyond the walls of Rome," he observed,
"is almost incredible and they are therefore open to every species of intrigue." While the pope's manner inspired confidence, he added, "I
doubt . . . if he is not wanting a little in the firmness which the present
circumstances of his position require, and his fear of offending the Jesuits and others who are already his bitter enemies leads him occasionally
to risk the loss of his friends and supporters."[23]

Here Minto shared the widespread belief that the Jesuits exercised a
pernicious influence on the pope. The religious order had long been accused of meddling in politics to advance their reactionary ends. The
French government had initially sent Rossi to Rome, in 1845, to protest
the Jesuits' reappearance in France. In the first year of Pius IX's reign,
anti-Jesuit feeling got a boost with the publication of a five-volume work
by Vincenzo Gioberti, a priest and one of the intellectual leaders of the
movement to unify and modernize Italy. His 1843 book, *On the Moral
and Civil Primacy of Italians,* calling for a confederation of Italian states
presided over by the pope, became one of the most influential texts of the
Italian unification movement. At the same time, Gioberti identified the
Jesuits as Italy's greatest enemies. His 1846 book, *The Modern Jesuit,*
continued his merciless attack on the order, portraying it as the source of
all evil, part of an unholy alliance with Austria. "If I had to choose,"
Father Gioberti wrote in an 1847 letter, "between chasing out the Austri-

ans and banishing the Jesuits, I would rather do the latter, because without the Jesuits the Austrians can do little harm and would not last long."[24]

It was in November, too, that the Consultative Council, the pope's concession to the principle of lay government, first met. Although its members were laymen from the upper classes, the pope named a prelate to be its president. That man, Cardinal Giacomo Antonelli, would come to play a fateful role in Pius's papacy.

Although a cardinal, Antonelli was not a priest, for he had never been ordained and so could neither say mass nor take confession. Nor was he an aristocrat like most of the upper clergy. He came from a family of peasant origins that lived in the southern provinces of the Papal States. The Antonellis had grown wealthy, first by acting as agents for large landowners and then as merchants selling animals and agricultural goods. Although as a youth Giacomo showed no penchant for the religious life, his father saw advantages to having a younger son in the church and was willing to pay the fifteen hundred *scudi* per year required to have his son enter the prelature.

Giacomo's career got an early boost thanks to his older brother, whose wife's uncle was a cardinal, but his rapid rise through the papal government was largely thanks to his own talents. Among clergymen notorious for their administrative and financial ineptitude, he stood out as someone who knew how to get things done. He had absolutely no interest in religious questions, but when the conversation turned to financial matters, he became animated, full of enthusiasm for his work in putting the accounts of the Papal States in order. When Pope Gregory died in 1846, the forty-year-old Antonelli was already treasurer general of the Papal States. It was the following year that Pius, grateful to him for helping sort out the disastrous finances of his realm, made him a cardinal.[25]

Although Antonelli was successful, he was far from popular. One foreign observer likened the thin five-foot-nine-inch prelate, with his long yellow-complexioned face, to a bird of prey. "Cesare Borgia and Machiavelli," he wrote, "are united in his disturbing, diabolical person." His legs, observed a journalist, "are mere spindle shafts. . . . His eyes, of a jet black, express intelligence and decision. . . . The lips are very large. . . . A range of large white teeth is at each instant disclosed, which

Giacomo Antonelli

taken in unison with the expression of the eye, does not render the general effect one of overflowing benevolence."[26] Father Pietro Pirri, a prominent church historian, described Antonelli as "cold and calculating, not one to harbor illusions or infatuations." Nor did the other cardinals, put off by his low social origins, warm up to him. Although Antonelli would soon orchestrate the pope's dealings with the world's great powers, he himself had barely ever set foot outside the Papal States.

The cardinal's personality could not have been more different from the pope's. While Pius was emotional, quick to pour his heart out, and often overcome with doubts about whose advice to take, Antonelli had great self-assurance. And while the pope was incorruptible, rumors swirled both about Antonelli's efforts to enrich his family and his clandestine liaisons with women. A popular anecdote recounted how the pope once lit up a cigarette and then offered one to Antonelli.

"You know, Holiness, that I do not have that vice," Antonelli told him.

"You know, Eminence," replied the pope, "that if it were a vice, you would have it."[27]

On November 15, the pope welcomed the twenty-four newly selected members of the Consultative Council to the Quirinal Palace for their opening session. Four of the men had been chosen from Rome, two from Bologna, and one each from the other provinces. Following the pope's remarks, the deputies lined up to kiss his foot and receive his blessing. They then climbed into their carriages and rode to the Vatican for a mass in St. Peter's Basilica. It would take two hours for the carriages to travel the short distance, for the streets, strewn with yellow flowers, and adorned with festive tapestries hung from the windows, were mobbed with well-wishers. Every balcony was packed with spectators, eager to witness the historic event.

Like many of Britain's upper class, the twenty-seven-year-old Florence Nightingale had come to spend the winter in Rome to enjoy the mild climate and see the sights. Nothing she saw in her time there struck her more strongly than the explosion of joy that greeted the opening of the council. "If we live for 200 years," she wrote the next day to her father, "we never can see such another, such an occasion in such a place. . . . It is a day taken out of heaven and put down upon earth." Swept up in the crowd's enthusiasm, Nightingale thought there "was not the slightest doubt" that the new council would "ultimately become a House of Commons, as powerful, as effective as ours." Even the sophisticated French ambassador agreed. The day, Rossi observed in his report to Paris, marked "the funeral of the clergy's political power in Rome. The form will remain, more or less, but the content . . . will be different. There will still be some cardinals, some prelates employed in the Roman government, but the real power will lie elsewhere."[28]

Pius viewed the council differently, seeing it as a way of better learning his people's needs and getting advice from a body of distinguished subjects. The deputies were to advise him on a wide variety of questions, from legal and financial, to economic and military, but it was to be advice only. He would still make all decisions himself. In his remarks at the council's first meeting he did his best to get this message across. "Those who would see in the council that I have created the realization of their own utopias and the seed of an institution incompatible with papal sovereignty," he warned, "are greatly mistaken." Unfortunately, he added, some people, "having nothing to lose, love disorder and revolt, and abuse any concessions." Pius's remarks did not auger well for his relations with the council members. "Clearly," recalled Marco Minghetti, one of Bologna's two deputies to the council, "the pope repudiated any semblance of a constitutional government."[29]

Although Pius thought that he had matters in hand, this view was not widely shared by the high clergy or by the foreign ambassadors in Rome. Censorship remained in place, but the old controls were breaking down. All kinds of publications were flooding Rome's streets, expressing hopes for reform and for the end of clerical abuses. In the place of political parties—which were not so much illegal as inconceivable in the Papal States—clubs were springing up. The previous spring a group of young men, enthusiastic about ending priestly rule in Rome and dreaming of a unified Italian nation, founded the Roman Club. Although they elected a young prince as their president, most of their 350 members were lawyers, merchants, small landowners, and the like. The following year another club, the Popular Club, would be founded, having a less elite, more radical cast. Clubs like these, headquartered in the cafés where men gathered each night, became the first models of open, popular participation in the papal kingdom.[30]

If the pope's remarks to the Consultative Council sparked some doubts, they seemed to put little dent in the pontiff's popularity. Margaret Fuller's 1847 reports from Rome to the *New York Tribune* offered a glowing image of the man all Europe was talking about, the heroic figure who combined deep humanity and humility with a commitment to bringing the retrograde Papal States into modern times.

Pius, Fuller wrote, "has not in his expression the signs of intellectual greatness so much as of nobleness and tenderness of heart, of large and liberal sympathies." In a typical dispatch later in the year, she described encountering the pope as he stepped out of his carriage to take a walk outside the city walls. "He walked rapidly, robed in a simple white drapery, two young priests in spotless purple on either side; they gave silver to the poor who knelt beside the way, while the beloved Father gave his benediction." Seeing that one of the people looked ill, Fuller continued, the pope's face offered the "expression of melting love . . . which assures all who look on him that, were his power equal to his will, no living thing would ever suffer more." Fuller, like many others, would soon turn on the pope, but for now she could hardly have been more smitten: "He has shown undoubted wisdom, clear-sightedness, bravery and firmness; but it is, above all, his generous human heart that gives him his power over his people. His is a face to shame the selfish, redeem the sceptic, alarm the wicked, and cheer to new effort the weary and heavy-laden."[31]

Yet the signs of trouble ahead were not hard to see. "The retrograde or Jesuits party as it is called," reported Lord Minto to London, "still occupy most of the posts about the Palace." They were constantly trying "to alarm [Pius's] very scrupulous conscience with fears of encroachment upon the Papal authority which his duty to the Church required him to maintain unimpaired." "The Pope's head," observed the British envoy, "is less good than his heart, and he is sadly open to intrigue work-

Margaret
Fuller

ing upon his religious conscience." As a result of pressures from the prelates, Minto concluded, the pope had come to distrust the liberals and had decided to resist them.[32] Although Pius felt great affinity for the liberals—for the most part, men of the propertied classes—he did indeed resent what he saw as their constant badgering to move further than seemed right to him.[33]

Where would it all lead? Metternich was convinced that the pope was not up to his task, and perhaps he wasn't. "Warm hearted, with little imagination," observed the Austrian chancellor, "he has since his election to the papacy allowed himself to be entangled in a net from which he is no longer able to escape." But the pope was not the only one who would prove unable to escape the political earthquake that was about to shake Europe. In the end, not only Pius but Metternich as well would be driven into exile, and of the two, only one would return.[34]

CHAPTER 4

PAPAL MAGIC

EIGHTEEN FORTY-EIGHT WOULD PROVE A FATEFUL YEAR FOR Europe, a year of revolutionary violence, of monarchs overthrown and bloody wars for independence. To many, it seemed that an exhilarating new era of Enlightenment had dawned. People would be free to decide on their own rulers, free to say and think what they pleased.

Pius got a hint of the coming drama on the very first day of that year. The previous evening, New Year's Eve, Monsignor Domenico Savelli, his police chief, had come to see him. With a reputation for brutality and widely known as "Monsignor Bulldog"—for his face bore a remarkable similarity to that creature—Savelli was not a popular man. Revolutionaries, he warned the pope, planned to take advantage of the crowd at the pontiff's New Year's blessing to trigger a revolt. Perhaps Savelli even thought this was true, although in fact there was no such plot. He reminded Pius of the recent papal decrees forbidding popular demonstrations. The pope instructed him to be sure that all Romans knew that the policy remained in effect.

"But if they ignore this and persist in assembling," asked Savelli, "what should we do?"

"You have all the necessary means at your disposal," replied the pope.

Eager to assert the government's authority, Savelli ordered Civic Guardsmen dragged out of bed to report for emergency duty, along with the rest of the papal armed forces. In the rainy morning, as torrents of water, mixed with mud, ran down the cobblestone streets, people made their way to the Quirinal for the pope's blessing. To their surprise, they found cavalrymen blocking the palace doors and a large number of police and guardsmen ordering everyone to leave.[1]

The people were bewildered. Why had Pio Nono barricaded himself in his palace? Many, including Lord Minto, thought it was part of a conspiracy by reactionary forces to provoke a violent clash that would justify foreign military intervention. "It is difficult to say how much of these proceedings," Minto reported to London, "may be explained by the negligence, stupidity, and mismanagement pervading every department of the Roman administration; but the existence of a design, by any means, to bring about a rupture between the government and the people, is, I think, beyond all doubt."

On Sunday, January 2, a delegation from the new city council went to see the pope to assure him that there was no danger. They urged him to show himself in public to calm people's spirits. That afternoon, heeding their advice, Pius emerged from his palace into another gray, rainy day.[2]

What followed was described by the French ambassador's assistant as "a truly revolutionary scene, a parody . . . of the French Revolution." The pope climbed into his carriage and, without his usual escort, made his way slowly down the Corso through the main streets of the city. "Three hundred people of the worst type," wrote the disapproving Frenchman, surrounded his carriage, shouting "Death to the Jesuits!" Marching right behind the papal carriage was the popular hero Ciceruacchio, described by the French diplomat as "a kind of butcher turned into a tribune." He carried a huge placard bearing the words "Holy Father, Justice for the People." And so, observed the young diplomat, the Vicar of Jesus Christ made his way back to the Quirinal in a procession that was "half *sans culottes*, half Carnival." No one had witnessed such a humiliating spectacle, remarked the envoy, since 1792, when the Parisian sans-culottes—militants from the poorer classes—forced King Louis XVI to place the revolutionaries' cone-shaped red felt cap on his head in an inspired, if cruel, ritual of degradation.[3]

The dramatic events around New Year's Day had, thought the British Lord Minto, opened the pope's eyes to "the treachery by which he is surrounded." Yet, he observed,

> the virtuous Pope is not of sufficient calibre for his position, that is to say for the position of a Sovereign who has little also than fools and rogues to compose his government, and who chooses to be his own prime Minister. He wishes to make his people happy, to give them a good government, good laws, and all kinds of comfort and prosperity. He wishes above all to be beloved and trusted by them. But then he is resolved that they should hold all these good things solely at his will and pleasure. . . . What he would like is liberal measures and arbitrary rule.[4]

Pius wanted to please his people, and he sympathized with their impatience at the continuing incompetence, corruption, and cruelty of the ecclesiastical government. As an Italian, he was not immune to the emotional pull of the call for freedom from foreign rule in Italy. But surrounded by prelates reminding him of his duty to follow the path laid out by his predecessors, and plagued by self-doubt, he kept sending mixed signals. On January 10, as Pius raised his arms to bless a crowd outside his palace, the pontiff began with words that were music to the patriots' ears: "God bless Italy!" But shortly after becoming the first pope ever to bless "Italy," he added, by way of warning, "Do not ask of me that which I cannot, I must not, I wish not to do."[5]

ON JANUARY 9, a manifesto appeared on the walls of Palermo, Sicily's capital. It would prove to be the first spark in a fire that would burn through much of Europe.

> Sicilians! . . . The protests, the pleas, the peaceful demonstrations have all proved useless, Ferdinando II having shown only contempt for them, and we, a free people, have been reduced to chains and misery. Will we delay any longer in reconquering our legitimate rights? To arms, sons of Sicily, to arms!

The conspirators set the date of the uprising for January 12. On that morning, people began filling the streets, raising a flag bearing Italy's three colors—red, white, and green. The ringleaders hurriedly passed out what few arms they had been able to get their hands on.

The rebels' prospects seemed dim, the sides grotesquely uneven. Only a few hundred poorly armed, untrained insurgents, with little in the way of coordination, faced five regiments of Ferdinand's army, along with royal warships in the harbor and an assortment of castles having heavy artillery surrounding the city, not to mention the city's police force. But the military was not trained for guerrilla warfare, and shot at and assaulted on the city streets, the soldiers quickly fell back. At the heart of the uprising were Palermo's highly politicized artisans, with a long history of revolt, and they had the support of many of the city's poor, who suffered under the brutality of the Bourbon state.

With the king's army in retreat, the insurgents announced a provisional government. Mixed in with their demand for Sicily's freedom from Neapolitan rule were calls for democracy, and scattered among the shouts of *Viva l'Italia!* were cries of *Viva Pio Nono!* Continuing to invoke the pope's name, the rebels would drive the king's army from almost the entire island in the months to come.[6]

With the uprising soon spreading to the mainland, the pontiff began to worry that it might soon reach Naples itself. Meanwhile his penchant for losing secretaries of state was becoming something of an embarrassment. His first, Gizzi, had lasted only a year, and now his second—his cousin Ferretti—resigned, having served only six months. Both had despaired of the pope's need to try to please everyone. Pius's new choice for the position, Giuseppe Bofondi, made a cardinal only the year before, seemed no more likely to succeed than his predecessors, and indeed he would not last very long himself.[7]

The mood in Rome was not helped by the abysmal weather. It had rained for forty days, and the damp city reeked. "Pour, pour, pour again, dark as night," wrote Margaret Fuller on a late January afternoon. "Vegetables are few and hard to have, except horrible cabbage, in which Romans delight." Her nerves on edge from being cooped up, she lashed out at the "wicked organ-grinder" who stationed himself outside her window, hoping for some coins, endlessly replaying the Copenhagen Waltz.[8]

At the end of January, with protests now erupting in his own capital and desperate to placate his rebellious subjects, King Ferdinand of Naples reluctantly announced that he would grant his people a constitution, proclaiming it to be "the general wish of our beloved subjects." The constitution he outlined contained an elected lower assembly—a revolutionary innovation in the monarchy—as well as an upper body whose members he would appoint. Bells rang and celebratory masses were held in churches throughout the kingdom. Farther north in the Italian Peninsula, the news produced great excitement among those pushing for reform. If the Kingdom of Naples, long regarded as the most backward and repressive state in Italy, could embrace a constitution, how could rulers elsewhere refuse to do the same?[9]

To Metternich and those of his circle, news of Ferdinand's constitution came as a shock. "The game is up," wrote Prince Schwarzenberg, who would soon succeed Metternich as Austrian chancellor. "The king and his ministers have completely lost their heads." To this, Metternich replied, "I defy the ministers to lose what they have never possessed." Within weeks both the king of Sardinia, in Turin, and the grand duke of Tuscany in Florence granted constitutions as well, establishing elected legislative bodies and guaranteeing individual rights. The pressure on the pope to do the same was becoming unbearable, and the strain was showing.[10]

Pius had recently appointed the first layman, a Roman prince, to his cabinet as minister of war. Rossi, worried that the situation might soon escape the pope's control, pleaded with him to lose no time in naming other lay ministers to the cabinet. It was crucial, he thought, if the pope was to rally the moderate liberals to his side and isolate the radicals.[11]

THERE WAS NOW NO QUESTION that the nightly demonstrations in Rome were far from spontaneous affairs. Demonstrators carried copies of a printed "Proclamation of the People," which featured the upper-case demand "down with the priest-ministers." It called for a government of laymen, recommending men "most liberal, and most sincerely attached to Italy's cause, which is that of independence and freedom."

"The horrendous threats I heard," recalled the Dutch ambassador, who had gone outside one night to see what was going on, were "shouted by people who seemed to have blood in their eyes and were carrying long knives." Violence was averted only when Prince Corsini, senator of Rome, agreed to take a copy of the proclamation to the pope. The crowd waited impatiently until Corsini emerged from the palace and then surged behind him as he made his way to the Piazza del Popolo. There he mounted the platform surrounding the obelisk at the center of the piazza and told them that the pope had said he would soon reply to their demands.[12]

Two days later the pope's response came in the form of a large proclamation, a papal crest at its top, pasted on the walls of the city. "Romans!" it began. "The Pontiff is not deaf to your desires, to your fears." Over the previous two years, it went on to say, he had shown many signs of his love for his people, as he worked to improve the government within the confines of what his duties to the church allowed. He would continue along the same path. "Oh God in your Greatness!" he declared. "Bless Italy, and preserve your most precious gift, faith!"[13]

Again the pope's mixed messages, rather than keeping everyone happy, as he hoped, succeeded only in making things worse. Romans seized on his "Bless Italy" as a papal blessing for the war for Italian independence. Thousands gathered in Piazza del Popolo to show their support for driving the foreigners out of the peninsula. At five p.m. a hastily assembled procession set out for the pope's palace. Units of Civic Guardsmen marched with their banners, as did sympathetic priests, carrying the white-and-yellow papal flag to which they had added Italy's three colors: green, red, white. Musical bands added to the festivities, playing patriotic songs and odes to the pope. Onlookers crowded the roofs surrounding Quirinal Square. A procession of little children arrived, dressed in miniature Civic Guard uniforms, waving white papal banners.

Feeling beleaguered, Pius summoned his new minister of war, along with the head of the Civic Guard and the commanders of the pontifical army, to meet him in the Quirinal Palace. Asked if he could count on their loyalty, they assured him that he could. Using a phrase he was particularly fond of, Pius told them that he would rather be cut into little pieces than agree to anything that would weaken the church.

He then ordered the door to the balcony flung open. His attendants

Pius IX

carried out a red tapestry and placed it over the railing. A great roar
arose from the crowd, now grown to tens of thousands, as torch-carrying
prelates emerged onto the balcony, followed by a prelate bearing a cross.
Then, to thunderous cheers, out strode the pope himself, with the minister of war on his left and the head of the Civic Guard on his right.
When Pius raised his arms, silence spread through the piazza, and people fell to their knees. "Blessed be the name of the Lord," he intoned in
Latin. His rich, strong voice could be heard across the piazza. In chorus
the crowd responded, "Now and forever." "Our help is in the name
of the Lord," proclaimed the pope. "Who made heaven and earth,"
came the thousands of voices in reply, followed by an oceanic "Amen."

"I pray to God with all my heart to bless you. May this heavenly blessing be on all of you, on all the land, and on all of Italy." Although in blessing "Italy" the pope intended simply to bless the people of the peninsula, partisans of Italian unification again chose to believe he had something else in mind. As the pontiff prepared to continue his remarks, a shout rang out, "No more priests in government!"

Startled, the pope paused. "Some cries which are not from the people, but speak only for the few," he said, "I cannot, I must not, I will not allow."

"Yes, yes!" came the shouts from the crowd, moved by their love for the pope.

"On condition that you keep your promises to me," the pope continued as the people again quieted, "I bless you with all my soul."

At these words, it seemed that the fifty thousand people below would have gladly given up their lives for him. "He's an angel, he's an angel," someone shouted. People's faces, wet with tears, radiated joy.[14]

The pressure on the pope to grant a constitution kept growing. The British foreign minister and prime minister both wrote to Lord Minto to advise support for this path. Minto, with his firsthand view of the turmoil in Rome, was of a different opinion. Granting the constitution now, he feared, would "teach the people the bad lesson that they must threaten to obtain what they desire."[15]

The Dutch ambassador, longtime deacon of the foreign diplomatic corps in Rome, shared Minto's view. He, too, worried that the pope's vacillations and endless concessions to the demands of the crowd were undermining his authority. The similarities to what had happened in the early days of the French Revolution, he observed, were impossible to miss. Then, too, the king had been forced to accept a constitution limiting his powers, amid growing outbreaks of popular unrest.[16]

The pope's mood at the time can be judged by a conversation he had with the man he had recently appointed minister of commerce, Giuseppe Pasolini, a thirty-three-year-old moderate. In his first conversations with the pope, Pasolini recalled, Pius kept returning to his chagrin at his subjects' lack of appreciation for all the good he had already done for them. "What ingrates!" said the pope. Did people not appreciate how far he had already gone in bending church orthodoxy to please them? Another side to the naturally warm, generous, gregarious pope so beloved by his people had begun to emerge. This sense of indignation would only increase, as would the flashes of ill temper for which he would later become famous.[17]

ON FEBRUARY 22, DEMONSTRATIONS against King Louis Philippe erupted in Paris. Brought to power in 1830 by a revolt against the conservative reign of Charles X, Louis Philippe had cast himself as a more liberal king. His constitutional monarchy featured an elected assembly dominated by wealthy bourgeoisie. But economic crises, the growth of an industrial proletariat, rising prices for basic food, and the spread of new socialist and utopian ideas ate away at the French king's popularity. Students organized the first protests. With encouragement from left-wing parliamentary deputies, and helped by sympathy from the National Guard, the demonstrations quickly grew and were joined by large numbers of workers. When initial efforts to quell the protests led to the massacre of scores of protesters, the demonstrations turned into a full-scale revolt. Within days the king fled the country, and a provisional government was formed.[18]

Pius IX initially saw the French revolt as a personal vindication. Had he followed the cardinals' advice and rejected reform, he was convinced, he would have suffered the same fate as Louis Philippe. "That is what happens when you try to govern with force rather than with love," the pope told various visitors over the next month. But Pius was unduly optimistic or perhaps simply obtuse. "As to the poor Pope," observed the British foreign minister, "events have gone too fast for such a slow sailor as he is."[19]

The news from Paris spread panic in Vienna, where the rich rushed to withdraw their money from the banks. On March 13, in the face of large antigovernment demonstrations in Vienna, Prince Metternich resigned. The man who had dominated the continent for so many decades was forced to flee in disguise, heading for refuge in England. Large crowds of protesters filled Vienna's streets, demanding freedom of press and freedom of conscience. When a student leader, haranguing a crowd of supporters in the courtyard of the government palace, was arrested, his enraged compatriots pushed their way through the outnumbered defenders, smashing windows and wreaking havoc. On the other side of the city, protesters tried to seize the armory but were repulsed by the troops, leaving a trail of dead bodies in the streets.

As night fell in Vienna, demonstrators called on supporters to place candles outside their windows. As windows having no candles were being smashed by rocks, the papal nuncio judged it prudent to place candles on his own windowsills. Two days later, when the emperor agreed to provide the people with a constitution, thousands of demonstrators gathered outside the nuncio's palace. His initial fear over the crowd's intentions dissolved when, mixed with shouts of "Long live the emperor!" he heard "Long live Pius IX!"[20]

THE POPE DECIDED THAT, distasteful as it was to him, he had no choice now but to grant a constitution. Informed of the decision, Cardinal Bofondi, having become secretary of state only two months earlier, told the pope he would serve no longer. He refused to be party, he said, to the dismantling of church authority in Rome.

Needing to find yet another secretary of state, Pius decided to appoint Cardinal Giacomo Antonelli, a man he felt he could trust to stay with him regardless of what the future held. With his fourth secretary of state in less than two years, the pope formed a new government, composed of nine laymen and only three prelates.[21]

Pius entrusted the task of drafting his constitution entirely to clergymen. While it shared some features with constitutions promulgated in Naples, Turin, and elsewhere in Europe, it was unique in attempting to marry elective government and civil rights with continued theocracy. There would be an upper chamber, whose members would be appointed by the pope, and an elected lower house, or Chamber of Deputies, but there was a third, higher body as well. "The Sacred College of Cardinals, electors of the Supreme Pontiff," the constitution declared, "is the pope's indispensable Senate." And, of course, since not even the cardinals could constrain the pope under the top-down ideology of the Catholic Church, no action could be taken without the pope's approval.

Pius knew that constitutional government—and the civil rights that accompanied it—were incompatible with the doctrine of divinely ordained rule. Freedoms of speech, of assembly, and of the press went directly against centuries-old church teachings. In crafting his constitution, the pope had done his best to protect the prerogatives of the papacy and of the church hierarchy. But in granting it, he had nourished expectations among his people that their rights would be like those in other constitutional states. In granting a constitution, he was helping to feed a fire that he would not be able to contain.

The announcement of the constitution in mid-March produced a great outpouring of joy. As word spread, thousands filled every inch of vast, sun-drenched Quirinal Square, pleased, no doubt, after months of torrential rain in Rome, to be outside. When, preceded by a cleric bearing a large cross, Pius walked out onto his balcony, the thrill of the huge adulatory crowd was enough to sweep away his doubts, if only briefly. Every roof for as far as he could see was filled with excited spectators.

That night bands played in every corner of Rome and led festive marches through the brightly lit streets. Thousands of voices joined in odes of praise to the pope. Over the following days, more and more Romans appeared on the streets with tricolored Italian ribbons proudly displayed on their jackets. But the signs of the trouble ahead were not hard to see, as shouts of *Viva Pio Nono!* were increasingly accompanied by cries of "Death to the Austrians!" and "Death to the Jesuits!"[22]

Again fearing that he was losing control, the pope ordered a new message pasted on the city's walls. For the first time, he directly raised the possibility of using force against his own people: "Romans, and all those who are children and subjects of the pope, listen one more time to the voice of a father who loves you," he began. Rome, he reminded them, was the seat of the Church of Jesus Christ. "We invite and urge all of you to respect it, and never to provoke the terrible anathema of an outraged God, who would cast his holy revenge against those who would assault his Anointed ones." Should the disturbances continue, Pius warned, "we intend to rely on the loyalty of the Civic Guard, and all the forces that we have provided to maintain public order."[23]

As ROMANS WERE CELEBRATING their new constitution, the northeast of Italy—the Kingdom of Lombardy-Veneto, part of the Austrian

Empire—erupted in revolt. In Venice, insurgents drove out the Austrian troops and proclaimed the rebirth of the Venetian Republic. The uprising in Milan that month proved bloodier. The *milanesi* erected barricades and fought in the streets, facing fourteen thousand Austrian troops under the command of eighty-two-year-old General Joseph Radetzky. After five days of urban warfare—soon dubbed the Five Glorious Days—the Austrians retreated, and the rebels announced the formation of a provisional government. With the rest of Lombardy and Veneto also rising up, Radetsky withdrew his troops to a line of forts stretching from Mantua to Verona, midway between Milan and Venice.[24]

The vast Austrian Empire seemed on the verge of collapse. The first three months of 1848 had shaken Europe's rulers: to the north, revolt in Vienna had sent Metternich into exile; to the east, the Hungarians were demanding their own representative government; and to the south, not only Venice and Lombardy but Tuscany, too, were in revolt. In France, the monarchy had been overthrown and a republic proclaimed; in Berlin and in the Rhineland, revolution had broken out; in Frankfurt, hundreds of delegates had gathered in assembly to call for universal male suffrage and the unification of the many German states and principalities into a single German nation. Sicily was in open revolt, and King Ferdinand had been forced to grant a constitution for the Kingdom of Naples, as had King Charles Albert in the Kingdom of Sardinia.

News of the uprisings in Milan and Venice electrified Rome. The battle to drive the Austrians out of Italy had begun. People filled the piazzas and jammed the Corso. Church bells pealed, and Castel Sant'Angelo's cannon boomed. Rioters converged on Palazzo Venezia, home of the Austrian embassy, where they leaned ladders against the massive front door and went to work tearing off the Reichsadler, the coat of arms bearing the image of the Austrian two-headed eagle. Perched atop a ladder, a burly worker with a bushy beard crawled behind it, ax in hand, chopping it free, as his companions below pulled on the chains they had thrown around it. The crest soon came clattering down. People kicked and swore at it. They embraced one another and cried: "A miracle!" "A godsend!" They attached the double-headed eagle to the tail of a donkey and dragged it down the Corso as onlookers jeered and little boys ran alongside, hurling mud. Arriving at the Piazza del Popolo, at the other end of the Corso, the crowd applauded as the revelers placed the Reichsadler on a makeshift funeral pyre, where the ever-present Ciceruacchio helped feed the flames.[25]

The next day, March 22, Cardinal Antonelli, newly appointed secretary of state, sent a circular to Rome's entire diplomatic corps, expressing the pope's "bitterness and indignation" at the violation of the Austrian embassy at the hands of "an insubordinate multitude." Anarchy, or something close to it, now reigned in the capital of Christendom.[26]

All Italy seemed to be rising up. With the widespread clamor to drive the Austrians from the peninsula, King Charles Albert, the Sardinian monarch—who ruled over northwestern Italy—saw an opportunity to extend his kingdom to the northeast. He was, after all, the leader of the Italian state with the strongest army, and he shared a long border with Austrian-held Lombardy.

The king was a peculiar man, melancholy, reserved, austere, and ill at ease on social occasions. "There is no reckoning with certainty," observed the British foreign minister the previous October, "upon the future conduct of a man so unstable in the mind as the King of Sardinia." Rumors that the monarch spent his free time cutting out paper images of saints and playing with toy soldiers did not help.[27]

If there was one way for the king to inspire devotion in his subjects, it was to cast himself as military hero of Italian independence and champion in the battle against foreign armies. The time to fulfill Italy's destiny, he declared, had come. On March 24 he led his troops into Lombardy, aiming, he said, to defend its recent liberation from the foreigners. In doing so, he added, he trusted "in the aid of that God, who is clearly with us, of that God who gave Pius IX to Italy, of that God who in His wisdom has put Italy in a position of creating itself."[28]

As Charles Albert moved into Lombardy, invoking the pope to justify his cause, the Romans called for volunteers for an army to be sent north to aid their Italian brethren in expelling the Austrians from Lombardy and Veneto. Nearly forty thousand people flocked into the Colosseum on March 23, where the patriotic Barnabite monk Alessandro Gavazzi harangued them with calls for a "holy crusade," describing the Austrians as "a thousand times more barbarous than the Muslims." "Let

King Charles Albert of Sardinia

us carry the cross on our chests," the monk exhorted them, "just like the Crusaders!"[29]

Succumbing to popular pressure, Pius reluctantly agreed to allow the army and the new corps of volunteers to march north. He appointed Giovanni Durando as their head, giving him instructions to remain just north of Bologna, on the papal side of the border with Lombardy. Before they marched from the city, the soldiers gathered outside the pope's window, where they received his blessing. As they headed north, they sang a hymn to Pio Nono:

> *The arms are ready*
> *At Pius's signal*
> *Sent by God*
> *To save Italy*
> Viva Pio Nono!
> Viva l'Italia!
> Viva l'unione!
> *Libertà!*[30]

In authorizing the army to head north, the pontiff was simply acceding to what he felt powerless to prevent. Painfully aware that his hold on Rome was slipping away, he hurriedly prepared a secret document that offered instructions to the cardinals on holding a conclave in exile, should he die outside the Eternal City.[31]

The Roman Club, composed largely of professional men, along with some aristocrats, had become a center of anti-Austrian agitation in Rome. The members now sent the pope a plea. "The Italian peoples," they declared, "are all children of the same family" and should be gathered into a single nation. They urged the pope to summon an all-Italian parliament to meet in Rome under his leadership. "Blessed Father," they pleaded, "in this time in which all the powers of the earth are failing, in this sublime reordering of European nationalities, only one power survives." The pope alone represented God on earth. He had the opportunity to add "new splendor to the papacy and to religion . . . giving back to Rome its moral and civil primacy not only in Italy, but in Europe and the world."[32]

Awaiting a new attack from the powerful Austrian army, Milan's defenders sent Pio Nono their own plea for support. "The great cause of Italian independence, which Your Holiness has blessed," they wrote, "has triumphed in our city as well. . . . In your Name, Most Blessed Father, we prepare to fight. We have written your Name on our flags and on our barricades."[33]

The Sardinian king added his own request, asking Pius to publicly declare his support for the efforts to drive the foreigners from Italy. The pope demurred. "If I could still sign my name as 'Mastai,' " he responded, "I would take a pen, and in a few minutes it would all be done, because I too am an Italian. But I must sign as Pius IX, and this name obliges me to bow down before God and beg for his infinite Divine wisdom to guide me." Pius's remarks mirrored a conversation he had had with the Austrian ambassador a year earlier. "As an Italian," Pius told him, speaking of those clamoring to drive the foreigners from Italy, "I can't blame them. As sovereign, I desire good neighborly relations with Austria. As pope, I ask God for peace between the nations. But," he added, "above all I must do my duty." Torn by the conflict between his feelings as an Italian and his deep sense of duty as pontiff, and between the pleas of the Italian patriots and the calls to his responsibility as pope from so many of the prelates around him, Pius was growing ever more miserable. Worse was yet to come.[34]

WHILE SOME CLERGYMEN WERE swept up in the patriotic fervor, the Jesuits, the popular symbol of reaction, widely identified with the Austrians, struggled to defend the old order against the movement that, ever since the French Revolution, had threatened to undermine the marriage of church and state. The pope himself had mixed feelings about Jesuits, fed in part by his lack of sympathy for Jan Roothaan, their austere, humorless, Dutch superior general. Aside from the personal contrast between the gregarious, emotional pope, quick to smile and even to joke, and the reserved, methodical, ever prudent Roothaan, Pius was annoyed by the Jesuit leader's strident opposition to any hint of reform. In all his attempts to move his kingdom into modern times over the past months, he had faced the Jesuits' hostility. Opponents of the idea of progress, their members drawn disproportionately from the families of the elite, they had become a thorn in his side.[35]

In February, mobs chased the Jesuits from the two major cities of the island of Sardinia. Similar scenes were soon repeated on the mainland. Rome had remained one of the order's last refuges, but after earlier resisting the pressure to drive the Jesuits from the capital of Christendom, the pope, in late March, told their superior general he could no longer protect them. Their continued presence in Rome, he feared, would only provoke more public unrest. "The reins of the government," complained Roothaan, the Jesuit leader, "have fallen into the mud."[36]

Although he drew no small pleasure from being hailed from Sicily to the Alps as Italy's great hero, Pius was well aware that the movement invoking his name was far from religious in inspiration or intent. What could he do? He was not one to spend much time reflecting on history or on questions of political philosophy. He had never had much of an intellectual inclination, and his seminary education—not in any case geared to critical examination of the church's guiding assumptions—had been limited. It would not occur to him that there was a fundamental incompatibility between his role as spiritual leader and his role as king. For Pius, the pope-king was a position created by God, so such a question could not even be posed. That modern times would undermine rule from on high, that people would no longer be happy being told to leave government to the priests, were questions that he did not think deeply about. He had gone long past the point at which he thought the concessions he'd granted were wise. Fearful that bowing to the latest popular demands would only further undermine the church's authority, he did his best to hold out against them, but he was fighting a losing battle.

In his defense, Pius confronted a problem his recent predecessors had not. For decades, the Austrian rulers had dominated the Italian Peninsula, serving as the bulwark of the old order, and the main guarantor of papal rule. But now Metternich was in exile, the Austrian army was in retreat in northern Italy, and Austria's emperor, Ferdinand, was feebleminded. France, that other great Catholic power, had become a republic, and its sympathy for a state viewed as a client of its archrival, Austria, far from certain. To many it seemed that a new era was dawning in Europe, requiring the church to adapt to the times. Casting the church's lot with the Austrian Empire—as every pope since the Restoration in 1814 had done—was now not without risk. Pius was out of his depth. Only God, he thought, could save him.

CHAPTER 5

THE TIDE TURNS

T HE POPE COULD NOT HAVE BEEN ANY CLEARER. GENERAL Durando, commander of the papal forces now camped at the northern border of the Papal States, was not to cross into Austrian territory. But the general—formerly an officer in the Sardinian army—refused to stand idly by as the historic battle to drive the Austrians from Italy was waged. He ordered his troops to move north, issuing marching orders that cast their cause as a holy crusade:

> As long as Italy is unable to defend itself, it is condemned by the Austrian government to plundering, rape, the cruelties of a savage militia, to fires, to murders, to total ruin. It has seen Radetzky make war on the Cross of Christ, knock down the gates of the Sanctuary, send horses in to profane the altars, violate the mortal remains of Our Fathers. . . . The Holy Pontiff has blessed your swords, so that together with those of Charles Albert you move ahead to exterminate these enemies of God and of Italy and those who insult PIUS IX, profane the Churches of Mantua, murder the Lombard monks. . . . Such a war of Civilization against the barbarians is not only national but above all Christian.

Huge letters spanned the bottom of the marching orders: "GOD WILLS IT." As the men set out, each wore a tricolored cross on his chest.[1]

Fearful of antagonizing Austria, the Catholic state that had long been the Holy See's greatest defender, the pope did what he could to limit the damage, sending word to his nuncio in Vienna to tell the Austrians he had never authorized his army to leave papal territory.[2]

As the pope's message was making its way to Vienna, the nuncio there was writing his own report back to Rome. Word that the papal army was poised to attack the Austrians in Lombardy, along with news of the Austrian imperial crest's desecration in Rome, had roiled public opinion in Vienna. With menacing crowds gathering outside his residence, the nuncio reported, he had taken the precaution of having the papal coat of arms removed from above his door. The church's enemies, reported the nuncio, were fanning people's anger in their efforts to undermine it in Austria.[3]

The pope's lay ministers, in an attempt to calm him, agreed to draft a statement on his behalf, published in the government's newspaper, the *Official Gazette*, on April 10. "The marching orders given to the soldiers in Bologna," it read, "express ideas and sentiments as if they were given from the mouth of His Holiness. When the pope wants to make known his sentiments, he does so himself, not from the mouth of some subordinate."[4]

Although the statement put some distance between the pope and the men who were going into battle in his name, it was a less-than-ringing denunciation of the war of independence. In this, it reflected the ministers' sympathy with that war. Feeling that he had to do more, Pius decided to prepare a formal statement of his own to let the world know where he stood.

Learning of his plan, the Tuscan grand duke's ambassador went to see him. He urged the pope to include language reflecting "his aversion to the Democratic Spirit that threatens to undermine public order," a plea that caused Pius to reflect unhappily on all the reforms he had recently granted. Somehow his eagerness to please, coupled with the contrast between his own gregarious personality and that of his austere predecessor, had led to the widespread belief that he wanted to bring the principles that governed the Papal States into harmony with modern times. But he had never intended to change what he thought it was his sacred duty to uphold: rule of the papal lands by the pope and the church hierarchy. If King Ferdinand hadn't granted a constitution, and if Austria hadn't sent its troops into Ferrara, he explained to the ambassador, he would never have gone beyond his decision to create a merely advisory Consultative Council. But in short order he had granted a constitution, and now his own army was poised to attack Austria's despite his opposition. No army of the pope had taken part in a war since early in the previous century, and that war had been aimed against the Muslim Ottoman Empire. The idea that papal troops would wage war against a Catholic people, and a government that had long been the popes' most important defender, would have seemed, until the dizzying events of the previous months, inconceivable.[5]

On the morning of April 17, Pius met with the group of cardinals who advised him on matters of state. He posed a simple question: Should the papal government join the war against Austria? They were unanimous in their reply: It should not. Pius then posed a second question: If he did not agree to join in the war, how was he "to prevent the ruinous consequences that this would provoke from the party that now predominates in all of Italy?" To this, the cardinals answered simply, if not helpfully: *Deus providebit,* "God will provide."[6]

ROME'S HALTING MOVE FROM its medieval ways to modern times was, perhaps, most evident in the fortunes of its Jews. Popes had long insisted that they be closed up in ghettos, but following Rome's winter flood, Pius had allowed individual Jewish families to petition to live outside the ghetto walls. And pressure was mounting to provide more relief to the Jews, for the equality of all people before the law, regardless of religion, was one of the liberals' core beliefs.

On March 29, Charles Albert, at his war camp in Lombardy, signed a decree emancipating the Jews of his kingdom. They thus became the first Jews in Italy to enjoy equal rights with their Christian neighbors. Excited by the news, the head of Rome's Jewish community asked that a copy of the Sardinian king's decree be published in the city's official newspaper. The minister of internal affairs, to whom the request came, refused, fearful that its publication would enrage the clergy.[7] But only a few days later the government—dominated by liberals, yet with the apparent support of the pope—issued its own decree, removing some of the restrictions on the Jews. One of these was the practice of locking the ghetto gates each night. That evening ax-wielding Jewish men, together with some of their more sympathetic Christian neighbors, reduced the ghetto gates to rubble. It was the first night of Passover—the celebration of the Jews' liberation from Egyptian slavery.[8]

The next day a manifesto appeared on the city's walls, titled "The Gates of Rome's Ghetto Thrown to the Ground." Above it were the words *Viva l'Italia, Viva Pius IX, Viva Charles Albert.* It described the destruction of the ghetto gates as the most recent act of the enlightened and beloved pope.

In France, the foreign minister, champion of the newly proclaimed French Republic, was pleased to receive news of these reforms. The ending of the ghetto, he wrote his envoy in Rome, "is a measure much in harmony with the principles of religious tolerance and civil equality, and thus we applaud it whole-heartedly." But not everyone was as happy. How was it, asked some in Rome, that at the same time as the Jesuits were being driven from the capital of Christendom, the Jews were now being treated so well? For well over a millennium the church had blamed the Jews for the death of Jesus and taught that, as a result, they were condemned by God to wander the earth in misery. Priests had long warned their parishioners that Jews posed a great threat, eager to defraud and impoverish their Christian neighbors, and commanded by their most sacred text, the Talmud, to drain Christian children of their blood in order to make their Passover matzo. The notion that Jews should be treated no differently from Christians was, to many, a radical idea, associated with the sacrilegious teachings of the French Revolution.[9]

THE GOVERNMENT MINISTERS, LEARNING that the pope planned to make a major statement on the war, were nervous. They had not seen him for several days, as he had moved into the Vatican for Holy Week. On April 25, two days after Easter Sunday, the ministers, joined by Cardinal Antonelli, sent the pope a long plea, urging him to use his address to announce his support for the war. The insurrection in Lombardy, they argued, had triggered tremendous patriotic enthusiasm in the Papal

States. The people's drive to take up arms was unstoppable. To disown the army as it marched under his banner would be disastrous.

The ministers acknowledged that, from a religious point of view, war was evil, but in this case, they told Pius, it was the lesser evil. If he wanted to preserve the Papal States, joining the war against the Austrians was his only choice. Should he come out against the war, they warned, "You cannot imagine without feeling a chill of horror what reactions, what disorders would occur."[10]

Pius felt trapped. "You certainly know as well as I do, my dear Count," he told the Dutch ambassador that evening, "that my authority grows weaker each day."

> Do these men, whose overwrought patriotism knows no limits, not want me to declare war? Me, head of a religion that wants only peace and harmony? Well! I will protest. Europe will know the violence that they have done to me, and if they want to continue to force me to do things that my conscience rejects, I will withdraw . . . to a convent to weep there over all the misfortunes of Rome, given over to all the disorders of this anarchy. . . . For the rest, wherever one turns, no way out appears on the horizon. It is all the hand of God, which reaches visibly over us and, when He wants to teach us lessons, they are great and they are terrible.[11]

Why Cardinal Antonelli agreed to sign the ministers' letter pleading with the pope to join in the war remains something of a mystery. He had been present at the cardinals' meeting on April 17, and there is no indication that he opposed the advice they gave the pope. Nor was Antonelli among the small number of high-ranking prelates who were known to be sympathetic to the liberal cause. If he had any firm political principles of his own, it is not clear what they were. He had been close to the reactionary Pope Gregory, to whom he owed a great deal, but then had had no trouble adapting to his role mediating between the pope and the liberal lay ministers of his government. In his meeting with the ministers he suggested that the pope had not yet made up his mind, but that same day he had written the nuncio in Vienna informing him that the pope would soon announce his decision to remain neutral.[12]

In the end, the ministers would learn of the pope's decision only on Saturday, April 29, when they read his statement in the city's official newspaper. Pio Nono's remarks came in the form of an allocution, a formal address given by the pope, seated on his throne, at a private meeting—a "secret consistory," in the language of the church—of the Sacred College of Cardinals. Even those who suspected that the pope would disappoint the partisans of Italian independence were taken aback by his combative tone. He began with a long denunciation of those "enemies of the Catholic religion" who would spread the "calumny" that he supported the violent efforts aimed at driving the Austrian army out of Italy. Lest "some unwary and more simple men" believe such wicked tales, said the pope, he wanted to set the record straight.

Events in upper Italy had inflamed the passions of people throughout the peninsula, he acknowledged, but he had issued "no other command to our troops, sent to the border of the papal territories, than that they should protect the integrity of the Papal State." His fateful words followed: "But when now some desire that we, together with the other people and sovereigns of Italy, should undertake a war against the Germans,* we have at length thought it our duty to . . . clearly and openly declare that this is wholly abhorrent from our counsels, seeing that we . . . regard and embrace with equal paternal earnestness of love, all tribes, peoples, and nations." To this the pope added a rather plaintive note: "But if, amongst our subjects, nevertheless, they desist not, in what manner finally shall we be able to restrain their ardor?" He went on to warn against the "crafty counsels . . . of those who would that the Roman pontiff should preside over some new Republic, to be formed of all the people of Italy." To the contrary, advised the pope, all of Italy's peoples should "firmly adhere to their sovereigns."[13]

The allocution marked the turning point in Pius's papacy, for it made clear the incompatibility between the pope's roles as universal spiritual leader and as monarch of the Papal States. It also marked the end of the myth of the liberal, patriotic Pio Nono that had flourished since shortly after his ascension to St. Peter's throne. The Sicilians had revolted

---

* In the Papal States, Austrians and Germans were both indifferently referred to as "Germans." The German nation-state would be founded only some time later.

against the Bourbon monarchy with the pope's name on their lips. The Sardinian soldiers battling the Austrians in Lombardy had invoked the pope, as had the men of the Papal States who had rushed north to help drive the foreigners from the peninsula. Now Pio Nono stood exposed as the retrograde champion of the existing regimes, the friend of the Austrians. "Pius IX," reflected one of the leaders of Italian unification, "was made by others and was unmade by himself. Pius IX was a fairy tale conceived to teach the people a truth. Pius IX was a poem." Those who had cast the pope as the champion of an independent Italy, free from foreign rule, the man of God who would bring an end to rule by the priests in the Papal States, had imagined a pope who had never existed. A very different pope—and a very different myth—was about to be born.[14]

There to steer the unsteady pontiff through his transformation from Italian national hero to traitor was Cardinal Antonelli, "master," as the pope's great Jesuit biographer, Giacomo Martina, would put it, "of the double game." "Readiness to dissimulate and to pretend, the ability to avoid openly taking a position, the preoccupation with maintaining his own control in any eventuality," observed Martina, "constitute some of the salient traits of the cardinal's moral physiognomy." Eager to prove indispensable to the politically adrift pope, but not yet sure where events would lead, the cardinal had thought it prudent to keep on good terms with the liberal ministers as long as he could.

Although to the ministers Antonelli posed as a friend of Italian independence and an enemy of the Austrians, in fact it appears that it was Antonelli who took Pius's own first draft of the allocution and removed from it the kind words for Italian national aspirations that he had originally written. He changed its tone from paternal benevolence and even sympathy for the national desire to drive the Austrians from the peninsula, to unbridled condemnation. Although the pope could not have been entirely comfortable with Antonelli's changes, he by now was painfully aware that his sentiments as a patriotic Italian and his desire to please his subjects were interfering with his duties as Supreme Pontiff. In Antonelli he saw a much-needed check on the impulses of his heart.[15]

Marco Minghetti, then the pope's minister of public works, later to become one of Italy's first prime ministers, remembered the moment he first read the pope's address. "There was no longer any doubt. It was the victory of Europe's reactionary and clerical party over Italy and over the liberal party." That evening the lay ministers handed in their resignations. True to form, Antonelli expressed his regret at not being able to join them, citing his vow of ecclesiastical obedience. "He didn't stop complaining about Pius IX," Minghetti recalled. "Indeed, even more impertinently than we, he blamed him, through his indecision, for leaving us in this big mess, and shaking the flap of his priest's cassock, he bemoaned the fact that he was not, as we were, free to resign."[16]

Because the original text of the allocution was in Latin, it was only the following day, Sunday, April 30, that the news of what the pope said spread through Rome. People flooded the cafés, clustering around the men who held in their hands copies of the paper with the text of the pope's allocution. As the pope's words were read aloud, shouts of anger and stupefaction filled the air. Adding to people's outrage were their fears about what would happen to the young men they knew who were then fighting under the pope's banner in Lombardy. Should they be captured, they would now be treated not as enemy combatants but as outlaws, to be taken out and shot.

As shock turned to action, Rome edged closer to the brink of open revolt. The leaders of Rome's clubs called an unprecedented joint meeting. On the evening of May 1, fifteen hundred members packed into the main room of the Merchants' Club, which had been founded the previous year in a palace on the Corso. The motion to be debated was whether papal rule should be ended and replaced by a new provisional government. An immense crowd gathered outside. Inside, the club members stood arrayed in a huge semicircle, as five of their leaders, sitting at a raised table, debated what was to be done. A small honor guard headed by Ciceruacchio stood to one side. The mood was one of expectancy, a feeling that the people were finally about to decide their own destiny.

In the end, the motion to install a provisional government failed. In its place, the club members decided to send one of their leaders, Count Terenzio Mamiani, an amnestied returnee from political exile, to demand that the pope form a new government composed entirely of laymen. It must, they insisted, be committed to reform and be free to decide whether the Papal States should join the war for Italian independence.[17]

As the people poured out of the building, they saw uniformed, armed Civic Guardsmen everywhere. The guardsmen had wrested control of Castel Sant'Angelo and the armory at Porta San Paolo from papal soldiers and taken up positions at the other gates of the city as well. Fearing for his life, the forty-six-year-old Cardinal Della Genga, former archbishop of Ferrara and a widely reviled reactionary, tried to escape, but an angry crowd spotted his carriage and forced him out. He was saved only when a group of more levelheaded Civic Guardsmen rushed to the scene and escorted him back to his palace. It was a humiliation the cardinal would not forget, and the next year he would have ample opportunity to take his revenge.[18]

For the pope, the signs of revolt were but new proof of his folly in heeding popular calls for reform. He had authorized the formation of the Civic Guard—drawn from the educated classes of the population—over the objections of many prelates, including his own secretary of state, Cardinal Gizzi, who had resigned in protest. Many of these guardsmen, infected by the raging patriotic fever, had marched north with General Durando, literally singing odes to their beloved pope. Now they felt betrayed.[19]

Ciceruacchio, the popular hero who had so long sung the pope's praises, was among the many who now turned against him. He led his followers through the streets as they shouted their displeasure. Those members of the pope's regular army and police remaining in the city—the best army units having left for the fight up north—were proving no match for the combination of Civic Guardsmen and an enraged public.

ALTHOUGH HIS MINISTERS HAD warned him, Pius was surprised by the violent reaction to his allocution. On the morning of the thirtieth, he called them in to ask them to reconsider their resignations. "True, I rejected the war," said the pope, "because I am pontiff, and as such I must look on all Catholic peoples with equal affection and as my children." But this did not mean he was personally unsympathetic to the Italian cause. The pope, who had little understanding of constitutional government, could not understand why his ministers were resigning. "You are not responsible for my allocution," he told them. "You did not sign it.

And besides, if I am your sovereign, if I have confidence in my ministers, why would you want to disobey me?"[20]

Feeling some obligation to the pope and recognizing the danger of a complete breakdown in public order, the ministers agreed to stay in the Quirinal Palace while Pius put together a new government. Cardinal Antonelli was pleased to have them there, hoping that their presence would protect him from the angry crowd outside. In the hours they spent together, he regaled them with a description of his impressive collection of precious stones and minerals and complained that the pope had misled them all.

"You are the lucky ones, for you can leave," said the cardinal, distinctive among the laymen in his black cassock. "Ah! Pius IX will never take me back into his service!" he added. "If he commands me as pontiff to do something, I will obey, because my ecclesiastical vow obligates me to, but as prince, no, I won't stand with him again!" It seemed that there were no limits to the cardinal's duplicity.[21]

In an effort to restore order, Pius issued a new proclamation, convinced that if his subjects knew that he personally sympathized with the Italian national cause, they would calm down. His message appeared on Rome's walls on May 2. "We are opposed to a declaration of war," explained the pope, "but at the same time we recognize that we are incapable of restraining the ardor of those of our subjects who are animated by the same spirit of nationality as other Italians." Yet even on this occasion, Pius could not resist venting his frustration. After all the ways he had shown his benevolence toward his people, and all the times they had shown their love for him, how was it that they were now repaying him with bloodshed and threats? "Will this," he asked, "be the reward that a sovereign pontiff should expect for the many acts of love he has shown to his people?"[22]

His new statement did nothing to quell the unrest. Seeing no alternative, Pius agreed to the clubs' demand that he form a new lay ministry headed by someone of their choosing, and so on the afternoon of May 2 he called in Terenzio Mamiani and asked him to lead it. Mamiani had returned to Rome only a few months earlier following more than fifteen years in exile in France.[23]

The next day the pope decided to try another approach. He addressed a letter directly to the Austrian emperor, pleading with him to put an end to his bloody battle to retake Lombardy and Veneto and to let go of the empire's Italian lands.[24] Hoping to placate Charles Albert as well, he sent the king a copy of the letter and had Antonelli accompany it with a letter of explanation. "In his allocution," wrote the cardinal, "the Holy Father did not in any way express himself against Italian nationality. He only said that as prince of peace and common father of all the faithful, he could not take part in war, but that he did not see how he could stop the ardor of his subjects." His plea to the Austrians was of course doomed from the start, for it was folly to think that Vienna would abandon its claims to Lombardy and Veneto to extricate the pope from the impossible position in which he found himself.[25]

"It is clear that a war is being waged against the temporal dominion of the Church," wrote the pope in a May 5 letter to a trusted young prelate, "but it is a great comfort to me to know that the Church itself was always at its most glorious in times of persecution." Pius felt secure in his faith in God but much less so about whether he had made the right decision regarding the war against Austria. All the foreign ambassadors had complained of his tendency to waffle, which was nowhere more on display than in the aftermath of his allocution rejecting the war for Italian independence. On May 9, apparently in the hope of getting theological support for overturning his earlier decision, Pius contacted twelve prominent theologians. He was moved to write them, he explained, by the unrest that had swept the Papal States following his allocution. Anarchy and even civil war now threatened. "In order to avoid the above-described evils, which might easily occur," he asked them, "could and should the Holy Father take an active part in the war being waged against Austria to win Italian independence?"[26]

From the way Pius phrased the question, his preference for a positive response seemed clear, but ten of the twelve theologians answered in the negative. If he was hoping for justification to join the patriotic cause, he would not find it there.

An envoy from the Duchy of Modena, visiting Pius at the time, was struck by how distressed he seemed. His subjects, the pope complained, did not understand him. "But," said the pope, "I am not any the less at peace in my mind as a result, nor do I love Italy any the less, Italy which, after religion itself, has always been what I care most about." As he spoke these words, recalled the diplomat from Modena, Pius's eyes moistened, and his voice thickened with emotion. After a moment, he regained his composure. "I hope that all will work out for the greater glory of God . . . and that the clouds that now darken the horizon will give way to the majesty of the sun."[27]

To the foreign diplomats who visited him, Pius admitted that he had lost control of his kingdom. Among those who heard the pope's litany of woes, the Dutch ambassador voiced a common sentiment in Rome's diplomatic corps, predicting that Pius would prove unable to long resist popular pressure:

> His heart is so good, and in the end so Italian, he has such great need of being surrounded by the love and confidence of his sub-jects, he attaches such a great value to being greeted by their ap-plause, that I would not be surprised to see him, one of these days, act in ways that, little by little, will undermine the effect of his allocution of April 29.[28]

With the men of the papal army, shouting *Viva Pio Nono,* battling the Austrians in the northeast, the pope was in a ticklish position. Meeting with him on May 7, an envoy from the patriots in Venice put it this way: "We have from Your Holiness both a word"—the pope's recent allocution—"and a fact"—the papal army's entry into combat. "For what reason," asked the envoy, "should we renounce the fact in order to hold to the word?"

"They wanted to go. . . . I wasn't able to hold them back," protested the pope.

"We would believe such a thing of a prince who was not loved and not strong," replied the Venetian. "If you had firmly ordered them not to go, they would not have gone, and so we believe that Your Holiness's inaction is tantamount to an express command to fight for the Italian cause."

To this, the pope could respond only with a nervous smile. Allowing the troops to go off in his name had been a mistake, but it had reflected not only his feeling that he could not stop them but his own ambivalence as an Italian not wholly immune to the national cause.[29]

Desperate to find a way out, Pio Nono sent an emissary to King Charles Albert to ask that he incorporate the men from Rome into his own army, giving them proper military status. This would offer them a way to fight for the national cause without directly implicating the pope; it would also give them official combatant status in case they should be captured. In a mid-May address to his troops, General Durando cited this papal request and chose to interpret it as a papal blessing for their prosecution of the war against Austria, simply the pope's latest effort to cement his alliance with the Sardinian forces. "Long live Independence and Italian Union!" called the general. "*Viva Pius Nono! Viva Charles Albert!*"[30]

In the wake of the pope's allocution, Milan's provisional government sent an aristocrat as its envoy to Rome to implore him not to abandon the battle for Italian independence. Meeting with Pius on May 13, the envoy argued that joining the war against Austria was, in fact, the only way to preserve conservative rule in Italy. Should the efforts to create a strong constitutional monarchy uniting northern Italy under King Charles Albert fail, the result, he warned, would not be a return to the old status quo. Rather, people would turn to the only alternative available for a land free from foreign control, namely "a super-democratic, revolutionary republic that would turn all of Italy upside down."[31]

Still, the pope's allocution of late April had found favor among some. "It was as though it had been brought down to me by an angel for it could not have reached me at a more opportune moment," observed the greatly relieved nuncio in Vienna. He rushed to have the pope's text translated, then published in all of Austria's important newspapers. It made, the nuncio reported, a "most excellent impression."[32]

THE ALLOCUTION MIGHT HAVE made an even greater impression in Austria had the government's attention not been elsewhere. Huge student demonstrations in Vienna in mid-May led to new concessions from the emperor, including universal male suffrage and a single-chamber parliament. But the unrest only grew: fearing for their lives, the emperor and his court fled to Innsbruck. Thousands of workers joined the students in Vienna, building barricades and battling the imperial authorities for control. Over the next few months, while the battered Habsburg monarchy plotted its revenge from Innsbruck, the radicals ruled over the Austrian capital.[33]

In Naples, King Ferdinand likewise sat precariously on his throne. In mid-April the Sicilian rebels had named a provisional government, declared the end of the Bourbon dynasty, and announced their intention to create a constitutional government of their own. In an effort to win popular support, Ferdinand had earlier announced that he was sending some of his troops north to join the Italian national cause against the Austrians. His proclamation, affixed to the walls of Naples, had featured at the top the words *Viva Pio IX*. Having sent the troops in a moment of panic, Ferdinand leaped at the chance offered by the pope's April 29 allocution to change course. He recalled his army from the north and dissolved the recently formed parliament and National Guard. Proclaiming a state of siege in mid-May, he unleashed a fierce wave of repression.[34]

While the Neapolitan king was dissolving his parliament, the Papal States held a vote for its Chamber of Deputies, one of the two chambers mandated by the pope's new constitution. A moderate liberal sentiment pervaded the Upper Chamber, whose members, mainly rather modest aristocrats from the provinces, the pope had appointed. The deputies—aristocrats, large landowners, and a smattering of professionals—ranged from the liberal to the more radical. Pius viewed the chambers as advisory, their proposed laws and policies to be considered by the cardinals and by himself, but members of the two chambers saw their role very differently. In their view, they were at the heart of a new system of constitutional government meant to replace priestly rule. If some of the seeds of the coming disaster had been planted by Pius's disavowal of the papal army as it entered northern Italy, others were sown by the convening of these two chambers.[35]

In a two-month period, the pope's kingdom had been radically transformed. A constitution had been granted, an elected Chamber of Deputies established, and a papal army—against the pope's wishes—was poised to do battle against the Austrian Empire. Reporting for the *New*

York Tribune, Margaret Fuller, perhaps the first woman to serve as a foreign correspondent for a major American newspaper, captured the abrupt change in people's view of the pope. While some in Rome cried "traitor" and others "imbecile," she wrote, the Romans' overriding feeling was of loss, of grief, not unlike the feeling of losing a father. The previous year she had portrayed Pio Nono in the warmest tones. Now she offered a very different image: "Italy was so happy in loving him. . . . But it is all over. He is the modern Lot's wife and now no more a living soul, but cold pillar of the Past."[36]

The pope felt ill used. Eager to make life better for his subjects, he had agreed to the Consultative Council of talented laymen, yet he had never questioned the divinely ordained nature of his role as pope-king. His was an enlightened, paternalistic despotism, under the authority of the church hierarchy. As an Italian himself, he had clearly shown his people his sympathy for an Italy free of foreign armies, and he had hoped to find a way to persuade the Austrians to leave Lombardy and Veneto peacefully. Why could people not understand that as pope he was pastor of all the faithful and so could never lead his people into war against other loyal sons of the church?[37]

On May 17, the new provisional government of the Duchy of Modena—the duke having recently been overthrown—sent an envoy to see the pontiff. Pius quickly turned the conversation to what seemed to be becoming his favorite subject, his people's ingratitude. His voice grew louder as he allowed himself a moment to vent his frustration.

"But we must have patience," said Pius, as he calmed down. "I am not letting this leave me with less peace of mind, nor allowing this to make me wish any the less for Italy's well-being." As he said these words, his eyes moistened and his voice thickened with emotion. Composing himself after a few moments, the pontiff assured the envoy that all would work to the greater glory of God. The sun would soon return. Or so, he said, he hoped.[38]

CHAPTER 6

FENDING OFF
DISASTER

THE FUTURE WAS ANYTHING BUT CLEAR. DESPITE ALL THE POPE had done to try to stop them, the men of the papal army had now joined the battle against the Austrians. Throughout Europe, the old monarchies had either fallen or faced widespread revolt. Pius himself had, grudgingly, granted a constitution. But far from calming the public, his concession had only triggered further demands.

Romans followed the news from northern Italy with great excitement. The people of Lombardy and Veneto had held plebiscites, voting to join Charles Albert's Kingdom of Sardinia. In early June, news reached the Eternal City that papal forces, in alliance with the Sardinian army, had defeated the Austrians at Vicenza. The bell atop Capitoline Hill woke Romans from their sleep, the cannon of Sant'Angelo boomed, and the bell towers of Rome's many churches joined in, creating such a din that several of the city's infirm died from fright, and forty-two women miscarried, or so it was reported. But the celebration was short-lived, the news of military victory tragically mistaken. In fact, on June 9, the Austrians had massed forty thousand men and 150 heavy guns around Vicenza and attacked Durando's lightly equipped and poorly trained papal army of ten thousand. After taking heavy losses, Durando had surrendered.[1]

In Rome, Pio Nono's hold over his government was growing ever weaker. When Terenzio Mamiani, the new prime minister, brought the pope the text of his planned opening address to the Chamber of Deputies, Pius crossed out many objectionable passages but at the chamber's opening session, Mamiani gave the address as he had originally written it. When the newspapers reported that the pontiff had reviewed the speech in advance and approved it, Pius informed the nuncios what had really happened.[2]

The battle of wills continued as both the upper and lower chambers

Terenzio Mamiani

passed resolutions backing the war against Austria. Then in late June, when the pope refused to recognize the authority of the new lay minister of foreign affairs, insisting that all such matters be in the hands of the cardinal secretary of state and the nuncios, Mamiani handed in his resignation. Pius could not have been more eager to rid himself of his irksome prime minister, but his efforts to find someone more to his liking, without triggering popular revulsion, proved fruitless, and so Mamiani continued in office. Making matters worse, his fifth secretary of state, Cardinal Anton Orioli—who had been appointed less than a month earlier, resigned, saying that he was not up to the job. Only after two other cardinals turned the pope down did the sixty-eight-year-old Giovanni Soglia agree to fill the post. He would not last much longer than Orioli.[3]

IN MID-JUNE THE NEW FRENCH ambassador arrived in Rome. The sixty-one-year-old scion of one of the oldest houses of the French nobility, Duke François Harcourt seemed an odd fit for the new French Republic. Unusually short, his voice harsh, his disposition restless and prickly, he was not especially popular among his colleagues. "Everything is against him," the papal nuncio in Madrid had reported when Harcourt was posted there, "not excluding his face."[4]

The duke soon began sending Paris alarming accounts of the pope's tenuous hold on power. The prelates who surrounded the pontiff, he wrote, were a narrow-minded lot, devoted to the Austrians, and enemies of reform. The great majority of Romans, the illiterate *popolani*, had long been emotionally attached to the pope and had taken little interest in matters of state. The pressure for reform and for Italian independence came mainly from Rome's small middle class. For the most part, these were moderates who, while pressing for long-overdue reforms, sought to leave the pope in place as head of state. But they were being pushed to an extreme by the demands being made through the city's clubs, many of whose most active members, charged Harcourt, were not from the Papal States at all but were refugees from other parts of Italy. Rome's aristocracy, noted the French ambassador, was weak, and while it was for the most part open to moderate reform, it had little influence.

Harcourt's initial reports received little attention in Paris, for its streets were then soaked in blood. On June 23 rebellious workers, protesting the government's recent moderate turn, had erected barricades, and three days of savage fighting had followed. While pleading for peace with the rebels at the barricades at the Place de la Bastille, the archbishop of Paris was shot dead. Five thousand insurgents died, as did fifteen hundred policemen and soldiers. In crushing the revolt, the government arrested fifteen thousand men and deported thousands to the new French colony of Algeria.[5]

THE MEMBERS OF ROME'S newly elected Chamber of Deputies were, for the most part, men of means who hoped to drive the Austrians out of Italy and forge some kind of Italian unity. To them, the radicals—who threatened to undermine the social hierarchy along with the political order—were just as distasteful as those who opposed any reform. "A reactionary party definitely exists," observed one of the moderate deputies in early July. "On the other side is a party of anarchists and fanatics." The problem the pope faced was that these men, to whom he had previously turned for support and advice, now felt that he was abandoning them.[6]

Among the "fanatics," none was more vocal than Charles Bonaparte, Napoleon's nephew. In relentless pursuit of the limelight, Bonaparte rarely let a session of the chamber pass without offering his opinions, and no one was more bellicose in calling for military action against the Austrians. Bonaparte, wrote one of its members, "has become the buffoon of the chamber." Or as another member put it, telegraphically, "Inexhaustible loudmouth, incredibly opinionated, lacking in principles."[7]

The standoff could not last much longer. Pius had repeatedly made clear his opposition to joining the war against Austria, but the government ministers favored war, and the two legislative chambers had voted to fund it. Fearful that more forceful action would trigger open revolt, Pius dared not act more aggressively. The result, observed the Dutch ambassador, was that "everyone is acting as if the temporal Sovereign, absolutely shorn of his authority, exists in form only."[8]

Tensions in Rome ratcheted up further in mid-July, when someone intercepted a letter the secretary of state had sent to the nuncio in Vienna and posted copies of it on the walls of Rome. While partly written in numeric code, it spoke clearly of the pope's lack of confidence in his own ministers and told the Austrians to ignore what they said. Indignant, Mamiani rushed to see the pope and demanded that he publicly deny the authenticity of the letter, but Pius refused. The cabinet members handed in their resignations, but lacking other options, the pope refused to accept them.[9]

The pressure Pius felt to join the war against Austria soon grew even greater. On July 14 seven thousand Austrian troops had crossed south into the Papal States and marched into Ferrara, demanding provisions from the papal government to resupply them before they returned north to confront Charles Albert's army. Patriotic passions in Rome now reached a fever pitch. "These words, 'Italian independence,' 'Italian nationality,'" reported the Dutch ambassador, "are on everyone's lips here." Furious with the Austrians for putting him in an impossible position, and with his Italian patriotic sentiments provoked, the pope lashed out. "In the end," he warned, "they are going to force me to have to do something myself." Here, it seemed, was the invasion of papal territory that Pio Nono had cited as a pope's only grounds for waging war, but after his initial fit of temper passed, Pius confined himself to sending a letter of protest to all of Europe's governments. The Austrians ignored it.[10]

In the north, Charles Albert was proving to be an inept military commander, and his army suffered a humiliating defeat at Custoza, midway between Milan and Venice. Much to the consternation and outrage of Italian patriots in Lombardy and Veneto, the king sued for peace. In early August he agreed to the restoration of Austrian rule over northeastern Italy. Only Venice still held out.[11]

Rome remained rudderless. "A conspiracy has been hatched," began the remarkable message the cardinal secretary of state sent to the nuncios across Europe in late July. It was a plot aimed at stripping the pope of his sovereignty. "The force of the current government has entirely disappeared. . . . Everyone in the world knows that the current minister is entirely in disagreement with the pope." Pius wanted to form a new ministry, but the radicals were organizing public protests to hamper his efforts. Papal rule hung by a thread.[12]

With emotions running high, both the upper and lower chambers voted to mobilize military forces to fight the Austrians for Italian independence, even though, without Charles Albert, the pope's army alone stood little chance of success. When Pius refused to give his approval, Mamiani resigned, this time for good. The pope posted copies of a *motu proprio*—a "letter in his own hand"—on the walls of Rome urging calm, but angry protesters tore them down. The rumor spread that if the pope would not back the war effort, the Civic Guardsmen would remove him from the Quirinal Palace and take him to the St. John Lateran Basilica. There he could fulfill his duties as bishop of Rome and spiritual leader of the world's Roman Catholics and leave the governance of the Papal States to others. The pope, remarked the Sardinian ambassador, was now "everywhere being treated with contempt."[13]

The Austrian military presence in the Legations—the northernmost portion of the Papal States—was a fuse waiting to be lit. In early August, the people of Bologna drove Austrian troops out of the walled city. When the news reached Rome, thousands of people poured into the streets to celebrate. "One would truly think," observed the French ambassador, "that one was taking part in a comedy, and I truly fear that in this country people are incapable of doing anything else."[14]

If Harcourt thought it a farce, Jules Bastide, the French foreign minister, was taking recent events very seriously. He was most worried by the prospect that Austria, France's archrival, would take advantage of the chaos to spread its influence in Italy. When he learned of the fighting in Bologna, Bastide informed both the pope and the Austrian government that any attempt by Austrian troops to occupy the rest of the Papal States would be regarded as a casus belli, grounds for war. The French would not tolerate Austria extending its hold on the Italian Peninsula.[15]

Meeting in mid-August with a French diplomat who was passing through Rome, the pope again lashed out at his ungrateful subjects. "The people whom God has entrusted to me have only an indirect interest in the current war," he explained. "I allowed the enrollments, the sending of volunteers, I authorized the defense of our territory. But here," complained the pontiff, "people only know how to shout, how to hurl slanders in the street, in the newspapers, in the clubs, in the assemblies. The people pay me back only with their ingratitude. . . .

"Ah!" said the pontiff, as he brought the audience to an end, "forgive me for my emotion. I can't hide it. Never has a pope or a sovereign been more miserable than me."[16]

THE PREVIOUS DECEMBER, in a sign of the widespread enthusiasm generated by the new pope, President James K. Polk had asked the U.S. Congress to establish diplomatic relations with Rome. The United States had had a consul there since the late eighteenth century, but any moves to appoint an ambassador had been blocked by the Protestant majority. Sharing the president's enthusiasm for the reform-minded pope, Congress voted the necessary funds to send a chargé d'affaires, an envoy only a step below full ambassadorial rank.

Jacob Martin, the man selected for the post, reached Rome in early August, when news of the Austrian victory over King Charles Albert was still fresh. "Rome," he reported, is "in the greatest agitation, and threatened with riot if not revolution." Noting that he had endured a long and stormy transoceanic crossing, he added that he had arrived "at a season when even the most acclimated think it hazardous to encounter the scourge of the malaria." The pope soon agreed to meet him, taking him by the hand and telling him how pleased he was that the United States had agreed to establish diplomatic relations with the Holy See. Martin expressed his government's pleasure at the reforms the pope had initiated. "The interview was to me," the American reported, "a very pleasant one, and impressed me vividly with that benevolence of character and gentleness of demeanour for which Pius IX is proverbial."[17]

Martin's fears for Rome's malarial season proved tragically justified. His first report to the American secretary of state turned out to be his last. The next report Washington received arrived a week later and came not from Martin but from his assistant. "Sir," it began, "it becomes my painful duty to inform you of the death of J. L. Martin." The new ambassador had died that morning. He had been in Rome less than a month.[18]

In mid-August, casting about for support, Pius wrote to General Louis-Eugène Cavaignac, president of the new French Republic, asking for a few thousand French soldiers to help him. Cavaignac refused. If, the general explained, the pope was asking for help in driving the Austrian army out of Italy, he was asking too much. France did not intend to get involved in the Italian war. If, as seemed more likely, the pope wanted the troops to help repress outbreaks of violent protest in the Papal States, such a task—more suitable for a police force—was beneath the dignity of the French army. In any case, Cavaignac added, it went against France's policy of not interfering in the internal affairs of other countries. The pope was on his own.[19]

While the pope was desperately trying to attract foreign aid, Charles Albert, the Sardinian king, was looking to the pope to help him. A proud, reserved man, the king was already dreaming of revenge for the humiliating defeat he had suffered at the hands of the Austrian army. In late July he turned to Antonio Rosmini, a fifty-one-year-old abbot and highly respected church intellectual, to be his special envoy to the pope. Rosmini came from a noble family in Austrian-ruled northeastern Italy, and in his many publications he had urged the church to come to terms with modern times. A few months earlier the pope himself had begged Rosmini to come to Rome. The abbot had refused, citing the anarchy in Rome and his feeling that he would be of little use to the pope.

This time, although far from enthusiastic, Rosmini agreed to see if he could do some good. In early August he went to Turin to meet with Vincenzo Gioberti, the patriot-priest turned government minister whose books calling for an Italian federation under the pope and denouncing the Jesuits had been so influential. The goal, Gioberti explained, was to persuade the pope to help form a league of Italian states aimed at driving the Austrians from the peninsula. Rosmini met with Pius on August 17 and spent the next two months in Rome trying to sway him. To liberal champions of Italian independence, Rosmini was a hero, the patriotic abbot who had the pontiff's ear.[20]

WITHOUT A FUNCTIONING GOVERNMENT, Pius badly needed to find someone who could help him steer his chaotic Papal States out of the morass into which they had fallen, someone who could stand up to the fanatics who now seemed to own the streets, someone who could help bring the deputies into line. One name kept coming up: Pellegrino Rossi. Although Rossi had lost his position as ambassador with the fall of the French monarchy several months earlier, he had remained in Rome. In many ways, he would be an odd choice. The former ambassador was distrusted, if not despised, by the cardinals for his liberal politics and his earlier writings, some of which had been put on the Index of Forbidden Books. It did not help that Rossi's initial mission in Rome, in 1845, was to negotiate the banishing of the Jesuits from France, or that his wife was a Protestant.[21]

Antonio Rosmini

Nor was the French government pleased by the rumors of Rossi's possible appointment. This was, after all, the man who had until recently been the ambassador of the now-deposed French king. Harcourt, who had replaced Rossi, asked indignantly how he could be expected to deal with a head of papal government who was "a Frenchman whom my government fired, and all this without ever consulting me?" But if Rossi was a "Frenchman," he was an unusual one, having been born and lived in Italy well into adulthood, then serving in the Swiss legislature, before moving to Paris and accepting a university chair in political economy.[22]

The pope announced his new government in mid-September. While it was in theory presided over by the secretary of state, it was in fact led by Pellegrino Rossi, who was named both minister of internal affairs—in charge of the police—and minister of finance. "You need a body made of iron," remarked Rossi, "not to fall sick in these unhappy times." He vowed to do all he could to strengthen the papal government.[23]

Rossi went to see Harcourt and assured him that, far from being hostile to France's new republican government, he had expressed his support for it from the beginning. Harcourt remained skeptical but advised Paris that under the circumstances it might be best not to oppose Rossi's appointment. "Not only the cabinet," wrote Harcourt, "but the whole country is in a state of dissolution." There had been no government ministers for the previous six weeks, and what government there was seemed powerless to deal with the crisis it faced. Neither the pope nor the deputies seemed to have the least notion of what was involved in representative government. The police chief had thrown up his hands, saying he lacked the means to do his job. "More complete anarchy," remarked the French ambassador, "would be impossible to see." Under such conditions, he asked Paris, did they really want to tell the pope that France would oppose the appointment of the only man he thought could save him?[24]

Given the state of anarchy enveloping the country, Rossi's task was immense, made all the more so by the lack of men of stature for him to rely on. As Harcourt, the French ambassador, reporting on the members of the new papal cabinet, put it, "All these individuals are but satellites circling around the planet Rossi and have been chosen with this in mind."[25]

While Rossi began his work, Rosmini, the abbot representing King Charles Albert, met with various foreign envoys in Rome in an effort to generate support for an Italian league. Rosmini initially conceived of the league as being led, at least in name, by the pope, but new instructions from Turin insisted that Charles Albert himself must be its head. It was he, after all, who had led the battle to drive the foreigners from the peninsula, he who had the strongest Italian army, and he who ruled the most modern Italian state and the only one free from Austrian influence. But the idea had little appeal. Ferdinand, Bourbon king of Naples, certainly had no interest in placing himself under the Savoyard king of Sardinia; nor did he have any interest in the unification of Italy. In Venice, the provisional government that was still holding out against the Austrians prized its own independence, while nostalgia for the thousand-year-long independent Venetian Republic still ran strong. Nor would Rossi recommend such a plan on behalf of the pope's government, it being unthinkable that the pontiff would subordinate himself to the Sardinian monarch.[26]

Indeed, Rosmini himself found the idea distasteful. "I believe I would be lacking in my duties," he informed the Sardinian foreign minister in early October, "if I did not advise Your Excellency to send some other diplomat to Rome who is more expert and more able than I am, and who has the belief—which I do not share—in the wisdom and likely success of the new project." With this note, the abbot resigned.[27]

On an October afternoon, in one of the Roman Jewish ghetto's narrow streets, Angelo Moscati got into an argument with another man. As heated words gave way to blows, Moscati pulled out a knife and slashed at the man's head, opening up a gash. Two members of the Civic Guard arrived and tried to seize the blade, but Moscati wounded one of them before they succeeded in subduing him. The whole episode would not have attracted much attention—knife fights being common on the streets of Rome—but Moscati was a Jew, and his victims Christian.[28]

The news raced through the city. Soon a large, angry crowd, led by the cousin of one the injured men, and apparently encouraged by neighboring Catholic clergy, descended on the ghetto seeking revenge, members of the Civic Guard among them. The invaders waved clubs and knives and began raining cobblestones and sticks on the heads of the ghetto dwellers. Shouts of "Long live religion!" "Send the Jews to the flames!" "Down with the friends of the Jews!" and "Down with the enemies of the Holy Religion!" rang out, as rocks shattered windows. Some of the more enterprising among the intruders carried sacks, hoping for plunder.

The captain of the nearby Civic Guard station, alerted to the violence, rushed to the scene with a number of guardsmen and pleaded with his marauding comrades to obey their oath to preserve the peace. In response, the captain recalled, the rioting guardsmen "treated us as pigs and cowards, saying that it was absolutely necessary to defend our uniform and burn down the Ghetto." Rossi released a statement, plastered on the city walls, denouncing the violence as "unworthy of a cultured and generous people." In the nights to follow, dozens of guardsmen were sent to patrol the ghetto, although many sympathized more with the rioters than with the terrified Jews.[29]

In many ways, the Jews were the city's bellwether, the living indicator of the struggle to move Rome from its medieval theocratic ways to modern times. The Enlightenment ideals that had been spreading in Europe for the past decades called for treating all subjects, all citizens alike. A modern society had no place for a ghetto, no grounds for forbidding professions or education to people based on their religion.

For centuries, in order to survive, Rome's Jews had groveled before popes, praising the great goodness and generosity of even the most repressive pontiffs, for this was their only way to gain any relief. But the Jews did feel genuine appreciation for what Pius had done for them. He had allowed some to live and work outside the ghetto's cramped quarters. He had put an end to the centuries-old humiliating public spectacle of vassalage requiring the officers of Rome's Jewish community on the first Saturday of Carnival to pay an annual tribute to the Senator of Rome as a large, raucous crowd jeered and mocked them. He had granted permission to Jews who otherwise met the criteria to become members of the Civic Guard, and he had allowed the ghetto gates to be torn down, a symbolically weighty step even if few of the Jews had left the ghetto. In August, the Chamber of Deputies voted to extend the Jews full civil, although not political, rights.[30]

Yet, following centuries of demonization of the Jews, popular attitudes were far from uniformly benevolent. In their weekly sermons, parish priests railed against them as Christ-killers and dangerous enemies of Christian society. The pope, some were now convinced, had himself become a dupe of the Jews. The people of Rome needed little encouragement to turn against them.

IN OCTOBER, TOO, a new popular uprising erupted in Vienna. On October 6 protesters tried to block imperial troops who were being sent to put down revolt in Hungary. The confrontation quickly devolved into open rebellion, and rebels killed Austria's minister of war. The next day the imperial family fled to Olmütz, a town in Moravia that today is part of the Czech Republic. For Giuseppe Mazzini and his followers, the time to strike against the Austrians in northeastern Italy seemed to be at hand. In an open letter to the people of Lombardy and Veneto, prefaced with his watchwords, "In the Name of God and the People," the prophet of Italian independence issued a call for national insurrection. Romans were excited as well, hoping that the Austrian government would fall and its empire unravel. They would soon be disappointed. By the end of the month, seventy thousand imperial troops had surrounded Vienna and crushed the revolt.[31]

In Rome, Rossi, facing a thousand obstacles, forged ahead. He initiated the construction of rail lines and telegraphs. He ordered clergymen to pay taxes and tried to clean up the corrupt civil service, which was largely composed of priests. Although despised by the upper clergy, Rossi was winning few friends among the liberals. His opposition to having the pope join the war against Austria, and his former role as French ambassador under the now deposed monarchy, provoked the hostility of both liberals and radicals. Nor did his ill-disguised sense of superiority and contempt for hypocrisy help him win allies. "The coldness of his smile, the irony of his glance, the disdain evident in his gestures," observed one otherwise sympathetic chronicler of the time, "made him as many enemies as did the rapid rise in his political fortunes."[32]

Rossi found himself in an impossible situation. Although accused of being a friend of the Austrians, he was not. He had left Italy nearly three decades earlier, he confided in a letter to a friend in September, because he did not want to live in a country where "Austrian bayonets reigned." The job he had accepted at the pope's urging, he confessed, was thankless, but how, he asked, could he refuse to help a pontiff in whose land he lived and "who has given me so many proofs of his confidence and his kindness?"

Rossi's decision to accept the pope's offer had also been rooted in his belief that he was indeed the only man who had the knowledge of the world, the judgment, and the insight needed to prevent disaster. The problems facing the Papal States could be solved, he thought, by enlightened administration, by eliminating corruption, and by a program of modernization. It would not be an easy task. The clergy, who stood to lose their special privileges, would oppose him, as would the radicals. Rossi, it seemed, believed that by the very force of his will, and his clearsighted vision of the tasks to be done, he could somehow overcome all obstacles.[33]

Although Rossi was proving unpopular in many quarters, the pope was pleased with him, very pleased. At long last he had found a man capable of leading his government, a man of boundless self-confidence and vision, a man who understood public administration and finance and could steer the ship of state to safety. After enduring a government that continually pressed him to join the war for Italian independence, the pope felt great relief in having someone in charge who agreed that it was best to stay out. And in those parts of the Papal States where civil unrest was getting out of hand, as it was in the northern provinces, Rossi—in sharp contrast with his predecessor—did not hesitate to call on the army to restore order. In a mark of the unusual regard the pope had for his new minister, he invited Rossi to dine with him, a privilege almost unheard of for a layman.[34]

On November 4, the saint day for Carlo Borromeo, Pius, accompanied by cardinals and other church dignitaries, went in elaborate procession to the Roman church named in Borromeo's honor. Jeers and whistles greeted Cardinal Soglia, the secretary of state. "Into the sewer!" people shouted at the red-robed cardinals as they rode by in their gilded carriages. A crowd of three or four hundred young men stood provocatively along the pope's route on the Corso, their hats remaining firmly on their heads, cigars dangling provocatively from their mouths, ostentatiously blowing smoke as the pope passed. Pius, who had begun to raise his hand in benediction, lowered his arm and looked away.[35]

The next morning the pope called in his minister of arms, General Carlo Zucchi, appointed the previous month to try to instill some kind of discipline in the notoriously inept papal army. Zucchi was seventy-one years old, small, gaunt, and severe, and his best days were long behind him. Even for an abler man, the task would have been daunting. "I found the greatest disorder in the training, in discipline, and in the administration," remarked Zucchi on observing his new charges. "No one knew who was in command. Each person did what he pleased, paying no attention to his commanding officer."[36]

Having learned of new unrest in Bologna and Ferrara, Pius ordered Zucchi to go north. A few days later the report Zucchi sent back was not encouraging. Bologna was in a fearful state. Revolutionary passions ran high. The fiery sermons of a patriotic priest, Father Gavazzi, had stirred people into a frenzy. The pope responded with a request to have the monk arrested, but a bigger problem soon appeared. The notorious revolutionary leader Giuseppe Garibaldi and his large band of armed men had arrived at the Tuscan border of the Papal States, not far from Bologna. Fearing that they would further fan the flames of discontent, Rossi ordered the army to drive them back into Tuscany.[37]

Rossi alone stood between the pope and the abyss, but Rossi was ever more isolated. The cardinals had never liked the idea of having a layman in charge of the papal government, and Rossi's efforts to rein in their privileges only increased their resentment. On the other side, many viewed Rossi as a heavy-handed autocrat and traitor to the cause of Italian independence. Rossi would give no ground. "If they want to destroy the pope's authority," he told the Bavarian ambassador one day in mid-November, "they'll have to do it over my dead body."[38]

CHAPTER 7

THE ASSASSINATION

On November 15, 1848—A DAY THAT WOULD LONG BE REMEMbered—a large, restive crowd gathered in the piazza outside the Palace of the Chancellery, where Rossi was scheduled to address the Chamber of Deputies. Scattered groups of unarmed Civic Guardsmen took up their positions around the vast Renaissance palazzo that lay in the heart of the city. Some papal police units, under separate command, were also on hand. Ominously, many veterans of the papal legion that had recently been defeated by the Austrians also appeared, as did many of the city's best-known radicals.

Rossi spent the morning at home. He'd been receiving death threats for the past several weeks, and rumor had it that radicals were planning to take advantage of his public appearance that day to act on them. Friends warned him, but he brushed them off. At noon Rossi said goodbye to his nervous wife and two sons and headed for the Quirinal Palace to see the pope before his speech.

"For Heaven's sake, my dear count," said Pius, "take care! Your enemies are many, and in their anger capable of the most infamous crimes!"

"Holiness," replied Rossi, "they are too cowardly, I have no fear of them."

As Rossi descended the Quirinal stairs on his way out, an unfamiliar priest rushed up and seized him by the arm. The cleric had tears in his eyes. Do not get into that carriage, the priest pleaded. "If you leave, you are dead!" Rossi pulled his arm free and continued down the stairs.

The carriage slowed to a crawl as it approached the Chancellery Palace and made its way through the crowd, passing through the gate into the courtyard. As Rossi, elegantly dressed in a black suit, stepped out, sixty legionnaires lined the path that led to the stairway. The men's scruffy appearance and surly bearing were far from reassuring.[1]

From the crowd he could hear the boos and the ugly shouts: "Slit his throat! Slit his throat! Kill him!" Rossi did his best to maintain his dignity. As he passed through the legionnaires, those behind him turned to follow, so that he soon found himself surrounded. As he neared the stairway, a man suddenly emerged from the crowd and struck him on his left side. As he turned to see who had hit him, a short young man, beardless but with flowing mustache, rushed up on his right and sliced his neck with the long, sharp blade of a dagger. "It's done! It's done!" came the shouts, as the assassins melted back into the crowd. Rossi staggered forward, then collapsed, the blood that gushed from his neck forming a widening stain on the ground. He had but a few moments left to live.[2]

The deputies heard the commotion outside and soon learned the news. After long moments of alarm and uncertainty, they hurried out. A strange brew of fear, terror, and exhilaration swept the city. Rossi had been the government. Now that he was gone, a great void had opened up. A crowd somehow both festive and sinister soon gathered. Numbering in the hundreds, they began parading through the streets of Rome, stopping outside Rossi's home, along the Corso, beneath the window of his widow and two sons. "Blessed is the hand who stabbed Rossi!" they chanted. Later, as others joined them, they waved tricolored Italian flags. Amid the poles they held aloft, one attracted special attention. From it hung not a flag but what appeared to be the assassin's knife, covered with blood. "Blessed be the hand that stabbed the tyrant!" had by now turned from chant to song. The pope's defenders were nowhere to be seen.[3]

The men at the Popular Club, headquartered in a building at the midway point of the Corso, rushed to fill the vacuum. In the wake of the pope's allocution opposing the war with Austria, the recently formed club had become the epicenter of the movement for Italian independence, displacing the more moderate Roman Club. Many of its leaders came from other parts of the Papal States. The investigation into Rossi's murder would later focus its attention on the club, thought to be the

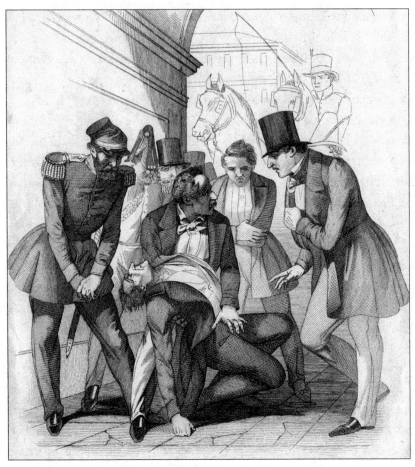

The death of Pellegrino Rossi

place where the assassination plot was hatched. Now it hummed with activity, as some members worked on a list of demands to present to the pope, insisting that men of their choosing be named to a new ministry, while others were out leading marches through the city's streets.[4]

THE PARALYSIS OF THE public authorities was complete. An official of the Civic Guard rushed to request instructions from its head, the duke of Rignano. In the absence of General Zucchi, who was up north dealing with the unrest there, the duke was also in charge of the army. "Act prudently" was the only instruction the duke gave before racing home with his servants to gather his belongings and flee to safety in Naples. Pius dispatched a messenger to General Zucchi, ordering him to return immediately to Rome.[5]

That night the pope asked to see Marco Minghetti, the moderate deputy from Bologna. "I found him sad and pensive, but calm," Minghetti recalled. "That mystical feeling that always dominated him, left him, even then, resigned to God's will." The pope spoke of the need to form a new government but did not explicitly ask Minghetti to head it. Minghetti advised the pope that a new ministry could survive only if it pronounced itself both liberal and committed to Italian independence. The pope asked him to return in the morning, when he expected to make a decision.[6]

Early the next day the leaders of both the Upper Chamber and the Chamber of Deputies received a request to meet with the pope at 8:45 that morning. "I finally found a man," Pius told them, "who not only knew how to determine what the state needs . . . but also told me what the remedies were. And now they have murdered him!"

Monsignor Muzzarelli, president of the Upper Chamber, tried to calm the pontiff. The people, he explained, despised Rossi. His death might in the end make things easier.

Standing behind his desk, Pius was indignant. "What?" he asked. "A monsignor, dressed in this color, a man whom I placed as head of the Upper Chamber, comes in here to make excuses to me for such an assassination?"[7]

The chamber leaders tried to turn the discussion toward practical issues. The pope had two choices, they told him. He could try to repress his subjects by force, or he could name a new government head who enjoyed popular support. They advised against the first option. Aside from other considerations, they warned, the pope could not count on the loyalty of his soldiers, many of whom had joined the demonstrators the previous evening.

What about the Civic Guard? asked Pius. Unlike the papal soldiers, they all came from the better classes. Surely they would defend him.

They were no more likely to be of help, advised the Upper Chamber president.

Pius told them he was thinking of asking Marco Minghetti to form a new government. That, the council leaders replied, would not be a good idea. Minghetti was seen as a friend of Rossi and would not help win the people's favor.

The Chamber of Deputies president then, unwisely, brought the conversation back to the assassination. Having the unpopular Rossi out of the way was not entirely a bad thing, he said, seconding the argument of his colleague of the Upper Chamber. At this, recalled one of the men at the meeting, "the pope became so overcome by emotion that the muscles in his face began to tremble horribly." Recalling that the pope had suffered from epilepsy as a child, his visitors suggested they leave him time to think about what they had said. They would await his summons to return.

As they left the room, they found Minghetti waiting outside. He would never be called in.[8]

THE PREVIOUS NIGHT, following the assassination, the Popular Club had posted a manifesto on the city's walls, proclaiming that in light of the emergency, it was taking upon itself the task of ensuring order until a new government could be formed. It called on the Romans to gather at Piazza del Popolo the next day to show their support for a program of national independence and a constituent assembly to devise a more democratic form of government. In response, many Civic Guardsmen and legionnaires joined the large crowd that streamed into the vast, round piazza. With the flag of the Popular Club at their head, they marched in rows, arm in arm, toward the pope's palace, drummers and a musical band leading the way. They looked, remarked one unsympathetic observer, "like ruffians in a melo-drama . . . the first act of which had been the foul murder of one old man, and this the second, an attack on another."

The demonstrators arrived at the Quirinal only to find its huge front door shut. After a delegation succeeded in entering and presenting the cardinal secretary of state with the document they had brought, they returned to the crowd to await the pope's response. Inside the palace the pope sat, surrounded by the members of the foreign diplomatic corps who had come to be with him in this moment of crisis. He read the list of demands, then sent his reply out to the crowd: Everyone should go home. Christ's vicar on earth could not bow to intimidation.[9]

Enraged by the pope's response, some men set fire to a side gate. Flames soon shot up over the door, and for a moment it seemed that the whole gargantuan palace might soon be ablaze. Men inside the building rushed to the gate with buckets of water and finally succeeded in extinguishing the fire. When others tried to reignite it, one of the Swiss Guards fired a shot at them. Hearing the sound, protesters with rifles of their own climbed up the bell tower and onto the roofs overlooking the piazza and shot at the palace windows. Monsignor Palma, the man responsible for preparing the Latin texts of the pope's official pronouncements, was hit in the chest by a bullet as he stood looking out from a window not far from Pius. "This is the second victim who dies for my cause," said the pope, "and I did not want to see a single drop of blood spilled for it!"[10]

By now, the crowd had grown to ten thousand, many armed. The demonstrators wheeled in carts and turned them on their sides to block off the streets leading into the piazza. Other carts were loaded with incendiary materials, threatening to set the palazzo afire. Men rolled in a cannon and pointed it at the main palace entrance. Pius, observed the French ambassador, had until then acted with admirable sangfroid, but he now realized the situation was hopeless. He would have to give in to the demand that he name new ministers agreeable to the clubs. As for their demand that he declare immediately for Italian independence and join the war against Austria, he would try to win some time by referring the matter to the two chambers.[11]

"You see the sorry state at which we've arrived," said Pius to the ambassadors. "Hope of resisting, none. Here in my own royal palace, a prelate has been killed. Shots are fired at us, cannons are aimed at us. Encircled, besieged by the rebels. We give in to avoid useless shedding of blood and even worse crimes, but only to force. You see, *signori*, we give in, but under protest. We give in only under threat of violence, and every concession we make is invalid, it is null and void."[12]

It was eight p.m. by the time the pope's decision to appoint new ministers was announced outside the Quirinal. Some of the legionnaires fired their rifles in the air in celebration. Others marched through the city's streets carrying torches and singing patriotic songs. Civic Guardsmen disarmed the pope's Swiss Guard and confined them to their barracks. As morning dawned, it was the Civic Guard and not the Swiss Guard who controlled access to the Quirinal. A new era, it seemed, had begun.[13]

IN THEIR SLATE OF PROPOSED government ministers, the protesters had listed a variety of prominent laymen known for their close ties to the radicals, some of whom were thought to have been involved in planning Rossi's murder. But one name struck the pope as offering some hope. The protesters had named Antonio Rosmini as a potential head of government. As a past envoy of the Sardinian king, known to have been urging the cause of Italian independence on the pope, the abbot was viewed as sympathetic to the patriotic cause. That night after the protesters had marched off, Pius sent word to him that he wished to appoint him to lead the government. Rosmini was shocked by the news and embarrassed that his name appeared on the radicals' list. He informed the pope that he would not serve. Pius understood and did not insist.[14]

Rome's streets were no longer in the pope's control. He could not count on the loyalty of the Civic Guard. The general in charge of his army was in the northern provinces of the Papal States, while the volunteers who had fought with the papal army against the Austrians had returned and were among the most hostile to his cause. The cardinals had largely deserted him. The aristocrats were nowhere to be seen.

In the wake of Rosmini's refusal, his options painfully limited, Pius turned to the head of the Upper Chamber, Monsignor Muzzarelli, whose cavalier attitude toward Rossi's assassination had so incensed him, as the best choice he had to head the government.

Shortly after announcing the new government ministers, drawn from the protesters' list, Pius called the ambassadors back to renew his protest. "I am like a prisoner," he told them. "They've taken my Guard away from me and replaced them with men of their own. What guides my action now that I lack any defense is the principle of doing all possible to avoid the shedding of fraternal blood. . . . But Europe and the world must know that I take no part in the acts of the new government, and I regard myself as entirely extraneous from it." The pope was especially eager for the ambassadors to tell their governments to ignore anything the new lay foreign minister of the Papal States said. Only the cardinal secretary of state could serve in such a role. In short, while Pius publicly authorized the new government, he was privately telling the foreign powers it had no legitimacy. "Given its current fanatical mood," worried the Sardinian ambassador, after his return from the papal palace, "if the public were to come to hear of this, it might well cause an outbreak even worse than what we witnessed yesterday."[15]

"Today," reported the French ambassador, the pope's "authority is absolutely gone, it no longer exists other than in name." "I must also tell you," he advised Paris, "that in this situation I have no doubt that sooner or later he will want to leave Rome, if it is possible for him, and in this case he will most likely go to Marseilles. However," he warned, "this is something that he must not let get out in order not to compromise his situation."[16]

CARDINAL LAMBRUSCHINI, SECRETARY OF STATE until Gregory's death two years earlier and widely reviled as the head of the pro-Austrian, reactionary faction of the Curia, became a particular target for the people's rage. On the night of November 16, the day after Rossi's murder, a group of legionnaires invaded his quarters in the Palace of the Consulta, the imposing Baroque building that bordered the same piazza as the Quirinal. Not finding him, they smashed his furniture and tore his bed to shreds with their daggers and bayonets. The cardinal meanwhile lay cowering beneath a pile of hay in the nearby palace stable. Two Civic Guardsmen—among the minority of their comrades who retained sympathy for his plight—had helped hide him there. They returned three hours later, after the legionnaires left, and, disguising the terrified cardinal in a heavy, ill-fitting soldier's coat, they put him in a carriage bound for Naples, where he would be out of harm's way.[17]

Nor were the aristocrats who had for so long enjoyed all the privileges of proximity to the pope anywhere around when he most needed their support. Curious to know the pope's situation but not inclined to risk going to see him, Prince Doria Pamphily asked the Belgian chargé d'affaires what he had seen in his recent visit to the Quirinal.

"You should ask me instead," he replied, "what I haven't seen, and that is the Roman princes."[18]

It did not take long for news of the shocking events in Rome to reach Paris. On the seventeenth, the French government sent warships to Civitavecchia, Rome's principal port, with instructions to do whatever was needed to save the pope's life but to avoid getting mixed up in "political" questions.[19]

The Spanish government was similarly eager to help the pope. Queen Isabel sat uneasily in power, having come to the throne fifteen years earlier at age two. Her long and flowery title, after all, began, "Isabel II by the Grace of God, Queen of Castile, Leon, Aragon, of the Two Sicilies, of Jerusalem, of Navarre, of Granada . . ." The list went on, including many lands—among them Sicily, Naples, Milan, and Sardinia—over which the Spanish monarchs had not in fact ruled for decades if not centuries. If she was queen by the grace of God, by divine right, she had, first of all, to ensure the reign of God's vicar on earth. She could not allow the pope to be driven in disgrace from his rightful throne.

During the siege of the Quirinal following Rossi's murder, Cardinal Soglia had turned at one point to the Spanish ambassador. What instructions, asked the secretary of state, had his government given him? "My orders and instructions," the ambassador replied, "are to put at His Holiness's disposition the army, the navy, and all the power of the queen of Spain." In fact, a few months earlier the pope had talked to the Spanish ambassador about the possibility that he might one day need to flee the city. The Spanish government had subsequently kept a ship at Civitavecchia for this eventuality, which Pius had found reassuring, but now that he needed it, the ship was gone. It had recently been sent back to Spain to be resupplied. The ambassador sent an urgent plea to Madrid to have the ship return quickly. Although he was undoubtedly concerned for the pope's welfare, he was likewise concerned that, should the Spanish ship not arrive quickly, one of Europe's other powers might get the pope in its hands and see its own influence and prestige rise accordingly.

He had reason to worry. The British government had sent its new steam-powered paddlewheel warship, the *Bulldog*, to Civitavecchia, where it would arrive on the twenty-third. In secret instructions, the *Bulldog*'s captain was told that, should "the commotions in Rome" place the pope in jeopardy and cause him to want to escape, "you will be ready to receive him . . . for conveyance to any port to which he may desire to retire."[20]

PIUS FELT PAINFULLY ALONE. Cardinal Soglia, appointed in June, his sixth secretary of state, had proven unequal to the task. Cardinal Antonelli, who had briefly been secretary of state the previous spring and now served as prefect of the sacred palaces of the Vatican, was the only man he felt he could rely on. Although hobbled by the gout that had confined him to bed much of the previous summer, Antonelli was now ever at the pope's side, urging him to flee.

Two days after Rossi's assassination, Pius secretly informed the few cardinals still in Rome of his intention to leave. Word that the pope might try to escape soon circulated among the diplomatic corps as well. In reporting this suspicion to Turin on the eighteenth, the Sardinian ambassador noted that, with the Quirinal surrounded by Civic Guardsmen, it would not be a simple matter. And if the pope did succeed in abandoning Rome, the ambassador worried, there was little to keep the radicals from declaring the end of papal authority and proclaiming a republic in its place. This was the last thing the Sardinian government wanted to see. King Charles Albert viewed the republicans as a greater threat than the Austrians and worried that if they succeeded in overthrowing the pope-king, his monarchy might well be the next to fall.[21]

On Tuesday, November 20, the lower chamber was at last called to order. Seeking to avoid a break with the pope, one of the moderates proposed that they send an official delegation to express the deputies' sense of devotion to him.[22]

At this point, Charles Bonaparte, encouraged by the packed gallery, rose to speak. As recently as August he had expressed his firm belief that the pope was essential to the Italian cause. "Pius IX," he had told the deputies then, "began the Italian movement. Only he was able to move the masses." Now the great Napoleon's nephew, an implausible revolutionary, sang a very different tune.[23]

"This is not the time, colleagues, to speak of thanks, still less of devotion," he said. "It is time for the promises that the people have obtained from the sovereign to be put into action." The people in the gallery roared their approval, but when the vote was first taken the moderates' motion to express solidarity with the pope passed. This provoked such an outpouring of abuse from the spectators that a new vote was called. This time the motion failed. Outraged, Marco Minghetti, committed to a constitutional monarchy under the pope, announced his resignation from the chamber and left Rome. The vote, he explained, had deprived the Chamber of Deputies of any legitimacy, for it contradicted the constitution on which the chamber was based, one that outlined a system in which the two chambers came under the pope's authority.[24]

It remains a matter of dispute whether the lack of public support for the pope in these tense days reflected the loss of the Romans' faith in him or simply intimidation by the radicals. In the years ahead, a Catholic account of this period would point to the latter, along with a belief among the more devout that the unfolding tragedy was some kind of divine punishment for a city that had strayed far from God's path. For the patriots, and for the Italian patriotic historians who would come to see the drama as the first step in the creation of modern Italy, it had a different meaning. It signaled the end of an era and of a theocracy that had its roots in the early Middle Ages. After centuries of oppression, the people were at last rising up to assert their rights. The tide of history had changed.

Pius IX had few moments of doubt. The Almighty, he was convinced, was testing his faith. As the Lord's vicar on earth, he vowed not to fail Him. God, he knew, would not long allow this sacrilege to endure.

CHAPTER 8

THE ESCAPE

Pius had been pondering the idea of exile for months. In March, on the day the pope granted his people a constitution, the Spanish envoy in Rome wrote an urgent note to Madrid asking for instructions should the pope decide to leave. Spain's foreign minister replied by offering the pontiff asylum on Spanish soil and suggested the Mediterranean island of Majorca; the offer was renewed by Francisco Martinez, the new Spanish ambassador, when he arrived in Rome in early August. Pius had also raised the subject of escape with the French ambassador during the summer, and at a meeting in late August, he had gotten yet another offer of help, this time from the commander of the British ship *Bulldog*.[1]

In October, Pius received a gift from the bishop of Valence, the French town where Pius VI had died in exile a half century earlier. It was a pyx, the small silver box in which Pius VI had kept the Eucharist. As the bishop explained in his accompanying note, it had been a great comfort to the exiled pope throughout his ordeal. Remarking that he hoped Pius IX would not suffer the same fate as his namesake, the bishop added, "But who knows God's secret plans, or the trials through which His Providence will lead Your Holiness?" Church history was filled with cases of popes living far from Rome. Seven successive pontiffs in the fourteenth century had set up their courts in France, at Avignon. More recently, both Pius VI and Pius VII had been forced into exile. Prone as he was to look for heavenly omens to help divine God's will, Pio Nono saw the gift of Pius VI's little box as a sign. He would hold it in his hands when the time came to leave his capital.[2]

With the Civic Guard now surrounding his palace, it was far from clear how he would be able to escape. Who could extract him from the Quirinal and get him out of the city? And assuming he could leave, where should he go? Several governments had offered him asylum, but which would let him act freely? Where would he be in the best position to try to persuade the other European powers to help restore him to his rightful place as pope-king in Rome?

The pope turned to Cardinal Antonelli to devise a plan. They needed to find people they could trust, for they could not make their escape on their own. The foreign ambassadors to the Holy See were among the few who had stood by the pope, and in the end, his escape depended on two of them: Duke Harcourt, the French envoy, and Count Karl von Spaur, from Bavaria.[3]

Remarkably, the secret was well kept. At four p.m. on Friday, November 24, the captain of the *Bulldog*, which was moored at Civitavecchia, came to see the pope to renew his offer of assistance. Pius told him that at present he had no plan to abandon Rome. He would leave all in God's hands. But the British officer had barely exited the Quirinal Palace when the pope set his escape plan in motion. The French ambassador entered the pope's quarters at five p.m. and pretended to talk to him while Pius hurriedly put on the black cassock and hat of a simple priest. He then rushed out the back entry into the awaiting two-horse carriage. It was only a short trip to the modest Church of Sts. Marcellino e Pietro, where Spaur, Bavaria's ambassador, awaited him. With a pistol in his right hand, the ambassador extended his left to help the pope into his carriage.[4]

At about the same time, back in the Quirinal, the French ambassador, judging the forty-five minutes he had spent in conversation with the absent pontiff to be sufficient, got up to go. He had done his part in the belief, encouraged by Antonelli, that Pius was now on his way north to the port of Civitavecchia. There, thought Harcourt, he would soon join the pope aboard the *Ténare*, the French warship that awaited them, and set sail for France.[5]

As the carriage carrying the disguised pontiff made its way out of the city, it turned not north toward Civitavecchia but south. While Harcourt was rushing to the Papal States' port, imagining his triumphal arrival with the pope in Marseilles, the Bavarian ambassador was hurrying the pope to the seaside fortress town of Gaeta in the Kingdom of Naples.

SPAUR KNEW ROME WELL, having served there for sixteen years as Bavaria's envoy and having married a young Roman woman well known in high society. Teresa Giraud, famed for her beauty and the niece of a prominent Roman playwright, had turned her home into one of Rome's most prominent salons for artists, politicians, aristocrats, and cardinals. A strong-minded woman accustomed to having her way, she had pried out of her husband the details of the pope's plan. She then insisted on accompanying the men to Gaeta.

In order not to attract attention, the Bavarian ambassador had fetched the pope in a small, nondescript, open carriage. Ten miles south of Rome, it came to a stop. Spaur explained to the pontiff that to make their way to Gaeta, they needed a more substantial carriage, and one was meeting them there. Much to Pius's astonishment, the large, luxurious carriage that greeted them contained the ambassador's elegantly dressed wife, along with her fourteen-year-old son. This, thought the pope, was only one more indignity he would have to bear, as he sat in the coach cooped up with the garrulous woman and her son, the ambassador having been relegated to a narrow, rear-facing bench on the back of the carriage with one of the servants.[6]

They traveled all night. In early morning, having gone close to ninety-five miles, they came to the small fishing village of Mola di Gaeta. There in the shadow of Gaeta, two men stood on the road awaiting them. Looking out from the carriage, the countess recognized one as the first secretary of Rome's Spanish embassy. The other, wearing a scarlet scarf that half covered his face and dressed as a layman, looked oddly familiar. When the pope saw him, he crossed his hands over his chest and, with some relief, said, "Lord, I thank you for having brought the good Cardinal Antonelli here safely." Antonelli carried a passport identifying him as the Spaniard's assistant.[7]

The cardinal led the group to a modest inn nearby. There he told Pius to pen a letter to the king of Naples, who knew nothing of the pope's plans. "Majesty," the pontiff wrote, "the Supreme Roman Pontiff, the Vicar of Jesus Christ, the Sovereign of the Papal States has found it necessary to abandon the capital of his dominions in order not to compromise his dignity, and lest he appear by his silence to approve the enormous excesses that have been and are being committed in Rome." He planned to remain in Gaeta, he added, "only for a brief time, not wanting to embarrass the king in any way." Count Spaur left for Naples immediately in his Spanish colleague's carriage, carrying the pope's letter to the king.[8]

LATER THAT AFTERNOON, the Bavarian ambassador's luxurious carriage appeared at Gaeta's gate. The officer in charge, checking the passengers' papers, was led to believe that the carriage contained the Bavarian ambassador and his wife, along with their son and the son's two tutors. The Spanish diplomat presented himself as Spaur to account for the fact that Spaur himself was on the road to Naples. They were not eager for too many questions to be asked about the two "tutors" accompanying them. Once inside the fortress city's walls, they checked into a

Gaeta

modest guesthouse. Fearing that someone might recognize him despite his disguise, the pope decided it best not to venture out.[9]

That night around midnight, a cannon blast from the port awakened the fortress commander. The *Ténare* had arrived from Civitavecchia and dropped anchor. The next morning two French officers rowed to shore, bringing with them a short, distinguished-looking visitor. The diplomat introduced himself as Duke François Harcourt, French ambassador to the Holy See.[10]

On exiting the Quirinal Palace, Harcourt had hurried to his residence, where his carriage and bags were waiting for him. In the carriage were two boxes of the pope's personal effects that Antonelli had entrusted to him to encourage his belief that he would soon be setting sail to France with the pope. Harcourt arrived at Civitavecchia at two a.m., expecting Pius to be waiting for him aboard the French ship. On learning that the pope had not only not arrived but was headed toward Gaeta with Spaur, Harcourt ordered the French captain to sail south, still hoping to persuade the pope to come with him to France.

A high-stakes tug-of-war was under way. For the leaders of any of Europe's Catholic nations, having the pope choose them to shelter him would be a great coup, bolstering the government's prestige both among its own Catholic population and among the governments of the world. To have the pope choose instead to turn to a rival was to compound the loss. Cardinal Antonelli had not only led Harcourt to believe that the pope was headed for France; he had at the same time assured the Spanish ambassador, Francisco Martínez de la Rosa, that the pope planned to accept his offer to take refuge on the Spanish island of Majorca. Pius was going to Gaeta, explained the cardinal, in order to board a Spanish ship there. As proof of his good faith, Antonelli had taken the ambassador's second-in-command with him to Gaeta.

Because Martínez was expecting the Spanish warship to arrive shortly at Civitavecchia, he had gone there, intending to board it and meet the pope in Gaeta. But on arriving at Civitavecchia on the morning following the pope's escape from Rome, two unpleasant surprises greeted him. Not only had the Spanish ship still not arrived, but the *Ténare* had sailed south for Gaeta with the French ambassador aboard. Martínez sent a frantic message to Madrid. The Spanish risked "seeing all their efforts of so many months lost in a moment." The great glory that would come to Spain as savior of the pope, of the papacy itself, now threatened to slip through their fingers.[11]

The pope was far from certain where he was going. He had acceded to Antonelli's advice to take refuge first at Gaeta but worried that casting his fate with the widely reviled king of Naples might be a mistake. Yet Gaeta did have some advantages for the pope. He would remain close to his own states, while the port allowed him easy access to the rest of Europe. There, too, he would avoid coming under the thumb of one of Europe's major powers and so would have more room for diplomatic maneuver. Gaeta would give him some breathing room and time to pray for divine inspiration.[12]

At about the same time as the French warship was laying anchor at Gaeta, the Bavarian ambassador, bearing the pope's letter, reached Naples. Spaur knocked on the door of the papal nuncio's palace and told the nuncio that he carried an urgent message from the pope to the king. The nuncio was initially unenthusiastic about waking the monarch at that late hour but, at Spaur's insistence, got into his carriage to go to the royal palace. Once there, he roused Ferdinand and relayed Spaur's request. The Bavarian had meanwhile gone to a nearby hotel to change from his dusty clothes into something more befitting a royal audience.

Sometime after midnight, to the astonishment of the rest of the royal household, the Bavarian ambassador appeared. Spaur handed King Ferdinand Pius's letter. The news that the pope was not in Rome but in the king's own fortress city, and was turning to the king to protect him, was both surprising and thrilling for the beleaguered monarch. He told Spaur to prepare to depart with him on the royal ship at six a.m., only a few hours away.[13]

In Rome, confusion reigned as news spread of the pope's disappearance. No one knew where he had gone. At noon, the government posted a dramatic announcement on the doors along the Corso. "Romans," it began. "We announce an unexpected event of the greatest importance, and one that can have the most serious consequences. Last night the Pontiff Pius IX silently abandoned Rome, and the exact direction he headed in is not known." The notice went on to assure the public that the government would maintain order.[14]

The pope's abrupt departure was met by "a general stupor," as one diplomat put it, but also by endless speculation. Mixed with people's uncertainty was a large dose of fear. Might foreign armies now try to retake the city for the pope?[15]

While some of the government ministers and many of the deputies feared they had gone too far, causing the pope to flee, others were excited. Among the latter was the irrepressible Charles Bonaparte, who that afternoon rose to speak in a hastily convened session of the Chamber of Deputies. "From this point on," he declaimed, "all thoughts of returning to the past are useless." In the new phase they had entered, declared the prince, the government bureaucracy had to be purged of the large number of "vicious parasites" whose loyalty was suspect and whose continued presence constituted a grave danger to the country. What was needed, concluded Bonaparte, was the immediate convocation of a constituent assembly, aimed at forming a new government of the people.[16]

ON THEIR ARRIVAL IN GAETA, King Ferdinand and Queen Maria Teresa of Naples got down on their knees as they neared the pope, who, to the stupefaction of the commander of the fortress, had emerged from the modest inn where he spent the night. After the tension, fears, and humiliation of the previous two days, Pius could not keep the tears from running down his cheeks. He placed King Ferdinand's hands in his, the first time the pope had ever felt the touch of a royal hand.

For Ferdinand, the pope's arrival was providential. Earlier in his reign, he had seemed open to the need to modernize his famously retrograde kingdom and had introduced railways and even elevators, but recent events had convinced him that his backward subjects could be ruled only by an iron hand. Having recently acquired the nickname "Bomb King" for his merciless bombardment of the rebellious Sicilian city of Messina, the king seized the chance to cast himself as the pope's savior.

Ferdinand's strongest source of support came from the upper clergy, although this had done little to boost his popularity. The king, reported the British envoy in Naples, "is above all a superstitious man and a faithful Catholic." From the perspective of Britain's Protestant envoy, the

Ferdinand II, King of the Two Sicilies

monarch was "enslaved to priestcraft in a degree beyond all belief." The king's confessor was one of the most detested men in the kingdom and, reported the envoy, "in league with the Minister of Police."[17]

Although Ferdinand was related through marriage to most of Europe's royal families, his cultural horizons did not reach much beyond Naples. The great intellectual movements of the times had totally passed him by. While his more enlightened royal counterpart in Turin saw the movement for Italian unification as a chance to enlarge his authority,

Ferdinand viewed it simply as a threat. The past year had been a nightmare, beginning with the revolution in Sicily and the revolt in Naples itself. Forced to grant a constitution, then soon reneging on it, he had in recent months been fighting a bloody battle to regain Sicily for his Bourbon kingdom and to bring his rebellious subjects on the mainland to heel.[18]

Before his early departure that Sunday morning, the king had arranged to have the *Giornale ufficiale,* Naples's official newspaper, announce the pope's arrival. "We have the joy of announcing," it read, "that the Holy Father is among us and has chosen Gaeta as his residence." After noting that Ferdinand was already on his way to greet him, the paper added, "We now raise our prayers to the One on high, that He may bless His vicar and deliver not only His states, but the other countries of Europe as well from anarchy."

In reporting all this to Paris on the twenty-sixth, the French ambassador to Naples, Alphonse de Rayneval, remarked that the news was making a huge impression, promising to strengthen the position of the king and his government. The next day the official Neapolitan newspaper described the pope's munificence in allowing all the members of the royal family and the senior Neapolitan military officers to kiss his foot. The pope had come out onto his balcony at the end of the day to bless the assembled troops and Gaeta's inhabitants. "All had tears of emotion in their eyes," reported the Naples paper, "and burst into shouts of love and devotion for the pope, mixed with cries of 'Long live the king! Long live Ferdinand II!'"[19]

THE KING HAD PIUS moved into his own royal quarters in the fortress town. The inn that had first hosted him would quickly become a sacred site, the bed in which the pope slept that one night left untouched. "A pilgrimage to Gaeta, in the eyes of the Neapolitan," the London *Times* correspondent in Naples later reported, "has nearly the same merit as a pilgrimage to Mecca to all true Mussulmans.* The people see before them

---

* Muslims.

a martyr, a suffering saint." Whole families would come to marvel at the modest room where Pius IX spent his first night in exile and the simple iron bed on which he had slept.[20]

After the drama of his escape from Rome, the pope began to settle into a new life, a life of waiting, of prayer, of hoping. A time of great uncertainty for the pope, it was no less so for Europe's other leaders. The Papal States remained one of the bulwarks of the existing order. The pope's absence from Rome was destabilizing, the establishment of the papal court under the protection of the king of Naples adding to the disquiet. The possibility that radicals might soon take over the Papal States in the pope's absence and turn them into a republic was deeply threatening. Yet the prospect that the pope might now call for an invasion by foreign powers to reinstall him in the Eternal City raised its own alarms.

Amid all the uncertainty, no one knew how long the pope would remain in Gaeta, or where he might go next, Pope Pius IX least of all.

PART TWO

—

THE
REVILED

CHAPTER 9

THE REACTIONARY
TURN

GAETA COULD NOT ABSORB ALL THE SOLDIERS, DIPLOMATS, cardinals, and royal familiars who now converged on it. Built into a natural amphitheater at the base of a high cliff, the fortress town was perched on a point of land stretching into the Tyrrhenian Sea. Other than an occasional potted orange tree, it had no vegetation. A single passable road led at either end to one of the fortress's two gates, one on the port side. Both were locked at night. Military barracks and storerooms lined one side of the road, the modest royal residence and other homes the other.

The ambassadors found local accommodations a painful contrast with their Roman palaces. Some stayed in the nearby fishing village of Mola di Gaeta, which soon filled with an assortment of clerics, diplomats, and other august visitors. The Belgian ambassador reported his horror at finding the woolen sheets of his bed there crawling with white lice. Twenty-seven cardinals would make their way to Gaeta over the next month, but few stayed long, most finding accommodations more to their liking in Naples.[1]

While Pius was no longer in the bare room in which he spent his first night, the quarters the king gave him were far from luxurious. The fortress's royal residence was in fact a modest building with five windows facing the street, distinguished from its neighbors only by its green shutters and its lesser degree of grime. It had a ground floor, a mezzanine, and a second floor. The mezzanine housed the captain of the papal guard, placed there by the king. The pope's sparsely furnished room on the second floor was the best available, but most who saw it thought it barely habitable. There Pius, not one to complain about his personal comfort, received visitors next to his simple bed. Cardinal Antonelli occupied a room down the hall—his, too, serving as both bedroom and study. Smaller rooms served as waiting and meeting rooms for diplomats and other visitors.[2]

Again the pope found himself in need of a new secretary of state. Cardinal Soglia had taken refuge in his diocese, near Ancona, and sent the pope his resignation from the safety of his new home. It was said that he had left Rome in such a hurry that he had a red knee sock on one foot, a white one on the other. In any case, it was by then clear to the pope who was best suited to deal with the extraordinary challenges he faced. Cardinal Antonelli had stayed by his side when others fled. He had masterminded the pope's escape, and his loyalty was beyond any doubt. In early December, Pius appointed him secretary of state.[3]

If Pius had no taste for the game of politics, with its strategizing, posturing, and undercutting of rivals, Antonelli was its master. Pius could not help but speak from his heart when visitors came to see him, but the steely Antonelli was adept at speaking at great length without saying anything. While the pope had a deep belief in his spiritual mission as pontiff and an unshakable faith in the Almighty, Antonelli gave no indication of having any spiritual life at all. A tireless worker, ever eager to gain more power, he was isolated, trusting no one outside his own family. He had no friends, not even among the other cardinals, perhaps especially not among the cardinals, for they resented his influence over the pope.[4]

The final weeks of 1848 would prove decisive for the future of Italy and for the future of the church. When the pope first arrived at Gaeta, neither he nor anyone else knew how long he was likely to remain or what would happen in Rome in his absence. Would chaos envelop the city? Would civil war erupt, pitting the pope's supporters against the radicals? Would the pope be able to overcome his anger at the Romans' betrayal of him and seek a compromise that would allow him to return peacefully to the Eternal City? Would, as some in the church feared, the people of Rome, disgusted with the Catholic clergy, turn to Protestantism?

Both the pope and Antonelli insisted that their arrival in Gaeta had been fortuitous. "We had planned to go in a very different direction on leaving from Rome," the cardinal told his nuncio in Paris. If the Spanish ship that was supposed to take him to Majorca had in fact been waiting for him, Pius told the Piedmontese envoy later in the month, that is certainly where he would have gone.

The choice of the Kingdom of Naples bore the unmistakable mark of Antonelli's calculating mind. In Gaeta, the pope came under the protection of one of the most retrograde monarchies in Europe. The papal party could be assured they would come under no pressure to meet the rebellious Romans halfway. Nor would the weak king of Naples hinder their efforts to play the powers of Europe off one another as they determined how best to restore papal rule to Rome.[5]

WHILE ANTONELLI HAD NO intention of allowing the pontiff to leave the Kingdom of Naples until such time as he could return to Rome, many were urging him to do just that.[6] The Sardinian ambassador pleaded with the pope to come to the Savoyard kingdom; the Spanish ambassador urged the pope to go to Majorca; and Britain's ambassador in Naples offered a ship to take him to Malta. The Portuguese queen sent her own emissary to Gaeta to invite the pope to Portugal, where, reported the papal nuncio in Lisbon, the sumptuous royal palace of Mafra could host him "with the dignity due his high rank." But no country was more eager to see the pope land on its soil than France.[7]

When the pope made his escape from Rome, France was in the midst of an election campaign. Nine months earlier the French king had fled and a republic had been proclaimed. Now a presidential contest pitted the current head of the government, General Cavaignac—a military man committed to republican principles but with little political experience—against Louis Napoleon, whose principles, other than his devotion to the glory of the Napoleonic name, were unknown. Cavaignac had the moderate republicans behind him but was eager to capture the Catholic vote, and nothing would help his cause so much as luring the pope to France.[8]

On November 27, unaware that the pope had left Rome three days earlier, the French government ordered Admiral Charles Baudin—veteran of the Napoleonic wars and commander of French naval forces in the Mediterranean—to take four steam frigates, with thirty-five hundred men, from Marseilles to Civitavecchia to bring the pope to safety in France. On the same day that he ordered the admiral into action, the French foreign minister wrote Harcourt, informing him that, along with the troops, the government was sending Francisque Corcelle, a member of the National Assembly and a longtime friend of Cavaignac, to be special political envoy.[9]

Corcelle's instructions were to extract the pope without getting involved in the political dispute under way in the Papal States. A devout Catholic, the forty-six-year-old Corcelle was thought to be someone who could win the pope's trust, but when Corcelle arrived in Marseilles, intending to board a ship to Italy, he was told that Harcourt had already engineered the pope's flight from Rome. Witnesses in Civitavecchia had spotted Harcourt—along, they said, with members of the pope's retinue—leaving on a French steamship, the *Ténare*. The pope, it was presumed, was on board with them, on his way to France.[10]

The French government hurriedly began making arrangements for the pope's arrival. On the first of December, the minister of education and religion left Paris for Marseilles to head the welcoming committee. That same day General Cavaignac read to the members of the French National Assembly a telegram that had been sent from Civitavecchia six days earlier. "The Pope has furtively departed from Rome on the 24th," it read. "Rome remains calm and indifferent. . . . The Pope is coming to France. The *Ténare* has gone to take him from Gaeta."[11]

Only on election eve did Cavaignac receive the unwelcome news that Pius had decided to stay in Gaeta. On that day, too, a letter by Louis Napoleon, addressed to the papal nuncio in Paris, appeared in the country's newspapers. He wanted to reassure the Catholic world, he said, that he had nothing to do with Charles Bonaparte, his revolutionary cousin in Rome. "I deplore with all my soul," wrote Louis Napoleon, "that he hasn't recognized that the maintenance of temporal rule by the venerable Head of the Church is intimately linked to the splendor of Catholicism." His letter seemed to have the desired effect. Unexpectedly, he won the election in a landslide.[12]

Louis
Napoleon
Bonaparte

Under five and a half feet tall, with a long body and short legs, Louis Napoleon had a large nose, pallid complexion, small dull gray eyes, an air of ennui, a thin mustache, and a pointed beard. Unlike his rabble-rousing Roman cousin, he bore no resemblance to his famous uncle. An acquaintance from his days in exile in London described the new French president vividly if not kindly: "At no time of his life could the Emperor have been handsome. . . . The ornithological resemblance . . . was to a sick eagle: his head held slightly on one side; an abstracted look, his eyes small, and not at all prominent; his hair of a fine texture, not profuse; and lying flat on his head. Hands large and muscular." Having been partly educated in Germany, he spoke French with a German accent, his voice thin and nasal, his words sparing and issued in a monotone. He did not rise before ten each morning and spent much time in the company of Miss Howard, his English lover, who had followed him to Paris, although his main passion in life was riding his horse, Lizzie. Not known for his intelligence, and with no previous experience with government, he was viewed with barely concealed disdain by the French elite. Karl Marx judged him "mediocre and grotesque." Cavaignac refused to shake his hand when the election results were announced. Exactly where the new president stood politically was not clear, but he was able to rise to power by trading on French nostalgia for the glory days of Napoleonic rule.[13]

News that the pope was indeed not on his way to France had meanwhile prompted a new diplomatic push. In early December, Harcourt, the French ambassador to the Holy See, and Alphonse de Rayneval, French ambassador to Naples, were joined in Gaeta by the new French envoy, Corcelle. Pius led the Frenchmen to believe he was open to going to France but said that one concern held him back. He worried about Louis Napoleon, who as a young man had taken part in the rebellion that rocked the Papal States in 1831. Did the pope really want to put himself in the position of depending on such an unreliable patron? Meanwhile King Ferdinand, the Frenchmen realized, was doing all he could to fan the pope's fears.[14]

Nor were others in the diplomatic corps sympathetic to the French proposal, least of all Count Spaur, who had taken the pope to Gaeta to escape their clutches. "Preoccupied with the idea that Duke Harcourt and the commander of the *Ténare* were resolved on kidnapping the pope," observed the Belgian ambassador, himself one of the more reactionary influences in Gaeta, Spaur "always had his pistols loaded to defend him. A very tall man, he would have thrown his little colleague in the gulf of Gaeta without batting an eyelid, and if he had been allowed to do it, he would have slept every night outside Pius IX's door, with a complete arsenal of deadly weapons."[15]

The French diplomats believed that the pope's stay in France would in any case not be long, for as they told him, it was important that he be able to return peacefully to Rome to continue his work bringing greater freedom to the people of his domain. Embracing the reactionary King Ferdinand, they warned, would be a grave mistake.

It had only been a small number of people, the pope assured them, who had caused his problems in Rome. Most of his subjects, he insisted, remained devoted to him. As for continuing his work of reform, he told the Frenchmen, he still believed that religion was not incompatible with freedom.[16]

Yet the longer the pope was away from Rome, the weaker the voices around him recommending compromise would become. With few exceptions, the cardinals and the foreign ambassadors urged a hard line. It was compromise, they argued, that had led to the current crisis.[17]

Like the French, the British despaired of the pontiff's ever greater identification with the despotic king of Naples. "He could not have found a worse adviser in Europe!" observed Astley Key, captain of the *Bulldog*. Key wished the pope well but thought his prospects poor. "Poor Pio Nono!" he wrote a friend at the beginning of December. "His sun is clouded, I think not set; but it will never shine brilliantly. His case shows clearly that good intentions with public men avail nothing. A line of conduct is required, not a benevolent wish. A better-hearted man—and a weaker—does not exist."[18]

RUMORS OF ALL KINDS raced through the Eternal City. Austrian troops were said to be massing on the northern border of the Papal States, ready to march on Rome to restore the pope. The king of Naples was said to be readying his army to attack from the south. A republic, some predicted, would soon be declared in Rome, with Prince Charles Bonaparte as its head. But what people most wondered about was the pope himself. What would he do next?[19]

While some in Rome were calling for an end to the pope's temporal powers, what remained of the government urged caution. The radicals, the moderates feared, had driven things too far. After the pope's flight in late November, the two chambers addressed a message to the Romans, linking their authority to the pope's: "If the pontiff has decided to leave his residence, no one less than he would want to abandon you to the evils of social dissolution. He himself, at the time of his departure, assigned the ministry the task of ensuring order and peace. . . . Even in the absence of the person of the Sovereign, his spirit, his name and his authority are not far from us."[20]

Made uneasy by the ambassadors' decision to follow Pius to Gaeta, and aware that calls for foreign military intervention were in the air, Terenzio Mamiani, newly appointed minister of foreign affairs, sent a plea to all of Rome's embassies. Rossi's murder, he told them, was an outrage and the government would quickly punish those found guilty. The pope himself, the minister stressed, had never been in danger. During the violence that broke out on the sixteenth, the men who were now government ministers had done all they could to calm the protesters' fury and bring about a peaceful resolution. The underlying problem, Mamiani argued, was the difficulty of combining the pope's role as spiritual leader with his role as temporal ruler. The only solution was to find a way to safeguard the pope's spiritual powers while transforming the priest-run government into one run by laymen in the pope's name. The foreign minister ended his message by invoking the love that Italians bore for the pope, praising Pius as the "August initiator of National regeneration."[21]

Pius was in no mood for compromise. Within two days of his arrival in Gaeta, he had prepared a proclamation of his own, penning several drafts, each more uncompromising than the last. The abbot Rosmini, who had rushed to Gaeta to be at the pope's side, urged him to soften his tone, but to no avail. With the pope were both his brother and his nephew, moderate men who, along with Rosmini, pleaded with Pius to be more conciliatory. Some blamed Antonelli for pushing the pope to take a more confrontational stance than was in his nature, and there is little doubt that Antonelli was feeding the pope's sense of outrage. But with memories of his humiliating escape from Rome still fresh, Pius was not inclined to extend an olive branch to the men he held responsible for betraying him.[22]

"The violence used against Us in the past days," said the pope in his address to his subjects, "and the clear wish for further such outbursts . . . have forced Us to temporarily separate from Our subjects and children, whom We have always loved and love still." He then introduced what would become a major theme as Catholics tried to explain how a pope could be driven from Rome: it was God's punishment: "In the ingratitude of the children We recognize the hand of the Lord that strikes Us, wanting satisfaction for Our sins and those of the peoples." Pius recalled that on November 16 and 17 he had protested to the diplomatic corps the "unheard of violence and sacrilege." "We therefore declare," he concluded, "that all the acts that derived from that violence are of no effect and no legality." The men who now ruled Rome, declared the pope, men whom he himself had appointed in the wake of Rossi's assassination, had no legitimate authority.[23]

STUNG BY THE POPE'S condemnation, Rome's government ministers submitted their resignations, but the Chamber of Deputies persuaded them to stay on. Mamiani and the other moderate members of the government then proposed that they send a delegation to urge Pius to return. Opposing them were the radicals, including Charles Bonaparte and Pietro Sterbini, a former political exile and leader of the influential Popular Club. Sitting on the extreme left of the Chamber of Deputies, Bonaparte and Sterbini argued that, rather than pleading with the pope to come back to Rome, the deputies should proclaim the end of papal rule and create a republic in its place.

As a young man, Sterbini had trained in medicine in Rome, but his two great passions in life were literature and politics. Having fled the Papal States after unsuccessfully trying to get the Romans to join in the revolts of 1831, he had spent years in exile in Corsica and Marseilles, writing plays and practicing medicine, before returning to Rome in 1846, a beneficiary of the papal amnesty. Like others of the time, he had literally written songs of praise to Pio Nono, joining the chorus calling for the pope to head a great confederation of Italian states. But following the pope's announcement that he could never take part in a war against Catholic Austria, Sterbini had become one of the fiercest voices calling for the end of priestly rule.

The moderates despised Sterbini. "I have known few men with greater intelligence or more horrible appearance," recalled Marco Minghetti. "There was no infamy of which he was not accused. He was not loved or esteemed, but feared." Luigi Carlo Farini, future prime minister of Italy, was even more caustic: "Boss or servant of the Popular Club . . . he did not tolerate contrary opinions. Sinister by nature, an odd fellow, lacking both courage and good sense, he had all the characteristics of the plebeian despot."[24]

Much to the radicals' displeasure, the deputies voted to send a delegation to plead with the pope to return. They chose men for the mission they thought most likely to be able to persuade him. Among them was the octogenarian Prince Corsini, not known for his democratic sentiments, along with another moderate aristocrat, and two priests.[25]

Pietro
Sterbini

As the delegation made its way south, Pius's attention was elsewhere. He had convoked the cardinals for a meeting whose subject reveals a good deal about him. Pius wanted to discuss not the unfolding political crisis but rather the need for an encyclical proclaiming the doctrine of the Immaculate Conception, the belief that the Virgin Mary was born free from original sin. Two years earlier, when Rossi had sent the French foreign minister news of Mastai's election as pope, he had begun his description of the cardinal by saying that he was "very pious" although little schooled in the world of politics. That observation now seemed more apt than ever. Pius was a pastoral, not a political, pope. He was more at home in the spiritual realm than in the harsh and messy world of politics, and he would rather confront the theological question of the circumstances of Mary's birth two millennia earlier than the question of what to do now about his rebellious kingdom. Pius ordered the Roman delegation that the Chamber of Deputies had sent turned back at the border.[26]

Around the same time, another of Rome's leading citizens received a cold shoulder from the pope. Before he left Rome, the pope had charged Marquis Giralomo Sacchetti, a nobleman who had served as steward of the papal palaces since 1840, with ensuring the sanctity of the papal palaces in his absence. Sacchetti now arrived in Gaeta carrying a variety of religious ornaments that he thought Pius would want to have with him. The pope, in a surprisingly foul mood, told the marquis that if he had wanted anything, he would have asked for it. Taken aback, Sacchetti then handed Pius a letter that Rome's city council had asked him to convey, urging the pope to return to Rome. It seems that it was knowledge of the letter that Sacchetti was carrying that had led the pope to greet him so coldly. On being given the letter, the pope lost his temper and ordered the nobleman out of his room. Late in the day a low-ranking aide came out to tell Sacchetti that the pontiff wanted him to leave Gaeta within the hour. Finding that the gates to the fortress were already locked, the humiliated marquis was obliged to pass the night in the guardhouse, able to leave only when the gate opened the next morning.[27]

IF THE POPE HAD any consolation, it was King Ferdinand's extraordinary devotion. The monarch had liked to boast that his kingdom was safe, for it was defended on three sides by salt water and on one side by holy water. With the pope no longer in Rome, his northern border had lost its divine protection, a situation he aimed to correct. Ferdinand practically moved into Gaeta to be at the pope's side. He and his family would spend more time in the next month in that small fortress than in their own vast royal palace, glad for the excuse to be far from Naples.

Although Ferdinand had recently acquired the nickname of "Bomb King," in Rome he was more commonly called "the Boor," a reputation nourished by the king's own boast of never having held a book in his hands. Thirty-eight years old, the king was tall but poorly proportioned, with a short torso and unusually elongated loins. His beard formed a crescent around the bottom half of his face, in an unsuccessful attempt to hide chubby cheeks and an oddly long face. His voice was nasal, some said feminine, although when he gave orders, which was often, he had the ability to raise his volume to a level that none could ignore. He came from royalty on both sides, his mother a Spanish Bourbon. Educated by priests, as had long been the royal practice, he had been named commanding general of the Neapolitan army at age seventeen. He loved to wear his military uniform, his chest covered with self-awarded medals, golden braids hanging from the elaborate epaulets on his shoulders. Born in exile in Sicily at a time when Napoleon's troops had seized the Neapolitan mainland, Ferdinand had good reason to feel nervous about the precariousness of his reign.[28]

The king was uncharacteristically happy while in Gaeta, where he delighted in parading his troops and casting himself as papal champion. Dining nightly with the pope, who otherwise normally followed the papal custom of dining alone, he had given up his own rooms in Gaeta to Pius and Antonelli and made his wife and children share a single room in the fortress.[29]

While comforted by Ferdinand's attentions, Pius realized that if he were to regain his lands, he could not rely on the king alone. Ferdinand's army, not known for its effectiveness, was in any case busy fighting the insurgency in Sicily. In fact, Pius had no clear plan, nor was he sure he needed one. The Lord, he thought, would not allow Rome to fall to the Godless. After all, only four decades earlier a much more powerful force had driven a pope from Rome, but Pius VII had returned in triumph, while his nemesis, Napoleon, had died in lonely exile.[30]

What most pained him, though, was that not a single Roman had lifted a finger in defense of his rule. In the place of the paternal love he had felt for his subjects in the first months of his papacy, a burning sense of betrayal now took root, fed by Antonelli and the other cardinals.[31]

WITH THE POPE IN EXILE, Rome was leaderless. To fill the void, on December 11 the Chamber of Deputies created a three-member executive to serve until the pope returned. Outside the Palace of the Chancellery, where the chamber met, the Popular Club organized a demonstration to show the people's support for the government. Ciceruacchio, the popular hero, gesticulating and declaiming from his perch on the palace steps, whipped the crowd into a frenzy. Along with the patriotic cries of

"Long live the Provisional Government! Long live Italy! Long live Uni-fication!" came more chilling calls: "Down with the rich! Down with the priests!" The people began singing the *Marseillaise*.

To add to the excitement, Giuseppe Garibaldi—veteran of the wars of independence in South America and, more recently, of the battle to drive the Austrians from Lombardy—rode into Rome on his white horse, having left his legionnaires back in Tuscany. "Long live the re-publican general!" shouted the people gathered at the Popular Club. But many Romans were relieved when, a week after his arrival, Garibaldi—dubbed a "foreign adventurer" by his detractors—left the city.

For the most part, calm prevailed. Most Romans still hoped they

Ciceruacchio speaks to the people

could keep a constitutional government with the pope at its head. What they worried about were their jobs, many of which had been lost with the departure of Rome's noble families. Astley Key, the British naval commander, visited Rome in mid-December and praised the people for showing such moderation. They had preserved the existing form of government and had urged the pope to return. "However," he added in a private letter, "it is impossible for this state of things to continue. Either the Pope must return to a part of his own dominions"—Key suggested—"or the form of government must be changed." Should the pope refuse to return, the Romans would have little choice, thought the naval officer, but to proclaim a republic.[32]

In Gaeta, the abbot Rosmini urged Pio Nono to find a peaceful solution to the crisis. The pope, who was fond of him, and whose moods lurched between stubborn intransigence born of a feeling of betrayal and an eagerness to regain the affection of his subjects, seemed finally to have softened. He asked Rosmini to prepare a message that he could use.

The people, wrote the abbot in his draft, had wronged their pontiff, a man who had done so much in his two years on St. Peter's throne to ensure their happiness. If they would simply recognize the wrong they had done, he would return to Rome, retain the constitutional guarantees he had granted the people, and all would be forgiven. Rosmini was not the only one who thought that such an approach had a good chance of success. The Sardinian envoy in the Eternal City reported that the Romans had had enough of turmoil and uncertainty. They feared that if the pope did not return peacefully, foreign armies would soon come to install him by force.

It was Antonelli, though, who lived with the pope and constantly had his ear, and Antonelli despised Rosmini, most of all because of the affection Pius clearly had for him. Although Pius did indeed like and respect Rosmini, a man of great intellectual stature, he depended on Antonelli. The descent from the splendor of papal Rome to the poverty of life in the fortress, the uncertainty of how or if he would ever return to the Eternal City, the nagging thought that he had failed in the awesome responsibility he had assumed in taking St. Peter's throne, all led him to find comfort in Antonelli's self-assurance. The abbot could not compete.

The cardinal persuaded Pius to jettison Rosmini's text. In its place, he talked him into issuing a very different message, denouncing Rome's new government as "a usurpation of Our sovereign powers." The statement made no mention of retaining any of the reforms that had so endeared Pius to the people, but if the cardinal prevailed it was because the pontiff himself was of two minds. Antonelli needed only fan the embers of betrayal already smoldering in Pius's heart.[33]

The London *Times* correspondent from Naples offered a bleak view. "In an ill-advised hour," he reported, "Pio Nono abandoned Rome . . . and . . . I cannot see how he is to get back. The diplomatic corps that surround him are more engaged in watching each other than in devising means for his restoration, and all appear, like cads of rival omnibuses at Charing-cross, on the alert to carry him off, each in his own conveyance."[34]

IN CITIES AND TOWNS throughout the Papal States, popular clubs clamored for a constituent assembly aimed at ending the pope's temporal power. In the absence of political parties, the clubs were the only organized form of popular participation in political life. In Rome, the fiery Charles Bonaparte seemed to be everywhere, urging an end to priestly rule. Mazzini, the exiled prophet of Italian independence, urged his supporters on: "Pius IX has fled, his flight is an abdication. . . . You are in fact now a republic." Abandoned by the pontiff, the moderates who had previously advised him now felt helpless. With the pope refusing to talk to the representatives of the government in Rome, they had no credible plan to propose. As one wrote from Rome on December 20, "We are witnessing the most miserable political spectacle imaginable. A people has become fully in charge of its own fate, and does not know what to do. . . . The fact is the manifestos of the Clubs are coming in from the provinces, calling for a Provisional Government and a Constitutional Assembly, and the same demands are being heard here as well, but no one really wants to proclaim either of them."[35]

Despite pressure from its more radical wing, the Chamber of Deputies was reluctant to act. On December 26 one of the chamber's moderates tried to make the case that it had no authority to create such a body. The angry crowd in the gallery shouted him down. Increasingly, even the moderates, forsaken by the pope and horrified by his embrace of King Ferdinand, felt no other path was open. "It was not the people who made the revolution," observed Charles Bonaparte, "but the Sovereign."[36]

No one better illustrates the radicalization of the moderates than Carlo Armellini. One of Rome's most prominent lawyers, a man known for his sober judgment, Armellini had become an influential member of the Chamber of Deputies. Called upon to help guide Rome in the power vacuum left by the pope's sudden departure, the seventy-one-year-old Armellini took the post of minister of internal affairs in a government still headed by Monsignor Carlo Muzzarelli.[37]

On December 28, it was Armellini who came to the podium and urged the Chamber of Deputies to authorize the convening of a constituent assembly. The man who had hailed Pius IX on his election, and upon whom the pope had relied in the first two years of his papacy, now turned against him. Those who sought to dethrone the pope were not, as some later defenders of the Papal States would suggest, troublemakers from outside the pope's lands but men who, like Armellini, were Romans to their core. As he spoke, the excited applause and supportive shouts from the gallery, packed with both men and women, forced Armellini to pause now and then to let the noise to die down:

> Can we or can we not continue at length in the current state of things, with a precarious Power, represented by a Sovereign who flees, who rejects every attempt to talk, and who, unwilling even to accept messages of peace, forces us to give up any hope of reconciliation? . . . Such a state of things cannot last; it must end. How however can one cope with it? Tell me what other means can be employed. Could there be anything more natural, surer, more legitimate, than a solemn call to the Nation? It must decide its own fate. . . . Can there be some other Lord more legitimate than the People, the People themselves?[38]

The following day the decision was made. Pietro Sterbini himself raced through Rome's streets in a carriage, directing the placement of the proclamation on the city's walls. A vote for members of the Constituent Assembly would be held on January 21, its two hundred members to be elected by universal male suffrage—a first in Italy. A hundred and one cannon blasts sounded from Castel Sant'Angelo, and for the next hour bells rang throughout the city. In the evening, festive crowds marched up Capitoline Hill, plastering the iconic equestrian statue of Marcus Aurelius with the tricolored flags of Italy so that no sign of the Roman emperor below could be seen. Bands played, and fireworks lit the sky. A patriotic priest from Venice stood up on the Aurelius pedestal to pronounce the creation of a government of the people to be an act blessed by God.

Yet amid all the festivity, signs of uncertainty were not hard to find. Hearing the blasts of the cannon coming from so close to the Vatican, some Romans thought they were signaling the pope's sudden return, and many rushed to the nearby city gate, eager to greet him.[39]

AMONG THE POPE'S LAST visitors in 1848 were two envoys sent by King Charles Albert, come to make one last attempt to persuade the pope to move to Piedmont. Their mission was destined to fail. Pius felt more secure where he was, and he was not well disposed to the Sardinian king. In recent months, the Sardinian government, now ruled by a constitution, had made efforts to limit the church's influence, including its hold over public education, and had also tried to curtail some of the clergy's privileges. It did not help that the newly appointed Sardinian prime minister was the patriotic priest Vincenzo Gioberti, scourge of the Jesuits. Nor was the pope pleased by the fact that the Sardinian government showed no interest in taking part in any military effort to restore him to Rome.[40]

In late December, Father Luigi Tosti, a Benedictine monk and old friend of the pope, came to visit him. Tosti was taken aback by the modesty of the pope's room. "On seeing me," recalled the monk, the pontiff "began to cry, something that had never happened before." He seemed not angry but depressed. How, Pius asked his friend, could a few demagogues have led the people so far astray?[41]

CHAPTER 10

REVOLUTION

I T HAD NOT BEEN SO MANY MONTHS SINCE ROMANS HAD PARADED through Rome's streets singing odes to the pope. The piazza beneath his window had filled with thousands of the faithful eager to glimpse his benevolent smile and to bask in the warmth of his blessing. Now Rome's streets once again became scenes of jubilation, but it was not the pope whose praises they were singing.

On January 2, 1849, in the wake of the announced plans for a constituent assembly, former papal soldiers marched through the streets, their artillery in tow, followed by Civic Guardsmen clutching their rifles. They converged on Piazza del Popolo, where armed men set a pile of wood afire to the sound of bands playing patriotic melodies. As sparks fluttered into the dark sky, drifting up toward the crescent moon, the men surged on to the Campidoglio, Capitoline Hill. There tricolored fireworks burst in the sky, illuminating the Italian flags that covered the bronzed Marcus Aurelius.

Not everyone was celebrating. The livelihood of many Romans depended on the presence of the pope, the cardinals, and the aristocrats. They looked on as others paraded, anxious about what was to come.[1]

Nor did the rest of the Papal States see a great outpouring of popular enthusiasm at the time. The moderates felt paralyzed, unhappy with the radical direction being taken but repelled by the pope's embrace of the reactionary king of Naples. "It is my firm conviction," wrote Captain Key on January 3, "that there exists a nearly universal wish for the

Pope's return, and that a very slight conciliatory disposition on his part would be responded to, and meet with favourable terms of accommodation, by his subjects."[2]

The pope, though, was in no mood for compromise. He used his New Year's address to condemn the sacrileges, murders, and other outrages that, he said, had swept Rome. His words were harsh, as he dismissed the "sterile invitation to return to Our Capital, without any word of condemnation of the above-mentioned attacks and without the least guarantee that assures Us against the illegalities, and the violence of this same bunch of lunatics, who still today tyrannize Rome and the Papal States with their barbarous despotism." He denounced the "detestable" decision to establish "a so-called National General Assembly of the Roman State" and warned the Romans that it would be a grave sin for anyone to support it.[3]

If the pope had any notion that this condemnation, widely viewed as a threat of excommunication, would help his cause, events would quickly prove him wrong. His vilification of those who favored change provoked widespread anger and, even worse, ridicule. Demonstrators broke into an ecclesiastical apparel store in Rome and made off with its stock of red cardinal hats along with a white papal skullcap. These they paraded through the streets to much hilarity before flinging them into the Tiber. Copies of the pope's address were ripped from the doors of Rome's basilicas and deposited in the city's latrines. Some of the more mischievous dressed up as priests, giggling as they mumbled irreverent imitations of priestly chants. "Long live the Excommunicated! *Bon voyage* to the pope and the cardinals!" they shouted. Large protest marches followed, and the pope's coat of arms was torn from government buildings and tossed from the Ponte Sisto into the Tiber.[4]

Rome's newspapers were unsparing in their attacks on the pope. Extracts were plastered on the city's walls and distributed as leaflets. Far from casting the new path as a rejection of religion, they portrayed it as following God's will:

Mastai Ferretti has raised his hand only twice, once to bless, and then to curse. He blessed a man who bombed his own people, and the men who enforced his brutal tyranny. He cursed his own people. Neither the one, nor the other, was the word of God.

Courage, Roman People! Have true faith, true love of the fatherland, conscience, and determination, and God will be with
you. One day the Pontiff, freed from his prison, will repent of his
error, a child of his weakness and of the overwhelming desires of
those who oppress and control him, and he will return to the love
of his children and to the duties of his heavenly mission.[5]

The pope's New Year's denunciation triggered a violent reaction in
other cities of the Papal States as well, prompting some bishops to judge
it prudent not to make it public. An article from one of Rome's major
newspapers, copies pasted on the city's walls, trumpeted the fact that
Bologna's archbishop had decided against promulgating "the act of excommunication." After consulting a group of distinguished theologians,
or so the article claimed, the archbishop had determined that the pope's
message was not in accord with Catholic doctrine.[6]

The American consul in Rome, Nicholas Brown, not averse to rhe-
torical flourishes, informed Washington that "in spite of the anile, tau-
tologous prolixity of this extraordinary document," he had decided to
send the full text of the pope's remarks. An abridgment, he explained,
"could hardly do justice to its imbecility."[7]

EUROPE'S POLITICAL SITUATION WAS far from stable. Less than a year
earlier, a revolution in France had toppled the monarchy and ushered in
a republic. In Naples, King Ferdinand had been forced to grant a constitution, Sicily was still in full revolt, and unrest continued to threaten the
capital itself. In the wake of Charles Albert's capitulation to the Austrian
army, the king of Sardinia was himself "very shaky on his throne," as
Captain Key put it. "Do not be surprised," the British naval officer added
in a letter to England, "if you hear of Charles Albert taking refuge on
board the *Bulldog*."[8]

Austria had seen Prince Metternich driven into exile the previous
year, and then at the close of that year, the feebleminded Ferdinand,
emperor since 1835, had abdicated, elevating his nephew, the eighteen-
year-old Franz Joseph, to the imperial throne. The new emperor—
destined to reign for almost seven decades—was something of a mystery.

"He is animated by good principles, the result of a Catholic education," observed the papal nuncio in Vienna, but "it is difficult to judge his intelligence, for he speaks very little."

Metternich's place had been taken by the forty-eight-year-old Prince Felix Schwarzenberg, a soldier at heart, of distinguished appearance, proud of his military bearing and cool under fire. Self-assured, some would say arrogant, he would continue to wear his military uniform even as prime minister. "Prince Schwarzenberg," recalled one of his friends, "had the greatest contempt for the human race, but he had not a profound knowledge of human nature." A loyal Catholic, firmly committed to the old order, and convinced that the papal theocracy was key to European stability, Schwarzenberg quickly became the point of reference for those of the cardinals—Antonelli very much included—who dreamed of restoration.[9]

Since the previous spring, when Vienna had ordered its envoy to leave Rome, Austria had had no ambassador to the Holy See. Given the pope's new circumstances, finding a replacement now became urgent. Count Moritz Esterházy seemed well suited to the job. He belonged to one of Hungary's most devout Catholic families and as a youth had spent several years in Rome. His principles, the nuncio reported in informing Antonelli of the appointment, were very Catholic and very conservative. Although not yet forty years old, Esterházy had already served as Austria's ambassador to the Netherlands.[10]

As the new ambassador prepared to set off for Gaeta, Schwarzenberg sent him instructions. Italians, complained the prime minister, thought Austria exercised undue influence in Italy. "Nothing," he remarked, "is more absurd, yet nothing is more generally believed in Italy. . . . The ignorance of the masses there and the bad faith of those who are educated . . . nourish a prejudice that, Monsieur* Count, you have been called upon to destroy wherever you encounter it." What Italy needed, Schwarzenberg was convinced, was a well-ordered society, where people respected the authorities. He was open to the idea, proposed the previous month by Spain, of a congress of the Catholic powers to jointly

---

* In these decades, Austrian diplomatic correspondence was written in French, not in German.

Felix Schwarzenberg

plan the pope's return to power. What could never be tolerated were French or British efforts to bring a peaceful end to the conflict by serving as mediators between the pope and his subjects. Pius, advised Schwarzenberg, must pay no attention to those who were trying to get him to leave Gaeta, nor to those urging him to negotiate with the men who had usurped his power.[11]

Distrustful of France and lacking confidence in the military abilities of the other Catholic states, Cardinal Antonelli hoped to persuade the Austrian government to take the lead in restoring the pope to Rome. Schwarzenberg opposed the idea, for he did not want to antagonize France, which had made its opposition to unilateral Austrian action clear. Austria's hold on northeastern Italy remained tenuous, the intentions of Louis Napoleon and France's republican government uncertain. The last thing Schwarzenberg wanted to do was push the new government in France to support King Charles Albert in an effort to drive the Austrians from the peninsula.[12]

While the Austrians' goals were clear—restoration of the Papal States under the pope's sole authority—the French government's were

not. Not long after his election, Louis Napoleon had sent the pope a letter that expressed concern for his well-being but, much to Pius's dismay,
said nothing about what aid France might offer to restore him to Rome.
The new French prime minister, Odilon Barrot, a strong supporter of
the popular uprising that had swept the Papal States in 1831, had no sympathy for the pope's role as king. To further complicate matters, there
was also a large and loud left wing in the French parliament. Fiercely
anticlerical, it saw the revolt in Rome as a sister movement, aimed at
bringing down the old autocratic order and ushering in a modern republic. In early January, Édouard Drouyn, the new French foreign minister
and himself unsympathetic to the pope's claims to temporal power,
warned that any unilateral military action by the Austrian government in
Rome risked provoking war with France.[13]

Pius briefly harbored the hope that he might avoid these foreign en-
tanglements by relying on his own army to retake his states for him. In
early January he sent word to General Zucchi, who had earlier helped
quell unrest in the northern provinces of the Papal States, to come to
Gaeta. But rather than agreeing to organize a military expedition on the
pope's behalf, as Pius had hoped, the general tried to convince him that
his wisest course would be to keep his constitution and find a peaceful
resolution to the conflict.[14]

While the French still held out hope that the liberal pontiff who had
earlier endeared himself to his people could somehow be brought back
to Rome, others recognized that the previous year's traumas had left a
permanent mark. "It is best not to have any more illusions about the
pope," observed Venice's envoy to the Holy See. "He is a man with good
intentions, but he sees himself solely as the representative and the guarantor of the Church. From such a man Italy can fear everything. And
one must not kid oneself. The pope is powerful. In Rome he is all powerful."[15]

JANUARY 21 WAS A beautiful sunny Sunday, and throughout the Papal
States men of all classes came to cast their ballots for the Constituent Assembly. A quarter of a million people—about a third of those eligible—
voted, in the first mass election in Italian history. A week later, at noon,

an immense crowd gathered in the piazza atop Capitoline Hill, as the names of the successful candidates were read from the balcony. Among those elected from Rome were the leaders of the interim government: the Latin-loving ecclesiastical lawyer Monsignor Muzzarelli; the radical poet-doctor Pietro Sterbini; the distinguished attorney Carlo Armellini; and the redoubtable rabble-rouser Prince Charles Bonaparte. Although the men of the lower, illiterate classes could vote, those elected all came from the middle and upper classes. No Ciceruacchio was among them. As the last name was pronounced, the city's bells began to ring and 101 artillery blasts sounded, with the cannon at Castel Sant'Angelo responding in kind.[16]

The large turnout for the Constituent Assembly elections deeply disturbed the pope. "In Rome," wrote Pius to one of the prelates closest to him, "the most deplorable acts are taking place. . . . Nonetheless, the Lord, who has always protected Rome from evil . . . will save it again: Let us hope and pray."[17]

To Harcourt, the French ambassador, who warned that relying on Austrian and Neapolitan armies to return him to Rome would bring disaster, Pius replied that he had heard no clear offer of help from France. Meanwhile the voices pushing a hard line were growing ever stronger. "It is necessary to use force, more force, always force," advised the Belgian ambassador. Feeling ever more isolated, the patriotic abbot Antonio Rosmini left Gaeta in late January. "As for me," he confided, "I was never asked my opinion about anything, and if sometimes I dared to give some advice, it was never followed."[18]

Cardinal Antonelli kept sending out apocalyptic warnings. Events in Rome, he told the nuncio in Madrid in late January, "are progressing each day toward total ruin by the growing audacity and impiety of that illegitimate and sacrilegious government." Every moment that passed without action, he charged, "is fatal to religion and the Church while the anti-Catholic party is doing all in its power to create absolute rule in Rome through arms and through terror."[19]

While the cardinal portrayed Rome as a theater of chaos and violence, Romans were in fact largely going about their business as before. Some priests refused to perform marriages for men who had voted in the recent elections, but many clerics spoke at public meetings in favor of a new order, one in which the pope's role would be confined to the religious sphere. "Whatever malevolence . . . may insinuate," reported the American consul in Rome, "order & peace never reigned more profoundly within her ancient walls." He had recently attended an opera performance of Verdi, to a packed house.[20]

Although hope for peaceful reconciliation was fast ebbing, a flicker still remained. At the end of January, Monsignor Muzzarelli, now a member of the provisional Roman government, summoned the British consul to the Quirinal Palace to give him a message for London. The members of Rome's government, he insisted, "had lost no occasion of assuring His Holiness that they were not only ready, but anxious to place into the hands of His Holiness all the power they held, provided His Holiness would return as a Constitutional Sovereign, and unaccompanied by the 'Camarilla'* at Gaeta." It was the pope's refusal to talk with the delegation they had sent the previous month that had forced them, said the monsignor, to take the course they had.[21]

While the political climate in Rome was uncertain, the weather was not. In contrast to the previous year's cold, rainy winter, this one was beautiful and sunny. With Carnival, always a high point of the year, approaching, the mood was festive, although some familiar elements were missing from the Carnival procession. The dukes and princes whose richly decorated carriages and fancily dressed attendants were normally among the main attractions were largely gone. Those who had stayed might have wished they hadn't. As the carriages of the few remaining aristocrats rolled along the cobblestone Corso, the people lining the way hurled insults, aimed not only at the noblemen but at their liveried attendants. "Down with the aristocrats! Off with the signs of servitude! Off with the fake hair braids!" they shouted. To mark the occasion, the gates to Rome's jail were opened, and the prostitutes imprisoned in them freed.[22]

AS THE DAYS PASSED in Gaeta, the foreign ambassadors—previously accustomed to spending their evenings in Rome traveling from one aris-

---

* The reference is to a small group of nefarious advisers.

tocrat's palazzo to another in their luxurious carriages—did their best to make do with the isolation and poverty of their new surroundings. Most days they ate lunch together and assembled again in the evening to dine. At eight p.m. some of them would change into their long tails and black ties for an hour's visit with the pope before returning to a new hand of whist, their cigars clouding the air. Their evening gatherings sometimes extended to one a.m.[23]

In early February, a new colleague arrived. Pius greeted Austria's new ambassador warmly. "I was being awaited," reported Moritz Esterházy, "like the Messiah. . . . It is on us, on Austria, that all hope for safety is placed." Short, slender, and well proportioned, Esterházy exuded energy. He was a man of good cheer, who projected a sense of elegance and distinction. He was "somewhat malicious like all very small men," commented an acquaintance, "but a pleasant talker."

Unlike his French colleagues in Gaeta, Esterházy was not one to suffer from illusions. He asked only one thing from the pope: in order for the emperor to justify sending his army, he would need an explicit request. There was unfortunately much ill will toward the Austrian army in the Papal States, so the pope's unambiguous call for Austrian military intervention was crucial.[24]

The next day Cardinal Antonelli, unhappy with the proposed conference of Catholic powers first suggested by Spain and now supported by Austria, wrote to his nuncio in Paris. "The immediate intervention of armed forces," insisted the secretary of state, "is an absolute necessity." He was especially upset that Austria was being so deferential to the French, having made known its reluctance to act alone. "If France does not judge it to be in its interests to join in participating in the necessary work with Austria and the king of Naples and others," complained the cardinal, "they should at least leave the field open for these powers."[25]

While Antonelli was unhappy, Count Esterházy thought all was going remarkably well. "The abbot Rosmini, Pius IX's evil genius and, without a doubt, our most formidable enemy," he reported to Vienna in mid-February, "is in Naples and has not reappeared at the Gaeta palace since my arrival." With Rosmini gone, he wrote, "Pius IX . . . is throwing himself in the arms of Austria! I believe his conversion to be sincere. . . . I would not say that it is deep, because I fear that there is nothing very deep to be found in this Prince."

Moritz
Esterházy

Although the new Austrian ambassador was not impressed with Pio Nono's strength of character, he had a very different opinion of the man who stood ever at his side: "We have acquired Cardinal Antonelli by conviction, as we have the great majority of the Sacred College [of Cardinals]." Praising the secretary of state's energy, and his analytical and political skills, Esterházy added, "It is in us alone that he puts his hopes." Antonelli had made clear he wanted the Austrians to launch their assault on the Papal States without delay. The less the unreliable French were involved, thought the secretary of state, the better.

MONDAY, FEBRUARY 5, MARKED the opening of the Constituent Assembly. Gathering at midmorning atop Rome's Capitoline Hill, the deputies—proudly wearing scarves bearing Italy's three colors—filed into the enormous Basilica of Santa Maria in Ara Coeli to begin the momentous day with a mass. Because the vice gerent, the prelate in charge of Rome's clergy in the absence of Rome's cardinal vicar, had forbidden the priests there to participate, a military chaplain presided.

A large, festive crowd joined the deputies when they emerged from the church. People from all fourteen of the city's *rioni* marched through the streets with them, each under its own banner, and delegations from all of Italy's regions marched too, flying their own flags. The banner of the veterans of the campaign in Lombardy was distinctive, covered in black crepe, a sign of mourning for their recent loss to the Austrian army. Political exiles from Naples and Sicily proudly carried their own flags aloft as well. Bringing up the rear were the various Roman clubs, militias, and the Civic Guard. Bands struck up the *Marseillaise*. Among those elected to the Constituent Assembly, Prince Charles Bonaparte marched alongside the Hero of Two Worlds, the swashbuckling Giuseppe Garibaldi, dressed in the military fatigues he had worn in his South American exploits. And while virtually all the ambassadors were in Gaeta with the pope, the American consul, Nicholas Brown, marched proudly, dressed in his formal diplomatic uniform. He apparently had not thought it necessary to await instructions from Washington, which, when they eventually arrived, would forbid him from recognizing Rome's new government.[26]

By the time the 140 deputies who made it to the opening day entered the Chancellery Palace—in whose courtyard the pope's prime minister had so recently had his throat slit—the gallery was crammed with spectators. Some might have noticed that the bust of Pius IX that normally adorned the hall was no longer there.

It was now more than two months since the pope had fled, leaving no government in place other than the one that he had no sooner named, following Rossi's murder, than he had, in exile, deemed illegitimate. The upper and lower chambers had been disbanded, and the administrative machinery of the Papal States lay in ruins. The various provinces of the Papal States had largely gone off on their own, and throughout the pope's kingdom, the merchants, the clubs, and the newspapers were all calling on the members of the newly elected Assembly to do something quickly to fill the void.

Amid this uncertainty, Carlo Armellini rose to give the opening address to the Assembly. The era of theocracy, of monarchs ruling by divine right, proclaimed the distinguished lawyer, was over. Pius had begun his papacy with great promise but then seemed increasingly ill at ease with what he had done. By rejecting the fight for Italian independence, he had betrayed the national cause. "You sit here, o Citizens, amidst the ruins of two great eras," concluded Armellini. "On one side lie the ruins of Italy of the Caesars, on the other the ruins of Italy of the Popes. It is your task to construct a building that can rise from that rubble."[27]

When the applause died down, the roll was called. Garibaldi then asked the Assembly to waste no time in debate and immediately proclaim a republic. Bonaparte rose to second him. "Do you not feel the sacred soil shake under our feet?" asked the prince. "It is the souls of your ancestors who tremble with impatience, and who shout in your ear: 'Long live the Roman Republic!' "[28]

The deputies did not delay long. At two a.m. on February 9, they voted a historic four-part decree:

1. The papacy no longer exercises temporal power over the Roman State either in fact or in law.

2. The Roman pontiff will have all the guarantees necessary to freely exercise his spiritual authority.

3. The form that the Government of the Roman State will have is pure democracy, and it will take the glorious name of the Roman Republic.

4. The Roman Republic will have with the rest of Italy those relations required by their common nationality.

The pope's temporal power was no more. Only an army could bring it back, if it could be brought back.[29]

That afternoon, from the city hall's loggia atop Capitoline Hill, leaders of the Assembly read the decree to the large crowd below, as Italian flags waved. News of the proclamation of the republic appeared on walls throughout the Papal States:

The great act has been accomplished. The National Assembly, sitting as your legitimate representatives, having recognized the sovereignty of the people, the only form of government congenial to us, that which made our fathers great and glorious. . . . After so many centuries we once again have our fatherland and our freedom. Let us show ourselves worthy of the gift that God has sent us.[30]

In one of its first acts, the Assembly decreed that all the new republic's laws would begin with the words "In the name of God and the People," a motto long championed by the prophet of a united republican Italy, Giuseppe Mazzini. The gold and silver coins to be minted would likewise bear the slogan "God wants Italy united." The republic's flag would consist of Italy's three colors—red, white, and green—with an eagle, symbol of ancient Rome, perched atop its staff.[31]

ON SUNDAY, FEBRUARY 11, an immense crowd, including the members of the new Constituent Assembly and many Civic Guardsmen and troops, packed into St. Peter's Basilica for a special Te Deum ceremony to thank God for the birth of the new republic. That same day the pope, following his own modest mass in Gaeta, summoned the new Austrian ambassador to his cramped room. Esterházy would be stunned by what the pope proposed in their two-hour meeting.

"Pope Pius IX," reported Esterházy to Vienna, "no longer today simply calls for our aid together with that of France, Spain, and Naples, but he is throwing himself entirely and with the greatest confident abandon into the arms of Austria and solicits, *through me*, its *immediate* armed intervention *alone* in favor of his cause." For the purpose of public consumption, the pope explained, he would formally address his plea to all four of the powers, but, he told Esterházy, this was simply for show. The pope, reported the ambassador, wanted Vienna to know "that all his hopes rested on Austria alone, that our intervention alone, if circumstances allowed it, would be the most desirable eventuality under all respects in his eyes."

In explaining his request to the Austrian ambassador, Pius admitted to considerable personal sympathy for Catholic France, but, he explained, "he could only view with repugnance the prospect of Republican France's armed intervention in his States." The pontiff—his worries fanned by Antonelli—feared that should French troops seize Rome, they would force him to return to constitutional rule. And how confident could he really be that France—which itself had overthrown its monarchy and proclaimed a republic only a year earlier—could be counted on to crush its sister republic in Rome and restore the papal monarchy?[32]

Three days after meeting with Esterházy, the pope summoned all the cardinals who could join him, nineteen in all, along with all the ambassadors to the Holy See, for a dramatic gathering at his room in Gaeta. The men formed a semicircle facing the pope and Antonelli, with the cardinals to one side, the ambassadors to the other. Pius branded the recent announcement of the end of papal rule in Rome as a product of "injustice, ingratitude, stupidity, and impiety." "You comfort our spirit in these dark days," he told the ambassadors. "You followed us to this land, where the Hand of God led us, the Hand that . . . never abandons those who trust in Him." Cardinal Antonelli then handed the ambassadors a copy of the papal protest to send their governments, before giving them a second document. It was the pope's written call for military intervention that the Austrian ambassador had requested, addressed to Austria, Spain, France, and Naples.

In reporting the papal call to arms, the Dutch ambassador pointed out that it failed to solicit aid from King Charles Albert's Savoyard kingdom—"that is to say," he noted, "the only government that still enjoys any popularity in Italy." With Austria and Sardinia having recently fought a war, the pope could hardly imagine involving both on his side. The choice was in any case not difficult, for the Sardinian government had made clear its opposition to having foreign armies return the pope to power.[33]

FOUR DAYS LATER, SEVEN THOUSAND Austrian troops crossed the Po River, headed toward Ferrara, the northernmost city of the Papal States. When Pius learned the news, he summoned the Austrian ambassador to express his gratitude. "All I ask now," the pontiff told Esterházy, "is that, for goodness sake, you do not turn back, but on the contrary, you bring more troops and advance as rapidly as possible."[34]

News of the Austrian invasion shook Rome. At a special midnight session of the Constituent Assembly, as the crowd in the gallery chanted *Viva la Repubblica!* Pietro Sterbini rose to speak. "The days that we all foresaw have arrived," proclaimed the fiery poet-doctor, "days of trial and of courage.

> The league between the priestly caste, Austria, and the Bourbon has been formed. . . . The Austrian has thrown down the gauntlet, challenging all of Italy, and it has done it with that insult that, if it is not washed away by blood, would make us the object of ridicule before all of Europe. . . . We gladly accept your challenge, o Vandal. You will have your war to the death and to extermination. Rise up, children of Italy. God wants to speed the day of our redemption. To arms![35]

Rome's new government now moved quickly against the church. In mid-February a printed warning had appeared on Rome's walls, urging priests to dispense with their triangular black hats and short pants, condemned as signs of reaction and ignorance. That day, too, Carlo Armellini, one of the three men newly elected to the executive, sent out an order to all ecclesiastical bodies demanding a full inventory of their property. Worried that this was the first step to confiscation of church holdings, the vice gerent instructed all religious institutions to reject the request. As a result, not a few priests and monks, refusing to cooperate with the new authorities, were marched off to jail.

In an act reminiscent of the French Revolution, when it was declared that each town needed only one church bell, the rest to be melted to make coins and weapons, Rome's new rulers ordered all the city's unused church bells melted down to forge cannons for the republic's defense. Ecclesiastical control of all schools and universities was ended, excluding only religious seminaries. All horses found in the Vatican and Quirinal Palaces were confiscated, as were all those owned by the pope's Noble Guard.[36]

No action in these first weeks was more fraught with symbolism than

the liberation of the Inquisition's prisoners. When the republican authorities arrived at the Inquisition Palace, a stone's throw from St. Peter's, they found the Dominican monk who held the keys to the cells
playing cards with two unsavory-looking jailers. Chained in the small,
dank cells were men and women who had been variously found guilty of
swearing, witchcraft, defamation of the Catholic religion, or, in the case
of two nuns, falling in love. Freed from their chains, they unsteadily
made their way into the glow of Rome's bright sun.

By the beginning of March, all special privileges for the clergy were
eliminated, as well as all ecclesiastical tribunals having jurisdiction over
laypeople. The church's vast landholdings were declared state property,
and censorship was abolished.[37]

These moves prompted furious denunciations from Gaeta. The
newly proclaimed Roman Republic, Cardinal Antonelli told all who
would hear, ruled only by fear, intimidation, and fraud. Other than a few
fanatics, he declared, and a small number of the credulous seduced by
their false promises, it lacked all popular support. As for the much-
ballyhooed popular vote, he claimed that it, too, had been a farce. "In the
capital," the cardinal advised the nuncios shortly after the Assembly
election, "they bought the votes of three thousand workers. . . . They
went through the hospitals, making the sick vote, they paid a huge number of people from the lower classes to vote multiple times at different
polling places, they made various men don clerical garb to give the impression that the clergy were in favor." The cardinal's allegations could
hardly have been more horrifying, albeit based for the most part on pure
invention.[38]

CHAPTER 11

PRESSURING
THE POPE

CARDINAL ANTONELLI KEPT UP THE DRUMBEAT OF DENUN-
ciations, bemoaning the chaos and violence reigning in Christendom's
capital. The men ruling Rome, he told Europe's diplomats, were seizing
priceless works of art from the churches and selling them to pay their
bills. Although this was untrue and his accounts of anarchy in Rome
were greatly exaggerated, Catholics throughout Europe spread these
tales.

The republic's ministers denied the charges and plastered the city
walls with pleas urging Romans to respect Catholic clergy and church
property, but violence against men of the cloth was not uncommon. In
one such incident, outrage at what had been found at the Dominican-run
Inquisition prison inspired a mob to light the Dominican monastery
afire. It took a large number of carabinieri to restore calm.[1]

Clerics brave—or foolish—enough to try to publicly defend the
pope risked their lives. In early March, a group of men angered by a
priest's loud complaints about the new order chased after him. When
they caught up with him, they made him stand on a table, where, to the
crowd's delight, they forced him to preach a sermon singing the praises
of the Roman Republic. Outside Rome, an archbishop who had forbidden his parish priests to administer the sacraments to those who voted in
the Assembly election was arrested and imprisoned, as was a bishop accused of trying to foment a counterrevolution. But for the most part,

bishops and parish priests of the Papal States lay low, avoiding acts openly hostile to the new government.[2]

The foundations of church power in Rome were rapidly eroding. The government declared the Vatican palaces and the Quirinal to be public property. Hospitals, public charities, and orphanages, all previously run by the church, were now in the hands of the republic, as were their endowments.[3]

The sessions of the Constituent Assembly were raucous affairs. "There is neither discipline nor dignity," observed the Tuscan envoy. "Disorder is frequent, the vain speeches and recriminations extremely frequent." As for the more moderate delegates, he added, they have "more heart than brains." "I must reluctantly tell you," reported one sympathetic observer, "that this Assembly seems to me to be a bunch of insolent and jealous children."[4]

Desperate for outside support, the Roman Republic sent secret emissaries to Paris to plead their case. After meeting with them in early March, the French minister of foreign affairs, Édouard Drouyn, was convinced that the men in power in Rome were willing to compromise. "Feeling themselves weak in the face of the storm that threatens them," Drouyn observed, "the authors of the revolution would be open to accepting a deal that would give them . . . an honorable way of getting out of the terrible situation in which they find themselves." If left to his own, thought Drouyn, the pope would certainly agree, judging a negotiated agreement preferable to "the cruel necessity of returning to Rome by directing the power of foreign arms against the Romans." "The pope," noted Drouyn, was, after all, "not only the head of government of a third-rate country. He is also, and above all, the head of the Catholic Church."[5]

IN VIENNA, LEARNING OF the pope's plea for Austrian troops alone to restore him to Rome, Schwarzenberg could not help but smile. The same pope who had blessed his troops the previous year as they marched northward to drive the Austrians from Italy was now begging the Austrian army to come to his rescue.

But it was not clear to the Austrian prime minister how he was to do what the pope asked. Pius had publicly called on all four Catholic powers to send their armies, and the French had warned Vienna against acting independently. With new signs of unrest in Austrian-controlled northern Italy, the last thing Austria needed was to give France a reason to support the northern Italians in the continuing conflict there.

It would be better, thought Schwarzenberg, to leave the taking of Rome to the French. It would undoubtedly be a messy business, and Austria had no interest in occupying Rome itself. What mattered to Austria was maintaining free rein over the Papal States' northern provinces and the eastern coast. The north helped protect Austria's southern boundary, while the coast allowed it to maintain control of the Adriatic.[6]

Although he knew it would anger the pope, Schwarzenberg decided to inform the French government of the pope's secret request to have Austria alone send its army. He knew that this would vindicate those in France who already suspected the pope of double-dealing, but by betraying the pope's trust, the Austrian prime minister hoped to win France's. He proposed a secret plan to the French foreign minister: Austrian troops would put down the revolt in the northern and eastern provinces of the Papal States. The French would land at Civitavecchia and march on Rome.

Not surprisingly, when Vienna's ambassador in Paris told Drouyn of Pius's proposed secret pact with Austria, he was outraged. In light of the pope's duplicity, said Drouyn, France would need to reconsider its commitment to helping him. As for the plan Austria was suggesting, he rejected it out of hand. Foreign armies, he was convinced, could never provide a durable solution to the problems the pope faced.[7]

IF THERE WAS ONE MAN WHO, for Pius, most incarnated the malevolence of the church's enemies, it was Giuseppe Mazzini. From his quarters in London, Mazzini had long championed a united Italy free from priestly and autocratic rule. Since 1831 he had had a hand in virtually every attempted uprising on the Italian Peninsula.[8]

Although unloved by the prelates, Mazzini had many admirers. William Lloyd Garrison, a leader of the American antislavery movement, had met Mazzini two years earlier on a visit to London and was immediately struck, as he put it, by "the brilliancy of his mind, the modesty of his deportment, the urbanity of his spirit, and the fascination of his conversational powers." I "felt drawn to him," recalled the American, "by an irresistible magnetism; in him there was not discoverable one spark of self-inflation, one atom of worldly ambition." He was, added Garrison, "a sublime idealist, but never transcending the bounds of reason," a man of "immense physical and moral courage."[9]

Thomas Carlyle, one of Britain's great literary figures of the time, befriended Mazzini in London, where, Carlyle observed, he lived "almost in squalor." He drank coffee with bread crumbled in it, smoked constantly, and preferred to speak in French, although he spoke English well, albeit with a strong Italian accent. "A more beautiful person," recalled Carlyle, "I never beheld, with his soft flashing eyes, and face full of intelligence."[10]

A sympathetic British biographer of a century ago captured his contradictions well. Mazzini, he wrote, "had a supreme confidence in his own thought. It was difficult for him to own an error, and hence he never learnt from his mistakes. . . . That very rigidity, that lifelong iteration of a few dominant ideas, carry force and conviction that a more agile intellect were powerless to give." But, he added, "absolute confidence in his own beliefs was joined to truest personal humility, and made the prophet. Humblest and least ambitious of men, he felt his call from God; and in God's name he was assertive, dogmatic. . . . Compromise in small or great seemed cowardice."[11]

Mazzini cast a special spell on women, and the American journalist Margaret Fuller proved an eloquent recruit, bombarding her American readers with adulatory accounts of the republican hero. Mazzini, she enthused, was a man of genius, yet one's first impression on seeing him "must always be of the religion of his soul, of his virtue." In mind he was a "great poetic statesman, in heart a lover." In her correspondence she confessed, "Dearly I love Mazzini, who also loves me. . . . His soft radiant look makes melancholy music in my soul."[12]

When this legendary prophet of Italian unity arrived in Rome on the evening of March 5, there to take up the Assembly seat he had recently won in a supplementary election, many in Rome greeted him as their savior. "He has the nature more of a priest than a statesman. . . . He is pontiff, prince, apostle, priest," observed Luigi Carlo Farini, who had served in Rome's Chamber of Deputies but then, along with Minghetti and other liberal dignitaries, left the city following Rossi's murder. Threatened by some of Europe's most powerful armies, its leaders under threat of excommunication, its government running badly, its treasury bare, its army small and ill equipped, Rome was in need of a hero. "It is to Mazzini alone that all eyes turn," observed the Swiss scholar Johann Bachofen, who was then living in Rome, "to him, the apostle of the revolution."[13]

Members of the Assembly were debating a banking bill on March 6 when a deputy's shout drew all eyes to the small, thin figure entering the hall. *"Viva Mazzini!"* he yelled, the cry becoming a chorus as a wave of applause from the deputies brought the debate to a halt. "I believe I speak for the sense of the Assembly," said Charles Bonaparte, sitting in the chair of the Assembly president, "inviting the deputy Mazzini to sit by the President's side." As the famed exile took his seat, a new round of applause greeted him. No one wanted to return to the banking bill. Mazzini needed little urging to come to the lectern to speak.

All the applause, the signs of affection that you give me, o colleagues, should instead be directed by me to you, for what little good I have not done, but tried to do, has come to me from Rome. Rome was always a kind of good luck charm for me. As a youth I studied the history of Italy, and I found that . . . only one city was favored by God in being able to die and then rise up even greater than before in fulfilling its mission in the world. . . . I saw that there first arose the Rome of the Emperors. . . . I saw Rome perish at the hands of the barbarians . . . and I saw it rise to even greater heights by conquering not by arms, but with words, rising in the name of the Popes to continue on its grand missions. I felt in my heart that it is impossible that a city that alone in the world has had two great lives, one greater than the other, does not have a third. . . . After the Rome of the Emperors, after the Rome of the Popes, will come the Rome of the People. . . . I cannot promise you anything from me, except my participation in all that you are doing for the good of Italy, for Rome, and for the good of Humanity. We may have to weather great crises. We may have to wage a holy battle against the only enemy that threatens us, Austria. We will fight it, and we will win.[14]

Mazzini, though a small man, spoke in a commanding voice, but when he finished, he looked exhausted, and despite the personal triumph of the moment, he seemed melancholy. "I am extremely nervous," he confided the next day. "Intentions here are good, but the capacity very little. Up until the day of my arrival, nothing was done to prepare for war. We have no arms, and virtually all of Europe's governments are working against us." Making matters worse, he added, the men with whom he had to work were strangers to him.[15]

Events from the north were about to produce another shock. Ever since his defeat at the hands of the Austrians the previous year, King Charles Albert had been biding his time, waiting for the moment to redeem himself. He now decided he could wait no longer. On March 17 word reached Rome that the king was again leading his army into Lombardy, but the king's attempt at redemption turned quickly to disaster. The 85,000 Sardinian troops had barely begun their attack, when they were outmaneuvered by a force of 59,000 Austrians. Soon it was the Austrians who were advancing into Sardinian territory. On March 23 Charles Albert surrendered to the triumphant eighty-three-year-old General Radetzky. Newly disgraced, the king quit his throne, ceding it to his son, Victor Emmanuel II. Accompanied by only a single aide, the fallen king departed at midnight, headed for France. He would die in exile, brokenhearted, before the year was out. He was fifty years old.[16]

When the news reached the Roman Assembly, its stricken members erupted in defiant shouts of *Viva l'Italia! Viva l'indipendenza!* The struggle for Italian independence, they vowed, would go on. But their future looked grim. Having crushed the Sardinian army, nothing now held the Austrians back from marching south into the Papal States.

Recognizing the need for stronger leadership in the face of this threat, the Roman Assembly voted to create a triumvirate and gave it unlimited powers to defend the republic. That Mazzini should be one of its members was never in doubt. The moderate, upright lawyer Carlo

The abdication of King Charles Albert

Armellini—whose brother and son were both Jesuits—was chosen as well. It was Armellini who had given the stirring opening address to the Assembly the previous month. The other triumvir, chosen to represent the north of the Papal States, was also a lawyer, Aurelio Saffi. A good man, well liked, from a noble family, he was only twenty-nine years old and still wrote a letter to his mother in Forlì every day. Although all three men would rule in name, only one would rule in fact. Mazzini alone had the drive, the intelligence, the fearlessness, the vast international network of contacts, and the credibility to lead a battle that would pit the largely defenseless republic against the combined armies of the continent's major powers.[17]

Although Mazzini had the reputation of a dreamer, once he had power in his hands he showed himself to be remarkably clear-eyed. He knew that his only hope lay with France. France was, after all, a sister republic, and France had long viewed Austrian military designs with suspicion. Reports from Paris offered Mazzini some encouragement. "The news that is coming from France," wrote one Assembly member in his diary in early April, "is comforting. That government finally seems disposed not only not to take part with the other Powers in an intervention against our state, but on the contrary to oppose it so that Austria is not tempted. May God will that it be so!"[18]

From Gaeta, Cardinal Antonelli was predicting a calamity of epic proportions should foreign armies not quickly come to the pope's rescue. "If the armed intervention we have requested is the only anchor against shipwreck," Antonelli wrote his nuncio in Madrid in mid-March, "let me add that without rapid action all is lost, while each moment that passes brings with it an abyss of irreparable harm." Later in March he issued similar warnings in letters to his nuncios in Vienna and Madrid: "Can it be possible," asked Antonelli,

for the Catholic powers to endure so many outrages against religion and its august Head without doing anything? . . . If the Catholic powers do not rush to our aid, they will be returning the

Triumvirate of the Roman Republic:
Carlo Armellini, Giuseppe Mazzini, and Aurelio Saffi

Pontiff not to his dominions, but rather to weep over a pile of rubble and abominations, and no longer to reside in Rome, the center of Christianity, but in a new Geneva.*

Over the course of the next month, Antonelli kept up his apocalyptic lament:

Rome's situation and that of the rest of the Papal States could not be worse. The impieties keep growing, the devastations, the plundering, the horrors. The seat of Christianity is being turned into theaters of crime and schools of irreligion. Thanks to their lethargy, the powers will have the Glory of restoring a Pontiff not to a State but to a mass of horrifying ruins.[19]

Although Antonelli adopted this dire tone for the benefit of his nuncios, he was in fact growing ever more confident. Austria, he was convinced, would not let the Roman Republic last long, now that its army was no longer held down by the Sardinian king in northern Italy. He knew Vienna had informed the French government of the pope's confidential request for Austrian aid, and he had let Esterházy know how disappointed he was at this violation of the pope's trust. But the French response to the news—threatening to rethink their pledge of support for the pope—had only confirmed his conviction that the pope should rely on Austria alone.[20]

Pius himself, so angry with Austria only a few months earlier, was now also counting on the Austrian army to save him. "The Pontiff is weak," observed the Sardinian envoy to Gaeta in late March, "and easily impressionable. Taking advantage of the right moment, one can get him to do things that don't seem to be in his nature." Or as a British envoy in Italy put it in a report to London, "the Pope had come to the determination to be for the future entirely guided by the advice of Cardinals Antonelli and Lambruschini."[21]

In Rome, the triumvirate issued a public call to rally support. "It is

---

* In A.D. 563 a huge wave in Lake Geneva, caused by a landslide, swept away churches, houses, and bridges in the city and killed a good part of the population.

our task to prove to Italy and to all of Europe that our cry, God and the People, is not a lie—that our work is religious, educational, moral to the highest degree—that the accusations of intolerance, of anarchy, of disorder are false." It was crucial to inspire confidence in the new government among people who had every reason to be skeptical about its prospects. "The Government of the Republic is strong," proclaimed Mazzini, who knew all too well that it was anything but.[22]

CARDINAL ANTONELLI HAD HOPED that the four-power conference that the Spanish had proposed would never have to meet. It would, he thought, only delay military action, offering France yet another opportunity to get in the way. But despite the cardinal's pleas, Austria insisted it would not act without the French. Reluctantly, Antonelli informed Austria, France, Spain, and Naples that the first session of the conference would meet in Gaeta on March 30. He also told them that he planned to chair the sessions himself.[23]

As the day of the conference approached, Harcourt complained to Paris that even the air they breathed in Gaeta seemed to be Austrian. There was little likelihood, he thought, that the four powers could ever reach agreement. The French government had to face the painful truth that the solutions it had been urging on the pope were no longer realistic. A negotiated settlement between the pope and Rome would, of course, be best, but Pius was unwilling to make any concessions, while the new authorities in Rome insisted that any settlement include the end of the pope's temporal power. Nor was there any chance that the people of the Papal States would themselves rise up and restore the pope's rule. As for the idea of having an all-Italian force come to the pope's aid, and so avoid invasion by foreign armies, this too was not going to happen. The Sardinian kingdom would not send its army to defeat the people who had long been pleading its cause in its fight with Austria, and King Ferdinand's army was still busy trying to put down the Sicilian revolt.

In short, Harcourt advised his foreign minister, France was left with only three options: it could simply leave the pope to his fate; it could allow the Austrians to act alone; or it could take military action by itself. "I recognize," he added, "that all three of these choices are bad, but I don't believe that it is possible to find any better." After having publicly proclaimed that France would defend the pope, how could the French do nothing while he spent the rest of his days in a small room in a Neapolitan fortress? Nor could they stand by while Austria acted alone, for that would mean allowing Austria to occupy all of the Papal States and to become the guarantor of Christendom's most sacred sites and of the pontiff himself. Only one option remained, unappetizing as it was. "We find ourselves," concluded Harcourt, "virtually forced by the fateful coincidence of circumstances to reestablish the pope ourselves."

For the French ambassador, there was an additional reason why it was so important that it be French armies that returned the pope to Rome. If the Austrians were to restore the Papal States, they would simply "reestablish the old state of things. . . . France alone," he argued, "can demand guarantees conforming to the principles of freedom that are in the true interests of the church itself."[24]

On March 30 Cardinal Antonelli called the first session of the four-power Gaeta conference to order. France alone had two representatives: Harcourt, ambassador to the Holy See, and Rayneval, ambassador to Naples. Count Esterházy represented Austria, Count Giuseppe Ludolf represented the Kingdom of Naples, and the Spanish ambassador to the Holy See, Francisco Martínez, represented Spain. Over the next months those six men would meet many times, but their often-heated arguments all took the same shape. The two Frenchmen found themselves isolated, facing the combined forces of Cardinal Antonelli and the Austrian, Spanish, and Neapolitan ambassadors. The division was clear from that first meeting, when Harcourt and Rayneval argued that restoring the pope through foreign armies would poison the people against him. Antonelli was dismissive. On first sight of a foreign army, insisted the cardinal, the pope's subjects would rise up against the small band of fanatics who oppressed them. "Even if the Turks were to come," said the cardinal, "the people would bless them."

Antonelli estimated that thirty thousand troops would be needed. The Neapolitan ambassador, Count Ludolf, enthusiastically supported armed intervention but noted that, given the ongoing revolt in Sicily, King Ferdinand did not have enough men available to do the job. The Spanish envoy likewise acknowledged that Spain could at best provide only a third of the needed troops. For his part, Esterházy informed his colleagues that Austria was prepared to send its army to restore the pope but would not act without first securing an agreement with France.

Cardinal Antonelli then offered his own proposal: each of the four powers would be responsible for reconquering one part of the Papal States. The Austrians would retake the northeast and the Adriatic coast; the Neapolitan army would take the southern provinces; the French would occupy the northwest; and the task of taking Rome would be given to Spain. Involving France would hopefully satisfy the Austrians, while the plan would keep France out of any of the major cities of the Papal States. The meeting ended without reaching any decision.[25]

Antonelli again felt frustrated. His hope of being able to rely on Austrian arms alone had been rebuffed by Prince Schwarzenberg, and France refused to take part in any jointly planned invasion. The cardinal vented his anger in a letter to his nuncio in Vienna:

It is therefore to be deduced that by virtue of France's action alone the Head of the Church is not to be restored to his full freedom and independence, and thanks to the obstacles placed by a Catholic Power the cause of religion cannot prevail.

And so the revolutionary party, perhaps aware of France's reluctance to intervene, while it places obstacles to the joint action of Austria with Spain and Naples, becomes ever bolder, tyrannizing ever more, oppressing, satiating its impious desires. Therefore as long as France does not quickly intervene in the Papal States, or does not agree to have Austria do so . . . the Church will continue to suffer under a most cruel servitude.[26]

CONCERNED THAT THE POPE's absence from Rome for the popular Easter rites might provoke unhappiness among the Romans, Mazzini was eager to ensure that a proper Easter mass be held at St. Peter's. The occasion would also show the people that the republican government posed no threat to their religion. Doing all this over the strong objection of the prelate in charge of St. Peter's, the republicans arranged the ceremony on their own. On Easter Sunday thousands of Romans, mingling with brightly dressed peasants who had come into the city for the occasion, crowded into the vast basilica and overflowed into the piazza. A patriotic Venetian priest, assisted by a dozen other priests, chaplains in the various militias that had recently formed throughout Italy, said the mass. Members of the Cappella Giulia, the regular Vatican choir, sang, dressed not in their customary white linen surplices but in street clothes. Nor were all the words they sang familiar ones. *Salvam fac Republicam nostrum*—"Save our republic"—they chanted to close the mass, echoing the words that, in the wake of the French Revolution, had replaced "God save the king" in concluding the mass in France.

Following the ceremony, the priest who had presided over the mass emerged onto the balcony above the great door of the basilica, festooned with Italy's tricolored banners, and offered his benediction. Amid the thousands in the crowd below stood Mazzini. "It is useless," observed the Italian prophet, as he surveyed the people on their knees. "This religion lives and will yet live for long years to come." He could attack the corruption of the priests, but he knew he would not get far if he attacked the rites over which they presided.

While Mazzini's mood was melancholy, for most it was a time of celebration. From the windows of the Vatican palaces facing the piazza, members of the Constituent Assembly waved their handkerchiefs to the crowd. The cannon of Castel Sant'Angelo sounded as squads of the republican army, scattered through the piazza, raised their rifles and pointed their bayonets to the sky. That night, rather than the normal bright lanterns that illuminated the great dome of St. Peter's on such occasions, the dome flickered in the pulsating light cast by tricolored fireworks.[27]

In mid-April Admiral Baudin, head of French naval forces, met with the pope in Gaeta and told him that a French frigate was about to arrive there to be put at his disposal. It was large enough, said the admiral, to take the whole papal party to France. The pontiff had initially been in a good mood, but as he mulled his options, it darkened. He could go to France, he said, and he knew that if he went personally to request

French help in restoring him to Rome, it would undoubtedly be forthcoming. "But how would it look," he asked, "for the head of Catholicism and vicar of Jesus Christ to go begging on a foreign land for the means to make war against his own subjects?" It was best, thought the pope, to make his requests for military aid behind Gaeta's closed doors.[28]

The pope then met with Harcourt, again urging him to reach an agreement with Austria so that his kingdom could be restored. Only Austria and France, said Pius, had the military means to return him to power.

The French ambassador tried to explain the difficulty his government faced. "Even with all the good will in the world in wanting to restore the Holy Father," he told the pope, "it is impossible for us not to take account of the state of public opinion in France." The notion that France could act in league with archrival Austria to restore the papal theocracy, even were it desirable, was, said the French ambassador, wholly unrealistic. Nor, he tried to convince the pope, was it in the church's own interest. "Whether rightly or wrongly," said Harcourt, "people view Austria as representing the principle of absolutism and the Austrians as the oppressors of Italy. We, on the contrary, are seen as the defenders of freedom, as the protectors of the emancipation of peoples. . . . So it is very difficult to combine two such different elements, and to have them march under the same flag."

Should the pope embrace the Austrians, "well-known enemies of Italy," Harcourt warned him, "you will only be able to stay on your throne with cannons." The time would inevitably come when the cannons would be withdrawn, and when that day came, predicted the Frenchman, "your temporal power will disappear amid a shower of the curses of all of Italy." The pontiff had a fateful choice to make. He could either throw himself in the arms of Austria or follow the path urged by France.

How, asked the pope, could he be expected to depend on France? It was, after all, now a republic, and who was to say that whatever position it took today would not be changed as a result of the next election? The French said that they could not join forces with the Austrians in restoring his temporal reign, but what, asked the pope, would they do if they heard that the Austrians were marching on Rome themselves? Would they stand by and allow the Austrians alone to bask in the glory of rescuing the Holy See?[29]

Having failed to convince Harcourt, the pope turned to France's other ambassador, Alphonse de Rayneval, a man he found easier to deal with. "His Holiness," reported Rayneval, following their conversation, "was very upset and this time did not have the calm, the serenity that ordinarily surprises all those who have the honor of approaching him." "My heart bleeds," the pope told him, "seeing the infinite evils that pile up day after day on my unhappy subjects." Pius looked into the face of the French envoy. "It is up to you to bring an end to this cruel situation. Do it, I beg you in the name of God, in the name of humanity. I beg you with tears in my eyes. Put an end to this great tragedy!" As Pio Nono said these words, tears did in fact trail down his face and drip onto his clasped hands.

Rayneval again tried to persuade the pope to come to France, where he could rally the French people to his cause. "I understand that," replied the pope.

> But how do you imagine I can follow your advice? How do you think I can abandon the position that I have taken up to now, that I turn my back on those who have up to now constantly shown themselves ready to support me? Can I put the fate of the papacy in the hands of one Power without provoking the jealousy, the sensitivities of all the others? Wouldn't that compromise the exercise of my spiritual power? Note that the majority of Catholic nations are monarchies. Can I turn to the only European Catholic power that is republican? Do you believe that the result of this will not be unending mistrust and difficulties? And who is to say what conditions you would impose on me?

It was not a matter of imposing conditions, replied the French envoy. It was a matter of adjusting to the times and to the challenges the French government faced.

"Certainly," said the pope. "But how far would this go? Where did the previous attempts I made end up leading me?

"I promised to go to France," said the pontiff, "and I will go. But in the meantime, note how Rome is becoming the *rendez-vous* of all the most dangerous and worst elements in all of Italy. The remnants of the Lombard, Livorno and Sicilian bands, as well as the Neapolitan rebels who have been pushed out of their own land, are all flocking to Rome. That's where the resistance is finding its last source of support. Just think of all the tragedy that can result! Reach an agreement with Austria," urged the pope. "That's the whole question."[30]

That veterans of other uprisings against Italy's reigning monarchs— from Sicily to Florence and Milan—were streaming into Rome was very much on Antonelli's mind as well. The dithering of the great Catholic powers, the cardinal complained in a letter to the nuncio in Madrid, "is calamitous beyond belief." Now that the other parts of Italy had been pacified, he explained, "all the rebel leaders are turning to Rome." But it was another worry that had prompted the cardinal to write his letter: he had heard a rumor that France might try to take Rome alone. Antonelli urged the nuncio to get the Spanish government to help dissuade Paris. The last thing he wanted was to have Rome in French hands.[31]

Two days after his meeting with Rayneval, the pope called in the cardinals and gave an allocution that was among the most violent papal addresses of the nineteenth century. Rome, he charged, had turned into "a forest replete with furious beasts." Commerce was at a standstill, the public treasury was bare, private property and church possessions had been seized, churches had been profaned, nuns had been driven from their convents, "the most virtuous and distinguished ecclesiastics and religious [were] cruelly persecuted, put in chains, and slain; the . . . Bishops . . . [were] violently dragged away from their flocks and thrown into dungeons."

Again he gave vent to his bitterness about the Romans' "black in- gratitude." Early in his papacy, he recalled, he had granted amnesty to political prisoners and offered a raft of reforms aimed at bettering his subjects' lives. But, he lamented, "the concessions freely and willingly granted by us in the very beginning of our Pontificate, not only could never yield the wished-for fruits, but could not even take root, because those crafty architects of deceit abused them to excite new agitations." In an *apologia pro se*, aimed at counteracting what he knew to be the cardinals' belief that he was himself to blame for the disaster, the pope chronicled all the attempts he had earlier made to keep things from getting out of hand. He had recognized the danger of popular demonstrations and had tried to rein them in. He had seen the risk that the newly instituted Consultative Council might overstep its authority, and so at its very first meeting had warned that it would be only an advisory body. His list went on. Once again he called on the four Catholic powers—Austria, France, Naples, and Spain—to send their armies to restore him to Rome.[32]

LOUIS NAPOLEON, THE FRENCH PRESIDENT, was torn. Personally, he regarded the pope's political role as a vestige of the Middle Ages. As a young man, he had even taken up arms against it. But if there was one thing he did stand for, it was a return of France's glory. When Alfred de Falloux, his minister of public education, and a fervent Catholic, came to plead the pope's cause, he knew what note to strike. How, he asked the president, could he stand by and simply watch while the Austrian army marched down the Italian Peninsula and occupied Rome?

"You're right," replied Louis Napoleon, "France cannot remain as a mere spectator. . . . Facing the prospect of a triumphant Austrian flag in Italy," said the president, with a large dose of wishful thinking, "our own will be greeted with universal applause." The French had no territorial ambitions in Italy, nor did they have any economic interests to protect in the Papal States. What did matter to France was that the troops of archrival Austria, already in control of all northeastern Italy, not come to occupy all the pope's lands as well.[33]

Impetuous and inexperienced, the French president forged ahead despite having only the vaguest of plans. On the same day that Antonelli convened the first four-power conference in Gaeta, the French prime minister, Odilon Barrot, himself no more sympathetic than Louis Napoleon to the pope's rule, stood before the French National Assembly. He had come to ask for over a million francs to send an expeditionary corps to Italy for a three-month period. His explanation for its mission was anything but clear. "Before the Assembly," a colleague advised him, "be vague." Barrot took the advice.[34]

On April 16, as the motion authorizing the military mission was about to come to a vote, Barrot made his final plea to the National Assembly: Austria was on the march in Italy. Having crushed King Charles Albert, the Austrians now aimed to restore Tuscany's grand duke—uncle of the Austrian emperor—and would then move south on Rome. "France cannot remain indifferent," Barrot told them. "The right to maintain our legitimate influence in Italy, the desire to help ensure that the people of Rome obtain a good government founded on liberal institutions," all required the French to act without delay.

The leader of the radical left in France, Alexandre Ledru-Rollin, who had come in a distant third in the recent presidential election, angrily accused the prime minister of duplicity. Beneath all his fine-sounding democratic rhetoric, said the opposition leader, Barrot was seeking to use French military might to restore the pope to power in Rome. Ledru-Rollin and his colleagues on the left were, however, in the minority, and so the motion passed in the end, 395 to 283. French troops would soon be on their way to Italy, but what exactly they would do when they got there remained far from clear.[35]

Drouyn informed Austria's ambassador of France's decision to send an expeditionary force to Rome's port city of Civitavecchia. The reasons he gave for taking this step without first consulting Austria, observed the Austrian in his subsequent report to Vienna, were a mass of illogical and contradictory arguments.[36]

Drouyn meanwhile sent word of the military mission to his ambassadors in Gaeta. The goal, he explained, "is neither to impose any regime on the Romans that they would not freely accept, nor constrain the pope, when he is recalled, to adopt one form of government or another." The French government was convinced, he explained, "that Pius IX, in returning to his States, will bring back the generous, enlightened, liberal policies" that he had previously championed.

Harcourt was told to inform Antonelli of the French expedition and to explain that, for the pope to profit from it, "the Holy Father must hurry to publish a Manifesto that, in guaranteeing liberal institutions conforming to the people's wishes as well as to what the times demand, causes all resistance to crumble. This Manifesto, appearing at the very moment that our forces appear on the coast of the Papal States, would be

Édouard Drouyn de Lhuys, French foreign minister

a signal of a conciliation that would include all but a very small number of malcontents. . . . You cannot insist strongly enough," concluded Drouyn, "on the utility, the necessity for such an act."[37]

The instructions that the French foreign minister sent at the same time to General Charles Oudinot, the man chosen to lead the expedition, show how far removed from reality the government was in imagining the reception the French army could expect. "All the information we have received give us reason to believe that . . . you will be received eagerly, by some as a liberator, by others as a useful mediator against the dangers of reaction." But, advised Drouyn, should there be any attempt to prevent him from landing, "you should not be stopped by the resistance made in the name of a government that no one in Europe has recognized and that maintains itself in Rome, against the wishes of the immense majority of the population, only by the audacity of a small number of agitators, who for the most part are foreigners."

Only two days after assuring the French Assembly that the force they were proposing was not being sent to occupy Rome, the foreign minister made clear to the general that this was exactly his mission. "You will judge if the circumstances are such that you can enter there with the certainty not only of not encountering any serious resistance, but being welcomed so that it is clear that in entering there you are responding to the people's appeal." What he was to do if the people did not open their arms to the French army, the foreign minister did not say.[38]

Along with his official note of instructions, Drouyn sent a confidential addendum. Oudinot was to maintain good relations with the Austrian commanders in the Papal States. Should Austrian troops move into Bologna and Ancona, no move should be made to oppose them. As for the pope, it was important that he remain in Gaeta as briefly as possible. It would be better if he came to Marseilles or, once the French troops were landed, to Rome or Civitavecchia. "Avoid," he added, "having him go anywhere on the Adriatic coast. The Mediterranean is French. The Adriatic is Austrian."[39]

Three infantry brigades, totaling twelve thousand men, 250 horses, sixteen cannons, and two companies of engineers prepared for their mission. The first of the many ships required to carry them left France late at night on April 21, 1849. Of the disaster that lay ahead, they had no inkling.[40]

CHAPTER 12

THE FRIENDLY ARMY

ALL SORTS OF RUMORS RACED THROUGH ROME, ALTHOUGH FEW had to do with the French. The Austrians were headed south from Lombardy. The Neapolitan king was readying his troops to march north. Thousands of Spanish troops had recently landed and were joining them. In desperate need of more defenders, Mazzini called on patriots from throughout Italy to come to Rome. He needed an army of fifty thousand. The triumvirate asked the nearby coastal town of Fiumicino to provide sand to fill thousands of sacks so they could barricade Rome's streets.[1]

"Rome is very peaceable," reported a visiting Brit, who added that, while he had seen little enthusiasm for the Roman Republic, "neither do I hear as much complaint as might be expected." The visitor, Arthur Clough, a thirty-year-old poet, was surprised to find, on meeting Mazzini, that he was "a less fanatical fixed-idea sort of man than I had expected," and that he seemed remarkably at ease. But, Clough added, he had no illusions. With all the foreign armies headed toward Rome, Mazzini "of course thinks it likely enough that the Roman Republic will fall." He had spent his entire life dreaming of this moment, and if it came to it, it would be much better to die as a martyr for the Italian cause than to shrink in fear from those who would try to restore the papal regime by force.[2]

THE POPE'S SALVATION, it seemed, might finally be at hand, for now that France had decided to send troops, all four of the Catholic powers were on the move. Schwarzenberg had ordered the Austrian army under Radetzky to enter Tuscany to restore the grand duke, then march on to restore papal rule to the northern provinces of the Papal States. From the Kingdom of Naples, Ferdinand, at the head of five thousand men, had crossed northward into the Papal States and was sending back reports that the people were applauding his arrival amid shouts of *Viva Pio Nono!* On April 29 a Spanish flotilla docked on the southern coast of the Papal States, and thousands of Spanish troops began to disembark.[3]

A few days earlier, on Tuesday, April 24, the French steamship *Panama*, armed with sixteen cannons and carrying twelve hundred soldiers, set anchor in the Mediterranean harbor of Civitavecchia, as a crowd filled the beach to watch. A rowboat brought a French diplomat and two senior officers to land, where the city's republican governor nervously awaited them. "Animated always by a very liberal spirit, the government of the French Republic," proclaimed the diplomat, reading from a script he held in his hands, "declares its desire to respect the view of the majority of the Roman population, and comes on their land in friendship. . . . It is committed to not imposing on these people any form of government that they would not choose for themselves." Having read this misleading preamble, he asked permission for the troops to come ashore.

Under orders from the triumvirate not to allow any foreign military force to land, the governor asked for twelve hours so he could consult with Rome. This the Frenchman refused to grant. The governor hurriedly convened a meeting of civil and military leaders in Civitavecchia, but the overwhelming French force, and the panic in the population at the suicidal prospect of taking up arms against it, convinced them they had little choice but to yield.

It would take twenty-four hours for all eight thousand French troops aboard the twelve steam-powered warships that had followed the *Panama* into port to set up camp. A hundred horses, two dozen pieces of heavy artillery, and an immense quantity of foodstuffs, ammunition, and wine were unloaded. "The people of Civita Vecchia," reported a British journalist who witnessed the scene, "looked on with stupid amazement, and not one word of approbation or disapprobation was heard. There were no vivas for the French or for Pio Nono." French intentions were far from clear. Although they had said they had come in friendship, the

French lost no time imprisoning the city's governor. But while they hoisted their own flag, they left the flag of the Roman Republic flying alongside it. If they carried a papal flag with them, they did not raise it.[4]

BY NIGHTFALL, ROME'S WALLS were covered with the surprising news. "Romans!" began the notice, signed by the triumvirate. "A number of French soldiers have appeared at Civitavecchia." The next day Mazzini and colleagues addressed a longer message to the Romans:

> A foreign invasion threatens the territory of the Republic. . . . The Republic will resist. The people must show France and show the world that they are not children, but men. . . . Let no one say: *the Romans wanted to be free, but they did not know how to be.* By our resistance the French nation must learn . . . our inalterable resolution never again to subject ourselves to the abhorrent government that we have overthrown.

Until this moment, popular support for the republic had been uneven. People resented government by the priests, but after centuries of papal rule, identification with the papacy still ran deep. Now, although fearful, people were also angry. In the face of foreign invasion, Romans began to rally behind Mazzini's government. Four thousand partisans of the republic gathered outside the Chancellery Palace, urging the Assembly to stand firm in the face of the new threat. "Respect for religion!" shouted Charles Bonaparte, haranguing the crowd. "Eternal hatred for the government of the priests!"[5]

On the morning of April 26, amid great tension, Mazzini rose to address the Assembly. The previous evening, he told them, General Oudinot, commander of the French troops, had sent a delegation to meet with the triumvirate. The French claimed that they had been welcomed by the population of Civitavecchia and hoped for the same fraternal welcome when they came to Rome. When asked what their mission was, they replied that it was twofold. They had come first of all to save the people from an invasion from Austria or Naples. Their other goal was to

determine the will of the people and, on that basis, to find a way to mediate the dispute with the pope so that a peaceful resolution could be found.

If the French had come to prevent the Austrians and Neapolitans
from invading them, replied Mazzini, they were going about it in a
strange way. Why would they not first declare publicly that they were
determined to block such an attack and so perhaps prevent it from happening at all? And why, if this was why they had come, had they not
contacted Rome's government in advance? As for determining the people's will, Mazzini asked, were the French unaware that the Assembly in
Rome had been elected by universal suffrage? For the first time in the
thousand years of the Papal States, it could now be said that Rome was
in fact ruled by the will of its people.

Before reading their final resolution, the deputies opened the doors
of the hall so that the large, anxious crowd waiting outside could come
in. "After the communications received from the triumvirate," the resolution read, "the Assembly commits itself to saving the Republic and
responding to force with force." Hats flew into the air amid shouts of
Viva la Repubblica!

Of all the preparations Mazzini made to defend the city, none would
prove more important than summoning Garibaldi. In the absence of an
effective regular army, Garibaldi's legion, its core the men who had
fought with him in South America, was the most effective fighting force
the republic had. But until then, Mazzini had not been eager to have the
shaggy-haired warriors in Rome. Although the Hero of Two Worlds
had been elected to the Assembly and had attended its first session, he
was no politician; nor, as a military leader, was he comfortable taking
orders from others. Most of the exploits that would give him his worldwide fame were still ahead of him, but he was nothing if not confident.
"In a hundred battles," he informed the triumvirate, "I have never lost
one."

At six p.m. on April 27, Garibaldi led his fifteen hundred legionnaires
on horseback through Porta Maggiore into the Eternal City. It was a
memorable sight. The wild-looking men, sunburnt, wearing conical hats
with black plumes, their bearded faces covered with dust, their lower
legs bare, crowded around their leader. Word spread quickly through

the city. "He has come! He has come!" No one had ever seen such a sight. The whole company, observed a British sculptor living in Rome, looked more like a bunch of brigands than a disciplined military force. They wore loose-fitting jackets, with black knapsacks on their back. Some carried long lances, others rifles. In their belts, rather than the swords worn by the regular soldiers, they carried large daggers.[6]

The hero himself, on his magnificent white horse, was impossible to miss. Of medium height, Garibaldi had wide shoulders and a broad chest. His blue eyes seemed almost violet and for many had a mesmerizing effect. His chestnut-colored hair flowed down, unkempt, to rest on his shoulders. He had a bushy mustache together with a thick reddish beard that came down into two points. His darkly tanned face and large leonine nose were covered with freckles. He wore a red jacket with a short tail and a small black felt hat, from which two ostrich feathers stuck out. From his left hip hung a saber.[7]

Garibaldi's arrival electrified the anxious city. "When I saw him on

Giuseppe Garibaldi

his beautiful white horse in the market-place, with his noble aspect," recalled an Italian who enlisted in the defense forces on the spot, "his calm, kind face, his high, smooth forehead, his light hair and beard . . . reminded us of nothing so much as of our Savior's head in the galleries. . . . We all worshipped him." Or as another of his followers enthused, Garibaldi was "a man of war, of rare bravery. . . . The soldiers love him like a father, because he is just, human, severe, terrible . . . in his ardor to do good."

Adding to Garibaldi's mystique was the distinctive figure who was always at his side. Andrea Aguyar's black skin, along with his considerable height and muscular build, could not fail to draw people's eyes to him. Born to slave parents around Montevideo, he had committed his life to Garibaldi from the time he joined him in South America. Aguyar dressed no less dramatically than Garibaldi himself, in a dark blue poncho over a red tunic, a beret atop his head, wearing blue trousers with green stripes. He carried a long lance adorned just below its point with a red streamer. A lasso from the pampas of South America hung from his belt. The imposing, ebony-skinned legionnaire atop his jet-black charger, alongside the golden-haired Garibaldi, wearing his white poncho on his white horse, made an unforgettable sight. When Garibaldi and Aguyar rode through the streets, hundreds of people rushed to see them, women lifting their small children on their shoulders so they, too, could witness history.[8]

Also at Garibaldi's side was a bushy-bearded, forty-seven-year-old Barnabite monk from Bologna, Ugo Bassi. He cut a dramatic figure himself, with kind eyes and a high forehead, set off against his dark beard and thick dark curly hair that hung in long waves from his head. A passionate and wildly popular preacher as well as poet, Bassi had long railed against the corruption of the upper clergy that plagued the church. He had been a strong early supporter of Pius IX and the causes of Italian independence and liberty. When the pope crushed the hopes of the Italian patriots with his address in April, Bassi, crestfallen, initially defended him. In a dramatic sermon in Bologna's massive central church, he urged the huge crowd not to turn on the pontiff. Pius, said the monk, was not a villain but a victim of the villainy of the prelates around him. But by the end of the year, Bassi was calling for an end to papal rule. His sermons

Garibaldi and his comrade-in-arms,
Andrea Aguyar

and writings in early 1849 had helped galvanize popular support for the Constituent Assembly.

When he first met the legionnaires outside Rome in April, Bassi quickly came under their leader's spell. "Garibaldi is the Hero most worthy of poetry of any I can ever hope to meet in my entire life," the Barnabite wrote. "Our souls have been conjoined, as if we had been sisters in Heaven before finding ourselves living on earth." From that moment, Bassi became the chaplain of the legionnaires and the religious sidekick of the fiercely anticlerical Garibaldi. [9]

Passing through Rome's streets, Garibaldi and his ragtag troops made their way to the Convent of San Silvestro, designated by the triumvirate to be their quarters. As they arrived, the last of the nuns who lived there were packing up their belongings and hurrying away.[10]

RAYNEVAL AND HARCOURT RECEIVED news of the French expedition along with urgent instructions from Paris. The success of the French military mission rested on their shoulders, they were told. If the pope would announce his intention to return to his reforming path, the Romans would greet the French army with open arms. If not, the result could be disastrous.[11]

Rayneval went to see Cardinal Antonelli, who was far from pleased to learn of the French landing. The French ambassador stressed the importance of a papal pledge to keep to a reform path, but Antonelli was not encouraging. The decision, said the cardinal, would be up to the pope, but he doubted that any such statement would be made. "The clergy and the great majority of the people," explained Antonelli, "blame the reforms that Pius IX introduced for all their misfortunes."

Hoping that he would get a more sympathetic hearing from the pope himself, Rayneval then went to see him. In contrast to Antonelli's unhappiness on learning of the arrival of French troops, the pope initially greeted the news warmly. Encouraged, Rayneval explained that the French were eager to restore the pope, but to be successful, they would need him to do his part by pledging to maintain a liberal regime. Seeing the pope's dubious expression, Rayneval tried to reassure him. All that would be required, he insisted, was for "Pius IX to remain Pius IX, nothing more." He had to free himself from the reactionary influences that surrounded him.

"I know very well," replied Pius,

what you have to say on this subject. The Pope is Austrian, the cardinals are Austrians and reactionaries, the Pope's entourage is pushing him to return to the old ways, and the poor pope doesn't know enough to listen. . . . Don't worry, Pius IX will remain Pius IX. But haven't I gone through an unpleasant, sad experience? Should this experience count for nothing? Can I learn nothing from all the evils that I have suffered? Are there not a thousand precautions I should take? Should I not moderate the press? Close the clubs? Disarm most of the National Guard?[12]

For Rayneval, this was bad news indeed. If they could not change the pope's mind, the justification the French had given for their military mission—ensuring freedom for the Roman people—would be revealed to the world to have been a cruel hoax.

Harcourt was similarly discouraged. "We don't have much to be happy about from what is going on here," he reported from Gaeta. "We had barely landed in the Papal States when the recriminations against us began." With the French military expedition's success depending on the pope's cooperation, Harcourt offered a picture that could not have been more unwelcome in Paris. "As the Holy Father is much gentler and more moderate than those around him, I had wanted to learn from him directly whether he would listen to us at least on some points. I have to tell you frankly and with great sadness that I now have little hope in this regard."[13]

GENERAL CHARLES OUDINOT, son of one of Napoleon Bonaparte's most famous generals, had recently inherited his father's title of duke. A

General Charles
Oudinot

conservative man, he had a well-developed sense of pride, both in his own exalted name and in the name of France. Urged to move quickly on Rome, and encouraged to believe that he would find little resistance in doing so, he was not inclined to delay.

"The resistance that Mazzini and his party can attempt," the French chargé d'affaires, still in Rome, informed the general, "is based on only three or four hundred foreigners and the fanatics of the Popular Club." Romans, he assured him, were "timid by nature" and would give in at the first sight of the powerful French army. All the defensive efforts in Rome—the barricades, the cannons—were, he reported, purely for show, and Garibaldi's legionnaires were merely a bunch of undisciplined rabble. It was a view shared by many other foreign observers in Rome. "Barricades are erecting and the people preparing as for defence," the British artist, William Story, who lived in Rome, recorded telegraphically in his diary. "Scores of labourers and *contadini* standing round and sometimes pitching a shovelful of gravel into a wheelbarrow, but taking about three days to do what an hour did in Berlin."[14]

On April 26, only a day after Oudinot's troops disembarked at Civitavecchia, Rayneval and Harcourt wrote him with much the same message. "Onward, general!" urged Harcourt. "It is crucial that you hasten your march on Rome. Your sudden arrival has surprised and terrified. It is a situation you should take advantage of. If you leave enough time for the bad characters in Rome to recover from their initial shock, they will prepare the means of resistance and they will make blood flow, which it would be preferable to avoid."

"I do not think the idea of resistance is seriously entertained for a single moment, either by the authorities or the people," the recently arrived American chargé d'affaires advised Washington on April 27. "The hopelessness of a contest with France is apparent to all."[15]

Encouraged by these reports, Oudinot led his troops out of Civitavecchia on April 28 and marched south along the sea down Via Aurelia. He took fifty-eight hundred of his men and brought no heavy artillery. His soldiers carried only three days of provisions in their backpacks.

Early on that hot morning, in St. Peter's Square, Garibaldi, together with the recently installed minister of war, General Giuseppe Avezzana, reviewed their forces. In addition to Garibaldi's legionnaires, they included what remained of the regular papal army. The fifty-two-year-old Avezzana had had a swashbuckling career of his own. As a young man in Piedmont, he had taken part in the revolts that swept Italy in 1821 and, in the face a death sentence, had boarded a ship bound for America, where he had become a U.S. citizen. On learning of the revolts that were multiplying through his homeland a year earlier, Avezzana had rushed back to join in.[16]

On the other side of the Tiber from St. Peter's, several thousand National Guardsmen assembled in Piazza Santi Apostoli, not far from the Trevi Fountain. There Pietro Sterbini, the poet-physician who was now one of the Constituent Assembly's most vocal radicals, addressed them.

"Will you allow the clerical government to be reestablished?" bellowed Sterbini, as he gripped the railing of the balcony overlooking the piazza.

"No!" the men shouted, thrusting their rifles over their heads.

"Do you want to defend the freedom you have won with all your might?"

"*Viva la Repubblica!*" the men bellowed in an impressive roar.[17]

MARCHING SOUTH TOWARD ROME, the French soldiers could not help but notice the hand-lettered signs, written in French, affixed to trees and poles, that lined the roadway. Their large block letters spelled out article five of the French constitution: "The French Republic respects foreign nations, as it expects others to respect its own, not initiating any war of conquest, and never employing its forces against the freedom of any people."

The walls of Rome bore a different message:

Brothers! Rise up! The foreigners, the enemies of the Roman people, are advancing. They want to treat us, free men, as beasts at a market. They want to sell us. They insult us saying there will be no battle in Rome because the Romans don't have the guts to fight. . . . They come to destroy the government that you have created. . . . They want to trample our freedom and honor. . . . In the name of God and of the people, then, rise up o brothers![18]

The next evening Oudinot ordered his army to make camp on the western outskirts of Rome. The men, thought the general, were an impressive sight. The soldiers wore tall, cylindrical hats on their heads, gold epaulettes at their shoulders, and a ring of metal armor around their necks. Their long tunics, belted tight around their waists, went down almost to their knees, partially covering their red pants. The handles of their sabers protruded from the leather sheaths that hung from their belts. They carried their sleeping bags over their shoulders and their ammunition in a cartridge pouch hanging around their waist. Despite the intense heat, their spirits were good, not least because they expected to receive a warm welcome from the Romans. They had marched two days without encountering any unpleasantness and were now camped in sight of the city's walls.

A delegation of deputies from the Roman Assembly arrived at the French camp and urged Oudinot to call off his assault. If he were to attack, they warned, he would be met by fierce resistance.

"Nonsense," replied the general. "The Italians do not fight. I have ordered dinner at the Hôtel de Minerve, and I shall be there to eat it."[19]

CHAPTER 13

THE FRENCH ATTACK

O UDINOT WAS NOT OVERLY CONCERNED ABOUT THE THICK twenty-six-foot-high seventeenth-century wall that now loomed ahead. The Romans' unhappiness with their new government, together with the fear inspired by the sight of his army, he thought, would lead them to open the city gates without too much unpleasantness. He had brought with him neither large siege cannons nor ladders to scale the walls. At five a.m. on April 30, he ordered his men to break camp and march on Rome, heading for the northwestern corner of the city, near the Vatican palaces. As they approached the wall, in midmorning, the men, wearing heavy greatcoats, were sweating profusely in the growing heat of the day.

A mile from the wall they reached a fork in the road. To the right, a narrower path followed the ancient Acqua Paola aqueduct to the top of Janiculum Hill and the Porta San Pancrazio gate. To the left, the larger road led to a summit overlooking the Vatican before descending to end at Porta Cavalleggieri, not far from St. Peter's Square. Oudinot ordered the bulk of his troops to the left, toward the Vatican, sending a smaller detachment, of perhaps a thousand men, to the right to guard his flank.

The main French force was within a quarter mile of the wall when, to their surprise, two cannon blasts from a bastion along the wall sent a hail of grapeshot onto their advance guard. Having received a telegram earlier that morning telling him that the troops were on their way, General

Avezzana, head of the republican forces, had sent a captain to climb atop the great cupola over St. Peter's Basilica to look out for them. For his part, Mazzini had made sure that the city was prepared religiously as well as militarily. Ever eager to identify the defenders' cause with the Romans' religion, he ordered a "Decree of the Triumvirs for Public Prayer" posted on walls throughout the city. At the pealing of the church bells, sounding the alarm at the time of attack, the decree declared, "The Holy Sacrament will be exposed in all of the principal churches to pray for Rome's safety and victory of its good cause."[1]

Once it was clear that the Romans planned to fight, prudence might have led Oudinot to order a retreat to await reinforcements and the heavy artillery required for a siege. But the general still nourished the belief that once the Romans saw the full force of his army, their resistance would quickly fade. In any case, the prospect of having his army turn tail at the first sound of gunfire was too humiliating to consider.

When, in responding to the cannon blasts, the French marksmen's first shots produced a moment of confusion among the defenders atop the wall, Oudinot ordered his men to advance. His plan was to enter the city through Porta Pertusa, at the northwestern point of the wall, bordering the Vatican gardens, and he had brought bags of gunpowder to blow it up if necessary. But when the troops neared the wall, they discovered that there was no longer any gate there. Porta Pertusa had been walled over decades earlier, a fact that had not yet found its way onto French military maps.

By the time they discovered their error, the French were coming under heavy fire, as the city's defenders rained cannon shot and musket balls down on the exposed troops. The French hastily wheeled two small field cannons into position and began firing, but they could not long survive the return fire from the bastions. A few of the braver Frenchmen tried to scale the wall with spike nails, but the task was hopeless.

With the Porta Pertusa plan foiled, the French command ordered a brigade to move to the right along the wall to attack Porta Cavalleggieri. To reach it, the soldiers would have to go at least half a mile, passing down a steep hill through open vineyards within shooting range of the defenders perched atop the wall. The task, they soon realized, was impossible. A second brigade was directed to go left around the Vatican in an attempt to penetrate Porta Angelica. Needing a path wide enough for their horse-drawn artillery, the soldiers had to follow a ridge going north before then turning down into a valley approaching the gate. Five hundred feet from Porta Angelica, they came under heavy fire. The French artillery captain leading the assault was among the first to be killed, felled along with the four horses that pulled the lead cannon.

The French brigades that had earlier separated from the main force, following the aqueduct toward Porta San Pancrazio atop Janiculum Hill, never made it to the wall. Not wanting to allow the French to gain the protection offered by the aristocrats' villas outside the gate, Garibaldi had already led his men into the area. The Janiculum's relatively cool temperatures, and its dense, verdant gardens, had attracted noble families for centuries. Among the most prominent of these were the Corsinis and Pamfilis, and it was on the grounds of their estates that the day's bloodiest battle was fought. As a volunteer battalion of highly motivated, but only hastily trained, university students and artists moved through the Pamfili gardens, they ran straight into the oncoming force of French infantry. As the young men fell before the French assault, Garibaldi, wielding his saber and riding his white horse, led his bearded legionnaires into the fray. Garibaldi's officers, easily spotted in their long red blouses, led their men through the flowering rosebushes, using their bayonets to skewer the French troops as the attackers paused to reload their rifles. Along the way, a French bullet pierced Garibaldi's stomach, a wound that would nag him for months. Ugo Bassi, the revolutionary monk, never far from his hero, was nearby, tending to the wounded, until he had his horse shot out from under him.

The battle had begun in late morning. By five p.m., it was over. Instead of enjoying a fine dinner at the Hôtel de Minerve, General Oudinot found himself setting up camp back on the road to Civitavecchia, ministering to his many wounded men and, perhaps most painfully of all, preparing a report to send to Paris. Garibaldi meanwhile returned to Rome with three hundred captured French soldiers in tow. "Long live the republic," "Down with Pius IX!" cried the Romans as the French troops trod down the street. When a woman passed by carrying a rifle, the men of the National Guard* broke into applause. Everywhere people clamored to get weapons of their own.[2]

The Romans' support for the new regime was no longer in doubt. Their victory over the French, reported the otherwise unsympathetic consul of Württemberg a few days after the battle, "had a wholly unexpected result. . . . Since the other day a huge enthusiasm has suddenly appeared among a people who until then had seemed entirely apathetic. . . . All of a sudden there is a spirit of war among the people that seems incomprehensible and that must have entirely altered the expectations of the French army." The U.S. chargé d'affaires was similarly surprised by the swift transformation. "The appearance of a foreign enemy has accomplished for the republic what its own measures, papal abuses and the cause of liberty have hitherto failed to effect. It has converted thousands, who were indifferent as to its existence, into warm and strong supporters."[3]

In preparing for the battle, Mazzini had appointed a special medical force, naming as its head Cristina Belgiojoso, a woman who would become a legendary figure in the Italian struggle for independence. She organized twelve military hospitals in Rome and recruited women from the upper classes to staff them. From one of Milan's wealthiest noble families, the forty-year-old Belgiojoso had married a much older prince when she was sixteen but separated from him by the time she was twenty. Known for her beauty, her intelligence, her distinguished manner, and her dramatic dress, she was thin, her skin almost pallid, with large black eyes and black hair, and a narrow aquiline nose. She normally dressed all in white, set off by a necklace of black coral. A lifelong supporter of Italian independence, she had been exiled from Milan by the Austrians in 1831 and had made her Paris home into a meeting place for other Italian exiles, intellectuals, and artists. Like many Italian patriots exhilarated by the toppling of the papal government, she had rushed to the Eternal City to take part in the momentous events under way there.[4]

On the day of the French assault, Belgiojoso wrote to Margaret

---

* With the advent of the Roman Republic, the Civic Guard was transformed into the National Guard.

Fuller, placing the American journalist in charge of the women volunteers to tend to the wounded at one of Rome's major hospitals, Fate Bene Fratelli. "Go there at twelve," wrote the princess, "if the alarm bell has not rung before." She concluded her note simply, "May God help us."[5]

Women would play an important role in Rome's defense. As the battle raged on the thirtieth, they stood at the city's barricades, armed with muskets and knives. In the days that followed, piles of stones could be found along Rome's streets, bearing the inscription "Arms for women." On May 6 the barricades commission issued a call: "Women of Rome! Gather deadly rocks, relentless stones. . . . Lucretia* stabbed herself to defend your honor. You, beautiful Roman women, win to defend your honor."[6]

In the wake of their unexpected victory, the Romans showed new pride. "Yesterday," began a proclamation placed on the walls of the city, "the entry of the French in Rome began. They entered through Porta San Pancrazio . . . as our prisoners." Mazzini had notarized copies of the testimony of captured French troops posted through the city. They had been misled, the soldiers said, told that the Romans yearned for the pope's return, but as one put it, once they had arrived, "we heard everywhere: 'We don't want any more of the government of the priests. The pope can return for all we care, but only for religious matters.' We came as friends, we are brothers, because we are true republicans, and we fought only because we were betrayed."[7]

Mazzini himself had few illusions. Unless the French changed sides, he knew, the Roman Republic was doomed. King Ferdinand and his Neapolitan army were threatening from the south, and the Austrians were preparing to invade from the north. Nothing Mazzini could do would stop them, but the French were a different matter. Two months earlier, fifty-seven members of France's Assembly had sent the Roman Republic a letter of support. "The old tyrants," they wrote, "will think twice before attacking Romans and overturning their independence. If they ever dare to do it. . . . Citizens of Italy, the French democracy's

---

* Lucretia, wife of a Roman consul in the late sixth century B.C., committed suicide after being raped by an Etruscan king's son, leading, it was believed, to the overthrow of the monarchy and the advent of ancient Rome's republic.

sympathies are with you. Should you call for aid, its volunteers would come to help you chase the barbarians out." Back then, the French left could not imagine that it would be French and not Austrian "barbarians" who would attempt to crush Rome's new republic.[8]

The French government's duplicity had now been exposed. With new parliamentary elections scheduled to be held in France in two weeks, Mazzini had reason to think—or at least hope—that the left might win. If it did, the French army's mission would certainly change. Rather than plot with the three Catholic monarchies to crush the Roman Republic, the French forces might well come to their sister republic's aid.

Eager to win French sympathy in advance of the election, the Roman triumvirate ordered the release of the French prisoners. There was no basis for hostility between the two republics, said Mazzini, in announcing a festive send-off for the captured Frenchmen. "The Roman people," he explained, "will salute the brave soldiers of our sister republic with applause and a fraternal demonstration at noon." Preceded by a phalanx of National Guardsmen, the French soldiers marched down the Corso to the stirring sound of the *Marseillaise*. The Romans lining the way applauded, with some coming up to embrace and kiss the young Frenchmen, others handing them food. "Long live the French people!" they shouted. "Long live the two sister republics! Down with the government of the priests!"[9]

That same day, a week after the French defeat, Captain Key, the British naval officer, made his way to Rome. The city was a war zone, and he had heard that some of his compatriots were eager to escape. Villas outside Rome's gates were being blown up and trees chopped down to leave a clear line of fire against any invading army. People filled their homes with paving stones, ready to hurl them from their roofs should hostile troops succeed in penetrating the city's walls. Construction of the barricades continued at a frenetic pace. New rumors that Neapolitan troops were approaching from the south heightened the tension.

The captain went to see Mazzini, who spoke to him in his accented English. The past days had been trying for the Italian leader. He looked haggard, his beard grizzled. In exchange for a pledge that the horses they took would not end up in French hands, Mazzini granted Key's request to allow any foreigner who wanted to do so to leave.

The next day the captain returned to talk to Mazzini again, hoping to help find a way to avoid bloodshed. It was clear that Rome must fall, Key told the republic's leader, either to the French now or to the combined armies of the other Catholic powers later. Clearly it would be better to negotiate with the French than to have to deal with the Austrians and Neapolitans. Having suffered such a great stain on their honor as they had with their abortive initial attack, the French would never rest until they had taken Rome. "I used every argument," recalled the British captain, "to convince him of the folly of resistance," but Mazzini would not be moved. Soon, thought the Italian prophet, the French people would learn the news that, contrary to what they had been told, their troops had been sent to Italy to reconquer Rome for the pope. The storm of outrage this would provoke would, he hoped, transform France from enemy into ally.[10]

With the armies Pius had summoned on the move, popular anger at the pope and the Catholic clergy was running high. "The hatred that this population shows against the priests," wrote a member of the Constituent Assembly to his wife in early May, "is unimaginable. They have burned the carriages of the cardinals in the public squares, and woe unto anyone who speaks out in favor of the pope. He would be the immediate victim of popular furor." The destruction of the cardinals' magnificently painted, gilded carriages had become an elaborate popular spectacle. In one of these pantomimes, to the onlookers' delight, prostitutes dressed themselves in priests' garb. In another, a man clothed in a cardinal's rich red robe sat haughtily in a carriage, surrounded by others impersonating priests and servants. A faux supplicant then approached the cardinal, only to be contemptuously dismissed. Then the people went to work with their axes and clubs, amid a torrent of curses, smashing the carriage to pieces before setting it afire.

Republican officials visited each of Rome's many monasteries and convents to inform the monks and nuns that they were now free to break their religious vows. Cloistered nuns opened their doors only a crack to receive the news, but it seems none availed themselves of their new freedom.[11]

General Oudinot sent a telegram reporting news of his defeat to Paris. He did so with remarkable economy: "Our troops, having met with resistance under Rome's walls, have retreated to Castel di Guido where General Oudinot awaits reinforcements and heavy equipment for a siege." At the same time, he wrote a longer report. "The sympathies for the old government," he remarked, "are far from being as great as was supposed. . . . Pius IX is loved, but people dread the return of the clerical government." French honor was now at stake, but so was Oudinot's own reputation. "Have no concern," wrote the general. Once reinforcements arrived, he vowed, it would take him only a few days to conquer Rome.[12]

When he read Oudinot's telegram with the shocking news of the army's unexpected defeat at Rome, Odilon Barrot, the French prime minister, felt faint and collapsed into a chair. Members of the cabinet gathered around the stricken Louis Napoleon, all dreading the prospect of telling the Assembly the news. "A humiliation of our army that is not immediately remedied," argued Falloux, the Catholic minister, "would be a double defeat for French influence and for the liberal spirit in Italy." By the president's look, Falloux—whose concern for advancing the liberal cause in Italy could hardly have been less sincere—knew that he had hit the right note. For Louis Napoleon, nothing was more important than casting himself as the defender of French honor. Not eager to face the attacks the news would provoke in the Assembly, the ministers decided to remain silent until they had more details. When, two days later, word began leaking out, the government put out a short—wholly misleading—statement:

> It appears from a telegram received by the government that General Oudinot began to march on Rome where, following all available information, he was called by popular demand. But having encountered a more serious resistance than was expected from the foreigners who have occupied Rome, he took up a position a short distance from the city where he awaits the rest of the expeditionary corps.

The government's attempts to minimize the import of the disaster did little to head off what would be an exceedingly painful session of the

Assembly that same day. Had they not been told the previous month, asked Jules Favre, one of France's most influential moderate republicans, that they were voting to send the army to help protect Rome from the Austrians? Had the prime minister not assured the Assembly that the goal of the military mission was, in Barrot's own words, to guarantee a good government to the Roman people, founded on liberal institutions? "The blood of our officers," Favre charged, "the blood of our generous soldiers has been shed for the Pope. It has been shed for despotism." To the ministers' denials, Favre replied:

> You say: no. You will offer a justification for your behavior, I think, and the Assembly will assess it. I hope the Assembly will take this deplorable affair in hand, and will no longer continue to give you its confidence, because it knows what you have done, whether through incompetence or treason I do not know.

"It's treason!" shouted the deputies from the left.

Favre demanded that an envoy be sent to Rome to represent the Assembly. "It is important," he said, "that France's position be clearly separated from that of the men who have so disastrously conducted this mission. The Assembly must intervene to impose its will and its authority." The body then approved a motion demanding that the French troops' mission in Italy be limited to the one that the Assembly had authorized.[13]

WHILE THE FRENCH WERE licking their wounds, King Ferdinand and his Neapolitan army were marching through several towns in the south of the Papal States, headed toward Rome. On May 2 the triumvirate alerted the Romans to the threat. "His intent," they proclaimed, "is to reestablish the pope as absolute temporal ruler. His arms are persecution, brutality, plunder." In a letter to his mother the next day, Aurelio Saffi, Mazzini's fellow triumvir, put up a brave front. "Twelve thousand Neapolitans are now at Velletri, with the king . . . but they don't scare

anyone. . . . The *popolani* of Rome are saying: 'We've eaten the Gauls,*
now we'll eat the macaroni.' "[14]

On May 5, the Neapolitans entered Albano, fifteen miles southeast of
Rome. From his new outpost, King Ferdinand wrote to the pope, reporting that people there were greeting him as a hero. Captain Key met with
the king in Albano three days later but painted a very different picture
for his navy superiors in London. "The people at Albano, though not
republican," wrote Key, "are much dissatisfied with the Neapolitans,
who have enforced a cry of 'Viva il re'† everywhere, and imprisoned
many who were suspected of being averse to the intervention."[15]

Having beaten back the French, Garibaldi and his legion were now
free to take on the Neapolitans. On paper, it would seem no match. The
sixteen thousand finely uniformed men of King Ferdinand's army, with
their large cavalry and well-equipped artillery, faced a ragamuffin force
that, to the eyes of many, resembled nothing so much as an unusually
large band of brigands. Garibaldi's men wore no uniform, aside from the
scarlet shirts of their officers. Chosen by the men based on their courage
in battle, the officers wore no other sign of their rank. When they stopped
to rest, the legionnaires left their horses free to wander, then mounted
them without saddle or bit. For food, they chased down sheep, which
they dispatched with their bayonets, returning to camp to roast the car-
cass and share the meat. Garibaldi himself gave the impression of being
more of an Indian chief than a general. He sat on his horse, said one
observer, as if he had been born in the saddle. When not resting in the
tiny tent that he made out of his rifle and his coat, he could be seen atop
a hill with his looking glass, scouring the countryside for enemy positions. His troops were a collection of young men bursting with enthusiasm for the Italian cause, old soldiers loyal to the bold captain they had
followed from continent to continent, and some, less scrupulous, eager
for adventure and hoping for plunder.

---

* This is a play on words in Roman dialect: *Ce semo magnate li Galli, mo ce magneremo li
maccheroni*. The word *Galli* has the double meaning of "Gauls"—or Frenchmen—and
"roosters." Romans condescendingly viewed southern Italians as macaroni eaters.

† "Long live the king."

Ferdinand nervously followed Garibaldi's movements. On May 9 he sent some of his units to try to cut off the legionnaires' escape route, but in a three-hour battle, it was the outnumbered *garibaldini* who sent the Neapolitan army in embarrassing flight, leaving their cannons behind them in their haste. Having heard horrifying tales of the savage Garibaldi, the Neapolitan soldiers who were taken prisoner begged for mercy, colorfully cursing the pope in Neapolitan dialect. Enjoying a cigar in celebration of a good day's work, Garibaldi was eager to pursue his advantage, but he received word from Rome that the French might soon launch their second assault. He was told to bring his legionnaires back.[16]

The Spanish had meanwhile landed at the coastal town of Fiumicino, at the mouth of the Tiber, eighteen miles west of Rome. It was not the most propitious of sites, for its few hundred inhabitants abandoned it during the malaria season each summer, but it was there, with much fanfare, that the Spanish planted a papal flag. "And so the chorus is complete," the triumvirate proclaimed on posters all over Rome. "Austria, France and Spain make yet another attempt at the old story, responding to a pope's call."[17]

IN EARLY MAY, IN YET another attempt to get the pope to publicly pronounce his willingness to keep his reforms, Harcourt and Rayneval sent Cardinal Antonelli a formal document spelling out the French position. France had decided to send its army to Rome, they wrote, "full of confidence in the generous intentions that must be expected from the Holy Father concerning the maintenance of the liberal institutions in his states. . . . The thinking of the Government of the Republic is not to impose on the Roman population a regime that they would not accept of their own free will."

France's aim, explained the French ambassadors, was "to bring about a rapprochement, ensuring that the Holy Father, in entering Rome, finds himself once again in a situation that is satisfactory both for him and for his people, for only this will guarantee both Italy and Europe against new unrest." The ambassadors concluded by renewing the plea that the pope had heard so many times:

In order to facilitate the difficult task that it has undertaken, France is counting heavily on the assistance of the Pontifical Government. It would therefore hope that, without any further delay, His Holiness would deign to publish a manifesto that, in guaranteeing liberal institutions . . . as required by the times, would ensure that all resistance would crumble.[18]

If the French ambassadors had any hopes that this latest appeal would be any more successful than their earlier ones, they were quickly disappointed. It would be folly, Pius told Rayneval, for him to embark on the same road that had already once led him to the "edge of the abyss."

"So don't imagine," said the pope, "that the return to the old order of things is possible. I would never permit it."

Pius went on to explain that Italians were different from the French. It was not simply a question of the incompatibility of constitutional rule with church authority in the Papal States. "When France gets to see things close up," he said, "it will understand that the Italian peoples are not suited for representative institutions. They are not yet sufficiently educated. . . . They must first pass through an intermediate stage. The time will come when they will be capable of having, like others, a regime that offers freedoms. But they are not ready for it today."[19]

Rayneval was frustrated, but Harcourt was even more upset. If it were not for the unpalatable alternative of having the Austrians occupy Rome, he advised Paris, he would recommend having the French wash their hands of the matter. What loomed ahead was frightening: French soldiers would shed their blood to restore a government of priests despised by the Romans, and as thanks they would gain only the hatred of the people they had come to help.

"The pope," reported Harcourt, "is very good, but he has the disadvantages of his goodness: he is fickle, irresolute, and as a consequence not by his nature able to escape the influences that surround him, which are all obscurantist and reactionary. The whole clique around him are Austrian-lovers down to the marrow of their bones."[20]

In Paris, as the left continued to denounce the government's duplicity, the French foreign minister bombarded his ambassadors in Gaeta with ever more frantic pleas to get the pope to announce his plans for reforms. On May 10, he sent instructions to General Oudinot: "Tell the Romans that we do not want to join with the Neapolitans against them. Pursue negotiations. . . . Reinforcements are being sent. Wait for them. Try to enter Rome through an agreement with its inhabitants, or if you are forced to attack Rome, be sure it is with the greatest possible chance of success."[21]

DISTRUSTFUL OF THE FRENCH and having little confidence in the fighting capacity of either the Neapolitans or the Spaniards, Cardinal Antonelli continued to place his hopes in Austria. "It is a true scandal," he complained to his nuncio in Vienna, "to further postpone coming to the aid of the Center and seat of Christianity, which is in the grip of the fiercest enemies of religion and of humanity. I hope that Austria will not want to delay the time of its much desired liberation."[22]

Although Antonelli did not yet know it, good news was on its way. Prince Schwarzenberg had already sent fifteen thousand troops to retake Tuscany for the grand duke and to march on the walled city of Bologna in the Papal States as well.[23] On May 8 a division of the Austrian army, with seven thousand men and a dozen cannons, took up positions in the hills overlooking Bologna. Accompanying the Austrian army was Monsignor Gaetano Bedini, Pius's choice to reestablish papal government there. When the *bolognesi* refused to yield, the Austrians launched their attack, assaulting two of the city's gates before being driven away by musket fire from atop the wall. From their positions in the nearby hills, the Austrians then rained their deadly artillery on the town below. After eight days of bombardment, as fires ravaged the city, their situation hopeless, the people of Bologna surrendered.[24]

WHILE THE AUSTRIAN ARMY was bombing the *bolognesi* into submission, a new French envoy was on his way to the Papal States in an effort to avoid the need for the French army to do the same in Rome. The French Assembly had demanded that someone be sent to ensure that the

Ferdinand
de Lesseps

French army not exceed its charge. The man chosen for what would prove to be a thankless task was forty-three-year-old Ferdinand de Lesseps, a second-generation diplomat who had most recently served as the French ambassador to Madrid. Lesseps had previously kept his distance from the hothouse of French politics. He now entered a minefield of double-dealing and treachery from which he would not emerge unscathed.[25]

The French government's embarrassment over its plight in Rome could scarcely have been greater. "A more remarkable series of blunders and failures both political and military," huffed a May 11 London *Times* editorial, "it has seldom been our duty to record." The government's mendacity had not gone unnoticed: "The root of the mischief seems to be the extraordinary equivocation practiced by the French government to conceal their real object in this expedition. They had the courage to undertake it, but not to avow the reason. . . . [They] continued to assume the credit of a demonstration against Austria for what was in reality a demonstration approved by Austria for the restoration of the Pope." As a result of the government's duplicity, added the *Times* Paris correspondent, a coup in Paris might be imminent.[26]

At a chilly meeting with Vienna's ambassador in Paris, Drouyn, the French foreign minister, pleaded for Austria's help in getting the pope to break free of what he termed the "occult" influences surrounding him in Gaeta who were turning him against his earlier reform path. Otherwise, Drouyn warned, a war between Austria and France might erupt, one that might well turn into a Europe-wide conflagration. For more than an hour, the French foreign minister droned on, recalled the disapproving Austrian, "in a manner as verbose as it was confused."

Unable to contain himself any further, the Austrian ambassador broke in. "You speak of an occult influence in Gaeta. If you are referring to the Imperial Cabinet you are in error. Austria's agents have everywhere used the same language." It was rather the French government that was acting deceitfully. "In Paris," the Austrian diplomat pointed out, the French government "said that it was sending an expedition to Rome to safeguard the Romans' freedoms, and in Gaeta it said that the expedition's goal was to return the Holy Father to his throne." Paris had claimed that it was acting to stop Austria, but, said the Austrian, this had fooled no one. "You blame us for the pope's mistrust. . . . Do not fool yourselves. It is you yourselves who have caused it. The Holy Father believes the aims that you have offered to the National Assembly, and the National Assembly believes the aims that you have given the pope." The French government, complained the Austrian ambassador, was now trying to make the pope pay the price for its own incompetence, intimidating him in order to quiet the left opposition in the French Assembly. "You risk setting yourselves against the church and, in doing so," warned the Austrian, "forgetting the maxim that one must never have for enemies either women or priests."[27]

On May 9, Rayneval arrived at French military headquarters outside Rome for a meeting with General Oudinot. With reinforcements already arriving, the general was in a surprisingly good mood, confident that he would soon be able to redeem himself. Yet he realized that the task ahead was a delicate one. Taking Rome for the pope, he explained to the ambassador, was a far more complicated task than conquering any other city. To bombard it into submission would mean to destroy its churches and monuments, the pride of the civilized world. Nor could the French wage war through the city's barricaded streets, for the resulting bloodshed would hardly endear the pope to his people. Instead, Oudinot explained, he planned to bring an overwhelming force to the walls of Rome, use his heavy cannons to blast a hole in it, build bridges over the Tiber, and so force the renegade government to surrender. Rayneval agreed that this was a good plan. In the end, he thought, resistance would be limited.

This was a view shared by Captain Key, following his visit to Rome and his inspection of the French troops camped outside the city. The new attack, he told London on May 12, would likely come in a few days' time. "As there are many parts of the walls where half an hour's cannonading would completely demolish them," he predicted, "the French will enter the town with ease." The question for the British naval officer was not whether the French would succeed in taking Rome but what they would do once they took it. In the towns they had occupied, the French had hoisted their own flag alongside that of the Roman Republic. Nowhere had they put up the white papal flag.[28]

The next night Ferdinand de Lesseps, the new French envoy, landed in Civitavecchia and made his way south to French military headquarters. On arrival, he handed General Oudinot a letter from the French foreign minister explaining his mission. The letter said nothing about the uproar in the Assembly that had led to Lesseps's appointment. Rather, Drouyn simply explained that, given the unexpected resistance Oudinot had encountered, the government had decided to place a diplomat alongside him to be entirely dedicated to negotiations with the authorities in Rome.[29]

The general was not happy to be saddled with a diplomat whose authority risked putting his in question and whose mission of crafting a negotiated settlement seemed to conflict with his own. Nor was it clear that the French government in fact did seek a peaceful settlement, for Lesseps handed the general a second letter, this one written by the French president, Louis Napoleon.

My dear general,

The news by telegram announcing the unexpected resistance that you encountered beneath Rome's walls has pained me greatly. I would have hoped, as you know, that the residents of Rome, opening their eyes to the evidence, would eagerly receive a friendly and selfless mission. But it was otherwise. As our soldiers were greeted as enemies, our military honor is now at stake. I will not abide by it suffering such a blow. You will not lack for reinforcements. Tell your soldiers that I appreciate their bravery, that I share their pain, and that they will always be able to count on my support and on my appreciation.[30]

The next day Oudinot sent a telegram to Drouyn: "I will enter Rome with the agreement of the inhabitants and without firing a shot. At least, I have good reason to count on it."[31]

As his superiors would later complain, the French general appeared to have great difficulty learning from experience.

CHAPTER 14

NEGOTIATING IN
BAD FAITH

IN MID-MAY, GENERAL OUDINOT MOVED INTO HIS NEW HEAD-
quarters in a villa only two miles from Rome's gates. Thousands of reinforcements had arrived, and more were on the way, as French officers
planned for the siege that would begin should negotiations fail. What
worried Oudinot most was not the military might of the Roman Republic, for which he had little regard, but the approaching Roman summer.
A reporter at the French camp captured the sense of dread: "Already the
heat is great. . . . Even within the walls of Rome, sickness and fever fall
to the lot of every stranger, but without, the effects of malaria are so severe that no one can sleep abroad with impunity. What, then, is to become of the 20,000 men now encamped within a mile of Rome?" In a
report later in May, the correspondent added, "One hundred men swollen with the malaria fever came in here yesterday, and in another week
the hospitals will not contain the number of sick who will claim admit-
tance. Will the General-in-Chief, under such circumstances, hesitate
any longer? For my part, I think not."[1]

While the French were building up their forces west of the city, King
Ferdinand and his army were back in the Papal States, at Albano, only a
few miles south of Rome. The king was emboldened by the news from
Sicily, where, on May 15, his army had captured Palermo, ending the
yearlong revolt. Eager to cast himself as the pope's savior, he stood at
the head of ten thousand troops.

With Lesseps, the new French envoy, beginning negotiations with

Rome's triumvirate, the danger of an immediate French assault was much reduced. It was time, thought Mazzini, to again address the threat to the south. In mid-May, both Garibaldi's irregular forces and the regular army under General Pietro Roselli marched out of the city. Coordination of the two forces left much to be desired. Roselli had formal military training and deep knowledge of the history of warfare and strategy. He planned carefully and closely monitored troop movements. By contrast, Garibaldi had no formal military training, nor any use for it. He fought by intuition, guided in no small part by emotion. At Roselli's headquarters, Garibaldi was referred to as "the pirate," but once the battle was joined, it was Roselli who would prove slow to adapt to new developments, while Garibaldi was nothing if not agile on the battlefield. It was Garibaldi whom King Ferdinand most feared. At word that he was on his way, the Bourbon monarch moved his army south to take up a defensive position at Velletri, where the rumor quickly spread among Ferdinand's troops that the "red devil," as they called Garibaldi, was invincible. When Garibaldi's men attacked, the terrified Neapolitan soldiers once again quickly melted away, heading south across the border. The subsequent return of the humiliated king to Gaeta on May 21 would further dampen the pope's spirits.[2]

Ferdinand's setback reinforced the pope's belief that his salvation lay with the Austrian army alone, but Prince Schwarzenberg had other ideas. "All our efforts," he told Esterházy on May 19, "must be directed to prevent the Italian complications from provoking a conflict between us and France." The best way to do this, he wrote, was through the four-power Gaeta conference.

There was one other piece of advice that Schwarzenberg felt compelled to give. He had been shocked by word that the French envoys were urging the pope to visit France to win popular support for his cause. The proposal, he declared, "seems to me to prove yet once more that there is no idea so bizarre that it does not find some adherents in France, if it in some way flatters the nation's self-regard." When he had been in Rome years earlier, recalled the Austrian chancellor, the pope, amid the majesty of his monumental basilicas, had been an awe-inspiring figure. By contrast, remarked Schwarzenberg, "a tourist pope, traveling up and down a part of Europe by rail and stopping at each station to bless the crowds of the curious eager to enjoy this new spectacle would simply be . . . futile food thrown out to the frivolity and skepticism of the false spirits who abound everywhere."[3]

WHEN LESSEPS MOVED INTO a hotel in the center of Rome to begin negotiations, he saw firsthand how determined the Romans were to resist invasion and urged Oudinot to hold off his attack. There was still a chance, the envoy thought, that a peaceful solution could be found. Reluctantly, on May 17, Oudinot agreed to a cease-fire.[4]

Two days later the Roman government rejected Lesseps's first proposal, which reflected his understanding of what the French parliament had authorized in sending the army to Rome. The text called on the Romans to ask for the French Republic's "fraternal protection" and to welcome the French soldiers as brothers. It guaranteed the Romans' right to decide freely on their own form of government. Military action inside Rome was to be jointly coordinated by Roman and French forces, and Rome's civil authorities were to continue to function. What the proposal lacked, Mazzini pointed out, was any recognition that a legitimate government, the Roman Republic, freely elected by the people, already existed in Rome.[5]

The French elections for a new National Assembly had meanwhile taken place, giving a boost to Oudinot, who was fast losing patience with Lesseps. The conservatives had won a big victory, crushing Mazzini's hopes for greater French support for his republican cause. Continued negotiations, thought the general, were now useless. "If one sincerely wants peace," he told Lesseps on May 21, "let's enter Rome. The army's discipline and our government's generosity are the most powerful guarantees of order and freedom that the Romans could want." That same day, aboard the *Bulldog* at Civitavecchia, Captain Key sent the latest news to London. "The French," he predicted, "will undoubtedly have possession of Rome either by treaty or assault before the end of this week."[6]

The Eternal City was a portrait of contrasts. Shops remained open, and life went on, but the city gates were shut and people could leave only with the military's permission. The threat of foreign invasion had united the Romans, who were furious at the pope for trying to reestablish his rule by military conquest. Reports of the bombardment and fall of Bologna, the second city of the Roman Republic, had only made things worse.[7]

On the afternoon of May 20, Ciceruacchio—who the previous year had led marches through Rome's streets vowing loyalty to the pope—brought a hundred of his followers to Piazza del Popolo. There they tore down the papal crests that hung over the doors of the piazza's four churches before entering the sanctuaries and ripping out their wooden confessionals, to be added to the city's barricades. For the people of Rome, nothing symbolized the intrusion of the priestly gaze into their lives more than the confessionals, where they were pressured to reveal their illicit thoughts and deeds under threat of excommunication.[8]

Ciceruacchio and his men then made their way down the Corso, pulling confessionals from other churches along the way. Piling some of these back in the middle of Piazza del Popolo, the men planned to hold a celebratory bonfire after dark.

On learning of all this, Mazzini was dismayed. After ordering the National Guard to put a stop to it, he had a proclamation posted on the city walls the next day. "Romans," it read, "yesterday, in a moment of thoughtlessness, produced by the imminence of new dangers, some of you removed several confessionals from churches in order to find new materials for the barricades." Given the dangers they faced, their imprudent action could be forgiven, but, the triumvirs warned, "the enemies of our holy Republic are watching from all corners of Europe, looking for the chance to put our noble efforts in a bad light, and to accuse the people of irreverence and irreligion." It was important, the notice concluded, "that you yourselves replace the confessionals in the churches from which you took them yesterday."[9]

WHEN PIUS LEARNED THAT the French had sent a new envoy to negotiate with the men who ruled Rome, he was furious. Adding to his irritation were Harcourt and Rayneval's incessant pleas for him to commit to keeping his reforms. No matter how many times he rebuffed them, they kept pressing. Although he had earlier felt a closer emotional bond with France, it was becoming ever clearer to him that it was on Austria that he must depend.

"You can be sure," Pius told Rayneval on May 18, "that Austria does not push me one way versus another. . . . Austria is content to protect my independence and does not go beyond that."[10]

Rayneval found himself in an increasingly uncomfortable position. He had repeatedly told Drouyn that there was no way they could persuade the pope to embrace representative government in Rome, yet each letter of instructions from Paris carried the same refrain. Rayneval also resented his government's decision to send Lesseps to Rome, undercutting his own authority. "The question, my dear count," confided Rayneval to the Dutch ambassador in Gaeta, "is now so overloaded with complications that I admit that I no longer understand anything, and I leave the task of untangling it all to those more skilled than I, or to the natural course of events."[11]

Meeting in Cardinal Antonelli's room on Sunday, May 20, for the latest session of the Gaeta conference, the two French envoys again found themselves under attack. Why had France sent an envoy to negotiate with the criminal band who had taken Rome? Their claim that Lesseps had come simply to negotiate the city's surrender met unconcealed disbelief. As the meeting then turned to other recent developments, the Neapolitan ambassador had the unenviable task of explaining how Ferdinand's army had been so ignominiously routed by Garibaldi's irregulars. The debacle, Count Ludolf tried to convince his colleagues, was all the fault of the French. Not only had they refused to coordinate their actions with Ferdinand, but by negotiating with Mazzini, they had left Rome's military free to move south.

At least, remarked Ludolf, wherever Ferdinand had gone in the Papal States, he had raised the papal flag and immediately handed the local administration over to papal authorities. By contrast, wherever the French had gone, they had left the Roman Republic's flag up alongside their own and refused to allow Pius's emissaries to reestablish papal rule.

The Austrian ambassador then took his turn lambasting the French, accusing them of undermining the four-power Catholic conference.

Rather than coordinating their efforts with the others, the French had sent its army to Rome without any warning and were now preventing the other powers from intervening.

Following the meeting, Rayneval went to see the pope, whom he found in a bleak mood. What, asked Pius, would now happen to all those who had rallied to his cause in the southern towns of the Papal States that Ferdinand had abandoned? They were now at Garibaldi's mercy. That evening the Belgian ambassador tried to comfort him. "The Holy Father," recalled the diplomat, "shed his tears and told me . . . 'My dear prince, one can endure anything for oneself, but when others are suffering because of you, that makes the pain all the more bitter.'" At that moment, bellicose military music from the street outside came through the pope's window. "This contrast sickened him," reported the ambassador, "and he raised his eyes to the heavens. One has to have been with Pius IX often," observed the Belgian, "to know all the delicacies of his heart."[12]

FROM HIS HOTEL ON ROME's fashionable Via Condotti, Lesseps shuttled back and forth to French military headquarters to discuss the latest developments with General Oudinot. His first meeting with Mazzini could not have been more informal. The French envoy had made his way to the Palace of the Consulta, Mazzini's quarters, arriving there at one a.m. and asking where he could find the Italian prophet. He was directed to the far side of the second floor. Taking off his shoes so that he would make no noise, he walked down the long hall, peeking into rooms until he came upon Mazzini's modest quarters. There, on a simple iron bed, lay Mazzini, asleep. Pulling the room's only chair aside the bed, Lesseps sat down. He spoke Mazzini's name softly, but Europe's great theorist of nationalism did not stir. The Frenchman kept repeating his name in ever increasing volume until the exhausted triumvir finally awoke.

Mazzini, whose room was entirely unguarded, opened his eyes to the surprising sight of the French envoy sitting by his bed. Half awake, the Italian prophet asked the Frenchman if he had come to assassinate him.[13]

In the negotiations that followed, Lesseps swung from admiration for the Italian's integrity and courage to suspicions that Italy's prophet of independence was a "modern Nero." Mazzini, Lesseps complained in mid-May, "is nothing other than a vulgar man of ambition." It was clear to Lesseps that the Romans despised "priestly" rule and were outraged that the pope had called foreign troops to invade their city. But, he thought, few outside the educated elite could be said to be republicans or cared much about what happened in far-off parts of the peninsula. For most Romans, Sicilians and Venetians were as foreign as the French or Spaniards. It was only, he thought, Mazzini and his small band of enthusiasts—mostly drawn from the middle classes, and many from outside the Papal States—who dreamed of a unified Italy.[14]

Oudinot kept pushing for an immediate attack on Rome, his impatience growing with each report of the Austrian army's victorious march in the northern provinces of the Papal States. He knew that the Austrians wanted the French to take Rome, so he was not worried that they would try to beat him to it. But the contrast between his own army's inaction and the Austrian army's relentless march was humiliating. Even Harcourt, despite his frustration with the pope, urged the general to attack. "We have not led an army of 20,000 men into Italy to put it at the mercy of Monsieur Mazzini and his colleagues," he told Oudinot during a visit to the general's headquarters on May 22. Later in the day Oudinot sent a message to Lesseps at his Rome hotel: "You are, Monsieur, very seductive, no one knows that better than I. . . . But the status quo which you condemn us to is harmful and strikes a most serious blow against the dignity and the interests of France, no less than against our military honor." The triumvirate had rejected the French proposal. This meant, said Oudinot, that the truce they had announced was over. It was time to attack.[15]

That same day the Americans' recently arrived chargé d'affaires, Lewis Cass, Jr., offered himself to Oudinot and Lesseps as an unofficial mediator between the French and the Roman Republic. Cass, whose father, a U.S. senator, had been the unsuccessful Democratic Party candidate for president in 1848, replaced the unfortunate Jacob Martin, who had died within weeks of his arrival the previous summer. Cass brought

Oudinot a handwritten counteroffer from Rome, drafted by Charles Bonaparte, then acting as president of the Constituent Assembly. It contained three articles:

> The Roman Republic, accepting the French Assembly deliberations that authorized the sending of troops to Italy to prevent foreign intervention, will be grateful for the support that it will receive.
>
> The Roman people have the right to pronounce themselves freely on the form of their government, and the French Republic, which has never put this in doubt, will pledge to solemnly recognize it from the moment that the Constitution to be voted on by the National Assembly is approved by a popular vote.
>
> Rome will welcome the French soldiers as brothers. But the troops will enter Rome only at such time as, a threat being imminent, the Republic's government asks them.[16]

Although this counterproposal contained elements that Lesseps could not accept, it gave him hope that a peaceful solution to the crisis might be at hand. He doubted that Mazzini himself would bend but thought pressure could be put on the less ideologically driven members of the Roman government. On the twenty-sixth Lesseps wrote to Drouyn in Paris, begging him to prevent Oudinot from attacking before the negotiations had a chance to succeed. He realized, he said, that the French could not hold off long with the malaria season approaching, but he urged them to give him a few more days.[17]

WHILE THE FRENCH BICKERED at their military headquarters outside Rome, Austria's ambassador in Gaeta had the pleasure of presenting the pope with the keys to Bologna. Pius, reported Esterházy, was visibly moved by the gesture and expressed his admiration for the efficiency with which the Austrian army had reestablished papal rule in the second city of his lands. "The rapid success of our action . . . compared to the scandalous attitude of France . . . under Rome's walls," reported Esterházy, "presents a contrast that cannot fail to impress and is much appreciated in Gaeta."

Eager as he was to encourage this unflattering comparison, the Austrian ambassador soon found himself in the odd position of trying to cool the pope's anger at the French. Disturbed by the latest news about the ongoing negotiations in Rome, Pius told Esterházy that he planned to issue a public protest. The Austrian warned him against it. France was now, after all, a republic. If the pope pushed the French too far, he feared, they might be tempted to switch sides, and should the large, well-equipped French army come to the aid of its fellow republic in Rome, the results would be catastrophic.[18]

Esterházy also found himself having to dampen Cardinal Antonelli's increasingly belligerent attitude toward France. Angered by a recent memo from the two French ambassadors insisting that the pope declare his intention to retain his earlier reforms, Antonelli told the Austrian ambassador that he would demand that they formally retract it. Again, Esterházy cautioned against any hostile move. Instead, he offered to help Antonelli draft his reply to the Frenchmen, an offer Antonelli readily accepted.[19]

While the Austrians were guiding Antonelli, the cardinal was guiding the pope. That Pius was not going to do anything that the cardinal did not approve was evident to all in Gaeta. "Without passing through him," said the Sardinian envoy, "nothing gets done."[20]

"There was a time," observed Schwarzenberg in late May, "when Pius IX declared that he would rather be locked up in Castel Sant'Angelo or retire to a monastery than see a single foreign soldier, and least of all an Austrian, tread upon the soil of his fatherland. How times have changed! Today it seems that the pope is falling into the other extreme since he would like to see his states swarming with foreign—and above all, Austrian—soldiers."[21]

The chancellor urged caution. "The pope's cabinet," Schwarzenberg told Esterházy, "seems to be of the opinion that the best way to counter the dreadful aspects of French action would be to concentrate the forces of the other intervening powers, Austria among them, around Rome." That, he thought, would only make matters worse. Given French public opinion, the appearance of the Austrian army at Rome might well drive the French to take the Roman Republic's side. The result would be a European-wide war.

Indeed, the mood in France at the time was anything but calm. The victory of the right in the recent parliamentary elections had led large, angry crowds to gather in the streets of Paris every night. In a session of parliament on May 22, to the great embarrassment of the prime minister, a deputy of the left read a proclamation that the Austrian General Wimpfen had posted on the walls of newly conquered Bologna. It declared that the destruction of the Roman Republic had been decided upon by the "four great powers," thus making clear the complicity of republican France with the Austrian, Spanish, and Neapolitan monarchies.[22]

The pope and the Italian Peninsula were far from the only preoccupations of the Austrian government at the time, for the reverberations of the previous year's uprisings were still being felt in other parts of the empire. For help in quelling the continuing revolt in Hungary, the Austrians had turned to the Russian tsar. As a result, thousands of Russian troops had recently battled a large Hungarian revolutionary army, resulting in the loss of thousands of Russian soldiers.[23]

Despite these worries, the Austrian chancellor remained focused on the pope's plight. Rome, he observed, repeating an old adage, was where the pope was. If France took Rome, but then demanded that the pope accept its conditions for returning, Pius would be better off moving somewhere else in the Papal States. There he would be in a stronger position than if he were residing in Rome as the "docile instrument of the agitators with whom the French general seems ready to reach an understanding." And of course, most important, there the pope would remain firmly under Austrian influence, protected by Austrian troops. The French would have Rome, but the Austrians would have the pope.[24]

Returning to Gaeta on the morning of May 28 from his latest trip to French military headquarters, Rayneval found the harbor filled with Spanish ships. Three weeks earlier a Spanish warship had docked at Fiumicino. Now, a larger contingent of forces had arrived, as thirty-five hundred Spanish troops pitched camp outside Gaeta's walls.[25]

Rayneval went to bring Antonelli the latest news from Rome. He found the secretary of state in a foul mood. On his desk was a copy of a

Pius IX blesses Spanish troops at Gaeta, May 26, 1849

recent issue of Rome's official newspaper, which had published the latest correspondence between Lesseps and the triumvirate.

How, asked the cardinal, could Rayneval reconcile Lesseps's "incredible" proposals with what the French ambassadors had said at the Gaeta conference? Rayneval assured the secretary of state that the new French envoy had acted on his own. They were all awaiting further instructions from their government, said Rayneval, and he, too, had grown exasperated with Lesseps.[26]

In Rome, hopes mixed with fears, and rumors abounded. The new American chargé d'affaires found himself in the middle of the negotiations between the triumvirate and the French, although he denied this in his reports to Washington, rightly suspecting that his government would not be pleased. Having earlier expressed doubt that the Romans would oppose the French army, Cass had now come to a very different view. "The various factions," he reported, "have coalesced into one attitude, that of defence of the republic; and expressions of patriotism and resolutions to suffer to the last extremity, is the only language heard in the streets." Cass especially praised Rome's women, who were donating their jewels—"some of which are reported to be of enormous value"—to the cause. "This city," he added, "is the last foothold of thousands, who have been fighting for years, from Milan in the North to Palermo in the South, for independence and constitutional government." He estimated that there were eighteen thousand of these political refugees from other parts of Italy. "Rome," he observed, "has become their last rallying point, and may be their final resting place."[27]

The mood among Rome's defenders was determined, although they were painfully aware of the swelling numbers of French troops massing outside the city's walls. Camped out at the monastery of Porta San Pancrazio, atop Janiculum Hill, a young partisan, Leone Paladini, penned a letter to his parents in Milan. Alongside him were the three hundred other volunteers from Lombardy in a battalion composed of idealistic young men of noble and wealthy families. The monastery's gardens were planted with artichokes, which formed the major part of the men's diet, along with some bread, salami, and a little wine.

With sunset, a welcome coolness descended, and the music began. "Our company counts two or three excellent opera singers," Paladini told his parents. "As we are almost all students, in general we are good at modulating our voices, and we organize truly delightful choruses, alternating martial and patriotic arias with others that are more tender and melancholy." As they sang, the young men's thoughts turned to their families back home, bringing, he admitted, tears to their eyes. Many would soon lose their lives not far from where they now sang; others would lose an arm, a leg, an eye or two.[28]

FROM GAETA, HARCOURT WROTE a dramatic plea to Paris. The French forces had to take Rome immediately, peacefully if possible, by force if necessary. "Anything else would be a humiliation for us and will create impossible embarrassments." Their attempts to get the pope to keep a constitutional system were getting nowhere. A new strategy was needed. They should first take Rome and then, proposed Harcourt, "impose very clear conditions on him, because, if one does not impose them they won't do anything."[29]

Although time was fast running out for Lesseps in his efforts to avoid bloodshed, he was convinced that a deal could still be struck. "There exists in Rome," he wrote to Paris on May 29, "a complete division between Mazzini and the Romans, who want an arrangement made with France." Although Lesseps may have been exaggerating—the division was not "complete"—there is no doubt that many Romans saw the futility of a battle against the full force of the French army. The Austrians had taken Florence a few days earlier and were now marching through Umbria, to the north of Rome. That the French were coordinating their action with Austria in an effort to restore the pope could no longer be in doubt.

The same day that he wrote to Paris, Lesseps sent the triumvirate a final ultimatum. The French could wait no longer. He proposed four terms for an agreement:

1.   The Romans ask for the protection of the French Republic.

2.   France does not contest the Romans' right to freely decide on the form of their government.

3.   The Romans will welcome the French as a friendly army. The French army will position itself as it judges proper, both for the defense of the country and the welfare of its troops. It will stay out of the country's administration.

4.   The French Republic guarantees the land occupied by its troops against all foreign attack.

Lesseps ended with a warning: should these terms not be accepted, he would regard his mission as ended, and the French army would take immediate action.[30]

Although Lesseps led Mazzini to believe that he was acting in concert with the French general, he was not. Over the past several days, Oudinot's resentment of Lesseps's interference had blossomed into open hostility. When, a few hours after Lesseps made this latest offer, the triumvirate sent yet another counteroffer, Oudinot exploded. Mazzini's new proposal incorporated article five of the French constitution, whose language pledged France never to employ its force against the freedoms of another people. Mazzini also insisted that the stationing of French troops be decided on in consultation with the government of the Roman Republic.

Oudinot ordered his senior officers to prepare the troops to attack. Lesseps pleaded for more time but found the French command united against him. "Wait!" cried one of the generals incredulously. "Wait for the season of heat and fever to arrive? Wait until our soldiers are decimated?" Lesseps suggested that the army move into the hills to the south and so escape the heat and disease while also preventing the Neapolitans and Spanish from approaching. Oudinot rejected the idea. Such a move would be seen as a humiliating retreat.[31]

The next morning, as French troops moved into position outside Rome's walls, Lesseps, in full diplomatic uniform, went to meet with the triumvirate in a final, desperate attempt to reach an agreement. After a day of intense negotiations, he succeeded in striking a deal. Under the threat of imminent attack, Mazzini agreed to drop both the reference to the Roman Republic and to article five of the French constitution.[32]

Lesseps hurried back to French headquarters, bringing the new agreement to Oudinot to sign. He refused. "Ever since the seventeenth of this month"—the date of Lesseps's arrival—the general told him, "you have paralyzed all the movements of the expeditionary corps under my command." In a letter he hastily wrote to the triumvirate, Oudinot disavowed the accord and told them that Lesseps had exceeded his authority in signing it. "The instructions that I have received from my government," wrote the general, "formally forbid me from associating myself with this latest act."

Irate, Lesseps said he would board the next ship for France and take the agreement to Paris, where he was sure he would be vindicated. He then sent a note to Rome's triumvirate: "I have the honor of declaring to you that I stand by the agreement signed yesterday, and I am about to depart to Paris so that it can be ratified."[33]

Lesseps was packing his bags when a messenger rushed in with a telegram. Sent by Drouyn in Paris, it was brief, and brutally to the point: "The Government of the Republic has ended your mission. You will return to France as soon as you receive this message." At the same time, another telegram from Paris instructed Oudinot to launch his attack on Rome: "All further delay would be harmful given the approach of the fever-filled season. The path of negotiations has been exhausted. . . .

Concentrate your troops. Enter Rome as soon as the attack is virtually assured of success." Oudinot was told to summon Harcourt and Rayneval to his headquarters to better coordinate diplomatic and military action.[34]

Lesseps had been ill used. The government had sent him as a sop to the members of the Assembly, whose denunciations had showered down on Barrot and company, but in the wake of the army's humiliating defeat at the end of April, only a triumphal entry into Rome would serve Louis Napoleon's ambitions. The election of the new, more conservative National Assembly in mid-May had sealed Lesseps's fate.

ROME, THE BEACON OF CHRISTIANITY for so many centuries, had become remarkably hostile to the Roman Catholic Church. Father Faurs, confessor to Pius IX's predecessor and as opposed as he could be to the Roman Republic, offered an alarming account of how low the church had sunk in the Romans' eyes. Popular religion still flourished in the Eternal City, he observed. Indeed, it would be hard to find a door without a cross or a room or workshop without an image of the Madonna on its wall. But most Romans viewed government by the priests with repugnance, and as a result they had come to despise the clergy, and now even women, reported Father Faurs, rarely attended mass.[35]

Despite the high state of alert in Rome, the republic's leader remained shockingly exposed. A British visitor, who had dropped in unannounced on Mazzini several times, quipped, "I wonder no spirited Jesuit has yet looked in with a pistol." With his latest counteroffer to the French rebuffed, the Austrian army gobbling up the northern portion of the Roman Republic, and thousands of Spanish troops landing to the south, bolstering King Ferdinand's army, Mazzini felt painfully alone. "I found him haggard and worn in appearance," reported another British visitor. "Like almost all Italians," he added in a not entirely complimentary way, "he is a visionary."[36]

On June 2, as the overwhelming French force moved into position for its assault, Mazzini gave vent to his frustration in a letter to Garibaldi:

I am going mad and I feel like ending the defense of the City and everything else, and going off to Fuligno* or to the home of the devil and finishing it all with a rifle in hand. In these crucial moments I thought I would find men in whom I could entrust the fate of the country. . . . Instead I find diffidence, reaction, individualism.

With the future of Rome and Italy itself resting on his shoulders, Mazzini found relief only when, alone in his room at the Palace of the Consulta, often well past midnight, he picked up his guitar. An accomplished musician, he sang in a soft voice as he played. His threat that he might abandon his post was an idle one. After years in exile, years of pleas, years of dreams, and thousands of pages of correspondence, his moment had come. But whether he would live to see the next month, or even the next week, remained very much in doubt.[37]

* A town in the Umbrian hills.

CHAPTER 15

BATTLING
FOR ROME

I N ONE OF THE GREAT IRONIES OF EUROPEAN HISTORY, AS FRENCH troops launched their attack on Rome, Louis Napoleon appointed the forty-four-year-old Alexis de Tocqueville to replace Édouard Drouyn as his foreign minister. Tocqueville, one of Europe's most celebrated theorists of constitutional rights, suddenly found himself charged with crushing the Roman Republic and restoring priestly rule.

Tocqueville came from an aristocratic family. His great-grandfather, grandfather, grandmother, aunt, and uncle had all been guillotined during the French Revolution, and his parents had been imprisoned until the end of the Terror in 1794. In the decades following Napoleon's demise, Tocqueville's father served as prefect for several French regions. In 1831–32, Tocqueville spent a year in the United States. The trip was designed to study America's prison system, but along the way he filled his notebooks with observations about the young republic and accounts of his many conversations. Three years after his return to France, he published the first volume of his celebrated *Democracy in America*. Proclaiming himself a "liberal of a new kind," he chronicled how democracy worked in practice, and he warned of the threats that majority rule posed to personal liberty. Elected to the French Constituent Assembly following the 1848 revolution, Tocqueville praised America as a model for the new French government. In May 1849 he was elected to the National Assembly, the product of the republican constitution that he had helped write. Although known for championing a new, more democratic age, he struck his compatriots as a perfect example of the *gentilhomme de l'ancien régime*, a gentleman of the old stripe. He dressed elegantly, a small, delicate man with soft and somewhat dreamy but brilliant dark eyes and long black hair.[1]

Tocqueville entered the government, he explained to a friend, despite

Alexis de Tocqueville

himself. "They came to take me from my bed, where I lay sick, and they overcame my resistance by assuring me that they were acting to prevent an imminent crisis . . . and that my friends and I were in a better position than anyone else to avert the storm." He accepted on one condition: he would not be expected to defend the government's previous behavior toward Rome in the National Assembly. Odilon Barrot, who remained prime minister, agreed. "I do not know how long I will remain in power," confessed Tocqueville in mid-June, then added, "Undoubtedly, not long."[2]

At the time of his appointment, Tocqueville barely knew Louis Napoleon. Over the next months, he would get to know him well, concluding that people underestimated the president. Most of the men who had pushed Napoleon's candidacy, he thought, had done so not because they believed he was especially worthy but to the contrary, because of "his presumed mediocrity." He was a man who appeared to have no firm principles of his own. They were confident they could bend him to their will.

As a private person, thought Tocqueville, Louis Napoleon had much to recommend him. He was good-natured, a pleasant, even tender man. But one never knew what he was thinking, for after decades spent hatching plots in exile, he had learned to disguise his true thoughts. He spoke few words, and when he did speak, he said little of significance. His dull, opaque eyes offered no window into his mind. Heedless of danger, the great Napoleon's nephew showed courage during times of crisis, yet at the same time he veered recklessly from one position to another. "His intelligence," Tocqueville observed, "was incoherent, confused, filled with great thoughts poorly applied." While he was capable of perceptive insights, he was "always ready to place a bizarre idea beside a good one." What Louis Napoleon did have was a knack for political theater. He knew how to play his part.[3]

On June 7, in one of its last acts before being replaced by the newly elected National Assembly, the French Constituent Assembly voted to forbid the government from attacking Rome. The deputies did not know that Louis Napoleon had already ordered Oudinot to do just that.[4]

AS THE MOMENT OF the French assault neared, Romans ricocheted from cockiness to despair. Hadn't they already defeated the French? Hadn't Garibaldi twice sent King Ferdinand and his Neapolitan army into humiliating retreat? But it was hard to ignore the Austrian army's relentless recent march through the Papal States. Ferrara had fallen, Bologna had fallen, Perugia had fallen. The vise around Rome was tightening.[5]

Mazzini had summoned all the republic's remaining fighting forces to come to defend Rome. On June 1 Garibaldi and his legionnaires returned from their latest foray south. For Mazzini, the presence of the Hero of Two Worlds was a mixed blessing. "Here I cannot avail anything for the good of the Republic, save in two ways," Garibaldi informed Mazzini that day, "as dictator with unlimited plenary powers, or as a simple soldier. Choose." Mazzini was certainly not about to appoint him dictator, a certain disaster, but he recognized Garibaldi's military genius and knew that he would stand his ground as the French army prepared to attack. His ultimatum rebuffed, Garibaldi fell in line, although his relations with Mazzini remained tense.[6]

Among the others returning from battling King Ferdinand's troops in the south were six hundred young men from Lombardy. They followed their twenty-four-year-old leader, Luciano Manara, who had won fame the previous year in the five glorious days of fighting that had briefly driven the Austrian army from Milan. From a wealthy *milanese* family, a handsome man of average height with a thick beard, he inspired fierce loyalty in his followers. "Every feature of his face exuded nobility," observed one of his compatriots. "His every glance won people's allegiance." As the battle against the Austrians had moved out of Milan, Manara found himself at the head of a growing group of young volunteers who joined with the Sardinian king Charles Albert in an effort to drive the foreigners from Italy. Following the king's defeat in March and the return of Lombardy to Austrian control, they had sailed south to join in Rome's defense.[7]

"It is impossible for me to describe how true, how great, how deep is the hatred that all these people have shown against the priests and also in part against Pius IX," observed one of the moderate members of Rome's Constituent Assembly as the French invasion loomed. Few Romans were committed followers of Mazzini, he remarked, but they were united with the republicans in one respect—their "hatred for the government of the priests."

In contrast to the tense resolve among Rome's defenders, the mood of the pope's supporters was bright. "Sadness changes to joy," observed Father Vaure, Pope Gregory's old confessor, describing the impact made by news of the French order to attack. "One thanks God for having delivered us from the abyss."[8]

Oudinot now had more than 30,000 well-armed men, many battle-hardened veterans of the French colonial war in Algeria, and sixty cannons. He also enjoyed a steady stream of new supplies from France. Against them stood 18,000 defenders, a patchwork of hastily assembled Roman forces, including Garibaldi's 1,200 legionnaires, 600 Lombard volunteers, 700 carabinieri, a battalion of 350 Roman university students, and a smattering of other foreign recruits. They lacked an effec-

tive unified command and had few cannons, limited ammunition, and a
supply route that the French could easily cut.[9]

Oudinot's high command finalized their plan. They would try to
breach Rome's massive twenty-five-foot wall at its highest point, on
Janiculum Hill, at Porta San Pancrazio, on the west of the city, where
they had been repelled on their first assault in late April. In some respects, this seemed an odd choice, for they were attacking where the wall
was most imposing, but by breaking through there, they would enjoy a
commanding position looking over Rome. In explaining this rationale to
the French minister of war on June 2, the general who had designed the
plan added another consideration. "It is on this side that we run the least
risk of damaging the public monuments, a powerful consideration when
it is a matter of using cannons to attack a city like Rome, on which the
entire history of the world's civilization is inscribed."[10]

At two-thirty a.m. on June 3, only some 650 feet outside Porta San
Pancrazio, a French brigade raced into action, blasting its way through
the thirteen-foot-high wall that surrounded the Villa Pamfili. After a
fierce four-hour battle with its Roman defenders, they seized the villa
and took two hundred prisoners. French troops also attacked Roman
outposts at two other villas nearby, but there, after much bloodshed on
both sides, they were beaten back.

Garibaldi, unmistakable in his white poncho, red shirt, and ostrich-
feathered cap, led his men in battle, his faithful, slave-born aide-de-
camp, Andrea Aguyar, alongside him. Miraculously, amid all the
hand-to-hand fighting, Garibaldi, who had taken a bullet to his stomach
a month earlier, escaped further injury, but many of Rome's defenders
were killed or wounded in a space that was no more than six hundred
paces long by three hundred wide.[11]

That night, after an eighteen-hour battle, a seemingly endless line of
stretchers snaked through Rome's barricaded roads, carrying back the
wounded and the dead. In a city that had seen so many raucous processions through those same streets, the silence was overpowering, as the
tears of onlookers flowed freely. Only by watching the pitiful procession
did many mothers first see the pallid faces and lifeless bodies of their
sons. As the Romans considered how little chance they stood against the
might of the French army, more bad news arrived. Neapolitan troops

had retaken Velletri. Spanish troops, now nine thousand strong, were also moving north, planting the papal flag in towns along the coast.

On the bridge that spanned the Tiber in the shadow of Castel Sant'Angelo, a gaggle of Rome's defenders gathered around Ugo Bassi, Garibaldi's Barnabite monk, as he stood precariously atop a pillar, leading them in prayer. At great cost they had held off the French attack, but the enemy was now digging into positions only 650 feet from the wall, and the battle had only begun.[12]

IF FOR THE ROMANS it was a day of death and misery, for France's two ambassadors in Gaeta it was a good day. Harcourt and Rayneval had been anxiously awaiting word from Paris, worried that their government might reject their advice and embrace Lesseps's negotiated settlement. Earlier that morning they had learned that Lesseps had been recalled and the order to attack given. Harcourt rushed to see the pope. Having won the battle with Lesseps, he now needed to show Paris that he had been right in arguing that, by occupying Rome, they would finally be able to extract concessions from the pontiff.[13]

Harcourt began his report to Paris the next day by recounting the latest news of the Austrian, Neapolitan, and Spanish troops. "All these different movements," he wrote, "are done less to help us in taking Rome than to neutralize our influence and our demands once we have taken it." In this, he added, the three Catholic powers had the strong backing of the papal court.

In his long conversation that day with the pope, Harcourt, feeling his position greatly strengthened, pressed the case for reform, but Pius gave little ground. He was willing to place more laymen in government administration, he said, and would bring back his Consultative Council. But as for allowing a constitution—"real rights," as Harcourt put it— his rejection could not have been any clearer. He would grant no rights that he could not easily withdraw.

In Gaeta, observed the French ambassador, "there is such a cardinal-heavy atmosphere of purely mundane interests, dissimulation, petty intrigues, and absence of any higher sentiments that one cannot hope that the pope can pierce it, even should he wish to." Men such as the abbot

Rosmini had been "swept aside, forced to leave Gaeta, powerless against this self-interested, corrupt, unenlightened entourage who surround the pope." All that mattered to these high prelates, reported Harcourt, were "their worldly privileges and so, consequently, the only political program consists of trying to get people to believe that in attacking their privileges one is attacking the true interests of the church and of the religion that they themselves do so little to honor."[14]

If the French ambassador despaired over the cardinals' baleful influence, he would certainly have to include the most influential of them all. On the day of the French invasion, before news of the long-delayed assault reached him, Antonelli wrote his nuncio in Madrid to express his gratitude for the thousands of troops sent by the Spanish queen. "Their arrival," he wrote, "could not have come at a more opportune time, because, based on the French troops' behavior up to now, the Holy Father's retaking of his See, which could have already been accomplished, has been considerably delayed, and even now does not seem to be near." Nor was Antonelli simply upset by the fact that the French were moving so slowly, for he had strong doubts as to whose side they were on. The cardinal suggested that it might be better to have the pope, when he finally did return to his states, avoid Rome altogether and go instead to one of the small towns that the more congenial Spanish had occupied.[15]

Antonelli was doing all he could to keep the voices of compromise far from the pontiff. Months earlier the abbot Rosmini had left Gaeta, certain that Antonelli had poisoned Pius against him. On June 9, hoping that there might still be a chance to persuade the pope to find a peaceful means of returning to Rome, Rosmini came back to Gaeta. The abbot had barely greeted the pope when Pius warned him, "You now find me anti-constitutional." Rosmini tried to change the pope's mind. True, said the abbot, not all the people's rights could be restored immediately, but it was crucial to give them some hope.

Pius was unmoved. "Even if they were to cut me into pieces," he replied, "I would never again give them a constitution."

The abbot was not easily discouraged. The rulers of virtually all the other civilized countries, he argued, had granted constitutions, even the Austrians. How could the Papal States alone maintain absolutist rule? To this, Pius replied that the Papal States were unlike any other land. A constitution, he had come to realize, was incompatible with government by the church. He had concluded as well, he said, that freedom of the press, freedom of association, and the like were all inherently evil. These were propositions that in the past popes had barely felt the need to express, for they were part of the air they breathed. The notion that government should be by the people was completely foreign to them. Pius now realized that in allowing himself to be swept along with the changing times, he had strayed from the basic tenets of the church. He vowed he would not make that mistake again.

Although Rosmini was making little headway, Cardinal Antonelli, knowing how fond the pope was of the abbot, did not want to take any chances. On the evening of June 11, a Gaeta policeman came to Rosmini's room and demanded to see his passport. After examining it, the officer told him he lacked a proper Neapolitan visa and would have to leave Gaeta immediately. Rosmini expressed surprise that there was anything out of order with his documents. He had come at the pope's invitation, he insisted, and would not go unless asked by the pope himself. The officer left but then, near midnight, returned. Protesting that he was in his nightclothes and about to go to bed, Rosmini at first refused to open the door, but when the officer threatened to break it down, he relented. A ship, said the officer, would be waiting for him early in the morning. He would face dire consequences if he failed to board. Before leaving him, the officer let it be known that the orders had come from Cardinal Antonelli.[16]

FROM PARIS, TOCQUEVILLE FOLLOWED events in Rome with a mixture of desperation and dread. He was less worried about the French army's ability to subdue the city than about what would happen once they conquered it. For the French government to be seen as reinstalling a medieval theocracy and assisting its archenemy, Austria, in doing so would be a disaster. He also had to consider his own reputation as a man who had often urged the importance of constitutional guarantees of personal liberty.

On June 6 he wrote to his two ambassadors in Gaeta to inform them of his appointment as foreign minister and spell out the government's aims. "I find France already engaged," he wrote, "in a path that I would not myself have chosen." They would have to make the best of it. They had four goals, he explained. France must exercise appropriate influence in Italy. The papacy had to regain its independence and ability to freely exercise its religious mission. They had to prevent the return of the old absolutist regime in the Papal States. Finally, they needed to support the majority of the people of the Papal States in putting an end to the abuses that plagued past papal governments.[17]

All this came as no surprise to Harcourt and Rayneval, but what did take them aback was Tocqueville's additional note: the new foreign minister informed them that he was sending his own personal envoy, Francisque de Corcelle, to work with Oudinot as the army entered Rome.[18]

Corcelle, a close friend of Tocqueville, had spent several weeks in Italy the previous year, immediately after the pope fled Rome, in an unsuccessful mission to persuade Pius to come to France. Having only a few days earlier celebrated Lesseps's recall, Harcourt and Rayneval again felt slighted, their own roles reduced. In choosing Corcelle, Tocqueville selected not only someone he could trust but someone strongly identified as a Catholic, which he thought would help persuade a skeptical pope, and an even more skeptical papal entourage, to do what the French so badly needed them to do.[19]

To date, all France's efforts to get the pope to embrace reform had, Tocqueville told his new envoy, been in vain. The answer they kept getting was that they should trust in the pope's good nature. "But we also know," Tocqueville wrote, "the force of the influences that can lead the papacy along truly deplorable paths." The pope had to assure his subjects of his good intentions. "If the hatred that the anarchic regime inspires in the Roman people has not been expressed more actively up to now," wrote Tocqueville, "it is above all because care has not been taken to reassure them against the possibility of the return of a past that is no less odious to them." It was crucial for the pope to guarantee "seriously liberal institutions." France otherwise risked disaster. "It is not possible," observed the author of *Democracy in America*, "for us to accept, even in appearance, the role of restorers of an absolute power."[20]

With the full force of the French army aimed at the aged walls of the city, many thought that Rome could not hold out for more than a few days. Yet somehow it did. Initial French attempts to blast through the wall produced few results. With his accustomed theatrical flourish, Charles Bonaparte presented the Constituent Assembly with an unexploded bomb that had rolled to a stop on the city's streets. He proposed that they place it in the city's archive with a plaque: "In perpetual memory of a Pope who ordered the bombing of the Capital of his faithful subjects and children."

Bombs did explode in Trastevere, one of the city's poorest neighborhoods, which stretched between Janiculum Hill and the Tiber River. On June 7 a plea was sent to church officials on behalf of the cloistered nuns of Trastevere's Convent of Sant'Egidio, asking permission to move them to safety on the other side of the Tiber.[21] Near the convent, the sight of children burned alive in homes set afire by exploding French bombs or buried beneath the rubble of roofs collapsed by French cannon fire further enraged the Romans. This was all, they said, the work of the priests.

"There goes another Pio Nono!" shouted those who could still keep

The bombardment of Rome

some sense of humor, however sardonic, as they pointed to the incoming projectiles. In a similar attempt to buck up their spirits, the defenders atop the city walls had named their three cannons after a pope and two cardinals: Pio Nono, Antonelli, and Lambruschini. Women and children as young as eight years old rushed with pans of wet clay to extinguish the burning fuses of the unexploded bombs that fell to earth. On one defused bomb, someone had placed a piece of paper with a message written in simple block letters: "The Holy Father's first little present to his beloved children in Trastevere."[22]

Mazzini ordered all able-bodied men in Rome to join military units to defend the city, calling on all others—both men and women—to work on the fortifications. The government requisitioned carts and wagons and ordered that the aristocrats' palaces on the far side of the city be opened to refugees from the neighborhoods where bombs were falling. Women and men piled mattresses behind the city gates, from which the faces of sculpted angels poked out here and there. Men carrying muskets ran through the streets, some wearing uniforms, some not. On June 8, in a sign of how low the defenders' munitions were, the republic's minister of war sent out a plea to the Romans, offering to pay them, by the pound, for all cannonballs and unexploded bombs that had fallen on the city. "Oh Citizens," the minister concluded, "these projectiles would remain useless in your hands, while we, on the other hand, with our cannons and artillery would send them back to the enemy!"[23]

Meanwhile the casualties mounted. "Many of these young men, students from Pisa, Pavia, Padua and the Roman University," wrote Margaret Fuller, who spent her days at their bedsides, "lie wounded in the hospitals, for naturally they rushed first in the combat. One kissed an arm which was cut off, another preserves pieces of bone which are being painfully extracted from his wound, as reliques of the best days of his life." In a letter to Ralph Waldo Emerson, she explained:

> though I have suffered—for I had no idea before, how terrible gunshot-wounds and wound-fever are—yet I have taken pleasure, and great pleasure, in being with the men; there is scarcely one who is not moved by a noble spirit. Many, especially among the Lombards, are the flower of Italian youth. When they begin to get better, I carry them books, and flowers, they read, and we talk.[24]

For Mazzini, only one hope remained: news of the French attack, he thought, might trigger a popular revolt in Paris. He had reason to think that the assault on Rome had little public support in France. "Here," reported Austria's ambassador in Paris at the time, "the Catholic party is weak. The masses, the bourgeoisie of the towns, and above all, the National Guard in Paris are entirely indifferent in matters of religion or essentially hostile to what they refer to as the 'regime of the priests.'" It follows, he concluded, that "the French expedition aimed at reestablishing the Pope is unpopular in France."[25]

The French government had concealed news of the assault from the Assembly as long as it could. On June 11, when the deputies finally learned what was happening, outrage exploded on the Assembly floor. With his enormous, hoarse voice, the forty-two-year-old leader of the left, Alexandre Ledru-Rollin, a tall, big, broad-shouldered man, led the attack. Over the past months, he had been corresponding with Mazzini, assuring him that his French allies would not let him down.[26]

"Citizens," boomed Ledru-Rollin, "there are supreme moments when speech becomes completely useless. I believe that we are in one of those times." After the initial French assault, he observed, Rome's walls remained intact, its courageous defenders having so far held their ground. "But," he added as he gesticulated dramatically, his ruddy cheeks turning a shade of purple, "French blood and Roman blood have been flowing in torrents.

> It is certain that we promised Rome, as an Assembly, to protect its independence. . . . It is certain that by our vote of May 7 the Constituent Assembly decided that the Italian expedition could no longer stray from the mission it had been assigned. . . . Barrot and the other ministers have kept endlessly repeating the same thing: the goal of the expedition was not to put an end to the Roman Republic. . . . Its goal was to protect Rome, to ensure its liberal institutions against the prospect that the Austrians would try to seize Rome and try to impose an absolutist government on it.

The time to act had come, concluded Ledru-Rollin. It was time to remove the president and his ministers, guilty of the most egregious crime—violation of the constitution.[27]

When their motion of impeachment was defeated by the Assembly's conservative majority, leaders of the left called for a public demonstration to protest the government's treachery in sending France's army against Rome. When Ledru-Rollin later led demonstrators in their march through Paris, policemen and soldiers on horseback emerged from the side streets and charged the crowd. Ledru-Rollin found refuge with some of his colleagues in the Palais National, where they nervously debated what to do. Outside, bloodied, enraged demonstrators regrouped, some calling for armed revolt. Amid the chaos, Prime Minister Barrot told the members of the National Assembly that a conspiracy to overthrow the republic was in progress. He read a message from Louis Napoleon calling on the deputies to authorize a state of siege. In the absence of most of the deputies of the left, the motion passed overwhelmingly. Meanwhile, a contingent of army troops had cornered Ledru-Rollin and his colleagues. The redoubtable leader of the left later described the scene:

> We saw death very close, my friends and I. Lined up against a wall . . . we were placed six paces from the muskets of a half-company which had already taken aim and awaited only the final command. The officer, drunk with passion and with wine . . . lifted his sword to give the death order when a superior officer galloped up and had barely time to order the guns to be lowered.[28]

Summoned elsewhere, the soldiers left their prisoners, and Ledru-Rollin and his companions fled. After finding a safe hiding place to spend the night, the famed orator succeeded in escaping the city and making his way to London. There he would spend the next two decades in exile.[29]

NEWS OF THE EVENTS in Paris brought an abrupt end to Mazzini's dreams of salvation from France. The Roman Republic, it seemed, now faced certain defeat, but still the Romans fought on. In increasingly desperate attempts to keep the heavy French artillery from the city gates, the defenders staged nighttime forays outside the wall. Demonstrating "more bravery than military skill," in the words of Rome's British consul, they were repeatedly beaten back, forced to retreat inside the wall. On the evening of June 12, General Oudinot had sent a message to the Romans. "We have not come to bring war to you," he told them. "Our Government's intentions are misunderstood." Predicting "terrible calamities" if the gates of the city were not opened to his troops, he warned that he could restrain his forces no longer. "If you persist in resisting us," he said, "you alone will bear the responsibility for the irreparable disasters." He gave them twelve hours to surrender.[30]

Rebuffed, the French had renewed their assault. The American chargé d'affaires painted a dramatic picture from his position inside the besieged city. The Romans' initial success in repelling the French troops, he wrote, had led to ever-greater support for the republican cause:

> From dawn to the close of the day, the domes, cathedrals and parapets, are crowded with spectators, whose acclamation at every gallant action incites to deeds of most extraordinary daring. . . . The roads leading from the gates are planted with iron spears, rendering the movements of cavalry impossible. . . . The gates themselves are mined. . . . Every house in the streets through which the enemy must pass, after having forced the outworks, is provided with oil and stones, the former of which is directed to be kept boiling hot, to be cast from the windows.

Yet food was growing short, and the French had cut off the ancient Roman aqueducts, so fresh water had become scarce. Amid the deprivation and fear, many Romans were beginning to question their faith in the church, a faith that had nurtured Rome for so many centuries. "The contest," observed the American diplomat,

> is no longer between one army and another . . . but it is a struggle that embraces a whole moral world of ideas, hopes and faith, that may have an echo in the most distant generations. The actual object of the intervention is shaking the edifice of the Catholic religion to its very foundations, crushing that faith in thousands of

hearts. . . . The consequence, naturally, is that many are now asking themselves whether he who represents a religion of peace has
a right to reassert temporal power by force of arms; and . . . not a
few begin to doubt of the truth of the Catholic religion, in consequence of the acts of its head. They cannot conceive how a religion . . . is now changed into a weapon intended to transform
free men into slaves.[31]

Although faith in their cause may never have burned more brightly
among Rome's defenders, the inevitability of their defeat now seemed
hard to deny. There was no one left to come to their aid, and the wall that
stood between them and the powerful French army had not been built to
withstand the endless pounding of large modern cannons. The only
question that remained, it seemed, was whether their fall would come at
the hands of the French alone or whether Austria, Naples, and Spain
might join in. Despite it all, Mazzini would not hear of surrender. "There
are defeats that bring honor," he later observed, "and victories that bring
shame."

In a final attempt to avoid further bloodshed, Oudinot summoned
Enrico Cernuschi, the young head of Rome's barricades, and urged him
to allow the French troops to enter peacefully. "In Rome," Cernuschi
replied, "we produce tragedies, we do not produce comedies. . . . If we
cannot save Italy, we at least want to save the memory of Italy. Italy is
not going to end as a vaudeville show."[32]

In mid-June, with French artillery raining down on Chancellery
Palace, home of the Constituent Assembly, the deputies moved to the
relative safety of city hall, atop Capitoline Hill. Each day hundreds of
French cannon blasts sounded. Rushing through the streets amid men
in arms, women handed out rocks and ammunition and carried messages and materials to build up the barricades. An eerie calm hung over
the city center. In the evenings the Corso was still crowded with people escaping the heat of their homes, the streetlamps were lit, and
stores were open, although counters normally piled high with vegetables and meats were largely bare, the few remaining chickens selling
for astronomical prices. In the piazzas, musical bands still played, their

festive dance tunes forming a strange counterpoint to the cannons' distant rumble. But this attempt at normality could not hide the pall of dread. As a poor laundress headed to St. Peter's to pray, making her way through a group of young soldiers, one of them touched her on the shoulder. "Mamma," he said, "say three Ave Marias for me so that the Madonna sees that this all ends soon, because we can't go on like this anymore."

One of the young Lombard volunteers, posted near the center of fighting at Porta San Pancrazio, recalled what these days were like:

> You get used to anything with time. So that now we see the transport of the wounded, immersed in blood, almost with indifference, and we eat bread and salami without being bothered by the stench of over twenty cadavers that for the past sixteen days lie in the garden of Villa Corsini, unburied and unbandaged, as black as coal, and swollen as if they had been drowned.[33]

The vise around Rome continued to tighten. On June 19, after weeks of bombardment by land and sea, the Adriatic port city of Ancona surrendered to the Austrians. As in Bologna and the other cities the Austrians had seized, they immediately turned local administration over to a monsignor sent by the pope to restore his rule.[34]

By June 20, the French had positioned their large siege cannons within 350 yards of the wall. Under constant bombardment by a dozen twenty-four-pound cannons, it quickly began to crumble, opening up three breaches that would soon be wide enough for the final assault.[35]

In Paris, Tocqueville viewed the prospect of a bloodbath in the Eternal City with dread. The French had cast themselves as champions of freedom. "We attach the highest price," Tocqueville told General Oudinot, "to having the pope's banner hoisted up by Roman hands following a local demonstration. That is necessary to preserve for our expedition the character that the National Assembly gave it and the government wants to maintain." That same day he wrote to his personal envoy, Corcelle, expressing his unhappiness on learning that no moderate party could be found in Rome, only supporters of the republican government

French troops fire on Rome's wall, June 20, 1849

on the one side and a small band of reactionaries favoring the return of the old ecclesiastical order on the other. The French, Tocqueville insisted, had to enter Rome to the cheers of demonstrators clamoring for the pope's return. "If we can't have the reality," he advised Corcelle, "it is absolutely necessary, at least, to produce the appearance."[36]

Near midnight on June 21, the French intensified their assault. "The bombardment and the cannon fire," recalled one of the defenders, "could not have been more terrible than it was that night." As bombs fell on some of the city's most famous piazzas, French troops climbed through a breach in the wall and began digging in. Mazzini urged Garibaldi to organize a counterattack, but unwilling to be ordered around by someone who knew nothing of military matters, the Hero of Two Worlds held back. Furious, Mazzini dashed off a letter to Luciano Manara, head of the Lombard volunteers, venting his anger:

> The assault had to be launched this past night, half an hour after they climbed through the breach. . . . Tomorrow the attack will be impossible, the enemy artillery will be in place. The system is now entirely changed; let me say it, ruined. . . . I consider Rome as fallen. God willing the enemy will dare to attack us soon, while

the people will mount a good defense at the barricades. Everyone will take part. Later, we will not even have that.

"The sole satisfaction that remains for me," concluded the beleaguered prophet of Italian independence, "is not putting my name to the act of surrender that I predict is soon to come. But what importance is it to me?" he asked. "It matters for Rome and for Italy."[37]

CHAPTER 16

THE CONQUEST

THE CARDINALS WERE NOW IN A BETTER MOOD, INCREASINGLY confident that the Roman Republic's blasphemous reign was nearing its end. Most, shunning the modest accommodations available near Gaeta, had set up households in Naples. There they nursed their grievances, blaming their reduced circumstances on Pio Nono's ill-advised quest to curry popular favor and unhappy that he rarely sought their advice.

In late June, aware of the cardinals' murmurings, Pius wrote to their most influential member, his predecessor's notoriously hard-line secretary of state, Luigi Lambruschini. "From the news that reaches me from Naples," began the pontiff, "I hear, to my great displeasure, that some cardinals are complaining that they have been abandoned by Gaeta and left in the dark. . . . These complaints," warned Pius, "might prove prejudicial to those who repeat them."

The pope told Lambruschini that he was working on a plan for what to do when Rome was retaken, which he promised to discuss with the cardinals. He outlined the principles that would guide him. "Constitutional Government," he wrote, "NO." Here he used capital letters for emphasis, aware that this would come as a great relief to the cardinals. "But," he added, "it is indispensable to do something because . . . the people are in such a state of agitation that to deny them entirely is impossible."[1]

While the pope was writing to Lambruschini in Naples, Esterházy was preparing his latest report to Vienna. The Austrian chancellor had recently written to Esterházy to tell him how pleased he was to hear that the pope was holding out against French entreaties to embrace reform. "The firmness which Pius IX has had the wisdom to deploy in the face of the French pressures," wrote Schwarzenberg, "already seems to have borne its fruits."[2]

"Up to now," replied Esterházy, "all my efforts are aimed at encouraging and helping the Roman court in its legitimate resistance to France's arrogant demands." He had found a receptive audience.

Antonelli needed little encouragement to do all he could to thwart the French. In a circular to his nuncios in early July, he again criticized Oudinot for being too eager to avoid bloodshed. "This pernicious slowness," he wrote, "makes an all the more sinister impression if one considers the speed with which the Austrian army . . . has occupied much of the state, overcoming the strong resistance that it encountered in Bologna and in Ancona."[3]

The pope was of the same view. Why, Pius asked, were the French not raising the papal flag in the towns they occupied? Harcourt, who was shuttling back and forth between Gaeta and the French base outside Rome, offered a reply that could not have endeared him to the pontiff. They had very much wanted to raise the papal flag, he explained, but "we have made it a policy up to now not to impose anything on the population. We have been waiting for some demonstration in support of the pope so we can act, and we even have tried to provoke one in every way possible." Despite all their attempts, said Harcourt, they had been unable to spark even the most modest popular demonstration in favor of restoring papal rule.[4]

Outside Rome, the new French envoy was growing impatient with the army's plodding pace. "Imagine my surprise," Corcelle told Tocqueville on June 25, when, at a war council called by General Oudinot, "I learned that this council estimated that it would probably take another fifteen or twenty days to take possession of the right bank of the Tiber." There was no reason, thought Corcelle, why they should not break through immediately.[5]

Tocqueville was more cautious, urging that the city be bombarded only if absolutely necessary. The kind of all-out attack that might permit the speedy conquest of Rome risked producing a level of destruction to its buildings and monuments that would horrify the civilized world. "You can be sure," warned the French foreign minister, "that the noise of our bombs will be heard in all of Europe and that *nothing* will be more harmful for our expedition's honor than the explosion of these projectiles in Rome." Rome, he added, "is not like any other city."[6]

Tocqueville was also nervous about what would happen after the city was taken. They must, he told Corcelle, get the Holy Father to announce his intention to install "an enlightened, liberal government." How else could France justify to its own people, and to the rest of the world, what its army was doing in Rome?[7]

The French foreign minister had another concern as well. Radetzky, commander of Austria's troops in Italy, had recently announced that the pope intended to move to Austrian-held Bologna before returning to Rome. "I do not have to tell you," wrote Tocqueville, "how such a trip would be harmful, what a blow it would be to the Holy Father in the opinion of liberal Europe, and I must say, what a disaster it would be for us, making us look ridiculous."[8]

The French kept up their bombardment as they fortified their newly won position inside Rome's wall. "Bombs kept falling on the city all night long," wrote the Roman diarist Nicola Roncalli. "In just a quarter of an hour seventeen were launched. In all, it is estimated that over a hundred and fifty fell . . . for the most part on a line leading to Capitoline Hill."[9]

In an effort to save Rome from further destruction, a group of Rome's foreign diplomats gathered at the home of the British consul, John Freeborn, and drafted a protest addressed to General Oudinot. Signed by ten men—including the American consul, Nicholas Brown, as well as the Prussian, Dutch, Danish, and Swiss consuls—it expressed "their deep regret at his having subjected the Eternal City to a bombardment lasting several days and nights." The assault, they charged, "puts the lives and property not only of neutral and pacific residents in danger, but also those of innocent women and children." They added that bombs had already destroyed many priceless works of art. "We place our confidence in you," urged the consuls, "that in the name of humanity and of the civilized nations, you will want to desist from further bombardment, to spare from further destruction the monumental city, which is considered to be under the moral protection of all the civilized countries of the world."[10]

Oudinot's reply came quickly. "The bombardment of Rome," he acknowledged, "will cause the shedding of innocent blood and will destroy monuments that ought to be eternal." He reminded them that he had said as much in his June 12 ultimatum to the Roman government. "The longer the surrender of the town is delayed," warned the general, "the greater will be the calamity that you so justly fear. But the fault for such disasters will not lie with the French. History will absolve us from any such charge."[11]

Knowing how unhappy Tocqueville would be to learn of the consuls' protest, Corcelle hastened to offer his own gloss on the episode. If Oudinot had decided not to deny the foreign diplomats' accusation that he was destroying Rome, it was not because the charge had any validity. In the entire time of the siege, claimed Corcelle, "not a single bomb has been aimed at the city." All the French artillery had been directed at the wall, even if, he acknowledged, some might have overshot its mark and inadvertently hit homes in the neighborhood below. "One even speaks of a projectile falling on the Constituent Assembly," he added, "but that is the exception. Rome has not been bombed."

Why, then, did Oudinot appear to accept the charge? It was, argued the French envoy, a ploy aimed at instilling fear in the Romans. If he promised not to bomb them, he would only encourage further resistance and so cause more useless bloodshed.[12]

Notwithstanding Corcelle's denials, bombs continued to fall on Rome. The makeshift hospitals overflowed with the wounded and the dying, as the constant cannon fire gradually began to penetrate the city's thick walls.

"Nothing would be more welcome for me," said Ugo Bassi, "than to die for Garibaldi." It looked like the bearded monk would get his wish, for he was constantly in the midst of the fighting on Janiculum Hill, assisting the wounded and the dying. He rode a white horse, a red shirt over his black priestly tunic, his long dark hair flowing beneath his distinctive broad-brimmed black hat, armed only with the cross around his neck. "Italy," Bassi told the men, "needs martyrs, many martyrs, before it can be free and great."[13]

On June 26 Garibaldi was surprised to see his twenty-seven-year-old South American wife, Anita, appear in the doorway of his headquarters. Although he had told her not to come, she had left safety in Nice to join him. By the next day, although both Garibaldi and Anita somehow escaped unharmed, cannon fire had reduced Garibaldi's headquarters to rubble.

With the situation seemingly hopeless, the Hero of Two Worlds proposed a new plan. The Roman Republic's political leadership and military, he thought, should abandon Rome and continue their battle in the nearby mountains. Mazzini rejected the idea. It was in Rome, he insisted, that they needed to make their last stand. Their martyrdom would serve as a testament to the nobility of their cause, an inspiration to those who would follow them in fighting for freedom.

Angered by the rebuff, Garibaldi ordered his legionnaires to leave Janiculum Hill and follow him across the Tiber to the eastern side of the city. Those left behind to face the French assault alone were horror-struck. It took the pleading of Luciano Manara, the young head of the Lombard volunteers, to persuade Garibaldi to return to the front line the next day.[14]

June 29 honored Rome's two patron saints, Peter and Paul, and nothing, it seemed, could stop the Romans from celebrating. At eight p.m. a huge storm erupted, the thunder initially indistinguishable from the cannon blasts. But the torrential rains soon ended, and the *festa* got under way. Above St. Peter's Basilica, fireworks in Italy's three colors illuminated the massive dome. Torches were then lit atop the cupola. Throughout the city, Romans placed candles at their windows. In the piazzas, military bands played, although few others ventured into the streets.[15]

Romans grasped at any rumor that suggested help might be on the way. According to one, a joint British-American flotilla had arrived at Civitavecchia, aimed at blocking the French supply route. Another reported that a cholera epidemic had broken out among the French troops and that even General Oudinot had been stricken. But for the men on Janiculum Hill, there was little solace. Constant nighttime bombardments made sleep impossible. One comrade after another crumpled to the ground, hit by bullets or shrapnel. Wagons creaked by carrying the latest mutilated bodies. The overwhelming French superiority in arms and in fresh men became clearer by the day, as did their own lack of ammunition, food, and water.[16]

At two a.m. on the night following Rome's patron saints' day, the French finally poured through the breaches in the wall. With bayonets fixed and muskets firing, they charged at Rome's weary defenders. In the darkness, amid the mud and the smoke-filled air, it was hard to tell friend from foe. Garibaldi led his men, brandishing his heavy saber, soon dripping with blood. French troops surrounded Villa Spada, the command post of the young Lombard volunteers. As the encircled men stood at the windows shooting their rifles, many were struck by incoming fire. Others were crushed as the masonry above them collapsed, shattered by French cannon blasts. The previous day the idealistic leader of the Lombard legion, Luciano Manara, had sent a letter to a friend. "They will win," he wrote, "because materially forty large guns aimed at a single point demolish and destroy. But every bit of rubble will be defended. Every ruin that covers the cadavers of our men is mounted by others who die rather than surrender." He concluded, "Rome is great at this moment, as are its memories, great as the monuments that adorn it and that the barbarian is bombarding." In a second letter that he was somehow able to send off amid the slaughter, he wrote, "We must die to bring '48 to a serious conclusion. For our example to be effective, we must die!"[17]

On June 30, as the bearded Manara stood peering at enemy positions through his telescope, a bullet opened a hole in his chest. "I am a dead man," he muttered as he fell to the ground.

Garibaldi led one last desperate charge of his legionnaires into the French lines and somehow again escaped unscathed, but the man who had so long stood at his side was not so lucky. Fragments of an exploding bomb punctured the left side of Andrea Aguyar's head. Garibaldi's black bodyguard and companion would die within hours, his body placed alongside Manara's in one of Rome's overcrowded hospitals. The next morning a truce was declared, allowing both sides to gather up their dead and wounded.[18]

———

ATOP CAPITOLINE HILL, THE men of the Constituent Assembly watched as Mazzini came to the lectern. In title, Mazzini bore no greater authority than his two fellow members of the triumvirate, yet as all knew, it was Mazzini alone who had guided the republic's course. In the president's chair sat Charles Napoleon, cousin of the man whose armies were poised to conquer Rome. Although Mazzini's face was unusually pallid, he betrayed no other sign of tension. The heroism of Rome's defenders, he told the men, had won the world's admiration, but, he admitted, they could not hold the French off much longer.

They had a fateful decision to make, Mazzini said, for only three choices remained. The first, he told them, was surrender, a prospect he dismissed as too shameful to contemplate. The second was to stay and fight. After all, they had spent weeks building the barricades for just such an eventuality. In Rome's narrow streets, the French could not use their artillery and would have to fight house to house against an armed population. This offered one honorable alternative. The other, and the one, he told the Assembly, he hoped they would adopt, was a version of the path that Garibaldi had urged a few days earlier. The Assembly, along with the government and its military, could regroup in the provinces. There they would enlist the support of the local population and continue the battle for freedom.

Murmurs of unease and unhappiness greeted the prophet's remarks. Someone suggested that Garibaldi be summoned to tell them what he thought, and so a messenger was sent to get him. Before long the Hero of Two Worlds strode in to excited shouts and prolonged applause, his mud-encrusted clothes torn, his poncho soaked with blood, his face covered in dirt congealed with sweat. "He shook his thick blond hair," recalled one observer, "like a lion who senses he has been wounded. . . . His expression was, rather than sad, fierce." Asked how they could fight on, Garibaldi replied that they would have to evacuate Trastevere, the neighborhood on the French side of the river, and blow up all the bridges. That this would only delay the inevitable was clear to all. Asked about the possibility of continuing the fight through the barricaded streets of the city, Garibaldi replied that the plan would never work. The French would not risk street-to-street combat but would simply set up their cannons closer and closer to the city center, wreaking ever-greater carnage until the city capitulated. Romans, said Garibaldi, had already done all that a heroic people could do. He added his support for Mazzini's proposal: the government and the army should take to the hills.[19]

Mazzini's influence over the Assembly had dramatically weakened. His reputation as someone all too willing to sacrifice other people's lives to his grandiose theories was now again much on people's minds. To take to the hills—and who knew exactly where?—with four enemy armies on their trail, with a dispirited and depleted military, with few munitions, little food, and no money, expecting to be supported by impoverished peasants, seemed foolhardy, if not suicidal.

Twenty-eight-year-old Enrico Cernuschi, son of a wealthy Piedmontese family, a member of the Assembly and the man in charge of the barricade defense, rose to speak. "You are well aware," he began, "how devoted I have been to defending this unhappy land, this people. But now"—here his voice began to break as he struggled to keep composed—"I am the one to declare that the French now have their path clear, and that Rome, this good people . . . after all its efforts, must resign itself to being occupied." As tears flowed from Cernuschi's eyes, many of the deputies began to weep with him. "For several minutes," recalled one of the men there that day, "nothing could be heard in that hall but stifled sobbing."[20]

The resolution approved by the Constituent Assembly and posted throughout the city was brief:

> In the name of God and the People
>
> The Roman Constituent Assembly ends a defense that has become impossible, and remains at its post. The Triumvirate is charged with the execution of the present Decree.[21]

The Romans would not surrender, but they would no longer fight. Within hours another notice appeared on Rome's walls, announcing the triumvirate's resignation. After praising the Romans for their courage in fighting for freedom, their new message to the Romans concluded with a typically Mazzinian plea:

> A cloud rises over you today. It will not last long. Keep constantly in mind your rights and the faith for which so many of the best among you, armed apostles, have died. God, who has gathered up their blood, is your guarantor. God wants Rome to be free and to be great; and it will be. Yours is not defeat. It is the victory of the martyrs for whom burial is the stairway to heaven.[22]

THE NUMBER OF THOSE who died defending Rome from the French attack would never be known. Perhaps it was a thousand, although the figure cited by the French general in charge of the assault was 1,700 to 1,800. Many more were injured. The French, eager to minimize their own losses, officially counted 162 dead and 842 wounded.[23]

With Mazzini having resigned, the task of notifying Oudinot of the Assembly's decision to end all resistance fell to General Roselli, head of the Roman Republic's army. Roselli sent Oudinot a brief note, along with a copy of the Assembly's resolution. "I will immediately stop all hostilities," wrote Roselli, "as I hope you too, General, will do as well." He added that representatives from the city government would come to French headquarters that evening to discuss arrangements.[24]

The four-member delegation arrived at French headquarters outside the wall after midnight. Oudinot complimented them on the valor with which the Romans had fought, and he expressed regret at the damage and loss of life that had resulted. His demands, he said, were simple: The French army must be free to enter the city peacefully and to occupy those positions it judged useful. The delegates replied by saying they would consult with the city council and return the next evening.[25]

The next day, still harboring some hope that the French might content themselves with ensuring that the Austrians and other armies were kept out of Rome, the city council came up with its own additional terms of surrender. The Romans would be allowed to retain some of their armed forces, and these would work in concert with the French in ensuring public order. The National Guard would also be allowed to remain. In addition, the French would guarantee "individual freedom and property for all" and not involve itself in the city's "internal administration."[26]

That evening, when the delegation presented its proposal, Oudinot replied that he would need to consult with his colleagues and asked them to return the next morning. When, later that night, Corcelle arrived at the military headquarters, he found Oudinot preparing to sign the terms the Roman city council had proposed. Corcelle was dumbfounded. How could Oudinot countenance having the men who had deposed the pope retain any influence, much less permit a separate army created by the republic to continue to exist? The Roman Assembly had already declared all further resistance impossible. Why bargain with the Romans at all? After some hesitation, Oudinot agreed.

On the morning of July 2, with the French poised to enter the vanquished city, a haunting scene played out on Rome's streets. Women and men sank to their knees as the funeral cortege for Luciano Manara, twenty-four-year-old leader of the Lombard volunteers, passed through the flower-strewn street. Those of his comrades who had survived, their uniforms ripped and filthy from their uninterrupted weeks at the front, their faces burned by the sun and still covered in dust, marched behind the funeral bier, some limping on crutches, many with bandages wrapped around their heads. Manara's bloodstained tunic had been laid atop the coffin, but when it reached its destination, at the Church of San Lorenzo in Lucina, just off the Corso in the center of the city, the cover was removed, revealing Manara in his uniform, his sword still in his hand. "It was one of those scenes," recalled one of those present, "which leaves a life-long impression and cannot be recalled without a thrill of horror."[27]

With the French army poised to march into Rome at any time, Lewis Cass, the American chargé d'affaires, sought out Garibaldi and told him that the United States was putting a ship at his disposal at Civitavecchia. He, and those of his men who were most in danger with the arrival of the French, could escape. Garibaldi was not tempted. He summoned the republic's remaining armed forces to St. Peter's Square. There, on his white horse, amid a crowd of thousands in which military men were mixed in with women, the young, and the old, the Hero of Two Worlds made his way with difficulty to the obelisk at the center of the square, where he raised his hands, silencing the crowd. "To those who follow me," he shouted, so as to be heard in the vast square, "I demand great love for the fatherland. . . . I can promise no pay but only hardship, hunger, thirst, and all the dangers of war." In response, the grizzled men raised their rifles. "We'll all come! You are Italy! Long live Garibaldi!" they shouted. Where exactly he was headed, none of them knew; nor, it seemed, did he.[28]

By eight p.m. that evening, four thousand men had gathered in the piazza in front of St. John Lateran Basilica, on the eastern side of the city, ready to follow Garibaldi. For his own red-shirted legionnaires, it was not a difficult decision, but many others had agonized over what to do. They feared that once they were in the mountains, chased by enemy armies, and taking food from local peasants, they would be viewed as little more than brigands. But if they remained in Rome, they wondered, what would happen to them once the French army arrived?[29]

Among those in the crowd that evening was Margaret Fuller, who described the scene:

> Never have I seen a sight so beautiful, so romantic, and so sad. . . .
> The sun was setting, the crescent moon rising, the flower of the
> Italian youth were marshalling in that solemn place. They had
> been driven from every other spot where they had offered their
> hearts as bulwarks of Italian independence. . . . They must now
> go or remain prisoners and slaves. . . . I saw the wounded, all that
> could go, laden upon their baggage cars. . . . I saw many youths,
> born to rich inheritance, carrying in a handkerchief all their
> worldly goods.

Her image of Garibaldi remained as heroic as ever: "The wife of Garibaldi followed him on horseback. He himself was distinguished by the white tunic; his look was entirely that of a hero of the Middle Ages. . . . There is no fatigue upon his brow or cheek."

The caravan set out, thirty-seven mules carrying their modest provisions. Ciceruacchio, the hero of Rome's *popolani*, accompanied by his two young sons, helped guide them out of the city. The sight of Garibaldi's South American wife, Anita, dark-complexioned and slight of build, caught many eyes as she rode on horseback, her gaze one of steely resolve. When Garibaldi reached the gate, he paused, got off his horse, and embraced the members of the Constituent Assembly who had come to salute him, recognizable by the tricolored sash they wore across their chests. "Hard was the heart, stony and seared the eye," observed Margaret Fuller, "that had no tear for that moment."[30]

ROME'S CONSTITUENT ASSEMBLY HAD little time left, but there was one thing its members were eager to do before the French troops flooded into the city. For several weeks, a committee had been working on a new, republican constitution, one that would spell out the rights of a free people, to serve as a model for all Italy. Its final details had been decided on only a few days earlier.

At noon on July 3, with the French army expected to arrive at any moment, the deputies gathered in the piazza designed by Michelangelo atop Capitoline Hill. As a few hundred supporters looked on, the Assembly president read the new constitution aloud. It felt like a sacred moment, and people reached up to remove their hats from their heads.

"The democratic government," he read, "has as its basic rule equality, freedom, and fraternity. It does not recognize titles of nobility, nor privileges of birth or of caste." The text went on to proclaim all equal before the law, regardless of religion. The pope would enjoy "all the guarantees necessary for the independent exercise of his spiritual power." Capital punishment was abolished, freedom of speech and association assured, and privacy protected. An Assembly elected by universal male suffrage would make the laws.[31]

As the constitution was being read on Capitoline Hill, the first French troops moved into Piazza del Popolo. The main march into Rome began a few hours later when General Oudinot, followed by his senior officers and a division of French cavalry, led his men down the Corso. The shops were closed, the city in mourning. A French military marching band began to play, but unnerved by the hostile crowd, they soon gave up. The calls rang out: "Long live the Roman Republic!" "Death to Pius

IX!" "Soldiers of the pope!" As the general rode by on horseback, he was showered with abuse: "Cardinal Oudinot!" "Liar!" "Butcher of Rome!" A handful of papal loyalists who imprudently greeted the French troops with shouts of welcome ended up dead, victims of the people's wrath. Among them was at least one man of the cloth.[32]

That evening Oudinot had a message to the Romans pasted on the city walls, in both Italian and French. "The Army that the French Republic has sent to your land," it began, "has as its goal the reestablishment of the order desired by the will of the people. A sectarian, or corrupt, minority has forced us to attack your walls. We now control the city and intend to accomplish our mission." The Constituent Assembly was dissolved, clubs were banned, the barricades were being dismantled, and the flags of the Roman Republic torn down. Nothing could be published without prior permission of the military authorities.[33]

Although Garibaldi had led his men out of the city the previous day,

French
soldiers

more than ten thousand republican military veterans remained in Rome, and they were still armed. With no official surrender but instructed not to resist, the men who had until a few days earlier been battling the

French now waited in their barracks, many in the massive Castel Sant'Angelo. That first night, while Rome's soldiers slept in their barracks, the French were forced to sleep outside.

Reporting all this to Tocqueville on July 5, Corcelle did not conceal his anger. It was now several days since they had conquered Rome, yet large numbers of armed men remained in the city, and according to the Frenchman, they had already assassinated twenty people whose only crime was voicing their support for the pope. Tricolored flags kept appearing on the streets. "The surrender," wrote Corcelle, "has been a veritable defeat for us after the victory." He lashed into Oudinot. It would have been easy, he said, if, at the moment the French entered the city, they had simply surrounded the Roman forces and disarmed them, but the general had wanted to avoid a bloody confrontation.[34]

For Mazzini, the defeat was bitter. "Rome has given up," he wrote to his mother the day the French troops entered the city. "Its position, from a military point of view, was bad, yet it could have mounted a defense at the barricades that would have astonished the world. But the Assembly did not want to, and in a moment of fear, all was lost." He recounted how he had urged the Assembly to go with the army to continue the fight elsewhere, but this too it had opposed. "And so for now," concluded Mazzini, "the magnificent drama ends in the saddest way."

Margaret Fuller, who went to visit the defeated leader, was struck by how much he had changed. "In two short months he had grown old. All the vital juices seemed exhausted. His eyes were all blood-shot; his skin orange; flesh he had none." Yet the man whom Fuller idolized remained. "Sweet and calm, but full of a more fiery purpose than ever, in him I revered the hero and owned myself not of that mold."[35]

On July 4, the day after the French entered Rome, Oudinot sent his personal envoy, Adolphe Niel, colonel of the French engineering corps, to Gaeta, bearing the keys to the gates through which the French troops had entered the city. "Pius IX's face is very pleasing," reported Niel, recounting his visit in a letter to his brother in France. "You can read the most touching goodness on it. His voice is sweet, his manner simple yet marked by great dignity." Expressing his gratitude, Pius penned a letter to the French general. He wanted to congratulate Oudinot, he wrote, "not for the blood that has been shed, which is abhorrent to me, but for the triumph of order over anarchy, and for the restoration of freedom to the honest, Christian people." He concluded, "The triumph of the French army came against the enemies of human society and for this reason ought to earn feelings of gratitude from all honest men in Europe."[36]

At the same time as Pius received the keys to Rome, he got a letter from Cardinal Lambruschini, the Curia's preeminent hard-liner, a response to the pope's own letter of a week earlier. Praising Pius for rejecting the pleas of those who urged him to retain his reforms, Lambruschini expressed special pleasure with the pope's decision not to grant a constitution, which he dismissed as "entirely incompatible with the political condition of the Holy See." The cardinal also urged the pope to reject the demands that he replace clergy with laymen in the government and courts. To give ground, he warned, was to guarantee a repetition of their recent disaster. "The people must be treated with a brake," he advised. "The brake can be somewhat gentle, but it must be a brake. . . . The people must be made to know the enormous crime they have committed, and in some way they should be made to atone for it."[37]

No one better appreciated the pressure the cardinals were putting on the pope than Harcourt, who had spent months in Gaeta urging Pius to spurn their advice. Writing from French military headquarters in Rome on the day the city was taken, he sent Tocqueville an urgent report. The French would obtain nothing, he told the foreign minister, by dealing benevolently with the Holy Father. Pio Nono would merely keep offering vague expressions of his goodwill. He would say everything except the one thing they actually needed, assurances that he would grant the people "real rights." He and Rayneval had tried every possible argument to convince him but to no avail. When pressed, the pope simply repeated that his conscience would not permit him to act as the French wished. Pius even threatened that he might not return to Rome at all but could go elsewhere, "even to America," reported Harcourt, "if we sought to do violence to his conscience."

Harcourt had lost all patience. There were only two ways, he believed, that the French could avoid catastrophe. Both meant issuing an ultimatum. If it were possible to persuade Austria to join with them, France and Austria could together demand that the pope publicly state his intention to retain a constitutional government. Should he refuse, they would withdraw their armies "and abandon him to his own forces, washing their hands of all responsibility for the future." If, as seemed more likely, Austria would not agree to this plan, only one path remained. France would have to act alone and tell the pope that should he not "reestablish the institutions that he himself had previously given, including the constitution," they would not allow him to return to his capital.[38]

The French army now occupied Rome but had yet to hoist the papal flag over the city. Pius remained in his modest room in Gaeta. A war of nerves was about to begin, pitting the celebrated author of *Democracy in America* against the exiled pope-king. It was not at all clear who would win.

CHAPTER 17

THE OCCUPATION

L ACKING ANY COMMITMENT FROM THE POPE TO RETAIN HIS reforms, the French seemed in no hurry to restore papal government. "So far," observed the Austrian ambassador, "all I see is the occupation of Rome by the French," the third, he noted, in the past half century. In 1798 Napoleon had seized Rome and driven Pope Pius VI into exile. A decade later his armies returned and forced his successor, Pius VII, to abandon the city. Now the French army had again taken Rome, and again the fate of a Pope Pius rested in their hands. Austrian troops meanwhile patrolled the streets of Bologna, Ancona, Ferrara, and the many other towns they had recently restored to pontifical rule.[1]

Two days after French troops entered Rome, the French appointed General Louis de Rostolan, a hard-bitten and not terribly well-lettered veteran of the French war in Algeria, to serve as governor of the city. He immediately announced that all gatherings were forbidden and no one would be allowed on the streets after nine-thirty p.m. Any violence or insult aimed at French soldiers would be punished severely. "Inhabitants of Rome!" warned Rostolan. "You want order. I know how to guarantee it. Those who dream of prolonging your oppression will find in me inflexible severity."[2]

Among the new restrictions, it was the curfew that Romans most resented. By evening, the heat of the summer sun turned the windowless homes of the *popolani* into insufferable ovens. Outside, in the cooler evening air, twenty-three thousand French soldiers set up camp in the squares and marketplaces, hundreds of their horses tied up along the streets.[3]

Upset by his lack of official diplomatic standing, Corcelle, Tocqueville's personal envoy, demanded that his status as France's primary representative in Rome be made clear. In a letter to the foreign minister, Corcelle took aim at the three men who stood in his way. On Oudinot, he had been heaping abuse since his first reports in June. "I told you," he advised Tocqueville, "that General Oudinot was capable of every possible kind of mistake and even some that are impossible. In administration, as in war, you will find him always uncertain, equivocating, lacking any sense of proportion, vague, passionate for the details, ingenious in complicating everything, a veritable font of false ideas expressed in a most refined way." To allow Oudinot to remain at his post, he warned, would bring disaster.[4]

So much for the general in charge. As for Harcourt, Corcelle devoted few words to him, for bowing to Corcelle's earlier pleas, Tocqueville had already let the ambassador to the Holy See know that he was soon to be recalled. And so, wrote Corcelle, the foreign minister had to choose: was it to be "Rayneval or me"?

Admittedly, wrote Corcelle, Rayneval, unlike him, spoke Italian, knew many of the key people in Italy, and was expert in Italian affairs. No one could deny that he was an able man with good judgment. But, Corcelle charged, there was a problem. Having been outside France the previous year when the monarchy was overthrown and the republic proclaimed, Rayneval had little understanding of the new order in his homeland. "His education," observed Corcelle, "was formed at the court where ideas of freedom were not in favor." While Corcelle had portrayed Harcourt as ineffective because he lacked the necessary finesse—the pope found his pushiness grating—he criticized Rayneval for not pressing the Holy Father hard enough.[5]

"No one is more convinced than I am of General Oudinot's inadequacy," replied Tocqueville in mid-July. "In my view, it was a crime to have confided such an affair to such a man, and from the second day since my entry into the cabinet, I have demanded he be replaced." This would soon be done. "As for the multiplicity of negotiators," the foreign minister assured his friend, "I have begun to put things in order by recalling Harcourt. It will not surprise you that my principal aim in doing so was to leave you in charge in Rome."

Rayneval, observed the foreign minister, had to be handled more carefully, for he was clearly a man of great merit. If they were to remove him from Italy, they would first need to find a major post for him elsewhere in Europe. "I believe, as you do," concluded Tocqueville, "that the best thing would be for you to remain alone. Harcourt's departure already greatly simplifies matters."[6]

THE MOOD IN ROME was sullen, the future unclear. On July 11 a man hired by the French to paint over the tricolored decorations on Rome's roofs was hit on the head with a cobblestone and killed. His would not be the last of the violent deaths in the city that month. Periodically a French soldier or a priest guilty of being too loud in his praise of the French occupation would also be attacked. But the French were living up to their word. The guilty parties were seized, stood up against a wall, and shot.[7]

Rayneval's reports to Paris offered some encouragement. In the last few days, he wrote on July 9, the French had dissolved Rome's National Guard, confiscated arms, and arrested or expelled many of the men who were trying to turn the population against the new order. They were also returning the palaces of the French, Austrian, and Spanish embassies to their rightful owners. Increasingly, priests and monks who had previously remained indoors, or ventured outside only in disguise, were now willing to risk appearing in their clerical garb on Rome's streets. The great majority of the Romans with whom he had spoken, he reported, had no sympathy for the fanatics who had so recently ruled Rome, but they were wary about the pope's return. "At base," Rayneval recounted, "the revolution was made to chase the priests from power. That is the key idea, the popular idea, the idea that everyone understands. The particular form that institutions take matters much less."[8]

The Italian patriots who had converged on Rome to join in the intoxicating days of the republic now found themselves with nowhere to go. Nicholas Brown, the American consul, and John Freeborn, his British counterpart, handed out hundreds of visas to help them flee, some bound northward in Europe, some to the Americas, and some to North Africa. Both men acted against their governments' wishes. "These unhappy people," Freeborn told London in trying to justify the five hundred passports he had given out, "have implored this protection even on their knees." Lord Palmerston, the British foreign minister, reprimanded him for disobeying clear instructions. Washington, even less pleased by its consul's embrace of the Roman Republic, dismissed him from his post.[9]

Nicholas Brown set sail on July 9 aboard a ship bound for Genoa, accompanied by the notorious Pietro Sterbini, leader of the Popular Club and the accused mastermind of the assassination of Pellegrino Rossi. Traveling with them were many other republican veterans bearing passports that the American consul had given them.[10]

Mazzini was still in Rome but knew that he could not stay long. Having gotten an American passport—under the alias "George Moore"—from the U.S. chargé d'affaires, he asked his good friend, Margaret Fuller, for help. Did she know of any American or British family traveling to Switzerland that would be willing to take him with them? "Under a little disguise and with my American passport," he told her, he could "patiently await and keep myself concealed till the day of their departure." As Fuller could find no such family, Mazzini took another route, sailing incognito to Marseilles on July 12. From there he made his way, unrecognized, to Geneva, hiding from the Swiss police before making his way to London to continue his life in exile, dreaming up new plots for Italian independence.[11]

AFTER ALL FRANCE HAD done for him, Pius might have been more grateful. When the Tuscan ambassador, having heard that the French had presented the pope with the keys to Rome, came to congratulate him, he was surprised at the pontiff's reaction. Rather than express appreciation, Pius complained that the French were being too indulgent in dealing with those who had driven him out. How had they allowed Garibaldi and his men to escape? How could they have permitted

Mazzini to show his face in public unmolested? Why was only the French flag flying over the city?"¹²

Cardinal Antonelli was displeased as well. "Every Power that has occupied the other parts of the Papal States," he wrote to his nuncios, "has had the merit of raising the Pontifical flag and declaring that its occupation was aimed at restoring the Government of His Holiness." The French had acted very differently. "Up until now, in the many acts that they have published, not a word has been said about the Holy Father, nor about his Government, nor has his flag been raised." The demagogues, Antonelli complained, including those who had served on Rome's city council, continued to walk freely down the city's streets, while priests remained fearful of appearing in public in their clerical robes.¹³

The French had imagined that papal rule would return only after Pius announced his intention to retain constitutional rights. Now that their troops occupied Rome and the pontiff had still not made any such pledge, the French found themselves in an awkward position. After all the blood they had shed, how could they admit that the Romans did not want papal rule brought back? Their only alternative, it seemed, was to create a government of their own, but this would not only be a direct challenge to papal authority over Christendom's capital, it would antagonize the Austrians. It would also open up a drain on French finances without any end in sight.¹⁴

Bowing to the inevitable, on July 15 French troops hoisted the papal flag over Castel Sant'Angelo as a hundred cannon blasts sounded. Accompanied by his senior officers, General Oudinot then rode through thousands of his troops to St. Peter's Square. There he dismounted and climbed the stairs up into the basilica, where three cardinals awaited him. Following a holy mass paying tribute to the French for their conquest of the city, Cardinal Antonio Tosti climbed to the podium. "You will pass on to posterity," said the cardinal, looking straight at Oudinot,

the title of the liberator of Rome. . . . You have freed us from the oppression of monsters who dishonor mankind. . . . The good people still mourn for the small amount of French blood that was shed, but this blood, together with that of the innocent priests and upright citizens barbarously slaughtered by these monsters, will bring heaven's blessings to France, to you, and to your valiant soldiers.

As General Oudinot walked back through the cavernous basilica, the Romans who had come to celebrate shouted cries of gratitude and joy and rushed forward to kiss his hands. Many were employees of the Holy See and had lived through trying months. Carried away by the emotion of the moment, some went into the nearby streets of Trastevere, where they called on the residents to join them in shouting *Viva Pio Nono!* They did not get the reaction they hoped for. "The women of Trastevere," noted the Roman diarist Roncalli, "opposed them with nasty gestures and instead hurled abuse at Pius IX himself."[15]

Corcelle went directly from the ceremonies in Rome to Fiumicino to board a ship bound for Gaeta.[16] Pius greeted him with great warmth. "I will never forget this moment," reported Corcelle. The contrast between the new French envoy's warm attitude toward the pope and Harcourt's poor opinion of the pontiff could scarcely have been greater. "Those who have experienced the grace of his paternal tenderness," wrote Corcelle, "know how difficult it is not to respond with emotion." That Tocqueville had replaced Harcourt with Corcelle says much about Tocqueville. Corcelle was part of a small group of his close friends who had worked together on journalistic and political projects for a decade. Tocqueville thought him well adapted for the post both because of his interest in the church and because he had briefly been the French government's special envoy to the pope immediately after Pius fled Rome. But Corcelle had a very different attitude toward the pope and would, in the end, do much to undermine Tocqueville's efforts to prevent a return of the old theocracy.[17]

In Corcelle's first two-hour conversation with Pius in Gaeta, and a second of equal length the next day, he followed Tocqueville's instructions, warning Pius of the danger of continuing to follow a reactionary path. Although the pope offered no indication that he agreed with the French advice, Corcelle defended the pope. "I am convinced," he wrote Tocqueville, "that Pope Pius IX has remained what he was in 1847."

In marked contrast with Harcourt, who had shown little compunction in badgering the pontiff, Corcelle clearly remained under the pope's spell. When Corcelle urged the pope to appoint laymen along with priests to his government, Pius replied playfully, "Do you want to be my minister of finance?" He reminded the Frenchman that he had once appointed one of his compatriots, Pellegrino Rossi, to help him put things in order. "He was the only statesman that I could find capable of overseeing an entirely new political approach," remarked Pius, before adding, "and they killed him!"

Corcelle followed up each of his conversations with the pope by going to see Cardinal Antonelli. The French envoy tried to impress on him the importance of getting the pope to return to Rome immediately. Otherwise, he argued, what little enthusiasm the French had been able to drum up for the pontiff through their ceremonies of July 15 would soon wane. Yet Antonelli was unmoved. He was clearly in no hurry to have the pope return.

At the same time, he informed the new French envoy that Pius was preparing a proclamation addressed to his subjects. They would be the pope's first words to them since Rome had been retaken. It was crucial, replied Corcelle, that the pontiff strike the right tone.

Antonelli handed him a copy of the text, which he read with mounting dismay. The pope spoke of the need to reestablish his rule but said nothing about granting freedom to his subjects. Told that the message had already been sent to General Oudinot to place on Rome's walls, Corcelle rushed to Rome in an effort to intercept it. Should it be published as it was, without any mention of the pope's intention to keep his reforms, thought the French envoy, it would be a disaster.[18]

On his arrival in Rome on July 21, Corcelle found Oudinot uncooperative. Hadn't they, only a few days earlier, made a much-ballyhooed announcement of the restoration of the pope's authority? How could they now prevent publication of the pope's address to his people?

As it turned out, the question was moot, for copies of the pope's proclamation were already appearing on walls throughout Rome:[19]

Pope Pius IX
    To his most beloved subjects
    God hath lifted his arm on high and hath commanded the stormy sea of anarchy and impiety to cease. He hath guided the

Catholic arms to sustain the rights of humanity trodden under foot. . . .

My beloved subjects! If in the whirl of frightful events our heart has been overwhelmed with grief in reflecting on the many ills suffered by the Church, by religion, and by you, it has not failed in the love which it always had for you, and still bears you. Our prayers hasten the day that shall bring us again among you. . . .

In the meantime, in order to reorganize public affairs, we are about to name a Commission, which, being provided with full powers and aided by a Minister, shall regulate the government of the State.

That blessing of the Lord which we have always implored . . . we now implore with greater fervor, that it may descend in full measure upon you, and it is a great comfort . . . to hope that all those who were resolved to become incapable of enjoying the fruits thereof by their errors, may be made worthy of it by a sincere and constant repentance.[20]

In the days since the French seized Rome, the people had been anxiously awaiting some sign of what path the pope would take in returning to the city. They hoped that the old, benevolent, liberal-minded pope would return, but they feared that a now vengeful pontiff, spurred on by his evil advisers, would try to restore the despised government of the priests. This first papal declaration of purpose did nothing to allay their fears.

"What is most notable in this city is heartbreaking," observed the Tuscan ambassador that day. "I don't speak of the material damage, though it is certainly visible, but of something more important. The discontent is painted on people's faces . . . unwilling to submit themselves to a government that wants to push the Restoration back to times that are inconceivable today." Or as the London *Times* reporter in Rome put it, "The dread of the restoration of Church government . . . pervades all classes, except those immediately connected with the families of the Cardinals."[21]

If the Romans were discouraged, the French troops in Rome were unhappy as well. Resented by the locals, living in cramped temporary quarters in the sweltering summer heat, their mission unclear, they had heard all too often of the ravages that the malaria season brought to the Eternal City. "The summer is very unpleasant," wrote the French colonel Adolphe Niel to his brother in late July. It was Niel who had brought the pope the keys to Rome earlier in the month: "Matters are very muddled. The pope does not dare to return." In the evenings, he reported, with the curfew eased, the long, narrow, dust-filled Corso was jammed with carriages and pedestrians as the Romans tried to escape the heat. The piles of warm horse manure made the streets treacherous. "The cobblestones are so slippery for the horses," Niel observed, "that despite wearing spiked horseshoes, they often fall down."[22]

Rome's Jews nervously waited to see what the pope's restoration would mean for them. The constitution that the Roman Republic had announced the day of its demise granted them equal rights, but now nothing was clear. When a Jew tried to open a store in the town of Velletri, south of Rome, local merchants complained. In response, Cardinal Antonelli, writing from Gaeta, advised them that with the return of papal authority, Jews no longer had the right to open stores outside the ghettos and would soon be closed back within their walls.[23]

Duke Harcourt, the French ambassador to the Holy See, having been recalled by Tocqueville, left Rome on July 21. Two months later he would resign from the diplomatic corps.[24]

In Gaeta, Rayneval, unhappy that the pope's first address to the Romans after retaking the city made no mention of any plans to keep his reforms, went to talk to him.

"Do you want me to forget my dignity?" replied Pius. "Should I condemn myself to appear to be bowing to French pressure? . . . If I do something good," he asked the French ambassador, "shouldn't my acts be spontaneous and, above all, have the appearance of being so?"

As long as Pius had needed the French to get Rome back, he had left them some hope that he would meet them halfway. Although he was neither politically astute nor calculating, his natural desire to please, and his long-standing emotional preference for the French over the Austrians, had led him to humor them. Now that Rome had been retaken, he would not budge.

"You do not know my intentions," the pontiff told Rayneval. "You will not find them reassuring. I do not want any Constitution because a Constitution would be the end of the Papacy. But as for the reforms that you speak to me about so often, haven't I taken the initiative?" Here the pope spoke of his willingness to establish representative town and provincial councils and even an advisory state council. And, he added, he was well aware of various abuses that had long plagued the Papal States. "Do I not know," he asked, "that the judicial system leaves much to be desired? Do I not know that improvements are needed in finances and administration?

"Why doubt my intentions?" asked the pope. "Haven't I given great proof of my goodwill?"[25]

Rayneval then went to see Antonelli, who gave him more discouraging news. The pope had indicated that he was about to name three men to oversee the new papal government in Rome. He had initially spoken of appointing one cardinal and two laymen, but now Antonelli insisted that only cardinals could properly represent the pope. This, thought Rayneval, would send exactly the wrong message. Antonelli also told the French ambassador that he would soon be announcing the reestablishment of the old ecclesiastical tribunals. Rayneval was horrified.

The next day Rayneval again went to talk to the pope. "Pius IX," he observed, "has a sweet, conciliatory disposition that easily calms even the most agitated feelings. Unfortunately," the diplomat added, "he lacks firmness, and he doesn't know whom to believe." That same apparent lack of firmness, which the French had earlier seen as a weakness, now became the one thin reed on which their hopes rested. Rayneval tried to turn the pope's attention to the need to grant the broadest possible amnesty in returning to power. The alternative, to launch a repressive roundup of those associated in any way with the Roman Republic, would only further inflame public opinion against his return.

Pius was unmoved. "Do not forget who I am," said the pope. "It is certainly necessary for the worst to be punished. For the rest, the important thing is that they leave."

Rayneval then turned to the importance of appointing laymen to the government. All the men the pope had recently chosen to restore papal government in the various cities of the Papal States were clerics. "Your

Holiness," said the ambassador, anticipating the pope's response, "undoubtedly wishes to tell me that the duties of these prelates are temporary—"

"And that's a fact," interjected the pope.

"Well, that's good, but this important fact is completely unknown. . . . Would it not be a good moment to make it public?"

Pius said he would give the matter some thought.[26]

WHILE RAYNEVAL PLEADED WITH Pius in Gaeta, Romans nervously waited to learn the pope's choices for the new three-member governing commission. "The people's fears," reported the French chargé d'affaires in Rome, "are greater than their hopes." Their views of the prelates around the pontiff were less than flattering. "Pio Nono," reported the London *Times* correspondent in Rome, "is surrounded by persons . . . who have no other remedy to offer than the old ones—the dungeon and banishment."[27]

The Romans' fears would prove justified when the names of the members of the governing commission were announced. Cardinal Gabriele Della Genga, the best known of the three, had been appointed a cardinal in 1836 at age thirty-four, seven years after the death of his uncle, Pope Leo XII. In the first two years of his papacy, Pius IX had viewed the reactionary Della Genga as an adversary and removed him from his post as head of the papal government in Ferrara, where he was deeply unpopular. The cardinal was rigid, ambitious, and vindictive. He had not forgotten the humiliation he suffered the previous year in Rome when he was forced from his carriage by the angry mob following the pope's rejection of war with Austria. The Austrians were delighted to learn of the appointment. He would be the soul of the commission that was taking shape.[28]

The other two cardinals were less well known—Rayneval initially dismissed both as "nonentities." Luigi Vannicelli, forty-eight years old and a cardinal for the past seven, had been a favorite of Gregory XVI. Known for his reactionary zeal while serving as papal legate in Bologna, he had spent four years in charge of the papal police in Rome. He, too, was a welcome choice for the Austrians. "He is one of the favorites of

Cardinal Lambruschini," recalled the Austrian ambassador, "and he remains today, just as his colleague Della Genga, among the most intimate and devoted friends of the former secretary of state. His political tendencies and his feelings in *our* favor are, I believe, beyond any doubt."

The third member of the commission, forty-four-year-old cardinal Prince Lodovico Altieri, came from an old, aristocratic Roman family. Appointed archbishop at age thirty, he had served as papal nuncio to Vienna before, at thirty-five, becoming a cardinal. More easygoing than Della Genga, and more open to change, he was viewed warily by the Austrians. "Cardinal Altieri," Esterházy told Schwarzenberg after singing the praises of the other two members of the new commission, "most assuredly represents the other side of the coin. I greatly regretted his nomination, as did Cardinal Antonelli and all those of good sense." But they need not worry, remarked the Austrian ambassador. Altieri would have no influence, given the firm hand of Cardinal Della Genga, who knew what needed to be done and who would have the support of Cardinal Vannicelli.[29]

If Esterházy was pleased, Rayneval was not. On learning of the appointments, he went to complain to the pope. Curiously, rather than defend his choices, Pius blamed them on the lack of any good men for the job. In any case, he added, what had been done was done. "I did not insist," Rayneval recounted to Tocqueville. "Besides, I sympathized with all his embarrassments and with all the uncertainties that weighed on this upright and well-intentioned but vacillating and weak soul."[30]

"You French," said the pope, "you are always in such a hurry. You want to move too quickly. We Romans are different. We take our time, and sometimes, I admit, we take a great deal of time. But this shouldn't frighten you. Be patient."[31]

In Paris, Tocqueville read the reports from Italy with mounting anger. "It is clear," he complained to Corcelle, "that they are playing with you and they are laughing at us. The Roman court is making a fool of us with its promises, as if we were children, while by *faits accomplis* it resumes all its old abuses. The pope himself, believe me, is not being sincere." Perhaps, acknowledged Tocqueville, Pius thought that what he was doing was for the good. "But toward us," the foreign minister concluded, "he has that variety of *insincerity* that men who are good but weak have to compensate for—and to use their amiable appearances as much as possible to cover up for—the damage their actions have caused."

Tocqueville had finally had enough. The French could abide no further humiliation. If, after all they had done for him, the pope continued to refuse French requests, he vowed, he would publicly denounce the pontiff to all of Europe and to the whole Catholic world. *"Voilà,"* he told his old friend Corcelle, "for my part this is what I would do—alone from the tribune as minister or as a simple deputy—rather than suffer the shame and the ridicule that they are preparing for us."[32]

PART THREE

—

THE
FEARED

CHAPTER 18

APPLYING
THE BRAKES

THE GOVERNING COMMISSION OF THE STATE
IN THE NAME OF HIS HOLINESS
HAPPILY REIGNING
TO ALL THE SUBJECTS OF HIS TEMPORAL DOMINION

Divine Providence, through the unvanquished, glorious Catholic armies, has rescued the peoples of all the Papal States, and especially those of the City of Rome, seat and center of our most holy Religion, from the stormy vortex of the blindest and darkest passions. Thus, faithful to the promise announced in His venerated *Motu proprio*, dated from Gaeta the 17th of this past month, the HOLY FATHER now sends us among you with full powers in order to repair, in the best manner, and as quickly as possible, the grave damage wrought by the anarchy and the despotism of a few.

THE PROCLAMATION, DATED AUGUST 1, 1849, FROM THE QUIRinal Palace, signed by the three recently appointed cardinals, announced the return of papal government to Rome. Within hours, virtually all the copies posted along the Corso had been ripped from its walls, a fact the cardinals blamed on "the bile of the democrats."

Romans dubbed the cardinals' commission the "red triumvirate," a reference not only to the color of their robes but to their presumed thirst for the blood of those who would oppose them. People had hoped that there would be at least one layman among them. Instead, as many saw it, the pope had sent a group of retrograde clerics bent on bringing back the Inquisition. For their first public act on August 1, the cardinals had intended to go in solemn procession to St. Peter's Basilica, but both French army officials and the city's highest-ranking clergymen advised against it. Rome, they told the cardinals, had not yet been sufficiently "purged."[1]

The next day the commission announced its first decisions, nullifying all government measures put into effect since Rossi's assassination. It brought back the ecclesiastical tribunals, the courts presided over by priests that were so dreaded by the Romans. All government employees hired since November 15 were dismissed. All who had refused to serve the Roman Republic were welcomed back to work. A special council would determine which, if any, of those who had remained on the job during the republic would be allowed to stay. A day later the cardinals announced that the currency used by the Roman Republic would be recognized at only a fraction of its face value.[2]

Although the repressive powers of the church are most closely identified with the Inquisition, what most alarmed the Romans was the decision to bring back the cardinal vicar's tribunal. The Inquisition dealt mainly with disciplining the clergy. The vicariate tribunal dealt in good part with the people of Rome. With the power of the papal police behind it, and aided by the watchful eye of the lower clergy, the tribunal struck deep into people's private lives.[3]

Fearful that the new cardinals' commission would trigger disorder, on August 3 the French army made a great show of force. The city again took on a warlike appearance, with cavalry and infantry encamped overnight in the main squares, horses saddled, and guns loaded. The French wheeled three large pieces of artillery into the Piazza del Popolo, positioning them so that they aimed down the main streets that radiated out into the city. All this, observed the newly arrived Austrian consul, "did nothing to improve public attitudes." Nor did the cardinals' first meeting with the French generals go well. The Frenchmen knew no Italian and were surprised at the cardinals' lack of fluency in French. For their part, the cardinals, offended by the generals' failure to kiss their rings, thought them boorish.[4]

"If the Quirinal was not guarded by French soldiers," reported Rome's London *Times* correspondent, "it would not be safe for one hour. That unpopularity will be increased a hundredfold for all that may emanate from Gaeta, when it is seen that nothing in the shape of a benevolent promise can be extracted from the Pope." The British correspondent noted a change in local attitudes toward the French military. Before the cardinals' arrival, the Romans had viewed the French force as an extension of the pope's. Now they realized that only the French army stood "between them and the vengeance of the Cardinals."[5]

Tension between the French and the new papal government kept growing. The cardinals were eager to round up those they held responsible for the Roman Republic. This, Tocqueville was convinced, would be disastrous. If political trials were conducted under the protection of French troops, he warned Corcelle, "we would be dishonored before the entire world." He ordered Corcelle and Oudinot to make sure that no such trials were held.

But the persecutions soon began. On the night of August 8, two papal policemen barged into the home of Pietro Ripari, the doctor in charge of medical services for one of the military divisions of the republic. Imprisoned, he demanded to know what the charges were against him. They were based, he was told, on his correspondence with Mazzini, dating to the time they were both in Switzerland in 1848, and on his writings critical of the pope. Moved from prison to prison and subjected to a series of trials, the doctor was finally sentenced, two years later, to twenty years in jail for "illicit epistolary correspondence." The pope's dungeons were full of such unfortunate souls.[6]

Tocqueville was furious. The pope's refusal to agree to even modest reforms "is causing me," he confessed to Corcelle, "an irritation so great that I am unable to overcome it. . . . We have sacrificed money and soldiers for him. We have placed our worldwide reputation for liberalism in jeopardy. We have exposed ourselves to a revolution in which we could have all perished and, after all that, they are refusing us, can that be?"

France, he reminded his envoy, had had three goals in intervening in Rome. They had accomplished the first two: ensuring that France exercised its proper influence in Italy, and ensuring the pope's independence. But they could not leave Rome without accomplishing their third: the people of the Papal States had to be governed by "serious liberal institutions." France's honor, insisted Tocqueville, demanded it. "It would have been a thousand times better never to have undertaken this enterprise," he declared, "than to abandon it without having obtained the necessary result."[7]

As the first reports of repression came in, Tocqueville wrote General Oudinot, upbraiding him for failing to prevent it. "All the news I am receiving here from Italy," wrote the French foreign minister,

> convinces me more and more that you have not understood . . . your role since the restoration of papal authority in Rome. You seem to believe that there now remains nothing more to do than be a passive spectator to the acts of the Pontifical government. . . . I see from the newspaper and from correspondence that with your concurrence or at least under your eyes the institutions that have been denounced by all Europe, such as the Inquisition and the detestable jurisdiction of the tribunal of the cardinal vicar, have been reestablished.[8]

What Tocqueville did not tell Oudinot was that on the same day he wrote his letter, he had finally succeeded in getting Louis Napoleon to have him dismissed. "Every single day for the past month," he informed Corcelle, "I have demanded General Oudinot's recall, and only the force of inertia has kept him despite me. Today I declared that I would refuse to conduct this affair any longer if he were not recalled. They have finally agreed."[9]

Early that same morning, August 4, Oudinot, not yet knowing of his dismissal and feeling the time had come to finally meet Pius, arrived in Gaeta aboard a French ship. With a benevolent smile, the pope embraced the general and praised him for all he had done for the papacy and for the church.[10]

The next day Oudinot had a long conversation with the pontiff. Had the pope had a decent army in the first place, the general told him, his prime minister would never have been assassinated and the whole sad subsequent series of events would never have taken place. Oudinot offered his own services, and those of his senior staff, to advise the pope on how to put together a modern military. At the same time, he urged him to return quickly to Rome.

Pius demurred. The public mood there, he feared, remained too agitated for him to go back anytime soon. Again he bemoaned the Romans' ingratitude. Perhaps, he suggested, he would first move to Castel Gandolfo, the castle nestled in the hills outside Rome where the popes had long had a summer residence.[11]

IN PARIS, REPORTS OF the repression in Rome sparked anger in the National Assembly. In response to the deputies' demand for assurances that the goal of the French expedition was going to be met and that a medieval theocracy was not being restored, Tocqueville reluctantly got up to reply. Throughout his remarks, deputies of the left constantly interrupted him.

The French, said the foreign minister, were at that very moment in the midst of negotiations with the pope, aimed at ensuring that he retain the liberal institutions that he had earlier created. In light of their delicacy, he told the deputies, it would be inappropriate to discuss them publicly. Loud ironic laughter greeted these remarks from the left, while voices of approval rose from the right.

"I am authorized not only to believe, but to say in the most formal possible manner," concluded the foreign minister, rattled perhaps less by the jeers from the left than by his own discomfort at so brazenly lying to them, "that these are the firm intentions of the Holy Father. What Catholic, what man of good will could doubt the word of Pius IX? Based both on his firm will and on ours, we can affirm that our expedition in Italy will not lead to a blind and implacable restoration."[12]

DEEP IN THE APENNINE MOUNTAINS, it looked like the end might be near for Garibaldi and his men. Abandoning his earlier plan of establishing a base to the north of Rome, Garibaldi had fixed his sights on Venice, the last part of Italy still holding out against the Austrians. As the weeks passed, his army had dwindled. The sick, the injured, the hungry, and the discouraged stayed behind or drifted away.

In late July, Garibaldi had led his men to the tiny mountain principality of San Marino, cutting his own trail through thick woods and rushing waters, with Austrian soldiers close behind. There he released the men from their vow to fight to the death with him. "Remember," Garibaldi told them, "that it is better to die than to live as slaves to the foreigner." Leaving most of the men behind, he then set out with his pregnant wife and three hundred of his followers, still hoping to reach Venice. Through the mediation of the San Marino authorities, the Austrian army, camped nearby, offered to allow the remaining men to go home if they would throw down their arms. Nine hundred of them agreed to do so. They would soon come to regret the faith they had placed in Austrian honor.

When they reached the Adriatic coast, Garibaldi and his followers overpowered an Austrian outpost, seized thirteen fishing boats, and set sail for Venice. Having begun life as a sailor, Garibaldi felt at home on the sea, but before long the speedier Austrian warships caught up with them, guns firing. Most of the boats were seized, and the men were sent in chains to a nearby Austrian fort. Miraculously, Garibaldi, his wife Anita, the monk Ugo Bassi, and Ciceruacchio and his two sons escaped.

Making land in a desolate part of the coast north of Ferrara, Garibaldi decided it best if they broke into smaller groups. He and Anita headed toward Ravenna, hoping to find help there. On the third day of their flight, with the Austrians on their heels, Anita, seven months pregnant, could go no farther. Weakened by the frenzied flight through the mountains, she had grown feverish. A day later she died, in her womb their fourth child, never to be born. Distraught, Garibaldi pushed on. With the aid of sympathizers along the way, he made his way across the peninsula to the Tuscan coast and from there to safety in Genoa.[13]

As Garibaldi was making his escape, the men who had laid down their arms in San Marino were marched in chains into Bologna. A local diarist recorded the sight: "At noon today, the sixth, in the midst of a troop of infantry and cavalry, the unfortunates who were part of Garibaldi's militia began to arrive. . . . The poor men are all torn up, shoeless and reduced to such a state as to move even the most unfeeling to compassion. . . . No one knows what their fate will be."[14]

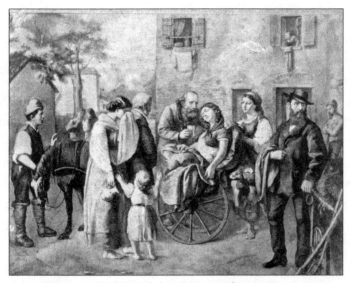

Garibaldi with his dying wife, Anita

Ugo Bassi had succeeded in reaching the town of Comacchio, along the coast east of Ferrara. There a local informer reported the monk to the police, who handed him over to the local Austrian commander.[15]

For the Austrian general in Bologna, the famed preacher, reputed to be Garibaldi's chaplain, was a prize catch. Frustrated that Garibaldi had eluded him, the general was determined to take his revenge. Using the bogus charge that the Barnabite monk had been found carrying arms, and without according him the benefit of a trial, the Austrian sentenced

The arrest of the monk Ugo Bassi

him to death. On August 8 soldiers hoisted the manacled Bassi onto a military wagon, and the procession began. A priest walked on either side of him, as a drummer pounded out a funereal beat. When they reached the site of the execution, Bassi got down on his knees to pray. A soldier came to put a blindfold over his eyes, but the monk asked that a priest put it on him instead, so it would be a priest's touch that the monk would last feel. The officer in charge raised his sword high. Bassi's voice could be heard, in prayer, as the Austrian lowered his arm. It was a moment that the patriotic monk from Bologna, who had braved French bullets to care for the wounded and bring God's words to Rome's weary defenders, had long envisioned. He crumpled to the ground as bullets pierced his body.[16]

Ciceruacchio, Rome's popular hero, met an even crueler fate. Together with his two sons, he was captured on August 9. With them were five other *garibaldini*, including a young priest who had, along with Ugo Bassi, ministered to the wounded and the dying. The next night the Austrian soldiers marched their eight prisoners, in four pairs, hands bound to each other, to the place of their execution. The Austrians made no pretense of a trial. Ciceruacchio, who was tied to his younger son, Lorenzo, begged the Croatian officer in charge to spare the boy—he was only thirteen years old. With an ironic smile, the officer instead ordered his men to shoot the child first. Only then did they aim their bullets at Ciceruacchio and his older son, Luigi.[17]

In Gaeta, in yet another effort to persuade the pope to embrace a path of reform, Rayneval brought Pio Nono a letter that Tocqueville had recently sent his ambassador, and read it aloud to him. It was unsparing in describing France's frustrations with the pope and warned of dire consequences should he fail to follow French advice.

"You don't trust me," said the agitated pontiff, interrupting Rayneval, "and it is not fair. My language has not changed. What I have promised, I will do. Why suppose that I would fail to honor my commitments?"

"France," replied Rayneval, "has waited a long time and has yet to see any result. . . . The old laws are being reestablished without any indication that they will soon be revised. Is it any surprise that the unhappiness and disappointment in Paris are so great?"

Spain, Austria, and Naples, the pope responded, were all pleased with the course he had taken. Why, he asked, should France alone find fault?

"France," said the ambassador, "risked its government's existence to save your Holiness." The French government had to answer to its people. "To whom," asked Rayneval, "do the King of Naples or the Emperor of Austria have to answer?"

"All in good time," said the pope.

Rayneval would not let the matter rest. "I don't see it that way," he countered. "Where I come from, when a new power is organized, there is nothing more pressing than announcing what it plans to do. We believe that uncertainty is the worst condition to be in when one wants to calm people's spirits, and we have quite a bit of experience in this regard. So we have been waiting for Your Holiness to lay this out from the very first day."

"There, where you say, Monsieur, that we should change our attitude," replied the pope. "*Voilà!* Your threats, your intimidation. Just because you have thirty thousand men behind you, do you think you can impose your will on me?"

"Your Holiness is mistaken," replied Rayneval, trying to cool the pope's temper. "We had begun by asking you for a constitution—"

"And if you had persisted," interjected the pope, "I would never return to Rome."

"We did not persist, but we came to content ourselves with what Your Holiness himself suggested to us. Is it possible to be any more moderate than that?"

Rayneval was growing ever more discouraged, as his report back to Paris made clear. "The history of these past years," he observed,

> shows us many examples of the complete uselessness of employing violent means with the pope. The pope, in these cases, displays the quintessential attitude of a priest. In saying nothing, he says everything. One exhausts oneself in vain. He remains un-

moved and, in the end, one is forced to compromise. We have no hold on him. Any other sovereign, once outside of his states, would no longer be anything. But this one loses little if he remains in exile. Our only means of action is persuasion. We can tell him of the dangers, and urge him to avoid them, but from the moment when we seem to want to impose on him, we can regard our cause as lost.[18]

WHILE THE FRENCH AMBASSADOR sparred with the pope in Gaeta, and as the executions were running their grisly course in the northern provinces of the Papal States, a change was under way in Rome. Oudinot was replaced by the fifty-nine-year-old general Louis de Rostolan. It was Rostolan who, the previous month, as head of the city's military government, had tried to quell the violence there. He was, an unenthusiastic Tocqueville told Corcelle, "a man of little consequence, it is true, but precise, punctual, and honest. Lacking anyone better, that will suffice, I hope."[19]

Tocqueville instructed the new army head to follow Corcelle's advice in all political matters, but this would not be easy to do, for Corcelle was bedridden. "My bowels have hardly any blood in them anymore," Corcelle reported to Tocqueville with some satisfaction in mid-August. He wrote to advise the French foreign minister that, following his doctor's advice, he was planning to move from Mola di Gaeta south to convalesce in Castellamare, on a point of the gulf of Naples where the heat was less oppressive. There he would be nursed by his wife, granddaughter of General Lafayette, French hero of the American Revolution.

Pius received a rather different account of Corcelle's indisposition. Although the French envoy was said to be suffering from inflammatory dysentery and cerebral fever, someone in the French legation informed the pope that the envoy's sudden departure was in fact caused by a mental, not a physical breakdown. It was not the first time, it was said, that this had happened to him.[20]

In mid-August, when Gaeta's four-power conference reconvened, Rayneval found himself fighting a lonely battle. Having abandoned the earlier French demand for a constitution, the ambassador urged that the pope at least create a lay council with authority to set taxes. Antonelli rejected the idea out of hand. Such a council, he explained, risked triggering "all the excesses and all the dangers that had led to the exile in Gaeta." Esterházy voiced strong support for Antonelli, as did Martínez, Spain's ambassador. Martínez was one of Spain's most prominent men of letters and had earlier been considered a political progressive. But for the Spaniard, the Roman question was unique, to be viewed in purely religious terms. A pope could not govern as a constitutional monarch. It was the church that properly ruled in the Papal States, and so laymen could never play more than a minor, supporting role. The combination of Martínez's geniality, literary sensibility, and clear devotion to the papal cause had made him one of Pius's favorites, and his support helped stiffen the pope's resolve.[21]

Rayneval was distraught. He had assured Tocqueville that, in compensating the French for his refusal to retain a constitution in Rome, the pope would allow this one fig leaf, the tax-setting council. Now this, too, was being rebuffed.

"The game is up," lamented Rayneval. "If they leave us some time to complain, it is only a courtesy."[22]

In Rome, all the repressive elements of the old papal theocracy were being brought back. In mid-August the cardinals announced the creation of a council to investigate all employees of the government, police, courts, and public administration to determine who among them merited punishment due to their participation in the "past political upheavals." It would also investigate all those on public pensions to determine whose payments should be stopped. Similar councils were established throughout the Papal States. The cardinals also reintroduced tight censorship, aimed at "preventing the damage that the periodical press, guided by a partisan spirit or infused with democratic passions, could cause to the public morality of these people, and to public safety."[23]

New government ministers were also being appointed. Of these the most important, and the only one with real power, was the man named minister of internal affairs, in charge of the police. For this the pope had brought back the infamous "Monsignor Bulldog," Domenico Savelli, the widely despised former police head. "A hard man, mean, vindictive," as one unsympathetic chronicler put it, the bulldog immediately came into conflict with the French. "An unfortunate choice," commented Rayneval. Within days of his appointment, Savelli was trying to get the French army's help in hunting down the former members of the Constituent Assembly.[24]

On August 23 the cardinals made a new public announcement. The crimes committed against the Catholic religion, its priests, and its august head in the recent rebellion, they told the Romans, had remained unpunished too long. They were creating a special commission to oversee the trials of all those charged, under the supervision of Monsignor Savelli.[25] The mood in Rome was gloomy, as Colonel Niel observed in a letter to his brother back in France:

> Political affairs are going poorly. The streets of Rome are paved with Capuchins, Dominicans, of priests in all kinds of outfits, whose haughty manners grate on the army. They are in every public place and are far from having the decent attitude of our priests in France. These are for the most part political men. They are clamoring for their old positions. On the other hand . . . the immense majority of the lay population is strongly opposed to the government of the priests and views the return of their political influence with disgust.[26]

Convinced that the pope and his entourage were taking them for fools, and in danger of appearing to the world—and to their own people—as allies of the Austrians in restoring autocracy to Rome, the French cabinet could hold back no longer. At a mid-August meeting, the French prime minister, who had long had doubts about the wisdom of their military mission in Rome, reviewed the latest outrages. The pope had promised that Rome's governing commission would be primarily composed of laymen. Instead, he had appointed three cardinals. On first receiving the French general and his senior staff in Rome, the cardinals had not even bothered to put on their formal scarlet robes, and they had made Oudinot and his men wait an unconscionable amount of time outside their door before allowing them in. When the French officers finally were admitted, the cardinals had greeted them coldly. The cardinals had then begun issuing their orders without consulting Oudinot, as the French had demanded. And then, in one of its first acts, the newly restored papal government announced it was bringing back the Inquisition. French honor, said Barrot, demanded that they suffer such abuse no longer.

Following the prime minister's tirade, Tocqueville read the cabinet a letter he had recently received from Lord Palmerston. The British foreign minister expressed doubts about whether the two governments could continue to collaborate, if the word of the French government— which had claimed it sent its army to Rome to defend freedom—meant so little. The Roman expedition, already a huge embarrassment, now threatened France's alliance with Britain, the centerpiece of French foreign policy. The French had shed much blood and spent an enormous amount of money to restore the pope to Rome, said Barrot, but rather than show his gratitude, Pius had treated them abysmally. The time had come to end the charade.[27]

Alarmed, Alfred de Falloux, French minister of education and religion and fervent papal defender, urged his colleagues not to take any precipitous action. When the meeting adjourned, postponing a final decision, Falloux rushed to see the papal nuncio. If he had not attended the cabinet meeting that day, he told the horrified nuncio, the decision to withdraw the French army from Rome would certainly have been made. As it was, he added, the president's good sense alone had saved them. Only Louis Napoleon, and to a lesser extent Tocqueville, he said, had any understanding of Roman affairs. As for the rest of the ministers, they knew neither "what the Pope is or what Religion is." He could not hold them off much longer. Falloux told the nuncio:

For the good of the church, I beg you to write to Antonelli to have him show at least some deference to France's envoys and, even more importantly, to indicate what political paths the Holy Father wants to follow. Whatever then happens will happen, but for heaven's sake, have him say it publicly and soon. If not, the government will feel obliged to take a measure that will be most grievous for every Catholic heart, and ruinous for the Holy Father's temporal government.[28]

WITH CORCELLE STILL CONVALESCING, Rayneval continued to meet with the pope but had little to show for it. Typical was Pius's response to the ambassador's complaint about the large number of arrests of the pope's political opponents. "In Rome, they think that [the arrests] are so numerous," said Pius, "but it's just the opposite, and I myself complain that there haven't been more." Far from excessive rigor, the problem was overindulgence. "The course of justice," complained the pope, "is at a standstill. Crimes remain unpunished. The men who have acted most openly against me walk freely through the streets of Rome. . . . What really should alarm us is the complete absence of repression and ensuring impunity for all crimes. In a situation like this," asked the pontiff, "can I offer an amnesty? Can I dream of returning to Rome?"

"The pope," recalled Rayneval, "was animated, and I recognized . . . clear signs of the feelings of bitterness that were beginning to get the better of him. He is getting tired of our demands. Our complaints are irritating him. He is no longer on the path that leads to concessions, but rather to resistance. . . . He has gone so far as to let it be known that as long as the French do not change their attitude, the pope would not return to Rome." Yet, wrote Rayneval, with the cardinals eager for revenge and the other foreign diplomats lining up behind Austria, "the pope is our only support. Besides him we have no one on whom we can count. He was always, deep in his heart, more French than Austrian. Soon," predicted the French ambassador, "it will be the reverse."[29]

CHAPTER 19

LOUIS NAPOLEON
AND THE POPE

A s Rayneval left the pope's quarters and made his way back to Rome, a French colonel was also headed there. He carried with him an ultimatum from Louis Napoleon.

Falloux had persuaded the French president to delay the army's withdrawal from Rome, but neither Louis Napoleon nor his prime minister was willing to leave matters as they were. It was the only time, recalled Barrot, that he had ever seen the normally placid Napoleon so emotional, angry at the pope for embarrassing him. Following that dramatic cabinet meeting, the president decided to deliver an ultimatum in the form of a letter addressed to his aide-de-camp, Colonel Edgar Ney, to be brought to General Rostolan in Rome.

> The French Republic did not send an army to Rome to extinguish Italian freedom but, on the contrary, to regulate it in order to preserve it from its excesses, and to give it a solid basis in returning to the pontifical throne the prince who first boldly placed himself at the head of all useful reforms. . . . It pains me to learn that the benevolent intentions of the Holy Father, as well as our own action, have been thwarted by the presence of hostile passions and influences of those who would instead like to make banishment and tyranny the basis for his return. . . . Make clear to the general [Rostolan] on my behalf that in no case can he allow any act to take place under the shadow of our flag that can alter the character

of our intervention. I would have the pope's temporal power resume in this way: general amnesty, secularization of the administration, and a liberal government.

The president also used his letter to complain of the poor way that
the three cardinals in Rome were treating French officers and their lack
of appreciation for the great sacrifices made by French soldiers. Ever
conscious that his own greatest strength lay in the power of his family
name, Louis Napoleon cast himself in his uncle's image:

When our armies made their way through Europe, they left everywhere, in their wake, the destruction of the abuses of feudalism and the seeds of freedom. It will not be said that, in 1849, a
French army could act in a different direction and lead to different
results.[1]

At a cabinet meeting the morning after Ney left Paris with the letter,
the prime minister passed a copy to Falloux. Realizing the enormous
storm it would provoke if it were made public, the Catholic minister
asked who in Rome would get to see it. The letter, Louis Napoleon assured him, was meant for General Rostolan alone.

"Well, then, Monsieur le Président," asked Falloux, "you promise
that it will never be published?"

"Oh! No! Never!" replied Louis Napoleon, who had already given
Ney instructions to do exactly that.[2]

Tocqueville himself only learned of the letter at that same meeting.
He wrote to alert Corcelle: "For several days all the news from Italy has
been disastrous. . . . They tell of the people's extreme discontent with
the papal government and of a perhaps even greater anger against us."
The result, reported the foreign minister, had been two cabinet meetings
where he had found himself trying to keep his colleagues from acting
precipitously. "They spoke of nothing less," Tocqueville recounted,
"than refusing to recognize the papal authorities in Rome and in the
provinces that we occupy."[3]

On his arrival in Rome on August 27, Colonel Ney showed the letter
to Rayneval—himself having just returned to Rome from Gaeta that

day—and informed him that the president wanted it published in Rome's official newspaper. The ambassador immediately recognized its importance. "It will produce a profound impression," Rayneval advised Paris, adding, "It is difficult to predict all the consequences this publication will have."[4]

The letter did not appear in the newspaper the next day, for General Rostolan refused to permit it. Given the tense state of public opinion, as well as the widespread discontent among his own troops, the general worried, it would be too dangerous to have the letter published.[5]

Rebuffed by the general, Colonel Ney made copies on his own, so that by the next day the letter was circulating throughout the city. No one, it seemed, was talking of anything else. Having gotten a copy themselves, the cardinals of the governing commission summoned Rayneval and told him that the letter not only offended the pope's dignity but risked stirring unrest among the people of the Papal States. If the French went ahead and published it anyway, they threatened, they would leave Rome and move the papal government to a part of the Papal States where the flag of a friendlier power flew.[6]

By the next day, as more illicit copies of the letter spread through Rome, papal police raided the city's cafés, destroying the copies they found, and searched for the clandestine printer. With the French president's rejection of the pope's plans now made public, reported the French newspaper *Débats*, a break between the pope and France seemed unavoidable. The correspondent speculated that instead of returning to Rome, the pope would likely move to one of the cities of his realm under Austrian control, perhaps Bologna or Ancona.[7]

Rayneval returned to Gaeta. His first report back to Paris struck a dark note:

Experience has counted for nothing. The real needs of society have counted for nothing. France's advice has counted for nothing. . . . The men the cardinals surround themselves with would render the most perfect institutions fruitless. . . . In Rome, where prominent, well-educated, distinguished lawyers are to be found in large numbers, they went and found a perfect unknown to be Minister of Justice. For Minister of Public Works they chose a contractor who had built a bridge, for Minister of Finance an accountant. This is what they have in mind by putting laymen in government.

It was now Esterházy who had the pope's ear. The Austrians had further strengthened their position a week earlier, when Venice, the last holdout against the Austrian army, finally surrendered, succumbing to prolonged bombardment, famine, and cholera. "Repression," Rayneval reported, "that is the key word for the Roman policy. . . . They are persuaded here that everything is going badly because they have not executed enough people, nor imprisoned enough, nor punished enough."[8]

Rayneval again went to see the pope, warning him that the number of his supporters in Rome was shrinking daily, and even the most moderate men there were despairing of the future. Only by leaving immediately for his capital, announcing a generous amnesty, and stating his intention to form an enlightened system of government could he avert disaster. How, asked Rayneval, would it look for the Supreme Pontiff to rule his people only by force of foreign arms? If the pope continued on such an ill-conceived path, the ambassador warned, he should not count on French arms to support him.[9]

The cardinals did not share the French ambassador's concerns. "We don't see people devoted to His Holiness's government," acknowledged Cardinal Della Genga, leader of the three-member governing commission, speaking to the Austrian consul in Rome in early September. "I have no illusions," he added, "and I see that the number of those desiring the government of the priests is very limited." The problem, he thought, lay not with ecclesiastical rule but with the heretical ideas that, thanks to the rabble-rousers, had spread among the unlettered population. The pope and the prelates ruled over the Papal States because it was what God intended. The disaster they had endured, charged Della Genga, was the pope's fault, for it was his "excessive leniency" that had undermined the people's affection for their rightful rulers.[10]

RATHER THAN RETURN TO his capital, as the French were urging, the pope decided to move farther away from it, finding more comfortable quarters near Naples. After spending nine months, nine days, and nine hours in Gaeta—or so a fawning Neapolitan chronicler calculated it—on the morning of Tuesday, September 4, Pius IX, in the company of the king and queen, became the first pope ever to travel on a steamship.

As they sailed down the coast, Ferdinand pointed out each landmark and noted the cloud of smoke wafting from Mount Vesuvius as it prepared for a new eruption. Their destination, a large royal palace that Ferdinand had reserved for the pope, was in Portici, a few miles past Naples. How long the pope would remain there, no one knew.[11]

In Rome, debris from what remained of the barricades and rubble from the bombed-out buildings still littered the streets. At night, those nostalgic for the days of the Roman Republic gathered in local *trattorie*, where they held seditious banquets and distributed contraband written accounts of those heady days. Four of Rome's theaters had reopened, although French authorities briefly shut one down when patrons hurled abuse at French officers in the audience.

Virtually all who had served in the Constituent Assembly were now gone. The French authorities had lured the last away on ships bound for Marseilles by leading them to believe they would be granted asylum in France. The French were eager to have them leave the Papal States rather than face the embarrassment of their imprisonment or execution at the hands of the restored papal government, but Louis Napoleon was not eager to have them settle in France. When their ships docked at French ports, they were kept aboard, to be sent on to America.[12]

In Rome, the mood remained fearful among the pope's partisans and sullen among the rest. "This swarm of idle priests that one runs into at every step, and who exploit the country, is an evil that is difficult to destroy," wrote Colonel Niel in a letter to his brother. "This is a population of sycophants and mendicants, who lack the habit of supporting themselves by their own work." What the Romans most needed, thought the French officer, was an efficient lay government. "But," he asked, "how could all this be reconciled with the authority of a pope who tends increasingly to give everything to the priests?"[13]

In Paris, Louis Napoleon was furious that his letter had still not been published, yet Rostolan threatened to resign rather than allow its publication, convinced that it would both undermine his troops' morale and encourage popular resistance to the new papal government.[14]

Rostolan was not alone in opposing the request. Corcelle vowed that if the French government continued to insist on having Napoleon's letter published, he, too, would resign. At the same time, Rayneval added a warning of his own. "Publishing it against the formal wishes of the papal government," he advised, "would put the government under our feet. The humiliation would be cruel."[15]

Among the reasons the French envoys gave for their reluctance to publish the letter was their wish that nothing happen to delay the pope's long-awaited address to his subjects on his plans for his new government. For weeks they had been telling the pope how important it was that he let his subjects know that he planned a broad amnesty for those who had participated in the revolt against him, that he would staff his government with laymen rather than priests, and that he would keep many of the liberal reforms he had earlier embraced. Now they nervously waited to see if he would heed their advice.

Shortly after arriving in Portici, the pope convened the cardinals to ask their opinion. Hostility toward the French ran deep. Promising concessions to his subjects, the cardinals argued, would give the appearance of weakness. People would see an embattled pope bowing to French pressure. Were he to bring back the Consultative Council, as the French were urging, Cardinal Lambruschini warned, all would be lost. That had been the first step on the road to revolution. The cardinals were no more enthusiastic about having the pope move to a city under French control. It would be better for him to go to one of the Austrian-occupied towns of the Papal States, for there he could do as he liked.

The pope seemed no longer the same man he was before. His subjects' rejection had stung him deeply. He never wanted to repeat that terrifying sense of helplessness he had felt amid the chaos in Rome in the days following Rossi's murder. He now clung to the one path in which he could comfortably place his faith, that of the eternal verities that his predecessors on St. Peter's throne had followed. Listening to those who told him he had to adapt to modern times had produced only heartache for him and disaster for the church he loved. Parliamentary government and individual freedoms, thought Pius, were not only incompatible with the divinely ordained nature of his own states but inherently evil. It was a belief that he would hold for the rest of his life.[16]

On September 17 the text of Pio Nono's long-awaited address to his subjects finally appeared on Rome's walls. Following a preface praising the "valorous armies of the Catholic Powers" for saving Rome from "tyranny" and restoring him to the plenitude of his powers, the pope described the features he intended to give the new papal government. There would be an advisory state council, whose membership and responsibilities he would announce at a later date. He would institute a financial council, whose members he would select. It would review state finances and offer its recommendations on taxes. He would also institute provincial councils, choosing their members from among names put forth by the town councils. Members of the town councils would be elected from local property owners. As for the judiciary, he would choose its heads and also appoint a commission to consider reforms.[17]

The last matter the pope addressed was the question of amnesty, stating simply that its terms would soon be published. The three cardinals announced the details the next day. Far from the broad, generous amnesty urged by the French, this one was limited at best. Among those excluded were the members of the republican government, the members of the Constituent Assembly, the heads of the various military units, and all those political prisoners and exiles who had previously been pardoned in the amnesty the pope had issued shortly after assuming the papacy in 1846.[18]

"In the whole history of amnesties," remarked Luigi Carlo Farini, a physician who had been in charge of public health in Pellegrino Rossi's government, and who had fled Rome during the republic, "one does not find a document like this, which can only jokingly be called by that name. Consider its terms, and you will see *no one* is amnestied."[19]

Writing to his nuncio in Vienna about the pope's amnesty, Cardinal Antonelli lashed out at the French, whom he knew would be displeased. The limits the pope placed on it, explained the secretary of state, were those demanded by justice and by the requirements of both morality and religion. He would have hoped, he told his nuncio, that now that the pope had announced his planned course for the restored government, the French would put an end to their constant demands. But, he added, "I cannot . . . hide from Your Reverence that each day such demands take on the nature of a violation of the rights of the temporal sovereignty of the Holy Father guaranteed by the Catholic Powers."[20]

In the battle of wills pitting Tocqueville and Louis Napoleon against the pope, the French had their army and their national pride at stake, but the pope had, in Antonelli, a man who well understood the political power of the church. Italy's more perceptive observers had little doubt who would prevail. Massimo d'Azeglio, the liberal Bolognese aristocrat whom the pope had originally wanted to head his government following Rossi's assassination, and who since May had become prime minister of the Kingdom of Sardinia, was among those who saw a bleak future ahead. "I continue to doubt," he confided in a letter to a friend, "that French influence will prove a match against priestly cunning."[21]

CHAPTER 20

THE UNPOPULAR
POPE

THE POPE'S LONG-AWAITED ADDRESS AND AMNESTY SERVED ONLY to further fuel what the Dutch ambassador called the "sentiment of aversion against the ecclesiastical government that exists here so generally." Grumbling among the French troops about serving as the wardens of the restored theocracy was growing as well.[1]

In reporting the pope's decree to Paris, Rayneval tried to give it the best face he could. The French had long ago abandoned their demands for a constitution. Even their modest request for a lay council to set tax policy had been rejected. But there were some positive elements, especially in municipal government, and the French could take credit for them, as they were due to French pressure alone. Modest as they were, the reforms upset the cardinals, who, the ambassador reported, "claim to see in them the germs of new misfortunes, the gateway to yet another exile. They regard (I do not exaggerate) the old Gregorian system as the only reasonable one.

"In the eyes of the Sacred College," the ambassador added, "Pius IX is a blind man who is bringing the temporal power to its ruin." The cardinals had employed every means they could—"intrigues, obsessions, expressions of bitterness, even threats"—to achieve their ends. "Who knows," asked Rayneval, "if, weak of character as he is, shaken beyond measure by the cruel experience that he has had, the Holy Father would not have yielded without the fear that France's attitude inspired in him? What he has done, he has done above all to please us. What he gives us costs him an enormous price, there is no doubt of it."

Aware that Tocqueville and his cabinet colleagues would be dismayed at how little ground the pope had given, Rayneval cautioned against any hasty action. "If we show that we are too unhappy," warned the French ambassador, "we would offend beyond measure the prodigiously sensitive nature of Pius IX, and it is in him alone that we can place any hope."[2]

Meanwhile in Paris, a new report had Tocqueville fuming. British and French newspapers were carrying a disturbing accusation made by the exiled Mazzini. "Rome's prisons," the Italian prophet charged,

> are packed full with people who, for the most part, are guilty of nothing more than having obeyed the existing government and having been singled out by some spies for the priests' vengeance. More than fifty ecclesiastics are imprisoned in Castle Sant'Angelo, guilty only of having offered their services to the hospitals of the Republic. Nor have the junior officers of the police been spared, and they have the cruelty to condemn them to life in prison.

"This would be very serious," Tocqueville told Corcelle, "if it is true, *even in part*." He asked him to determine how many people had been jailed for political crimes since the French had entered Rome, and how many were still being held. France, he declared, could not permit such imprisonments. If the cardinals complained that the French were encroaching on the pope's sovereignty, said the French foreign minister, "So be it." Tocqueville told his envoy,

> The only consolation that remains for us, the only excuse that we can present to the world amidst the ruin of the hopes for freedom that our expedition had aroused, is at least having saved some people. On these grounds we win universal sympathy. I repeat. Rather than let them defeat us, break off relations. This is not a suggestion. *It is an order.*[3]

It was while he was writing these words that the French foreign minister finally received a copy of the pope's message to his people on the form of government he was planning. Tocqueville had already resigned himself to the fact that the pope would not embrace the constitutional guarantees the French had been pressing on him, but now he was newly angered. Compared with the vindictive pope, he fumed, the Austrian emperor and the Neapolitan king were fonts of mercy. "I have said that France could not allow its expedition to bring about a blind, implacable restoration. It is even more blind than I had thought, and more implacable than I would have dared to imagine." The author of *Democracy in America* could take the embarrassment no longer. "I will have to reflect," he told Corcelle, "on whether I can, even in the interest of my country, remain in my position when the program that I have given to our policy has been so poorly fulfilled."[4]

AT THE POPE'S MAGNIFICENT new quarters in Portici, Rayneval told him how disappointed his government was with his recent address.

"Perhaps in France one can find some people who will take my defense, who recognize the innumerable difficulties that surround me," replied the pope. "I know very well that politically the institutions that I have given are very incomplete. The sovereign power remains intact. It is not shared. But I could not do anything more. Nor," he added, "is one convinced by many examples that Italy is made for, or at least is now ready for, democracy."

Pursuing this last point, Pius asked Rayneval how many of all the constitutions recently granted in Italy were still in effect. The king of Naples had jettisoned his, as had the grand duke of Tuscany. Only the Kingdom of Sardinia had kept its constitution, and it had proven disastrous for the monarchy, said the pope. In the past year and a half, the king had gone through eight different prime ministers. "If the purely temporal sovereigns have to suffer so much pain, given the difficulties of a regime that allows free speech in Italy," he asked, "how do you think the pope, who has so many interests to look after, could overcome it?"

As a proud Italian, Pius had once shared the dream of an Italy free of foreign rule, but he had never thought very deeply about how this might happen, much less pondered its implications for the papacy and the church. If he had, he would have realized that his beliefs in the prerogatives of the papacy clashed with the liberal ideals fueling the move for

Italian independence. In his first encyclical, in 1846, he had spoken of the divine right of Europe's monarchs. "We hope," he had said in *Qui pluribus*, "that Our political leaders will keep in mind in accordance with their piety and religion, that 'the kingly power has been conferred on them not only for ruling the world but especially for the protection of the Church.'" It was God who had entrusted the kings with the right to rule and, in granting them this great power, demanded that they protect the rights of the church and its pope-king. This was the world that Pius knew, the world that God had willed, and the only one in which the church would be safe. Should the forces propelling an independent Italy prevail, he now realized, the Papal States would not long survive.[5] Pius told Rayneval:

> Don't fool yourselves. The Italian liberals, the advanced liberals, those who would most quickly come to power, have only one idea in their heads: unification. An impractical idea, an idea that will lead only to heartbreak here and perhaps in the end to foreign domination. Just because France succeeded in establishing its unity, should it be assumed that Italy can do the same? Is it in its nature? Is it something it needs? . . . You French, you have your faults, most certainly, but you have a prodigious instinct for nationality. You are always ready to sacrifice yourselves for your country. Have you seen anything similar in Italy? Unification is a wild dream, but a dream that the advanced party pursues relentlessly. . . . And the sovereigns among whom Italy is divided are obstacles that they must remove. . . . But among these obstacles the greatest of all is the Pope. Putting an end to the Pope's sovereignty is, for them, to accomplish three-quarters of their goal.[6]

As he often did after visiting with the pope, Rayneval went to see Antonelli. Again, Rayneval tried to persuade the cardinal not to delay the pope's return to Rome. Now that those whom the pope had been so worried about were in exile or in prison, what reason could there be to wait any longer?

The problem, the cardinal replied, was that their treasury was bare.

The pope could not return empty-handed. He had to be able to pay government employees, fund rebuilding projects, and distribute charity. In short, he needed a large loan. During Gregory's papacy, the Holy See had taken out several such loans, most from the Rothschild banking family, lenders to governments throughout Europe. Antonelli had again turned to the Rothschilds, and until those talks were concluded, he said, Pius could not return. So it was that, in another of history's ironies, at the same time that he was forcing the Jews back into the ghetto, the pope was counting on Europe's most prominent Jews to come to his rescue.[7]

In late September, General Rostolan renewed his request to Paris to accept his resignation. At the same time, Corcelle told Tocqueville that he wanted to resign as well, saying that he no longer had confidence in the course that the foreign minister was asking him to pursue. "Replace me," he wrote his old friend on October 2, "as soon as possible." In two weeks, he said, he could tie up loose ends and be ready to leave. "I write you with this firm decision with much calm and without the least bitterness. We have not had the same opinion on this immense and difficult affair. That is all. It will not in the least harm our good friendship."[8]

As Corcelle waited for a response, he continued to pepper the foreign minister with his complaints. "I still find in your personal letters very little goodwill toward the Church," he wrote. "How could you compare the Church to a Turkish camp on the banks of the Bosporus? That is not worthy of you. I no longer understand anything of your witticisms on this question. . . . To deal with the Church, the first requirement is to know the Church, and I should even add . . . to love it. . . . What a shame that you are Protestant!"[9]

On receiving Corcelle's letter of resignation, Tocqueville, who, while not a very observant Catholic, was hardly a Protestant, hurriedly penned a reply. He could only hope, he wrote, that Corcelle's decision was not irrevocable. Everyone knew that he was Tocqueville's close friend. To have him so publicly repudiate Tocqueville's policies would be deeply harmful.[10]

Tocqueville's letter had the desired effect. After vowing that he would never do anything to hurt his friend, Corcelle agreed to stay. But the tension between the two remained.[11]

———

IN ROME, MONSIGNOR SAVELLI, the bulldog, had been wasting no time putting the pope's plan into action. On September 24 he sent a new order to Rome's police:

> By force of that Notification issued by His Holiness's express wish, all individuals who are excluded from the pardon that has been conceded, either because they had taken part in the provisional government, or taken part in the deliberations of the Constituent Assembly, or been members of the republican Triumvirate, or heads of military units, or those who, having given their word after the earlier amnesty, got involved in the recent political unrest . . . must be immediately arrested and subjected to the justice of the competent Criminal Tribunal.[12]

Two weeks later a new body, a board of censors, was created. It was to identify all those teachers and professors who had taken part in the recent "political turmoil" and judge whether they should be allowed to continue to occupy their positions.[13]

Among the problems facing papal authorities was reining in the city's youths, many of whom had been enthusiastic participants in the battle against the priests. In mid-October, Rome's cardinal vicar received an anonymous complaint about Rome's night schools for children, established by the republican government but still in operation after its fall.

> It was as beautiful for a Republican as it was painful for a true Catholic to see bands of these young people prancing through the streets loudly shouting songs against Religion, against the Holy Father, and against all of the Ecclesiastical Hierarchy. . . . After the entry of the French, and the restoration of the Papal Government, they had the temerity in one of the night schools to shout *Papal Pig! Long Live the Roman Republic.*

That the schools were still allowed to operate, complained the informer, was a scandal.[14]

A religious revolution was under way, Rome's police prefect confided to the French colonel Niel. Disgusted with the papal regime, many Romans now, he thought, wanted to become Protestant. Niel, in relating this conversation to his brother, said it brought to mind the story about the Jew who came to Rome. The man was so struck by the amount of corruption among the priests there that he decided to be baptized on the spot. This must be the true religion, he explained, if it could have survived for so long with such horrendous ministers.[15]

"The greatest discontent prevails at Rome," reported a British envoy in early October, as each new action of the cardinals' commission generated greater hostility. "Every act of theirs has shown the strongest tendency to retrograde principles and to the adoption of the abuses of the old priestly rule. . . . The Pope is now undoubtedly swayed by entirely opposite principles to those formerly entertained by him."[16]

Nor was the pope's popularity in Rome being helped by his recent move into the Neapolitan king's magnificent palace outside Naples. "His continuous excursions, his sumptuous visits," observed the Austrian consul, "while Rome's ruins still smolder . . . are interpreted in a way that is most harmful to the affection and respect that these people were accustomed to show the heads of the Church." Why, the Romans asked, did the pope not do as Pius VII, driven into exile by Napoleon, had done and live simply, spending his days praying to God to protect his people? "Pio Nono," observed a British journalist of the time, "has taken a fancy to the Neapolitan soil, as well as, I fear, an aversion to his own, and he seems too happy in the quiet and security of the one to be in any hurry to engage in the turmoils of the other." There was some truth to this picture, for the pope did view the prospect of returning to his restive capital with great trepidation. Although he was not entirely comfortable living in Ferdinand's palace, he basked in the flattery and the attention the royal family showered on him there.[17]

Others were coming to the same conclusion: the pope's embrace of King Ferdinand was taking a toll. "I am again the witness of horrors," observed the British naval captain Key in Naples on October 6. "This ill-advised King of Naples is arresting everyone who took part, or is supposed to have wished to take part, in any of the disturbances which have taken place since January '48. A reign of terror exists. No one on going to bed feels sure that he will not be in prison before morning." The French ambassador was of the same view: "The terror is always at a fever pitch. Everyone feels threatened, pursued. They are living in a state of siege, war councils, and bloody executions." The police and courts, Rayneval reported, "display the most uncontrollable zeal and strike . . . at the most honorable of men." In the pope's frequent trips into Naples to visit the city's convents, he observed, "one is always struck by how little enthusiasm, how little sign of veneration one finds along the way."[18]

IN MID-OCTOBER, LOUIS NAPOLEON's need to get a new round of funding for the Roman expedition led to another lengthy debate in the French Assembly. Among those speaking in opposition to the request was Victor Hugo. Gesturing dramatically, the famed author spoke warmly of the letter the president had sent to Rome, contrasting it with the pope's response, in the form of his recent *motu proprio* outlining his plan for restored papal government.

> A huge distance separates them. The one says yes, the other says no! It is impossible to escape the dilemma posed by these things. You absolutely have to say that one of them is wrong. If you approve the letter, you disapprove the *motu proprio*. If you accept the *motu proprio*, you disavow the letter. You have, on one side, the president of the Republic, calling for freedom for the Roman people, in the name of a great nation that, for three centuries has brought enlightenment . . . to the civilized world. On the other side, you have Cardinal Antonelli, refusing, in the name of the clerical government. Choose![19]

"Pope Pius IX," wrote Hugo some time later, "is simple, sweet, timid, fearful, slow in his movements, negligent about his person . . . one would say a country priest." He added, "Beside him, Antonelli, in his red stockings, with his look of a diplomat and the eyebrows of a spy, resembles nothing so much as an unsavory bodyguard."[20]

After three days of debate, Tocqueville—not known for his skills as an orator—got up to speak. He had dreaded this moment. He certainly could not tell the truth. How could he tell the deputies that the pope was committed to a return to the old theocracy and that the French government had, against the express wishes of the Assembly, used the nation's military might to destroy a republic, end constitutional rule, and restore a government widely viewed as a vestige of medieval times? How could he admit that far from acting to thwart the ambitions of Austria, France's bitter rival, the government had done exactly what the Austrians wanted it to do?

The French government, Tocqueville told the members of the National Assembly, had made a series of demands. The basic principles contained in Rome's 1848 constitution had to be retained, most important those protecting individual freedoms. The courts had to guarantee people's basic rights. Municipal and provincial assemblies, composed of members elected by the people, had to be created. Laypeople must replace priests in the government.

Tocqueville then went on to say that, while negotiations were still in progress, the pope—despite all appearances—had made known his intention to embrace the path of reform. At that point, the voices of derision from the left became too loud for the foreign minister to continue.

"Can you, messieurs, doubt the word of the Holy Father?" Tocqueville asked when he could once again be heard. On saying these words, pronounced in the purest bad faith, Tocqueville became overcome with emotion, or perhaps simply by a guilty conscience. He struggled to regain his composure.

Because he had faith in Pius IX, said Tocqueville when he was able to continue, he was confident that the French mission would succeed. "I believe it," he told the deputies, "because in answering our prayers, he will only be persevering in this grand design . . . of reconciling freedom with faith and continuing to play the great role that he has so gloriously begun." Here again Tocqueville had to stop amid the laughter from the benches on the left. Only repeated calls to order by the Assembly president allowed the foreign minister to complete his remarks.

Two days later, following hours of raucous debate, the deputies cast their votes. Although the voices from the left had been loud, their numbers were far too few to carry the day. The motion to continue funding the Rome mission was approved.[21]

ON THE MORNING OF October 28, Rayneval, in Naples, having received word of the French Assembly vote, rushed to Portici, where he found the pope with King Ferdinand. Both were pleased to hear the news, the pope especially effusive. "It is very clear," said Pius, "that God is protecting us."[22]

Rayneval had new worries. He had recently heard rumors that the pope, his fears fanned by Cardinal Antonelli, had decided not to return to Rome until he could find a way to get other, more congenial military forces to replace the French troops there.

The ambassador sought out the secretary of state. "Waiting for the French to cede their position to others," he warned Antonelli, "is to count on the impossible. We will withdraw when the pope is in a position to rule by himself and when the other armies have also left. How," he asked, "could we imagine leaving the Papal States as long as the Austrian army continues to occupy it?" The pope needed to get back to Rome and, with French help, organize his own papal army so that all the foreign forces could go. "What then are the difficulties?" asked Rayneval. "Show us the obstacles, and we will make them disappear."

Finding the cardinal inscrutable, the ambassador went to see the pope. "Don't worry," said the pontiff, trying to calm him down. "I will return to Rome, and I will return there soon. I am not talking about January or February. That would be much too late. The time has come." This, however, did not mean that he no longer had any concerns, for, he told Rayneval, he had recently learned of "sinister" plots aimed against him in Rome. "Not that I fear for my own person," Pius quickly added. "I am in God's hands. But it is necessary to prevent new misfortunes."[23]

Despite all the unhappiness in Rome, the pope did have some reason to believe that people would be glad to have him back. Many Romans' livelihoods depended on having the papacy in Rome, for the city's role as the worldwide center of Roman Catholicism was its lifeblood. The Austrian consul in Rome explained:

I am convinced that the Holy Father will be received with all the dignity and demonstrations of respect that are due to him, for it is an indisputable fact that the people are all more or less "papal." Their interests are too tied to the presence of the head of the Church. They are too frustrated by his absence, and the habits, the way of life, even their customs are too linked to the specialty of ecclesiastical government to be able to give it up all at once. Moreover, today the Romans are everywhere eager to return to the old state of tranquility which promises them the advantages of a comfortable life. This desire can only be realized by the presence of the pope in Rome. Today everyone understands this truth, and though the government is doing little to end the abuses of the previous administration—something in truth not easy to do— and while the organization of the different branches of the judiciary and of finance are regulated on the most intolerable basis, he will find sympathy everywhere.[24]

AMONG ROME'S MOST ANXIOUS inhabitants, the city's four thousand Jews, now crowded back into their insalubrious ghetto, waited to learn their fate. The freedom that Pius IX had once granted them to leave the ghetto without getting a special license had been revoked. Once again, in order to travel they needed to get a special permit from the Holy Office of the Inquisition to be shown to the authorities at every town they passed through. For the Jews, it was a source of mortification. The Roman Republic's proclamation of freedom for all was now only a memory.[25]

The raid on the ghetto began early one morning when it was still dark. At four a.m. on October 25, French troops took up positions at the ghetto's gates, preventing anyone from entering or leaving. Along the Tiber, which bordered the ghetto on one side, several police boats docked. The papal officers stepped out of their boats and entered the ghetto's narrow, labyrinthine streets. There they barged into homes, ransacking them in search of goods that had been taken from church property and from aristocrats' palaces during the recent months of republican rule.[26]

Identifying the Jews with the forces that had overthrown the pope's rule offered the papal government a means of winning back the support of Rome's *popolani*. The *Giornale di Roma*, the city's official paper, gave prominence to the story. "It being notorious that many objects stolen in the days of the past anarchy were sold to the Jews," reported the paper, "in the night preceding the 25th the police surrounded the Ghetto and proceeded to search the homes."

The searches lasted two full days. In homes where police found suspicious objects, they arrested the Jewish family head and marched him to jail. Protests that the items were their own availed the Jews little. Church officials were eager to publicize all the treasures said to have been discovered in the ghetto. The list was long although rather modest: cardinals' red skullcaps, linens from church altars, lace surplices of priests, copper dishes, and many silver vases, sugar bowls, forks, spoons, and knives.[27]

Curiously, the police report on the raid justified it not by any evidence that stolen goods had been found in the ghetto but by anger at the Jews for having embraced the recent republican government. "The Jews in general nourished an indescribable hatred for the Pontifical Government," charged the police report, "and a true pleasure for the Anarchic Government, not showing any shame in being in the first ranks of the Demagogues, in the city government, in the clubs, and in other places where the sects meet." It could not have escaped the notice of papal authorities that two Jews had been elected to the Constituent Assembly, and three others had served on Rome's city council.[28]

Aware that Tocqueville would be newly outraged by this news, Corcelle—perhaps sharing in the popular prejudices against the Jews but in any case eager to keep Tocqueville's unhappiness with the pope from growing even greater—wrote to assure him that the searches had been prompted by reasonable suspicions and were in full compliance with the law. The ghetto raid, the French envoy added, was met by "the great applause of the entire population, who were beginning to think that [the Jews] were being treated as a privileged class."[29]

———

By the time Corcelle's note arrived in Paris, his old friend was in fact no longer foreign minister. In a move that would prove to be the first step on a course that would soon lead to the French Republic's demise, Louis Napoleon announced that he wanted a ministry that better reflected his own views. His existing cabinet was composed in good part of the men he had appointed shortly after becoming president, when, as a little known newcomer, he needed the support of notables from some of the most influential groups in the Assembly. Now that he felt more secure, he was eager to free himself from men who had their own political followings and their own agendas. His new cabinet would be composed of men of little political weight, many drawn from the military, accountable to him alone. Odilon Barrot, the defenestrated prime minister, expressed alarm at what he referred to as Napoleon's "coup d'état." But while many members of the French Assembly were shocked by the move, they made little effort to oppose it.[30]

Louis Napoleon also decided to dismiss Corcelle, whom he viewed as too close to Tocqueville, and to recall General Rostolan from Rome as well. The roles of head of the expeditionary army and ambassador to the Holy See were to be combined and placed in the hands of a career military officer. For this, the president chose a man of the monarchist right, fifty-four-year-old General Achille Baraguey d'Hilliers.

Surprisingly, Napoleon announced his intention to replace Tocqueville, his foreign minister, not with a military man or with someone known to be close to him but rather with the French ambassador in Naples, Alphonse de Rayneval.

Rayneval was in bed in Naples with a painful case of gout when he received the unexpected news. The honor of an appointment to be foreign minister was great, the confidence shown by the president flattering. But the uncertainties over what path Louis Napoleon planned to follow, the risks of casting himself as the architect of a foreign policy whose outlines he did not know, and the fact that he personally knew none of the military men who would be his cabinet colleagues all made him uneasy. The courier returned to Paris not with Rayneval but with

General
Achille Baraguey
d'Hilliers

the ambassador's note explaining why he could not accept the appointment. He gave as his excuse his lack of parliamentary experience and his unfamiliarity with the political situation in France, having been abroad for so long. Spurned by Rayneval, Louis Napoleon would turn to yet another general to replace Tocqueville. A new era was about to begin.[31]

CHAPTER 21

"THOSE WICKED ENEMIES OF GOD"

HE MEN AROUND THE POPE CONTINUED TO WARN HIM AGAINST returning to Rome, reluctant to move to a city seething with hostility to the clergy and under French control. In November they had told him that Mazzini had dispatched twenty-four assassins to Rome from his hideout in Switzerland. That same month Roman police arrested eleven people planning a banquet to celebrate the first anniversary of Rossi's assassination. "The return to Rome," observed Rayneval, "is the object of great repugnance and great terror."[1]

General Baraguey, the new French ambassador, had arrived in mid-November and moved into the imposing Colonna Palace in the center of Rome. He was eager to present his credentials to the pope but was delayed by a quarantine in effect in Naples, aimed at preventing the spread of France's cholera epidemic. As he waited for clearance for his visit, he sent his first impressions to Paris. They were not encouraging:

> The Holy Father ought not to ignore the fact . . . that people's misery and disaffection are growing every day, not only in Rome but also in the provinces. . . . The prolongation of the absence of the head of the state reinforces the opinion that has already spread among many people that his presence is not indispensable for the conduct of public affairs. The numerous arrests are everywhere making him enemies, because the three cardinals justify their ac-

tions as based on his orders. It seems that everything is being done to alienate people.[2]

Winning a reduction of quarantine to ten days, Baraguey was allowed to disembark at Naples on November 29. The next morning he met the pope for the first time. "I was well received, if a bit coolly," he reported. Baraguey was a general, not a diplomat. What he lacked in tact, he made up for by a highly developed sense of French national honor. His failure to show deference either to cardinals or to aristocrats would lead both to regard him warily.

As Baraguey entered, the pope held in his hand a recent letter from Louis Napoleon. It made clear that Napoleon would no longer be pressing his earlier list of demands and so, in effect, repudiated his August letter. The French president had jettisoned Barrot, his prime minister, a longtime opponent of the temporal power of the papacy, and Tocqueville, his foreign minister, who had been so embarrassed to find himself overseeing the restoration of the papal theocracy. Given his own efforts to reduce the power of France's National Assembly, Louis Napoleon no longer had much interest in trying to limit the pope's authority over his subjects. Instead, his letter simply called on the pope to show mercy.

"The President urges me to show leniency," said the pope, annoyed. "But he also speaks of justice." Justice, Pius told Baraguey, required that those guilty of rebelling against him be punished.

"The pope now fears the Roman people," concluded the general. He had tried to reassure the pontiff that the French had matters firmly in hand and that no harm would befall him should he return to his capital. But, reported the new French ambassador, rather than showing gratitude for all that the French had done for him, the pope—and Cardinal Antonelli with him—had only complaints.[3]

Returning two days later, Baraguey pressed the pontiff to set a date for his return. Again Pius gave voice to his fears. "He tells me of the stilettos, the daggers, of the large number of malicious subjects in the city, of the need to disarm them. . . . In vain I tried to reassure him, saying 'I accept all responsibility.'" Baraguey told the pope he would take "the most severe measures" to guarantee his safety, but, the general reported, "my pleas were useless. He is surrounded by bad advisors who take advantage of his terrors."[4]

IF THERE REMAINED ANY doubts that Pius was now committed to a path of reaction, he dispelled them early in December with his first encyclical since regaining control of Rome. Addressed to all Italy's archbishops and bishops, its language could hardly have been harsher. His first sentences offer something of its flavor:

> You know as We do, venerable brothers, the recent wrongdoing which has strengthened some wretched enemies of all truth, justice, and honor, who strive both openly and deceitfully with plots of every sort to spread their disorders everywhere among the faithful people of Italy. These disorders include the unbridled license of thinking, speaking and hearing every impious matter. They spread these like the foaming waves of a savage sea, and they exert themselves not only to shake the Catholic religion in Italy itself but if possible to utterly destroy it.

While, thanks to "God's mercy and the arms of Catholic nations," Rome and the Papal States had been restored, said the pope:

> Nonetheless, those wicked enemies of God and men still continue their lawless work, if not by open force, at least in other deceitful ways. . . . We cannot restrain Our tears, when We see that some Italians now are so wicked and so wretchedly deceived that they admire the vile teachings of impious men. In fact, they are not afraid to plot with them for this great destruction of Italy.

The pope's embrace of a medieval vision of society could not have been clearer. Quoting the New Testament (Romans 13:1–2), he told Italy's bishops: "There is no authority except from God. . . . Therefore he who resists authority resists what God has appointed, and those who resist will incur their own condemnation." He turned as well to Saint

Augustine, reminding the bishops of Augustine's admonition that the Catholic Church

> teaches slaves to remain true to their masters, not as much from the compulsion of their state as from delight in duty, and makes masters kind to their slaves by the thought that the supreme God is their common Lord. . . . It teaches kings to take care of their people, and people to submit to their kings.[5]

Although the pope mentioned men many times in his encyclical, he made only one reference to women, and that in his opening paragraph. "In their wicked recklessness," said the pope, the rebels in Rome had pushed aside the loyal clergy. "Consequently, when some of their own number fell sick and struggled with death, they were deprived of all the help of religion and compelled to breathe their last in the arms of a wanton prostitute." The pope appeared to refer here to the women who had served as nurses to the wounded and dying in Rome. In the lands ruled by the popes, nuns served as nurses but only for female patients. Those few orders that allowed their nuns to minister to sick men did so only when they could act through a male intermediary.[6]

The following month, the former head of the Roman Republic's nursing corps, Princess Cristina Belgiojoso, stung by the pope's words, responded in a letter. "Holy Father," she wrote:

> I read in a French newspaper part of Your Holiness's encyclical to the bishops of Italy in which . . . Your Holiness adds that those victims were forced to die in the arms of prostitutes. As the introduction of women into Rome's hospitals was my work . . . I believe it my duty to respond to Your Holiness's accusations. . . . The hospitals were all always provided with priests, and . . . not one of the many victims, so rightly lamented by Your Holiness, died without the assistance of a priest and the comfort of the sacraments. If Your Holiness is unaware of this fact, your representatives certainly are not because, no sooner had the Cardinals assumed the powers that Your Holiness conferred on them, than all the priests who had exercised their sacred ministry in the hos-

pitals were thrown into the prisons of the Holy Office of the Inquisition.[7]

The arrests and imprisonments continued. "The accounts I receive
from Rome," reported the British ambassador to Turin, "are deplorable.
'La vendetta Pretina' [the priests' revenge] is in full operation, and the
French are there, tranquil spectators of all that occurs. I hear nothing
about the Pope's return and indeed, how can he shew his face at Rome,
when such excesses are committed with his sanction, and such an insane
course of policy is followed by those acting in his name."

The patriot
princess
Cristina
Belgiojoso

For his part, Cardinal Antonelli, mastermind of the repression, was frustrated by the continuing interference of French authorities. When Baraguey attempted to prevent the arrest of papal army officers compromised by their participation in the Roman Republic, Antonelli complained to Rayneval. Had French officers acted as these men had, he told the ambassador, you "would have simply taken them out to be shot."[8]

THE POPE DECIDED TO spend the Christmas holidays with King Ferdinand in his palace at Caserta, twenty-two miles north of Naples. As Pius prepared to leave on December 24, he met with Rayneval, who again asked when he would return to Rome. Again the pope cited the need for the loan from the Rothschilds, but it was something else that most worried him. "The hatred of the priests," confided the pope, "is still very much alive."[9] The cardinal deacon of the Sacred College had himself recently cautioned Pius against returning. Rome, warned the cardinal, was still filled with many

> demagogues and not a few individuals capable of committing any crime, with the police not free to do their work. People speak publicly in the cafés against the pope, against the cardinals, and against the clergy, and the revolutionaries are still bold and threatening. I know that they want Your Holiness's prompt return to Rome to remedy so many evils. But will You have the means to put an end to so much discord, and to reestablish good religious, moral and political order, lacking the material force sufficient to ensure that You are obeyed?[10]

In their efforts to prevent the pope from returning to Rome, the cardinals got strong support from King Ferdinand, eager to continue to benefit from his status as the pope's royal protector. "There is a powerful party, with the King as its head," reported Rayneval on the last day of 1849, "that is trying to keep the Pope far from his States." They were using all sorts of pretexts, but, the French ambassador observed, their true motivation was one they would not admit. "They do not trust the

Pope, his instincts, his tendencies. . . . They fear, in a word, that he may pass from one camp to the other."[11]

To MARK NEW YEAR'S Eve, Rome's new city government ordered the Corso festively decorated and papal banners hung. But people were not in a festive mood, and well-aimed rocks smashed the lanterns bearing the papal coat of arms that the pope's supporters had placed in their windows.

Having returned to Portici, Pius hosted the members of the diplomatic corps on New Year's Day, as was his custom. His tone was uncharacteristically chastened. "We must have confidence in Providence," he said, "but it is wise not to have any illusions. . . . Many difficulties and many dangers remain."[12]

As 1850 began, Luigi Carlo Farini—medical doctor, historian of Italian unification, and, in the early 1860s, one of the Kingdom of Italy's first prime ministers—captured the sense of repression felt in the newly restored Papal States:

> Both education and charity governed and administered by the clergy. Clerical police and French police in Rome, clerical police and Austrian police in the provinces. Censorship of the press administered . . . not by any law, but by the whim of the Holy Office of the Inquisition, the bishops, the police. . . . All the old civil, communal, ecclesiastical, mixed, and exceptional tribunals restored. . . . All the old immunities and privileges of the clergy restored. . . . The Jesuits resurgent and more powerful. . . . The prisons full.[13]

If the pope worried about his subjects' hostility to papal rule as the New Year dawned, he also remained nervous about his financial situation. Discussions with the Rothschilds had begun almost a year earlier and had continued in Paris, where James Rothschild, head of the banking family in France, met frequently with the papal nuncio.[14]

"It seems more and more clear to us," the new French foreign minister, General Jean-Ernest de la Hitte, wrote to Baraguey on the first of the year, "that the question of the Holy Father's return to his states is tied to the conclusion of a loan. So we continue to do all that we can to facilitate it and speed it." A few days later he sent an update from Paris: "I have just learned that Monsieur Rothschild is motivated by the best intentions for the conclusion of the loan negotiated with the Holy See. He has received a very favorable impression of the news that he received about the Pope's intentions with regard to his fellow Jews."[15]

The pope, who had ordered the Jews of the Papal States back into their ghettos, now depended on the goodwill of Europe's most prominent Jews to be able to return to his capital. The Rothschilds, for their part, found themselves under great pressure from their coreligionists. It was not a new position for them. Ever since the Rothschilds had become bankers to the popes, Jewish communities of the Papal States had begged them to use their influence to relieve their suffering. In the first year of Pius's reign, the officers of Rome's Jewish community had sent the pope a petition asking for modest improvement in the condition of the ghetto. Having gotten no reply, they had sent a copy of the petition to Salomon Rothschild, director of the bank in Vienna, pleading for his aid. In response, Rothschild met with the papal nuncio and urged him to persuade the pontiff to help Rome's Jews. Perhaps it was this request that prompted the pope to take the modest actions he did in the first two years of his reign, allowing some Jews to leave the ghetto and tearing down the ghetto gates.[16]

"The pope's return to Rome is decidedly dependent on the conclusion of the loan," wrote the French foreign minister to Rayneval on January 10, 1849. "The discussions [in Paris] with Monsieur [James] Rothschild continue. His pretentions are a little much. Cardinal Antonelli has urged me to see him and convince him to be more moderate." Rothschild's "pretentions" were aimed at the pope's treatment of the Jews. Before making the loan, he wanted Pius to agree to abolish Rome's ghetto and allow Jews to own real estate, practice commerce freely, and attend the university.[17]

In trying to get Rothschild to drop these demands, the papal nuncio in Paris, acting as an intermediary in the negotiations, rehearsed arguments long used by the Holy See to justify its treatment of the Jews. The popes, the nuncio argued, were acting only in the Jews' own best interests. If the popes closed the Jews in the ghetto, it was only to protect them from the hostility of their Christian neighbors.[18]

As a man for whom French pride loomed larger than Catholic devotion, General Baraguey was quickly becoming disenchanted with the pope. The papal court, he thought, was using the loan negotiations merely as a pretext to keep Pius from Rome. The French had expected him to return to his capital as soon as they reestablished papal rule there. It was a great embarrassment that he seemed so reluctant to leave the embrace of the king of Naples, a disinclination that could only be seen as a vote of no confidence in the French. Now, months after Harcourt had argued that they could persuade the pontiff to do what was needed only by giving him an ultimatum, Baraguey reached the same conclusion: "The only means to get [the pope] to follow a policy in keeping with our dignity and our interests would be, I believe, . . . to set a date beyond which our troops would be withdrawn to Civitavecchia. At the same time we would warn the courts of Vienna and Portici of our firm intention not to allow any foreign force to replace us here."

On issuing such a declaration, Baraguey realized, France would have to be prepared to wage war should the other powers not heed their warning. He acknowledged that France might well not want to take this risk but argued that there was no honorable alternative.

There was another reason, suggested Baraguey, why France should follow this course. The pope and a number of the foreign ambassadors had made clear their desire to have some combination of the armed forces of Austria, Naples, and Spain replace the French in safeguarding papal rule in Rome. The offense to French national honor of withdrawing from Rome, only to see their rivals' armies occupy the city, would certainly be too great to bear.

"Naples," added Baraguey, "seems to me to have become a center of evil designs against us. They work to spread rumors of the instability of the French government. Each day they spread word of a new revolution, and everyone is united in urging the Holy Father to put off his return." He concluded his letter to the French foreign minister, a fellow general, with a rousing call to arms:

If France does not take a vigorous stance, if, despite the fact that it is able to, it does not speak loudly and firmly, if it does not say that it is ready to support its will by the force of arms, but instead goes from one concession to another, I do not know where it will all lead us.

You ask me to have patience and perseverance. I believe, thank God, I possess both these qualities. But when this patience takes on the appearance of self-deception, I do not believe in giving it new opportunities, because in this case, patience and forbearance greatly resemble weakness.[19]

"It is a heart-rending spectacle," observed Rayneval in early February, "to see the Holy Father's never-ending uncertainties. . . . To see such great matters entrusted to a person so unsure of himself, so influenced by the least incidents, one feels that doubts and fears for the future are all too well founded." Having heard from Antonelli that the Rothschild loan now seemed likely, he had held two long meetings with the pope, trying to get him to commit to a date to return to Rome.

Before entering Pius's room for the second of these meetings, Rayneval saw a delegation of Roman Jews leaving. What, asked the ambassador, had they wanted? The Jews, replied the pontiff, had come to complain about the police incursions into the ghetto and to ask for "privileges." As he spoke, Pius became ever more animated. The Jews had believed—or at least hoped—that the pope's dependence on the Rothschilds for a loan put them in a position to make demands on him. In fact, although it is not clear if either the pope or Rayneval knew it, before visiting the pope the Jewish delegation had first gone to Naples to meet with Charles Rothschild, head of the local family bank branch. They had begged the Rothschilds not to make the loan unless the pope first agreed to significant concessions.

"I urged these men," Pius told the French ambassador, "not to get too excited by Mr. Rothschild. I swear to you that if there is the least bit of a question of concessions to make to the Jews as a condition of the loan, three things would result: I would do nothing for the Jews; I would not take the loan; I would not return to Rome."

The pope added that even if he were inclined to grant the Jews any new rights, the anger that such a move would provoke among his Christian subjects would give him pause. When, in the early months of his papacy, he had authorized a few Jewish families to reside outside the ghetto, he recalled, "the complaints from the tenants in the buildings where the Jews lived were incessant. The same thing happened where they were allowed into public schools." Nor could the pope imagine allowing the Jews to own property, for soon, he feared, they would buy up much of the land in the Papal States, and that was unthinkable.[20]

With no other source in sight for his loan, a great deal depended on whether either side would back down. In the end, it was the Paris-based James Rothschild, the most influential of the brothers, who did. Under pressure from both the French and Austrian governments, and eager to keep both indebted to him, Rothschild agreed to settle for a generic papal promise. It came not directly from the pope or Antonelli but through French intermediaries. The pope, they said, could not be seen to condition a matter of theological importance—the treatment of the perfidious Jews—on receiving money from a Jewish family. But once he had the loan, he would, they assured Rothschild, relieve some of the restrictions on his Jewish subjects.[21]

Those who met with the pope in these weeks were struck by how changed he seemed. A monsignor from one of the offices of the Curia in Rome, having come to visit the pontiff, was surprised to find the formerly benevolent pope so sour. The first thing the pope asked him was whether he had purged his office of all the miserable men who had continued to work there during the republic.[22]

Pius dreaded the prospect of returning to his capital. The contrast between the early days of his papacy, when he was the object of popular adulation, and the sullen population he knew he would face on his return upset him. He nursed a strong sense of outrage at how poorly the people had repaid him for all he had done for them and embarrassed by how few of his subjects had spoken up for him, how readily they had abandoned him. At the same time, he was surrounded by cardinals who faulted him for his earlier concessions and his weakness. One of the few of their number sympathetic to Pius's plight tried to defend him to the French: "What do you want the poor pope to do? He is a prisoner, surrounded by his enemies who only let those who are hostile to him or who can redouble his fears get near him." So battered was the pope, recalled the cardinal, that when he last went to see him, he found him weeping in his oratory. How, the pope had asked him, could he ever return to a city that was full of his enemies?[23]

Pius seized on one excuse after another to delay his return. "Every day," lamented the pope's nephew, who had been pushing his uncle to move back to Rome, "another mushroom sprouts up."[24]

CARNIVAL, NORMALLY A TIME for joyous abandon, was fast approaching, but as the repression ground on, Rome was not in a festive mood. Antonelli had ordered the mail addressed to those of questionable sympathies opened and anything interesting sent to him in Portici. On their arrival in Rome, all foreign newspapers were read by censors before—if deemed inoffensive—they were sent on to their subscribers. The French placed warnings on the walls that anyone found with a gun or a knife would be summarily executed, but the notices were ripped down as quickly as they could be put up. In mid-February a man from Trastevere was placed in front of a firing squad in Piazza del Popolo, charged with having killed a French soldier. The next week, in another piazza, a large crowd gathered to watch the execution of a forty-year-old man caught the night before carrying arms.[25]

While the French were having difficulty keeping their notices affixed to Rome's walls, the papal authorities were having trouble taking down all the subversive messages that were pasted up each night under cover of darkness. On the first anniversary of the proclamation of the Roman Republic, a message from Mazzini appeared:

Romans

You were great in your uprising, and you remain great in this time of disaster. Europe admired you as combatants for your freedom and for Italy's honor. . . . It admires you today for suffering with dignity without having any cowardly dealings with the internal enemy, and without dishonorable contact with the foreign armed forces that alone govern you. . . . Freedom shines forever and, sooner than others think, will wash away the tyrannical filth that now weighs you down. . . .

God blesses you o Romans! Your exiles today feel joined together with you in spirit on this first anniversary of the Republic. They will celebrate the second with you in the exhilaration of the common victory of the Campidoglio.

Long Live the Republic![26]

Eager to show that life in Rome was back to normal, papal authorities saw the traditional eight days of Carnival celebrations as an important test. The past year's festivities, shortly after the proclamation of the republic, had been an especially joyous affair, embarrassing to the official papal narrative of a people suffering under the yoke of a small band of cutthroat foreign fanatics. Now, hearing mutterings of a planned boycott of the first celebration following the return of papal rule, the government ordered all residents of the Corso—the main parade route—to cover their homes with decorations. Parish priests, who in previous years had warned their flock against the evils of Carnival celebration—traditionally a time of license and debauchery—now urged them to take part.

Despite all these efforts, the festival was an embarrassing failure. Few people decorated their homes, and in place of the endless parade of richly adorned carriages, the Corso seemed eerily empty. Those who might have been inclined to take part were warned off by clandestine flyers. In desperation, the police offered to pay some of the *popolani* to put on Carnival masks and hop into the carriages they provided, but the effect was more sordid than uplifting.[27]

Foolishly, a young aristocrat decided to brave the jeering crowd, climbing into his luxurious carriage and telling the driver to pass down the Corso. Alongside him sat his sixteen-year-old sister. As the horses pulled the carriage along, a large bouquet of flowers landed at the prince's feet. Picking it up to hand it to his sister, he noticed that it felt strangely heavy, for buried in the bouquet was a glass-covered bomb. It exploded, sending shrapnel into the prince's face, hand, and thigh and slicing through his sister's leg.[28]

CHAPTER 22

RETURNING TO ROME

On Monday, March 11, 1850, Cardinal Antonelli summoned the ambassadors of the four powers for the long-awaited announcement. Pius, he told them, would leave for Rome in early April, the week after Easter.[1]

Following the meeting, Rayneval went to see the pope, who clearly had mixed feelings about returning to his capital. "I cannot hide the fact," said Pius, "that I tread into dangers, or at least into embarrassments and countless difficulties. There is no worse task," he added, "than governing people as demoralized as the people are at the moment. Between the republicans, the constitutionalists, and the absolutists, each more extreme, more passionate than the other, my road ahead will be hard to travel." This time, it seemed, there would be no turning back. "The ordeal is inevitable," said the pope. "If I don't face it today I will have to face it tomorrow. There is no way to postpone it further, and with God's help, I will go at the announced time to take this heavy burden up once more."[2]

Declining the ship the French had offered for the voyage, Pius decided to travel by land. He felt confident that the rural people of the southernmost Papal States would greet him affectionately, offering proof that his subjects were eager to have him back. He was less confident about the reception that would greet him in Rome.

Antonelli threw himself into the work of ensuring the trip's success, bombarding the cardinals of Rome's governing commission with instructions. "News received by the police in Naples," wrote Antonelli in one of his memos, "express the certainty that, on the Holy Father's reentry into his dominion, the Roman demagogues plan to greet him with festive demonstrations of affection, thus gathering a large crowd, and then start shouting 'Long live the Constitution and the National Guard!'" The police, instructed Antonelli, had to find a way to thwart "their perverse plan."[3]

On April 3, the day before the pope's departure, Rayneval again went to see him, telling him how pleased France was that, despite all those who kept trying to frighten him, he was finally returning to Rome.

The pope remained nervous. "They have even told me," said the pontiff, "that France would return to its old demands, that it would impose a constitution and all that follows from it on me."

Rayneval reassured him. The French had long ago abandoned their demand that he reign as a constitutional monarch.[4]

THE DAY OF THE POPE's departure from Portici finally arrived. He first set out for the king's palace outside Naples to thank him for sheltering him for his many months in exile. On Pius's arrival, Ferdinand bowed and kissed the pope's foot and his hand. Pius remained with the royal family that night.[5]

The next morning the pontiff stepped onto the external balcony of Ferdinand's palace to offer his blessing to the small crowd that had gathered outside. He then walked down the grand marble staircase, pausing to let the members of the royal family, on their knees, kiss his foot. According to the official Neapolitan chroniclers, the princesses all had tears in their eyes. With royal troops lining its path, the richly adorned carriage carrying the pope and the king led a procession of seven carriages, each pulled by six horses. A long phalanx of Neapolitan cavalry rode in front and behind them. As the pope's carriage passed through the fields north of Naples, peasants took their hats into their hands, dropped to a knee, and bowed their heads.[6]

Ferdinand made the most of his final hours with the pope. Naples's official newspaper published a rapturous account of their parting at the northern border of the Neapolitan kingdom on April 6:

His Holiness, the king, and the duke . . . had barely gotten out of the carriage, when the king and the duke threw themselves at the Holy Father's feet, which they devoutly embraced. Then the king, still on his knees, asked for the sacred blessing. "Yes," said the Holy Father, "I bless you, I bless your family, I bless your kingdom, I bless your people. I cannot properly express to you my gratitude for the hospitality you have given me." "I only did my duty as a Christian," the king replied. "Yes," responded the pontiff, his voice heavy with emotion, "your filial affection was great and sincere." He then made the king rise. . . . He embraced him effusively and got back into his carriage, where the king, the royal prince and their entourage all kissed him on the foot.[7]

As Pius then made his way through the southernmost towns of his states, he passed through hastily erected triumphal arches, choirs singing odes of praise to him, and official delegations from nearby towns who came to pay their respects. Bishops and local elites jostled one another in efforts to greet him.

At Velletri, a town nestled in the Alban Hills thirty miles southeast of Rome, General Baraguey and his entourage met the pope to escort him the rest of the way to his capital. The general was eager, as he put it, "to completely banish the terrors that [the pope] has not stopped having."[8]

It was at Velletri, a year earlier, that Garibaldi had dealt King Ferdinand such an embarrassing blow. The scene now was very much changed. People's excitement that the pope would be coming to their town was great, the preparations frenetic. Local would-be sculptors fashioned faux classical figures, fastening them onto a hurriedly constructed triumphal arch. Over the doors of the city hall, half a dozen painters were inscribing paeans to Pius IX. One, in his enthusiasm, simply wrote, "Pio Nono. Immortal! Immortal! Immortal!" Others painted allegories of the pope, in one of which, oddly, he appeared in the shape of a female angel with her foot on a demon bearing the label "rebellion." A huge effigy of the pope, made of numerous sheets attached to wooden planks, hung atop the triumphal arch, fluttering perilously in the hill town's afternoon wind. A half-dozen town dignitaries milled about in evening dress, looking out of place among the roughly dressed peasants and artisans.

At last, in late afternoon, following a line of cavalry, the pope's carriage rolled into town. As Pius passed by, the troops presented arms, and the people knelt. The pontiff stopped in front of the town hall, but the awestruck local dignitaries were too tongue-tied to deliver the speeches of welcome they had so carefully prepared. The carriage door opened, and the pope put out his foot, as people elbowed their way to get close enough to kiss it. After a brief mass of thanksgiving in the cathedral, Pio Nono made his way to the palace perched at the crest of the town, in front of which thousands of people from Velletri and its hinterland had converged. Cannons blasted and music blared. Surrounded by priests holding torches aloft, Pius emerged on the balcony. As the people quieted, the pontiff stretched out his arms to bless them.[9]

There was reason to doubt that the pope would receive such a warm welcome when he reached his capital. "The people's mood is not favorable to any demonstrations of joy," reported the Tuscan ambassador in Rome. He explained:

> The remnants of the destruction and the disasters they have suffered are largely still there. Rome's appearance saddens any who see it again, even in these moments preceding the pope's return. The population, decimated by the war, by the banishments, by the jailings, and by the voluntary emigrations, makes the city seem empty. . . . Sadness and discouragement reign.[10]

The French were on high alert, as signs of trouble ahead abounded. Roman women, police were told, were planning a protest to embarrass the pontiff on his arrival. Leaflets containing Mazzini's calls for resistance had mysteriously appeared on city walls, and police interrupted three men as they piled pieces of wood against the door of the pope's Quirinal Palace, preparing to set it ablaze.[11]

At midafternoon on Friday, April 12, Pius finally appeared at the city's western gate. The last time he passed through one of Rome's gates, seventeen months earlier, he had been disguised as a country priest. Now on his triumphal return, the pealing of Rome's church bells greeted him, punctuated by the sound of 101 cannon blasts from Castel Sant'Angelo. The lumbering procession made its way to the vast sun-bathed piazza in front of the pope's cathedral, St. John Lateran, where a large crowd awaited. When the pope stepped out of his carriage, a cheer went up and handkerchiefs were waved, but as the London *Times* correspondent noted, "the enthusiasm that is valuable is that which does not boast of such a luxury as handkerchiefs. Very few people seemed to think it necessary to kneel, and, on the whole, the mass were more interested in the pageant itself." As Pius entered the vast cathedral, Rome's cardinal vicar, along with the three cardinals of the governing commission, greeted him. Prostrating themselves, members of the diplomatic corps, in their dark uniforms, kissed the pope's hand. Pius could not hide his emotion. Entering the nave of the church, he sank to his knees at the tomb of Peter and Paul to pray.

The papal procession then set out on its course to the other side of the city. Richly dressed papal soldiers led the way, followed by French cavalry, a detachment of Noble Guardsmen, and then the pope's own closed carriage, General Baraguey riding on one side, Prince Altieri, head of the Noble Guard, on the other. The French senior command followed on horseback, then other French troops, eight cardinals, each in his own luxurious carriage, members of the city government, and finally the twenty members of the diplomatic corps. Colorful tapestries and garlands of flowers adorned the buildings along the way. Lining the route, French troops dropped to a knee as the pope passed. The procession finally crossed the Tiber and reached St. Peter's Basilica, where other cardinals were waiting. Thousands of people were already inside, along with a line of French troops positioned against either wall. The pope entered, and a mass of thanksgiving was said. The cardinals then escorted the pope to his apartment in the adjoining Vatican Palace.

Pius IX would remain in Rome for another quarter century, but never again would he live in the Quirinal Palace. Its memories were too painful. His change of residence signaled something else as well. The Quirinal was first of all the symbol of political power, of the pope as king of the Papal States. The Vatican was the center of the pontiff's religious authority, worldwide in reach. The Pius who returned to Rome wanted as little as possible to do with the political role that had caused him so much heartache. For those matters, he would let Antonelli, more suited to that other world, take charge. Over the next years, as momentous historical changes took shape around him, the pope would retreat ever more into his religious role, finding solace in the spiritual realm. No more would he allow himself to be tortured by doubts about how best to deal with his people's endless political demands.[12]

The popular excitement that had greeted the pope in the hill town of Velletri was not repeated in Rome, although bright banners waved overhead and flowers littered the pope's path. Romans could not forget the recent bloodshed, and the sight of the pope, protected by the French army that had so recently conquered the city, produced mixed emotions. "Things went reasonably well," remarked the Dutch ambassador, "but without any enthusiasm, above all on the part of the population. . . . The Romans participated in this entry, or rather this return, as one takes part in a spectacle, guided by a simple instinct of curiosity, and the same as if tomorrow they were to take part in those that the Republic offered them, if it were to arise from its ashes."[13]

The French had hoped that once the pope was free from King Ferdinand's influence and firmly ensconced in his French-held capital, he would come around to their point of view. Although Louis Napoleon had reduced his pressure on the pope, the full-scale return of a medieval theocracy would still be a great embarrassment. But initial reports from Rome were not encouraging. Pius was showing no sign that the move to Rome had made him any more eager to follow French advice. "The conversations that I have had on this subject with the pope and Cardinal Antonelli," reported the French ambassador in late April,

are scarcely more satisfying than the reality, and I greatly fear that the status quo will be embraced for a long time to come as far as reforms of any kind are concerned. Moreover, I cannot repeat too often, the Holy Father is personally sympathetic to France, but the milieu in which he lives is profoundly hostile. In this respect nothing has changed. The pope is no freer in Rome than he was in

Gaeta or Portici. On the contrary, they are redoubling their efforts to diminish the influence that the Holy Father's return to Rome ought naturally have given to France.

All this, Baraguey predicted, augured poorly for the future, for unless the pope made significant reforms, he would never be able to rule except by foreign arms.[14]

The London *Times* correspondent in Rome painted a similar picture. "I am sorry to commence by saying that hitherto the Holy Father has, since his return, disappointed all his friends, and that not a single step has been taken to inspire confidence or hope. . . . The enthusiasm which the Pope's presence inspired is fast wearing away. . . . He is constantly in public, but the people scarcely notice his passing by."[15]

Caught up in the daily struggle to feed their families, most Romans wished only for the returned pope to be the same benevolent pontiff they had known from the early days of his papacy. But the flame of Italian patriotism still burned in the hearts of many, and the occasional murder of a French soldier or of a particularly reviled clergyman—their bloated black-robed bodies periodically fished out of the Tiber—kept tensions alive.

On April 30, the first anniversary of their victory over the initial French assault, Romans awoke to see a message painted in large red letters on the walls of several churches: "Priests, the blood of the martyrs screams for revenge!" A new leaflet flooded the city, with an ironic ode to the pope-king:

> *Rejoice o Pope, you are in Rome, you are on the throne, you are*
> *   king . . . your hands are soiled with blood. . . .*
> *So Rejoice o Pope, you are king. Like all the other Popes, you have*
> *   betrayed the fatherland, handing it over to foreigners. . . .*
> *You have called for war and carnage. . . . You have given your*
> *   blessing to a massacre! . . . So rejoice, o Pope, you are king!*[16]

Among those waiting in vain for signs of papal benevolence were the three thousand political prisoners languishing in the Papal States' jails. Five or six prisoners lived in a dark cell intended for one, with no blanket to keep them warm at night, breathing air rancid with the stench that wafted from their lidless latrines. Living on a diet of stale bread and beans, they quickly fell prey to disease. Among them were fifteen priests, found guilty a few weeks earlier of *lesa maestà*—revolt against the monarch. Monsignor Carlo Gazzola, a prominent Catholic intellectual, was imprisoned in Castel Sant'Angel, having been given a life sentence for "injuries to the person of the pope," inflicted through articles in a newspaper he edited. Hair-raising stories spread through Italy, such as the case of Giovanni Marchetti, director of a center for exercising horses, accused of having blackened the nose of a statue of Cardinal Lambruschini with the flame of a candle. Jailed in 1849, he was still awaiting trial two years later. Coughing up blood from the tuberculosis he had contracted in prison, he begged to be released to his family. His request was denied.[17]

On the pope's return to Rome, the cardinals' governing commission was disbanded. One man alone ran the papal government, the formidable Cardinal Antonelli. "Hated by many," as church historian Giacomo Martina described him, he was "virtually omnipotent in economic-administrative matters and in the defense of temporal power."[18]

While Antonelli grew in confidence, the pope himself also seemed changed. He was no longer so good-natured or eager to please. To the secretary of the city government who came humbly to beg for his old job back—having been dismissed for failing to abandon it when the pope had fled—Pius replied, "The time for mercy is over, it is now the time for justice." Visibly aged, prone to bouts of melancholy, apt to be more cautious and suspicious, Pius, who celebrated his fifty-eighth birthday shortly after his return to Rome, was also more given to outbursts of temper.[19]

Antonelli moved quickly to consolidate his power. In late June he began talking about reinstating the long-abandoned practice of allowing cardinals to visit the pope only by previous appointment. As it was, any cardinal could come to the pope's quarters and expect to see him. "The Sacred College, already not well disposed to Cardinal Antonelli," observed the Neapolitan envoy to Rome, in reporting the plan, "would with this new measure be even less well disposed. However, this shows that he feels strong and secure in his Sovereign's favor."[20]

Feeling considerably less secure in the pope's favor were the French. Rather than appreciate the protection that French troops now offered him, the pope made known how much he resented their embrace. "In short," complained Pius to Esterházy in late May, "in whose hands am I? In the hands of the French!" Just as the pope had feared, the French ambassador kept pushing him to announce reforms, warning that popular unhappiness was growing ever greater.[21]

Pius pushed back. Despite what the ambassador kept telling him, the pope told Baraguey, the fact that he had not yet announced any reforms was not causing any problems. Said the pope,

> I have now seen many delegations. Not one has uttered a word about it. When they have come to see me . . . it was to tell me: "in heaven's name, Holy Father, don't go and fall again into new dangers by establishing municipal elections on too broad a basis at a time when spirits are not yet sufficiently calmed down for general elections to lead to good results."[22]

It was now summer, a time when Romans who were wealthy enough escaped malaria season by retreating to their country estates in the hills. By the end of August, twelve hundred of the ten thousand French soldiers who remained in Rome were bedridden, feverish with the disease. Meanwhile the relentless pace of the arrests continued. "They imprison many," complained Rayneval, and "they only begin their interrogations months later."[23]

The executions continued as well. Before the recent upheavals, capital punishment had been meted out in Rome by a guillotine placed in the middle of a large piazza, as a crowd of the curious and the horrified looked on. Pius IX had had his first experience with the guillotine when, as bishop of Imola, he gave last rites to two convicted murderers moments before their execution. "I have seen the guillotine for the first time," he wrote a friend at the time. "The image is still with me, and I believe I will not forget the spectacle that I witnessed for many years."[24]

Rome's guillotine was among the casualties of the Roman Republic, demonstrators in those heady days having burned it in a celebratory blaze, retrieving the warm pieces of iron that remained from its ashes and throwing them into the Tiber. Forced as a result to rely on firing squads, papal officials discovered that their former method was much more reliable. One early October morning, in a particularly embarrassing episode, six men found guilty of committing a murder during the days of the republic were taken to the piazza facing the Church of Santa Maria in Cosmedin, famed for its *Bocca della Verità*, the Mouth of Truth. The pope had refused the men's appeal for leniency. A crowd gathered to watch. The signal sent, the soldiers opened fire, but their aim was poor. One of the condemned men found to his surprise that he had been only lightly wounded in a rib. *"Grazie,"* he said, apparently thinking that he was now spared. The officer in charge then ordered a second round fired. Only after a third round ripped through the survivors were all the men dead.[25]

When the pope first returned to Rome, Lewis Cass, the American chargé d'affaires, expressed hope that things would soon improve. Cardinal Della Genga had told him that Pius was a great admirer of the United States and its institutions, a statement the American reported credulously to Washington, along with assurances from another cardinal that the pope was eager to adopt a liberal constitution. When, shortly after Pius's return, Cass—who at that point had been in Rome for a year—finally got to meet him, the pope's warmth won him over. "He took me by the hand," recalled the ambassador:

> He spoke of his late efforts to introduce liberal reforms to his States and of the difficulties which he had encountered, adding that he had learned by painful experience that it required much caution and prudence to prepare his people for an order of things to which they had not been accustomed. Far from being disheartened, however, by the late untoward result of his political experiments, he stated, with a firmness and consistency which does him no small honor, it to be his intention to pursue the same course in the future, and on all practicable occasions to introduce into his government salutary measures of reform, which he admitted to be much needed.[26]

Over the following months, as all signs pointed to the return to the old theocratic ways, the American ambassador's optimism faded. What obedience to authority could be found in Rome, remarked Cass, was simply the result of coercion. The French troops had retreated from any involvement in public affairs, and, he reported, "the papal functionaries are no longer, in the slightest degree, restrained in the exercise of their accustomed duties."[27]

NONE IN ROME FELT more fearful than the Jews. With the founding of the Roman Republic, all legal restrictions on the Jews had been lifted, but they had barely begun to enjoy their freedom when the French army brought the pope back to power. Now the Jews lived in great anxiety. Would the old, benevolent Pius IX be returning, or would the chastened pope embrace the repressive measures of the past?

With evidence quickly accumulating that it was to be the latter, Rome's Jews turned once again to the Rothschilds. A week after the pope's return to Rome, the officers of the Jewish community sent a letter to Baroness Rothschild in Vienna. "In this state of painful uncertainty about our affairs, alternating between resignation and hope," they wrote, "we send you the present letter, praying that you will want to address a letter to Prince Schwarzenberg, minister of foreign affairs at the imperial court of Vienna, encouraging him to have the goodness to write an official note." Schwarzenberg, they hoped, would urge the pope to reinstate the concessions he had previously granted Rome's Jews.[28]

A few months later officers of the Jewish community prepared another long plea to the Rothschilds. After chronicling all the restrictions on the Jews that previous popes had imposed, they praised Pio Nono for having earlier had the goodness and the courage to abolish a number of them, "to the applause of all of civilized Europe." Now, they lamented, these same restrictions were being brought back.

The Jews expressed the hope that they might keep the freedoms that they had enjoyed under the Roman Republic. They wanted again to be able to live and work outside the ghetto. They wanted to be free to practice a wide variety of occupations and to be able to own real property.

They also wanted their children to be able to attend universities. They sought to end other humiliations they suffered, including the law forbidding Jews from giving testimony in civil trials and the requirement that they pay a large sum each year to support the House of the Catechumens, the church institution dedicated to their conversion. They did not ask to be allowed to have access to positions in the city administration, for this they thought would be too much, but they did ask that the menial jobs sponsored by the municipal government, available to the city's poor, be opened to them.[29]

The Jews' pleas did them little good. Pius IX had never been comfortable challenging the old orthodoxies and was certainly not about to do so now. He regretted that he had ever agreed to the requests that, in his first months as pope, had led him to grant the Jews so many freedoms. Over the next months, as reports of Jews remaining outside the ghetto's walls streamed in to Rome's cardinal vicar, Jewish stores were shuttered and Jewish families forced back into the ghetto.[30]

THE ARRESTS IN ROME continued at a brisk pace. Those known to be critical of the papal regime lived in fear of the hand on the shoulder, the manacles on the wrists, and the trip to the prison where beatings were common. Michelangelo Caetani, the duke of Sermoneta, a literary man from one of Rome's preeminent noble families, explained to a British visitor in early 1851 what life was now like in the Eternal City. Ten people a day, he said, were arrested, "to be confined for a few weeks in a damp, filthy dungeon, among wretches swarming with vermin and allowed to perpetrate on a new comer any atrocities that they think fit." It was a method, he said, the police used to make people think twice before criticizing the papal regime.

Pius, explained the duke, believed firmly in the right God had bestowed on him to wield absolute power. It was a trust that he was charged with transmitting intact to his successors, as his predecessor had to him.[31]

Marble genitalia offer a good barometer of the state of repression in Rome. Ever since Michelangelo painted a bevy of nude figures on the walls of the Sistine Chapel, covering up the naked human form had periodically become a papal crusade. Now Pius IX, bent on restoring morality in his capital, entered the fray. "At St. Peter's," reported one observer in April 1851,

> they continue to put clothes on the angels, the genies. The Genies of the Monument to the Royal Stuarts by Canova have all received little tunics. On the pilaster to the left as you enter there is a large medallion of Saint Leo supported by angels, one of which has no pants. They have been busy covering it a bit. What they have done most dramatically is this: at the foot of the statue of a pope, there was a woman nursing a child. They have hidden the breast, but what to do about the child? They cut off his head and put it back on facing in the other direction.[32]

Around this time Nassau William Senior, a prominent British lawyer and economist, visited Rome. Eager for insight into the political situation, he went to see Alphonse de Rayneval, who months earlier had become the new French ambassador to Rome. The unflattering view of the Romans that Rayneval conveyed was equaled only by his dim view of the pope's prospects. "If 500 foreign republicans were to come in, I do not think that they would find 500 Romans to join them," said Rayneval, before adding, "but I do not think that they would find fifty to oppose them. The Romans would run into their houses, lock the doors, and peep through the keyholes to see what would happen."

The next day Senior went to see the British consul, John Freeborn, who had been an enthusiastic supporter of the short-lived Roman Republic. Senior told him what the French ambassador had said. "Rayneval," replied the disapproving consul, "is utterly mistaken. He does not know the feelings of the middle classes here; for he does not mix with them. I do; and I can assure you that in three hours after the French left us, there would be a sanguinary revolution."[33]

This was the American chargé's view as well. "The tendency now," Lewis Cass reported to Washington in May, "is to return to the old system, with all its abuses. . . . The feeling against the Vatican . . . is as strong as ever, and I have every reason to believe, that a great majority of the inhabitants of the Papal States are willing, in their desire for a change in the political economy, to encounter the horrors of a second revolution. . . . Hatred to Church government and dread of despotic power appear to animate every breast."[34]

Nor did Cardinal Antonelli himself have any illusions. "The Roman people," he confided in a mid-1851 memo to his nuncio in Vienna, "is in general radically corrupted, or inept, and incapable of giving the government the least shadow of support." The ideas spread during the revolution, and the propaganda sneaked into the city in the months since, had, he wrote, "perverted the ideas and the sentiments of this people to such a degree, that," should the French troops leave Rome, "the government of His Holiness would find itself abandoned to passionate hatred in the womb of its own capital."[35]

The pope sat uneasily on his throne. It was not only the Romans' hopes that had been crushed in the time since those exhilarating days when festive crowds had marched through the city's streets singing his praises. The pope's dreams, too, had faded. Pio Nono had wanted to be a benevolent ruler and had delighted in his people's praise. In those early, heady days of his papacy, the tears he shed were tears of joy at the outpourings of people's love for him. What a contrast with the tears that had so often moistened his eyes during his humiliating exile, as he heard reports of the curses hurled at him in Rome and contemplated his return with the greatest trepidation. It was only by weaning himself from what he now recognized as his weakness, his great desire to be loved by his people, that he could face the future. He would need to develop a protective shield, to turn not to the people for approval but to God alone.

A new, more spiritual, yet stronger-minded pope was beginning to emerge. Over the next years, he would face challenges no less daunting, no less consequential for the future of Italy and the church than those he had faced in these early years of his papacy. God, as he would see it, was not finished putting him to the test. He vowed he would prove worthy of the divine judgment that surely would come.

EPILOGUE

———

Thanks to the bishop of Marseilles, who sent the pope two new guillotines, executions in the Papal States could once again proceed in a more dignified manner. In 1851 officials carted one of them from town to town, stopping long enough at each place to sever the heads of those condemned to death by the local ecclesiastical tribunals.[1]

Three years later, following a long trial, eight men were found guilty of Pellegrino Rossi's murder. Two, Luigi Grandoni, a forty-year-old Roman, and the twenty-eight-year-old sculptor, Sante Costantini, were sentenced to death. Grandoni, who in fact had played no part in the plot, committed suicide in prison while awaiting execution. On Saturday, July 22, 1854, Costantini, proclaiming his innocence, was alone marched to the place of his decapitation. Accompanying him were a priest, a monk, and members of the religious confraternity devoted to assisting in such executions. They headed toward the *Bocca della Verità*, whose piazza was one of the three sites for capital punishment in papal Rome. Catching sight of some of his friends among the crowds of the curious who lined the way, Costantini shouted, "They're sending me to the slaughterhouse!" Rebuffing all pleas that he confess and take last rites, Costantini said that he was tired of suffering in the dungeons and simply wanted to get the execution over with. The confraternity leader recorded what happened next:

6:15 p.m. The patient* is taken to the platform of the guillotine. On mounting it he shouted, in a loud voice, "Viva la Repubblica!" at which the drums sounded. As the condemned man persisted in his final refusal to repent, he received the mortal blow with that wicked defiance that regrettably one must recognize in many of the condemned men who have been sent to the guillotine for crimes committed in the heat of the rebellion.[2]

Over the following years, many heads rolled into the guillotine's bucket. Among them, three years later, severed at the same spot, was that of Antonio de Felice. The thirty-five-year-old hatmaker had accosted Cardinal Antonelli on a Vatican stairway, brandishing a small pitchfork, but attendants had subdued him before he could do any harm. In a final act of bravado, on mounting the platform, De Felice kissed the executioner before placing his head beneath the blade.[3]

Two weeks after De Felice's execution, Charles Bonaparte, the revolutionary prince-naturalist, died a beaten man, in Paris. After enjoying the limelight in the fiery days of the Roman Republic, he had lived his last years in painful obscurity, spurned by his Catholic wife, who had remained in Italy, and barely tolerated by his cousin, Louis Napoleon, whose army had caused his misfortune.[4]

Despite their hopes of help from the Rothschilds and their pleas to the pope, Rome's Jews, after their brief liberation, found themselves again confined to lives of poverty in the ghetto, objects of scorn and abuse. Worst of all, they lived in fear that their children might be taken from them, for should any Christian think to baptize a Jewish child, under the laws of the church, that child had to be removed from his Jewish family to be raised a Catholic.[5]

French troops remained in Rome throughout the decade to protect the pope from his restive subjects. The French continued to plead with him to replace priests with laymen in the government and the courts of the Papal States, but Pius held firm.

---

* Curiously, the head of the confraternity here refers to the condemned man as *il paziente*, "the patient," employing a medical metaphor and giving a new meaning to the phrase "The operation was a success, but the patient died."

The pope's worldly kingdom would not last long. In 1859, with Louis Napoleon—having in the meantime pronounced himself Emperor Napoleon III—feeling emboldened, and Charles Albert's son, King Victor Emmanuel II, eager to avenge his father's ignominious defeat of a decade earlier, the French and Sardinian forces combined in a new effort to drive the Austrians from the peninsula. With the Austrian army in retreat, the people in the Austrian-occupied provinces of the Papal States tore down the papal banners and drove out the clerics who ruled in the pope's name. The day of Italian independence was finally at hand, as patriots from the newly liberated papal lands organized referenda to join the expanding Savoyard kingdom. Victor Emmanuel II had shown no desire to have the southern portion of the peninsula join his realm, but the omnipresent Garibaldi forced his hand, sailing with a thousand armed volunteers to Sicily and then marching northward, through the Kingdom of Naples. In late 1860, fleeing his capital, the twenty-four-year-old Francis II—who had ascended to the Neapolitan throne on the death of his father, Ferdinand II, a year earlier—decided to make a last stand at the fortress of Gaeta, where as a child he had so often gone with his family to visit the pope. After a bloody siege, he surrendered early in 1861. Later that year the Kingdom of Italy, under Victor Emmanuel II, was proclaimed, encompassing the entire Italian Peninsula except for Venice, still in Austrian hands, and Rome and the region surrounding it, left to the pope in deference to French Catholic sensibilities and the continuing role of French troops in the capital of Christendom.

Rebuffing the Italian king's efforts to negotiate, Pius, in a January 1860 encyclical, demanded the "pure and simple restitution" of the Papal States. Excommunicating those guilty of usurping the papal lands, Pius expressed his faith that God would not long allow the outrage to stand. After all, little more than a decade earlier, the pope's defeat had proven short-lived, the Italian patriots crushed.

Committed to continued papal rule in the Eternal City, the French kept their army there and extracted an agreement from the Italian king to leave Rome alone. Pius could take some solace from the fact that none of the continental powers seemed eager to see the emergence of a strong, unified Italy. Both he and Antonelli bided their time, hoping that the pope's rightful realm might soon be restored. "Like the Pope," reported

Britain's envoy in Rome in early 1865, "Antonelli hopes in a European war to set matters right again in the Holy See!"[6]

Pius was once again plagued by the sense that he had failed in his duties as Supreme Pontiff, having presided for a second time over the loss of much of the papal kingdom. Again his temper battled with his good nature. "How is it," Pius asked Britain's envoy at the beginning of 1866, "that the British can hang two thousand Negroes to put down an uprising in Jamaica, and receive only universal praise for it, while I cannot hang a single man in the Papal States without provoking worldwide condemnation?"

"His Holiness," recounted the envoy, "here burst out laughing and repeated his last sentence several times holding up one finger as he alluded to hanging one man, so as to render the idea still more impressive."[7]

For the patriots, there could be no true Italian nation without Rome, and the king came under intense pressure to take it. Reluctant to provoke a war with France by launching a direct attack on the Eternal City, the king secretly sent funds there to try to prompt "spontaneous" popular uprisings, which he might then use to justify intervening. Much to the king's dismay, the Romans, having so often seen the workings of the guillotine, showed little interest in sticking their necks out.

In March 1868 the British envoy again met with the pope. Buoyed by France's recent reinforcement of its garrison in Rome, and by the large number of Catholic volunteers who had poured into Rome to join the papal army from France, Ireland, Germany, and as far away as Canada, Pius was feeling increasingly confident. In proportion to his state's population, he told the envoy with a chuckle, he now had the largest army in the world.[8]

The pontiff made full use of his spiritual arsenal as well. In December 1864 he issued what would become one of the most important encyclicals of modern times, *Quanta cura*, with an accompanying Syllabus of Errors. No Catholic, he warned, could believe in freedom of speech, freedom of the press, or freedom of religion. Catholics had to believe that the pope must rule over a state of his own. All Catholics, he declared, were bound to reject the view that "the Roman Pontiff can and should reconcile himself to progress, liberalism, and modern civilization."[9]

Visiting Rome early in 1869, the American poet Henry Wadsworth

Longfellow found the city "beleaguered" and "depressing." "I look out of the window this gray, rainy day," he wrote to an American friend, "and see the streets all mud and the roofs all green mould, and the mist lying like a pall over the lower town, and Rome seems to me like king Lear staggering in the storm and crowned with weeds." What most struck Longfellow was how little Rome had changed in the forty years since he had first visited it, an observation he shared in his meeting with Cardinal Antonelli. "Yes, thank God!" replied the cardinal, pausing to put a pinch of snuff to his nose.[10]

A few months later Rome witnessed something it had not seen for 350 years. The pope summoned all the world's bishops, cardinals, and heads of the religious orders to St. Peter's for a Vatican Council. The timeless truths of Christianity, as he saw it, were under assault from the godless forces that had emerged from the French Revolution. The principle of separation of church and state had been making its way into the European states' new constitutions, along with guarantees of freedom of expression and the press that went directly against church doctrine. Pius wanted to show the world that he had the church's full support in his battle against these modern heresies. He had a second goal as well, eager to strengthen his position by having the pope, for the first time, officially declared infallible. "Religion," Pius explained in a public address he gave in the midst of the council, "is immutable; not an idea, but the truth. Truth knows no change."[11]

On December 8, 1869, the 774 bishops and several hundred other church dignitaries who had flooded into Rome for the council gathered in St. Peter's for the inaugural ceremony. Since seven in the morning, the basilica had been packed, many foreigners having come to witness the historic event. In a separate reserved section sat the various sovereigns of Europe, including Elizabeth, empress of Austria, Francis II, the deposed king of Naples, Leopold II, deposed grand duke of Tuscany, and the deposed duke of Parma. In a special position of honor sat General Kanzler, head of the papal army, and General Du Mont, commander of the French expeditionary force patrolling Rome.

Having decided that the battle for the church's survival depended on the proclamation of papal infallibility, Pius pressed the bishops to support his cause, and those opposed felt his anger. He branded one "evil," another "a madman," and a third an "incorrigible, schismatic snake." His campaign came as the culmination of a centuries-long battle aimed at wresting power away from the cardinals and bishops and from the national churches. Over the next months, in Latin speeches few could have understood even if the acoustics had not been so wretched, the church fathers continued their debate.[12]

Europe's rulers, fearing that the doctrine of papal infallibility might lessen their hold over their Catholic subjects, looked on in horror. Napoleon III, the pope's great protector, was so enraged that he threatened to pull all French troops from Rome. But as a man of faith and decidedly not of realpolitik, Pius pushed forward. On July 18, 1870, as a thunderstorm outside darkened the midday skies, the prelates cast their votes. Of those who had misgivings, many in the end voted in favor, fearful of incurring Pius's wrath. The pope's pronouncements on matters of faith would now be deemed infallible.

The vote proved to be unfortunately timed. Two days earlier France had declared war on Prussia, and Napoleon was eager to marshal all the forces he could for the fighting ahead. The declaration of papal infallibility gave him all the excuse he needed to abandon the pope to his own devices. On July 27 the emperor ordered the withdrawal of all French troops from Rome.[13]

The pressure on Victor Emmanuel to take Rome now became irresistible. Amid the excitement, Giuseppe Mazzini, unhappy that the Italian nation he had long dreamed of had embraced monarchy, decided to return to Italy in hopes of triggering a republican uprising. Disguised as an Englishman named John Brown, Mazzini traveled on a ship bound for Sicily but was recognized and seized by Italian police. Ironically, they imprisoned the prophet of Italian unity in the fortress of Gaeta, where Pius had taken refuge two decades earlier. The Italian prime minister meanwhile ordered police in Sardinia to arrest Garibaldi, the other patriotic hero of the Roman revolution, should he make any move to leave his remote island home off the Sardinian coast.[14]

Before daybreak on September 20, the Italian army began its assault on Rome's walls. What two decades earlier had taken the French weeks to do, now, in the face of only halfhearted defense, took the Italians a few hours. The American consul to Rome observed the scene:

The old walls generally proved utterly useless against heavy artillery, in four or five hours they were in some places completely swept away, a clear breach was made near the Porta Pia fifty feet wide, and the Italian soldiers in overwhelming force flowed through it and literally filled the city. . . . A white flag was hoisted over from the dome of St. Peter's. After the cannonading ceased the papal troops made but a feeble resistance, and they who a moment before ruled Rome with a rod of iron were nearly all prisoners, or had taken refuge in the Castle of St. Angelo, or St. Peter's square.

The disinclination of the papal forces to fight more fiercely, in the American consul's view, was fed by their realization that the Romans welcomed the Italians as their liberators, for "no private citizens made the least effort or demonstration in favor of the Papal Government." In short, he reported:

It was an easy victory for the Italians, and the loss, in killed and wounded, on both sides, was not great, they were in overwhelming force, with very heavy artillery and they knew that the mass of Romans were their friends; the Zouaves [the papal troops], on the other hand, although they never could have imagined how much they were detested, must have, at heart, feared the people and could not fight their best.[15]

The following year Victor Emmanuel made his triumphal entry into Italy's new capital. Bowing to the pleadings of the Holy See, the European powers boycotted the ceremony. "Today," the eminent historian of medieval Rome, Ferdinand Gregorovius, then living in the city, wrote in his diary, "is the close of the thousand years' dominion of the Papacy in Rome." The Castel Sant'Angelo cannon sounded. "How the Pope's heart must have quailed at every shot!" wrote Gregorovius. "A tragedy without a parallel is being enacted here."[16]

In an encyclical issued a month later, Pius reiterated his excommunication of the leaders of the new nation and declared the Italian occupation of the Papal States null and void. The Holy See, proclaimed the pope, would never compromise. "Despite our advanced age," he wrote, "we prefer . . . , with divine aid, to drink the cup to the dregs rather than accept the iniquitous proposals which have been made to us."[17]

The pontiff hoped that 1870 would prove to be a repeat of 1848, as 1848 had proven to be a repeat of 1798 and 1809. "That they will leave Rome is a certainty," wrote Milan's Catholic daily newspaper, "just as the Napoleonics, the Mazzinians, and before them all the other enemies of the Church. How and when they will leave, it is not yet possible to say. Probably they will leave soon and they will leave badly."[18]

Pius now cast himself as a prisoner. Although he had control of the hundred acres of the Vatican, with its magnificent palaces and gardens, and no one would stop him from leaving were he so inclined, images of his imagined imprisonment spread quickly. Mass-produced cards bearing an image of the pope behind jail bars circulated from Ireland to Poland, and in France, priests, monks, and nuns sold, as holy relics, straw that the pope, they said, had slept on in his cell.

Rome was now the capital of the Italian king, capital of a modern constitutional monarchy, and seat of Italy's bicameral legislature. The Quirinal Palace from which Pius had made his daring escape in 1848 was now the king's home. But the king never felt comfortable in the Eternal City, with the man who claimed to be its legitimate ruler—and who had excommunicated him—living as a self-proclaimed prisoner barely a mile away. Victor Emmanuel spent as little time as he could there, preferring to spend his days at one of his country estates, riding his horse and hunting. Indeed, the king feared that he was now cursed, and perhaps he was, for in early January 1878, at age fifty-seven, he fell sick and died a few days later. The Catholic press made much of this evidence of divine punishment, although it might have made more of it had the elderly Pius IX not died four weeks later.

Pius IX's long struggle in life continued after his death. In 1881 his successor, Leo XIII, judged that tensions had cooled enough to allow him to grant Pius's wish to be buried in the Basilica of San Lorenzo, on the other side of Rome. To minimize the possibility of any unpleasantness, Leo had the procession with the pope's remains set out at midnight, its route a secret. But mixed in with the thousands of the faithful who came to honor the martyred pope were large numbers of anticlerics. As the procession reached the bridge over the Tiber at Castel Sant'Angelo, hundreds of protesters, shouting "Into the river!" tried to break through the police escort and send the papal bier plunging into the Tiber's yellow waters. Many were injured in the resulting melee, but the pope's mortal remains made their way safely to their final resting place.[19]

It would take more than half a century after Pius IX's death for a pope to recognize the legitimacy of the Italian state and its claim over Rome. Until that year, 1929, when the Italian dictator Benito Mussolini reached a deal with Pope Pius XI and Vatican City was formally created, no pope would ever set foot outside the Vatican walls.[20]

In 2000, to mark the end of the second millennium, Pope John Paul II decided to beatify two of his predecessors. In an apparent effort to keep all in the church happy, he combined the beatification of Pope John XXIII, convener of the Second Vatican Council and hero of the liberals, with that of Pius IX, convener of the First Vatican Council and hero of the conservatives. In his remarks that day, John Paul II explained why he regarded Pius IX as worthy of sainthood:

> Amid the turbulent events of his time, he was an example of un-conditional fidelity to the immutable deposit of revealed truths. Faithful to the duties of his ministry in every circumstance, *he always knew how to give absolute primacy to God and to spiritual values*. His lengthy pontificate was not at all easy and he had much to suffer in fulfilling his mission of service to the Gospel. He was much loved, but also hated and slandered.
>
> However, it was precisely in these conflicts *that the light of his virtues shone most brightly*: these prolonged sufferings tempered his trust in divine Providence, whose sovereign lordship over human events he never doubted. This was the source of Pius IX's deep serenity, even amid the misunderstandings and attacks of so many hostile people.[21]

The man on whom Pius IX relied so heavily in those troubled times, Giacomo Antonelli, has not, in death, been treated so kindly. He served as the pope's guide from the time he stood at Pius's side in their Gaeta exile until his death in 1876. He piloted the Holy See through times when its very survival seemed in doubt. For the easily excitable and naïve pope, more comfortable in the spiritual than the political realm, he was the invaluable steady hand who remained cool in every crisis.

Few would mourn the cardinal's death. To the partisans of the new Italian nation, of course, he was a villain, but he was scarcely better liked within the church. Rumors of his alleged mistresses had long circulated, along with gossip about his collection of precious gems, his love of wealth, and his penchant for using his position to enrich members of his family. Nor was his reputation helped by rumors that he had left little of his large fortune to the church. It suffered a further blow when, sometime after his death, a young woman, claiming to be his illegitimate daughter, sued the Antonelli estate. Although she lost the case in the end, the gleeful attention given the proceedings in the press did nothing to help the cardinal's cause.[22]

THE STORY TOLD IN THESE PAGES recounts the death throes of the popes' thousand-year kingdom. But it reaches far beyond, for it is also the story of the death of a doctrine of faith that had a huge impact on the course of Western civilization. If the pope himself could no longer claim to have been divinely ordained to rule his land, how could any other monarch claim such a right?

This world of the divine right of rulers, its roots in ancient times, first came under threat by the subversive ideas of the Enlightenment, its flames then fanned by the French Revolution. The marriage of aristocracy and church that had for centuries proved such a durable basis for rule began to give way amid calls for popular sovereignty, rule by and for the people. With the fall of the pope-king, the rationale for people elsewhere to accept their humble places in society as God's will, their leaders as supernaturally sanctioned, could not long survive.

The Enlightenment transformed the West but passed other parts of the world by. Claims to rule by religious authority are not hard to find today; nor are movements that justify their own pretensions to power as acting as God's agents on earth. The baleful results of this continued brew of religious and political authority are all too clear, whether in the cold repression enforced by religious police or in the bloody battles waged in God's name.

But before we in the West become too smug in dismissing such ideas as medieval, and congratulate ourselves for having long championed religious freedom and the separation of church and state, we might take a closer look at our own history. Well into the latter half of the nineteenth century, Pius IX and the Roman Catholic Church condemned ideas of religious freedom, of freedom of speech and of the press, and of the separation of church and state as incompatible with Christianity. It was only in the 1960s, with the Second Vatican Council, that the Roman Catholic Church fully rejected this medieval vision.

Nor does one have to look hard to find many in the West today who lament the abandonment of the old verities, who look back nostalgically to the not-so-long-ago days when government was guided by religious authority. Like Pius IX, they fault modern times for turning away from God. The pope-king's rearguard battle is far from over. Throughout much of the world, it continues still.

ACKNOWLEDGMENTS

———

I AM GRATEFUL TO THE MANY PEOPLE WHO HELPED ME ALONG the way as I plunged into one of Europe's great historical dramas. I also feel thankful that, working in the second decade of the twenty-first century, I have resources for shedding light on this history that my predecessors of the nineteenth and twentieth did not.

There is no better example of this than the Google digitization project, which has resulted in the electronic availability of the hundreds of published memoirs and other published materials of mid-nineteenth-century Europe that illuminate the events described in this book. To consult them in the past, I would have had to wander the libraries of the United States and Europe, in many cases only to find fragile volumes, able only to scribble notes by hand. What in the past would have taken years to accomplish can now be done in a few days. One need only have access to the HathiTrust database, look up the books or periodicals needed from the nineteenth century, and download them. As they are fully searchable, tracking down relevant material in many cases is a matter of minutes rather than hours.

The modern digital age has transformed archival work as well. Rather than keeping notes on thousands of cards or, as more recent historians did, making thousands of photocopies, we can now make (or have made) digital copies of all archival documents of interest. Having thousands of documents on the computer, retrievable instantly, offers unparalleled possibilities for analysis.

Let me begin my thanks by acknowledging the great research help given me by two Italian historians, Alessandro Visani and Roberto Benedetti. Their work in the archives was invaluable. Tragically, Alessandro died recently.

I would also like to thank all the archivists who helped facilitate this research, including those at the Archivio Segreto Vaticano at Vatican City, and the archivists at the two branches of the Archives du ministère des Affaires étrangères at La Courneuve and at Nantes. Special thanks to the director of the historical archive of the Museo Centrale del Risorgimento at Rome, Marco Pizzo, for his generosity and his deep expertise in the archival sources for this history. Thanks, too, to the director of the Archivio Storico della Comunità Ebraica di Roma, Silvia Haia Antonucci, and to Gabriella Franzone, Micol Ferrara, and the late Giancarlo Spizzichino for their help with my research there.

I am indebted to John Davis and Roberto Benedetti for their comments on an earlier draft of this book, and to friends who answered questions that came up along the way, including Massimo Riva, Kevin Madigan, and Carl Kramer. Thanks as well to Nina Valbousquet and Gilles Boquerat for their help in dealing with the French archives, and to the Department of Sociology and Social Research at the University of Trent and Francesca Decimo for hosting me there as a visiting professor while I was finishing this book.

For the past quarter century, I have had a most congenial academic home at Brown University, which has offered great support for my research efforts. Special thanks are due to Paul Dupee, Jr., for establishing the chair that first brought me to Brown and that has continued to support my work. Thanks also to the staff of the anthropology department—Matilde Andrade, Mariesa Fischer, and Marjorie Sugrue—for all their help. I am grateful to the staff at the Brown University libraries and at the Watson Institute for International and Public Affairs at Brown, and to its director, Ed Steinfeld, for providing me with a congenial and supportive environment. I would also like to thank my talented undergraduate research assistant, Talia Rueschemeyer-Bailey, for all her good efforts.

For their support and advice on this book project, I am indebted to my literary agent, Wendy Strothman, and also to David Ebershoff, my former editor at Random House who has now turned his attention full-time to his own writing. Thanks as well to my astute editor, Hilary Redmon, and to Caitlin McKenna, at Random House, for their help shaping this book, and to Laura Hartman Maestro for the two impressive maps she prepared for these pages.

I dedicate this book to my two new granddaughters, Anouk, born while I was in the midst of writing it, and her little sister, Naho, born just in time.

ABBREVIATIONS
USED IN NOTES

———

THE FOLLOWING ABBREVIATIONS ARE USED IN THE ENDNOTES

ARSI   Archivium Romanum Societatis Iesu, Roma

ASCER   Archivio Storico della Comunità Ebraica di Roma

       CO.   Corrispondenza

ASR   Archivio di Stato di Roma

ASV   Archivio Segreto Vaticano

       ANH   Archivio, Nunziatura di Madrid

       ANN   Archivio, Nunziatura di Napoli

       ANV   Archivio, Nunziatura di Vienna

       SEGR. ST.   Segreteria di Stato

ASVR   Archivo Storico del Vicariato di Roma

BFSP   British and Foreign State Papers

BSMC   Biblioteca di Storia Moderna e Contemporanea, Roma

       FS   Fondo Spada, BSMC, online at www.repubblicaro mana-1849.it/index.php?4/fondospada

DRS   *La diplomazia del Regno di Sardegna durante la Prima Guerra d'Indipendenza*, 3 vols. (see References)

MAEC   Archives, Ministère des Affaires Étrangères, La Courneuve (France)

       CP   Correspondance Politique: Autriche, Espagne, Naples, Rome

MD   Mémoires et Documents, Rome

PAR   Papiers d'Agents, Rayneval

PAW   Papiers d'Agents, Walewski

PDI   Personnel, Dossiers Individuels de Carrière

MAEN   Archives, Ministère des Affaires Étrangères,
Nantes (France)

RSS   Rome Saint-Siege

MCRR   Archivio, Museo Centrale del Risorgimento, Rome

TL   *Times* of London

CITATIONS OF ARCHIVAL SOURCES

An.	Anno/year
b.	busta/box
bis	supplementary page or volume
f.	foglio/page
fasc.	fascicolo/folder
ff.	fogli/pages
ms.	manuscript
n.	number
r.	recto
Rubr.	rubrica/heading
v.	verso
vol.	volume

NOTES

———

PROLOGUE

1. Gutierez de Estrada a Lützow, ministro d'Austria presso la Santa Sede, Roma, 26 novembre 1849, in Blaas 1973, pp. 28–31; Liedekerke à Monsieur le Baron, Rome, 24 novembre 1848, reproduced in Liedekerke 1949, pp. 115–20.

2. This description is based on the account provided in the Dutch ambassador's March 18, 1848, letter to his foreign minister, reproduced in Liedekerke 1949, pp. 21–22.

3. Harcourt au ministre des affaires étrangères, 17 novembre 1848, MAEC, CP, Rome, vol. 988, ff. 146–47.

4. The pope's prayer is from Psalm 51, Miserere. The quote from the New Testament is from Matthew 26:39–41. This scene is described by Filippani's daughter, Cittadini 1989, p. 99.

5. There are many contrasting accounts of the pope's escape from Rome. Some of the disparities can be explained by the political motives of the chroniclers, not least those linked to the French ambassador who, in retrospect, looked so naïve. Others may simply reflect the chaos enveloping Rome at the time. British readers were told that, with the French ambassador in the pope's bedroom, Pius donned the livery of the Bavarian legation, disguising himself as the Bavarian ambassador's servant: "The Escape of the Pope," *Times*, December 7, 1848. The primary sources employed in my account are Berra 1957; Cittadini 1989, pp. 99–101; Mollat 1939, pp. 277–79; Spaur 1851, pp. 17–21; Lancellotti 1862, p. 25; Simeoni 1932, p. 255.

CHAPTER 1: THE CONCLAVE

1. Wiseman 1858, pp. 420–22, 504–6; Martina 1974, pp. 60–61. Johan Koelman, a Dutch painter living in Rome at the time, remarked that he had

never heard anyone say a good word about the pope: Koelman 1963, vol. 1, pp. 29, 32–33.

2. Herzen's (1996, pp. 72–75) comments were made in December 1847. More brutally, in April 1849, another foreign visitor of the time, the English poet Arthur Clough (1888, p. 146), wrote: "Rome in general might be called a rubbishy place."

3. Story 1864, vol. 2, pp. 38–52.

4. "The barber," observed a Frenchman in Rome, "accomplishes his task in open air with a speed that would do honor to Figaro himself." Toytot 1868, p. 33.

5. Moroni 1851, pp. 239–48 ("Parrocchia"); Demarco 1949, pp. 188–90; Desmarie 1860, pp. 29–31.

6. Half of the Papal States' population of three million consisted of peasants who worked in the fields, and another quarter million were employed as servants. Demarco 1947, pp. 25–29; Demarco 1949, pp. 24–29; Negro 1966, p. 149.

7. Desmarie 1860, p. 40; Gillespie 1845, pp. 157–59.

8. Desmarie 1860, pp. 27–30.

9. "Conclave de 1846," MAEN, RSS 588; Gizzi 1996–97, pp. 111–14; Martina and Gramatowski 1996, p. 163; Gajani 1856, pp. 294–95.

10. Oxilia 1933, p. 583; Chiron 2001, p. 41; Matsumoto-Best 2003, pp. 12–14.

11. Roncalli 1972, p. 190.

12. On the veto, see "Veto," MAEN, RSS 588; Gillespie 1845, p. 150. On Metternich, see Nunzio di Vienna a Lambruschini, Vienna, 19 febbraio 1836, doc. 30 in Manzini 1960, pp. 597–98; Ward 1970, pp. 50–53; Dumreicher 1883, pp. 96–117.

13. For Metternich's letter to the Belgian king, see Manzini 1960, pp. 603–4. Metternich sent instructions to the cardinal archbishop of Milan—which, along with the rest of northeastern Italy, was then part of the Austrian Empire—to use Austria's veto to prevent the election of Cardinal Bernetti, Pope Gregory's first secretary of state. It seems what Metternich wanted above all was a pope who regarded Vienna as his best friend and kept a distance from Austria's archrival, France. Metternich thought Bernetti too close to France. In any case, Metternich's veto arrived in Rome only after the new pope had been elected. Martina 1974, p. 87; Bortolotti 1945, pp. 83, 114–22.

14. François Guizot à Pellegrino Rossi, letters of instructions dated June 8 and June 17, 1846, MAEN, RSS 272. See also Ideville 1887, p. 142; Bortolotti 1945, pp. 11–12. None of the French cardinals made it to Rome in time for the conclave, so the question of the French veto was moot.

15. Foreign minister, Naples, to Giuseppe Ludolf, ambassador, Rome, June 6, 1846, in Cipolletta 1863, pp. 231–32; Arcuno 1933, pp. 4–11.

16. Count Ludolf to foreign minister, Naples, June 6, 1846, in Cipolletta 1863, pp. 229–30; Bortolotti 1945, pp. 97–99, 108–13.

17. Giampaolo 1931, pp. 1, 8–9, 81–82; Monsagrati 2004; Regoli 2011, p. 313; Manzini 1960, pp. 448, 488–90, 653–55; Piscitelli 1953, p. 159. Lützow to Metternich, 23 août 1842, in Bortolotti 1945, pp. 99n–103n. On Lambruschini, see Giampaolo 1931; Regoli 2011; Monsagrati 2004. That Lam-

bruschini's fame as an inflexible reactionary lives on in the Vatican can be seen by the reaction in 2005 of the then newly appointed secretary of state Tarcisio Bertone, when asked about being the first monk appointed to that office since Lambruschini. "For goodness sake," replied Bertone, "don't compare me to Lambruschini!" (Regoli 2011, p. 309).

18. "Conclave de 1846," MAEN, RSS 588; Gajani 1856, pp. 308–12; Pelczar 1909, pp. 104–9; Balleydier 1847, pp. 17–18; Martina and Gramatowski 1996, pp. 206–7; Gizzi 1996–97, pp. 183–86. The cardinals in conclave were not completely cut off, for they each had their meals prepared by their own servants and brought to them every day in a large basket containing tablecloth, silverware, plates, and the meals themselves. Ventura 1848, p. 74.

19. Ventura 1848, pp. 72–82.

20. The detail on the condition specified by Pius VII is given in Chiron 2001, p. 24. Much of my description of Mastai's early years relies on Chiron's biography, but also useful was Falconi 1981.

21. Chiron 2001, pp. 41–43.

22. Lützow to Metternich, Rome, 23 août 1842, in Bortolotti 1945, p. 104n; Chiron 2001, pp. 46–47.

23. Martina 1974, pp. 89–90.

24. Martina 1974, p. 92; Gizzi 1996–97, pp. 197–98; Cittadini 1986, p. 23. Historical accounts contain many dramatic descriptions of this scene that appear to be apocryphal, including ones claiming that Cardinal Mastai fainted on realizing he was to be pope, and Lambruschini passing out for the opposite reason. Cardinal Bernetti, who had reason to think he might himself be elected, is said to have uttered, as the vote was cast electing Mastai, "Oh great! After a cop, we'll have a little girl!" Bianchi 1869, vol. 5, pp. 8–9; Pio 1878, p. 31. The previous conclave, which had elected Gregory XVI, had lasted fifty days.

25. Martina and Gramatowski 1996, pp. 210–11; Ventura 1848, pp. 6–7, 97–99; Martina 1974, pp. 93–94; Koelman 1963, vol. 1, pp. 43–45; Minghetti 1889, vol. 1, p. 190; "Conclave de Pie IX, 1846," 7 octobre 1891, MAEN, RSS 588. The delay between the election of the new pope and the public announcement caused an embarrassing spectacle for one of the conclave's most prominent cardinals. Fifty-eight-year-old Pasquale Gizzi, of noble family and having served in many important diplomatic posts for the Holy See, returned from the Quirinal following the conclave to find his servants, still drunk following a night of celebration, smashing all his crockery, judged too modest for his exalted new status. They had already thrown all of his cardinal robes into the fire. The rumor had reached them the previous night that it was their master who had been elected pope, and following custom, they had celebrated by burning his now no-longer-needed cardinal's attire. They had also gotten word to his hometown, south of Rome, where the overjoyed inhabitants had likewise spent the night in wild celebration. Gizzi 1995, p. 133; Gizzi 1996–97, p. 200; Koelman 1963, vol. 1, pp. 44–45.

26. Rossi à Guizot, Rome, 17 juin 1846, in Ledermann 1929, pp. 332–34. In his response to Rossi, Guizot, the French foreign minister, adopted a

tone of guarded optimism, expressing the hope that the new pontiff might quickly adopt needed reforms that were well overdue. Guizot à Rossi, 27 juin 1846, MAEN, RSS 272.

27. Lützow to Metternich, 17 June 1846, quoted in Bortolotti 1945, pp. 122–23.

28. Metternich à Lützow, Vienne, 23 juin 1846; Metternich à Lützow, Vienne, 28 juin 1846, in Metternich 1883, pp. 247–48, 248–50.

29. Martina 1974, p. 95; Gizzi 1996–97, pp. 202–5.

CHAPTER 2: THE FOX AND THE CROW

1. The original Italian text is found in Ventura 1848, pp. 361–62; the British envoy in Rome sent London an English translation, found in Freeborn to Viscount Palmerston, Rome, July 18, 1846, BFSP, vol. 36 (1861), pp. 1196–98. The internal discussions leading to the decree are examined in Pirri 1954, pp. 207–23; Gizzi 1995, pp. 134–35; and Gizzi 1996–97, pp. 33–34.

2. Giovagnoli 1894, p. 68; Roncalli 1972, pp. 198–200; Gizzi 1996–97, pp. 36–37; De Broglie 1938, pp. 132–33.

3. Rossi à Guizot, Rome, 18 juillet 1846, in Ideville 1887, p. 149; Guizot à Rossi, Paris, 5 août 1846, MAEN, RSS 272.

4. Metternich à Lützow, Vienne, 12 juillet 1846, in Metternich 1883, pp. 251–56; Pirri 1954, pp. 208–12; Gizzi 1996–97, pp. 33–34; Bortolotti 1945, pp. 160–63; Martina 1974, p. 110. "Je n'aime pas le peuple," one of the prelates attached to the French embassy in Rome remarked on seeing the imposing crowd. De Broglie 1938, p. 133.

5. Bortolotti 1945, pp. 174–76.

6. Martina 1974, pp. 113–15; Gizzi 1995, pp. 132–33; Demarco 1947, p. 12; Giovagnoli 1898, p. 137.

7. Guizot 1872, p. 345; Ideville 1887, pp. 151–53, 198; Fraser 1896, pp. 159–60; Gemignani 1995, pp. 16, 100.

8. Arcuno 1933, pp. 12–14.

9. Gizzi 1995, p. 136. Martina (1974, p. 109) quotes the September 19, 1846, letter from Cardinal De Angelis to Cardinal Amat.

10. Mack Smith 1994; Matsumoto-Best 2003, p. 17; King 1911. Mazzini's letter is quoted in Quazza 1954, vol. 1, pp. 69n–70n.

11. De Broglie 1938, pp. 139–41.

12. Roncalli 1972, p. 219; Spada 1868–69, vol. 1, pp. 113–14.

13. Pius IX al Conte Gabriele Mastai, 5 novembre 1846, in Monti 1928, p. 248; Gizzi 1995, p. 137.

14. Balleydier 1847, pp. 164–73; Roncalli 1972, pp. 220–21.

15. Ludolf a Scilla, Roma, 21 novembre 1846, in Arcuno 1933, pp. 122–23. The democrat's quote is from Filippo de Boni, cited in Candeloro 1972, pp. 29–30.

16. An English translation of *Qui Pluribus* is found at http://www.papalen cyclicals.net/Pius09/p9quiplu.htm.

17. Minghetti 1889, vol. 1, pp. 213–15.

18. Ranalli 1848–49, vol. 1, p. 77; Roncalli 1972, pp. 225–26; Ventura 1848, pp. 139–43; Martina 1967b, p. 211.

19. Lützow's letters of August 8 and December 26 and 31, 1846, quoted in Bortolotti 1945, pp. 182, 201–2.

20. Minoccheri 1892, pp. 35–36; Aubert 1990, p. 38; Ventura 1848, pp. 7–14, 180–81; Desmarie 1860, p. 39.

21. D'Azeglio's account of his March 13, 1847, meeting with the pope is found in his letter to Cesare Balbo, reproduced in Predari 1861, pp. 188–91.

22. Quazza 1954, vol. 1, p. 44.

23. A few months later, Gizzi followed up this edict with a new public warning. Every printed page or image that was not submitted to the censorship board for prior approval would be declared clandestine. The authors, printers, and hawkers of such materials would be punished by imprisonment of six months to a year and subject to a large fine. Jankowiak 2007, pp. 144–50; Candeloro 1972, p. 37; Petre to Hamilton, Rome, August 26, 1847, attached to n. 103, Sir George Hamilton to Viscount Palmerston, Florence, August 30, 1847, BFSP, vol. 36 (1861), pp. 1257–58; Farini 1850–53, vol. 1, pp. 313–14.

24. Pareto al Solaro, 1 aprile 1847, quoted in Quazza 1954, vol. 1, pp. 80–81.

25. Bortolotti 1945, p. 202; Pareto a Solaro, 6 aprile 1847, quoted in Quazza 1954, vol. 1, pp. 82–83; Giovagnoli 1898, p. 137; Gualterio 1851, pp. 111–14; Gizzi 1995, p. 140; Minghetti 1889, vol. 1, pp. 216–17.

26. Badie 2012, p. 31.

27. Fuller, May 1847, Rome, letter XIV in Fuller 1856, pp. 224–25. For a recent biography of Fuller, see Marshall 2013.

28. Farini 1850–53, vol. 1, pp. 192–93; Martina 1974, p. 130; Roncalli 1972, pp. 257–58; Liedekerke, 26 avril 1847, quoted in Martina 1974, p. 131.

29. De Broglie 1938, pp. 144–45 (28 avril 1847).

30. Metternich added that the revolutionaries' next step would be to institute a Civic Guard as a means of ejecting the Swiss Guard who protected the pope. For these conspirators, he warned, "the cries of *Railroads!* and of *Gas lamps on the Streets!*" were only a ruse. Metternich à Lützow, à Rome, Vienne, 15 mai 1847, in Metternich 1883, pp. 410–13.

31. In sending an English translation of this edict to London the next day, the British envoy in Rome added his own note of approval. "With regard to these public meetings and processions," he wrote, "it was certainly desirable that they should be put an end to." While initially spontaneous, they were now, he warned, "gradually getting under the management of 200 or 300 individuals" with clearly seditious intent. Moreover, added the envoy, the repeated gatherings in front of the papal palace and appearances of the pope to bless them were "little suitable to his dignity." George B. Hamilton, Florence, to Viscount Palmerston, June 28, 1846. Hamilton, the British consul in Florence, received the report from the British envoy in Rome, William Petre, and sent it on with the English translation of the edict to the British foreign minister. BFSP, vol. 36 (1861), pp. 1218–21; Chantrel 1861, p. 32.

32. Pareto, 26 giugno 1846, quoted in Quazza 1954, vol. 1, pp. 167–68.
33. Lützow à Metternich, 2 juillet 1847, excerpted in Quazza 1954, vol. 1, pp. 173–74.

CHAPTER 3: AN IMPOSSIBLE DILEMMA

1. In Guizot 1872, p. 350.
2. Lützow à Metternich, 2 juillet 1847, quoted in Quazza 1954, vol. 2, pp. 5, 20.
3. Freeborn to Viscount Palmerston, Rome, July 5, 1847, BFSP, vol. 36 (1861), pp. 1221–22; Francia 2012, p. 41. A parallel demand for citizen militias was sweeping the Grand Duchy of Tuscany at the same time. Francia 2012, pp. 65–70. In Tuscany, as in the Papal States, many property owners saw the guard as a means of protecting them against popular unrest that seemed to be getting out of hand. Candeloro 1972, pp. 38–39.
4. In Gizzi 1995, p. 143. On hearing the news of Gizzi's resignation, Metternich had a similar reaction. Things were spinning out of control, and God alone knew how it would all end. "Cardinal Gizzi's successor," he told his ambassador in Rome, "will have a difficult task to accomplish. I just hope that it does not become impossible." Metternich à Lützow, Vienne, 18 juillet 1847, in Metternich 1883, pp. 413–14.
5. In Natalucci 1972, p. 431. This is the text of the pope's message as found in the Ferretti family private archive. Curiously, a different text, seeming to reflect the pope's sometimes mischievous sense of humor, is reported by Sardinian ambassador Pareto: "Most Eminent Cousin, The Most Eminent Gizzi for the second time has given his resignation, and we could do no less than accept it. Do you know who is the new Secretary of State? The Most Eminent Ferretti. Come immediately to Rome. Have courage that God is with us." Attachment to Pareto report of July 17, in Quazza 1954, vol. 2, p. 15.
6. Martina 1974, pp. 172–73; Martina 2004, pp. 190–91; Giovagnoli 1894, pp. 73–76.
7. Quazza 1954, vol. 2, p. 30.
8. Giovagnoli 1894, pp. 73–76; Modena 2011, pp. 29–35; Trebiliani 1972; Francia 2012, pp. 80–81; Ranalli 1848–49, vol. 1, pp. 56–57; Ventura 1848, pp. 210–11; Quazza 1954, vol. 2, p. 4; Roncalli 1972, pp. 261–62. Or as the Sardinian prime minister put it, "Modern Rome could boast of its Ciceruacchio as ancient Rome could boast of Cicero." Britain's consul in Rome likewise reported in July that "the influence of 1 individual of the lower class, Angelo Brunetti, hardly known but by his nickname of Ciceruacchio, has for the last month kept the peace of the city more than any power possessed by the authorities, from the command which he exerts over the populace." Mr. Petre to Sir George Hamilton, July 21, 1847, BFSP, vol. 36 (1861), p. 1226.
9. Florence Nightingale to Miss Nightingale, Embley, Rome, November 26, 1847, letter XIII in Keele 1981, p. 65.
10. Martina 1967b, pp. 200–201; Story 1864, vol. 1, pp. 54–55.

11. "I popolani di Roma e l'Università Israelitica," Roma, 6 luglio 1847, signed "Uno Spettatore," BSMC, FS, n. 1236457; Roncalli 1972, pp. 267, 269–70.

12. Metternich was also worried that if he waited until revolution erupted in Rome itself and then sent troops there, it might provoke a war between Austria and France. Candeloro 1972, pp. 45–46.

13. The Austrian troop entry into Ferrara is recounted in Pareto a Solaro, Roma, 21 luglio 1847, in Quazza 1954, vol. 2, pp. 38–39; and Candeloro 1972, p. 48. The Austrian diplomatic correspondence regarding Metternich's intentions is examined in Quazza 1954, vol. 2, pp. 40–41.

14. Lützow à Metternich, 25 juillet 1847, excerpted in Quazza 1954, vol. 2, p. 43.

15. The quotes are from Metternich's two letters to Count Rodolphe Apponyi, the Austrian envoy to Paris, both dated August 6, 1847, in Metternich 1883, pp. 414–16. Keeping Britain, Europe's other great power, informed, Metternich justified his troops' movements in the Papal States on the grounds that a revolution had already begun. Britain's foreign minister, Lord Palmerston, judged such concerns "extremely exaggerated." "Whatever may be passing in the minds of some few enthusiasts," he observed, "nothing has yet happened which can justly be called a revolution, or which can indicate any probability of an attempt to unite Italy under one authority." He acknowledged that "deep, widely spread, and well-founded discontent exists in a large portion of Italy." But for this very reason, he argued, the new pope's interest in correcting many of the abuses that had produced the discontent was to be praised and encouraged. Metternich à Dietrichstein, 2 août 1847 (communicated by Dietrichstein to Viscount Palmerston, August 11), in BFSP, vol. 36 (1861), pp. 1231–32; Viscount Palmerston to Viscount Ponsonby, Foreign Office, August 12, 1847, and August 13, 1847, in BFSP, vol. 36 (1861), pp. 1232–34. The Roman situation took on a new complexion for the British foreign minister when he later received word that Pius IX had sent a messenger to the Sardinian king, Charles Albert, in Turin, asking if he might take refuge in his lands should the Austrians decide to occupy all of the Papal States. He asked, Palmerston was told, that a ship of war be sent by Charles Albert to Civitavecchia, Rome's port city, to await his orders. R. Abercrombie, Turin, to Viscount Palmerston, 18 August 1847, in Palmerston Papers, online.

16. Ferrari 1926, pp. 32–98; Bartoccini 1969; Stroud 2000.

17. "Protesta del Governo Pontificio contro gli Austriaci," 10 agosto 1847, BSMC, FS; Pareto a Solaro, 9 settembre 1847, doc. IV in Ferrari 1926, pp. 95–96; Ventura 1848, pp. 265–66. Amid the ferment, the pope received a most unusual piece of unsolicited advice. It came in the form of a long letter from Giuseppe Mazzini, the best known—and in many courts of Europe, the most despised and feared—champion of government by the people and exponent of Italian nationalism. If there was a man capable of taking advantage of the pope's political naïveté and desire to please his subjects, it was the infamous exile in London.

"Most Blessed Father," Mazzini began, "Permit an Italian, who has studied your every step for some months with great hope, to address you . . . some free and profoundly sincere words." What the pope had likely heard of him, the Italian patriot advised, was in error. "I am not a subverter, nor a communist, nor a man of blood, nor a hater, nor intolerant. . . . I adore God, and an idea which seems to me to come from God: Italy an angel of moral unity and of progressive civilization to the nations of Europe. . . . There is no man not only in Italy but in all Europe, more powerful than you." Thanks to the depredations of his predecessors, Mazzini told the pope, "Catholicism is lost in despotism. . . . Look around you; you will find the superstitious and the hypocritical, but not believers." For the pope to fulfill his divinely ordained mission, wrote Mazzini, he must lead the fight to unify Italy. "Take no counsel except from God, from the inspirations of your heart. . . . God will protect you. . . . Unify Italy, your country." Giuseppe Mazzini, "A Pio IX, Pontefice Massimo," Londra, 8 settembre 1847, in Mazzini 1912, pp. 154–60.

18. The conversation, with the prominent Jesuit philosopher, Father Luigi Taparelli, is recounted by Martina 1974, p. 118. As Taparelli reported it only years later, under very changed political circumstances, there is some reason to treat it with caution.

19. Engel-Janosi 1952, p. 13; Metternich à Apponyi, 7 octobre [1847], in Metternich 1883, pp. 341–43. Britain's envoy in Rome, by contrast, reported the creation of Rome's city council enthusiastically: "This is without a doubt the first great reform effected by Pius IX." Mr. Petre to Sir George Hamilton, Rome, October 4, 1847, BFSP, vol. 36 (1861), pp. 1291–92.

20. Another visitor to Rome at the time, the Russian author Alexander Herzen, then thirty-five years old, got to see Cardinal Lambruschini, former secretary of state, as he approached the pope. The cardinal "looked like an old jackal," recalled Herzen. "I waited for him to bite the holy father, but they embraced each other most peacefully." His impression of the other cardinals curiously mirrored Montanelli's, although their backgrounds could scarcely have been more different: "what faces they were, carrying the scent of unhappiness and recalling the Inquisition. . . . Each gesture of these old men without families expresses a life led in duplicity and solicitation, a hatred for everything free, love for power, envy." Herzen 1996, pp. 81–82. Herzen, an early socialist and not a Roman Catholic, was in any case not positively disposed to the Catholic Church, as is evident in his description of witnessing a special papal ceremony at the Basilica of Santa Maria Maggiore in late 1847: "Pius IX was borne through the church in an armchair under varicolored fans. This Indian appearance in no way suited him. It was terribly hot in the church, the pope swayed as on a boat, and, pale from oncoming seasickness, his eyes closed, he dispensed blessings right and left. Soldiers lined both sides of the path, the red *guardia nobile* and the varicolored Svizzeri in medieval dress. At the approach of the cortege, the officers commanded '*Armi!*' and in the middle of the church rifles were presented with a clatter; the officers commanded '*Ginocchio,*' and the soldiers knelt at the beat. I cannot get used to the military setting. . . . Add to them the unpleasant sing-

ing of the castrati, the crowd of fattened monsignors and sated canonists . . . along with the dry and jaundiced Jesuits and the half-savage monks from remote monasteries, and you will understand what the impression must have been." Herzen 1996, p. 82.

21. Montanelli 1853, vol. 2, pp. 54–58.

22. Like other Protestant countries, including the United States, Great Britain had no formal diplomatic relations with the Papal States and so had no ambassador in Rome. Queen Victoria herself had doubts about the wisdom of getting involved in what was going on in the Papal States and so had to be persuaded to allow Lord Minto to be sent. Prince Albert had reminded the prime minister that it was a crime under English law to have any relationship with the Holy See. Queen Victoria to Lord John Russell, 29 August 1847, with Memorandum of Prince Albert, doc. 4 in Curato 1970, vol. 1, pp. 39–41 et passim. Among the main goals of Minto's mission was to enlist the new pope's aid in preventing priests in Ireland from helping to foment revolt. Palmerston's instructions regarding Ireland are expressed in an October 29 letter: "We are entitled I think to make to the Pope the plain and simple and reasonable request that he would exert his authority over the Irish priesthood to induce them to abstain from meddling in politics, but on the contrary . . . to exhort their flocks to . . . obedience to the law and abstinence from acts of violence." Palmerston to Minto, 29 October 1847, doc. 64 in Curato 1970, vol. 1, pp. 128–30; Wallace 1959, p. 15.

23. Minto created quite a stir when he arrived at the Quirinal for his first audience with Pius IX. The proper male dress for a papal audience was a formal morning coat, a dark suit with a long tail, and a vest. Minto came dressed in clothes that the papal entourage deemed more appropriate for a foxhunt. Minto's diary entry for November 8, 1847, is found in Curato 1970, vol. 2, pp. 238–40; see also Minto to Palmerston, Rome, 14 November 1847, doc. 103 in Curato 1970, vol. 1, pp. 190–94.

24. Candeloro 1972, p. 113; Hales 1962, pp. 39–43; Whyte 1930, pp. 9–10; Traniello 2001; Borutta 2012, pp. 192–93. Rossi's original instructions regarding the Jesuits is found in "Instructions de M. Rossi," 15 mars 1845, MAEN, RSS 272. Some sense of the reaction to these attacks by the Jesuits in Rome at the time can be found in ARSI, Ital 1015 0145 (24 dicembre 1847).

25. Minghetti 1889, vol. 1, p. 219.

26. "Rome, Naples, and Sicily," TL, September 17, 1849.

27. See Coppa's (1990) biography of Antonelli, as well as Pirri (1958, p. 81); Martina (2004, pp. 194–96); Falconi (1983, p. 144); Aubert (1961, p. 2); and Hales (1962, pp. 157–58). The cigarette anecdote is given by Ward (1970, p. 98). It may well be apocryphal, but it is revealing of popular perceptions nonetheless. The bird of prey quote is from Adolph Mundt (Negro 1966, p. 161). Coppa (1990, p. 20) provides the information on the payment required for entering the prelature.

28. Mr. Petre to Sir George Hamilton, Rome, November 17, 1847, BFSP, vol. 36 (1861), pp. 1347–49; Minto to Palmerston, Rome, 18 November 1847, doc. 112 in Curato 1970, vol. 1, pp. 205–6; Florence Nightingale to

W. E. Nightingale, Rome, November 16, 1847, letter X in Keele 1981, pp. 46–51; Rossi à Guizot, Rome, 18 novembre 1847, in Ideville 1887, pp. 172–75; Coppa 1990, p. 42; Francia 2012, pp. 62–63; Chantrel 1861, p. 33. Rossi's report on the day to Guizot, dated November 18, 1847, is reproduced in Guizot 1872, pp. 389–92.

29. The pope, Rossi told the new secretary of state, showed great naïveté in telling the new body of laymen that they would have only consultative power: "It is too little. It might have been possible a year ago . . . when hopes were modest, and the rest of Italy had still not awakened. Today is something else. The time for illusions is over. . . . The radicals are knocking on your door. You must stand up to them. You clergy cannot do it alone. You have to have the help of the laity." He added, "It is now more than a year that I have said the same thing and I repeat: if you do not strengthen yourselves by calling laymen to positions that have nothing to do with religious or Church matters, everything will become impossible for you and all will become possible for the radicals. You will throw the Consultative Council into their arms." Chantrel 1861, pp. 33–34; Minghetti 1889, vol. 1, pp. 295–96.

30. Gabussi 1851–52, vol. 1, p. 57; Roncalli 1972, p. 93; Farini 1850–53, vol. 1, p. 279; Spada 1868–69, vol. 1, pp. 286–97.

31. Fuller, Rome, October 18, 1847, and December 17, 1847, letters XVII and XIX in Fuller 1856, pp. 242, 263–64.

32. Minto diary entry for December 19, 1847, in Curato 1970, vol. 2, pp. 242–48; Minto to Palmerston, Rome, 31 December 1847, doc. 160 in Curato 1970, vol. 1, pp. 282–86. Giacomo Martina (1974, p. 183), Pius IX's great biographer, and himself a Jesuit, offers a different view of the pope's attitude toward the Jesuits, arguing that he was in fact not well disposed to the order.

33. These tensions were now playing out in the new council. Members wanted their debates to be published, a measure the pope rejected. "I am convinced," wrote Massimo d'Azeglio, council member from Bologna, in a letter barely a month after its first meeting, "and it hurts me terribly to have to say so, that Pius IX's magic will not last. He is an angel, but he has to deal with demons who are too cunning. His state is disorganized, with many parts corrupt, and he will not be able to overcome the obstacles he faces." Candeloro 1972, pp. 110–11. For an analysis of the pope's plight at the time, see also Rossi à Guizot, Rome, 18 décembre 1847, n. 61, MAEN, RSS 409.

34. Metternich à Ficquelmont, à Milan, Vienne, 9 décembre 1847, in Metternich 1883, pp. 442–44; Coppa 2003, p. 675.

CHAPTER 4: PAPAL MAGIC

1. Minto to Palmerston, Rome, January 13, 1848, doc. 168 in Curato 1970, vol. 1, pp. 296–97; Minto diary entry, 8 January 1848, Curato 1970, vol. 2, pp. 290–92; "I primi due giorni del 1848 in Roma," 1 e 2 gennaio 1848, BSMC, FS; De Cesare 1907, pp. 23–24.

2. Rossi à Guizot, Rome, 8 janvier 1848, MAEN, RSS 409; Minto to Palm-

erston, Rome, 13 January 1848, doc. 168 in Curato 1970, vol. 1, pp. 296–98.

3. De Broglie 1938, pp. 176–77. Not all had the same impression of the procession as De Broglie. According to Margaret Fuller's account, Pius "passed through the principal parts of the city, the people throwing themselves on their knees and crying out 'Oh Holy Father, don't desert us; don't forget us, don't listen to our enemies.' . . . The Pope wept often and replied, 'Fear nothing, my people, my heart is yours.'" She concluded, "For the moment the difficulties are healed, as they long will be whenever the Pope directly shows himself to the people. Then his generous affectionate heart will always act and act on them, dissipating the clouds which others have been toiling to darken." "The Pope and His People," Rome, New Year's Eve of 1847, dispatch 21, in Fuller 1991, p. 188. Worried about the rumors that were quickly spreading, the secretary of state sent a letter on January 4 to his nuncios. The pope, the secretary explained, had decided to prevent the usual New Year's Day gathering partly because of the bad weather that had been plaguing Rome, and partly because the pope had been suffering from a bad cold. In explaining the subsequent papal procession, while admitting that some "hateful shouts" were heard along the way, he informed the nuncio that there had been no disturbance. On the contrary, he concluded, the people showed themselves as affectionate as ever to the pope. ASV, ANV, b. 329, ff. 2r–3r; ASV, ANM, b. 312, ff. 28r–29v.

4. Minto to Palmerston, Rome, 13 January 1848, doc. 168 in Curato 1970, vol. 1, pp. 296–98; Minto to Palmerston, Rome, 16 January 1848, doc. 178 in Curato 1970, vol. 1, pp. 309–10.

5. Rossi à Guizot, Rome, 8 janvier 1848, MAEN, RSS 409; Curato 1970, vol. 1, p. 298; Martina 1974, p. 203; Viaene 2001, p. 475; Minghetti 1889, vol. 1, p. 327.

6. Francia 2012, pp. 99–105; Ward 1970, pp. 122–23; Arcuno 1933, pp. 50–51; Scirocco 1996.

7. Rossi à Guizot, Rome, 18 janvier 1848, MAEN, RSS 409; Rossi à Guizot, Rome, 28 janvier 1848, MAEN, RSS 409. Bofondi had a background in law and spent time in administration in the northern provinces of the Papal States, but he had no experience in central government or foreign affairs, and spoke no language other than Italian. Martina 2004, pp. 191–92; Liedekerke à Monsieur le Comte, Rome, 29 janvier 1848, doc. VII in Liedekerke 1949, p. 9.

8. Fuller 1856, pp. 296, 300.

9. Francia 2012, pp. 108–9; Candeloro 1972, pp. 130–31; Quazza 1952, pp. xi–xxii; Martina 1974, pp. 197–98.

10. Ward 1970, p. 124; Martina 1974, p. 229. Insight into Metternich's view of the granting of the Naples constitution can be seen in the lengthy report that the French ambassador to Vienna sent to Guizot on his conversations with the Austrian chancellor, a copy of which Guizot sent to Rossi in Rome. Ambassade de France à Vienne, à Guizot, Vienne, 5 février 1848, MAEN, RSS 273.

11. Rossi à Guizot, Rome, 8 février 1848, MAEN, RSS 409.

12. Rossi à Guizot, Rome, 11 février 1848, MAEN, RSS 409; Viaene 2001, p. 476.

13. A copy of "Pius Papa IX. Proclama rivolto ai romani" is found in BSMC, FS.

14. Rossi à M. le Président du Conseil, Rome, 14 février 1848, MAEN, RSS 409; Saint-Albin 1870, p. 41; Farini 1850–53, vol. 1, pp. 340–43. Pius spoke, recalled Florence Nightingale, who stood in the crowd below, "with that voice which no one who has heard it can ever forget, it has a fervor of love and truth in it." Florence Nightingale to Miss Nightingale, Embley, Rome, February 12, 1848, letter XLV in Keele 1981, pp. 234–39. Two days later the pope replaced three of the prelates who served as government ministers with laymen. Demonstrators greeted the news with renewed celebration. This time, along with many white-and-yellow papal flags, the tricolored Italian flag led the way as, an hour before sunset, the people flooded into the square facing the pope's quarters. Long processions of soldiers, students, priests, women, and musical bands converged, with Ciceruacchio leading his own group of followers into the piazza. When the pope came out to bless the multitudes, shouts of *"Viva Pio Nono!"* were mixed with shouts of "Constitution!" and, in a tribute to the exiled, charismatic prophet of republicanism and Italian independence, *"Viva Mazzini!"* Pasolini 1887, pp. 77–79; Radice 1972, p. 26.

15. In his letter to Minto, the prime minister added, "But whether the Pope will be as wise as we are I much doubt. He surely might reserve his ecclesiastical and spiritual power, and yet have a constitution for his temporal government." Russell, prime minister, to Minto, Downing Street, 12 February 1848; Palmerston to Minto, Foreign Office, 12 February 1848; Minto to Russell, Naples, 15 February 1848, docs. 250, 251, and 258 in Curato 1970, vol. 2, pp. 30–31, 43; Rossi à M. le Président du Conseil, Rome, 17 février 1848, MAEN, RSS 409.

16. The pope, observed the Dutch ambassador, was a good man, his intentions pure. But, he added, the ability to govern was "entirely lacking in him." Liedekerke à Monsieur le Comte, Rome, 12 février 1848, doc. XI in Liedekerke 1949, pp. 13–15; Liedekerke 1949, pp. ix–xii.

17. Pasolini 1887, p. 83.

18. News of the French king's flight and the proclamation of a French republic arrived in Rome in early March. Initial shock was followed by an outpouring of joy. Rossi got official word that he was to report to a new foreign minister, the poet and diplomat Alphonse de Lamartine. "Monsieur," wrote the new minister, "you know of the events of Paris, the people's victory, their heroism . . . France is Republican." Lamartine à Rossi, Paris, 4 mars 1848, Choffat 2008, p. 95.

19. The French assistant to the ambassador, Albert de Broglie (1938, pp. 189–90), interpreted this as another example of the pope's naïveté. Pius IX may also have been encouraged by the positive attitude of the French clergy to the new regime; Collins 1923, pp. 48–53. For Palmerston's comments, see Palmerston to Minto, 24 February 1848, doc. 276 in Curato 1970, vol. 2, p. 76.

20. Nunzio Viale, Vienna, a Antonelli, Roma, 12 marzo 1848, 14 marzo 1848,

and 18 marzo 1848, docs. 11, 12, and 16 in Lukács 1981, pp. 233–35, 235–237, and 242–44; Stearns 1974, pp. 95–98.

21. Pareto al Conte di S. Marzano, Roma, 10 marzo 1848, doc. 8 in DRS 1949–51, vol. 2, pp. 78–80. Antonelli was also someone who at the time seemed to have the people's favor, for on the proclamation the people had presented the pope the previous month, they had placed Antonelli's name alongside those of the laymen they had called on the pope to appoint to his government. Antonelli's popularity would not last long.

22. Liedekerke au Comte, Rome, 18 mars 1848, doc. XVI in Liedekerke 1949, pp. 21–24. On March 29, Margaret Fuller lamented Rome's weather that winter: "rain was constant, commonly falling in torrents from the 16th of December to the 19th of March. Nothing could surpass the dirt, the gloom, the desolation, of Rome. Immense mistake to come to Rome in winter. Glorious sun finally returned." Letter XXIII in Fuller 1856, p. 303.

23. Candeloro 1972, pp. 174–76; Farini 1850–53, vol. 1, pp. 351–66. The text of the papal warning is given in Spada 1868–69, vol. 2, pp. 118–20.

24. Candeloro 1972, pp. 161–76; Ward 1970, pp. 166–73; Johnston 1901, pp. 115–17; Francia 2012, pp. 134–35.

25. Herzen 1996, pp. 114–15; DRS 1949–51, vol. 2, pp. 88–90; Fuller, March 29, 1848, Rome, letter XXIII in Fuller 1856, p. 306.

26. Cardinale Antonelli, "Circolare. Dalle stanze del Quirinale, 22 marzo 1848, a S.E. il Sig. Ministro Plenipot. di S.M. Sarda," DRS 1949–51, vol. 2, p. 91; Liedekerke à Monsieur le Comte, Rome, 24 mars 1849, doc. XVII in Liedekerke 1949, p. 24.

27. Palmerston to Minto, 29 October 1847, doc. 64 in Curato 1970, vol. 1, p. 128; Stroud 2000, p. 165; Giovagnoli 1894, pp. 28–29; Vecchi 1851, pp. 20–23.

28. Candeloro 1972, pp. 180–82, 204. The reference to Italy creating itself was added in part to discourage the Milanesi from turning to the new French Republic for help rather than to him.

29. Francia 2012, p. 144.

30. Ordini del Ministro delle Armi, 23 marzo 1848, doc. XI in Ovidi 1903, p. 307; Demarco 1947, pp. 62–63; Hales 1962, pp. 78–79. Domenico Pareto a Lorenzo Pareto, Roma, 24 marzo 1848, doc. 25 in DRS 1949–51, vol. 2, pp. 92–93; Agresti 1904, p. 29; Spada 1868–69, vol. 2, pp. 151–53. The text of the Inno a Pio Nono is found in the unpublished manuscript of Antonio Bonelli, *Privato giornaletto d'un Legionario Romano nella campagna del Veneto della Militare Divisione Pontificia*, MCRR, "Archivio Michelangelo Pinto," b. 887, f. 33.

31. Liedekerke à Monsieur le Comte, Rome, 24 mars 1849, doc. XVII in Liedekerke 1949, p. 28; Minghetti 1889, vol. 1, p. 362; Martina 1966, pp. 552–53. The pope's secret instructions were dated March 25.

32. Spada 1868–69, vol. 2, pp. 141–42.

33. "Il Governo provvisorio di Milano alla santità di Papa Pio IX," Milano, 25 marzo 1848, BSMC, FS.

34. Candeloro 1972, pp. 208–10; Martina 1974, p. 152.

35. Martina 1974, p. 183.

36. Boero 1850, pp. 82–83; Rocca 2011, pp. 75–78; Candeloro 1972, pp. 138, 211; Demarco 1947, p. 70; Martina 1974, p. 220; Engel-Janosi 1952, p. 18. The pope had a notice printed in the official government gazette on March 30 whose language offers insight into his bitterness at being forced to drive the Jesuits—described as "tireless collaborators in the Lord's vineyards"—from Rome. Farini 1850–53, vol. 2, pp. 16–17. But at his December 8, 1846, meeting with Pellegrino Rossi, Pius, in justifying the moves he would be making against the Jesuits, explained, "Public opinion is a fact; one must accept it." Engel-Janosi 1952, p. 8.

CHAPTER 5: THE TIDE TURNS

1. "Ordine del Giorno al Corpo d'Operazione," Durando, Bologna, 5 aprile 1848, BSMC, FS. The rather literary language of the general's orders may be attributed to the fact that they were drafted by Massimo d'Azeglio. Minghetti 1889, vol. 1, p. 364. That the men under Durando viewed their venture in the same way is evident from a statement put out by the Civic Guard units, whose address to their families was plastered across the walls of Rome in early April: "Parents, wives, brothers! Have no fear. . . . Our flag is the flag of PIO IX, and glory and victory will always follow it. . . . If the hated enemy dares to confront us . . . One shout alone will come from our lips: Viva Pio Nono!" It concluded: "Viva l'Italia, viva Pio IX, long live a Free Lombardy!" "Indirizzo dei Civici partiti da Roma alle loro famiglie," da Fuligno, 2 aprile 1848, BSMC, FS; Zeller 1879, pp. 73–74; Farini 1850–53, vol. 2, p. 57; Ward 1970, p. 119; Demarco 1947, pp. 62–63.

2. Antonelli a Viale Prelà, Roma, 4 aprile 1848, doc. 1 in Martina 1967a, p. 42.

3. Viale a Antonelli, Vienna, 4 aprile 1848, and 5 aprile 1848, docs. 19 and 21 in Lukács 1981, pp. 250–52, 253–54; Giovagnoli 1894, p. 514.

4. Minghetti 1889, vol. 1, pp. 366–67. On the same day as the pope's statement appeared in the *Official Gazette,* Durando issued new marching orders. His men were to go into battle on the pope's behalf: "Soldiers! I remain certain that on this occasion, as always, you will show yourselves worthy of the name of soldiers of PIUS IX, and of the holy cause of Italian independence." Candeloro 1972, pp. 216–17; "Ordine del Giorno del General Durando," Bologna, 10 aprile 1848, BSMC, FS.

  "Here we have our dear Pope," remarked the Austrian ambassador to Paris, "who is a real Anti-Christ. He will also receive his due . . . he will lose everything in the war waged against us in Italy." Count Rudolf Apponyi, Paris, April 13, 1848, in Lukács 1981, p. 50. While news of the spreading anger in Austria nagged at the pope, he was also bombarded with requests from Piedmontese moderates to more explicitly take their side. The alternative to having the Piedmontese and the pope drive the Austrians from Lombardy, they argued, was allowing the radical movement—the republicans who would overthrow all of Italy's monarchs and ruling families—to have the field to itself. An April 11 letter

from the Sardinian foreign minister to his ambassador in Rome com-
plains of the "inaction" of Durando's troops. Doc. 5 in DRS, vol. 2, p. 7.
See also the ambassador's account of his attempts to convince the pope in
his April 15 letter, doc. 6, pp. 7–8. King 1911, p. 116.

5. Bargagli, 20 aprile 1848, in Martina 1966, pp. 543–45.

6. "Interrogativi proposti alla Commissione Cardinalizia, sulle ragioni pro
   e contro l'intervento pontificio," s.d., doc. III in Martina 1966, pp. 563–
   65; see also pp. 541–42. The pope had much on his mind at the time, for
   not only did he face momentous questions of war and peace, but it was
   the start of Holy Week. It would be a week dense with rituals at which he
   was at the center, from the blessing of the palms at St. Peter's to the con-
   ducting of several masses and solemn processions, to the rite of the washing of the feet of twelve men, recalling Jesus's washing of the feet of his
   twelve apostles.

   A less than sympathetic account of these Holy Week ceremonies is
   given by the American artist William Story, who recounted his experience in Rome in a letter to James Lowell. "I have seen the Pope wash the
   feet of twelve fellows in white foolscaps, and at peril of my life have obtained over the heads of a garlic-smelling, fetid crowd a sight of the same
   august person serving at the apostles' table twelve fat fellows who eat
   away like mad. . . . It was with difficulty that the Pope himself could keep
   his countenance while he was performing this solemn farce." Story to
   J. R. Lowell, Rome, April 28, 1848, in James 1903, pp. 99–100.

7. It is notable that the minister who refused the Jews' request was the
   prominent liberal Luigi Carlo Farini, future Italian prime minister.

8. The request of the secretary of the Jewish community of Rome to publish King Charles Albert's emancipation decree was sent by Salvatore
   Betti to Farini on April 9, 1848. Betti, who had been one of the official
   Papal States censors of the press the previous year, was a liberal and had
   been a member of the Consultative Council. He urged Farini to approve
   publication, arguing that "the absolute civil emancipation of all religious
   dissidents among us is a great act of justice." Betti a Farini, Roma, 9
   aprile 1848, doc. LXXV in Giovagnoli 1894, p. 514. On Betti, see Giovagnoli 1894, pp. 154, 229, 366n3.

   There are conflicting accounts of the destruction of the ghetto gates,
   with many later chroniclers and historians claiming that Ciceruacchio
   and his Christian compatriots took on the task as the Jews looked on. A
   contemporaneous observer's account, however, records that it was the
   Jews of the ghetto themselves who tore down the gates. Carlo Gilardi a
   Rosmini, 19 aprile 1848, doc. VIII/4 in Rosmini 1998, pp. 194–85.

9. "Le porte di ghetto in Roma gettate a terra," BSMC, FS, s.d., but April
   18, 1848. Lamartine à Forbin Janson, chargé d'affaires, 1 mai 1848,
   MAEN, RSS 273. For a history of the demonization of the Jews in Italy
   in the nineteenth century, see Kertzer 2001.

10. The document is reproduced in Paoli 1880, pp. 375–78. At the same time,
    the Sardinian ambassador also met with the pope to discuss his upcoming
    allocution. What was important that the pope could bring to the battle,

argued the ambassador, was not so much his material resources as his moral authority. His support could prove decisive. The ambassador was eager not only to get the pope to back the war against the Austrians but also to encourage the Lombards and Venetians to cast their lot with the Sardinian king and not try to go their own way. D. Pareto a L. Pareto, Roma, 24 aprile 1848 and 25 aprile 1848, docs. 50 and 51, DRS, vol. 2, pp. 119–21; Minghetti 1889, vol. 1, pp. 368–71.

11. Liedekerke à Monsieur le Comte, Rome, 28 avril 1848, doc. XXII in Liedekerke 1949, pp. 38–39.

12. Martina 1966, p. 547; Pasolini 1887, p. 101; Minghetti 1889, vol. 1, pp. 371–72. That Antonelli, however, realized that a papal statement opposing the war with Austria would trigger disorders is clear from his remark in a letter he wrote to the nuncio in Paris at the time, warning him that they should expect "a rapid reaction and one not without unfortunate consequences." Martina 1966, p. 566.

13. I here use the official British foreign ministry English translation of the pope's allocution. Johnston 1901, pp. 357–61.

14. The quote is from Carlo Cattaneo. Giovagnoli 1894, p. 48.

15. Martina 1966, pp. 558–59.

16. Minghetti 1889, vol. 1, pp. 372–73.

17. Leti 1913, p. 36; Spada 1868–69, vol. 1, p. 301.

18. These events are described in detail in a dispatch sent by Cardinal Orioli to the nuncios. ASV, ANM, b. 312, ff. 95r–98r. See also Ventura 1848, pp. 353–55; Pasolini 1887, pp. 104–5; Gennarelli 1863, pp. xix–xxii; Gabussi 1851–52, vol. 1, pp. 236–39; Koelman 1963, vol. 1, pp. 143–45; Annuario 1847, pp. 46–47. The pope's allocution came as a blow to King Charles Albert as well. Not only might he now not get reinforcements from the pope's army, but he had been casting the battle with the Austrians as a holy crusade, blessed by the pope. His ambassador sent a strong note of protest to Cardinal Antonelli: "The presence of [the pope's] troops on the battlefield and the words full of unequivocal expressions by his chief general Durando . . . could not give rise to even most remote suspicion on the nature of his frank and loyal intentions as befitting a Regenerator of the Peninsula." The letter was also signed by Bargagli, the Tuscan ambassador to the Holy See. Pareto e Bargagli al Cardinale Antonelli Segretario di Stato, Roma, 30 aprile 1848, doc. 56 in DRS 1949–51, vol. 2, pp. 128–29.

19. "Our flag is the flag of PIUS IX, and glory and triumph will follow it always," the guardsmen had proclaimed in a printed address to their families as they had marched northward on April 2. "Pius IX's blessing has spread over all of Italy. . . . Long live Italy! Long live Pius IX!" "Indirizzo dei Civici partiti da Roma alle loro famiglie," BSMC, FS.

20. Minghetti 1889, vol. 1, pp. 376–77.

21. Pasolini 1887, p. 106; Minghetti 1889, vol. 1, pp. 379–81.

22. "Oh Lord," concluded the pope's message, "save your Rome from so many evils; enlighten those who do not want to listen to the voice of your Vicar, bring them all to heed sager advice." Text in Paoli 1880, pp. 383–85.

23. Spada 1868–69, vol. 2, pp. 297–300; Candeloro 1972, pp. 223–24, 311–12; Brancati 2007.

24. "We appeal to your piety and religion," wrote the pope, "and exhort you with paternal affection to put a halt to the arms of a war that, without being able to regain the spirits of the Lombards and the Venetians for the Empire, brings with it a disastrous series of calamities." Text in Farini 1850–53, vol. 2, pp. 120–21. In late May the pope sent a special envoy, Archbishop Carlo Morichini, to Vienna, to communicate his peaceful intentions to the emperor. Card. Orioli a Monsig. Delegato Apostolico, Madrid, Roma, 26 maggio 1848, ASV, ANM, b. 312, ff. 115r–115v.

25. Text in Paoli 1880, pp. 386–87. "I will be very happy to see a good end to the armed struggle of King Charles Albert, and the enlargement of his territories," wrote the pope to his confidant, Cardinal Amat, in early May. Still stung by the dramatic shift in the Romans' feelings for him, he added, "It is false that I condemned Italian nationalism and called the present war unjust. I pronounced not a word nor a judgment on this question, but unfortunately some have claimed to find both the one and the other in my allocution." Martina 1974, pp. 246–47n.

    With the protesters shouting death threats to Cardinal Antonelli, widely suspected of having persuaded the pope to betray the Italian cause, Pius decided he also needed a new secretary of state, his fifth in less than two years. That the man he appointed, a sixty-nine-year-old monk, Antonio Orioli, was not up to the task would be apparent soon enough—he would last only a month. Martina 2004, pp. 192–93.

26. Martina 1974, pp. 248–49.

27. The pope's audience was with Giuseppe Tabboni. Bianchi 1869, vol. 5, pp. 239–40.

28. Liedekerke à Monsieur le Comte, Rome, 28 mai 1848, doc. XXVIII in Liedekerke 1949, p. 51.

29. Martina 1974, pp. 247–48.

30. "Notizie della mattina," Roma 17 maggio 1848, BSMC, FS.

31. Curiously, Pius had a word of advice of his own for the Milanese count. Rather than try to get the Lombards to embrace the Savoyard king in Piedmont, wouldn't it be better, he asked, for them to find a monarch of their own? "Estratto di una conversazione avuta dal Conte Luigi Litta con Sua Santità nell'udienza del 13 maggio 1848," doc. 75 in DRS 1949–51, vol. 2, pp. 147–48.

32. Viale Prelà a Orioli, Vienna, 13 maggio 1848, doc. 25 in Lukács 1981, pp. 313–14.

33. Stearns 1974, pp. 102–15.

34. "Proclama di S.M. Il Re Ferdinando II. Napoli 9 Aprile," BSMC, FS; Francia 2012, pp. 230–31; Di Rienzio 2012, p. 43; Rossi 2001, pp. 32–34; Ward 1970, pp. 186–87.

35. Farini 1850–53, vol. 2, pp. 144–45; Demarco 1947, pp. 77–79; Patuelli 1998, pp. 27–32, 38–39.

36. Datelined Rome, December 2, 1848, letter XXV in Fuller 1856, p. 328; Fuller to Elizabeth Cranch, Rome, 14 May 1848, letter 718 in Fuller 1988, p. 65. The reference to Lot's wife is from Genesis 19:26. Fuller's Decem-

ber 2 report was her first from Rome in six months. Having become pregnant as a result of her romance with a Roman man, she had gone into seclusion to escape notice while she prepared to bear her child. Leaving her infant son with a wet nurse shortly after his birth, she returned to Rome and resumed her reporting.

37. "In pronouncing that allocution," the pope told the Dutch ambassador, "which has now unleashed against me so much passion, I was simply responding to the voice of my conscience. Ah well! If it must come at the cost of my temporal power, let God's will be done." Liedekerke à Monsieur le Comte, Rome, 8 mai 1848, doc. XXV in Liedekerke 1949, pp. 42–44.

38. Martina 1966, p. 559. Giuseppe Tabboni's account of his papal audience is in Bianchi 1869, vol. 5, pp. 239–40.

CHAPTER 6: FENDING OFF DISASTER

1. Mount Edgcumbe 1850, pp. 8–9; Farini 1850–53, vol. 2, p. 203; Johnston 1901, p. 164; Candeloro 1972, p. 205.

2. Soglia a Mons. Brunelli, delegato apostolico, Madrid, Roma, 17 giugno 1848, ASV, ANM, b. 312, ff. 57r–58r; Panigada 1937, p. 1795.

3. Liedekerke à Monsieur le Baron, Rome, 7 juin 1848, doc. XXX in Liedekerke 1949, pp. 57–58; Candeloro 1972, pp. 312–13; Farini 1850–53, vol. 2, p. 145; Martina 2004, pp. 193–94. "Here," wrote one deputy from Rome on June 23, "things couldn't be going worse. The Minister Mamiani is an incompetent nonentity." Panigada 1937, p. 1795.

4. Ghisalberti 1958, p. 73n; Engel-Janosi 1950, pp. 139–40; Leflon 1963, p. 385n; Liedekerke 1949, pp. 72–73.

5. Harcourt à Bastide, Rome, 28 juin 1848, n. 2, MAEC, CP, Rome, vol. 988, ff. 65r–67r; Agulhon 1983, p. 61; Milza 2004, p. 147; Chantrel 1861, p. 55. The nuncio in Paris offered his own account of the fighting in a letter to the nuncio in Madrid, describing the archbishop as "a true victim of his pastoral zeal, sacrificed to the cannibals' fury." ASV, ANM, b. 312, ff. 55r. It appears that the archbishop was hit by a stray bullet. Collins 1923, pp. 128–31.

6. The letter quoted is by F. Mayr al cugino, 8 luglio 1848, doc. IV in Panigada 1937, p. 1798. Mayr adds, "The Pope is not with us."

7. To this could be added the description left by Marco Minghetti, then a fellow deputy, and no admirer of the prince: "He had in his face—and also in the intonation of his voice—something of the characteristics of the Bonaparte family. . . . He was fat, ruddy, and showy. He busied himself in and made a great din about everything. He was a man of acute intelligence, highly cultured, indeed a scholar of natural history, lively and facetious in conversation, but his character was ugly, and all the more repugnant the greater were the advantages of his intelligence and his class."

     For attitudes in the Chamber to Charles Napoleon, see Panigada 1937, p. 1796; Zucconi 2011, p. 112; Giovagnoli 1894, pp. 218–19; Bartoccini 1969. Minghetti (1889, vol. 1, pp. 203–4) observed that so great was the prince of Canino's reputation for lying that telling a great falsehood in Rome came to be referred to as telling a "caninata."

8. Liedekerke à Monsieur le Baron, Rome, 7 juillet 1848, doc. XXXV in Liedekerke 1949, p. 72.

9. Harcourt à Bastide, Rome, 14 juillet 1848, MAEC, CP, Rome, vol. 988, ff. 73r–74r; Quazza 1952, p. lxxiii.

10. The pope's quote is from D. Pareto al Ministro L. Pareto, Roma, 17 luglio 1848, doc. 133 in DRS 1949–51, vol. 2, p. 201. The quotes from the Dutch ambassador are found in Liedekerke 1949, p. 80. These events are also described in Harcourt à Bastide, 18 juillet 1848, MAEC, CP, Rome, vol. 988, ff. 80r–80v; Pasolini 1887, pp. 116–18; Farini 1850–53, vol. 2, pp. 264–70; Candeloro 1972, p. 314. The letter of protest was signed by the secretary of state.

11. Roncalli 1972, p. 303; Ward 1970, pp. 205–8; Mack Smith 1994, p. 62; Francia 2012, pp. 188–89.

12. Chantrel 1861, p. 55; Card. Soglia al nunzio a Madrid, 29 luglio 1848, ASV, ANM, b. 312, ff. 71r–72r. Pásztor (1966, p. 334) cites the copy of this circular sent to the Vienna nuncio.

13. "Unfortunately," the ambassador added, "the state of despondency in which the pope has now for some time found himself, deepened even further following the latest news, does not permit him to make use of those powerful moral means that he would have in his power, nor does he ever seem to be planning to use them." D. Pareto al Ministro L. Pareto, Roma, 3 agosto 1848, 7 agosto 1848, docs. 148 and 152 in DRS 1949–51, vol. 2, pp. 217–18, 221; Liedekerke à Monsieur le Baron, 3 août 1848, doc. XLI in Liedekerke 1949, pp. 83–84.

14. Harcourt à Bastide, Rome, 11 août 1848, MAEN, RSS 409.

15. Bastide à Harcourt, 18 août 1848, MAEN, RSS 273; D. Pareto al Marchese L. Pareto, Roma, 17 agosto 1848, doc. 164 in DRS 1949–51, vol. 2, pp. 230–31.

16. De Reiset 1903, pp. 167–70; DRS 1949–51, vol. 2, p. lxxvi.

17. Jacob L. Martin to James Buchanan, Rome, 20 August 1848, in Stock 1933, pp. 8–15; Rossi 1954, p. 62.

18. J. C. Hooker to James Buchanan, Rome, 26 [August] 1848, in Stock 1933, pp. 15–16; Marraro 1944, p. 490. Martin was buried in Rome's Protestant cemetery. For a rich description of the impact of malaria in Rome around the time, see Desmarie 1860, pp. 51–58.

19. Bastide à Harcourt, Paris, 25 août 1848, MAEN, RSS 273.

20. Ministro a Marchese Pareto, 6 agosto 1848, doc. 18 in DRS 1949–51, vol. 2, pp. 18–19; Capograssi 1941, pp. 1–3; Radice 1972, pp. 60–65. The government's instructions for Rosmini can be found in Rosmini 1998, pp. 12–14. "It would be difficult to say," observed Luigi Carlo Farini, prominent patriotic member of the Chamber of Deputies in Rome, "which was greater," Rosmini's "religiosity, knowledge and intelligence, or his modesty, goodness, and love for Italy." Farini 1850–53, vol. 2, p. 335.

21. "Most of the cardinals," observed the Sardinian ambassador of Rossi in Rome in early August, "don't hide their disapproval of him, and those who as a result of the positions they hold have to meet with him, com-

plain loudly about the ambiguity of the way he works." D. Pareto al Ministro L. Pareto, Roma, 4 agosto 1848, doc. 150 in DRS 1949–51, vol. 2, pp. 219–20.

22. Jules Bastide, the French foreign minister, whose response would arrive too late to do any good, called the notion of Rossi's appointment "so extraordinary, it would be an act so gratuitously offensive to the French Republic and its Government . . . that I do not understand how the thought could have occurred to the Holy Father." Harcourt à Bastide, 24 juillet 1848, MAEN, RSS 409; Bastide à Harcourt, 3 août 1848, MAEN, RSS 273.

23. "I know how hard the task I have taken on is," Rossi confided in a letter to a friend at the time. "I know that I will encounter obstacles and impediments even where I should find encouragement and aid. I will do all I can to satisfy my conscience as a man, as a citizen, and as an Italian." Rossi a Vincenzo Salvagnoli, Roma, 10 settembre 1848, doc. C in Salvagnoli 1859, pp. 123–24.

24. If Harcourt now took a less belligerent attitude to his predecessor, it was because Rossi had been able to change his mind. The pope's choice, Rossi argued, was a clear sign of his intention to look to France rather than to Austria for support. "The Holy Father," explained the French ambassador, "has very good intentions, but he is weak and irresolute, and his entourage is in general despicable, which is to say, devoted to the Austrians and retrograde." One could never be sure that what the pope promised one day he would do the next. Given all this, said Harcourt, France could only benefit by having Rossi appointed. "The greatest danger," Harcourt concluded, "is that the situation has already become more than he can handle, and drags him down like all the rest." Harcourt au ministre des affaires étrangères, Rome, 4 septembre 1848, MAEN, RSS 409.

25. Liedekerke à Monsieur le Baron, Rome, 15 septembre 1848 and 24 septembre 1848, docs. L and LII in Liedekerke 1949, pp. 102–3, 106–8; Harcourt au ministre des affaires étrangères, Rome, 24 septembre 1848, n. 17, MAEC, CP, Rome, vol. 988, ff. 125r–125v; Cittadini 1989, pp. 134–35.

26. Harcourt au ministre des affaires étrangères, Rome, 4 octobre 1848, MAEN, RSS 409.

27. Rosmini al ministro degli affari esteri in Torino, Roma, 4 ottobre 1848, in Paoli 1880, pp. 401–3; Rosmini 1998, pp. 74–77.

28. Citoyen romain 1852, pp. 102–3; Comando generale della Guardia Civica, Roma, 23 ottobre 1848, doc. LVIII in Giovagnoli 1898, pp. 378–79.

29. Ferdinando Lefèvre, capitano a S. E. il Comandante generale della Guardia Civica, 28 ottobre 1848, doc. IX in Giovagnoli 1898, pp. 379–80; C. Terzi, capitano di guardia, rapporto, Guardia Civica, battaglione 5, 28 ottobre 1848, doc. XL in Giovagnoli 1898, pp. 394–95; Giovagnoli 1898, p. 243; Citoyen romain 1852, pp. 103–4.

30. Laras 1973, pp. 515–16. On allowing Jews into the Civic Guard, see ASCER, Co. 48, f2, Rb, 9 sup. 2, f. 3 for June and July 1848. Demarco 1947, pp. 70, 104; Capuzzo 1999, p. 273. A brief attempt to convince the pope to fully emancipate the Jews of his domains, which appears to date from these months, titled "Memoria sulla Emancipazione degli Ebrei

negli Stati Pontifici considerata nel punto di vista dell'interesse della Chiesa Cattolica," is found at ASCER, Co. 48, f2, Rb, 9 sup. 2, p1, f. 11.

31. Stearns 1974, pp. 119–21; Candeloro 1972, pp. 284–85; Roncalli 1972, p. 309; "Lettera di Giuseppe Mazzini, Insurrezione nazionale," 29 ottobre 1848, BSMC, FS; Harcourt au ministre des affaires étrangères, 4 novembre 1848, MAEN, RSS 409.

32. The quote is from Balleydier 1851, vol. 1, pp. 229–30. The text of the ministerial order establishing the first two telegraph lines in the Papal States, dated 29 settembre 1848, is found in Stato pontificio 1850–51, pp. 256–57. Typical of the hostility Rossi inspired was the reaction of Andrea Bonfigli, a prominent layman then responsible for the papal government in Rieti, north of Rome. Paying a visit to the capital in October, he went to introduce himself to the new minister. Rossi, he recalled in his diary, treated him as if he were a "vassal, with such a tone of arrogance and supremacy that I have myself never treated a prison guard." His next meeting with Rossi was even more humiliating, as Bonfigli came to see him before leaving Rome. "He made me wait three hours in the antechamber, always standing, he never looked me in the face, and after a few brief questions he dismissed me." From Bonfigli's diary, in Cittadini 1989, pp. 134–35.

33. Rossi à Vincent Salvagnoli à Florence, doc. LXXII in Ledermann 1929, pp. 346–47; Trevelyan 1907, pp. 74–75.

34. Harcourt au ministre des affaires étrangères, Rome, 14 octobre 1848, Harcourt au ministre des affaires étrangères, Rome, 4 novembre 1848, MAEN, RSS 409; Pareto a Perrone, Roma, 14 ottobre 1848, doc. 212 in DRS 1949–51, vol. 2, p. 273; Rossi a Cardinale Amat, Roma, 17 ottobre 1848, doc. LXXV in Ledermann 1929, pp. 349–50; Martina 1974, pp. 280, 287; Trevelyan 1907, pp. 74–75; Rossi 2001, p. 40. The meal is reported by the Sardinian ambassador in Rome, who noted that Rosmini was also invited. Pareto a Perrone, Roma, 14 ottobre 1848, doc. 212 in DRS 1949–51, vol. 2, p. 273.

35. Roncalli 1972, p. 312; Liedekerke à Monsieur le Baron, Rome, 11 novembre 1848, doc. LV in Liedekerke 1949, pp. 112–13; Lancellotti 1862, p. 7; Cittadini 1989, p. 138.

36. Zucchi 1861, p. 146; Cittadini 1989, pp. 137–38.

37. Zucchi 1861, pp. 146–50; Pareto a Perrone, Roma, 13 novembre 1848, doc. 229 in DRS 1949–51, vol. 2, pp. 286–87; Giovagnoli 1898, p. 244n; Candeloro 1972, pp. 275–79.

38. Bianchi 1869, vol. 6, p. 16.

CHAPTER 7: THE ASSASSINATION

1. Marco Minghetti, who passed them as he made his way into the building that day, was himself taken aback, describing the legionnaires as "sinister looking thugs." Minghetti 1889, vol. 2, p. 122; Farini 1850–53, vol. 2, pp. 366–67.

2. There are numerous accounts of the morning of Rossi's murder and of the murder itself, and many are clearly unreliable. I have tried here as

best I can to stick closely to eyewitness sources and to avoid the many embellishments the story has acquired. Among those I've used is the description given in Michelangelo Pinto's unpublished manuscript, MCRR, Fondo Pinto, b. 887, pp. 139–43; also Ideville 1887, pp. 231–50; Arrigoni 1996, pp. 71–72, 80–85; Roncalli 1972, pp. 315–16; Nicefero 1899, pp. 165–67; Rosmini alla cognata Adelaide Cristiani, Gaeta, 29 novembre 1848, doc. XLII in Rosmini 1998, pp. 338–39; Pasolini 1887, p. 145n; Martina 1974, pp. 289–90. The account that seems most credible, and the one largely employed by Martina (1974, pp. 289–90), is offered by Giovagnoli (1898, pp. 266–71). In this recounting, seven men met in a little tavern the evening of November 14 to plan the murder. The mastermind was Pietro Sterbini—the exiled doctor-poet who had returned to Rome following Pio Nono's amnesty, and who had months earlier written one of the most popular songs of praise to the pope. It seems that at a meeting on the evening of November 12, Pietro Sterbini, Charles Bonaparte, and Ciceruacchio decided that Rossi should be killed. On the fourteenth, Sterbini, appealing to the young man's commitment to the cause of freedom and challenging him to show his courage, convinced Luigi Brunetti, Ciceruacchio's elder son, to do the deed. The investigation of who killed Rossi, begun immediately after the murder but then suspended until September 1849, lasted until 1854. For diplomatic reasons, the pope decided to repress all direct mention of the role of Charles Bonaparte, the cousin of the ruler of France. There remains some uncertainty about the details. Bartoccini (1969, p. 8), in his examination of the evidence, argues that Charles Bonaparte bore only moral responsibility for the murder and was not directly involved in planning it. See also Niceforo 1899, pp. 165–66.

3. Giovagnoli 1898, p. 281; Ideville 1887, pp. 257–58.
4. Giovagnoli 1911, pp. 23–24, 38; Boero 1850, p. 138.
5. Giovagnoli 1898, pp. 282–87; Farini 1850–53, vol. 2, pp. 373–75; Martina 1974, pp. 290–91; Pasolini 1887, p. 145n.
6. Minghetti 1889, vol. 2, p. 125.
7. Carlo Muzzarelli, president of the Upper Chamber, was a cleric of a peculiar stripe. Although addressed as monsignor and wearing black clerical gowns, the sixty-one-year-old Muzzarelli was not an ordained priest. From a noble family in Ferrara, he had worked as an ecclesiastical lawyer in the administration of the Holy See in Rome while pursuing his literary interests, including a passion for Latin. Although no radical, he had over the past months been won over to the patriotic cause; Bustico 1939.
8. Minghetti 1889, vol. 2, pp. 123–25; Pasolini 1887, pp. 144–49; Gabussi 1851–52, vol. 2, pp. 216–20.
9. Giovagnoli 1898, p. 289; Lancellotti 1862, p. 15. The quote is from Mount Edgcumbe 1850, p. 14.
10. Rosmini a Donna Adelaide Cristani, Gaeta, 29 novembre 1848, doc. XLII in Rosmini 1998, pp. 339–40; Liedekerke à Monsieur le Baron, Rome, 24 novembre 1848, Liedekerke 1949, p. 117. That Margaret Fuller's reports of events were not always accurate is evident in her own report of the death of Monsignor Palma, which she did not witness.

"This man," wrote the American correspondent, "provoked his fate by firing on the people from a window." Deiss 1969, p. 185.

11. Harcourt à Bastide, 17 novembre 1848, Rome, MAEC, CP, Rome, vol. 988, ff. 146r–147v; Foramiti 1850, p. 13.

12. Farini 1850–53, vol. 2, p. 380. A slightly different version of the pope's remarks is given in Spada 1868–69, vol. 2, p. 524.

13. Pareto a Perrone, Roma, 17 novembre 1848, doc. 234 in DRS 1949–51, vol. 2, pp. 289–90; Gaillard 1861, pp. 419–23. The disarming of the Swiss Guard is chronicled in "Parlamento del Corpo Diplomatico a S. Sanità presso il Quirinale ed altre notizie del giorno," Roma, 17 novembre [1848], MCRR, ms. 126/33, Nicola Roncalli, documenti a stampa, 1848.

14. Rosmini a Donna Adelaide Cristani, Gaeta, 29 novembre 1848, doc. XLII in Rosmini 1998, p. 340; Rosmini a Puecher, Gaeta, 19 dicembre 1848, doc. XLV/2 in Rosmini 1998, pp. 354–55.

15. Pásztor 1966, pp. 334–35; Camarotto 2012; Pareto a Perrone, Roma, 17 novembre 1848, doc. 235 in DRS 1949–51, vol. 2, p. 291. The pope's remarks are taken from the Tuscan ambassador's report, quoted in Ferrari 2002, p. 127.

16. Harcourt à Bastide, 17 novembre 1848, Rome, MAEC, CP, Rome, vol. 988, ff. 146r–147v. By the seventeenth, Cardinal Soglia was already sending out letters to the nuncios recounting these events, the violence used against the pope on the sixteenth, and his ceding to force with the approval of the diplomatic corps. Card. Soglia al Nunzio Apostolico, Madrid, ASV, ANM, b. 313, f. 70r. The text of the program presented to the pope by the newly appointed government ministers on November 17, then published the next day in Rome, can be found in Miraglia 1850, pp. 36–37. It focused on plans to have the Papal States take part in the battle for Italian independence, with the pope joining with the rulers of the other states of Italy in some kind of political union.

17. Roncalli 1972, p. 320; Liedekerke à Monsieur le Baron, Rome, 24 novembre 1848, doc. LVIII in Liedekerke 1949, p. 119. For the cardinal's later remarks citing the protection that Holy Mary gave him that day, and the symbolism of his possible death in the hay in the manger, see the passage from his letter quoted in Manzini 1960, p. 401.

18. Liedekerke à Monsieur le Baron, Rome, 24 novembre 1848, doc. LVIII in Liedekerke 1949, p. 119.

19. The letter of Jules Bastide, the French foreign minister, to Harcourt in Rome, recounting these instructions, is reproduced in Leflon 1963, p. 388.

20. "It is extremely unfortunate," Madrid's ambassador reported to his government, "that on an occasion as serious as this, the steamship that was sent to Civitavecchia is not there. . . . Today, I briefly got to see His Holiness who was so pleased by my offers in the name of Her Majesty's government that he could not hold back his tears." De Chambrun 1936, pp. 330–31; Key 1898, pp. 117–18, 175.

21. Pareto a Perrone, Roma, 18 novembre 1848, doc. 236 in DRS 1949–51, vol. 2, pp. 291–92; Aubert 1961, p. 3; Coppa 1990, p. 59. That morning, having heard the same rumors, Rosmini went to see the pope. Cardinal

Antonelli, whom he found waiting outside the pope's door, pretended to know nothing about any plan for escape. But, he asked Rosmini, did he think leaving Rome was a good idea? Yes, replied the abbot. Pius was no longer safe in Rome. He had come not to dissuade the pope from leaving but to ask whether the pontiff would want Rosmini to join him wherever he went. Antonelli agreed to ask and went into the pope's quarters. He returned a few minutes later, with the pope's reply: the pope would be very grateful if Rosmini would join him at his destination. Rosmini 1998, pp. 88–89.

22. Pareto a Perrone, Roma, 21 novembre 1848, doc. 238 in DRS 1949–51, vol. 2, pp. 294–95; Minghetti 1889, vol. 2, p. 128.
23. Spada 1868–69, vol. 2, p. 443.
24. Minghetti 1889, vol. x, pp. 128–31; Spada 1868–69, vol. 2, p. 534.

CHAPTER 8: THE ESCAPE

1. Flint 2003, pp. 109–10; De Chambrun 1936, pp. 327–29.
2. The letter from the bishop of Valence is dated October 15, 1848, and reproduced in Orbe 1850, vol. 1, pp. 1–2; Jankowiak 2008, p. 131n; Pelczar 1909, p. 406; Martina 1974, p. 298; Berra 1957, p. 684.
3. This had the advantage of enlisting the aid of the two major Catholic powers in Europe, for in the absence of the Austrian ambassador, withdrawn earlier from Rome in protest, Spaur represented Austrian interests in Rome. De Chambrun 1936, p. 339; Spaur 1851, pp. 16–17; Simeoni 1932, p. 255; Berra 1957, p. 672.
4. Key 1898, p. 176.
5. The *Ténare* had been at Civitavecchia for more than a month at that point, left there at Harcourt's disposal. De Chambrun 1936, p. 335.
6. Monsagrati 2014, pp. 5–6; Spaur 1851, pp. 17–21. According to the Belgian ambassador, on seeing that he would have to get in the carriage with Spaur's wife, the pope exclaimed, *"Je dois donc boire le calice jusqu'à la lie"* (And so I must drink the chalice to the dregs). She would come to be known in diplomatic circles, with not a little sarcasm, as "Our Lady of Gaeta." De Ligne 1929, pp. 170–71, 181. For more on Teresa Spaur, see Berra 1957, p. 672; Silvagni 1887, pp. 281–86.
7. Piscicelli 1978, p. 28.
8. The text of the pope's letter is found in Spaur 1851, pp. 33–34; De Chambrun 1936, pp. 345–47.
9. Blois 1854, pp. 7–9.
10. Ibid., pp. 9–10.
11. De Chambrun 1936, pp. 333–34.
12. Martina 1974, pp. 299–300. In an early December letter to the nuncio in Paris, Antonelli described his arrival with the pope in Gaeta as "truly by chance, because we had planned to go in a very different direction on leaving from Rome." Pásztor 1966, p. 340n. However, the evidence suggests that it was Antonelli who steered the pope to Gaeta and made sure he remained there. Liedekerke à Monsieur le Baron, Rome, 27 novembre

1848, 10 a.m., doc. LIX in Liedekerke 1949, p. 120; "Preciso ragguaglio dell'imbarco di S.S. a Civitavecchia," BSMC, FS; Pareto a Perrone, Roma, 25 novembre 1848, docs. 243 and 244, in DRS 1949–51, vol. 2, pp. 298–99.

Before Harcourt set sail from Civitavecchia to Gaeta, he had sent a message to the French foreign minister. The pope had left Rome the previous evening, he reported, "and his intention is to go to France. He has gone to Gaeta, a convenient place for embarking on the *Ténare*." Why the pope would have gone to Gaeta in order to board the French ship Harcourt did not explain. De Chambrun 1936, pp. 338–39; Mollat 1939, p. 276.

13. Blois 1854, pp. 10–11; Filipuzzi 1961, vol. 1, pp. 364–65.

14. Roncalli 1972, p. 324; "Romani," 25 novembre 1848, BSMC, FS. In a second moment, a somewhat less breathless version was posted: "Romans, The Pontiff left Rome this past night, taken in by pernicious advice." The government, the ministers went on to say, would continue to function and ensure public order. "Romans!" it concluded, "have faith in us, show yourselves worthy of the name you bear, and respond with the highest standards of character to the calumnies of your enemies." "Lettera lasciata di Pio Nono," 24 e 25 novembre 1848, BSMC, FS.

15. Forbin-Janson à Bastide, 25 novembre 1848, MAEC, CP, Rome, vol. 988, ff. 150r–152r.

16. Bonaparte 1857, pp. 229–33.

17. Nor was Ferdinand helped by the portly papal nuncio in Naples, a man who was, reported the British diplomat, good-humored and kindhearted but "much engrossed with eating; I will not say that his belly is his God, but it is certainly his diocese." Napier, chargé d'affaires, Naples, to Minto, 15 November 1847, in Curato 1970, vol. 1, p. 200.

18. Radice 1972, p. 84; Spaur 1851, pp. 47–49; Ward 1970, pp. 125–26; Candeloro 1972, pp. 70–71; Giovagnoli 1894, p. 26; Scirocco 1996, p. 7.

19. Rayneval à Bastide, Naples, 26 novembre 1848, MAEC, PAR; De Chambrun 1936, p. 352.

20. "Rome, Naples, and Sicily," datelined Naples, December 2, TL, December 13, 1848; Radice 1972, pp. 84–85n.

CHAPTER 9: THE REACTIONARY TURN

1. De Ligne 1923, p. 319; Ghisalberti 1958, p. 56n; Spada 1868–69, vol. 3, pp. 73–83.

2. De Ligne 1929, pp. 186–88; De La Rochère 1853, pp. 176–77.

3. Cittadini 1989, p. 139; Pásztor 1966, p. 337. Antonelli's actual title was "pro-secretary of state," the "pro" referring in this case to the provisional nature of an appointment made outside Rome. Coppa 1990, p. 66. Antonelli sent the nuncios and ambassadors accredited to the Holy See word of his appointment on December 6. Antonelli a Mons. Giovanni Brunelli, nunzio apostolico, Madrid, ASV, ANM, b. 313, f. 3r; Antonelli a Domenico Pareto, Gaeta, 7 dicembre 1848, doc. 257 in DRS 1949–51, vol. 2, p. 316.

4. The very fact that Antonelli's traits were so different from the pope's is what most recommended him to the pontiff. "Pius IX," wrote Father Martina, the pope's biographer, "emotional, impulsive, optimistic, little inclined to examine the big political problems in depth, found in Antonelli not only a man extremely able in practical matters, but also the expert, discreet politician, with that sense for judging men and their motives which too often the Pontiff himself lacked." Dalla Torre 1979, pp. 144, 193; Martina 2004, p. 194; Martina 1974, p. 309.

5. Pásztor 1966, p. 340n; Montezomolo al Signor Presidente del Consiglio, Mola di Gaeta, 30 dicembre 1848, doc. 105 in DRS 1949–51, vol. 2, pp. 477–79.

6. Amid the uncertainty, journalists and diplomats spread the latest rumors of the pope's imminent departure. The London *Times* went so far as to report, on December 5, that Pius had already left Gaeta and arrived in Malta, under British protection. "Arrival of the Pope in Malta," TL, December 5, 1848. The *Times* published a story the next day confirming the pope's arrival there.

7. Flint 2003, p. 118; Pirri 1949, p. 9. On the invitation of the Portuguese queen, see the letter of the nuncio in Portugal to the nuncio in Madrid: Lisbona, 23 dicembre 1848, ASV, ANM, b. 313, f. 42r.

8. Agulhon 1983, pp. 69–71; Milza 2004, pp. 152–53; Collins 1923, pp. 158–60.

9. Lespès 1852, pp. 247–49; Bastide 1858, pp. 211–13; Boyer 1956, pp. 244–45; Bastide à Harcourt, Paris, 27 novembre 1848, MAEN, RSS 274; Bastide 1858, pp. 199–201; De Chambrun 1936, pp. 357–64.

10. Leflon 1963, pp. 389–90.

11. De Chambrun 1936, p. 481. Bishops throughout France, hearing the news of the pope's impending arrival, competed with offers of hospitality. Among those that the nuncio communicated to the pope was one from the French department of Vaucluse, where the governing council unanimously voted to invite the pope to reestablish the papal residence—after an absence of four and a half centuries—in Avignon. The papal nuncio communicated these offers to the pope through the secretary of state, writing from Paris on December 8. ASV, Segr. Stato, An. 1848–50, Rubr. 248, fasc. 2, ff. 83r–84r.

12. Louis Napoleon had spent a good part of his youth in Italy and, along with his brother, had gone off to join in the revolt against papal rule in 1831, during which his brother died. In late October 1848, the leader of the Catholic party in France met with Louis Napoleon to determine if he merited Catholic support. Confronted with his antipapal past, Louis Napoleon replied: "I understand your scruples. . . . I have indeed taken part in insurrections against the Holy See, and I have had the misfortune to lose my brother thereby. But that is one of the deeds that I regret most. I shall repair it, if God spares my life. . . . I am a Catholic, not perhaps as good a one as you, but still I am one, and I revere all the traditions." Collins 1923, pp. 175–77; Choffat 2008, pp. 94–95.

13. As Tocqueville put it, Louis Napoleon was backed by his supporters from the elite "not because of any merits, but due to his presumed medi-

ocrity. They believed they found in him an instrument which they could use at their discretion." Tocqueville 1893, pp. 313–18. See also Bastide 1858, p. 191; Milza 2004, pp. 167–68; Choffat 2008, pp. 92–93, 102; McMillan 1991, pp. 32–35; Agulhon 1983, pp. 71–73; Yvert 2008, p. 107; Barrot 1876, pp. 28–29; Fraser 1896, p. 114. The text of Louis Napoleon's letter is found in Spada 1868–69, vol. 3, pp. 54–55.

14. Rayneval, who had inherited the title of count on his father's death a dozen years earlier, had long experience in Italy, having earlier served for five years as first secretary to the French embassy in Rome. He had been appointed French ambassador to the Kingdom of Naples only a few months before the pope's surprising appearance at Gaeta. MAEC, PDI, 29 juin 1848. The same archival collection has other, undated documents recounting the diplomatic postings of Rayneval.

15. Blois 1854, pp. 23, 26; De Chambrun 1936, pp. 485–86, 492–94; Leflon 1963, pp. 396–97; Rayneval à Bastide, Naples, 7 décembre 1848, n. 49, MAEC, PAR; De Ligne 1929, pp. 180–81. To the Spanish ambassador, who tried to dissuade the pope from going to France by warning him against trusting in a republican government, Pius replied that in any case he had not intended to go to Paris. He was thinking, he said, of first going to Marseilles but only for a short time. The Spaniard urged him to take refuge in Majorca under Spanish protection.

16. Harcourt à Bastide, Gaëte, 2 décembre 1848, MAEN, RSS 409; Boyer 1956, p. 246; Rayneval à Bastide, Naples, 30 novembre 1848, MAEC, PAR.

17. The Sardinian ambassador was among the few who supported the French position that the pope seek compromise. But in early December, the Sardinian ambassador to Naples reported that Pius was now surrounded "by all those who had always reproached him for his path of reform." Only by extracting the pope from Gaeta, and ideally having him come to Piedmont, thought the diplomat, could disaster be averted. Collobiano à Perrone, Naples, 4 décembre 1848, doc. 224 in DRS 1949–51, vol. 3, p. 219; Pareto a Perrone, Gaeta, 5 dicembre 1848, doc. 253 in DRS 1949–51, vol. 2, p. 311.

18. Key 1898, p. 178. The quote is from Key's letter dated December 1, 1848. Antonelli called on all the ambassadors to leave Rome and join the pope at Gaeta. When the Sardinian government initially balked at this move, their ambassador informed Turin that virtually all the other foreign envoys to Rome had gone to be with the pope. To remain in Rome would be viewed as a huge affront to the papacy. He too quickly joined his colleagues. Pareto a Perrone, Roma, 2 dicembre 1848, doc. 250 in DRS 1949–51, vol. 2, p. 309. Antonelli's circular to the foreign emissaries, dated Gaeta, 27 novembre 1848, is reproduced in DRS 1949–51, vol. 2, p. 310.

19. As the French envoy in Rome reported at the beginning of December, "The city's tranquility has never been greater. Maintaining it, though, will depend on the pope's first declarations, which people await with extreme impatience." Forbin Janson à Bastide, Rome, 1 décembre 1849, MAEC, CP, Rome, vol. 988, ff. 157r–158r. A few days later the Sardinian

envoy remaining in Rome offered similar observations: "So far the city is perfectly tranquil, yet in extreme anxiety over the uncertain future." Della Minerva al ministero degli affari esteri, Roma, 5 dicembre 1848, doc. 272 in DRS 1949–51, vol. 2, pp. 334–35. On the rumors, see Lancellotti 1862, p. 31; "The Escape of the Pope," TL, December 7, 1848.

20. Severini 1995, pp. 135–36.
21. Terenzio Mamiani al Marchese Pareto, Roma, 29 novembre 1848, appendix to doc. 248 in DRS 1949–51, vol. 2, pp. 305–6. The text received by the French embassy is found at MAEC, CP, Rome, vol. 988, ff. 159r–161r. Mamiani had written on November 27 to the various papal nuncios of Europe informing them that he should be regarded as the foreign minister of the Papal States, although none of the nuncios would agree to his request. Mamiani al nunzio di Napoli, Roma, 27 novembre 1848, ASV, ANN, b. 392, ff. 52r–52v; Mamiani al nunzio di Madrid, Roma, 27 novembre 1848, ASV, ANM, b. 313, ff. 47r–48r.
22. Rosmini 1998, pp. 99–100; Martina 1974, pp. 544–45.
23. A printed copy of the pope's address to his subjects was sent to the nuncios. ASV, ANM, b. 313, f. 69r; Pie IX 1855, pp. 2–5; Blaas 1973, p. 36; Della Minerva al ministero affari esteri, Roma, 4 dicembre 1848, doc. 271 in DRS 1949–51, vol. 2, pp. 332–33. After dismissing the government in Rome as illegitimate, the pope, almost as an afterthought, announced the creation of a government commission to ensure public order in Rome. He listed its members, headed by a cardinal, with one other prelate, four aristocrats, and the head of his army, General Zucchi. But when the members learned of their appointment, the only three who remained in the city fled. The cardinal was left alone to figure out what to do, but the task the pope had assigned him was clearly impossible and the commission never convened. It seems that the cardinal was more inclined to take a conciliatory approach to the governing institutions in Rome than Antonelli and the pope were willing to abide. Pásztor 1966, pp. 340–43. Few of Rome's aristocrats remained in the city. Captain Key (1898, p. 177), in explaining their departure, remarked that "their excuse is, that they cannot recognize the existing ministry; their reason is fear."
24. "Gl'inni e il maestro Magazzari," Il vero amico del popolo, 29 dicembre 1849, p. 130; Martina 1974, pp. 289–90; Pierre 1878, pp. 50–51; Gemignani 1995, p. 234; Farini 1850–53, vol. 3, pp. 105–6.
25. Pareto a Perrone, Roma, 2 dicembre 1848, doc. 250 in DRS 1949–51, vol. 2, pp. 308–9; Farini 1850–53, vol. 3, pp. 20–21; Candeloro 1972, pp. 337–38; Ideville 1887, pp. 145–46.
26. Martina 2000, p. 353; Jankowiak 2008, p. 143; Gabussi 1851–52, vol. 2, pp. 265–66.
27. Palomba, console generale d'Austria a Civitavecchia a Lützow, Civitavecchia, 8 dicembre 1848, doc. 6, allegato E, in Blaas 1973, p. 36.
28. Brevetti 2014, p. 185; Di Rienzo 2012, p. 15; Scirocco 1996, pp. 1–2; Arcuno 1933, p. 11.
29. Rayneval à Bastide, Naples, 2 décembre 1848, 12 décembre 1848, 14 décembre 1848, MAEC, PAR; Montezemolo à Gioberti, Mola di Gaeta,

31 dicembre 1848, doc. 106 in DRS 1949–51, vol. 2, p. 480; De Ligne 1929, p. 176; Blois 1854, pp. 27–29; Koelman 1963, vol. 1, p. 179; Scirocco 1996, p. 7.

30. Rayneval à Bastide, Naples, 14 décembre 1848, MAEC, PAR; Pareto al ministro degli affari esteri, Torino, 16 dicembre 1848 and 18 dicembre 1848, docs. 260 and 261 in DRS 1949–51, vol. 2, p. 316.

31. The pope greeted visitors in his bedroom while sitting at a small writing table covered with papers and a crucifix. "Seeing him again in a foreign land, after being forced into exile from his own States," recalled the Dutch ambassador following his first meeting with the pope at Gaeta, "and observing the profound alteration of his features, on which it was all too easy to read all that he had endured and was still enduring in moral suffering, I could not help but experience great emotion to the point where at first I was unable to respond to the words of goodness and affectionate welcome that the pope, as in better days, deigned to address to me." "Even the coldest heart is moved," remarked the Belgian ambassador after his first meeting with the pope in Gaeta. Liedekerke à Monsieur le Baron, Mola-de-Gaëte, 13 décembre 1848, doc. LXIV in Liedekerke 1949, pp. 129–30; De Ligne 1929, pp. 175–76.

32. Key (1898, pp. 179–89) could not be accused of having an overly generous view of Romans in general. In that same letter, while praising their recent behavior, he confessed his belief that their character was "cowardly and contemptible." At the same time, the Sardinian envoy in Rome came to a similar conclusion about the untenable position of the moderates. Della Minerva al ministero degli affari esteri, 18 dicembre 1848, Roma, doc. 283 in DRS 1949–51, vol. 2, p. 345. On the anxiety in Rome, see also Della Minerva's report of the next day in doc. 284, p. 348.

It is reported—although the account seems suspiciously apocryphal, that when Garibaldi arrived in Rome, Ciceruacchio, former indefatigable organizer of celebrations honoring Pius IX, approached him and said, in rhyme: *"Un fatto d'armi io vorrei; Non più paternostri e giubilei"* (I would like to take up arms if you please; enough of the *pater nosters* and jubilees). Spada 1868–69, vol. 3, p. 60; Roncalli 1997, pp. 46, 52; Lancellotti 1862, pp. 41–42, 48; Foramiti 1850, p. 29; Della Minerva al ministero degli affari esteri, Roma, 12 dicembre 1848, doc. 278 in DRS 1949–51, vol. 2, pp. 340–41.

33. Making a similar point, Coppa (1990, p. 68) writes that Antonelli "pandered to the Pope's change of heart rather than provoking it."

34. The text drafted by Rosmini as well as the final text of the papal protest of December 17 are found in Martina 1974, pp. 546–47. Minerva a Gioberti, Roma, 24 dicembre 1848, doc. 288 in DRS 1949–51, vol. 2, pp. 351–52; Rosmini 1998, pp. 101–7; "Rome, Naples, and Sicily," Naples, datelined December 21, TL, January 3, 1849.

35. Candeloro 1972, p. 343; Ferrari 2002, p. 132; Monsagrati 2014, p. 37. The letter is from Giuseppe Pasolini to Marco Minghetti, dated Roma, 20 dicembre 1848, in Pasolini 1887, pp. 162–63.

36. Panigada 1937, pp. 1790–92; Bartoccini 1969, p. 10.

37. Severini 1995, p. 141.

38. In Saffi 1898, pp. 101–4. See also De Felice 1962; Severini 1995, p. 141; Severini 2002b, p. 10.

39. Minerva a Gioberti, Roma, 30 dicembre 1848, doc. 294 in DRS 1949–51, vol. 2, p. 357; Koelman 1963, vol. 1, p. 188; Lancellotti 1862, pp. 54–55; Roncalli 1997, p. 61; Key 1898, pp. 182–83; Vecchi 1851, p. 268. The text of the proclamation is found in Patuelli 1998, pp. 40–41.

40. Montezemolo a Gioberti, Mola di Gaeta, 30 dicembre 1848 and 31 dicembre 1848, docs. 105 and 106 in DRS 1949–51, vol. 2, pp. 477–9, 479–80; Martina 1974, pp. 315–16, 350. On Gioberti's role at the time, see Capograssi 1941, pp. 21–22; Farini 1850–53, vol. 3, pp. 128–31; Saffi 1898, vol. 3, pp. 90–93; Rosmini 1998, pp. 126–29.

41. Inguanez 1930, pp. 93–94.

CHAPTER 10: REVOLUTION

1. Roncalli 1997, p. 68; Demarco 1944, p. 63; Deiss 1969, p. 194.

2. Key 1898, p. 184.

3. "Adding iniquity to iniquity," the pope protested, "the authors and supporters of the demagogic anarchy are trying to destroy the temporal authority of the Roman Pontiff over the Domains of the Holy Church." People, he charged, were being "deluded by fallacious seductions and by preachers of subversive doctrines." An original copy of the pope's address is found in ASV, ANM, b. 313, f. 153r; a published copy can be found in Cittadini 1989, pp. 223–25.

4. Palomba, console generale d'Austria a Civitavecchia, a Lützow, 12 gennaio 1849, doc. 10 in Blaas 1973, pp. 43–44; Pasolini a Minghetti, 8 gennaio 1849, doc. VII in Pasolini 1887, p. 168; Citoyen romain 1852, pp. 146–47; Foramiti 1850, pp. 40–42; Roncalli 1997, p. 72; Fuller 1991, p. 253. That in fact the pope intended his denunciation as an excommunication for any who took part in the election of the Constituent Assembly is made clear in the summary of events sent by Cardinal Antonelli to the nuncios. Antonelli al nunzio, Madrid, Gaeta, 18 febbraio 1849, ASV, ANN, b. 392, ff. 252r–254v, 265r–267r.

5. "Pio IX e la scomunica," articolo estratto dall'*Alba*, 11 gennaio 1849, BSMC, FS.

6. It was hoped, the article concluded, that the archbishop's example would soften the heart of the pontiff, "liberating him from the men around him with their earthly, avaricious, blood-stained advice, and causing him to remember that the Reign of Christ is not of this world." MCRR, ms. 660/41, "Atto del Card. Oppizzoni riguardo la scomunica," estratto dalla *Gazzetta di Roma*, 22 gennaio 1849.

7. Brown to James Buchanan, Rome, January 16, 1849, in Stock 1945, p. 144. "The Pope, to the astonishment of everybody, and to his own detriment," observed a British envoy, "has excommunicated those who have taken part in the Roman government since his departure, and threatens those who may take part in the constituent with the like penalty. Who

would have thought this possible in 1849?" R. Abercrombie to Palmerston, Turin, January 13, 1849, Palmerston papers, online at http://www .archives.soton.ac.uk/palmerston/search.php?agree=Y. Even the most moderate of the city's citizens, reported the Sardinian envoy in Rome, felt that they had a right to provide themselves with a government, and so the pope's order had given "immense force" to Rome's new government. Berghini, 23 gennaio 1849, Roma, doc. 112 in DRS 1949–51, vol. 2, p. 489.

8. Key 1898, p. 188. His letter was sent in February 1849.

9. Lukács 1981, pp. 384–85; Schwarzenberg 1946, pp. 8, 33–35; Chantrel 1861, p. 57; Engel-Janosi 1950, p. 138; Dino 1910, p. 260; Ward 1970, pp. 226–27. Schwarzenberg's friend, Count Friedrich von Beust (1887, pp. 91, 97), added, "Prince Schwarzenberg despised men but did not know them." Schwarzenberg served as foreign minister as well as prime minister. For the Vienna nuncio's characterization of the new Austrian leader, see Lukács 1981, pp. 385–86. Lord Palmerston had referred to Austria under Ferdinand as a "government where the sovereign is an idiot." Ward 1970, p. 112. Apparently Ferdinand resisted the idea of abdicating but was convinced by his wife, the Empress Maria Anna, herself the daughter of King Victor Emmanuel I of Sardinia, whom King Charles Albert succeeded. Schwarzenberg 1946, pp. 33–35.

10. Annuario 1847, pp. 69–70; Schwarzenberg 1946, pp. 93–94n. Nunzio Viale à Antonelli, Vienna, 26 dicembre 1848, doc. 57 in Lukács 1981, pp. 315–16; de la Cour à Drouyn, Vienne, 25 décembre 1848, 30 décembre 1848, MAEC, CP, Austria, vol. 437, ff. 191r–199r, 202r–203r; Nunzio Viale à Antonelli, Vienna, 7 gennaio 1848, doc. 58 in Lukács 1981, pp. 316–18. At first, it looked as though Schwarzenberg might name his own younger brother, Friedrich, who had been made cardinal in 1845 at age thirty-seven, to be the new ambassador to the Holy See. Harcourt, from Gaeta, predicted as much. Harcourt à Drouyn, 11 janvier 1849, MAEN, RSS 410.

11. Schwarzenberg à Esterházy, Vienne, 23 janvier 1849, docs. 12 and 13 (both containing the same date) in Blaas 1973, pp. 52–53, 56–57.

12. An additional factor was that Austria viewed Great Britain as its most powerful rival in Europe and was not eager to encourage a British-French, anti-Austrian alliance. Druidi 1958, p. 221.

13. Drouyn à de la Cour, Paris, 3 janvier 1849, MAEN, Vienne, Article 33, ff. 02r–07r; Pierre 1878, p. 58; Bourgeois and Clermont 1907, pp. 7–8; Falloux 1888, pp. 437–40. Tocqueville, who beginning in June would become Falloux's colleague in the cabinet, characterized Falloux's role in the cabinet by saying "he represented . . . the Church alone." Bourgeois and Clermont 1907, p. 9. Harcourt reported to Paris that it was hard to believe that the pope could be so obtuse as not to see that being brought back to Rome by the Austrian army would cause irreparable harm to the Holy See. Harcourt à Drouyn, Gaëte, 3 janvier 1849, MAEN, RSS 274.

14. Zucchi was among the many who saw Pio Nono as well-meaning but under the spell of the evil Cardinal Antonelli. The pope, Zucchi recalled,

said nothing against his suggestions, yet "in reality the good-hearted but weak Pius IX had already been duped by the ambitious cunning of Cardinal Antonelli and by the freedom-destroying schemes of Austria. They wanted to ensure that this Pontiff—of such good but indecisive nature, unsophisticated in political matters, but boiling with religious zeal—close his eyes to the true situation and render his heart insensitive to any peaceful path toward harmony and forgiveness toward his subjects." On January 5, the pope had sent General Zucchi a letter lamenting the treasonous behavior of the papal troops in Rome following Rossi's assassination. In it he made a distinction between the troops who had betrayed him and those who had simply been momentarily "seduced" by the rebels. Lettera di Pio IX al General Zucchi, MCRR, ms. 129/26, Nicola Roncalli, "Cronaca di Roma," documenti a stampa, 1849. Francisque Corcelle, the French envoy to the pope, later recalled that in early 1849 Pius still harbored the hope of being restored by General Zucchi and his troops, sharing the belief held by many in Gaeta that the temporary government in Rome would prove incapable of mounting any significant defense. Senior 1872, vol. 2, pp. 10–11.

15. Druidi 1954, p. 301.

16. Nicholas Brown to James Buchanan, Rome, January 24, 1849, in Stock 1945, pp. 145–49; Harcourt à Drouyn, Gaëte, 21 janvier 1849, MAEN, RSS 410; Giannini 2009, p. 3; Monsagrati 2014, p. 49; Severini 2011, p. 17; Foramiti 1850, p. 48; Roncalli 1997, p. 80. As the parish priests had the only existing lists of local inhabitants, thanks to the census they conducted each year before Easter, the organizers of the vote turned to the priests for help in putting together the voting rolls. Where priests refused to cooperate, the officials often simply seized the parish documents.

17. Martina 1974, pp. 324–25.

18. Mellano 1987, p. 31.

19. Martina 1974, pp. 324–25; Harcourt à Drouyn, 23 janvier 1849, Gaëte, MAEN, RSS 410; Viaene 2001, p. 497; Capograssi 1941, pp. 18, 33; Antonelli al nunzio di Madrid, Gaeta, 26 gennaio 1849, ASV, ANM, b. 313, ff. 7r–7v.

20. Nicholas Brown to James Buchanan, Rome, February 1, 1849, in Stock 1945, pp. 149–55; Cittadini 1968, p. 274; Roncalli 1997, p. 83; Demarco 1944, pp. 66–67.

21. John Freeborn to Viscount Palmerston, Rome, February 2, 1848, doc. 2 in Parliament 1851, pp. 1–2. Popular belief that the king of Naples and the pope's evil advisers were holding Pius back from acting on his natural benevolent inclinations was also slow to die. In late January a notice appeared on the walls of Rome, claiming that the pope, dressed in disguise, had tried to flee Gaeta on the night of January 21 but had been thwarted in his attempt by the king. "La fuga da Gaeta tentata da Pio IX e impedita dal Governo Napoletano," MCRR, ms. 127/27, Nicola Roncalli, "Cronaca di Roma," documenti a stampa, 1849.

22. Fuller, Rome, February 20, 1849, letter XXVII in Fuller 1856, pp. 346–47; Lancellotti 1862, pp. 86–87.

23. De Ligne 1929, pp. 187–88.

24. Esterházy à Schwarzenberg, Gaëte, 7 février 1849, doc. 15 in Blaas 1973, pp. 60–64; Dumreicher 1883, pp. 22–23; Beust 1887, pp. 315–18; Dino 1910, p. 68. Some years later, when Esterházy joined the Austrian cabinet, a fellow minister would observe of him, "In sharp criticism Moritz Esterházy is a master, and he cannot deny himself the pleasure of critically illuminating every opinion, every proposal of another's." Engel-Janosi 1950, pp. 140–41.

25. Martina 1974, p. 341. In response to the Austrians' request that he issue a written plea for military intervention, the pope convened the twenty cardinals with him in Gaeta in a secret consistory. They enthusiastically gave their support. The great majority of the cardinals agreed that the pope should turn first and foremost to Austria, proposing that his request be addressed to the Austrian emperor, with copies sent to the other Catholic powers with the suggestion that they join in as well. However, the temporary presence of a French cardinal in Gaeta, on a mission partly motivated by the French government's attempt to use him to plead restraint, apparently led the cardinals to instead approve having the pope address his plea equally to Austria, France, Naples, and Spain. Esterházy à Schwarzenberg, 8 février 1849, doc. 16 in Blaas 1973, pp. 64–67. Gioberti's letter to Martini, from Turin, 15 febbraio 1849, is extracted in Bianchi 1869, vol. 6, pp. 42–43; Farini 1850–53, vol. 3, pp. 192–93.

26. Foramiti 1850, pp. 51–52; Gabussi 1851–52, vol. 3, pp. 5–6; Fuller 1856, p. 357; Roncalli 1997, p. 84; Rossi 1954, p. 64; Loevinson 1902–4, vol. 1, p. 132. Brown's account of the procession is found in Nicholas Brown to James Buchanan, Rome, February 12, 1849, in Stock 1945, p. 156. On February 11, Brown sent his "warmest congratulations" to the new government of the Roman Republic. Marraro 1932, p. 70.

27. Severini 1995, pp. 154–56. The Dutch ambassador described Armellini as one of the most distinguished members of the Roman bar, with a large clientele. Liedekerke à Monsieur le Ministre, Molo-de-Gaëte, 9 février 1849, doc. LXXIV in Liedekerke 1949, p. 153. Armellini's wife was less than pleased with his newfound political passion, constantly reminding him of the pope's excommunication and, allegedly, keeping a copy of it under his pillow when he slept. Lancellotti, diary entry for February 12, 1849, in Cittadini 1968, p. 281.

28. Charles Bonaparte would continue to be front and center at the Assembly, although he would increasingly try the patience of his colleagues. "The penchant for adventures and eccentricity," recalled one of the men who would soon lead the government, "guided him in all political matters, as in every other sphere of his life. He always needed to create trouble, to insert himself, to act theatrically, to do the unexpected. For him the revolution was just a game and an opportunity to call attention to himself." But while many took a dim view of the prince-naturalist, the deputies soon elected him vice president of the Assembly, and in the weeks ahead he would often preside over it. Farini 1850–53, vol. 3, p. 205; Saffi 1898, p. 152; Casanova 1999, p. 116; Roncalli 1997, p. 87.

29. Rusconi 1879, pp. 40–42; Foramiti 1850, p. 52; Demarco 1944, p. 95; Repubblica romana 1849, pp. 3–5; Spada 1868–69, vol. 3, p. 221. Garibaldi

recalls in his memoirs that due to a flare-up of his rheumatism, he had to be carried into that historic session of the Assembly on the shoulders of his assistant. Garibaldi 1888, p. 222.

30. Foramiti 1850, pp. 53–54.

31. Cittadini 1968, p. 281; Nicholas Brown to James Buchanan, Rome, February 12, 1849, in Stock 1945, p. 156; République romaine 1849, pp. 5–6; Repubblica romana 1849, p. 83.

32. Esterházy's account of his conversation with the pope is found in Esterházy à Schwarzenberg, Gaëte, 11 février 1849, doc. 20 in Blaas 1973, pp. 77–81. His earlier reports are found in his letters to Schwarzenberg dated 10 and 11 février 1849, docs. 18 and 19 in Blaas 1973, pp. 72–77. "Regardless of the strength of religious interests there," the pope explained to Rayneval, the French ambassador to Naples, at their February 14 meeting, "France cannot fight in Rome the same principle which was the basis of the government in Paris." The pope had good reason to doubt that the French would help him. Only the previous month France had adopted a new constitution. The fifth article of its preamble pronounced that it would "never employ its forces against the freedom of any people." As for Naples, the pope explained that while he appreciated Ferdinand's generous support, he had no confidence in the king's ability to take the military action needed to restore him to Rome. Still less, the pope added, could he count on the aid that Spain was offering. He appreciated the Catholic devotion of the Spanish court but doubted Spain's military capacity. Rayneval à Drouyn, Naples, 14 février 1849, n. 72, MAEC, PAR.

The pope's doubts about Spain's capacity to help reflected a more widespread view. "Spain, with the munificent liberality which generally accompanies those deeply in debt, and who have in reality nothing to give," the London *Times* Naples correspondent had written in late December, "has instructed her Minister to offer her fleet, her armies, and her treasury to His Holiness. Such generosity has touched the old man's heart." "Rome, Naples, and Sicily," datelined Naples, December 21, TL, January 3, 1849. The text of the French constitution adopted on November 4, 1848, is found at http://www.conseil-constitutionnel.fr/conseil-constitutionnel/francais/la-constitution/les-constitutions-de-la-france/constitution-de-1848–iie-republique.5106.html.

33. Harcourt à Drouyn, Gaëte, 14 février 1849, MAEN, RSS 410; Antonelli al nunzio apostolico, Vienna, Gaeta, 14 febbraio 1849, ASV, ANV, b. 330, ff. 34r–35r; Liedekerke à Monsieur le Ministre, Molo-de-Gaëte, 16 février 1849, doc. LXXVII in Liedekerke 1949, pp. 156–57. The copy of the papal protest sent to Madrid can be found at ASV, ANM, b. 313, f. 111r; a published version can be found in Rusconi 1879, pp. 49–50. The copy of the papal call for four-power intervention that was sent to Vienna is found in ASV, ANV, b. 330, ff. 40r–45r.

When Vincenzo Gioberti, the Sardinian prime minister and a priest himself, learned that the pope had snubbed his government despite the fact that it boasted Italy's largest and strongest army, he was irate. "The Roman court," he wrote to his envoy in Gaeta, "does not know its true friends. . . . The Gaeta government, rebuffing any ideas of reconciliation, and putting in their place only vendetta and blood, seems not to realize that it is repudiating Christ's teachings, and substituting those of Mohammed." Sardinia would never permit Austrian troops to intervene in Roman affairs, threatened Gioberti. "We have a hundred thousand men who can fight against the Germans in the Papal States." The pope, though, was by now dead set against Sardinia, regarding Gioberti as a renegade priest and a dangerous apostle of Italian unity. Rayneval à Drouyn, Naples, 24 février 1849, n. 77, MAEC, PAR.

34. Esterházy à Schwarzenberg, Gaëte, 16 février 1849, doc. 15 in Blaas 1973, p. 90; Gabussi 1851–52, vol. 3, p. 123. Schwarzenberg à Esterházy, Vienne, 25 février 1849, doc. 30 in Blaas 1973, pp. 108–9; Esterházy à Schwarzenberg, Gaëte, 26 février 1849, doc. 31 in Blaas 1973, pp. 113–15.

35. In Spada 1868–69, vol. 3, pp. 240–41.

36. On the French case, see "Secularization and the Fate of Church Bells During the Revolution," Newberry Library, at http://publications .newberry.org/frenchpamphlets/?p=1130.

37. Repubblica romana 1849, pp. 19–20, 32, 95–101; Spada 1868–69, vol. 3, pp. 221–22; Roncalli 1997, p. 86; Boero 1850, pp. 261–62; Demarco 1944, pp. 107–10; République romaine 1849, pp. 10–15; Koelman 1963, vol. 1, pp. 205–7. The cardinal vicar archives of Rome contain a copy of the printed circular sent on February 19 to all religious bodies instructing them to refuse to cooperate in the republic's attempts to conduct an inventory of their property. ASVR, Decreta, 1849, f. 65v—65r.

38. Martina 2000, p. 360. Antonelli's notes to the nuncios in Madrid and Naples on these developments can be found at ASV, ANM, b. 313, f. 131r and ASV, ANN, b. 392, f. 10r; his protest to the diplomatic corps at ASV, ANN, b. 392, f. 4r.

CHAPTER 11: PRESSURING THE POPE

1. Harcourt sent Paris a copy of the Roman Republic's foreign minister's response to the "calumnies" against the Roman Republic in early March. Harcourt à Drouyn, Gaëte, 3 mars 1849, MAEC, CP, Rome, vol. 989, ff. 72r–74r; Miraglia 1850, pp. 160–61; République romaine 1849, p. 28; Foramiti 1850, pp. 65–66, 69–70; Fiorentino 1999, p. 36n.

2. Roncalli 1997, pp. 93, 99, 103; Candeloro 1972, p. 433.

3. Repubblica romana 1849, p. 155; *Diurno* 1849, p. 7.

4. Bianchi 1869, vol. 6, pp. 451–52; Ghisalberti 1965, pp. 142–43n.

5. Drouyn à Harcourt, Paris, 6 mars 1849, MAEN, RSS 274. The latter quote is from a letter written the same day to Harcourt, informing him that Rayneval would also represent France at the Gaeta conference. Drouyn had replaced Bastide as French minister of foreign affairs in late December 1848. Barrot 1876, p. 29.

6. Schwarzenberg à Esterházy, Olmütz, 5 mars 1849, doc. 35 in Blaas 1973, pp. 128–31.

7. The meeting of the Austrian ambassador with the French foreign minister is recounted both from the French side (Drouyn à de la Cour, Paris, 13 mars 1849, MAEN, Vienne, Article 33, ff. 67r–70r) and from the Aus-

trian side (Thom à Schwarzenberg, Paris, 14 mars 1849, doc. 48 in Blaas 1973, pp. 161–64). On April 13, the day after the dramatic meeting, the French foreign minister outlined the French position: best would be some kind of peaceful negotiation leading to an agreement between the pope and his subjects. Second-best would be a revolt by the people of the Papal States on behalf of the pope. Only if that too were not forthcoming should military action be resorted to, and in such an eventuality intervention by an all-Italian—Sardinian and Neapolitan—force would be greatly preferable. Of all possible solutions, what was least desirable was any role for the Austrian army. 13 mars 1849, MAEC, CP, Espagne, vol. 834, ff. 317r–320r.

8. In a typical clerical view, one papal partisan of the time, while admitting Mazzini's "vast intelligence," added immediately that it was "an intelligence impregnated with evil." For Mazzini, he wrote, "humanity is nothing, the idea is everything." "You have sent your young friends to die in Italy," Francesco Guerrazzi, leader of the short-lived republican government of Tuscany and onetime political ally of Mazzini, told him accusingly on his return to Florence earlier in 1849. Ghisalberti 1965, p. 144.

9. The William Lloyd Garrison quotes are drawn from Mack Smith 1994, p. 53.

10. In Mack Smith 1994, p. 31.

11. King 1911, pp. 331–37.

12. Fuller 1856, p. 367; Fuller 1988, p. 210.

13. Ghisalberti 1965, p. 144; Arrigoni 1996, p. 145n; Vecchi 1851, pp. 101–4; Vecchi 1911, pp. 36–37; Balleydier 1851, vol. 1, pp. 363–65. The first quote is from Farini (1850–53, vol. 3, pp. 275–76). Bachofen's remarks are quoted in Arrigoni 1996, 145n.

14. Saffi 1898, pp. 217–18.

15. Fuller 1988, p. 5:201; Ghisalberti 1965, pp. 150–51; Severini 2011, p. 43.

16. Rusconi 1879, pp. 73–76; D'Ambrosio 1852, p. 10; Farini 1850–53, vol. 3, pp. 307–8; Johnston 1901, pp. 248–49.

17. Arrigoni 1996, pp. 145–47; Martina 2000, p. 356; République romaine 1849, pp. 35–36; Repubblica romana 1849, pp. 260–61; Giannini 2009, p. 4; Saffi 1898, pp. 182, 246–48; Bratti 1903, p. 71; Vecchi 1851, pp. 392–93. With his appointment, noted the liberal patriot, Farini, no friend of the republican prophet, Mazzini became the absolute ruler of Rome. "The legislative assembly remained, but he governs the assembly and the people through flattery, by sectarian bands, with an unperturbed fanaticism which through his courage and his faith reassures the weak and the simple. He governs with the aid of those faithful to him, with the hope of worldwide revolts, through his prophecies." The Roman revolution, concluded Farini, "is incarnated in Mazzini." Farini 1850–53, vol. 3, p. 313.

18. Lazzarini 1899, p. 66.

19. Antonelli al nunzio di Madrid, Gaeta, 14 marzo 1849, ASV, ANM, b. 313, ff. 551r–551v; Antonelli al nunzio di Vienna, Gaeta, 26 marzo 1849, ASV, ANV, b. 330, ff. 85r–86r; Antonelli al nunzio di Madrid, Gaeta, 26 marzo

1849, ASV, ANM, b. 313, ff. 101r–102r. The April 23 Antonelli letter, to the nuncio in Lisbon, is quoted in Jankowiak 2008, p. 132n.

20. Martini al Ill.mo Signore, Gaeta, 26 marzo 1849, doc. 71 in DRS 1949–51, vol. 2, p. 451; Esterházy à Schwarzenberg, Gaëte, 26 mars 1849, doc. 46 in Blaas 1973, pp. 154–56.

21. Esterházy à Schwarzenberg, Gaëte, 24 mars 1849, doc. 45 in Blaas 1973, pp. 152–53; Martini al Ill.mo Signore, Gaeta, 26 marzo 1849, doc. 71 in DRS 1949–51, vol. 2, p. 453; Ralph Abercrombie to Viscount Palmerston, Turin, April 4, 1849, Palmerston Papers online.

22. Mazzini, Roma, 5 aprile 1849, in Repubblica romana 1849, pp. 282–86.

23. Drouyn was displeased when he learned that Antonelli insisted on chairing the four-power conference. He did not believe Antonelli should even be attending the conference, whose discussion would be constrained by his presence. Drouyn à Harcourt, Paris, 15 avril 1849, MAEN, RSS 274.

24. Harcourt à Drouyn, Mola di Gaeta, 29 mars 1849, MAEN, RSS 410.

25. The French delegation wrote up the minutes of the session, but there was one paragraph of their draft that the other ambassadors insisted be deleted. It noted the French recommendation that in returning to Rome, the pope pledged to keep the constitution and his reforms. Neither Cardinal Antonelli nor any of the other three envoys would agree to this. The pope, whose goodness and concern for the welfare of his people was beyond doubt, they argued, could not have foreign powers dictate to him how to run his own land. He could be counted on to do what was right once he was back in Rome. Rayneval à Drouyn, Gaëte, 31 mars 1849, MAEC, PAR; Capograssi 1941, pp. 101–7; Druidi 1958, p. 231; Ludolf a Cariati, Gaeta, 2 aprile 1849, doc. IIc in Cipolletta 1863, pp. 10–11; De Ligne 1929, p. 182; Meriggi 2006.

26. Antonelli went on to update his litany of the outrages under way in Rome, claiming that even the Sistine Chapel had been sacked. (It hadn't.) He urged the nuncio in Vienna to employ all his "zeal and energy to remove all further pernicious delays to the requested armed intervention." Antonelli al nunzio di Vienna, Gaeta, 2 aprile 1849, ASV, ANV, b. 330, ff. 91r–92r.

27. Martina 2000, pp. 362–64; Agresti 1904, pp. 42–43; Roncalli 1997, pp. 101–2; Lazzarini 1899, pp. 71–72.

28. Boyer 1956, p. 250.

29. Harcourt à Drouyn, Mola de Gaëte, 13 avril 1849, MAEN, RSS 410.

30. Rayneval à Drouyn, Naples, 19 avril 1849, MAEC, PAR.

31. Antonelli al nunzio di Madrid, Gaeta, 19 aprile 1849, ASV, ANM, b. 313, ff. 812r–813v.

32. The Italian text of the papal allocution is reproduced in Blois 1854, pp. 108–28. An English translation is found in Parliament 1851, pp. 73–84; Rayneval à Drouyn, Naples, 19 avril 1849, n. 99, MAEC, PAR. The pope's allocution was remarkable in being one of the earliest attempts to discredit the church's enemies by linking them to communism. The first Communist League had been formed in London only two years earlier, and its mention by the pope—who seems unlikely to have been so famil-

iar with the still small and obscure workingmen's association in England whose manifesto Marx and Engels had recently drafted—seems to reflect some other, more sophisticated hand. The reforms that the troublemakers in Rome were demanding, said the pope, "have no other object in view than to foment incessant agitation; that all the principles of justice, virtue, honor, and religion may be everywhere totally swept away, and the horrible and most lamentable system which they style Socialism or Communism, entirely adverse as it is even to reason and the law of nature, may, to the greatest detriment and ruin of the whole of human society, in all directions, be spread and propagated, and prevail everywhere." Bourgeois and Clermont 1907, pp. 30–31; Lodolini 1970, pp. 138–40; Viaene 2001, p. 499.

33. Falloux 1888, pp. 391–99, 444–45; Barrot 1876, p. 145.
34. In a report to his prime minister, the Austrian ambassador in Paris explained the sudden shift in the French position. The decision was taken on April 14 in a heated five-hour cabinet meeting pitting Falloux against Drouyn. Falloux threatened to resign if France did not answer the pope's call. Knowing of the disaster that had befallen his predecessor when the pope failed to appear on French soil, Louis Napoleon became convinced that being hailed as the pope's savior and consolidating Catholic support would help pave his path to glory. But the French president nonetheless remained troubled. "As the son of revolution and representing, nominally at least, the republican regime of France," reported the Austrian ambassador, "Louis Bonaparte felt a great repugnance about going to make war in Rome against a revolution and a republic." Hübner à Schwarzenberg, Paris, 18 avril 1849, Paris, doc. 74, allegato B, in Blaas 1973, pp. 229–32.
35. Pierre 1878, pp. 68–74; Jolicoeur 2011, p. 518; Bourgeois and Clermont 1907, p. 11; Collins 1923, pp. 216–17; Gaillard 1861, pp. 159–61; Bittard des Portes 1905, pp. 10–12; Barrot 1876, pp. 193–99; Calman 1922, pp. 308–9.
36. The Austrian ambassador had a dim opinion of the French foreign minister. Drouyn, he told Schwarzenberg, had argued against sending French troops to Italy. He was "very unhappy that in the cabinet the opinion of his colleagues demanding intervention prevailed over his, and was clearly suffering. He attributed his indisposition to the influence of a recent case of cholera, but I believe that it was the natural result of his political situation, caught between a defeat suffered in the cabinet and the need to conduct a battle to support the mission in the assembly." Il consigliere di Legazione Hübner à Schwarzenberg, Paris, 18 avril 1849, doc. 260, allegato A, in Filipuzzi 1961, vol. 2, pp. 81–84. A new epidemic of cholera had broken out in Paris in the spring. Falloux 1888, p. 453. Austria's military situation at the time was complicated by the fact that the revolt in Hungary was still very much alive. Engel-Janosi 1950, pp. 144–45.
37. Drouyn à Harcourt, Paris, 18 avril 1849, MAEN, RSS 274.
38. Drouyn à Oudinot, Paris, 18 avril 1849, MAEN, RSS 537 bis.

39. Drouyn à Oudinot, Paris, 18 avril 1849, Particulière e confidentielle, MAEN, RSS 537 bis. That same day Drouyn summoned the Austrian envoy to tell him something of the instructions he had just sent to Oudinot. He told him that the French would make no complaint if the Austrian army took Bologna, and that they would issue only the mildest of complaints if the Austrian army moved farther into the northern provinces of the Papal States. Il consigliere di Legazione Hübner à Schwarzenberg, Paris, 18 avril 1849, doc. 260, allegato B, in Filipuzzi 1961, vol. 2, p. 84.

40. Thiry 1851, p. 3; Barrot 1876, pp. 202–3; Bourgeois and Clermont 1907, pp. 24–25.

CHAPTER 12: THE FRIENDLY ARMY

1. Spada 1868–69, vol. 3, pp. 371–79; Clough 1888, p. 146; Lancellotti 1862, pp. 9, 117; République romaine 1849, pp. 59–61.

2. Curiously, Clough ended his letter by concluding, "It is a most respectable republic; it really (ipse dixit) thought of getting a monarch, but couldn't find one to suit." Clough to Palgrave, Rome, 23 April 1849, in Clough 1888, pp. 147–49.

3. Rayneval à Drouyn, Gaëte, 30 avril 1849, MAEC, PAR; Candeloro 1972, p. 424. Schwarzenberg's letter informing the British of his ordering of Austrian troops into Tuscany and the Papal States, and giving its justification, can be found in Schwarzenberg to Count Collerato, Vienne, 29 avril 1849, in Parliament 1851, p. 21. King Ferdinand wrote the pope from Terracina on April 29 to report having hoisted the papal flag at the fort there and having taken down the republic's. Ferdinando II a sua Santità Pio IX, Terracina, 29 aprile 1849, in Cittadini 1968, pp. 137–38.

4. Lesseps 1849, pp. 9–10; Mannucci 1850, pp. 119–31; Boulangé 1851, pp. 9–16; A. Cialdi, comandante del corpo, Marineria militare, Civitavecchia, al ministro della guerra, Roma, 24 aprile 1849 and 25 aprile 1849, docs. LII and LIII in Torre 1851–52, vol. 1, pp. 343–45; Palomba, console generale d'Austria a Civitavecchia, a Schwarzenberg, 25 aprile 1849, doc. 55 in Blaas 1973, pp. 186–88; U.S. consul, Civitavecchia, to Nicholas Brown, April 25, 1849, in Rush Hawkins Papers, vol. 4, John Hay Library, Brown University; Torre 1851–52, vol. 1, pp. 341–43; "State of Rome," TL, May 8, 1849; Marraro 1943, pp. 472–73.

5. Koelman 1963, vol. 1, p. 261; Roncalli 1997, pp. 107–8; République romaine 1849, pp. 65–66; Gabussi 1851–52, vol. 3, pp. 332–37.

6. Beghelli 1874, vol. 2, pp. 134–36; Loevinson 1902–4, vol. 1, p. 152; Bittard des Portes 1905, p. 52; Trevelyan 1907, p. 111; Beseghi 1946, vol. 2, p. 76.

7. Koelman 1963, vol. 1, pp. 243–46.

8. Vecchi 1851, p. 176; Trevelyan 1907, pp. 119, 141; Hoffstetter 1851, pp. 29–32; Loevinson 1902–4, vol. 2, pp. 226–27; Hibbert 1965, p. 50; Balleydier 1851, vol. 2, p. 34.

9. Trebiliani 1970; Beseghi 1946, vol. 2, pp. 66–67, 261–62; Hoffstetter 1851, p. 272; Facchini 1890, p. 171.

10. Boero 1850, pp. 272–73.

11. "I hope that it will be possible for you to convince the Roman court," Drouyn advised, "to publish a Manifesto that, in reassuring [the Romans] against the possibility of the return of reaction, deprives the anarchists of their force and prevents all serious resistance on their part." Rayneval à Drouyn, Naples, 24 avril 1849, MAEC, PAR; Drouyn à Harcourt, Paris, 25 avril 1849, MAEN, RSS 274.

12. Rayneval à Drouyn, Gaëte, 25 avril 1849, MAEC, PAR.

13. "One can be certain that every time we negotiate with people here, we will lose," wrote Harcourt. "There is only one way to accomplish something, namely, to know clearly what we want and to declare clearly what we want to obtain. If we don't act this way, we may well find ourselves one day in the situation of having come to reestablish the absolutism of the Papal States and leaving amid the curses of those same people who had called for our help." Harcourt à Drouyn, Gaëte, 30 avril 1849, MAEN, RSS 410.

14. Forbin-Janson to Oudinot, Rome, April 26, 1849, quoted in Pierre 1878, pp. 79–80; James 1903, pp. 152–53.

15. Gaillard 1861, pp. 168–69; Rayneval à Drouyn, Gaëte, 27 avril 1849 MAEC, PAR; Lewis Cass, Jr., to John Clayton, Rome, April 27, 1849, in Stock 1933, pp. 32–33.

16. Lerro 1962; Pierre 1878, pp. 82–83; Trevelyan 1907, pp. 123–24; Loevinson 1902–4, vol. 1, p. 160; Vecchi 1911, pp. 81–82.

17. Thiry 1851, pp. 6–7; Bittard des Portes 1905, pp. 63–66; Gabussi 1851–52, vol. 3, pp. 350–51; Rusconi 1879, p. 112. The Venetian envoy, Giovanni Castellani, describing public opinion in Rome at the time, reported, "I can assure you that in the Papal States no one wants the government of the priests, and everyone wants the pope." Ghisalberti 1965, p. 170n.

18. Spada 1868–69, vol. 3, pp. 420–21.

19. This, at least, was the account that Rayneval later gave to Nassau Senior of the conversation. Senior 1871, vol. 2, pp. 123–24. See also Foramiti 1850, pp. 85–86; Bittard des Portes 1905, pp. 63–68; Boulangé 1851, pp. 18–19.

CHAPTER 13: THE FRENCH ATTACK

1. Text in Repubblica romana 1849, pp. 536–37.

2. Lecauchois-Féraud 1849, pp. 25–32; Vaillant 1851, pp. 7–11; Hoffstetter 1851, pp. 19–21; Torre 1851–52, vol. 2, pp. 28–34; Gabussi 1851–52, vol. 3, pp. 354–57; Thiry 1851, pp. 9–11; Spada 1868–69, vol. 3, pp. 438–41; Key 1898, p. 197; Saffi 1898, pp. 291–94 (Saffi's letters to his mother from Rome on April 30, 1849); Loevinson 1902–4, vol. 2, p. 198; Trevelyan 1907, pp. 125–34; Monsagrati 2014, pp. 108–10; Beseghi 1946, vol. 2, pp. 77–79; Rossi 2001, pp. 309–12. On April 30 Pius IX issued a message addressed "to his most beloved subjects" in the Papal States. He offered an explanation of his decision to rely on foreign armies to return him to power in Rome: "The many evils that afflict the temporal Dominion of the Holy See . . . have persuaded us to turn to all the powers invoking

from them the opportune relief." Doc. 102 in Cittadini 1968, p. 140. For its part, the Roman Republic likewise justified its defense as doing the Lord's work. On the day of the French assault, Mazzini's government put out a proclamation: "He who dies for the fatherland carries out his duty as a man and as a Christian. Temporal rule by the priests is contrary to the doctrine of Christ." Repubblica romana 1849, p. 544.

3. Freeborn to Palmerston, Rome, May 1, 1849, doc. 23 in Parliament 1851, p. 16; Candeloro 1972, pp. 444–45; Cass to Clayton, Rome, May 8, 1849, in Stock 1933, p. 36.

4. Proia 2010; Bittard des Portes 1905, p. 98; Giorcelli 2000, p. 79n; Montesi 2002, pp. 152–54; Whitehouse 1906.

5. Christine Tivulze, of Belgiojoso, to Miss Fuller, Comitato di Soccorso pei Feriti, April 30, 1849, in Marraro 1944, p. 498. That same day the republican government put out a call for women to help tend the wounded, expressing satisfaction at all the women who had already volunteered. It concluded by specifying that "we are looking, above all, for women of robust health." "Avis aux femmes de Rome," *Moniteur romain* du 30 avril, in République romaine 1849, pp. 81–82.

6. "The State of Europe," TL, May 14, 1849; Repubblica romana 1849, p. 620.

7. Repubblica romana 1849, pp. 566–67; Beghelli 1874, vol. 2, pp. 182–83; the text of the notarized French soldiers' statement, dated May 5, 1849, is published as doc. 4 in Del Vecchio 1849, pp. 133–34.

8. Ghisalberti 1965, p. 160.

9. Repubblica romana 1849, p. 627; Del Vecchio 1849, p. 42; Lazzarini 1899, pp. 113–14; Key 1898, p. 198; Bourgeois and Clermont 1907, pp. 76–77.

10. Key 1898, pp. 197–99; Freeborn to Palmerston, Rome, May 5, 1849, doc. 28 in Parliament 1851, p. 19; James 1903, pp. 156–57.

11. Lazzarini 1899, pp. 110–12; Severini 2002c, p. 122; James 1903, p. 155; Repubblica romana 1849, pp. 499–500; Boero 1850, pp. 270–72; Rocca 2011, pp. 155–59. Letters from convents to the cardinal vicar of Rome telling of these visits can be found in ASVR, Segreteria, Atti, b. 62, fasc. 3. Priests thought to be spying for the pope's foreign armies were at risk of their lives, and not a few were killed in these weeks. Roncalli 1997, pp. 113, 118; Severini 2002a, pp. 114–15; Monsagrati 2014, pp. 89–91. The British ambassador to Florence, reporting on events in Rome at the time, informed Lord Palmerston that "hatred of Priestly Government seems to be deeply rooted in the minds of the great mass of the people." He added, "The dislike of the cardinals and priests is unbounded." George Hamilton to Viscount Palmerston, Florence, May 3, 1849, doc. 25 in Parliament 1851, p. 17.

12. Le préfet maritime, Toulon, au ministre de la marine, 4 mai 1849, MAEC, CP, Rome, vol. 993, ff. 24r–24v; Bittard des Portes 1905, pp. 103–6; Bourgeois and Clermont 1907, p. 76.

13. Séance du 7 mai 1849, Assemblée nationale 1849a, pp. 469–90; Bourgeois and Clermont 1907, pp. 47–51; Barrot 1876, pp. 208–11; Lesseps 1849, pp. 7–8.

14. Repubblica romana 1849, p. 576; Saffi 1898, p. 307.

15. D'Ambrosio 1852, p. 22; Key 1898, p. 198; Ferdinando II a Pio IX, Albano, 5 maggio 1849, in Cittadini 1968, pp. 138–39.
16. Farini 1850–53, vol. 4, pp. 85–86. For the gloss the Neapolitans tried to put on the encounter, see the account of a Neapolitan officer in Piscicelli 1978, pp. 1–3; and Hoffstetter 1851, pp. 28–59. That Ferdinand was putting out glowing stories of his victories over Garibaldi's "bands" is evident from Rayneval's reports from Gaeta. Rayneval à Drouyn, Gaëte, 20 mai 1849, MAEC, PAR. Captain Key wrote on May 12, following his visit to Ferdinand's camp: "The Neapolitan army at Albano and Velletri are in great fear of Garibaldi, and very anxious to join their forces with the French." Commander Key to Vice-Admiral Parker, aboard *Bulldog*, Palo, May 12, 1849, in Parliament 1851, pp. 29–31.
17. Repubblica romana 1849, pp. 628–29; Farini 1850–53, vol. 4, p. 52.
18. Note des plénipotentiaires Français au Cardinal Antonelli, Gaëte, 3 mai 1849, signed Harcourt and Rayneval, MAEC, PAR.
19. Rayneval à Drouyn, Gaëte, 3 mai 1849, MAEC, PAR.
20. Harcourt à Drouyn, Mola-de-Gaëte, 4 mai 1849, n. 46, MAEN, RSS 410.
21. Drouyn à Oudinot, Paris, 10 mai 1849, MAEN, RSS 537 bis; Télégraphie, Drouyn à Oudinot, Paris, 10 mai 1849, MAEN, RSS 537 bis.
22. Antonelli a Viale, Gaeta, 7 maggio 1849, ASV, ANV, b. 330, ff. 112r–112v.
23. Viale a Antonelli, Vienna, 3 maggio 1849, ASV, ANV, b. 322, f. 25r; Esterházy à Schwarzenberg, Gaëte, 4 mai 1849, doc. 60 in Blaas 1973, pp. 196–97. King Ferdinand was meanwhile doing his part, reported Esterházy, leading eight thousand Neapolitan troops across the border, headed north. The king's goal, Esterházy explained in a dispatch to Vienna, was "to use his presence on Roman territory to counterbalance the equivocal attitude of the French army."
24. The Austrian commander Marshal Franz von Wimpffen issued a proclamation: "Residents of the Papal States! In execution of the supreme orders received from Field Marshal Count Radetzky, I have entered your territory with the imperial troops. I come, together with the special commissioner of His Holiness, to restore the legitimate government of His Holiness Pius IX, who was overthrown by a perverse faction." On May 5, as the Austrian army crossed into Tuscany, its commander, Baron D'Aspre, addressed a similar proclamation to the people: "Tuscany! I have entered your territory with the troops under my command, to defend the rights of your legitimate Sovereign . . . Grand Duke Leopold II. . . . Tuscans! A perverse faction had overthrown public order among you . . . to satisfy its private objects, its criminal passions, the yoke of the most insufferable anarchy. . . . Let no idea of resistance enter your minds, as it would place me in the disagreeable and hard necessity of using force." The English translation appears in "Tuscany," TL, May 16, 1849. For the text of Wimpffen's Bologna declaration, see Foramiti 1850, pp. 95–96. On the assault on Bologna, see Torre 1851–52, vol. 2, pp. 143–53, 381; Pisacane 1851, pp. 263–65.
25. Diesbach 1998, pp. 23–41.
26. "The situation of the French expedition," TL, May 11, 1849; "France,"

TL, May 14, 1849. The text of the Assembly debate that day can be found in Assemblée nationale 1849a, pp. 549–67.

27. "You speak of war," the Austrian ambassador went on to tell Drouyn, "but I ask you, against whom? Against us? But what for? The Pope has approached us as he has you to help him against the anarchists. We are in the midst of doing this, frankly, sincerely, and without any ulterior motive. . . . Is this a cause for war? I cannot think so. It must then be the pope whom you want to wage war against. But that is an eventuality that does not even merit serious examination. The fact is that in dissimulating the true mission of the expedition to Civitavecchia at the National Assembly, you have placed yourselves in an untenable position." Hübner à Schwarzenberg, Paris, 11 mai 1849, doc. 75 in Blaas 1973, pp. 235–37.

28. Rayneval à Drouyn, Terracina, 10 mai 1849, MAEC, PAR; Key 1898, pp. 199–200.

29. "I told him," Drouyn wrote to Oudinot, explaining Lesseps's mission, "to maintain the most intimate and confidential relations with you, and I ask you to do all you can to facilitate the accomplishment of the delicate task he has been given." Drouyn added that the Neapolitan army's intervention in the south of the Papal States and the expected intervention of the Austrians from the north were an unfortunate complication. Oudinot was to take care that no one think that there was any coordination between the French army and the others, adding: "I do not need to tell you the many serious disadvantages that would result." Drouyn à Oudinot, Paris, 8 mai 1849, MAEN, RSS 537 bis; Edgar-Bonnet 1951, pp. 88–89. Lesseps had traveled on a naval ship put at his disposal. With him was a member of the Roman Constituent Assembly whom Drouyn thought would help him establish relations with the triumvirate, a move that was not destined to make a good impression on the pope. Diesbach 1998, pp. 91–92.

30. Barrot 1876, p. 219.

31. Dépêche télégraphique, Oudinot à Drouyn, Maglianella, 14 mai 1849, MAEC, CP, Rome, vol. 993, ff. 57r–57v. Given all the mixed signals, the French officers could be forgiven if they were not entirely sure who exactly their enemy was. A British reporter was dining with French officers at their camp outside Rome when one of their comrades rushed in. "Gentlemen," exclaimed the officer excitedly, although inaccurately, "I have the honor to inform you that the destination of our expedition is changed. We are here now to defend the Roman Republic. . . . We are at war with Austria and Naples!" Frantic cheers met the news, as the officers stood up, shouting *"Vive la République!"* "The Intervention in the Papal States," TL, May 22, 1849; Antonini a Cariati, Parigi, 15 maggio 1849, doc. IX in Cipolletta 1863, p. 30.

CHAPTER 14: NEGOTIATING IN BAD FAITH

1. Thiry 1851, pp. 13–14; Vaillant 1851, p. 13; Boulangé 1851, pp. 44–47; Hibbert 1965, p. 65; "French Intervention in the Roman States," TL, May 29, 1849; "The French Intervention in the Papal States," TL, June 6, 1849.

The term *malaria* comes from the Italian for "bad air," and indeed at the time the mosquito-borne source of the disease was unknown. Thousands were affected in Rome each summer, the season beginning in June and at its worst from July to October. Desmarie 1860, pp. 51–58; Niel 1961, p. 478; Tommasi-Crudeli 1892, pp. 53–80; Hoolihan 1989, p. 481.

2. Pisacane 1849, pp. 14–15; Pisacane 1851, pp. 301–2; Scirocco 1996, p. 19; Demarco 1944, p. 140; Gouraud 1852, pp. 271–73; Pierre 1878, p. 95; Roselli 1853, pp. 56–60; Gabussi 1851–52, vol. 3, p. 404n; Rossi 2001, p. 140; Liedekerke 1949, p. 185; Repubblica romana 1849, pp. 4–8; Torre 1851–52, vol. 2, pp. 372–77; Rayneval à Drouyn, Gaëte, 22 mai 1849, MAEC, PAR.

3. Schwarzenberg à Esterházy, Vienne, 19 mai 1849, doc. 74 in Blaas 1973, pp. 226–29.

4. Lesseps à Drouyn, Rome, 16 mai 1849, doc. 4 in Lesseps 1849, pp. 75–77; Repubblica romana 1849, p. 727.

5. Mazzini à Lesseps, Rome, 19 mai 1849, doc. 12 in Lesseps 1849, pp. 90–91. The text of the proposed accord is found in République romaine 1849, pp. 104–5.

6. Oudinot à Lesseps, Villa Santucci, 21 mai 1849, doc. 18 in Lesseps 1849, pp. 96–97. On the French elections, see Pierre 1878, pp. 137–47; Bourgeois and Clermont 1907, pp. 98–101; Agulhon 1983, pp. 75–78; Milza 2004, pp. 173–75; Calman 1922, pp. 307–9; Key 1898, pp. 201–2.

7. Giannini 2009, p. 5; Brown to Clayton, Rome, May 19, 1849, in Stock 1945, pp. 173–75.

8. Matsumoto-Best 2003, p. 75. Individuals who failed to take part in confession at least once each year risked excommunication. Moroni 1851, pp. 239–48.

9. Roncalli 1997, p. 141; Boero 1850, pp. 251–53; Torre 1851–52, vol. 2, p. 359; Lancellotti 1862, p. 150; Spada 1868–69, vol. 3, pp. 555–57; "Proclamation sur les confessionnaux," *Moniteur romain* du 21 mai, in République romaine 1849, pp. 114–16. It would appear unlikely that the confessionals that had been removed were in any condition to be returned to use in the churches.

10. Rayneval à Drouyn, Gaëte, 18 mai 1849, n. 121, MAEC, PAR.

11. Liedekerke à Monsieur le Ministre, Mola-de-Gaëte, 20 mai 1849, doc. XCV in Liedekerke 1949, p. 184.

12. Rayneval à Drouyn, Gaëte, 20 mai 1849, n. 125, MAEC, PAR; Capograssi 1941, pp. 133–40; Rayneval à Drouyn, Gaëte, 22 mai 1849, n. 127, MAEC, PAR; De Ligne 1929, p. 191.

13. Diesbach 1998, pp. 94–95.

14. Ghisalberti 1965, pp. 146–47. Lesseps's remarks on Mazzini as a vulgar man are found in his May 20 report to Drouyn. Diesbach 1998, p. 99; Lesseps 1849, p. 32; Vecchi 1851, pp. 101–4; Bittard des Portes 1905, p. 171. In characterizing Mazzini, Lesseps remarked, "Il voudrait régénérer les hommes en passant sur des ruines e sur des cadavres." It was a charge commonly made against Mazzini, even by some of his compatriots. Francesco Guerrazzi, an old follower of his who had become head of the short-lived republican government in Tuscany earlier in 1849, once told

him: "You have sent your young friends to die in Italy, yet your head remains on your shoulders." Ghisalberti 1965, p. 144. Lesseps also suspected Mazzini of favoring a religious schism in Italy, seeking to draw Italians away from the Catholic Church into a kind of Protestantism.

15. Bourgeois and Clermont 1907, pp. 120–21, 126; Lesseps 1849, p. 87; Oudinot à Lesseps, 22 mai 1849, in Lesseps 1849, pp. 151–52. Mazzini wrote a letter to his mother reflecting his sense of isolation and betrayal: "It is truly shameful," complained the republican champion, "that while we hold on against three Powers, the rest of Italy does nothing." Severini 2011, p. 145n.

16. Lesseps 1849, pp. 26–28; Humphreys 1956, pp. 24–26.

17. Lesseps 1849, pp. 34–35; Lesseps au Triumvirat, Villa Santucci, 26 mai 1849, doc. 28 in Lesseps 1849, pp. 112–13. On May 27 Rayneval arrived at the French headquarters and spent four hours in uncomfortable conversation with Lesseps. "Everyone is against him," observed Rayneval. Generals and soldiers alike were angry at him for holding them back. Rayneval à Lesseps, Quartier Général sous Rome, 27 mai 1849, joint au no. 130, MAEC, PAR; Rayneval à Drouyn, Quartier Général sous Rome, 27 mai 1849, n. 130, MAEC, PAR. Harcourt made similar points from Gaeta in his letter to Drouyn a few days later. Harcourt à Drouyn, Gaëte, 30 mai 1849, MAEN, RSS 410.

18. Esterházy à Schwarzenberg, Gaëte, 23 mai 1849, docs. 78 and 80 in Blaas 1973, pp. 240–43, 249–50.

19. Esterházy à Schwarzenberg, Gaëte, 24 mai 1849, doc. 82 in Blaas 1973, pp. 252–54.

20. He added, "True, the pope is more tractable, but then the others do not let him realize that which was hoped." Balbo al ministro degli affari esteri, Mola di Gaeta, 28 maggio 1849, doc. 120 in DRS 1949–51, vol. 2, p. 500.

21. Schwarzenberg à Esterházy, Vienne, 31 mai 1849, doc. 89 in Blaas 1973, p. 265.

22. Bourgeois and Clermont 1907, pp. 101–5.

23. Report to the ministère de la marine et des colonies, Ancône, 27 mai 1849, République romaine 1849, pp. 127–28.

24. Schwarzenberg à Esterházy, Vienne, 31 mai 1849, doc. 86 in Blaas 1973, pp. 260–63. That the desirability of having the pope move to Bologna, under Austrian control, was being discussed at the time in confidential discussions between Schwarzenberg and the papal nuncio in Vienna is clear from Schwarzenberg to Esterházy, Vienne, 31 mai 1849, doc. 88 in Blaas 1973, p. 265.

25. Spada 1868–69, vol. 3, pp. 429–30; Foramiti 1850, p. 94.

26. Rayneval à Drouyn, Gaëte, 28 mai 1849, n. 131, MAEC, PAR; Balleydier 1851, vol. 2, pp. 153–55. Both French ambassadors in Gaeta were making known their displeasure with Lesseps and hinted that he might soon be recalled by the French government. Bargagli al ministro, Mola di Gaeta, 31 maggio 1849, in Bianchi 1869, vol. 6, p. 547.

27. Severini 2002a, pp. 142–43; Cass to Clayton, Rome, May 23, 1849, in Stock 1933, pp. 39–40. Margaret Fuller pictured the mood in Rome even

more starkly: "When I first arrived in Italy, the vast majority of this people had no wish beyond limited monarchies, constitutional governments. . . . It required King Bomba . . . it required Pio IX . . . and finally the imbecile Louis Bonaparte . . . to convince this people that no transition is possible between the old and the new. The work is done; the revolution in Italy is now radical, nor can it stop till Italy become independent and united as a republic. Protestant she already is." Fuller, report of May 27, 1849, Rome, in Fuller 1991, p. 278. Or as the Dutch ambassador's informant in Rome put it on May 22, "Our excellent pope and the upper clergy are fooling themselves, or they have been fooled by false reports, if they ignore the immense change that, in these last months, has altered the views of the great majority of the Roman population." Liedekerke au Monsieur le Ministre, Mola-de-Gaëte, 6 juin 1849, doc. XCIX in Liedekerke 1949, p. 191n.

28. Leone Paladini, Roma, 25 maggio 1849, in Paladini 1897, pp. 37–40.

29. Harcourt à Drouyn, Gaëte, 28 mai 1849, n. 48, MAEN, RSS 410. Some sense of the pressure on the French comes from the report sent by the London *Times* correspondent with the French army outside Rome on May 29. The army, the *Times* reporter argued, was in a dishonorable position. "Austria and Naples have been openly deceived, the Roman people deluded, the Pope treated as if he were a fool, a French army has been ignominiously repulsed." Only an immediate occupation of Rome could begin to repair the damage. "The French Intervention in the Papal States," TL, June 6, 1849.

30. Lesseps à Drouyn, quartier général devant Rome, 29 mai 1849, MAEC, CP, Rome, vol. 991, ff. 77r–78r; Lesseps 1849, pp. 36–37.

31. Bittard des Portes 1905, pp. 179–82; Bourgeois and Clermont 1907, p. 143.

32. Repubblica romana 1849, pp. 78–79.

33. Diesbach 1998, pp. 102–3; Repubblica romana 1849, pp. 100–101. In a colorful account, the London *Times* correspondent reported that Oudinot told Lesseps he should be shot, while Lesseps replied by telling the general that he would pay dearly for his action. "Papal States," TL, June 12, 1849.

34. Drouyn à Lesseps, Paris, 29 mai 1849, MAEC, CP, Rome, vol. 991, f. 102r; Drouyn à Oudinot, Paris, 28 mai 1849, MAEN, RSS 537 bis; Drouyn à Oudinot, Paris, 1 juin 1849, MAEN, RSS 537 bis; Drouyn à Oudinot, Paris, 29 mai 1849, n. 5, MAEN, RSS 537 bis. In two sharply worded letters to Lesseps, Drouyn chastised him for exceeding the authority he had been given. "The government of the Holy Father never ceased being the Roman government in our eyes," wrote the French foreign minister. Drouyn à Lesseps, Paris, 25 mai 1849 and 26 mai 1849, MAEN, RSS 537 bis.

35. Briffault 1846, pp. 171–83; Niel 1961, p. 470.

36. Clough 1888, p. 154; James 1903, pp. 156–57.

37. Severini 2006, p. 111n; Monsagrati 2014, p. 123.

CHAPTER 15: BATTLING FOR ROME

1. Tocqueville 2004, pp. 678–904; Senior 1872, vol. 1, pp. iv–v.
2. Tocqueville's letter, dated June 15, was written to Paul Clamorgan. Reverso 2009, p. 309n.
3. Tocqueville 1893, pp. 313–18.
4. Tocqueville 1893, pp. 318–21; Lesseps à Tocqueville, Paris, 7 juin 1849, MAEC, CP, Rome, vol. 991, ff. 137r–137v. Adding to the sense of crisis, Paris was in the midst of a terrible outbreak of cholera. Hundreds were dying each day. Pierre 1878, pp. 159–60; "The Cholera in Paris," TL, June 13, 1849.
5. Candeloro 1972, p. 446. On June 1, Captain Key (1898, p. 202) observed, "The Romans are evidently aware that nothing decided will be attempted by the French until the opinion of the new National Assembly is ascertained, and they are so elated with the flight of the King of Naples to his own dominions . . . that their confidence in their own strength has passed all reasonable bounds."
6. Garibaldi 1889, p. 101.
7. Oudinot himself had briefly detained the Lombard volunteers at Civitavecchia as they appeared in the port city shortly after his own arrival in April. "You are Lombards, and so what do you have to do with the affairs of Rome?" Oudinot asked Manara. To this, the young Milanese leader replied with a question of his own: "And you, General, are you from Paris, Lyon, or Bourdeaux?" Farini 1850–53, vol. 4, pp. 3–4. Although they would pay a heavy price for their role in defending the Roman Republic, the Lombard Volunteers were in fact not generally well disposed to Mazzini or republicanism. Rather, they claimed allegiance to the Savoyard monarchy. Dandolo 1851; Hoffstetter 1851, pp. 22–25.
8. The assemblyman's remarks are by D. Pantaleoni. Demarco 1944, pp. 339–40. Vaure's letter, from Civitavecchia on June 1, is found in Bourgeois and Clermont 1907, p. 170.
9. Farini 1850–53, vol. 4, pp. 168–69; Borie 1851, pp. 239–40; Severini 2011, p. 148.
10. Johnston 1901, p. 299; Vaillant au ministre de la guerre, au quartier général de Santucci, 2 juin 1849, in Gaillard 1861, pp. 467–68.
11. Delmas 1849, pp. 5–6; Thiry 1851, pp. 31–38; Hoffstetter 1851, pp. 120–23; Hibbert 1965, pp. 81–83; Trevelyan 1907, pp. 189–90; Dandolo 1851, pp. 239–41; Rusconi 1879, pp. 127–32; Freeborn to Palmerston, Rome, June 8, 1849, doc. 66 in Parliament 1851, p. 43. In an effort to reassure the Romans, the day after the initial assault the triumvirate put up notices claiming that on June 3, only three of the defenders had been killed and fewer than a hundred injured. "Cittadini," Roma, 4 giugno 1849, MCRR, ms. 129/10, Nicola Roncalli, "Cronaca di Roma," documenti a stampa, 1849.
12. "His fiery speeches and his bravery in the face of death surprised everyone," observed one of Garibaldi's volunteers of the monk, adding, "No handshake ever did me as much good as did his!" Rusconi 1879, pp. 132–

33; Lancellotti 1862, p. 136; D'Ambrosio 1852, p. 60; Hoffstetter 1851, p. 272.

13. Cesare Balbo al ministro degli affari esteri [Torino], Mola di Gaeta, 3 giugno 1849, doc. 121 in DRS 1949–51, vol. 2, pp. 501–2.

14. It would be necessary, advised Harcourt, to "reduce this mass of Italian cardinals, who come to their positions not through any merit, but solely because their name ends in an 'o' or an 'i,' and who would like to make their religion into a sort of Italian sect." One day, he speculated, the church would decide instead to draw its cardinals from the most distinguished and honest Catholics around the world. But in the sorry state in which the church now found itself, the Sacred College, observed Harcourt, consisted of Italy's "most ignorant and most retrograde." Harcourt au ministre des affaires étrangères, Gaëte, 4 juin 1849, MAEN, RSS 410. Harcourt wrote this letter before learning that Tocqueville had replaced Drouyn as French foreign minister.

15. Antonelli al nunzio, Madrid, 3 giugno 1849, Gaeta, ASV, ANM, b. 313, ff. 860r–861r; Cesare Balbo al ministro degli affari esteri, Mola di Gaeta, 9 giugno 1849, doc. 123 in DRS 1949–51, vol. 2, p. 504. At the same time, the papal nuncio in Vienna wrote to offer his strong support for Antonelli's suggestion that the pope should go not to Rome but to another city in the Papal States. Placing the pope in a city under French control, he thought, would be too risky. Viale a Antonelli, Vienna, 5 giugno 1849, ASV, ANV, b. 322, ff. 34r–34v.

16. Rosmini's opinion of the pontiff had dimmed. Pius, he observed several months later, "is prone to both likes and dislikes, and for this reason has little consistency. He has little education and for that reason feels obligated to remain noncommittal and vague so as not to go out on a limb, which nonetheless he frequently does." Radice 1972, p. 24.

17. Tocqueville à Rayneval et Harcourt, Paris, 6 juin 1849, n. 39 and 40, MAEC, CP, Rome, vol. 989, ff. 261r–263r, 264r.

18. On the same day, Tocqueville also sent this news to General Oudinot, instructing him to defer to the new envoy on measures to adopt in Rome once it was taken. Tocqueville à Oudinot, Paris, 6 juin 1849, MAEN, RSS 537 bis.

19. That the new envoy was someone Tocqueville felt very close to is evident from the fact that from the time of Corcelle's first reports, he addressed a separate stream of private letters to Tocqueville, which he began with the salutation "My dear friend" and, in the case of the first letter, closed with *"Je vous aime de tout mon coeur"* (I love you with all my heart). Corcelle à Tocqueville, Civitavecchia, 12 juin 1849, doc. 101 in Tocqueville 1983, vol. 15/2, pp. 253–55. Eight years earlier the two men had toured Algiers and its hinterland together. Tocqueville 2004, p. 896. In a dispatch to the Austrian prime minister telling of Corcelle's appointment, Austria's ambassador in Paris reported that the French government had replaced Lesseps—"who became crazy"—with Corcelle, "belonging to the Catholic party." Hübner à Schwarzenberg, Paris, 6 juin 1849, doc. 97 in Blaas 1973, p. 276.

20. Tocqueville à Corcelle, Paris, 6 juin 1849, MAEN, RSS 274. As Corcelle made his way to Rome, Tocqueville, eagerly awaiting word from Oudinot, thought that the city had likely already fallen. If it had not, he worried, the government might not be able to survive the outrage another botched attack would trigger in Paris. On June 10, Tocqueville wrote his ambassador in Vienna to inform him of the invasion, adding "one can assume that Rome is in the hands of our troops." He added that the French had a moral responsibility not to allow the return of the "detestable regime" of the kind that Pius IX's predecessor had presided over. Tocqueville à La Cour, Paris, 10 juin 1849, MAEN Vienne, Article 33, ff. 147r–151r.

21. "Our nuns of Sant'Egidio, placing their faith in Divine Providence," read the message to Rome's vice gerent, "were determined not to abandon their Convent. But seeing that the ruins are constantly growing, with 28 cannon balls and bombs already having fallen on them, causing much damage to the Convent, they have decided to . . . join their sisters in our other Convent of Santa Teresa at the Four Fountains." P. Preposito Generale de' Carm.ni Scalzi a Mons. Francesco Anivitti, Pro-Vicegerente di Roma, 7 giugno 1849, ASVR, Segreteria, Atti, b. 62, fasc. 3.

22. Roncalli 1997, p. 159; Foramiti 1850, p. 121; Fuller 1991, p. 299; Koelman 1963, vol. 2, pp. 333–42, 352–53, 367–68. The active role taken by Rome's women in the city's defense was especially striking to the men who came from farther north in Italy. In mid-June, one of the Lombard volunteers observed that "although the women of the lower classes are uncouth and ignorant, they nonetheless demonstrate and flaunt a virile courage. Roman pride shines in their eyes." Paladini 1897, p. 59.

23. Giuseppe Avezzana, ministro di guerra, Roma, 8 giugno 1849, in République romaine 1849, pp. 139–40; République romaine 1849, pp. 150–54; Lancellotti 1862, p. 163; Trevelyan 1907, p. 196; Deiss 1969, p. 259; Koelman 1963, vol. 2, p. 331.

24. Fuller 1991, pp. 298–300.

25. Hübner à Esterházy, Paris, 13 juin 1849, doc. 97 in Blaas 1973, pp. 274–75.

26. On his trips to Paris seeking to gain French support for the Roman Republic, Carlo Rusconi, the republic's foreign minister, visited Ledru-Rollin in his home. He was shocked by its magnificence: "satin and gold everywhere, not an object on which one passed one's eye that was not valuable, splendid paintings in gilded frames on the walls. . . . Turkish carpets under foot." Rusconi 1883, p. 100.

27. Ledru-Rollin, observed Victor Hugo, a fellow member of the Assembly, was "a sort of bastard Danton," having "a certain lawyerly tact mixed with the violence of a demagogue." Barrot, who was the object of Ledru-Rollin's ire, was no more charitable in his description. The leader of the left was, said the prime minister, "a vehement orator in whom the demagogue and the statesman combined in such a way as to make him a redoubtable adversary. . . . He belonged to that class of men," he added, "in whom ambition and pride are restrained neither by the brain nor by

the heart." Calman 1922, p. 250n, 256–57, 264; Senior 1871, vol. 1, p. 122. The text of Ledru-Rollin's June 11 remarks is found in Assemblée nationale 1849b, pp. 191–92.

28. In Calman 1922, p. 389.

29. Three months earlier, shortly after Mazzini had made his way to Rome, Ledru-Rollin had sent him a letter offering his advice: "Tell our brothers: Do you want to live? Then know how to die!" Now he seemed disinclined to take his own advice. Calman 1922, pp. 374–96; Pierre 1878, pp. 169–200; Agulhon 1983, p. 79; Beghelli 1874, vol. 2, pp. 100–101. Barrot's depiction of the events of June 13, cast in terms of an abortive insurrection, can be found in his memoirs. Barrot 1876, pp. 297–312. For Tocqueville's account, see Tocqueville à Harcourt, Paris, 15 juin 1849, MAEN, RSS 274.

30. Freeborn to Palmerston, Rome, June 16, 1849, doc. 67 in Parliament 1851, pp. 43–44; Niel 1961, p. 473; République romaine 1849, p. 167; Rusconi a Pinto, Roma, 13 giugno 1849, n. 55, MCRR, "Archivio Michelangelo Pinto," b. 884, fasc. 5, f. 11r.

31. Cass to Clayton, Rome, June 14, 1849, pp. 42–44. In a June 12 dispatch, Rusconi reported that the French "have cut off an extremely useful, not to say indispensable, aqueduct." MCRR, "Archivio Michelangelo Pinto," b. 884, fasc. 5, f. 10r.

32. Gabussi 1851–52, vol. 3, p. 465; Farini 1850–53, vol. 4, pp. 183–84. Tocqueville himself thought that when news of the French left's defeat reached Rome, it would severely undercut the will to continue the fight. Tocqueville à Oudinot, Paris, 20 juin 1849, MAEC, CP, Rome, vol. 993, f. 127r; Monsagrati 2014, p. 169.

33. Foramiti 1850, p. 125; De Longis 2001, p. 265; Paladini 1897, pp. 59–60; Severini 2002c, pp. 179–80.

34. Hearing a report that the Romans had mined St. Peter's Basilica, Margaret Fuller went to ask Mazzini if this were true. That even Fuller, one of the people in Rome he felt most fond of, would think such a thing possible of him was more than the Italian prophet could bear. "It is written that none will trust me," he replied. "You too! Can you believe for a single moment such nonsense as that of St. Peter being mined, whilst *I* am here? Have I proved a vandal?" Two days after Mazzini's outburst, a priest, disguised in the uniform of a National Guardsman, was found with a map showing republican positions and numbers. Garibaldi ordered him taken out and shot. Capograssi 1941, pp. 152–53; Lodolini 1970, p. 75; D'Ambrosio 1852, p. 71; Deiss 1969, p. 264; Roncalli 1997, p. 181.

35. "The Papal States," datelined Monte Mario, June 19, TL, June 30, 1849; Hoffstetter 1851, pp. 240–41; Harcourt à Tocqueville, Fiumicino, 20 juin 1849, MAEN, RSS 410.

36. Gaillard 1861, p. 274; Tocqueville à Corcelle, Paris, 20 juin 1849, doc. 108 in Tocqueville 1983, vol. 1, pp. 275–78.

37. Hoffstetter 1851, pp. 242–49; Clough 1888, pp. 158–59; Beghelli 1874, vol. 2, pp. 373–74; Adolphe Niel, San Carlo devant Rome, 22 juin 1849, doc. 8 in Niel 1961, p. 474.

CHAPTER 16: THE CONQUEST

1. The text of the pope's letter from Gaeta to Cardinal Lambruschini in Naples, dated June 26, 1849, is reproduced in Manzini 1960, pp. 405–6.
2. Schwarzenberg à Esterházy, Vienne, 16 juin 1849, doc. 99 in Blaas 1973, p. 282.
3. Esterházy à Schwarzenberg, Gaëte, 27 juin 1849, doc. 103 in Blaas 1973, pp. 288–90; Martina 1974, p. 347. "The pope and the cardinal," observed the Sardinian ambassador, shortly after meeting with them in late June, "are more stubborn than ever and do not want to speak of a Constitution, at least for the time being." Balbo al ministro degli affari esteri, Mola di Gaeta, 28 giugno 1849, doc. 133 in DRS 1949–51, vol. 2, p. 515.
4. Harcourt à Tocqueville, Quartier général Santucci, 29 juin 1849, n. 53, MAEN, RSS 410. Following a long meeting with Harcourt and Rayneval on June 29 to discuss how to go about reestablishing papal authority, Corcelle sent what he termed a "delicate question" to Tocqueville. Which pontifical flag were they supposed to raise? Would the one adopted by the pope in 1847 be acceptable? Along with its venerable white papal emblem that flag contained the tricolored symbol of a united Italy. Corcelle à Tocqueville, Civitavecchia, 25 juin 1849, doc. 113 in Tocqueville 1983, vol. 1, p. 291.
5. Corcelle à Tocqueville, Civitavecchia, 25 juin 1849, n. 5, MAEN, RSS 411.
6. Tocqueville à Corcelle, Paris, 23 juin 1849, MAEN, RSS 411; Tocqueville à Corcelle, Paris, 26 juin 1849, doc. 111 in Tocqueville 1983, vol. 1, pp. 284–85.
7. Tocqueville à Corcelle, Paris, 23 juin 1849, MAEN, RSS 411. He wrote separately to Oudinot and Harcourt with the same instruction, adding, "Take the necessary measures to inspire that large portion of the population that desires the Holy Father's return, but is afraid of compromising itself, with the courage to organize a clear demonstration." Tocqueville à Harcourt, Paris, 26 juin 1849, MAEN, RSS 274; Tocqueville à Oudinot, Paris, 26 juin 1849, MAEN, RSS 537 bis.
8. Tocqueville à Corcelle, Paris, 24 juin 1849, doc. 111 in Tocqueville 1983, vol. 1, pp. 280–81. The London *Times* reported a letter from Rome, dated June 26, telling of the departure of a deputation from Bologna bound for Gaeta to convince the pope to move to Bologna until better times allowed his return to Rome. "Rome," TL, July 5, 1849.
9. Roncalli 1997, p. 179; Polidori's diary entry for June 23 makes a similar observation about the French bombardment of the city that night. Severini 2002a, p. 205.
10. République romaine 1849, pp. 161–62.
11. Oudinot's text, dated June 25, is found in Torre 1851–52, vol. 2, pp. 253–54.
12. If anyone should be the object of the consuls' denunciations, argued Corcelle, it was not the French but the "enemy bands" in Rome who, in digging in to face the French outside Porta San Pancrazio, had, he claimed, devastated the famous basilica of the same name that stood

there. The savages had "mutilated all the statues of St. Pancrazio . . . lacerated the paintings, opened the tombs, overturned the altars, and made latrines at the entry of the catacombs, indeed in the middle of the church in the place where, tradition has it, the saint was martyred." There seemed to be no limit, in Corcelle's view, to the depravity of the men who stubbornly held out against the highly principled forces of the French army. He sent two letters to Tocqueville on this matter on the same day: Corcelle à Tocqueville, Civitavecchia, 27 juin 1849, n. 6, MAEN, RSS 411; Corcelle à Tocqueville, Civitavecchia, 27 juin 1849, doc. 112 in Tocqueville 1983, vol. 1, pp. 285–88. Corcelle blamed the British consul, Freeborn, for instigating the protest. Freeborn and most of the other consuls, claimed Corcelle, were businessmen who were profiting from the current government in Rome and were motivated purely by the desire for personal gain.

13. White Mario 1888, pp. 141–43; Severini 2002a, pp. 214–15; Clough 1888, p. 159; Paladini 1897, pp. 86–87; Dandolo 1851, p. 263. Garibaldi himself was struck by Bassi's fearlessness: "You can't imagine how much this man saddens me," he told one of his men, "because I see that he wants to die." Hoffstetter 1851, pp. 271–72; Facchini 1890, p. 180; Koelman 1963, vol. 2, p. 331; Beseghi 1946, vol. 2, p. 87.

14. The story spread that the legionnaires had come into town simply so that they could change out of their tattered clothes into their colorful new, red-bloused uniforms. Loevinson 1902–4, vol. 1, pp. 258–59; Trevelyan 1907, pp. 212–16; Dandolo 1851, p. 263.

15. Lancellotti 1862, p. 180; Vecchi 1851, p. 485; Foramiti 1850, p. 132; Roncalli 1997, p. 186.

16. Severini 2002a, pp. 217–19.

17. Monsagrati 2014, p. 184.

18. Loevinson 1902–4, vol. 2, pp. 227–28; Trevelyan 1907, pp. 217–24; Hoffstetter 1851, pp. 292–306; Vaillant 1851, pp. 132–44; Balbiani 1860, pp. 430–33. There are contrasting accounts of Aguyar's death, many casting it in especially dramatic fashion. The day after Aguyar's death, Garibaldi eulogized him in a public statement: "Yesterday America gave up with the blood of its valorous son, Andrea Aguyar, a proof of the love of free men of all lands for our beautiful and unfortunate Italy." Repubblica romana 1849, pp. 244–45.

19. Paladini 1897, p. 98.

20. Rusconi 1879, pp. 199–202.

21. Repubblica romana 1849, p. 238.

22. Ibid., pp. 239–40.

23. Spada 1868–69, vol. 3, pp. 676–81; Delmas 1849, p. 33; Severini 2011, p. 151.

24. Pisacane 1849, p. 13. For its part, on July 2 the city council voted a resolution "to receive the French in the city impassibly, protesting that we cede only by force." Beghelli 1874, vol. 2, p. 403.

25. Giuntella 1949, pp. 132–37; Del Vecchio 1849, p. 193.

26. "Capitulation qui M.r de Corcelles n'a pas acceptée," MAEC, PAW, ff. 99 bis r–99 bis v.

27. Koelman 1963, vol. 2, pp. 446–47; Dandolo 1851, pp. 282–83; Roncalli 1997, p. 191. Amid the sense of sorrow, and the bewilderment at what was to come, the momentary power vacuum also led some to give vent to their sense of helplessness by turning on a popular target, the city's Jews. A small group of disbanded soldiers and others set out to sack the stores of the ghetto. The city's police had not yet been pulled from duty and so were able to stop the violence before it had gone far. Giuntella 1949, p. 125.

28. Garibaldi 1888, p. 239; Hoffstetter 1851, pp. 323–26; Koelman 1963, vol. 2, p. 453; Roncalli 1997, p. 197. Many different versions of Garibaldi's remarks at St. Peter's Square exist, partly because they were not easy to hear in the crowd, some undoubtedly made all the more eloquent in retrospect. The text of the letter Cass sent on July 2, written in French, asking Garibaldi to come see him, is reproduced in Marraro 1943, p. 483.

29. Paladini 1897, pp. 100–101; Dandolo 1851, pp. 284–85.

30. Fuller 1856, pp. 412–13; Vecchi 1851, p. 489; Candeloro 1972, p. 453; Hoffstetter 1851, pp. 326–41; Trevelyan 1907, pp. 229–34. The day after Garibaldi led his men out of the city, Mazzini, unaware that Ciceruacchio had gone with Garibaldi, wrote to Margaret Fuller to ask for her help in getting the American chargé d'affaires, Cass, to provide Ciceruacchio and one of his sons with U.S. passports under assumed names. Humphreys 1956, p. 44.

31. République romaine 1849, pp. 184–95; Giuntella 1949, p. 135; Gabussi 1851–52, vol. 3, p. 476. In late June, the Assembly had debated its recommendations. Among the last points of contention was the proposed language regarding religion. The draft had declared that "the Catholic religion is the religion of the state," although it had also specified that "the exercise of civil and political rights does not depend on religious belief." But at the urging of the ever-vocal Charles Bonaparte, the full Assembly voted down the first phrase, adopting the second alone. The Roman Republic would privilege no religion above any other. Grilli 1989, pp. 288–96. The Assembly approved the text of the constitution unanimously at its July 1 session. Repubblica romana 1849, pp. 247–57.

32. Thiry 1851, pp. 152–53; Paladini 1897, pp. 104–5; Koelman 1963, vol. 2, pp. 460–69; Clough 1888, pp. 162–63; Del Vecchio 1849, p. 119; Rusconi 1879, pp. 286–87. In his report to Tocqueville, Corcelle, who rode along with Oudinot in his entry to the city, acknowledged that the reaction of the people was "hostile" but blamed this on outsiders, not Romans. Corcelle à Tocqueville, Rome, 4 juillet 1849, n. 8, MAEN, RSS 411.

33. The text of Oudinot's proclamation is found in ASV, ANN, b. 392, f. 90r.

34. Corcelle à Tocqueville, Rome, 5 juillet 1849, n. 9, MAEN, RSS 411. In the first days of the occupation, the two French ambassadors—Harcourt and Rayneval—had formed a kind of political brain trust with Corcelle, advising Oudinot on the measures to take. Harcourt now headed to Gaeta to fill the pope in on what was happening in Rome and to try to convince him to take those measures the French desired. Rayneval was also eager to return to the pope, but Corcelle depended on him for his knowledge of Italy and asked him to stay by his side. It was not by chance that

Corcelle asked Rayneval, rather than Harcourt, to remain with him. He viewed Rayneval as a man of similar opinion and similar character. Harcourt, thought Corcelle, was not only overly emotional but also overly enthused with republican principles.

35. Mazzini's letter to his mother is found in Severini 2011, p. 153. Fuller reported her meeting with Mazzini in a letter to William Henry Channing, quoted in Deiss 1969, p. 270.

36. Niel 1961, p. 476n; Antonelli al nunzio Vienna, 4 luglio 1849, Gaeta, ASV, ANV, b. 330, f. 171r; Martina 1974, p. 348.

37. Lambruschini a Pio IX, Napoli, 2 luglio 1849, in Manzini 1960, pp. 406–8.

38. Harcourt à Tocqueville, au quartier général, n. 54, 3 juillet 1849, MAEN, RSS 410. In a postscript, Harcourt added that a delegation of prominent citizens from Bologna had come to Gaeta to invite the pope to move to Bologna, but on the condition that he retain the constitution. This, Harcourt reported, the pope would refuse.

CHAPTER 17: THE OCCUPATION

1. Martina 1974, p. 379.
2. Stato pontificio 1850, pp. 30–31; Ghisalberti 1949, pp. 150–51.
3. Fuller 1991, p. 306; Cass to Clayton, Rome, July 6, 1849, in Stock 1933, pp. 45–46.
4. That doubts about Oudinot's abilities were widespread at the time can be seen by a July 5 London *Times* editorial: "When the French Government selected a cavalry officer of no previous reputation in war or in politics to take command of the Roman expedition," the *Times* asserted, "they gave a very strong proof that their invasion of the Papal States was not expected to assume the character it has since acquired, or to call for any great amount of military skill or resolution. General Oudinot was chosen for this duty because he was the son of one of Napoleon's Marshals and man of good connexions in French society."
5. Corcelle à Tocqueville, Rome, 10 juillet 1849, doc. 118 in Tocqueville 1983, vol. 1, pp. 300–302.
6. Tocqueville went on to express his great unhappiness with the situation in Rome, although assuring Corcelle that he blamed it all on Oudinot. Oudinot, complained Tocqueville, was so dense that he was unable to keep two ideas in his head at the same time: putting an end to the "terror" exercised by the "demagogues," while, at the same time, lifting up the "liberal party." These were the two aims of French policy and, the foreign minister insisted, one could not be imagined without the other. Tocqueville à Corcelle, Paris, 18 juillet 1849, doc. 124 in Tocqueville 1983, vol. 1, pp. 322–26.
7. Corcelle à Tocqueville, Rome, 8 juillet 1849, n. 11, MAEN, RSS 411; Ferrari 2002, p. 140.
8. Rayneval à Tocqueville, Rome, 9 juillet 1849, n. 144, MAEC, PAR; Lancellotti 1862, p. 194.
9. Marraro 1932, p. 71; Palmerston to Freeborn, Foreign Office, July 23,

1849, doc. 93, and Freeborn to Palmerston, Rome, August 4, 1849, doc. 108 in Parliament 1851, pp. 84, 100.

10. Zucconi 2011, p. 119; Casanova 1999, pp. 155–56; Humphreys 1956, p. 45. "The English and American consuls," reported Corcelle on July 9, "are very malicious and tied to the fanatics. They are giving many passports to Romans and foreigners. While they think that in doing so they are thwarting us, they are actually rendering us a service." Corcelle à Tocqueville, Rome, 8 et 9 juillet 1849, n. 11, MAEN, RSS 411; Virlogeux 2001, pp. 5–7. Among the letters from these days in the Nicholas Brown archives at Brown University are various letters of Cristina Belgiojoso asking for Brown's help. Also found in that archive is a July 12 letter from Massimo d'Azeglio, then minister in the Sardinian government, responding to Brown's plea to aid the refugees.

11. Humphreys 1956, pp. 44–45; Candeloro 1972, pp. 453–54; Cass to Clayton, Rome, September 20, 1849, in Stock 1933, p. 59.

12. Bargagli al ministro degli affari esteri, Mola di Gaeta, 7 luglio 1849, in Bianchi 1869, vol. 6, pp. 548–50. In a letter at the time thanking the grand duke of Tuscany for his recent letter of congratulations on the taking of Rome, the pope expressed his satisfaction but warned that the city would not be healthy until it was "purged." As they were "still very far from seeing such a purge carried out," the pope added, "the elements of corruption . . . will continue to exhale their sickening vapors." Bianchi 1869, vol. 6, p. 270.

13. Antonelli al nunzio di Madrid, Gaeta, 13 luglio 1849, ASV, ANM, b. 313, ff. 951r–952r; Antonelli al nunzio di Napoli, Gaeta, 14 luglio 1849, ASV, ANN, b. 392, ff. 85r–85v.

14. Ever since the French troops had liberated them from a regime of oppression and anarchy, declared Oudinot, the Romans had repeatedly demonstrated "their loyalty and their gratitude to the generous pontiff to whom they were indebted for their new freedom." Apparently unaware of the concept of protesting too much, the general added, "France has never placed in doubt the existence of these sentiments." Stato pontificio 1850, pp. 62–63.

15. Beghelli 1874, vol. 2, pp. 433–34; Spada 1868–69, vol. 3, pp. 711–14; Roncalli, 1997, p. 202. According to a former member of the Constituent Assembly, on the evening of the hoisting of the papal flag, demonstrators paraded through the Corso, amid the French patrols, singing a parody of the *Marseillaise*: "*Allons enfants de la sacristie*. . . ." Citoyen romain 1852, p. 218. The French also organized a ceremony of thanksgiving in Civitavecchia to mark the restoration of papal rule there. "The Papal flag," reported a British naval officer who witnessed the ceremony, "was rehoisted here under a salute of 100 guns." He added, "There was not on the part of the people the slightest manifestation of joy on the occasion." Lieutenant Willes to Vice Admiral Parker, Civitavecchia, July 21, 1849, doc. 103, inclosure 2, in Parliament 1851, pp. 93–94.

16. The ship Corcelle boarded was on its way from France to Naples. When they arrived at the Neapolitan port, Corcelle and his fellow shipmates were informed that due to the cholera epidemic in France, King Ferdi-

nand had ordered all ships from France to spend fourteen days in quarantine in the harbor before anyone could disembark. Corcelle demanded to see the government minister in charge, who ultimately consulted the king himself. Corcelle was allowed to get off the ship, but without his two secretaries and without his papers. Corcelle à Tocqueville, Rome, 20 juillet 1849, n. 13, MAEN, RSS 411.

17. While Corcelle was in Rome he kept up a secret correspondence with Falloux, the pope's great defender in the French cabinet. A number of Corcelle's letters to Falloux from Rome can now be found online at: http://correspondance-falloux.ehess.fr/index.php?958.

18. Corcelle à Tocqueville, Rome, 20 juillet 1849, doc. 125 in Tocqueville 1983, vol. 1, pp. 326–28; Corcelle à Tocqueville, Rome, 20 juillet 1849, n. 13, MAEN, RSS 411.

19. Corcelle à Tocqueville, Rome, 20 juillet 1849, doc. 126 in Tocqueville 1983, vol. 1, pp. 328–30.

20. Both the original Italian text and an English translation, which I have used here with minor modifications, are found in Parliament 1851, doc. 99, pp. 86–87. An original copy of the proclamation can be found in ASV, ANN, b. 392, f. 84r. Oudinot, in his letter to Barrot of July 22, 1849, reports that the appearance of the papal address on walls throughout the city caused "a general anxiety in the public." Barrot 1876, pp. 405–6.

21. Roncalli 1997, p. 205; Martina 1974, p. 380; Farini 1850–53, vol. 4, pp. 240–43; "The French in Rome," TL, July 30, 1849. "Rome," reported Prince Odescalchi (1851, p. 4), made head of a new provisional municipal commission by Oudinot in mid-July, "was squalid, beaten down, fearful." A July 16 internal report of the Holy See's secretary of state office offers details of the destruction caused by the battle over Rome. "Stato materiale di Roma" Bullettino n. 2, Roma, 16 luglio 1849, ASV, Segr. Stato, An. 1849, Rubr. 155, fasc. 1, ff. 20r–22r.

22. Colonel Adolphe Niel to Gustave Niel, Rome, 28 juillet 1849, doc. 11 in Niel 1961, pp. 477–78.

23. Martina 1974, p. 411n.

24. Belcastel à Tocqueville, Rome, 24 juillet 1849, n. 1, MAEN, RSS 410. Baron de Belcastel served as chargé d'affaires for France in Rome from July to September of that year. Tocqueville 1983, vol. 1, p. 322n.

25. Rayneval à Tocqueville, Gaëte, 24 juillet 1849, n. 150, MAEC, PAR.

26. Rayneval à Tocqueville, Gaëte, 27 juillet 1849, n. 151, MAEC, PAR. As their discussion moved to the names of the men who might serve in the new papal government, the ambassador expressed his displeasure at the pope's insistence that the minister of internal affairs—in charge of the police—be a prelate. "A fatal idea," observed Rayneval. As for the minister of foreign affairs, said the pope, this, too, had to remain in a prelate's hands, for it was properly the job of the cardinal secretary of state.

27. Belcastel à Tocqueville, Rome, 24 juillet 1849, MAEN, RSS 410; "The French in Rome," TL, August 1, 1849.

28. Rayneval à Tocqueville, Gaëte, 20 juillet 1849, n. 147, MAEC, PAR; Belcastel à Tocqueville, Rome, 24 juillet 1849, n. 1, MAEN, RSS 410; "The

French in Rome," datelined July 21, TL, August 1, 1849; Annuario 1847, pp. 46–47; Falloux 1888, p. 524; Jankowiak 2007, p. 170n. "As to what concerns us," the Austrian ambassador in Gaeta reported to Vienna, "we could not have wished for anyone better than Della Genga." Engel-Janosi 1950, p. 153. Luigi Carlo Farini (1850–53, vol. 4, pp. 245–46), a liberal who would later become one of Italy's first prime ministers, described Della Genga as "Proud, rash, frank in his hatred for liberty and liberals, and for all that was new."

29. Altieri, observed Rayneval, was "proud, as his name [meaning 'proud' in Italian] would seem to indicate." Rayneval à Tocqueville, Gaëte, 28 juillet 1849, n. 152, MAEC, PAR. Annuario 1847, p. 55; Giuntella 1960; Farini 1850–53, vol. 4, p. 246; Jankowiak 2007, p. 171n; Esterházy à Schwarzenberg, Gaëte, 13 août 1849, doc. 119 in Blaas 1973, pp. 338–39.

30. Rayneval à Tocqueville, Gaëte, 29 juillet 1849, n. 157, MAEC, PAR. On July 30, as the three cardinals were about to arrive in Rome, Rayneval wrote to Oudinot to alert him. The French ambassador's main worry was that the cardinals would try to arrest people guilty only of having supported the Roman Republic, and he advised Oudinot to do what he could to prevent this from happening. Rayneval à Oudinot, Mola-de-Gaëte, 30 juillet 1849, in Gaillard 1861, pp. 488–90. At this time, Corcelle was sick in bed, and so Rayneval alone was dealing with the pope and his entourage at Gaeta.

31. Count Esterházy offered similar advice. "Don't worry," he told Rayneval. "Things are going well. You don't need to keep pressing. These people attach a great importance to their dignity. They are surrounded by people who every day incite them to move in the opposite direction to yours." Nonetheless, predicted Esterházy, the pope would end up adopting many of the reforms the French were pushing on him. Rayneval à Tocqueville, Gaëte, 31 juillet 1849, n. 158, MAEC, PAR.

32. France's foreign minister reserved special disdain for Cardinal Antonelli, who had been giving Corcelle a hard time about the fact that he lacked any official diplomatic status. Unlike the pope, wrote Tocqueville, Antonelli "does not even try to keep up any pretense. I find nothing more impertinent and more puerile than the complaint he has made about your powers. . . . Such an incident was, in truth, the last of all the ecclesiastical ruses I would have predicted." Tocqueville à Corcelle, Paris, 30 juillet 1849, doc. 131 in Tocqueville 1983, vol. 1, pp. 340–43. While the pope's great defender in the French cabinet, Alfred Falloux, viewed developments in Rome very differently from Tocqueville, the two agreed in taking a dim view of Antonelli. The secretary of state, Falloux later recalled, was the very opposite of the pope. He tried to cast himself as working only for the best interest of the church. "Yet those perceptive enough get a glimpse of his drive for domination and lucre. . . . He is as prone to cold calculation as Pius IX is to spontaneous action. His haughty immobility stood in contrast with Pius IX's smiling warmth." Falloux 1888, p. 517.

CHAPTER 18: APPLYING THE BRAKES

1. An original copy of the cardinals' proclamation is found at ASV, Segr. Stato, Spoglio Pio IX, 3, f. 270r; Farini 1850–53, vol. 4, pp. 246–48; Martina 1974, p. 380; Barrot 1876, pp. 408–10. The tearing down of the proclamation, and the advice the cardinals received regarding their planned procession to St. Peter's, are recounted in a report of the secretariat of state: ASV, Segr. Stato, An. 1849, Rubr. 155, fasc. 2, ff. 2r–11v. The French chargé d'affaires in Rome reported to Tocqueville on the Romans' negative reaction to the cardinals' initial announcement. Belcastel à Tocqueville, Rome, 4 août 1849, MAEN, RSS 410. Rayneval, in reporting on these developments, concurred in his estimation of the negative popular reaction to the news, added that Cardinal Della Genga in particular was "decidedly very unpopular." Rayneval à Tocqueville, Gaëte, 4 août 1849, n. 161, MAEC, PAR.

2. An original copy of the "notification" is found at ASV, ANM, b. 313, f. 205r.

3. Petre to Palmerston, Rome, July 25, 1849, inclosure 1 to doc. 102 in Parliament 1851, pp. 91–92.

4. Palomba, console generale d'Austria a Civitavecchia, a Schwarzenberg, Civitavecchia, 7 agosto 1849, doc. 118 in Blaas 1973, pp. 328–32; De La Rochère 1853, pp. 180–81; "The Papal States," letter dated August 5, TL, August 14, 1849.

5. "We are here perfectly tranquil, under the influence of 30,000 French bayonets, but men, though they speak not above their breaths, grind their teeth, and vow vengeance." "The French and the Pope," datelined Rome, August 7, TL, August 18, 1849.

6. Ripari (1860) recounts his experience in an open letter to Cardinal Antonelli. He would spend seven years in jail.

7. Tocqueville à Corcelle, Paris, 2 août 1849, doc. 132 in Tocqueville 1983, vol. 1, p. 346; Tocqueville à Rayneval, Paris, 4 août 1849, MAEN, RSS 274.

8. Tocqueville à Oudinot, Paris, 4 août 1849, MAEN, RSS 411. Rayneval shared Tocqueville's view of the vicariate tribunal. In his letter to Tocqueville later in the month, he noted that these tribunals operated throughout the Papal States, each under the supervision of the local bishop, aimed at policing people's morals. It was, reported the French ambassador, "the most detestable invention in the world." Rayneval à Tocqueville, Gaëte, 24 août 1849, particulière, MAEC, PAR.

9. Tocqueville à Corcelle, Paris, 4 août 1849, doc. 133 in Tocqueville 1983, vol. 1, p. 348.

10. Rayneval à Tocqueville, Gaëte, 4 août 1849, n. 161, MAEC, PAR.

11. Rayneval à Tocqueville, Gaëte, 6 août 1849, n. 163, MAEC, PAR.

12. The transcript of the National Assembly session of August 6 is found in Assemblée nationale 1849c, pp. 250–68. The next day La Presse praised Tocqueville for the frankness of his speech but observed that while he was no doubt sincere in describing his efforts to ensure that the pope did not return to the abuses of the past, he was naïve in thinking he would be

successful. "He has inflicted a wound on the majority, and he has not satisfied the minority. His speech is one which does honour to the man, but which diminishes the influence of the Minister." "France," TL, August 9, 1849.

13. Farini 1850–53, vol. 4, pp. 220–26; Hoffstetter 1851, p. 450; Vecchi 1851, pp. 509–10; Garibaldi 1888, p. 252.

14. The diarist is Bottrigari, quoted in Beseghi 1946, vol. 2, p. 220.

15. Among the personal items they took from Bassi, a prolific poet, was the draft of his latest poem, "The Victorious Cross." Informed of Bassi's arrest, the local vicar general, acting in place of the absent bishop of Comacchio, demanded that he be turned over to him, for as a monk Bassi enjoyed ecclesiastical immunity and, in the Papal States, could only be disciplined by church authorities. When the Austrian commander refused, the cleric sent an urgent letter to the archbishop of Bologna informing him what had happened. Meanwhile news of the famed monk's arrest reached Monsignor Bedini, the papal commissioner in charge of Bologna. He made no move to save the monk but had news of Bassi's arrest placed in the official Bologna newspaper. The next day Austrian soldiers put the manacled monk in a cart, bound for Bologna. Luigi Carlo Farini (1850–53, vol. 4, p. 250) observed that Bedini, who would head the temporary government in Bologna following the fall of the papal states a decade later, "seemed more like a pupil of Austria than a pontifical prefect."

16. Beseghi 1946, 2, pp. 221–48. The people of Bologna had a new martyr and new cause for their hatred of the Austrians and their own newly restored papal government. The place of the monk's execution and nearby burial quickly became a pilgrimage site, the people piling flowers high over the newly sacred ground. Alarmed, Monsignor Bedini, the pope's commissioner for Bologna, decided to act. On August 19 he sent a letter to the cardinals' commission in Rome reporting that "it was thought prudent to move the cadaver secretly in the night to the cemetery of Certosa, placing it in a secluded spot unknown to the public." The monsignor added with evident satisfaction that they had accomplished their mission "with great circumspection and discretion, in such a way that most people believe that it was not the work of the Government, but was done by those devoted to the person of Father Bassi." Mons. Bedini alla Commissione Governativa di Stato, 19 agosto 1849, in Gualtieri 1861, pp. 187–88.

17. Beseghi 1946, vol. 2, p. 86n; Modena 2011, pp. 192–97.

18. Rayneval à Tocqueville, Gaëte, 9 août 1849, particulière, MAEC, PAR.

19. Tocqueville added, "What an appalling scarcity of good men! . . . That's the first thing that one learns when one arrives in power." Tocqueville à Corcelle, Paris, 8 août 1849, doc. 135 in Tocqueville 1983, vol. 1, pp. 350–51; Ghisalberti 1949, pp. 150–51.

20. Esterházy thought Corcelle not up to the task he had been given. Corcelle, the Austrian ambassador observed, had won the pope's sympathy through his "religious sentiments and his pious admiration for Pius IX." But, thought Esterházy, the new French envoy was painfully naïve. Corcelle had asked the Austrian ambassador for his help in "giving an

amiable physiognomy to the Church." Esterházy was not impressed: "M. de Corcelle displayed an ardor and insistence which gave evidence of zeal rather than ability, and certainly not of familiarity with the conditions of the terrain on which he moved." Esterházy à Schwarzenberg, Gaëte, 13 août 1849 and 18 août 1849, docs. 119 and 125 in Blaas 1973, pp. 333–34, 355–57; Engel-Janosi 1950, p. 152. Illness was a constant fact of life in Gaeta, with both Rayneval and Esterházy also often being ill for various stretches of time. Esterházy à Schwarzenberg, Gaëte, 14 août 1849, doc. 120 in Blaas 1973, p. 342; Corcelle à Tocqueville, Mola-de-Gaëte, 14 août 1849, doc. 137 in Tocqueville 1983, vol. 1, pp. 355–57; De Chambrun 1936, p. 490. The pope's account of Corcelle's mental breakdown was reported by Esterházy. Esterházy à Schwarzenberg, Gaëte, 18 août 1849, doc. 124 in Blaas 1973, pp. 355–56.

21. Antonelli recounted what happened at the session in a memo to his nuncio in Vienna. After rehearsing the reasons why the pope could not agree to a council with decision-making power over finances, he added: "Only the French envoy, caring little for these serious concerns, did not stop strongly insisting that the decision-making vote be allowed." Antonelli al nunzio di Vienna, Gaeta, 14 agosto 1849, ASV, ANV, b. 330, ff. 211r–212r. Rayneval offers his own analysis of the Spanish ambassador, Martínez, and his relationship with the pope in an early September report to Paris. Rayneval à Tocqueville, Gaëte, 3 septembre 1849, n. 180, MAEC, PAR.

22. Rayneval à Tocqueville, Castellamare, 19 août 1849, n. 169, MAEC, PAR. Rayneval had gone to Castellamare to confer with the bedridden Corcelle.

23. An original copy of the *notificazione* on the councils is found at ASV, ANN, b. 392, f. 136r. The names of the ten men appointed to the Central Council of Censorship were not made public but are found in ASV, Segr. Stato, An. 1849, Rubr. 155, fasc. 2, ff. 73v–74r. They included two prelates. On the censorship of newspapers, see ASV, Segr. Stato, An. 1849, Rubr. 155, fasc. 2, ff. 91v–92r.

24. De Cesare 1907, pp. 23–24; Gabussi 1851–52, vol. 2, p. 502; Rayneval à Tocqueville, Gaëte, 24 août 1849, MAEC, PAR. "My government's formal instructions," Oudinot informed Savelli in turning down his request, "oppose having the French army collaborate in purely political arrests." Oudinot à Tocqueville, Rome, 16 août 1849, MAEC, PAW, ff. 37r–37v.

25. Stato pontificio 1850, pp. 50–51.

26. Adolphe Niel à Gustave Niel, Rome, 19 août 1849, doc. 12 in Niel 1961, p. 478. On August 22 the British naval captain Key reported that "the detestation of the cardinals and priests, and a dread of their return to power, is openly expressed by the Roman people of all classes." Key 1898, p. 207.

27. Conservative British sentiment of the time might be judged by an editorial the London *Times* ran on August 20, blasting the reactionary nature of the pope's restoration: "He has kept himself aloof from his kingdom; has garrisoned his capital with foreign bayonets, and has commissioned

a Triumvirate, whose very names are symbolical of misgovernment and tyranny, to dispose of the liberties and fortunes of his people."

Heedless of French warnings, the pope was bringing back all the old abuses. "With so weak a man as Pius IX," Tocqueville wrote to his good British friend, Nassau William Senior (Senior 1872, vol. 1, p. 237), "the influence of those immediately around him is omnipotent. The cardinals, old, ignorant, timid and selfish, detest all change, and he does not venture to differ from them."

28. Should the French government recall its troops, predicted Falloux, "all the Holy See's enemies would rejoice and perhaps, after a few weeks, a new revolution would erupt in the certainty that France would not return." Nunzio, Paris, a Antonelli, 15 agosto 1849, ASV, Segr. Stato, An. 1849, Rubr. 165, fasc. 2, ff. 115r–118v. On receiving the nuncio's report, Antonelli quickly wrote to the three cardinals in Rome, sending them a copy and recommending that they help Falloux by being sure to inform the French commander in Rome in advance of any important measure they planned to take. Antonelli, Gaeta, ai Cardinali Componenti la Commissione Governativa, Roma, 25 agosto 1849, ASV, Segr. Stato, An. 1849, Rubr. 165, fasc. 2, ff. 113r–114r.

29. Rayneval à Tocqueville, Gaëte, 26 août 1849, n. 173, MAEC, PAR. Although it appears that Rayneval had not yet received the news, on August 22, with Harcourt having been dismissed and no longer in Rome, and Corcelle still indisposed, he had been named interim ambassador to the Holy See. MAEC, PDI Rayneval, 22 août 1849.

CHAPTER 19: LOUIS NAPOLEON AND THE POPE

1. A copy of Louis Napoleon's letter is found in MAEC, MD, 121, ff. 328r–329v. It can also be found in Barrot 1876, p. 414. See also Barrot 1876, pp. 430–44.

2. Falloux 1888, pp. 527–30. Falloux reports that he was not completely naïve and so imagined that the letter might well end up being shown to the three cardinals in Rome. This, he thought, might not be such a bad thing, as it would vindicate what he had said about the depth of French government anger toward the pope and the prospect that the government might well withdraw its troops from Rome.

3. Tocqueville à Corcelle, Paris, 18 août 1849, doc. 139 in Tocqueville 1983, vol. 1, pp. 360–63. Tocqueville's account differs from Falloux's in asserting that Louis Napoleon's letter was only sent off after they had seen it. Hoping to stave off disaster, Tocqueville wrote a new set of directions to Rayneval. As the pope kept citing the continued presence of former members of the Constituent Assembly in Rome as a reason why he could not return, the French needed to see that the men were safely removed from the Papal States. For this purpose he had ships ready at Marseilles to take them to America. At the same time, Rayneval and Rostolan were charged with seeing that the inquisitorial courts that the papal government was trying to put into action in Rome were stopped, and the prac-

tice of using ecclesiastical courts to try laypeople ended. Rayneval was also to convince the pope that his planned amnesty be as broad as possible. Only a small number of people should be excluded. Otherwise, wrote the foreign minister, the amnesty would be "illusory." While Tocqueville reluctantly accepted the pope's insistence that he would not tolerate a constitution, the French, the foreign minister instructed, needed to ensure that people's rights be as similar to those found in constitutional governments as possible. Tocqueville à Rayneval, Paris, 29 août 1849, MAEN, RSS 411.

4.   Rayneval à Tocqueville, Rome, 28 août 1849, n. 175, MAEC, PAR.

5.   Rostolan à Tocqueville, Rome, 30 août 1849, MAEN, RSS 537 bis.

6.   Rayneval à Tocqueville, Rome, 30 août 1849, n. 176, MAEC, PAR; Rostolan à Tocqueville, Rome, 30 août 1849, MAEN, RSS 537 bis.

7.   Palomba, console generale d'Austria a Civitavecchia, a Schwarzenberg, Civitavecchia, 5 settembre 1849, doc. 129 in Blaas 1973, pp. 364–68. An English text of the *Débats* August 31 letter from Rome was published in "The Papal States," TL, September 10, 1849. At five p.m. on August 31, the second day Louis Napoléon's letter was being circulated in Rome, General Rostolan ordered a proclamation to be posted on the city's walls reiterating the warning that any public gathering or demonstration would be immediately put down by the military and its promoters tracked down and punished. Repubblica romana n. 15, Roma, 31 agosto 1849, ASV, Segr. Stato, An. 1849, Rubr. 155, fasc. 2, ff. 123r–128v. Resentment against France by the cardinals of the Sacred College, already great, now grew even more. "This sentiment of ill will for France that animates all the men who want to see the Holy Father return with the plenitude of his absolute powers," the French chargé d'affaires in Rome reported on the thirty-first, "is expressed in all circumstances." Belcastel à Tocqueville, 31 août 1849, Rome, n. 8, MAEC, CP, Rome vol. 989, f. 366r.

8.   The French, Rayneval added, are being blamed for the failure to establish order in Rome. "It is indeed remarkable," he observed, "that the Sacred College [of Cardinals] has a deeply engrained hatred for the only power that is truly Catholic, truly dedicated to the Catholic cause." Rayneval à Tocqueville, Rome, 31 août 1849, n. 179, MAEC, PAR. On Venice, see Chantrel 1861, p. 61; "Venice," TL, September 5, 1849. If Esterházy seemed to the French to be resolutely on the side of reaction, Schwarzenberg's position was more nuanced. Meeting with the papal nuncio in Vienna in late August, he expressed his own displeasure with reports that all the old abuses of ecclesiastical government were being restored to the Papal States and urged that some effort be made to institute reform without threatening the pope's absolute power. Viale Prelà, Vienna, a Antonelli, 28 agosto 1849, ASV, ANV, b. 322, ff. 55v–57r.

9.   "Monsieur," wrote the despondent ambassador in concluding his report to Tocqueville, "what little optimism I still had deserts me now. To get more than we have gotten so far is not possible. Our role, in continuing to insist . . . would only make us look ridiculous. . . . These people are blind. They don't see the sun shining in the middle of the day. They have

a different language from us. Only one man is for us: the pope, and he is slipping out of our hands. He is becoming bitter. They are surrounding him, they are turning him against us." Rayneval à Tocqueville, Rome, 3 septembre 1849, n. 180, MAEC, PAR.

10. Palomba a Schwarzenberg, Civitavecchia, 5 settembre 1849, doc. 129 in Blaas 1973, p. 367.

11. "Diario della venuta e del soggiorno in Napoli di sua Beatudine Pio IX," settembre 1849, ASV, ANN, b. 392, ff. 187r–188v; Blois 1854, pp. 200–207. At the time, Antonelli predicted that the pope's stay in his new quarters would last only a matter of weeks. Antonelli a Cardinal Patrizi, Gaeta, 28 agosto 1849, ASVR, Segr. Vicariato, Atti, b. 8, fasc. 12, ff. 1r–2v.

12. Bollettino n. 17, Roma, 15 septembre 1849, ASV, Segr. Stato, An. 1849, Rubr. 155, fasc. 2, ff. 186r–193v; Palomba a Schwarzenberg, Civitavecchia, 15 settembre 1849, doc. 135 in Blaas 1973, pp. 384–85; Prefettura di polizia, 30 agosto 1849, ASV, Segr. Stato, An. 1849, Rubr. 155, fasc. 2, ff. 121r–121v. Rayneval advised Tocqueville not to let the refugees know they were in fact bound for America lest they refuse to leave. Rayneval à Tocqueville, Naples, 11 septembre 1849, n. 185, MAEC, PAR.

13. Adolphe Niel à Gustave Niel, Rome, 20 septembre 1849, doc. 13 in Niel 1961, p. 479.

14. By this time, the letter had been published in several French newspapers, provoking positive comments. In an editorial printed alongside it, the French *Débats* added its words of approval for the president's message: "All that has been done at Rome since we re-established the Pontifical authority there has been done in spite of us. . . . It was a state of things which could not continue. . . . It would be to inflict a mortal insult on the Sovereign Pontiff to go and re-establish in the capital of his States those institutions which he had himself destroyed. . . . We have given an army to Pius IX, and not to Gregory XVI." The text of the *Débats* article is reported in "France," TL, September 10, 1849. Louis Napoleon's letter to Ney was also published in *Le Moniteur* on September 7. Milza 2004, pp. 182–83.

15. Corcelle à Tocqueville, Naples, 20 septembre 1849, doc. 154 in Tocqueville 1983, vol. 1, p. 415; Rayneval à Tocqueville, 20 septembre 1849, n. 147, MAEC, PAR. That same day, Rostolan renewed his request: "I once again beg the minister of war," he wrote, "to put an end to my mission. I am not the right man for the government's current policy." Rostolan à Tocqueville, Rome, MAEC, CP, Rome, vol. 993, f. 226r.

16. The Austrian ambassador reported on this meeting of the cardinals, expressing his own view—shared by Schwarzenberg—that the pope should move to an Austrian-held area only as a last resort. It was better if some kind of understanding could be reached with the French. The possibility of conflict between Austria and France following a move of the pope to Austrian-held territory, leaving the French to rule Rome, was too great. Esterházy à Schwarzenberg, Naples, 11 septembre 1849, doc. 133 in Blaas 1973, pp. 380–82. On the pope's political change of heart, see Martina 1974, pp. 366–67. On Lambruschini's warnings, see Rayneval à Tocqueville, Naples, 13 septembre 1849, n. 186, MAEC, PAR.

17. A copy of the original document is found in ASV, ANN, b. 392, ff. 175r–176v. Although first appearing in Rome on the seventeenth, it carried the date of September 12.

18. The text is found in Stato pontificio 1850, pp. 169–70.

19. Farini is quoted in Ghisalberti 1949, p. 143. In meeting with Cardinal Antonelli in late September, Rayneval complained about the pope's limited amnesty. If they had listened to the French, replied the secretary of state, they would not have ended up excluding anyone from the amnesty. "Ah," responded the French ambassador, "then so much the better, that would do honor to the Holy Father. He would show himself to be merciful and generous." "Not at all," replied Antonelli. "A general pardon would, at the same time, be both unjust and immoral." Rayneval à Tocqueville, Naples, 30 septembre 1849, n. 198, MAEC, PAR.

20. "The French military authorities in Rome," Antonelli went on to complain, "want to exercise their influence in the most important areas, especially with regard to the police." Antonelli a Viale, Portici, 17 settembre 1849, doc. 49 in Lukács 1981, pp. 369–70. Antonelli sent the same letter to the nuncio in Madrid, along with a copy of the *motu proprio*. Antonelli al nunzio di Madrid, Portici, 17 settembre 1849, ASV, ANM, b. 313, ff. 707r–712r.

21. Quoted in Ghisalberti 1949, p. 143.

CHAPTER 20: THE UNPOPULAR POPE

1. Liedekerke, September 22, 1849, in a report excerpted in Ghisalberti 1949, pp. 147–50.

2. Rayneval à Tocqueville, Naples, 23 septembre 1849, n. 192, MAEC, PAR.

3. Tocqueville à Corcelle, Paris, 24 septembre 1849, doc. 155 in Tocqueville 1983, vol. 1, pp. 416–23. The following day Tocqueville wrote to Rostolan to inform him of Mazzini's accusation and to give him similar instructions. Tocqueville à Rostolan, Paris, 25 septembre 1849, MAEN, RSS 537 bis.

4. Tocqueville à Corcelle, Paris, 26 septembre 1849, doc. 157 in Tocqueville 1983, vol. 1, pp. 429–30.

5. The English text of *Qui pluribus* is found at http://www.papalencyclicals .net/Pius09/p9quiplu.htm. In this passage, Pius IX quotes from his sainted fifth-century predecessor, Pope Leo the Great.

6. Rayneval à Tocqueville, Naples, 30 septembre 1849, n. 198, MAEC, PAR.

7. Rayneval à Tocqueville, Naples, 27 septembre 1849, n. 196, MAEC, PAR; Lukács 1981, p. 31n.

8. On Rostolan's request, see Rayneval à Barrot, Rome, 24 septembre 1849, in Gaillard 1861, pp. 500–502. Two days after his initial letter to Tocqueville, Corcelle advised the foreign minister that he would keep the matter of his resignation confidential. He said he did not want to undermine his own authority in the interim, nor did he want to encourage Rostolan to stick by his decision to resign. Corcelle also feared the im-

pact that the news of his resignation would have on the papal court. Nor, he added, did he want to embarrass his good friend. "If you think that my resignation for political reasons looks badly for you," he told Tocqueville, "attribute it to reasons of health and the expiration of the natural term of six months." Corcelle à Tocqueville, Rome, 24 septembre, 2 octobre, 4 octobre 1849, docs. 155, 161, 162 in Tocqueville 1983, vol. 1, pp. 427, 444.

9. Corcelle à Tocqueville, Rome, 10 octobre 1849, doc. 164 in Tocqueville 1983, vol. 1, pp. 449–51.

10. The foreign minister sent the letter to the warship he kept at Toulon for emergencies and ordered the captain to set sail immediately to rush it to Corcelle. Tocqueville à Corcelle, Paris, 9 octobre 1849, doc. 164 in Tocqueville 1983, vol. 1, pp. 448–49.

11. Corcelle à Tocqueville, Rome, 13 octobre 1849, doc. 165 in Tocqueville 1983, vol. 1, pp. 451–54. "The limited concessions that your repeated entreaties and those of M. de Rayneval have obtained from the Holy See," Tocqueville wrote Corcelle in mid-October, "have been unable to modify more than minimally the harsh judgment of the amnesty decree." The foreign minister urged him to keep up the battle. Tocqueville à Corcelle, Paris, 15 octobre 1849, n. 12, MAEN, RSS 274; Tocqueville à Corcelle, Paris, 30 octobre 1849, n. 18, MAEN, RSS 274.

12. D. Savelli al Sig.r Assessore gen.le di Polizia, 24 settembre 1849, ASV, Segr. Stato, An. 1850, Rubr. 165, fasc. 3, ff. 76r–76v. It appears that due to French pressure, Savelli was not entirely able to have his way, and many of those excluded from the amnesty were given until the end of September to leave the Papal States. Frantic attempts to flee followed, often to destinations unknown. Bollettino n. 22, Roma, 29 settembre 1849, ASV, Segr. Stato, An. 1849, Rubr. 155, fasc. 2, ff. 228v–229r.

13. Segreteria della S. Cong.ne degli Studi a Bonaventura Orfei, 9 novembre 1849, MCRR, ms. 40, Consiglio di censura per l'Università romana, 1849–50, ff. 21r–22v. There may have been no clearer sign of how far unhappiness had spread in Rome than the revolt in the city's foundling home. The mammoth thirteenth-century Santo Spirito complex, aside the Vatican's walls, housed hundreds of girls who had been abandoned at birth. Those for whom a husband could not be found were forced to spend the rest of their lives there. During the republic, laywomen had replaced the nuns who ran the home. When, on October 1, the nuns returned, the *bastarde,* as they were called, erupted in protest, their shouts of "Long live the Republic!" and "Death to the priests!" creating a huge din. Only through the intervention of French troops were the nuns and calm restored. Roncalli 1997, p. 235. On infant abandonment in nineteenth-century Italy, see Kertzer 1993.

14. ASVR, Vicariato, Documenti particolari, Istituti diversi, Dossier F, fasc. 11.

15. Adolphe Niel à Gustave Niel, Rome, 4 octobre 1849, doc. 14 in Niel 1961, p. 481.

16. "Although the character of the Pope, so remarkable for personal piety, is respected, yet all enthusiasm and even interest in his cause has ceased to exist." Hamilton to Palmerston, Florence, October 6, 1849, doc. 120 in

Parliament 1851, p. 114. The Austrians, too, were under no illusion. The corruption that came with the return of priestly rule, the new Austrian consul to Rome reported, was producing "general unhappiness in the lower classes, which the ill-intentioned are adroitly turning against the clergy and against the Sacred College, accusing them of blocking the concessions promised by the old constitution and thwarting the Holy Father himself." Schnitzer-Meerau à Schwarzenberg, Rome, 6 octobre 1849, doc. 140 in Blaas 1973, pp. 394–97.

17. "Rome, Naples, and Sicily," TL, September 11, 1849. "The Pius IX of 1849," reported the consul, describing what the prelates were telling him, "is as far as we are concerned the same person he was in 1847, blessing 'Italy.'" It is well known, he added, that Gregory XVI hesitated a long time before naming Mastai a cardinal. To all those who asked him why he was so hesitant, Gregory gave the same reply: "In the Mastai family home, even the cats are liberals." Schnitzer-Meerau à Schwarzenberg, Rome, 18 octobre 1849, doc. 150 in Blaas 1973, pp. 413–16.

18. Rayneval à Tocqueville, Naples, 24 septembre 1849, n. 194, MAEC, PAR; Key 1898, p. 209; Rayneval à Tocqueville, Naples, 10 octobre 1849, n. 203, MAEC, PAR; Rayneval à Tocqueville, Naples, 24 septembre 1849, n. 194, MAEC, PAR. Corcelle, too, could not imagine how the pope could place himself in the hands of a king who seemed to be growing ever more paranoid. "It is evident," observed the French envoy, "that the King of Naples has a frightful system, which can have no reasonable result, because he extends the number of the people he goes after in proportion to his fear, and his fear grows with the number of men who are being pursued. . . . It is difficult to believe that the Holy Father feels at ease in the midst of such abominable follies." Corcelle à Tocqueville, Rome, 15 octobre 1849, MAEN, RSS 411.

19. Barrot 1876, pp. 454–55.

20. Jankowiak 2007, p. 222.

21. The vote in favor was 469 to 168. Assemblée nationale 1849d, pp. 86–91, 147.

22. Rayneval à Tocqueville, Naples, 28 and 31 octobre 1849, nn. 210, 211, MAEC, PAR.

23. Rayneval au ministre des affaires étrangères, Naples, 4 novembre 1849, n. 212 bis, MAEC, PAR. News of the appearance of half a dozen cases of cholera among the French troops in Civitavecchia, and the fear that it might spread quickly to Rome, further increased the French diplomats' sense of urgency. Corcelle à Tocqueville, Rome, 30 octobre 1849, n. 36, MAEN, RSS 411.

24. Schnitzer-Meerau à Schwarzenberg, Rome, 24 octobre 1849, doc. 153 in Blaas 1973, pp. 419–20.

25. ASCER, Co. 48, f. 2, Rc, 9 sup. 2, fasc. 3, 7 settembre 1849.

26. The raid did not come as a surprise to the people of Rome. Rumors that Jews had made off with sacred objects of immense value had been circulating since the French entered the city. In September, word spread that the police were going to surround the ghetto and search its homes. People attributed the fact that this did not then happen to General Rostolan's

opposition. Rumors spread that the Jews had paid him six thousand *scudi* to buy his support. Roncalli 1997, p. 231.

27. The police reports are reproduced in Grantaliano 2011, pp. 120–27. The secretary of state report on the importance of publicizing what was found in the ghetto, and warning of the need to counter charges of religious prejudice against the Jews, is found in ASV, Segr. Stato, An. 1849, Rubr. 155, fasc. 3, ff. 71v–73v. On these events, see also Carpi 1849, pp. 5–13.

28. A copy of the Roman police report, dated October 30, is found in the archives of the Rome Jewish community. ASCER, Co. 48, f.2 Rc, 9 sup 2, fasc. 6, estratto dal "Times" del 12 novembre 1849. On the election of the Jews to the Constituent Assembly and to Rome's city council, see Capuzzo 1999, p. 279.

29. From the beginning of July, explained Corcelle, the authorities had asked all Romans to return any objects taken from public establishments during the previous months. "A large number of restitutions were made by the Christians in the time we had allotted," he reported, adding, "It is remarkable that the Jews did not return a single thing." A delegation from the ghetto had come to complain to Corcelle about the raid, but he told them he had had nothing to do with what had happened. He did, though, go together with General Rostolan to speak with the cardinals of the governing commission. The cardinals assured the Frenchmen that "there did not exist any plan of persecution nor any exceptional measure to be taken against the Jews." Corcelle à Tocqueville, Rome, 31 octobre 1849, n. 37, MAEN, RSS 411. Rome's Jewish community later sent Corcelle a formal written protest about the ghetto raid. He sent it on to Paris with the comment that it should not be taken seriously. Corcelle au ministre des affaires étrangères, Rome, 10 novembre 1849, n. 39, MAEN, RSS 411.

30. Barrot's anger was all the greater because one of the men who piloted the "coup" was his own brother, Ferdinand. It was from this time that Ferdinand Barrot, previously the president's general secretary and now his new minister of the interior, came to be referred to behind his back as "Cain." Barrot 1876, pp. 470–84; Agulhon 1983, p. 120; Martina 1974, p. 390.

31. Esterházy à Schwarzenberg, Naples, 14 novembre 1849, doc. 157 in Blaas 1973, pp. 427–28.

CHAPTER 21: "THOSE WICKED ENEMIES OF GOD"

1. Mercier à d'Hautpoul, Naples, 18 novembre 1849, n. 215, MAEC, PAR; Rayneval au ministre des affaires étrangères, Naples, 24 novembre 1849, n. 216, MAEC, PAR; Roncalli 1997, p. 239. Rayneval remained convinced that deep down the pope was eager to do good, but, he again observed, "he is indecisive by nature and lacks the resolution needed to push back against the mistaken and unreasonable objections of his entourage." Rayneval à d'Hautpoul, Naples, 4 décembre 1849, n. 218, MAEC, PAR.

2. Baraguey au ministre des affaires étrangères, Rome, 24 novembre 1849, n. 1, MAEN, RSS 411.

3. Baraguey à de la Hitte, Naples, 2 décembre 1849, n. 4, MAEN, RSS 411; De Cesare 1907, pp. 34–36. In response to the letter from Louis Napoleon that Baraguey gave the pope, Pius sent a letter to the French president in mid-December. There he further argued against broadening his amnesty. "The pardon that I already gave, in a spontaneous manner, on another occasion, shows clearly enough that my soul is disposed to clemency. But this act had only very bad effects, being followed only by a most cruel reciprocity." A copy of Pius IX's letter to Louis Napoleon, dated Portici, 16 dicembre 1849, is found attached to de la Hitte à Baraguey, Paris, 22 décembre 1849, MAEN, RSS 274.

4. Baraguey à de la Hitte, Naples, 4 dicembre 1849, n. 5, MAEN, RSS 411. In fact, the most influential of these "bad advisors," Cardinal Antonelli, was at that time trying to arrange the replacement of the French troops in Rome with a battalion of eight thousand Spanish volunteers. This came as an alternative to Antonelli's preferred plan of substituting the Spanish army for the French army in Rome, given the Spanish government's decision to withdraw its troops from the Papal States. Antonelli al nunzio di Madrid, 5 dicembre 1849, Portici, ASV, ANV, b. 330, ff. 381r–382r.

    The next day the new French envoy had a testy exchange with Austria's ambassador. It was beneath the pope's dignity, Esterházy told him, to return to a Rome that was flooded with French troops. "I am surprised by what you say," replied the general, "because France has only undertaken this expedition to Rome in order to reestablish the pope in all the plenitude of his temporal power." The troops were there to ensure order. If the Austrians were concerned about reducing the number of foreign troops in Italy, he added, they should begin with their own army of occupation. They had twelve thousand men in Tuscany and another twelve thousand in the Papal States. "The Holy Father's dignity," said Baraguey, "may be just as compromised by the pressure that you exercise on him."

    Tuscany, replied Esterházy, was a whole other matter. Austria had a special relationship with the grand duchy and, indeed, it could be considered to be Austrian. Nor did the Austrian want to discuss reducing the imperial troops in the Papal States. Baraguey à de la Hitte, Naples, 4 décembre 1849, n. 5, MAEN, RSS 411. That the general's first encounter with the influential Austrian ambassador did not go well is evident from Esterházy's report to Vienna. "The impression I got from this conversation," he observed, "was that the French cabinet did not make a happy choice." Baraguey, thought the Austrian, "had a great deal more ambition than real merit. He has little experience and very little knowledge of political affairs." Esterházy à Schwarzenberg, Naples, 17 décembre 1849, doc. 172 in Blaas 1973, p. 472.

5. I here use the English translation of *Nostis et nobiscum* at http://www .papalencyclicals.net/Pius09/p9nostis.htm.

6. Rocca 2011, pp. 105–7; De Longis 2001, pp. 276–78.

7. Belgiojoso's letter is excerpted in Rocca 2011, p. 106n. Dated January 20, 1850, it was published in the *Giornale di Gorizia*. The patriotic princess ended her letter on a caustic note: "The accusation pronounced by Your

Holiness will not stand in the face of my denial, and those who once again have defamed pious Roman women with the false accusation of being 'prostitutes' will be few, hardhearted, and closed-minded." Proia 2010, pp. 172–73.

8. R. Abercrombie to Lord John Russell, Turin, December 2, 1849, in Palmerston Papers online, #Docref=PP/GC/AB/210; Rayneval à de la Hitte, Naples, n. 223, 31 décembre 1849, MAEC, PAR. Romans found some solace in humor. A prominent pharmacist in Rome, it was said, took great pride in his parrot's speaking ability. Earlier in the year he had taught it to repeat "Long live the Roman Republic, Death to Pius IX." What the pharmacist had not taught his prize parrot to do was to unlearn what it had learned, causing, or so it was said, much malicious mirth. Roncalli (1997, p. 242), in relating this seemingly apocryphal account of the parrot in his diary entry for December 1, 1849, swears that it was true.

9. Rayneval à de la Hitte, Naples, n. 222, 24 décembre 1849, MAEC, PAR.

10. A week later Cardinal Della Genga, the leading member of the red triumvirate overseeing papal administration in Rome, offered his own warning. Although he began by expressing his hope that the pope might be able to return before long to his capital, he immediately added: "However, I cannot hide the fact that, while the boiling spirits of the Republic and of the time of anarchy have calmed down considerably, nonetheless . . . the multitudes have not yet returned to that religious and political sense that is so much to be desired for the benefit both of people's souls and of civil society." The quotes from Cardinal Della Genga's letter of January 8, 1850, and from Cardinal Macchi's December 30, 1849, letter to Pius IX are found in Martina 1974, pp. 406–7.

11. For his part, Rayneval saw not the least sign that these fears were justified. "It is true that deep down Pius IX is liberal," reported the ambassador, "but he was sorely tested, and for a person of his nature, uncertain and fearful, lessons of this kind will always exert a profound influence." Rayneval à de la Hitte, Naples, n. 223, 31 décembre 1849, MAEC, PAR.

12. Lancellotti, 31 dicembre 1849, in Cittadini 1968, p. 264; Lodolini 1970, p. 103; Martina 1974, pp. 414–15.

13. Farini 1850–53, vol. 4, p. 295.

14. Gille 1967, pp. 68–70. In mid-December, Rayneval reported on Antonelli's eagerness to get the loan from the Rothschilds and his expectation that a member of the banking family would soon come to meet with him. Rayneval à de la Hitte, Naples, 14 décembre 1849, n. 220, MAEC, PAR. On December 21, the French foreign minister, de la Hitte, sent a note to Antonelli on the Rothschild negotiations via Baraguey, stressing how crucial it was that they be successful. De la Hitte à Baraguey, Paris, 21 décembre 1849, n. 8, MAEN, RSS 274.

15. De la Hitte à Baraguey, Paris, 5 janvier 1850, n. 2, MAEN, RSS 274; de la Hitte à Rayneval, Paris, 5 janvier 1850, MAEN, RSS 274.

16. Laras 1973, pp. 515–19; Martina 1967b, pp. 211–12.

17. De la Hitte à Rayneval, Paris, 10 janvier 1850, n. 2, MAEC, CP, Naples, vol. 180, ff. 14r–14v.

18. Martina 1974, pp. 410–12. Rayneval reported in mid-January on his conversation with Antonelli about the Rothschilds' requests for better treatment of the Jews. Rayneval à de la Hitte, Naples, 15 janvier 1850, n. 3, MAEC, CP, Naples, vol. 180, ff. 16r–19v.

19. Baraguey à de la Hitte, Rome, 14 janvier 1850, n. 13, MAEN, RSS 412. Baraguey is reported to have declared, "I would a thousand times rather have to deal with the Bedouins than with the cardinals!" Citoyen romain 1852, p. 224. At the same time as the French general was casting the blame on the men of the papal court, the men in the papal administration were heaping abuse on the French. In his weekly report, Rome's police chief attributed the continuing hostility of large parts of Rome's population to the return of the ecclesiastical regime to the "dubious policies" pursued by France. The report also chronicled the latest of a series of rumors swirling around the pope's return. "Those who out of deep malice nurse hatred in their hearts for the pontiff . . . have not failed in recent days to spread the rumor in Rome that the papal steamship that is being awaited from Naples, along with a portion of the Holy Father's crew, was shipwrecked and sunk in the sea along its route." Direzione generale di polizia, Bollettino politico dello Stato pontificio dal giorno 10 al 16 Gennaio, Roma, 18 gennaio 1850, ASV, Segr. Stato, An. 1850, b. 155, fasc. 1, ff. 36r–36v.

20. Rayneval à de la Hitte, Naples, 4 février 1850, n. 6, MAEC, CP, Naples, vol. 180, ff. 29r–34v; Gille 1967, p. 2:70.

21. De la Hitte à Baraguey, Paris, 23 février 1850, n. 10, MAEN, RSS 274; Gille 1967, pp. 70–71.

22. Martina 1974, p. 395.

23. Baraguey à de la Hitte, Rome, 5 février 1850, n. 17, MAEN, RSS 412.

24. Falconi 1983, pp. 232–33.

25. Martina 1974, pp. 399–401.

26. The text is taken from the version found in the Vatican archives: ASV, Segr. Stato, An. 1850, Rubr. 155, fasc. 1, ff. 180r–181r.

27. Jan Koelman, the Dutch painter living in Rome, described the scene: "Packed into five or six crude carriages, dressed in squalid, patched-up costumes, they went up and down through the silent street" shouting "Long live the Holy Father! Long Live Pius IX!" As they left, having pocketed the money, they added shouts of ironic appreciation, "Long live the Holy Father's police!" Koelman 1963, vol. 2, pp. 498–99; Roncalli 1997, pp. 256–57.

28. Baraguey à de la Hitte, Rome, 9 février 1850, n. 19, MAEN, RSS 412. The young man in question was none other than the prince of Musinano, son of Charles Bonaparte. He had sided with his devoutly Catholic mother in repudiating his father, who was then living in exile.

CHAPTER 22: RETURNING TO ROME

1. Conférence de Portici, Compte rendu de la 15ème séance, 11 mars 1850, MAEC, CP, Naples, vol. 180, ff. 76r–78r; Rayneval à de la Hitte, Naples, 14 mars 1850, n. 17, MAEC, CP, Naples, vol. 180, ff. 70r–75v.

2. Rayneval à de la Hitte, Naples, 14 mars 1850, n. 17, MAEC, CP, Naples, vol. 180, ff. 71r–71v.
3. Antonelli ai Cardinali Componenti la Commissione Governativa, Portici, 16 marzo 1850, ASV, Segr. Stato, An. 1850, Rubr. 1, fasc. 2, ff. 45r–45v. Antonelli had written the three cardinals in Rome in early January asking them to begin making preparations for security along the pope's intended land route to Rome. Antonelli ai Cardinali componenti, Commissione Governativa, Portici, 10 gennaio 1850, ASV, Segr. Stato, An. 1850, Rubr. 1, fasc. 2, ff. 4r–4v. Although he had not yet informed the diplomats, Antonelli had told the three cardinals in Rome on March 7 of the planned date and route of the pope's return. Della Genga, Vannicelli, e Altieri al ministro del commercio, Roma, 11 marzo 1850, ASV, Segr. Stato, An. 1850, Rubr. 1, fasc. 2, ff. 33r–33v.
4. Rayneval à de la Hitte, Naples, 4 avril 1850, n. 21, MAEC, CP, Naples, vol. 180, ff. 99r–104r.
5. Even at the time the pope set out, not all were sure he would actually return to Rome. Reporting from Caserta on April 4, the London *Times* correspondent wrote: "I am acting on the persuasion that Pio Nono will this time keep his word, but I do so in defiance of my better judgment, and of that of many true friends of the Church, who cannot yet be convinced that he seriously intends to go so far. In fact, I shall not believe that the Pope is at Rome until I see him there." "The Return of the Pope to Rome," TL, April 13, 1850.
6. Barluzzi 1850, pp. 1–7; Blois 1854, pp. 216–20.
7. Univers 1850, p. 4.
8. Baraguey à de la Hitte, Rome, 10 avril 1850, n. 30, MAEN, RSS 412.
9. "Affairs of Rome," datelined Velletri, April 11, TL, April 23, 1850.
10. From Bargagli's letter from Rome to the Tuscan minister of foreign affairs, April 9, 1850, quoted in Martina 1974, p. 416.
11. Carlier, le Préfet de police, au ministre intérieur, 12 avril 1850, MAEC, CP, Rome, vol. 994, ff. 157r–158r; lettres de Rome, 12 avril 1850 in Univers 1850, pp. 27–28.
12. Cuneo 1850, pp. 35–37; "Affairs of Rome," datelined Rome, April 12, TL, April 24, 1850; de la Rochère 1853, pp. 474–75; Falconi 1983, p. 258.
13. Liedekerke's April 13 report to the Dutch foreign minister is quoted in Ghisalberti 1949, p. 175. Both Esterházy's report to Vienna, and Ludolf's to Naples, tell of the subdued popular mood amid the splendor of the papal procession into Rome. Engel-Janosi 1950, p. 159; Ludolf al ministro degli affari esteri in Napoli, Roma, 13 aprile 1850, doc XLIII in Bianchi 1869, vol. 6, pp. 552–53.
On the very day of the pope's entry into Rome, the police prefect there sent an urgent warning. Police sources had learned that Mazzini had organized a conspiracy, they reported, to take advantage of the chaos in Rome to murder the pope. Mazzini's initial aim, said the police prefect, had been to assassinate Louis Napoleon, but his fellow refugees in London had dissuaded him. Instead, he now hoped that the murder of the pope would trigger a new uprising in Rome. The principal agents of the assassination plot were to be a group of women, headed by the wife of

one of the chief officers of the *garibaldini*. Although her husband was in exile, she remained in Rome, minding the family's jewelry business. Carlier, le Préfet de police, au ministre intérieur, 12 avril 1850, MAEC, CP, Rome, vol. 994, ff. 157r–158r.

14. Baraguey à de la Hitte, Rome, n. 33, 30 avril 1850, MAEN, RSS 412.

15. "Affairs of Italy," datelined Rome, April 30, TL, May 11, 1850.

16. De Cesare 1907, pp. 10, 25–29; Citoyen romain 1852, p. 226.

17. Ghisalberti 1949, p. 172; Burdel 1851, pp. 8–19; Laureano 1970, pp. 226–30. On Gazzola, see Monsagrati 1999. A year after his trial, Gazzola escaped from Castel Sant'Angelo, helped by French soldiers guarding the castle. For a first-person account of years spent in the pope's prisons, see Tergolina 1860.

18. The appointment, on the pope's return to Rome, of Antonelli's brother to head the Bank of Rome only served to increase animosity toward the all-powerful secretary of state. Ghisalberti 1949, pp. 176–77; Falconi 1983, pp. 258, 264; Martina 2004, p. 195; Cipolletta 1863, pp. 43–47.

19. Martina 1974, pp. 395–96.

20. Bianchi 1869, vol. 6, pp. 560–61.

21. Esterházy's May 28, 1850, report to Schwarzenberg is quoted in Ghisalberti 1949, p. 177.

22. Having recently heard rumors that the pope was under pressure from the cardinals to dismiss Antonelli, Rayneval then turned to the subject of the secretary of state, arguing that the pope had no one capable of replacing him. Rayneval had become one of Antonelli's greatest supporters, believing—mistakenly—that it was the other cardinals who were trying to prevent any liberal reforms from taking place, and that only Antonelli promised to move the Papal States into modern times. The cardinal, the ambassador told the pope, must be allowed to finish the work he had started. For his part, the pope dismissed the rumors, and said he had complete confidence in Antonelli. Rayneval à de la Hitte, Rome, n. 12, 30 juin 1850, MAEN, RSS 412.

23. Rayneval à de la Hitte, Rome, , n. 11, 24 juin 1850, MAEC, PAR; Rayneval à de la Hitte, Rome, n. 26, 31 août 1850, MAEC, PAR; Rayneval à de la Hitte, Rome, n. 18, 20 juillet 1850, MAEC, PAR; Rayneval à de la Hitte, Rome, n. 19, 24 juillet 1850, MAEC, PAR; Viaene 2001, p. 505. In these months, too, whenever the pope planned to visit a church in Rome, Antonelli would first alert the French general in charge of security to provide the pope with a French cavalry escort. A series of reports of this kind can be found in ASV, Segr. Stato, An. 1850, Rubr. 1, fasc. 1 for August and September 1850.

24. Chiron 2001, p. 49; Roncalli 1972, pp. 32–33; Gillespie 1845, p. 161. That not all the upper clergy at the time shared Mastai's sensitivities about the guillotine is evident from the discussion that Cardinal Giuseppe Sala had with Pope Gregory XVI in the wake of the revolt that greeted Gregory's election. In arguing that it was only by executing the rebels that they would quell the unrest, he told the pope that he would be happy to perform the executions himself if only he could receive dispensation from the "irregularity" of having a cardinal perform such a task. Morelli 1953,

pp. 98–99. Apparently this made an impression on the pope, for the following year he appointed the cardinal to be prefect of the Congregation of the Index (of forbidden books).

25. Rayneval à de la Hitte, Rome, n. 39, 10 octobre 1850, MAEC, PAR; Roncalli 1997, pp. 292–93; Citoyen romain 1852, pp. 233–40.

26. Cass to John Clayton, Rome, September 4, 1849, n. 13; Cass to John Clayton, Rome, September 20, 1849, n. 14; and Cass to John Clayton, Rome, April 20, 1850, n. 24; Stock 1933, pp. 54–59, 66–67.

27. Cass to Daniel Webster, Rome, October 15, 1850, n. 34, Stock 1933, pp. 75–77.

28. S. Alatri and A. Rapelli to Baronne de Rothschild, Rome, 19 avril 1850, ASCER, Co 50–51, f2, Rd. 9, sup. 2, p4, fasc. 6.

29. "Memoria sugl'Israeliti," al ministro della Repubblica francese e March. de Rothschild, novembre 1850, ASCER, Co 50–51, f. 2, Rd. 9, s. 2, p4, fasc. 15. An undated document, "Note sur la situation des Israélites des États Pontificaux, et sur ceux de Rome in particulier," found in the same folder as the document cited above, and possibly an appendix to it, further chronicles the restrictions reimposed on Rome's Jews following the restoration.

30. Story 1864, vol. 1, pp. 81–82. One example comes in an early 1851 letter from the police head for the Regola *rione* of Rome, addressed to the cardinal vicar, complaining bitterly of the scandal of still seeing Jews living in the same buildings as Catholics. Francesco Soderini a Cardinale Patrizi, 15 gennaio 1851, ASVR, Segreteria, Atti, b. 76, fasc. 28. There is even some evidence of the attempt to reintroduce the forced sermons, held at a church bordering the ghetto. Jewish men were forced several times a year to attend the conversionary sermons, given by a Dominican, on Saturday afternoons. The semiofficial Rome almanac for 1851 identifies Sant'Angelo in Pescheria as the "Church where sermons for the Jews are held," and lists the three priests charged with the sermons. *Notizie* 1851, p. 371.

31. Senior 1871, vol. 2, pp. 113–15. Caetani had been one of Rome's noblemen called into service by Pius IX. He had also served as the president of the Roman Club. Caetani 1974, p. 33.

32. Viaene 2001, p. 505.

33. Senior 1871, vol. 2, pp. 93–94 (Senior's diary entry is dated March 3, 1851).

34. Cass to Webster, Rome, May 24, 1851, n. 42, in Stock 1933, pp. 85–86.

35. Quoted in Viaene 2001, p. 505.

EPILOGUE

1. Gajani 1856, p. 422; Citoyen romain 1852, pp. 233–40.

2. Marchese G. Sacchetti, provveditore, Arciconfraternità di San Giovanni Decollato, in Colonna 1938, pp. 277–81. On the Rossi murder trial, also see Giovagnoli 1911. The court findings in the case are found in ASR, Tribunale supremo della Sacra consulta, Processi politici, b. 217, fasc. 132, Pellegrino Rossi.

3. Ghisalberti 1965, pp. 236–48.

4. Less than five months after Charles Bonaparte died, his son, Lucien, re-nounced his newly acquired title of prince of Canino to enter the priest-hood. A decade later Pius IX appointed him a cardinal. Casanova 1999, p. 169; Bartoccini 1969, p. 13.

5. Story 1864, vol. 2, pp. 81–87. The most notorious forced baptism case in these years involved the six-year-old Edgardo Mortara, taken from his parents on orders of the inquisitor in Bologna in 1858 and sent to Rome, where Pius IX himself became intimately involved in resisting pressures for the child's return. Kertzer 1997. For other cases of forced baptism in nineteenth-century Rome, see Kertzer 2001, pp. 38–59.

6. Odo Russell to Earl R., 17 January 1865, in Blakiston 1962, n. 310.

7. Odo Russell to Earl of C., 22 January 1866, in Blakiston 1962, n. 335.

8. Odo Russell to Lord S., 16 January 1868, and Odo Russell to Lord S., 26 March 1868, in Blakiston 1962, nn. 349 and 383.

9. The English text of *Quanta cura* can be found at http://www.papalen cyclicals.net/Pius09/p9quanta.htm; the text of the Syllabus of Errors is found at http://www.papalencyclicals.net/Pius09/p9syll.htm.

10. Longfellow to George W. Greene, Rome, January 30, 1869, in Longfel-low 1886, p. 450.

11. Mozley 1891, vol. 2, p. 103.

12. The best discussion of the pope's role in the Vatican Council is found in Martina 1990, pp. 111–232.

13. See Kertzer 2004, pp. 33–35.

14. Mack Smith 1994, pp. 204–11; Cadorna 1889, pp. 28, 35.

15. D. M. Armstrong to Hamilton Fish, U.S. consulate, Rome, 23 September 1870, in Stock 1945, pp. 354–56.

16. Gregorovius 1907, pp. 404–5.

17. The encyclical, *Respicientes ea omnis,* was released on November 1, 1870. Halperin 1939, pp. 101–2.

18. Martina 1971, pp. 316–17.

19. For a full description of the fraught funeral procession, see Kertzer 2004, pp. 179–97.

20. Kertzer 2014, pp. 98–113.

21. "Homily of His Holiness John Paul II," 3 September 2000, Beatifica-tion of Pius IX, John XXIII, Tommaso Reggio, William Chaminade, and Columba Marmion, found at http://w2.vatican.va/content /john-paul-ii/en/homilies/2000/documents/hf_jp-ii_ hom_20000903_beatification.html.

22. Negro 1966, p. 162; Coppa 1990, p. 179. Although the woman lost her suit, many believed she deserved to win. For more on the case, see Pirri 1958, pp. 105–17. Coppa (1990, p. 181) disputes the allegation that An-tonelli had acquired a fortune through illicit means while secretary of state and also disputes the widespread belief that he left little to the church in his will.

REFERENCES

———

About, Edmond. 1859. *La question romaine*. Lausanne: Corbaz & Fouiller.

Achilli, Giacinto. 1851. *Dealings with the Inquisition, or, Papal Rome, Her Priests, and Her Jesuits, with Important Disclosures*. New York: Harper and Brothers.

Agresti, Olivia Rossetti. 1904. *Giovanni Costa: His Life, Work, and Times*. London: Gay and Bird.

Agulhon, Maurice. 1983. *The Republican Experiment, 1848–1852*. Cambridge: Cambridge University Press.

Annuario Pontificio. 1847. Notizie per l'anno 1847. Roma: Stamperia Cracas.

Arcuno, Irma. 1933. *Il regno delle Due Sicilie nei rapporti con lo Stato pontificio (1846–1850)*. Naples: Perrella.

Arrigoni, Giampiera. 1996. *La fidatissima corrispondenza: Un ignoto reportage di Johann Jakob Bachofen da Roma nel periodo della rivoluzione romana (1848–1849)*. Florence: Nuova Italia.

Assemblea costituente. 1849. *Ai governi ed ai Parlamenti di Francia e d'Inghilterra*. Rome, opuscolo, http://www.repubblicaromana-1849.it /index.php?9/opuscoli/ieio138196.

Assemblée nationale. 1849a. *Compte rendu des séances de l'Assemblée nationale. Du 16 avril au 27 mai*. Paris: Panckoucke.

———. 1849b. *Compte rendu des séances de l'Assemblée nationale. Du 28 mai au 20 juillet 1849*. Paris: Panckoucke.

———. 1849c. *Compte rendu des séances de l'Assemblée nationale. Du 21 juillet au 10 octobre 1849*. Paris: Panckoucke.

———. 1849d. *Compte rendu des séances de l'Assemblée nationale. Du 11 octobre au 30 novembre 1849*. Paris: Panckoucke.

Aubert, Roger. 1961. "Antonelli, Giacomo." *Dizionario biografico degli italiani*, online.

———. 1990 [French orig. 1964]. *Il pontificato di Pio IX. Storia della Chiesa*. Vol. 21/1. Edited by Giacomo Martina. Rome: Edizioni Paoline.

Badie, Bertrand. 2012. *Diplomacy of Connivance*. Translated by Cynthia Schoch and William Snow. New York: Palgrave Macmillan.

Balbiani, Antonio. 1860. *Storia illustrata della vita di Garibaldi*. Milan: Inversini e Pagani.

Balleydier, Alfonso. 1847. *Roma e Pio IX*. Naples: Borel e Bompard.

———. 1851. *Histoire de la révolution de Rome*. 3rd ed. 2 vols. Paris: Comon.

Barbagallo, Francesco. 2000. "The Rothschilds in Naples." *Journal of Modern Italian Studies* 5 (3): 294–309.

Barluzzi, Giulio. 1850. *Relazione storica del viaggio di Sua Santità papa Pio IX da Portici a Roma nell'aprile dell'anno 1850*. Rome: Tip. delle Belle Arti.

Barrot, Odilon. 1876. *Mémoires posthumes de Odilon Barrot*. Vol. 3. Paris: Charpentier.

Bartoccini, Fiorella. 1969. "Bonaparte, Carlo Luciano, principe di Canino." *Dizionario biografico degli italiani*, online.

Bastide, Jules. 1858. *La République française et l'Italie en 1848. Récits, notes et documents diplomatiques*. Brussels: Meline, Cans.

Baudi di Vesme, Carlo. 1951. *La diplomazia del Regno di Sardegna durante la prima guerra d'indipendenza*. Vol. 2, *Relazioni con lo Stato pontificio (marzo 1848–luglio 1849)*. Turin: Istituto per la storia del Risorgimento italiano.

Beghelli, Giuseppe. 1874. *La Repubblica romana del 1849*. 2 vols. Lodi: Società Cooperativa-Tipografica.

Berra, Francesco L. 1957. "La fuga di Pio IX a Gaeta e il racconto del suo scalco segreto." *Studi romani* 5:672–86.

Bertotti, E. 1927. *Goffredo Mameli e la Repubblica romana nel 1849*. Genoa: Studio editoriale genovese.

Beseghi, Umberto. 1946. *Ugo Bassi*. 2 vols. Florence: Marzocco.

Beust, Friedrich Ferdinand, Count von. 1887. *Memoirs*. London: Remington.

Bianchi, Nicomede. 1869. *Storia documentata della diplomazia europea in Italia dall'anno 1814 all'anno 1861*. Turin: Unione tipografico-editrice.

Bittard des Portes, René. 1905. *1849: L'expédition française de Rome sous la Deuxième république d'après des documents inédits*. Paris: Émile-Paul.

Blaas, Richard, ed. 1973. *Le relazioni diplomatiche fra l'Austria e lo Stato pontificio*. 3rd series. Vol. 1. Rome: Istituto storico italiano per l'età moderna e contemporanea.

Blakiston, Noel, ed. 1962. *The Roman Question: Extracts from the Dispatches of Odo Russell from Rome, 1858–1870*. London: Chapman & Hall.

Blois, Giovanni. 1854. *Narrazione storica, religiosa, politica, militare del soggiorno nella Real piazza di Gaeta del Sommo pontefice Pio IX dal dì 25 novembre 1848 al dì 4 settembre 1849*. Naples: Reale Tipografia Militare.

Boero, Giuseppe, S. J. 1850. *La rivoluzione romana al giudizio degli imparziali*. Florence: Birindelli.

Bonaparte, Charles Lucien. 1857. *Discours, allocutions et opinions de Charles Lucien prince Bonaparte dans le conseil des députés et l'Assemblée costituante de Rome en 1848 et 1849*. Leiden: Brill.

Borie, Victor. 1851. *Histoire du pape Pie IX et de la dernière révolution romaine (1846–1849)*. Brussels: Tarride.

Bortolotti, Sandro. 1945. *Metternich e l'Italia nel 1846*. Turin: Edizioni Chiantore.

Borutta, Manuel. 2012. "Anti-Catholicism and the Culture War in Risorgimento Italy." In *The Risorgimento Revisited,* ed. Silvana Patriarca and Lucy Riall, pp. 191–213. London: Palgrave Macmillan.

Boulangé, Théodore (l'Abbé). 1851. *Rome en 1848–1849–1850: Correspondance d'un officier français de l'armée expéditionaire d'Italie.* Vol. 2. Limoges: Barbou.

Bourgeois, Emile, and E. Clermont. 1907. *Rome et Napoléon III (1849–1870).* Paris: Colin.

Boyer, Ferdinand. 1956. "Pie IX à Gaète et l'amiral Baudin." *Rassegna storica del Risorgimento* 43:244–51.

Brancati, Antonio. 2007. "Mamiani della Rovere, Terenzio." *Dizionario biografico degli italiani,* online.

Bratti, Daniele Ricciotti. 1903. *I moti romani del 1848–49 dal carteggio di un diplomatico del tempo.* Venice: Pellizzato.

Brevetti, Giulio. 2014. "Il Re Bomba e l'eclissi della natura." In *Per la conoscenza dei beni culturali,* vol. 5. Seconda Università di Napoli, dottorato in metodologie conoscitive per la conservazione e la valorizzazione dei beni culturali. Santa Maria Capua Vetere: Edizione Spartaco.

Briffault, Eugène. 1846. *Le secret di Rome au XIXme siècle.* Paris: Boizard.

Burdel, Ernest. 1851. *Le prigioni di Roma nel 1851.* Translated by F. Foce. Turin: Demaria.

Bustico, Guido. 1939. "Un ministro ferrarese di Pio IX, Carlo Emanuele Muzzarelli." *Rassegna storica del Risorgimento* 26: 459–75.

Cadorna, Raffaele. 1889. *La liberazione di Roma nell'anno 1870.* Rome: Roux.

Caetani, Michelangelo. 1974. *Lettere di Michelangelo Caetani duca di Sermoneta. Cultura e politica nella Roma di Pio IX.* Edited by Fiorella Bartoccini. Rome: Istituto di studi romani.

Calman, Alvin R. 1922. *Ledru-Rollin and the Second French Republic.* Ph.D. diss., Political Science, Columbia University.

Camarotto, Valerio. 2012. "Muzzarelli, Carlo Emanuele." *Dizionario biografico degli italiani,* online.

Candeloro, Giorgio. 1972. *Storia dell'Italia moderna.* Vol. 3, *La Rivoluzione nazionale (1846–1849).* Milan: Feltrinelli.

Capograssi, Antonio. 1941. *La conferenza di Gaeta del 1849 e Antonio Rosmini.* Rome: Proja.

Capuzzo, Ester. 1999. "Gli ebrei e la Repubblica romana." *Rassegna storica del Risorgimento* 86:267–86.

Carpi, Leone. 1849. *Blocco dei francesi al ghetto di Roma nell'anno di grazia 1849 e secondo della loro repubblica.* Turin: Stamperia sociale degli artisti.

Casanova, Antonio G. 1999. *Carlo Bonaparte: Principe di Canino, scienza e avventura per l'unità d'Italia.* Rome: Gangemi.

Chantrel, J. 1861. *Annales ecclésiastiques de 1846 à 1860.* Paris: Gaume Frères et J. Duprey.

Chiron, Yves. 2001. *Pie IX, pape moderne.* Suresnes: Clovis.

Choffat, Thierry. 2008. "Louis Napoléon candidat élections législatives et présidentielles de 1848." In *Napoléon III, l'homme, le politique,* ed. Pierre Milza, pp. 85–104. Navarre: Napoléon Éditions.

Cipolletta, Eugenio. 1863. *Memorie politiche sulla restaurazione e decadenza del governo di Pio IX compilate su documenti segreti diplomatici rinvenuti negli Archivi degli affari esteri delle Due Sicilie.* Naples: Morelli.

Citoyen romain. 1852. *Les mystères du clergé romain . . . par un citoyen romain.* Lausanne: Weber.

Cittadini, Giovanni. 1986. *Il conclave dal quale uscì Giovanni M. Mastai-Ferretti Papa.* Naples: Laurenziana.

————. 1989. *La fuga e il soggiorno di Pio IX nel Regno di Napoli.* Naples: Laurenziana.

Cittadini, Giovanni, ed. 1968. *Carteggio privato di papa Pio IX e Ferdinando II re di Napoli esistente nell'Archivio statale di Napoli coll'aggiunto del diario della rivoluzione di Roma del marchese Luigi Lancellotti.* Macerata: Opera "Mater misericordiae."

Clough, Arthur. 1888. *Prose Remains.* London: Macmillan.

Collins, Ross W. 1923. *Catholicism and the Second French Republic.* Ph.D. diss., Political Science, Columbia University.

Colonna, Gustavo Brigante. 1938. *L'uccisione di Pellegrino Rossi (15 novembre 1848).* Milan: Mondadori.

Coppa, Frank J. 1990. *Cardinal Giacomo Antonelli and Papal Politics in European Affairs.* Albany: State University of New York Press.

————. 2003. "Pio Nono and the Jews: From 'Reform' to 'Reaction,' 1846–1878." *Catholic Historical Review* 89 (4): 671–95.

Cuneo d'Ornano, Marquis. 1850. *Retour de Pie IX à Rome 1850.* Rome: Salviucci.

Curato, Federico. 1970. *Gran Bretagna e l'Italia nei documenti della missione Minto.* 2 vols. Rome: Istituto storico italiano per l'età moderna e contemporanea.

Curci, Carlo M., ed. 1849. *La quistione romana nell'Assemblea francese il 14, 18, 19, 20 ottobre, preceduta da un'avvertenza e con note.* Paris: Lecoffre.

Dalla Torre, Paolo. 1979. "Il Cardinale Giacomo Antonelli fra carte di archivio ed atti processuali." *Pio IX* 8:144–95.

D'Ambrosio, Gaetano. 1852. *Relazione della campagna militare fatta dal corpo napolitano negli Stati della Chiesa l'anno 1849.* Naples: Tipografia Militare.

Dandolo, Emilio. 1851. *The Italian Volunteers and Lombard Rifle Brigade.* London: Longman.

De Broglie, Albert. 1938. *Mémoires de Duc de Broglie, avec un préface di son petit-fils.* Vol. 1. Paris: Calmann-Lévy.

De Cesare, Raffaele. 1907. *Roma e lo Stato del Papa dal ritorno di Pio IX al XX settembre.* Vol. 1. Rome: Forzani.

De Chambrun, Gilbert. 1936. "Un projet de séjour en France du pape Pie IX." *Revue d'histoire diplomatique* 50:322–64, 481–508.

De Felice, Renzo. 1962. "Armellini, Carlo." *Dizionario biografico degli italiani,* online.

Deiss, Joseph J. 1969. *The Roman Years of Margaret Fuller.* New York: Crowell.

De La Rochère, Eugénie Dutheil, comptesse. 1853. *Rome: souvenirs religieux, historiques, artistiques de l'expédition française en 1849 et 1850.* Tours: Mame.

De Ligne, Eugène (Prince). 1929. "La Pape Pie IX à Gaète. Souvenirs inédits." *Le Correspondant,* 25 avril 1929, pp. 172–95.

De Ligne, Princesse. 1923. *Souvenirs de la princesse Ligne née princesse Lubomirska.* Brussels: Van Oest.

Delmas, E. 1849. "Relation du siège de Rome en juin 1849." *Spectateur Militaire* 48: 259–92.

De Longis, Rosanna. 2001. "Tra sfera pubblica e difesa dell'onore. Donne nella Roma del 1849." *Roma moderna e contemporanea* 9 (1–3): 263–83.

Del Vecchio, B. 1849. *L'assedio di Roma. Racconto storico.* Capolago: Elvetica.

Demarco, Domenico. 1944. *Una rivoluzione sociale, la Repubblica romana del 1849 (16 novembre 1848–3 luglio 1849).* Naples: Gufo.

———. 1947. *Pio IX e la rivoluzione romana del 1848: saggio di storia economico-sociale.* Modena: Società tipografica modenese.

———. 1949. *Il tramonto dello stato pontificio. Il papato di Gregorio XVI.* Turin: Einaudi.

De Reiset, Comte. 1903. *Mes souvenirs.* Vol. 1. Paris: Plon-Nourrit.

Desmarie, Paul [pseud.]. 1860. *Moeurs italiennes.* Paris: Poulet-Malassis et de Broise.

Diesbach, Ghislain de. 1998. *Ferdinand de Lesseps.* Paris: Perrin.

Dino, Duchesse de. 1910. *Memoirs of the Duchesse de Dino, 1841–1850.* Edited by Princess Radziwill. New York: Scribner's.

Di Rienzo, Eugenio. 2012. *Il Regno delle Due Sicilie e le potenze europee 1830–1861.* Soveria Mannelli: Rubbettino.

Diurno repubblicano: in cui si pongono, giorno per giorno, tutti gli avvenimenti. . . . che avvennero in Roma, dal 14 novembre 1848 al 2 luglio 1849. 1849. Rome: Ajani.

DRS. 1949–51. *La diplomazia del Regno di Sardegna durante la prima guerra d'indipendenza.* 3 vols. Turin: Istituto per la storia del Risorgimento italiano. For vol. 1, see Pischedda 1949; for vol. 2, see Baudi di Vesme 1951; for vol. 3, see Quazza 1952.

Druidi, Maria Cessi. 1954. "Intorno alla conferenza di Gaeta." *Rassegna storica del Risorgimento* 41:299–303.

———. 1958. "Contributo alla storia della Conferenza di Gaeta." *Rassegna storica del Risorgimento* 45:219–72.

Dumreicher, Alois. 1883. *Portraits par un diplomate.* Paris: Plon.

Edgar-Bonnet, George. 1951. *Ferdinand de Lesseps.* Paris: Plon.

Engel-Janosi, Friedrich. 1950. "The Return of Pius IX in 1850." *Catholic Historical Review* 35:129–62.

———. 1952. "French and Austrian Political Advice to Pius IX, 1846–1848." *Catholic Historical Review* 38:1–20.

Facchini, Didaco. 1890. *Biografia di Ugo Bassi.* 2nd ed. Bologna: Zanichelli.

Falconi, Carlo. 1981. *Il giovane Mastai: Il futuro Pio IX dall'infanzia a Senigallia alla Roma della Restaurazione 1792–1827.* Milan: Rusconi.

———. 1983. *Il Cardinale Antonelli. Vita e carriera del Richelieu italiano nella chiesa di Pio IX.* Milan: Mondadori.

Falloux, Alfred Pierre Frédéric, comte de. 1888. *Mémoires d'un royaliste.* Vol. 1. Paris: Perrin.

Farini, Luigi Carlo. 1850–53. *Lo stato romano dall'anno 1815 all'anno 1850*. 4 vols. Florence: Monnier.

Ferrari, Federica. 2002. "Dai rapporti della legazione toscana a Roma e a Gaeta: Un'immagine della Repubblica romana." In *Studi sulla Repubblica romana del 1849*, ed. Marco Severini, pp. 123–49. Ancona: Affinità elettive.

Ferrari, Rina. 1926. *Il Principe di Canino e il suo processo*. Rome: Libreria di scienze e lettere.

Filipuzzi, Angelo. 1961. *Le relazioni diplomatiche fra l'Austria e il Regno di Sardegna, e la guerra del 1848–49. Granducato di Toscana*. 3rd series. 2 vols. Rome: Istituto storico italiano per l'età moderna e contemporanea.

Fiorentino, Carlo M. 1999. "La politica ecclesiastica della Repubblica romana." *Rassegna storica del Risorgimento* 86 (supp. to no. 4): 33–48.

Flint, James P. 2003. *Great Britain and the Holy See: The Diplomatic Relations Question, 1846–1852*. Washington, D.C.: Catholic University Press.

Foramiti, Nicolò. 1850. *Fatti di Roma degli anni 1848–49*. Venice: Cecchini.

Francia, Enrico. 2012. *1848: La rivoluzione del Risorgimento*. Bologna: Il Mulino.

Fraser, William (Sir). 1896. *Napoleon III (My Recollections)* 2nd ed. London: Sampson Low, Marston.

Fuller, Margaret. 1856. *At Home and Abroad*. Edited by Arthur Fuller. Boston: Crosby, Nichols.

———. 1988. *The Letters of Margaret Fuller*. Vol. 5. Edited by Robert N. Hudspeth. Ithaca, N.Y.: Cornell University Press.

———. 1991. *These Sad but Glorious Days: Dispatches from Europe, 1846–1850*. Edited by Larry J. Reynolds and Susan B. Smith. New Haven, Conn.: Yale University Press.

Gabussi, Giuseppe. 1851–52. *Memorie per servire alla storia della rivoluzione negli Stati romani*. 3 vols. Genova: R. I. de' Sordo-Muti.

Gaillard, Léopold de. 1861. *L'expédition de Rome en 1849*. Paris: Lecoffre.

Gajani, Gugliemo. 1856. *The Roman Exile*. Boston: Jewett.

Garibaldi, Giuseppe. 1888. *Memorie autobiografiche*. Florence: Barbèra.

———. 1889. *Autobiography of Giuseppe Garibaldi*. Vol. 3. Translated by A. Werner with supplement by Jessie White Mario. London: Smith and Innes.

Gemignani, Beniamino. 1995. *Pellegrino Rossi 1787–1848*. Carrara: Società internazionale Dante Alighieri.

Gennarelli, Achille. 1863. *Le sventure italiane durante il pontificato di Pio Nono*. Florence: Bettini.

Ghisalberti, Alberto. 1949. "Una restaurazione 'reazionaria e imperita.'" *Archivio della Società romana di storia patria* 72:139–78.

———. 1958. *Roma da Mazzini a Pio IX: ricerche sulla restaurazione papale del 1849–1850*. Milan: Giuffrè.

———. 1965. *Momenti e figure del Risorgimento romano*. Milan: Giuffrè.

Giampaolo, Maria A. 1931. "La preparazione politica del Cardinal Lambruschini." *Rassegna storica del Risorgimento* 18:81–63.

Giannini, Giorgio. 2009. "Storia della Repubblica romana." Online at http://www.instoria.it/home/repubblica_romana_1849.htm.

Gille, Bertrand. 1967. *Histoire de la maison Rothschild*. Vol. 2. Geneva: Librairie Droz.

Gillespie, William H. 1845. *Rome: As Seen by a New Yorker in 1843–44*. New York: Wiley and Putnam.

Gilson, Bonaventure, and Pierre Kersten. 1894. *Mémoires pour servir à l'histoire du traditionalisme et de l'ontologisme en Belgique de 1834 à 1864. Correspondance de l'abbé Gilson avec Mr. Kersten*. Alost: Vernimmen.

Giorcelli, Cristina. 2000. "La Repubblica romana di Margaret Fuller: tra visione politica e impegno etico." In *Gli americani e la Repubblica romana del 1849*, ed. Sara Antonelli, Daniele Fiorentino, and Giuseppe Monsagrati, pp. 53–88. Rome: Gangemi.

Giovagnoli, Raffaello. 1894. *Ciceruacchio e Don Pirlone. Ricordi storici della rivoluzione romana dal 1846 al 1849 con documenti nuovi*. Rome: Forzani.

————. 1898. *Pellegrino Rossi e la rivoluzione romana*. Vol. 1. Rome: Forzani.

————. 1911. *Pellegrino Rossi e la rivoluzione romana*. Vol. 3. Rome: Voghera.

Giuntella, Vittorio Emanuele. 1949. "Il municipio di Roma e le trattative col general Ouidnot (30 giugno–2 luglio 1849)." *Archivio della Società romana di storia patria* 72:121–37.

————. 1960. "Altieri, Ludovico." *Dizionario biografico degli italiani*, online.

Gizzi, Stefano. 1995. "Il Cardinale Tommaso Pasquale Gizzi, Segretario di Stato di Papa Pio IX." *Pio IX* 24:117–46.

————. 1996–97. "Il Conclave del 1846 e l'elezione di Papa Pio IX." *Pio IX* 25:111–43, 183–209; 26:12–43.

Gouraud, Charles. 1852. *L'Italia. Sue ultime rivoluzioni e suo stato presente. Versione con annotazioni critiche e documenti di Mario Carletti*. Translated by Mario Carletti. Florence: Mariani.

Grantaliano, Elvira. 2011. "Gli ebrei di Roma tra repressione e integrazione." In *Judei de Urbe. Roma e i suoi ebrei*, ed. Marina Caffiero and Anna Esposito, pp. 103–27. Rome: Ministero per i beni e le attività culturali, direzione generale per gli archivi.

Gregorovius, Ferdinando. 1907. *The Roman Journals of Ferdinand Gregorovius, 1852–1874*. London: Bell.

Grilli, Antonio. 1989. "Riflessioni in tema di rapporti tra stato e chiesa nella Repubblica romana del 1849." *Rassegna storica del Risorgimento* 76:283–96.

Gualterio, Filippo A. 1851. *Gli ultimi rivolgimenti italiani. Memorie storiche con documenti inediti*. Vol. 1. Florence: Le Monnier.

Gualtieri, L. 1861. *Memorie di Ugo Bassi apostolo del Vangelo, martire dell'indipendenza italiana, coll'aggiunta di lettere e di preziosi documenti relativi alla vita e morte del Martire non che ai principali avvenimenti politici del 1848*. Bologna: Monti al Sole.

Guizot, François. 1872. *Mémoires pour servir à l'histoire de mon temps*. Vol. 8. Paris: Lévy.

Hales, Edward E. Y. 1962. *Pio Nono: A Study in European Politics and Religion in the Nineteenth Century*. Garden City, N.Y.: Image.

Halperin, William. 1939. *Italy and the Vatican at War*. Chicago: University of Chicago Press.

Herzen, Aleksandr. 1996. *Letters from France and Italy, 1847–1851*. Translated and edited by Judith E. Zimmerman. Pittsburgh: University of Pittsburgh Press.

Hibbert, Christopher. 1965. *Garibaldi and His Enemies*. London: Longmans.

Hoffstetter, Gustavo von. 1851. *Documenti della guerra santa d'Italia: Giornale delle cose di Roma nel 1849*. Turin: Cassone.

Hoolihan, Christopher. 1989. "Health and Travel in Nineteenth-Century Rome." *Journal of the History of Medicine and Allied Sciences* 44 (4): 462–85.

Humphreys, Sexson E. 1956. "Lewis Cass Jr. and the Roman Republic of 1849." *Michigan History* 40:24–50.

Ideville, Henry, comte de. 1887. *Le comte Pellegrino Rossi, sa vie, son oeuvre, sa mort (1787–1848)*. Paris: Michel Lévy Frères.

Inguanez, Mauro. 1930. "Il racconto di due fatti dettati dal P. Tosti al Caravita, cioè, l'incontro del Tosti con Pellegrino Rossi e la fuga di Pio IX a Gaeta." *Rassegna storica del Risorgimento* 17:91–95.

James, Henry. 1903. *William Wetmore Story and His Friends*. Vol. 1. Boston: Houghton Mifflin.

Jankowiak, François. 2007. *La curie romaine de Pie IX à Pie X*. Rome: École française de Rome.

————. 2008. "La Curie et le gouvernement central de l'Église sous la République romaine de 1849." In *La Répubique romaine de 1849 et la France*, ed. Pierangelo Catalano, pp. 129–47. Paris: L'Harmattan.

Johnston, R. M. 1901. *The Roman Theocracy and the Republic 1846–1849*. London: Macmillan.

Jolicoeur, Nicolas. 2011. "Être allies sans le montrer: l'Autriche, la France et la restauration du pouvoir temporal du pape." *Rassegna storica del Risorgimento* 98:515–32.

Keele, Mary, ed. 1981. *Florence Nightingale in Rome: Letters Written by Florence Nightingale in Rome in the Winter of 1847–1848*. Philadelphia: American Philosophical Society.

Kertzer, David I. 1993. *Sacrificed for Honor*. Boston: Beacon Press.

————. 1997. *The Kidnapping of Edgardo Mortara*. New York: Knopf.

————. 2001. *The Popes Against the Jews*. New York: Knopf.

————. 2004. *Prisoner of the Vatican*. Boston: Houghton Mifflin.

————. 2014. *The Pope and Mussolini*. New York: Random House.

Key, Astley Cooper (Admiral). 1898. *Memoirs of Sir Astley Cooper Key*. Edited by Vice Admiral Philip Colomb. London: Methuen.

King, Bolton. 1911. *The Life of Mazzini*. London: Dent.

Koelman, Jan Philip. 1963. *Memorie romane*. 2 vols. Edited by Maria Luisa Trebiliani. Rome: Istituto per la storia del Risorgimento italiano.

Lancellotti, Luigi. 1862. *Diario della rivoluzione di Roma dal 1 novembre 1848 al 31 luglio 1849*. Naples: Guerrera.

Laras, Giuseppe. 1973. "Ansie e speranze degli ebrei di Roma durante il pontificato di Pio IX." *Rassegna mensile d'Israele* 39 (9): 512–31.

Laureano, Edoardo. 1970. "Il clero e la Repubblica romana del 1849." *Rassegna storica del Risorgimento* 47:226–32.

Lazzarini, Giovita. 1899. *Diario epistolare di Giovita Lazzarini, ministro di grazia e giustizia nella Repubblica romana, Roma dal 10 febbraio al 7 luglio*

1849. Edited by Giuseppe Mazzini. Rome: Società Editrice Dante Alighieri.

Lecauchois-Féraud, Marc-Valérie. 1849. *Précis historique et militaire de l'expédition française en Italie, par un officier d'état major.* Marseille: Carnaud.

Ledermann, László. 1929. *Pellegrino Rossi, l'homme et l'économiste, 1787–1848.* Paris: Librairie du Recueil Sirey.

Leflon, Jean. 1963. "La mission de Claude de Corcelle auprès de Pie IX après le meurtre du Ministre Rossi." *Archivum Historiae Pontificiae* 1:385–402.

Lerro, Luigi. 1962. "Avezzana, Giuseppe." *Dizionario biografico degli italiani,* online.

Lespès, Léo. 1852. *Histoire politique, anecdotique et philosophique de la 1er présidence du Prince Louis-Napoléon Bonaparte: depuis le 10 décembre 1848 jusqu'au 20 décembre 1851.* Paris: Ploche.

Lesseps, Ferdinand de. 1849. *Ma mission à Rome, mai 1849: Mémoire présenté au Conseil d'état.* Paris: Giraud.

Leti, Giuseppe. 1913. *La rivoluzione e la Repubblica romana (1848–1849).* Milan: Vallardi.

Liedekerke de Beaufort, Augusto de. 1949. *Rapporti delle cose di Roma (1848–1849).* Rome: Vittoriano.

Lizzani, M. 1949. "Gli ultimi giorni di Mazzini a Roma." *Capitolium* (settembre-dicembre): 207–14.

Lodolini Tupputi, Carla. 1970. *La Commissione Governativa di Stato nella Resataurazione pontificia (17 luglio 1849—12 aprile 1850).* Milan: Giuffrè.

Loevinson, Ermanno. 1902–4. *Giuseppe Garibaldi e la sua legione nello Stato romano 1848–49.* 2 vols. Rome: Società Editrice Dante Alighieri.

Longfellow, Henry Wadsworth. 1886. *Life of Henry Wadsworth Longfellow.* Vol. 2. London: Kegan Paul.

Lukács, Lajos. 1981. *The Vatican and Hungary, 1846–1878: Reports and Correspondence on Hungary of the Apostolic Nuncios in Vienna.* Budapest: Akadémiai Kiadó.

Mack Smith, Denis. 1994. *Mazzini.* New Haven, Conn.: Yale University Press.

Mannucci, Michele. 1850. *Il mio governo in Civitavecchia e l'intervento francese, con note e documenti officiali.* Turin: Arnaldi.

Manzini, Luigi M. 1960. *Il cardinale Luigi Lambruschini.* Vatican City: Biblioteca Apostolica Vaticana.

Marraro, Howard R. 1932. *American Opinion on the Unification of Italy, 1846–1861.* New York: Columbia University Press.

———. 1943. "Unpublished American Documents on the Roman Republic of 1849." *Catholic Historical Review* 28 (4): 459–90.

———. 1944. "American travelers in Rome, 1848–1850." *Catholic Historical Review* 29 (4): 470–509.

Marshall, Megan. 2013. *Margaret Fuller.* Boston: Houghton Mifflin.

Martina, Giacomo. 1966. "Nuovi documenti sull'Allocuzione del 29 aprile 1848." *Rassegna storica del Risorgimento* 52:527–82.

———. 1967a. "Ancora sull'allocuzione del 29 aprile e sulla politica vaticana in Italia nel 1848." *Rassegna storica del Risorgimento* 53:40–47.

———. 1967b. "La lotta per l'emancipazione ebraica." In *Pio IX e Leopoldo II*, ed. Giacomo Martina. Rome: Pontificia Università Gregoriana.

———. 1971. "La fine del potere temporale nella coscienza religiosa e nella cultura dell'epoca in Italia. *Archivum Historiae Pontificiae* 9:309–76.

———. 1974. *Pio IX (1846–1850)*. Rome: Università Gregoriana Editrice.

———. 1990. *Pio IX (1867–1878)*. Rome: Università Gregoriana Editrice.

———. 2000. "La Repubblica romana e le carte dell'Archivio segreto vaticano." *Rassegna storica del Risorgimento* 86:351–68.

———. 2004. "I segretari di stato di Pio IX." *MEFRIM: Mélanges de l'École française de Rome* 116 (1): 1000–1009.

Martina, Giacomo, and Wiktor Gramatowski. 1996. "La relazione ufficiale sul conclave del 1846." *Archivum historiae pontificiae* 34:159–212.

Matsumoto-Best, Saho. 2003. *Britain and the Papacy in the Age of Revolution, 1846–1851*. Rochester, N.Y.: Royal Historical Society.

Mazzini, Giuseppe. 1912. *Scritti e ricordi autobiografici di Giuseppe Mazzini, scelta con note storiche a cura di Alessandro Donati*. Milan: Dante Alighieri.

McMillan, James F. 1991. *Napoleon III*. New York: Longman.

Mellano, Maria F. 1987. *Lo scontro Rosmini-Antonelli nel '48–'49 secondo il memoriale del filosofo e alla luce della realtà storica*. Stresa: Sodalitas.

Meriggi, Marco. 2006. "Ludolf, Giuseppe Costantino." *Dizionario biografico degli italiani*, online.

Metternich, Klemens von. 1883. *Mémoires, documents et écrits divers laissés par le prince de Metternich*. Vol. 7. Edited by Prince Richard de Metternich. Paris: Plon.

Milza, Pierre. 2004. *Napoléon III*. Paris: Perrin.

Minghetti, Marco. 1889. *Miei ricordi*. 3 vols. Turin: Roux.

Minoccheri, Francesco. 1892. *Pio IX ad Imola e Roma, memorie inedite di Francesco Monoccheri, di lui famigliare segreto*. Edited by Antonmaria Bonetti. Naples: Festa.

Miraglia, Biagio. 1850. *Storia della rivoluzione romana*. 2nd ed. Genova: Ponthenier.

Modena, Claudio. 2011. *Ciceruacchio: Angelo Brunetti, capopopolo di Roma*. Milan: Mursia.

Mollat, Guillaume. 1939. "La fuite de Pie IX à Gaète (24 novembre 1848)." *Revue d'histoire ecclésiastique* 35:265–82.

Monsagrati, Giuseppe. 1999. "Gazzola (Gazola), Carlo." *Dizionario biografico degli italiani*, online.

———. 2004. "Lambruschini, Luigi." *Dizionario biografico degli italiani*, online.

———. 2014. *Roma senza il papa. La Repubblica romana del 1849*. Rome: Laterza.

Montanelli, Giuseppe. 1853. *Memorie sull'Italia e specialmente sulla Toscana dal 1814 al 1850*. 2 vols. Turin: Società editrice italiana.

Montesi, Luana. 2002. "Tracce femminili nella Repubblica romana." In *Studi sulla Repubblica romana del 1849*, ed. Marco Severini, pp. 151–63. Ancona: Affinità elettive.

Monti, Antonio. 1928. *Pio IX nel Risorgimento italiano con documenti inediti*. Bari: Laterza.

Morelli, Emilia. 1953. *La politica estera di Tommaso Bernetti, segretario di stato di Gregorio XVI.* Rome: Storia e letteratura.

Moroni, Gaetano. 1851. *Dizionario di erudizione storico-ecclesiastica.* Vol. 51. Rome: Emiliana.

Mount Edgcumbe, Ernest Augustus, Earl of. 1850. *Extracts from a Journal Kept During the Roman Revolution.* 2nd ed. London: Ridgway.

Mozley, Thomas. 1891. *Letters from Rome on the Occasion of the Oecumenical Council, 1869–70.* 2 vols. London: Longmans, Green.

Natalucci, Mario. 1972. "Un segretario di stato di Pio IX: il card. Gabriele Ferretti di Ancona (1795–1860)." *Pio IX* 1:413–32.

Negro, Silvio. 1966. *Seconda Roma, 1850–1870.* Milan: Hoepli.

Niceforo, Nicola [pseud. Emilio del Cerro]. 1899. *Cospirazioni romane (1817–1868).* Rome: Voghera.

Niel, Françoise. 1961. "Lettres inédites du Général Niel à sa famille pendant la campagne de Rome (13 mai 1849–10 janvier 1850)." *Rassegna storica del Risorgimento* 48:463–86.

Notizie per l'anno MDCCCLI. 1851. Rome: Salviucci.

Noto, Adolfo. 2011. "Il ministro Tocqueville e la restaurazione pontificia." In *Un laboratorio politico per l'Italia. La Repubblica romana del 1849,* ed. Laura Rossi, pp. 65–76. Rome: Biblink.

Odescalchi, Pietro. 1851. *Rapporto fatto al consiglio dal presidente della commissione provvisoria municipale di Roma sull'azienda del comune da lei amministrata dal 15 luglio 1849 al marzo 1851.* Rome: Salviucci.

Orbe (L'). 1850. *L'orbe cattolico a Pio IX Pontefice Massimo, esulante da Roma (1848–1850).* 2 vols. Naples: Civiltà Cattolica.

Ovidi, Ernesto. 1903. *Roma e i romani nelle campagne del 1848–49 per l'indipendenza italiana (con documenti inediti).* Rome: Roux e Viarengo.

Oxilia, Ugo. 1933. "Tre conclavi." *Rassegna storica del Risorgimento* 20:563–84.

Paladini, Leone. 1897. *La difesa del Vascello o Villa Giraud—fuori Porta S. Pancrazio fatta dal Comandante Giacomo Medici e la sua legione durante l'assedio di Roma.* Rome: Stamperia Reale.

Panigada, Costantino. 1937. "Governo e Stato Pontificio nei giudizi d'un deputato del '48." *Rassegna storica del Risorgimento* 24:1773–802.

Paoli, Francesco. 1880. *Della vita di Antonio Rosmini-Serbati. Memorie.* Rome: Paravia.

Parliament (U.K.). 1851. *Correspondence Respecting the Affairs of Rome, 1849.* House of Commons Parliamentary Papers, online.

Pasolini, Pietro. 1887. *Giuseppe Pasolini. Memorie raccolte da suo figlio.* 3rd ed. Turin: Fratelli Bocca.

Pásztor, Lajos. 1966. "La segreteria di stato di Pio IX durante il triennio 1848–1850." *Annali della Fondazione italiana per la storia amministrativa* 3:308–65.

Patuelli, Antonio. 1998. *1848–49: Le costituzioni di Pio IX e di Mazzini.* Florence: Le Monnier.

Pelczar, Giuseppe (Bishop). 1909. *Pio IX e il suo pontificato.* Vol. 1. Turin: Berruti.

Pie IX. 1855. *Recueil des actes de Pape Pie IX (texte et traduction).* Vol. 13. Paris: Lecoffre.

Pierre, Victor. 1878. *Histoire de la République de 1848*. Vol. 2. Paris: Plon.

Pio, Oscar. 1878. *Vita intima e pubblica di Pio IX*. Milan: Guglielmini.

Pio IX. 1851. *Moto-proprio emanato dalla Santità di N. Signore Papa Pio IX a dì 12 settembre 1849 in Portici: coi successivi, e relativi ordinamenti pubblicati a tutto l'anno 1850*. Benevento: Camerale.

Pirri, Pietro, S.J. 1949. "Relazione inedita di Sebastiano Liebl sulla fuga di Pio IX a Gaeta." In *Miscellanea Pio Paschini. Studi di storia ecclesiastica*, pp. 421–51. Rome: Facultas Theologica Pontifici Athenaei Lateranensis.

———. 1954. "L'amnistia di Pio IX nei documenti ufficiali." *Rivista di storia della chiesa in Italia* 8:207–32.

———. 1958. "Il cardinale Antonelli tra il mito e la storia." *Rivista di storia della chiesa in Italia* 12:82–120.

Pirri, Pietro, S.J., ed. 1944. *Pio IX e Vittorio Emanuele II dal loro carteggio privato*. 2 vols. Rome: Università Gregoriana.

Pisacane, Carlo. 1849. *Rapido cenno sugli ultimi avvenimenti di Roma, dalla salita della breccia al dì 15 luglio 1849*. Lausanne: L'Unione.

———. 1851. *Guerra combattuta in Italia negli anni 1848–49*. Genoa: Pavesi.

Pischedda, Carlo, ed. 1949. *La diplomazia del Regno di Sardegna durante la prima guerra d'indipendenza*. Vol. 1, *Relazioni con il Granducato di Toscana (marzo 1848–aprile 1849)*. Turin: Istituto per la storia del Risorgimento italiano.

Piscicelli Taeggi, Oderisio. 1978. *Si scopron le tombe. Pio IX, Ferdinando II e Garibaldi 1848–1849*. Naples: Ediz. del Delfino.

Piscitelli, Enzo. 1953. "Il Cardinal Lambruschini e alcune fasi della sua attività diplomatica." *Rassegna storica del Risorgimento* 40:158–82.

Predari, Francesco. 1861. *I primi vagiti della libertà in Piemonte*. Milan: Vallardi.

Proia, Gianna. 2010. *Cristina di Belgiojoso: dal salotto alla politica*. Rome: Aracne.

Quazza, Guido, ed. 1952. *La diplomazia del regno di Sardegna durante la prima guerra d'indipendenza*. Vol. 3, *Relazioni con il regno delle Due Sicilie (gennaio 1848–dicembre 1849)*. Turin: Istituto per la storia del Risorgimento italiano.

Quazza, Romolo. 1954. *Pio IX e Massimo d'Azeglio nelle vicende romane del 1847*. 2 vols. Modena: Editrice Modenese.

Radice, Gianfranco. 1972. "Pio IX e Antonio Rosmini alla luce di nuovi documenti d'archivio." *Pio IX* 1:22–97.

Ranalli, Ferdinando. 1848–49. *Storia degli avvenimenti d'Italia dopo l'esaltazione di Pio IX*. 2 vols. Florence: Batelli.

Regoli, Roberto. 2011. "Il cardinal Luigi Lambruschini tra Stato e Chiesa." *Barnabiti studi* 28:309–32.

Repubblica romana. 1849. *Bollettino delle leggi, proclami, circolari, regolamenti ed altre disposizioni della Repubblica romana*. Edizione officiale. Rome: Tipografia nazionale.

République romaine. 1849. *Actes officiels de la République romaine depuis le 9 février jusqu'au 2 juillet 1849*. Paris: Amyot.

Reverso, Laurent. 2009. "Tocqueville et la République Romaine de 1849: Les apories du libéralisme." *Revue française d'histoire des idées politiques* 30: 299–325.

Ripari, Pietro. 1860. *Pietro Ripari al Cardinale Antonelli.* Milan: Fratelli Borroni.

Rocca, Giancarlo. 2011. "Religiosi e religiose nel '48–'49." *Barnabiti studi* 28: 61–159.

Roncalli, Nicola. 1972. *Cronaca di Roma.* Vol. 1, *1844–1848.* Edited by Maria Luisa Trebiliani. Rome: Istituto per la storia del Risorgimento italiano.

———. 1997. *Cronaca di Roma.* Vol. 2, *1848–1851.* Edited by Anna Franca Tempestoso and Maria Luisa Trebiliani. Rome: Istituto per la storia del Risorgimento italiano.

Roselli, Piero. 1853. *Memorie relative alla spedizione e combattimento di Velletri avvenuto il 19 maggio 1849.* Turin: Pons.

Rosmini, Antonio. 1998. *Della missione a Roma di Antonio Rosmini-Serbati negli anni 1848–1849.* Edited by Luciano Malusa. Stresa: Edizioni rosminiane.

Rossi, Augusto. 2001. *Pio IX e la distruzione della Repubblica romana: 1849: Una pagina nera nella storia del papato.* Rome: Serarcangeli.

Rossi, Joseph. 1954. *The Image of America in Mazzini's Writings.* Madison: University of Wisconsin Press.

Rusconi, Carlo. 1879 [1850]. *La Repubblica romana del 1849.* 3rd ed. Rome: Capaccini & Ripamonti.

———. 1883. *Memorie aneddotiche per servire alla storia del rinnovamento italiano.* Rome: Sommaruga.

Saffi, Aurelio. 1898. *Ricordi e scritti.* Vol. 3. Florence: Barbèra.

Saint-Albin, Alex de. 1870. *Histoire de Pie IX et de son pontificat.* 2nd ed. Vol. 1. Paris: Palme.

Salvagnoli, Vincenzo. 1859. *Della indipendenza d'Italia.* Florence: Le Monnier.

Schwarzenberg, Adolph. 1946. *Prince Felix zu Schwarzenberg, Prime Minister of Austria, 1848–1852.* New York: Columbia University Press.

Scirocco, Alfonso. 1996. "Ferdinando II di Borbone, re delle Due Sicilie." *Dizionario biografico degli italiani,* online.

Senior, Nassau W. 1871. *Journals Kept in France and Italy from 1848 to 1852.* Edited by M. C. M Simpson. 2 vols. London: Henry & King.

———. 1872. *Correspondence and Conversations of A. de Tocqueville with N. W. Senior.* Edited by M. C. M. Simpson. 2 vols. London: Henry & King.

Severini, Marco. 1995. *Armellini il moderato.* Rome: Istituti editoriali e poligrafici internazionali.

———. 2002a. *Il diario di un repubblicano: Filippo Luigi Polidori e l'assedio francese alla Repubblica romana del 1849.* Ancona: Affinità elettive.

———. 2002b. "Il corso degli eventi." In *Studi sulla Repubblica romana del 1849,* ed. Marco Severini, pp. 3–23. Ancona: Affinità elettive.

———. 2002c. *Studi sulla Repubblica romana del 1849.* Ancona: Affinità elettive.

———. 2006. "Nascita, affermazione e caduta della Repubblica romana." In

La primavera della nazione: la Repubblica romana del 1849, ed. Marco Severini, pp. 15–123. Ancona: Affinità elettive.

———. 2011. *La Repubblica romana del 1849*. Venice: Marsilio.

Silvagni, David. 1887. *Rome: Its Princes, Priests and People*. Translated by Fanny McLauglin. Vol. 3. London: Stock.

Simeoni, Luigi. 1932. "La fuga di Pio IX a Gaeta nella relazione del ministro di Baviera conte Spaur." *Rassegna storica del Risorgimento* 19 (4): 253–63.

Spada, Giuseppe. 1868–69. *Storia della rivoluzione di Roma e della restaurazione del governo pontificio dal 1 giugno 1846 al 15 luglio 1849*. 3 vols. Florence: Pellas.

Spaur, Contessa Teresa Giraud. 1851. *Relazione del viaggio di Pio IX. P.M. a Gaeta*. Florence: Galileiana.

Stato pontificio. 1850. *Raccolta di leggi, ordinanze, regolamenti e circolari dello Stato pontificio*. Vol. 3. Rome: Giornale del Foro.

———. 1850–51. *Raccolta delle leggi e disposizioni di pubblica amministrazione nello Stato pontificio*. Vol. 2. Rome: Stamperia della R.C.A.

Stearns, Peter N. 1974. *1848: The Revolutionary Tide in Europe*. New York: Norton.

Stock, Leo F. 1933. *United States Ministers to the Papal States. Instructions and Despatches 1848–1868*. Washington, D.C.: Catholic University Press.

———. 1945. *Consular Relations Between the United States Ministers and the Papal States. Instructions and Despatches 1848–1868*. Washington, D.C.: Catholic University Press.

Story, William W. 1864. *Roma di Roma*. 4th ed. 2 vols. London: Chapman and Hall.

Stroud, Patricia T. 2000. *The Emperor of Nature: Charles-Lucien Bonaparte and His World*. Philadelphia: University of Pennsylvania Press.

Tergolina, Vincenzo, conte di. 1860. *Quattro anni nelle prigioni del Santo Padre*. Turin: Cerutti, Derossi e Dusso.

Thiry, Charles-Ambroise. 1851. *Siège de Rome en 1849, par l'armée française. Journal des opérations de l'artillerie et du génie, publié avec l'autorisation du Ministre de la Guerre*. Paris: Imprimerie Nationale.

Tocqueville, Alexis de. 1893. *Souvenirs de Alexis de Tocqueville*. Paris: Lévy.

———. 1983. *Œuvres complètes*. Vols. 15/1 and 15/2, *Correspondance d'Alexis de Tocqueville et de Francisque de Corcelle*. Paris: Gallimard.

———. 2004. *Democracy in America*. Translated by Arthur Goldhammer. Edited by Olivier Zunz. New York: Library of America.

Tommasi-Crudeli, Corrado. 1892. *The Climate of Rome and the Roman Malaria*. Translated by Charles Dick. London: Churchill.

Torre, Federico (General). 1851–52. *Memorie storiche sull'intervento francese in Roma nel 1849*. 2 vols. Turin: Progresso.

Toytot, Ernest de. 1868. *Les romains chez eux: Scènes et moeurs de la vie romaine*. Paris: Albanel.

Traniello, Francesco. 2001. "Gioberti, Vincenzo." *Dizionario biografico degli italiani*, online.

Trebiliani, Maria Luisa. 1970. "Bassi, Ugo." *Dizionario biografico degli italiani*, online.

————. 1972. "Brunetti, Angelo, detto Ciceruacchio." *Dizionario biografico degli italiani*, online.

Trevelyan, George Macaulay. 1907. *Garibaldi's Defence of the Roman Republic (1848–49)*. 2nd ed. London: Longmans, Green.

Univers (l'). 1850. *Pie IX et l'armée française. Lettres de Rome (Correspondance de l'Univers)*. 2nd ed. Paris: Lecoffre.

Vaillant, Jean-Baptiste (General). 1851. *Siège de Rome en 1849 par l'armée française*. Paris: Imprimerie Nationale.

Vecchi, Candido Augusto. 1851. *La Italia. Storia di due anni 1848–49*. Turin: Perrin.

————. 1911. *Le vicende della Repubblica romana narrate dal rappresentante del popolo*. Florence: Quattrini.

Ventura, Gioacchino (Padre). 1848. *Pio IX e l'Italia ossia storia della sua vita e degli avvenimenti politici del suo pontificato seguita da molti documenti ufficiali*. Milan: Turati.

Viaene, Vincent. 2001. *Belgium and the Holy See from Gregory XVI to Pius IX*. Brussels: Institut historique Belge de Rome.

Virlogeux, Georges. 2001. "La 'vendetta pretina' e i diplomatici statunitensi nel 1849." *Italies* 5, http://italies.revues.org/2025.

Wallace, Lillian Parker. 1959. "Pius IX and Lord Palmerston, 1846–1849." In *Power, Public Opinion and Diplomacy*, ed. Lillian Wallace and William Askew, pp. 3–46. Durham, N.C.: Duke University Press.

Ward, David. 1970. *1848: The Fall of Metternich and the Year of Revolution*. London: Hamish Hamilton.

White Mario, Jesse. 1888. *Agostino Bertani e i suoi tempi*. Vol. 1. Florence: Barbera.

Whitehouse, H. Remsen. 1906. *A Revolutionary Princess: Christina Belgiojoso-Trivulzio, Her Life and Times, 1808–1871*. London: Unwin.

Whyte, A. J. 1930. *The Political Life and Letters of Cavour*. Oxford: Oxford University Press.

Wiseman, Nicholas Patrick (Cardinal). 1858. *Recollections of the Last Four Popes and Their Times*. London: Hurst and Blackett.

Yvert, Benoît. 2008. "Le président oublié." In *Napoléon III, l'homme, le politique*, ed. Pierre Milza, pp. 105–22. Navarre: Napoléon Éditions.

Zeller, Jules. 1879. *Pie IX et Victor-Emmanuel*. Paris: Didier.

Zucchi, Carlo. 1861. *Memorie del Generale Carlo Zucchi*. Edited by Nicomede Bianchi. Milan: Guigoni.

Zucconi, Antonietta Angelica. 2011. "I Bonaparte tra rivoluzione e reazione." In *Un laboratorio politico per l'Italia. La Repubblica romana del 1849*, ed. Laura Rossi, pp. 109–24. Rome: Biblink.

ILLUSTRATION CREDITS

Illustrations 1–5, 7, 10–25, 31–34, 36: Museo Centrale del Risorgimento, Roma

Illustrations 6 and 35: © Sovrintendenza Capitolina ai Beni Culturali—Museo Napoleonico

Illustrations 26, 28, 30: Bibliothèque nationale française

Illustration 27: Portrait by Hughes Foureau, 1853, Les Musées de la ville de Châteauroux

Illustration 8, 9, 29: U.S. Library of Congress

INDEX

Acqua Paola aqueduct, 190
Adriatic Sea, 160, 169, 177, 278
agriculture, 6, 8
Aguyar, Andrea, 183, *184*, 227, 246, 406*n*
Alban Hills, 324
Albano, 199, 207
Algeria, xxiii, xxvi, 89, 226, 257
Altieri, Lodovico, 268, 326, 411*n*
Amat, Luigi, 371*n*
amnesties, 19–25, 27, 43, 416*n*, 418*n*, 419*n*, 422*n*
anarchy, 67, 81, 82, 96, 397*n*
Ancona, 8, 126, 177, 238, 242, 257, 289
anti-clerical sentiment, 70–71, 143, 148–49, 156–59, 196, 221, 226, 255, 259, 261, 274, 284, 296, 300–302, 321, 328, 344–45
anti-Semitism, 41–42, 74–75, 97–98, 305–6, 318–19
Antonelli, Giacomo, xix, xx, xxiii, 49–51, *50*, 64, 67, 75–76, 78, 79, 81, 82, 111, 114, 115, 117, 118, 126–27, 132, 136, 138–39, 145, 146, 148, 150–51, 155, 157, 158, 165–66, 167, 168, 169, 173, 174, 175, 185, 200, 202, 211, 215, 216–17, 229,

230, 232, 242, 261, 263, 265, 266, 268, 283, 284–85, 293–94, 298–99, 302, 304, 310, 314, 318, 319–20, 322–23, 327–28, 329, 335, 338, 339–40, 341, 345–46, 363*n*, 366*n*, 367*n*, 368*n*, 370*n*, 371*n*, 377*n*–78*n*, 379*n*, 380*n*, 381*n*, 383*n*, 384*n*, 385*n*–86*n*, 388*n*, 389*n*, 390*n*, 391*n*, 396*n*, 402*n*, 408*n*, 409*n*, 411*n*, 414*n*, 415*n*, 417*n*, 418*n*, 422*n*, 423*n*, 424*n*, 425*n*, 426*n*, 429*n*
Apennine Mountains, 277–78
Apostles, 16
Apponyi, Rodolphe, 362*n*
archbishops, xx, 89, 144, 311
aristocracy, xx–xxi, 4–5, 49, 53–54, 60, 69, 85, 89, 109–10, 138, 149, 192, 233, 252, 310, 321, 346
Armellini, Carlo, 140, 148, 153, 156, 163–64, *165*, 387*n*
artillery, 141, 190–92, 200, 202, 227, 232–33, *232*, 236–38, *239*, 242–48, 274, 326, 403*n*
assassinations, 102–5, *104*, 110, 111, 131, 152, 162, 260, 274, 276–77, 292, 294, 309, 337, 375*n*–76*n*, 425*n*–26*n*

assembly, freedom of, 65, 230, 252

Augustine, Saint, 311–12

Austrian Empire:

ambassadors of, 22–23, 30, 35–36, 70, 150–51, 301, 392*n*, 417*n*; *see also specific ambassadors*

emperor of, xxiii, 81–85, 99, 144–45, 150, 297, 385*n*

imperial government of, xxiii, 84–85, 98–99

Italian states invaded by, xxiii, 12, 13, 14, 16, 32–33, 35–36, 42–45, 90–91, 92, 93, 111, 150–56, 159–60, 277, 278, 280, 289, 304, 317, 361*n*, 413*n*

military forces of, 14, 16, 35–36, 42–44, 65–66, 69, 71, 90–91, 94, 144, 150, 152

Pius IX supported by, xix, xxii–xxiii, xxvi, 10–12, 20, 22–23, 24, 30, 35–38, 109, 145–46, 147, 150–51, 154, 155, 159–60, 167, 171–73, 174, 265, 267–68, 281, 283, 284, 286, 290, 297, 374*n*, 386*n*, 420*n*

territories of, 65–66, 356*n*, 361*n*

Avezzana, Giuseppe, 187–88, 190–91, 403*n*

Avignon, 113, 380*n*

Azeglio, Massimo d,' 31, 41, 294, 359*n*, 364*n*, 368*n*, 409*n*

Bachofen, Johann, 162, 390*n*

banking, 162, 299, 315–19, 332–33, 338, 423*n*

baptisms, 338, 428*n*

Baraguey d'Hilliers, Achille, xxiii, xxvi, 307–11, *308*, 314, 316, 317–18, 324, 326, 328, 330, 421*n*, 422*n*, 423*n*, 424*n*, 425*n*, 426*n*

barbers, 6

Barnabite monks, xx, 67, 183, 228, 279

barricades, 210, 227, 237, 239–40, 247–48, 291

Barrot, Odilon, 147, 174–75, 197–98, 221, 224, 234, 235, 285, 287, 307, 310, 381*n*, 389*n*, 392*n*, 393*n*, 395*n*, 397*n*, 403*n*–4*n*, 410*n*, 412*n*, 415*n*, 418*n*, 420*n*, 421*n*

basilicas, 143, 151–52, 344, 262*n*; *see also specific basilicas*

Bassi, Ugo, 183–84, 192, 228, 244–45, 278, 279–80, *279*, 406*n*, 413*n*

Bastide, Jules, 92, 374*n*

Baudin, Charles, 127–28, 170

Bavaria, xxix–xxx, 101, 114, 115, 116, 117, 118, 130, 355*n*

beatification, 345

Bedini, Gaetano, 202, 413*n*

beggars, 6, 7

Belgiojoso, Cristina, xx–xxi, 193, 312–13, *313*, 395*n*, 409*n*, 422*n*–23*n*

Belgiojoso, Emilio Barbiano di, xx–xxi

Belgium, 10, 11, 23, 110, 130, 212, 356*n*

benedictions and blessings, xxix, 27–28, 30, 46, 51, 52–56, 57, 60–62, 68–69, 100, 121, 208–9, *217*, 323, 325, 359*n*, 369*n*

Bernetti, Tommaso, 356*n*, 357*n*

Bertone, Tarcisio, 356*n*–57*n*

Betti, Salvatore, 369*n*

Bible, 311, 371*n*

bishop of Rome, 27, 92

bishops, 20, 27, 92, 144, 158–59, 173, 311, 341–42

blasphemy, 28–29

Bocca della Verità ("Mouth of Truth"), 331, 337

Bofondi, Giuseppe, 58, 64, 365*n*

Bologna, 8, 9, 29, 32, 51, 73, 92, 101, 144, 177, 183, 202, 210, 214, 216, 225, 238, 242, 243, 257, 267, 278, 279, 280, 289, 393*n*, 399*n*, 405*n*, 408*n*, 413*n*, 428*n*

"Bomb King," 119, 135, 400*n*

Bonaparte, Charles, xxi, 44–46, *45,* 90, 111–12, 119, 128, 129, 131, 133, 139, 140, 148, 152, 153, 154, 162, 180, 213–14, 232, 247, 338, 376*n,* 387*n,* 407*n,* 424*n,* 428*n*

Bonaparte, Louis Napoleon, Emperor of France (Louis Napoleon Bonaparte), xxiii–xxiv, xxvi, 127–30, *129,* 146–47, 174, 197, 205–6, 221, 223, 224–25, 235, 276, 285, 287, 288–89, 291–92, 294, 302, 307–8, 310, 327, 338, 339, 342, 380*n*–81*n,* 392*n,* 400*n,* 415*n,* 416*n,* 417*n,* 422*n,* 425*n*

Bonaparte, Lucien, xxi, 44, 428*n*

"Boor, the," 135

Borgia, Cesare, 49

Borromeo, Saint Carlo, 27, 100

Bourbon dynasty, xxii, 12, 24, 58, 77–78, 85, 121, 136

British envoys, 47–48, 51, 63, 111, 113, 114, 131, 146, 166, 209, 296, 301, 340, 361*n,* 363*n,* 414*n*–15*n*

Brown, Nicholas, 144, 152, 243, 260, 386*n,* 387*n,* 409*n*

Brunetti, Angelo (see Ciceruacchio)

Brunetti, Lorenzo, 280*n*

Brussels, 23

Bulldog, 111, 113, 114, 131, 144, 209

bureaucracy, 4, 57, 99–100, 119, 183, 228–29, 298–99, 301, 364*n,* 420*n*

Caetani, Michelangelo, duke of Sermoneta, 333, 427*n*

Caffé delle Belle Arti, 44

Calabria, 47

"Camarilla," 149

Campidoglio (see Capitoline Hill)

Canino, 44, 372*n*–73*n*

cannons, 141, 190–92, 200, 202, 227, 232–33, *232,* 236–38, *239,* 242–48, 274, 326, 403*n*

Canova, Antonio, 334

capital punishment, 252, 330–31, 337–38, 340, 426*n*

Capitoline Hill, 87, 141, 142, 148, 151–52, 153, 237, 243, 247, 252, 321

capopopolo (popular leader), 39–41

Cappella Giulia, 170

Capuchins, 284

carabinieri, 158, 226

cardinal advisers, xx, 21–25, 30, 31, 32, 37–38, 47, 51–52, 63, 64, 74, 75–76, 85, 88–89, 101, 108–9, 125, 130–31, 134, 138–39, 145, 150–51, 155, 173–74, 185–86, 241, 255, 261, 264, 266–68, 273, 283–86, 288, 294, 295, 309–14, 322–23, 326, 373*n*–74*n,* 385*n*–86*n,* 402*n,* 411*n,* 415*n,* 424*n,* 426*n*

cardinal deacons, 18

cardinals, 143, 196, 341–42
    see also specific cardinals

cardinals commission (red triumvirate), 273–74, 282–85, 289, 290, 423*n*

Carlyle, Thomas, 161

Carnival, 98, 149, 320–21

Carrara, 24

Caserta, 314, 425*n*

Cass, Lewis, Jr., 213–14, 217–18, 250, 331–32, 334–35, 394*n,* 395*n,* 399*n,* 404*n,* 407*n,* 408*n,* 409*n,* 427*n*

cassocks, 114

Castel di Guido, 196–97

Castel Gandolfo, 277

Castellamare, 282

Castel Sant'Angelo, 18, 27, 66, 80, 87, 141, 148, 169, 170, 197, 215, 228, 254, 261, 296, 326, 329, 343, 344–45, 426*n*

Catholic Church:
  authority of, 8–9, 34, 64–65, 71,
    156–57, 201–2, 231, 293, 311–12,
    345, 362n, 407n, 417n
  beatification in, 345
  clergy of, 6–10, 49, 97, 156–57, 284;
    see also nuns; priests
  as commonwealth, 28–29
  conservatives vs. moderates in,
    14–15, 17, 20, 112, 139–40, 185–86,
    231–32
  ecclesiastical rule in, 6–8, 17, 23, 25,
    26–27, 29, 35–36, 183, 188, 283–84,
    415n–16n
  excommunication from, 143, 144,
    162, 210, 339, 343–44, 384n–85n
  feast days of, 30, 32, 269–70; see also
    specific feast days
  hierarchy of, 8–9, 64–65
  Holy See of, xxii–xxiii, xxiv, xxv,
    xxvi, xxviii, xxix, 17, 18–19,
    22–23, 24, 72–73, 93, 94, 106–9,
    114, 117, 130, 145, 147, 155, 168,
    172, 229, 255, 258, 262, 265, 299,
    307, 316–17, 340, 343–46, 357n,
    363n, 376n, 380n, 385n, 394n–95n,
    415n
  Latin as language of, xxviii, 61, 79,
    342
  laymen in, 48, 49, 51–54, 59, 108–9
  in military conflicts, 74, 77–78, 399n
  monarchs as supporters of, xxii,
    xxiv, 74, 77–78, 83–84, 110, 117,
    119–20, 122, 127–28, 132, 136,
    139–40, 144–46, 150, 154–55,
    165–66, 170–75, 178–79, 195–96,
    201–2, 214–15, 228, 293–94, 304–5,
    385n, 387n, 391n, 392n; see also
    specific monarchs
  ordination in, xx, 15
  papal rule in, see specific popes
  property of, 141, 156–57, 158, 159,
    169, 170, 173; see also specific
    basilicas and churches
  relics in, 344
  sacraments of, 113, 158, 191
  secularization opposed by, 287–88
  theology of, 28–29, 82, 134, 144,
    156–57, 170, 277, 283, 295, 298,
    311–12, 340, 341–42
Cavaignac, Louis-Eugène, 93, 127,
    128, 129
Cernuschi, Enrico, 237, 248
Chamber of Deputies, 59, 64, 85,
    87–88, 90, 98, 102–3, 105–6, 107,
    108, 111–12, 119, 131, 133, 134,
    136–40, 151–55, 162, 373n, 376n
Chancellery Palace, 102–5, 136, 152,
    180, 237
chaplains, 184, 279
charity, 31, 39–40, 159
Charles Albert, King of Savoy, xx,
    xxii, 66, 67, 68, 72, 74, 75, 82, 84,
    87, 91, 93, 94, 96, 111, 141, 144,
    146, 155, 163, 164, 175, 226, 339,
    361n, 369n, 370n, 371n, 385n
Charles X, King of France, 13–14, 63
children, 232–33, 243
Chile, 16
cholera epidemic, 245, 309, 392n,
    401n, 409n–10n, 420n
Christianity, 70, 165–66, 202, 221, 341
  see also Catholic Church
"Christ-killers," 41–42, 98
church property, 141, 156–57, 158, 159,
    169, 170, 173
Ciceruacchio (Angelo Brunetti), xxi,
    39–41, 40, 56, 67, 79, 80, 136–37,
    137, 148, 210, 251–52, 278, 280,
    360n, 366n, 369n, 376n, 382n,
    383n
city councils, 45–46, 56, 135, 250, 261,
    262–63, 266, 267–79, 273, 283–84,
    289, 295, 315, 322–23, 329, 414n

Civic Guard, xxvii, xxviii, xxix, 16, 38, 44, 55–56, 60–61, 65, 80, 91–92, 97–98, 102, 104–6, 108, 109, 111, 114, 142, 152, 154, 359n, 360n, 368n

Civitavecchia, 110–11, 114, 117–18, 128, 160, 175, 177, 179, 180, 187, 192, 205–6, 209, 245, 250, 317, 377n, 378n, 379n, 397n, 401n, 409n, 420n

clerical rule, 6–8, 17, 25, 27, 32–33, 59–60, 62, 71, 75, 78, 85, 126, 139, 156–59, 160, 180, 188, 194, 196, 197, 201, 213, 221, 223, 226, 264, 266–68, 274, 290, 295, 321, 386n, 420n

Clough, Arthur, 178, 356n, 393n

clubs (political), 52, 69, 79, 81, 89, 92, 103–4, 106, 133, 136–37, 139, 186, 187, 253, 260

Colonna Palace, 309

Comacchio, 279, 413n

Communist League, 391n–92n

conclaves, 3–20, 23, 69, 357n

confederations, 48, 96–97, 133

confession, 49, 210, 221, 226

confessionals, 210

confessors, 221, 226

Congress, U.S., 92–93

Congress of Vienna (1815), 10–11

constitutional monarchy, xxii, 63, 84, 85, 112, 149, 283, 323, 344, 365n

constitutional rule, xxvii–xxviii, 34, 62, 64–65, 66, 85, 106, 112, 113, 149, 201, 228, 229–30, 241, 255, 257, 261, 265–66, 281–83, 295, 296–97, 366n

Consultative Council, 33–34, 49, 51–54, 74–77, 79, 86, 174, 228, 292, 364n, 369n

contraband, 291

convents, 184–85, 232–33, 403n

"Copenhagen Waltz," 58

Corcelle, Francisque de, xxiv, xxv, 128, 130, 231, 238–39, 242–43, 244, 250, 254, 258, 262–63, 268, 269, 275, 276, 282, 286, 288, 292, 296, 297, 299, 306, 307, 386n, 402n, 403n, 404n, 405n–8n, 409n, 410n, 411n, 412n, 413n–14n, 415n, 417n, 418n–19n, 420n, 421n

corruption, 4, 57, 99–100, 183, 228–29, 301, 364n, 420n

Corsica, 133

Corsini, Prince, 60, 133, 192

Corso, 22, 29, 33, 39, 44, 56, 66–67, 79, 100, 103, 118, 195, 210, 237, 250, 252–53, 265, 273, 315, 321, 409n

Costantini, Sante, 337–38

Counter-Reformation, 27

Croatians, 42

Crusades, 67–68

curfews, 257–58

Curia, 17, 109, 255, 319

currencies, 274

Custoza, 91

Czech Republic, 99

Dante, 24

Danton, Georges, 403n

de Angelis, Filippo, 25

death penalty, 252, 330–31, 337–38, 340, 426n

Débats, 289, 417n

de Broglie, Albert, 365n, 366n

"Decree of the Triumvirs for Public Prayer," 191

de Felice, Antonio, 338

Della Genga, Gabriele, xix, 80, 267, 268, 290, 331, 411n, 412n, 423n

democracy, xx, 28, 33–34, 58, 84, 223–24, 231, 242, 331, 346

Democracy in America (Tocqueville), xxvi, 223, 232, 257, 297

dictatorship, 225

divine punishment, 132

divine right, 14, 36, 64–65, 110, 132, 311–12, 333, 335

Dominicans, 157, 158, 284

Drouyn de Lhuys, Édouard, xxiv, 147, 159, 160, 175–77, *176,* 204–6, 211, 214, 220–21, 223, 385*n,* 386*n,* 388*n,* 389*n,* 391*n,* 392*n,* 393*n,* 394*n,* 396*n,* 397*n,* 398*n,* 399*n,* 400*n,* 402*n*

Du Mont, General, 341

Durando, Giovanni, 68, 72, 80, 84, 87, 368*n*–69*n,* 370*n*

Dutch ambassadors, 33–34, 59–60, 62, 76, 83, 90, 91, 155, 210, 295, 327, 366*n,* 372*n,* 382*n,* 400*n*

Easter Sunday, 32, 75, 169–70

ecclesiastical courts, 415*n*–16*n*

ecclesiastical tribunals, 156–57

education, xx, xxvi, 9–10, 156, 300–301, 319, 333

elections, 157, 158, 161–62, 195, 214

Elizabeth, Empress of Austria, 341

Emerson, Ralph Waldo, 233

encyclicals, 28–29, 134, 298, 311–13, 339, 340, 343–44

Engels, Friedrich, 392*n*

Enlightenment, 9, 98, 346

epilepsy, xx, 15, 16, 36, 106

esaltati (fanatics), 24–25

Esterházy, Moritz, xxii–xxiii, 145, 150–51, *151,* 154, 155–56, 166, 168–69, 208, 214–15, 241–42, 268, 283, 290, 291, 330, 385*n,* 387*n,* 388*n,* 389*n,* 391*n,* 396*n,* 398*n,* 399*n,* 403*n,* 405*n,* 411*n,* 413*n*–14*n,* 416*n,* 417*n,* 421*n,* 422*n*

Eucharist (Holy Sacrament), 113, 191

excommunication, 143, 144, 162, 210, 339, 343–44, 384*n*–85*n*

exiles, xxi, xxii, 15–16, 21–23, 34, 152, 233, 259–60

Falloux, Alfred de, xxiv–xxv, 174, 197, 285, 287, 288, 385*n,* 392*n,* 410*n,* 411*n,* 415*n*

Farini, Luigi Carlo, 133 162, 293, 315, 369*n,* 371*n,* 390*n,* 413*n*

Fate Bene Fratelli, 194

Faurs, Father, 221

Favre, Jules, 198

feast days, 30, 32, 269–70
see also specific feast days

Ferdinand I, Emperor of Austria, 385*n*

Ferdinand II, King of Naples and the Two Sicilies, xxii, 12, 57–59, 66, 71, 73–74, 85, 96–97, 115–16, 118, 119–21, *120,* 130, 131, 135–36, 139–40, 142, 144, 150, 167, 168, 179, 194, 198–200, 207, 208, 210, 211, 212, 221, 225, 226, 291, 297, 301–2, 304, 314–15, 317, 323–24, 327, 339, 371*n,* 379*n,* 385*n,* 388*n,* 393*n,* 396*n,* 401*n,* 409*n*–10*n,* 420*n,* 421*n*

Fermo, 25

Ferrara, 8, 42–45, 73–74, 80, 91, 101, 155–56, 225, 257, 267, 278, 279, 361*n,* 376*n*

Ferretti, Gabriele, 27, 38–39, 58

Ferretti, Giovanni Maria Mastai, *see* Pius IX, Pope

feudalism, xxi

Filippani, Benedetto, xxviii–xxix

firing squads, 331

Fiumicino, 178, 200, 262, 404*n*

Five Glorious Days, 65–66

flooding, 29–30, 39–40, 41, 58, 74

Florence, 59, 173, 219, 390*n,* 395*n*

Foligno, 16

forced conversions, 333, 338, 427*n,* 428*n*

foreign ministers, 67, 108–9, 131–32

foreign residents, 5–6, 51, 178, 187, 195, 259–60, 369n

Forlì, 23, 164

fortifications, 156, 120, 190, 196–97, 205–6, 214–15, 218, 220, 227, 228, 232–33 *232*, 234, 235–36, 238, *239*, 243–44, 246, 341–42

four-power conference, 167–68, 173–75, 208, 210, 282–83, 391n

France:
ambassadors of, xxvi, xxviii, xxx, 22, 24, 34, 51, 56, 89, 92, 95, 107, 109, 113, 114, 117, 148, 200–201, 212–13, 228–31, 295–97, 302, 307–8, 315–16, 355n, 374n, 381n, 390n; *see also specific ambassadors*

Constituent Assembly of, xxiv, 213–14, 220, 223, 225

constitution of, xxiv, xxvi, 199, 213–14, 219, 220, 223, 225

empire and monarchy of, 12, 13–14, 24, 56, 63, 339

flag of, 261, 287–88

French Revolution (1789) in, 8, 44, 56, 62, 70, 75, 156, 170, 223, 341, 346

French Revolution of 1830 in, 14

French Revolution of 1848 in, xxiv, xxvi, 63, 66, 144

government of, xxiv–xxv, 71, 75, 89, 96, 146–47, 174–77, 202–25, 302–10, 403n–4n

military forces of, 8, 63, 170–71, 179

Napoleonic period of, xxi, xxiii, xxv, 8, 10–11, 12, 15–16, 44, 46, 90, 112, 129, 130, 136, 186, 223, 225, 257, 288, 301, 344, 372n, 408n

National Assembly of, xxvi, 147, 174–77, 194–98, 202–3, 204, 205,
209, 213–16, 219–21, 223, 224, 225, 233–35, 238–39, 302–4, 307, 310, 403n–4n

naval forces of, 170–71, 179

Papal States and relations with, xxiii–xxvi, 10, 12, 13–14, 18–20, 22, 26–27, 32–33, 34, 48, 95, 114–15, 117, 127–28, 131, 134, 146–47, 150, 154–55, 159–60, 165–66, 167, 170–75, 177, 208–10, 230–31, 241–42, 254–55, 258–69, 274–77, 280–86, 289–90, 294, 295–98, 302–4, 314, 319–20, 330, 332, 335, 338, 380n, 385n, 387n, 391n, 392n, 394n, 415n–16n

Pius IX supported by, xxiii–xxvi, 10, 12, 13–14, 18–20, 22, 26–27, 32–33, 34, 48, 95, 114–15, 117, 127–28, 131, 134, 146–47, 150, 154–55, 159–60, 165–66, 167, 170–75, 177, 208–10, 230–31, 241–42, 254–55, 258–69, 274–77, 280–86, 289–90, 294, 295–98, 302–4, 314, 319–20, 330, 332, 335, 338, 380n, 385n, 387n, 391n, 392n, 394n, 415n–16n

as republic, xxvi, 71, 75, 89, 96, 146, 154–55, 171–72, 175–76, 179, 194–98, 214–16, 219–21, 230–31, 233–35, 253, 307, 366n, 385n, 392n, 411n

Roman attack of, 189, 190–243, 397n, 400n, 403n, 405n–6n, 408n, 409n

Roman conquest and subjugation by, 190–97, 205–6, 235–55, 256

Roman military headquarters of, 255, 264–65, 274–75, 288, 291

Roman military intervention of, xxiii, xxvi, 155, 164, 166, 168, 169–72, 175–239, *232*, *239*, *254*, 290, 295, 307

France (*cont.*):

  Roman occupation by, xxv, xxvi, 174–77, 213, 249, 252, *254*, 257, 274–77, 284, 302–4, 305, 309–10, 314, 317–18, 324, 325, 327, 328, 335, 338, 340, 341, 342, 420n

  Tocqueville as ambassador and envoy for, xxiv, xxv, xxvi, 223–25, *224*, 230–31, 238, 239, 242–43, 244, 254, 255, 257, 258–59, 262, 265, 268–69, 275–76, 277, 280, 282, 283, 285, 288, 294, 296–97, 299, 303, 306–8, 310, 380n–81n, 385n, 402n, 403n, 405n, 406n, 408n, 412n–19n

Francis II, King of Naples, 339, 341

Frankfurt, 66

Franz Joseph I, Emperor of Austria, 144–45, 150

Freeborn, John, 243, 260, 334, 358n, 360n, 386n, 395n, 401n, 404n, 406n, 408n–9n

French Revolution (1789), 8, 44, 56, 62, 70, 75, 156, 170, 223, 341, 346

French Revolution (1830), 14

French Revolution (1848), xxiv, xxvi, 63, 66, 144

Fuller, Margaret, 33, 52–53, *53*, 58, 85–86, 161, 193–94, 233, 251, 252, 254, 260, 359n, 364n, 365n, 367n, 371n–72n, 376n–77n, 384n, 386n, 387n, 390n, 395n, 399n–400n, 403n, 404n, 407n, 408n

Gaeta, 115–19, *116*, 121, 122, 125–28, 130–32, 135, 136, 138, 145–50, 152, 154, 155, 157, 165–68, 170, 171, 174, 175, 177, 186, 202, 204, 208, 211, 214–17, *217*, 218, 228–30, 241, 242, 254–56, 262, 265, 267, 273, 275, 276, 280, 282, 283, 288, 289, 291, 328, 339, 342, 345, 376n, 377n,

378n, 379n, 380n, 381n, 382n, 383n, 385n, 386n, 387n, 388n–89n, 390n, 391n, 396n, 399n, 402n, 405n, 407n, 409n, 411n, 414n

Garibaldi, Anita, 245, 252, 278, *279*

Garibaldi, Giuseppe, xxi, 101, 137, 152, 153, 154, 181–85, *182*, *184*, 187–88, 192, 199–200, 208, 211, 212, 221–22, 225–26, 227, 228, 239, 244–48, 250–54, 260, 277–79, *279*, 280, 281, 324, 339, 342, 383n, 387n–88n, 396n, 401n, 404n, 406n, 407n, 413n, 425n–26n

garibaldini (legionnaires), xxi, 183–84, 187–88, 192, 199–200, 210, 225, 226, 244–45, 250–51, 277–78, 280, 425n–26n

Garrison, William Lloyd, 160–61, 390n

gates, 190, 195, 207, 209–10, 233, 236, 254, 255, 260, 265, 325–26

"Gates of Rome's Ghetto Thrown to the Ground, The," 75

Gavazzi, Alessandro, 67–68, 101

gazettes, 73, 368n

Gazzola, Carlo, 329, 426n

Genesis, Book of, 371n

Geneva, 24, 166, 260, 278

Genoa, xx, xxii, 13, 26, 260

gentilhomme de l'ancien régime ("gentleman of the old stripe"), 223–24

German confederation, 66, 77n, 129

ghettos, 29–30, 41–42, 74–75, 97–98, 265, 299, 301, 305–6, 315–19, 332–33, 338, 369n, 374n, 407n, 420n–21n, 427n

Gioberti, Vincenzo, 48–49, 94, 141, 387n, 388n–89n

Giornale di Gorizia, 422n–23n

Giornale di Roma, 306

Giornale ufficiale, 121

Giraud, Teresa, 115

Gizzi, Pasquale, 23–24, 25, 30, 31, 32, 35, 37–39, 41, 58, 80, 356n, 357n, 358n, 359n, 360n

Grandoni, Luigi, 337–38

Great Britain, 67, 127, 149, 166, 260, 359n, 360n, 363n, 384n–85n, 395n, 409n,

Gregorovius, Ferdinand, 343, 428n

Gregory XVI, Pope, xx, 4, 8, 9–10, 13, 16–17, 28, 31, 33, 44, 49, 76, 226, 267, 299, 356n, 357n, 417n, 420n, 426n

Guerrazzi, Francesco, 390n, 398n–99n

guerrilla warfare, 58, 180

guillotine, 330–31, 337–38, 340, 426n

Guizot, François, 356n, 357n–58n, 360n, 364n, 365n, 366n

Habsburg monarchy, 85

Harcourt, Duke François, xxv, xxviii, 89, 92, 95, 96, 114–15, 117, 128, 130, 148, 167–68, 170, 171, 172, 175–76, 185, 186, 187, 200–201, 210–11, 213, 218, 221, 228–29, 231, 242, 255–56, 258–59, 262, 265, 317, 355n, 372n, 373n, 374n, 375n, 377n, 378n, 379n, 380n, 381n, 385n, 386n, 388n, 389n, 391n, 392n, 394n, 396n, 399n, 400n, 402n, 404n, 405n, 407n–8n, 415n

Herzen, Alexander, 5, 356n, 362n–63n

Hitte, Jean-Ernest de la, 315–17

Holy Father, 9, 22, 24, 47, 82, 121, 171, 175, 186, 200, 204, 212, 229, 233, 243, 255, 258, 261, 273, 277, 285–86, 287, 294, 295, 300, 303, 304–5, 309–10, 312, 316, 317–18, 323–24, 327–28, 330, 365n, 374n, 400n, 405n, 416n, 418n, 420n, 422n, 424n

Holy Sacrament (Eucharist), 113, 191

Holy See, xxii–xxiii, xxiv, xxv, xxvi, xxviii, xxix, 17, 18–19, 22–23, 24, 72–73, 93, 94, 106–9, 114, 117, 130, 145, 147, 155, 168, 172, 229, 255, 258, 262, 265, 299, 307, 316–17, 340, 343–46, 357n, 363n, 376n, 380n, 394n–95n, 415n

Holy Week, 75, 369n

hospitals, 159, 246, 296, 312–13

Hôtel de Minerve, 189, 192

House of the Catechumens, 333

Howard, Harriet, 129

Hugo, Victor, 302, 403n

Hungary, 42, 66, 98–99, 145, 216, 392n

Immaculate Conception, 134

Imola, xx, 16–17, 18, 19, 20, 330

industrial proletariat, 63

infallibility doctrine, 341–42

Innsbruck, 85

Inquisition, 156–57, 158, 274, 276, 305, 312–13, 315, 362n

Ireland, 340, 344, 363n

Isabel II, Queen of Spain, 110

Italian League, 24, 96–97

Italian Peninsula, 8, 9, 46, 59, 71, 92

Italy:

    Austrian occupation of, xx, xxi, xxii–xxiii, 9–10, 11, 49, 65, 66–71, 80–84, 86, 87, 88, 89, 90–91, 93, 102, 103, 108, 133, 137, 144, 339, 368n–70n, 374n, 393n

    confederation of, 48, 96–97, 133

    constitutional monarchy for, xxii, 63, 84, 85, 112, 149, 283, 323, 344, 365n

    democracy in, xx, 28, 33–34, 58, 84, 223–24, 231, 242, 331, 346

    flag of (tricolor banner), 58, 65, 103, 141, 142, 151, 154, 170, 180, 210, 245, 252, 253, 254, 259

    formation of, xxii, 338–44

Italy (*cont.*):

freedom in, xx, 23, 59, 65, 230, 252, 287–88, 292–93, 302–4, 305, 340, 346–47, 388*n*, 414*n*–15*n*

French occupation of, xxv, xxvi, 174–77, 213, 249, 252, *254*, 257, 274–77, 284, 302–4, 305, 309–10, 314, 317–18, 324, 325, 327, 328, 335, 338, 340, 341, 342, 420*n*

Garibaldi's leadership in, xxi, 101, 137, 152, 153, 154, 181–85, *182*, *184*, 187–88, 192, 199–200, 208, 210, 211, 212, 221–22, 225–26, 227, 228, 239, 244–48, 250–54, 260, 277–79, *279*, 280, 281, 324, 339, 342, 382*n*, 387*n*–88*n*, 396*n*, 401*n*, 404*n*, 406*n*, 407*n*, 425*n*–26*n*

as "geographic expression," 43

guerrilla warfare in, 58, 180

independence movement in, xx–xxii, xxv, 43, 44–45, 66–67, 79, 82–83, 89, 90–91, 99, 100, 101, 103, 139, 153, 160–67, 172–73, 193, 239–40, 260, 297–98, 339, 361*n*, 377*n*

majority rule in, 223, 231

manifestos and pamphlets of, xxi, 43, 57–58

map (1848) of, *xv*

Mazzini's leadership in, xxi, xxii, 25–26, *26*, 99, 139, 154, 160–67, *165*, 169, 170, 178, 180, 181, 187, 191, 193, 194, 195–96, 208, 209, 210, 211, 212–13, 214, 218–19, 220, 221–22, 225–26, 233–34, 235, 237, 239–40, 245, 247, 248, 249, 254, 260–61, 296, 309, 320–21, 325, 342, 344, 358*n*, 361*n*–62*n*, 366*n*, 375*n*, 390*n*, 391*n*, 395*n*, 398*n*–99*n*, 404*n*, 407*n*, 408*n*, 418*n*, 425*n*

military forces of, xxi, xxvii, xxviii, 68–69, 183–84, 187–88, 192,

199–200, 210, 225, 226, 244–45, 250–51, 277–78, 280, 425*n*–26*n*

nationalism in, xx, xxi, 3, 23, 25–26, 43–44, 59–62, 67, 68–70, 77–78, 79, 81, 83–84, 94, 105, 106, 108, 112, 131, 140, 154, 165–66, 297–98, 339–40, 361*n*–62*n*, 368*n*–70*n*, 394*n*

popular revolts in, 32, 133, 188, 223, 302, 344

private property in, 53–54

republican ideals of, xxiii, 136–41, 152–54, 156, 158–70, 178–80, 214–16, 219–20, 223, 230–31, 234, 235–39, 245, 247–52, 260, 265–67, 274, 275, 291, 293, 332, 334, 338, 387*n*, 392*n*, 395*n*, 400*n*, 401*n*, 407*n*, 411*n*, 419*n*, 423*n*

revolutionary movements in, xxi, xxii, xxiv, xxvi, 3–4, 25–26, 32, 44–45, 55, 63–66, 69–71, 99, 112, 126, 133, 136, 188, 223, 246, 275, 302, 339–40, 344

separation of church and state in, 3–4, 33, 340, 341, 346–47

suffrage (popular vote) in, 66, 84–85, 140–41, 157, 181, 252, 386*n*

unification of, 25, 43, 46, 60–62, 69, 78, 96–97, 120–21, 339–46

Jamaica, 340

Janiculum Hill, 190, 192, 218, 227, 232, 244–45

Jesuits, 43, 45, 48–49, 53, 56, 65, 70–71, 75, 78, 94, 141, 164, 221, 315, 363*n*, 364*n*, 368*n*

Jesus Christ, 41, 42, 75, 369*n*, 384*n*, 389*n*

Jewish population, 29–30, 41–42, 74–75, 97–98, 265, 299, 301, 305–6, 315–19, 332–33, 338, 369*n*, 374*n*, 407*n*, 420*n*–21*n*, 427*n*

John, Saint, 30
John XXIII, Pope, 345
John Paul II, Pope, 345
judicial system, 9–10, 57, 415*n*–16*n*
July Monarchy, xxiv

Kanzler, Hermann, 341
Key, Astley, 131, 138, 142–43, 144,
    195–96, 199, 205, 209, 301–2,
    377*n*, 378*n*, 381*n*, 382*n*, 383*n*,
    384*n*, 385*n*, 394*n*, 395*n*, 396*n*,
    397*n*, 398*n*, 401*n*, 414*n*, 420*n*
keys (Roman gates), 254, 255, 260, 265
Koelman, Johan, 355*n*–56*n*

Lafayette, Gilbert du Motier, Marquis
    de, xxiv, 282
Lake Geneva, 166*n*
Lamartine, Alphonse de, 366*n*, 369*n*
Lambruschini, Luigi, xx, 13–14, 15,
    17, 21, 22, 23, 37, 47, 109, 166,
    232, 241, 255, 267–68, 292, 329,
    356*n*–57*n*, 362*n*, 405*n*, 408*n*, 417*n*
Latin language, xxviii, 61, 79, 342
lay ministers, 33–34, 49, 51–54, 59,
    74–77, 79, 80–81, 86, 87–88, 90,
    101, 104, 108–9, 119, 131–32, 133,
    174, 228, 262–63, 274, 283–84,
    291, 292, 366*n*
leaflets, 143–44
Ledru-Rollin, Alexandre, 175, 234–35,
    403*n*–4*n*
legates (papal), 23, 267–68
Legations (region), 92
legionnaires (*garibaldini*), xxi, 183–84,
    187–88, 192, 199–200, 210, 225,
    226, 244–45, 250–51, 277–78, 280,
    425*n*–26*n*
legionnaires (papal), 102–5, 106, 108,
    109
Lent, 7
Leo XII, Pope, xii, 44, 267

Leo XIII, Pope, 344
lesa maestà, 329
Lesseps, Ferdinand de, xxv, 203–4,
    205, 207–8, 209, 210, 211, 212–13,
    214, 216–20, 221, 228, 231, 393*n*,
    395*n*, 397*n*, 398*n*, 399*n*, 400*n*,
    401*n*, 402*n*
liberalism, 29, 37–38, 46, 53–54, 59,
    74–77, 85, 99–100, 105, 112, 131,
    133, 138, 139–40, 142, 175, 185–86,
    231–32, 243, 262–67, 275–76, 277,
    280–82, 288, 293–98, 331, 340,
    420*n*
Lizzie (Louis Napoleon's horse), 129
Lombard volunteers, 226, 238,
    239–40, 245, 246, 250, 401*n*, 403*n*
Lombardy, xxi, xxii, 4, 8, 11, 12,
    65–69, 72, 73, 74, 75–78, 79, 82,
    86, 87, 91, 99, 137, 152, 163, 173,
    178, 218, 225, 226, 233, 238,
    239–40, 245, 246, 250, 368*n*, 370*n*,
    371*n*
Lombardy-Veneto, Kingdom of, 8,
    65–66
London, xxii, xxiv, 25–26, 53, 56, 121,
    129, 139, 149, 160, 161, 166, 199,
    203, 205, 209, 235, 260, 264, 267,
    275, 326, 358*n*, 361*n*, 380*n*, 388*n*,
    391*n*, 400*n*, 405*n*, 408*n*, 414*n*,
    425*n*
Longfellow, Henry Wadsworth,
    340–41
Lot's wife, 371*n*
Louis XVI, King of France, 12, 56
Louis Philippe, King of France, 12,
    14, 24, 63
Lowell, James, 369*n*
Lucerne, 23
Lucretia, 194
Ludolf, Giuseppe, 168, 211, 356*n*,
    358*n*, 391*n*, 425*n*
Lützow, Rudolf von, 20, 22–23, 43

Machiavelli, Niccolò, 49

Madonna (Virgin Mary), 7–8, 134,
    221, 238, 377*n*

Madrid, xxiv, xxv, 89, 110, 113, 117,
    148, 165, 173, 203, 229, 377*n*, 388*n*,
    389*n*, 418*n*

Mafra, 127

maggiordomo, 30

Majorca, 113, 117, 127, 381*n*

majority rule, 223, 231

Mamiani, Terenzio, 79, 81, 87–88, *88*,
    90, 91, 131–32, 133, 382*n*

Manara, Luciano, 226, 239–40, 245,
    246, 250, 401*n*

Mantua, 66, 72

map (Rome), *xvi–xvii*

Marchetti, Giovanni, 329

Marcus Aurelius, Emperor of Rome,
    141, 142

Maria Anna, Empress of Austria, 385*n*

Maria Teresa, Queen of Naples, 119

Marini, Cardinal Pietro, 47

marriage ceremonies, 148

Marseillaise (French patriotic song),
    137, 152, 195, 409*n*

Marseilles, xxviii, 109, 114–15, 128,
    131, 177, 260, 291, 337, 381*n*, 415*n*

Martin, Jacob, 93, 213

Martina, Giacomo, 78, 329, 355*n*,
    356*n*, 357*n*, 358*n*, 359*n*, 360*n*,
    362*n*, 363*n*, 364*n*, 365*n*, 367*n*,
    368*n*, 369*n*, 370*n*, 371*n*, 372*n*,
    375*n*, 376*n*, 378*n*, 380*n*, 382*n*,
    383*n*, 384*n*, 386*n*, 387*n*, 389*n*,
    390*n*, 391*n*, 405*n*, 408*n*, 410*n*,
    417*n*, 421*n*, 423*n*, 424*n*, 425*n*,
    426*n*, 428*n*

Martinez, Francisco, 113

Martínez de la Rosa, Francisco,
    117–18, 168, 283

martyrs, 121–22

Marx, Karl, 129, 392*n*

Mass, xix, 46, 59, 113, 151–52, 154, 261,
    325, 326

matzo, 75

Mazzini, Giuseppe, xxi, xxii, 25–26,
    26, 99, 139, 154, 160–67, *165*, 169,
    170, 178, 180, 181, 187, 191, 193,
    194, 195–96, 198, 208, 209, 210,
    211, 212–13, 214, 218–19, 220,
    221–22, 225–26, 233–34, 235, 237,
    239–40, 245, 247, 248, 249, 254,
    260–61, 275, 296, 309, 320–21, 325,
    342, 344, 358*n*, 361*n*–62*n*, 366*n*,
    375*n*, 390*n*, 391*n*, 395*n*, 398*n*–99*n*,
    401*n*, 404*n*, 407*n*, 408*n*, 418*n*,
    425*n*

Mediterranean Sea, 177

mercenary forces, 37–38

Merchants' Club, 79

Messina, 119

Metternich, Klemens von, xxiii,
    10–12, *11*, 13, 17, 20, 34, 38, 42,
    43–44, 46, 54, 59, 63, 66, 71, 144,
    145, 356*n*, 357*n*, 358*n*, 359*n*, 360*n*,
    361*n*, 362*n*, 364*n*, 365*n*

Michelangelo, 252, 333–34

Middle Ages, xxi, 9, 12, 14, 112, 174

Milan, xx–xxi, 13, 66, 69, 84, 91, 110,
    173, 193, 218, 226, 344, 356*n*

milanesi (Milan residents), 66

Minghetti, Marco, 29, 52, 78–79,
    105–6, 112, 133, 162, 357*n*, 358*n*,
    359*n*, 363*n*, 364*n*, 365*n*, 367*n*,
    368*n*, 370*n*, 372*n*–73*n*, 375*n*, 376*n*,
    378*n*, 383*n*, 384*n*

Minto, Lord, 48, 53, 56–57, 62, 363*n*,
    364*n*, 365*n*, 366*n*, 367*n*, 379*n*

Modena, 11, 83–84, 86

Modern Jesuit, The (Gioberti),
    48–49

Mola di Gaeta, 115, 125, 282, 380*n*,
    382*n*–83*n*, 384*n*, 391*n*, 399*n*, 402*n*,
    405*n*, 409*n*

monarchy, 10–12, 24–25, 34, 57–59, 66, 77–78, 127, 144, 258, 297–98, 342
see also constitutional monarchy
monasteries, 158, 196
monks, xx, 6, 7, 13, 17, 47, 67, 72, 156, 157, 158, 183, 196, 228, 279, 344, 363n
Montanelli, Giuseppe, 46–47, 362n, 363n
Montevideo, 183
monuments, 5, 227, 242–44, 333–34
Mortara, Edgardo, 428n
Moscati, Angelo, 97
motu proprio ("letter in his own hand"), 91–92, 273, 302
Mount Vesuvius, 291
mushrooms, 6
Musinano, prince of, 424n
Muslims, 67–68, 74, 121, 389n
Mussolini, Benito, 345
Muzzarelli, Carlo, 105, 108, 140, 148, 149, 376n

Naples (city), 28, 58, 64, 85, 104, 109, 116, 118, 121, 125, 139, 152, 241
Naples, Kingdom of, xxv–xxvi, 8, 10, 12, 16, 24, 28, 34, 58, 59, 64, 66, 85, 96, 104, 109, 110, 115, 116, 118–22, 125, 127, 130, 131, 135, 139, 142, 144, 150, 152, 154, 155, 167–69, 174, 179, 180, 237, 241, 281, 282, 291, 297, 301, 302, 304, 307, 309, 310, 314, 317, 318, 323, 339, 341, 365n, 381n, 386n
Napoleon I, Emperor of France, xxi, xxiii, xxv, 8, 10–11, 12, 15–16, 44, 46, 90, 112, 129, 130, 136, 186, 223, 225, 257, 288, 301, 344, 372n, 408n
nationalism, xx, xxi, 3, 23, 25–26, 43–44, 59–62, 67, 68–70, 77–78, 79, 81, 83–84, 94, 105, 106, 108, 112, 131, 140, 154, 165–66, 297–98,

339–40, 361n–62n, 368n–70n, 394n
Neapolitan dialect, 200
Neapolitan troops, 178, 179, 180–81, 194, 195, 196, 198–200, 202, 207, 208, 210, 212, 216, 220, 225, 227–28, 237, 317, 390n, 396n
Netherlands, xxii, xxiii, xxiv, 33–34, 59–60, 62, 76, 83, 90, 91, 155, 210, 295, 327, 366n, 372n, 382n, 400n
newspapers, 73, 143–44, 216–17, 289, 306, 321, 329, 368n
New Testament, 311
New Year's Day address, 55, 56–57, 143, 144, 315, 365n
New York Tribune, 52, 85–86
Ney, Edgar, 287–89
Nice, xxi, 245
Niel, Adolphe, 254–55, 265, 284, 291, 301, 398n, 400n, 404n, 408n, 410n, 414n, 417n, 419n
Nightingale, Florence, 41, 51, 360n, 363n, 364n, 366n
night schools, 300–301
Noble Guard (guardia nobile), xxvii, 20, 156, 326, 362n
nuncios, papal, xx, 10, 13–14, 64, 73, 76, 89, 90, 118, 127, 145, 148, 150, 157, 159, 169, 173, 229, 268, 284, 293, 315, 316, 355, 377n, 378n, 382n, 391n, 415n
nuns, 6, 196, 232, 312–13, 344, 403n, 419n
nurses, 312–13

Official Gazette, 73, 368n
Olmütz, 99
On the Moral and Civil Primacy of Italians (Gioberti), 48
ordination, xix, 49
original sin, 134

Orioli, Cardinal Anton, 88–89, 370n,
    371n
orphanages, 159
Ottoman Empire, 74
Oudinot, Charles, xxv, xxvi, 176, 177,
    180, 186–87, 186, 189, 190, 191,
    192, 196–97, 202, 204–6, 207, 209,
    212, 213–14, 219–20, 221, 225–27,
    231, 236, 237, 238, 242, 243, 244,
    245, 249–50, 252, 253, 254, 255,
    258, 261–62, 263, 275, 276–77,
    282, 284–85, 392n, 393n, 394n,
    396n, 397n, 398n, 399n, 400n,
    401n, 402n, 404n, 405n, 407n,
    408n, 409n, 410n, 411n, 412n,
    414n

Palace of the Consulta, 109, 212, 222
Paladini, Leone, 218, 400n, 403n,
    404n, 406n, 407n
Palais National, 235
Palazzo Venezia, 66
Palermo, 4, 57–58, 207, 218
Palma, Monsignor, xxvii, 107,
    376n–77n
Palmerston, Henry John Temple,
    Lord, 260, 285, 361n, 363n, 385n,
    395n
Pamphily, Doria, 110
Panama, 179
Pantheon, 5
Paolina Chapel, 15–18
papal crests, 210
papal nuncio (Lisbon), 127
papal nuncio (Madrid), 89, 148, 173,
    229
papal nuncio (Naples), 118, 379n
papal nuncio (Paris), xx, 128, 150, 159,
    284, 316, 378n
papal nuncio (Vienna), 10, 64, 73, 76,
    90, 145, 169, 268, 293, 316, 335,
    391n, 399n, 402n, 416n

papal nuncios, xx, 10, 13–14, 64, 73,
    76, 89, 90, 118, 127, 128, 145, 148,
    150, 157, 159, 169, 173, 229, 268,
    285, 293, 315, 316, 355, 377n, 378n,
    379n, 380n, 382n, 391n, 399n,
    402n, 415n, 416n
Papal States:
    administration of, xix, 4, 17, 23, 43,
        49–54, 56, 57, 99–100, 119, 151–55,
        183, 228–29, 265–66, 298–99, 301,
        364n, 420n
    agriculture of, 6, 8
    anarchy in, 67, 81, 82, 96, 397n
    anti-Semitism in, 41–42, 74–75,
        97–98, 305–6, 318–19
    aristocracy of, xx–xxi, 4–5, 49, 53–54,
        69, 85, 89, 109–10, 138, 149, 346
    armed forces of, 14–15, 16, 20, 23,
        55–56, 60–61, 72–74, 80–84, 85,
        100–101, 102, 154, 162, 163, 280,
        341
    Austrian ambassadors to, 22–23, 30,
        35–36, 70, 150–51, 301, 392n, 417n;
        see also specific ambassadors
    Austrian invasion of, xxiii, 12, 13, 14,
        16, 32–33, 35–36, 42–45, 90–91,
        92, 93, 111, 150–56, 159–60, 277,
        278, 280, 289, 304, 317, 361n, 413n
    banking in, 162, 299, 315–19, 332–33,
        338, 423n
    Bavarian ambassador to, xxix–xxx,
        101, 114, 115, 116, 117, 118, 130,
        378n
    borders of, 12, 42, 101, 131, 135, 160,
        323–24
    British diplomatic relations with,
        47–48, 51, 63, 67, 111, 113, 114, 131,
        146, 166, 209, 296, 301, 340, 361n,
        363n, 414n–15n
    bureaucracy of, 4, 57, 99–100, 119,
        183, 228–29, 298–99, 301, 364n,
        420n

capital punishment in, 252, 330–31, 337

cardinals as officials in, xxvii, 6, 7–10, 12–13, 14, 51, 85, 100, 111

cardinals commission (red triumvirate) for, 273–74, 282–85, 289, 290, 423*n*

Catholic monarchs as supporters of, 10–12, 21–23, 80–83, 130

censorship in, 14, 52, 156–57, 283, 300–301, 315, 321, 333–34, 359*n*

Chamber of Deputies of, 59, 64, 85, 87–88, 90, 98, 102–3, 105–6, 107, 108, 111–12, 119, 131, 133, 134, 136–40, 151–55, 162, 376*n*

clerical rule in, 6–8, 17, 25, 27, 32–33, 59–60, 62, 71, 75, 78, 85, 126, 139, 156–59, 160, 180, 188, 194, 196, 197, 201, 213, 221, 223, 226, 264, 266–68, 274, 290, 295, 321, 386*n*, 420*n*

commemorative poem for, ix

corruption in, 4, 57, 99–100, 183, 228–29, 301, 364*n*, 420*n*

Dutch ambassador to, 33–34, 59–60, 62, 76, 83, 90, 91, 155, 210, 295, 327, 366*n*, 372*n*, 382*n*, 400*n*

ecclesiastical courts of, 415*n*–16*n*

education in, xx, xxvi, 9–10, 156, 300–301, 319, 333

exiles from, xxi, xxii, 15–16, 21–23, 34, 152, 233, 259–60

finances of, 4–8, 13, 24, 49, 162, 298–99, 315–19, 332–33, 338, 414*n*, 423*n*

foreign ambassadors to, 14, 52, 67, 83, 111, 130–31, 145, 149–50, 154–55, 243–44, 258, 259, 266–68, 326, 369*n*–70*n*; *see also specific ambassadors*

foreign intervention in, 32–33, 34, 35–36, 57, 86, 119, 165–66, 297–98, 394*n*–95*n*

foreign ministers of, 67, 108–9, 131–32

French ambassadors to, xxvi, xxviii, xxx, 22, 24, 34, 51, 56, 89, 92, 95, 107, 109, 113, 114, 117, 148, 200–201, 212–13, 228–31, 295–97, 302, 307–8, 315–16, 355*n*, 374*n*, 381*n*, 390*n*; *see also specific ambassadors*

French relations of, xxiii–xxvi, 10, 12, 13–14, 18–20, 22, 26–27, 32–33, 34, 48, 95, 114–15, 117, 127–28, 131, 134, 146–47, 150, 154–55, 159–60, 165–66, 167, 170–75, 177, 208–10, 230–31, 241–42, 254–55, 258–69, 274–77, 280–86, 289–90, 294, 295–98, 302–4, 314, 319–20, 330, 332, 335, 338, 380*n*, 385*n*, 387*n*, 391*n*, 392*n*, 394*n*, 415*n*–16*n*

government of, 12–13, 24, 32–34, 35, 46, 55–57, 64, 74, 79, 91–92, 94, 95–96, 99–100, 103, 105–9, 118–19, 229–31, 342–44, 366*n*, 379*n*, 382*n*, 424*n*

in Italian unification, 25, 43, 46, 60–62, 69, 78, 96–97, 120–21, 339–46

judicial system of, 9–10, 57, 415*n*–16*n*

as medieval institution, 9, 12, 14

mercenary forces in, 37–38

National Guard of, 63, 85, 186, 188, 192–93, 195, 210, 250, 404*n*

Neapolitan ambassadors to, 24–25, 28, 154, 155, 167, 169, 174, 281, 297, 301–2

newspapers in, 31–32, 34–35

official gazette of, 73, 368*n*

political prisoners in, 19–23, 34, 152

Papal States (*cont.*):

political situation in, 17, 23, 48, 51, 52–54, 62–63, 78, 126, 139, 147, 345–46, 380*n*, 411*n*

Pope as ruler of, xxvii–xxviii, 3–4, 32–33, 35, 43, 51–52, 64–65, 77–78, 87–88, 90, 99–100, 108–9, 111–12, 128, 131–32, 138–39, 140, 148–49, 154, 158–59, 160, 165–66, 171–74, 199, 200–201, 209–10, 228–31, 255–56, 263–64, 265, 273, 283, 285–88, 292–94, 295, 297–98, 304–5, 326–27, 339–40, 346–47, 394*n*

poverty in, 4–8, 29–30, 41–42, 74–75, 97–98

prime minister of, 87–88, 90, 91

prisons in, 19–23, 34, 149, 152, 156–57, 195, 275, 283–84, 296, 312–13, 328–29, 333, 337, 343

property ownership in, 53–54, 141, 156–57, 159, 169, 170, 293

provinces and territories of, 8, 33, 77, 91, 152, 160, 174

republican movement in, 12–13, 42, 90, 91, 111, 122, 131, 136–41, 151–55, 212

revolution in (1848), xxii, 9, 16, 42, 82–83, 90, 91, 99–100, 101, 102–5, 130, 202, 210, 212

Rome as capital of, 3–4, 66–67, 70, 158, 166, 167–68, 221, 261, 407*n*

Rothschild loan for, 299, 315–19, 332–33, 338, 423*n*

Sardinian ambassador to, 127, 381*n*–82*n*, 383*n*, 405*n*

social order of, 8–9, 13–14

sovereignty of, 51–52, 77–78, 80–81, 86, 90, 99–100, 111–12, 115–16, 122, 131, 138–39, 140, 296–97, 333, 339–40, 346–47

taxation in, 7, 99, 283, 293, 295

theocratic rule of, xx, xxvi, 9–10, 12, 34, 64–65, 112, 145, 170, 262, 295, 302–4, 310, 311–12

treasury of, 13, 162, 298–99

U.S. diplomatic relations with, 93, 149, 152, 187, 193, 213–14, 217–18, 236–37, 243, 250, 260, 331–32, 334–35, 342–43, 363*n*, 409*n*

Pareto, Lorenzo, 360*n*

Paris, xx, 13, 63, 89, 110, 127, 150, 159, 233–34, 284, 315–16, 378*n*

Parma, 11, 341

Pasolini, Giuseppe, 62–63, 383*n*

Passover, 75

passports, 260, 409*n*

paternalistic despotism, 86

Paul, Saint, 245, 246, 326

peasants, xix, 8

pensions, 283

Perugia, 16, 225

Peter, Saint, 10, 47, 245, 246, 326

Piazza del Popolo, 33, 39, 44–45, 60, 66–67, 106, 142, 210, 252–53, 274, 320

Piazza Navona, 6

Piazza Santi Apostoli, 188

Piedmont, 141, 188, 368*n*, 371*n*

Pirri, Pietro, 50, 358*n*, 363*n*, 380*n*, 428*n*

Pisa, 46, 233

Pius VI, Pope, 15, 113–14, 257

Pius VII, Pope, 15–16, 18, 113, 136, 257, 301

Pius IX, Pope:

absolutism supported by, 170, 229–31, 333, 394*n*

allocutions of, 77–84, 85, 103, 173, 369*n*–70*n*, 371*n*, 372*n*, 391*n*

amnesties granted by, 19–25, 27, 43, 416*n*, 418*n*, 419*n*, 422*n*

as archbishop of Spoleto and bishop of Imola, xx, 16–17, 18, 19, 20, 330 assassination plots against, 309, 425n–26n

audiences granted by, 30–31, 47, 92, 141

Austrian support for, xix, xxii–xxiii, xxvi, 10–12, 20, 22–23, 24, 30, 35–38, 109, 145–46, 147, 150–51, 154, 155, 159–60, 167, 171–73, 174, 265, 267–68, 281, 283, 284, 286, 290, 297, 374n, 386n, 420n

background of, xx, 15–16, 57, 70, 360n

beatification of, 345

benedictions and blessings given by, xxix, 27–28, 30, 46, 51, 52–56, 57, 60–62, 68–69, 100, 121, 208–9, 217, 323, 325, 359n, 369n

biographies of, 78, 380n

birthday of, 40

birth of (May 13, 1792), xx, 15

British relations with, 47–48, 51, 63, 111, 113, 114, 131, 146, 166, 209, 296, 301, 340, 361n, 363n, 414n–15n

bust of, 152

cabinet of, 59, 90, 96, 215

as cardinal, xx, 3–20, 357n, 420n

cardinal advisers of, xx, 21–25, 30, 31, 32, 37–38, 47, 51–52, 63, 64, 74, 75–76, 85, 88–89, 101, 108–9, 125, 130–31, 134, 138–39, 145, 150–51, 155, 173–74, 185–86, 241, 255, 261, 264, 266–68, 273, 283–86, 288, 294, 295, 309–14, 322–23, 326, 373n–74n, 385n–86n, 402n, 411n, 415n, 424n, 426n

carriages and coaches used by, xxix–xxx, 27–28, 46, 52–53, 56, 114–15

cast of characters for reign of, xix–xxx

Catholic monarchs as supporters of, xxii, xxiv, 74, 77–78, 83–84, 110, 117, 119–20, 122, 127–28, 132, 136, 139–40, 144–46, 150, 154–55, 165–66, 170–75, 178–79, 195–96, 201–2, 214–15, 228, 293–94, 304–5, 385n, 387n, 391n, 392n

charitable acts of, 31, 39–40

coffee enjoyed by, 30, 31

conclave for, 3–20, 23, 69, 357n

constitutional rule as viewed by, xxvii–xxviii, 34, 62, 64–65, 66, 85, 106, 112, 113, 149, 201, 228, 229–30, 241, 255, 257, 261, 265–66, 281–83, 295, 296–97, 366n

Consultative Council of, 33–34, 49, 51–54, 74–77, 79, 86, 174, 228, 292, 364n, 369n

coronation ceremonies for, 20

correspondence of, 27, 81–82, 118, 135, 254–55

daily routine of, 30–31, 117, 135–36, 141, 301

death of (February 7, 1878), 69, 344–45

decrees and proclamations of, 35, 55, 65, 132, 175–76, 368n

depressions of, 36, 141, 329, 373n

disguise worn by, xxvii–xxx, 114–15, 117, 325–26, 386n

divine right of, 8–12, 23, 33, 71, 112, 113–14, 118, 298, 346

edicts issued by, 35, 65, 368n

election of (1846), xxvii, 3–20, 21, 23, 40, 44, 45, 54, 134, 357n

encyclicals of, 28–29, 134, 298, 311–13, 339, 340, 343–44

entourage of, 30, 185, 228–29, 231, 284, 363n, 374n, 411n

epilepsy of, xx, 15, 16, 36, 106

escape of, xxvii–xxx, 114–15, 117, 122, 132, 139, 140, 152, 262, 325–26, 344, 355n, 386n

Pius IX, Pope (*cont.*):

excommunication by, 143, 144, 162, 210, 339, 343–44, 384n–85n

excursions and processions of, 30–31, 46, 52–53, 231, 326–27, 362n–63n, 365n

exile of, xx, xxv–xxx, 54, 69, 109, 128, 169–73, 177, 257, 290–302, 304, 307, 309–10, 314–15, 318, 322–24, 335, 424n

fifty-eighth birthday of, 329

French exile proposed for, 113, 170–73, 177, 380n

French support for, xxiii–xxvi, 10, 12, 13–14, 18–20, 22, 26–27, 32–33, 34, 48, 95, 114–15, 117, 127–28, 131, 134, 146–47, 150, 154–55, 159–60, 165–66, 167, 170–75, 177, 208–10, 230–31, 241–42, 254–55, 258–69, 274–77, 280–86, 289–90, 294, 295–98, 302–4, 314, 319–20, 330, 332, 335, 338, 380n, 385n, 387n, 391n, 392n, 394n, 415n–16n

funeral of, 344–45

Gaeta residence of, 115–19, 116, 121, 122, 125–28, 130–32, 135, 136, 138, 145–50, 152, 154, 155, 157, 165–68, 170, 171, 174, 175, 177, 186, 202, 204, 208, 211, 214–17, 217, 218, 228–30, 241, 242, 254–56, 262, 265, 267, 273, 275, 276, 280, 282, 283, 288, 289, 291, 328, 339, 342, 345, 378n, 379n, 380n, 381n, 382n, 386n, 388n–89n, 405n, 407n

governments appointed by, xxvi, 26–27, 33–34, 49, 51–54, 74–77, 79, 86, 174, 228, 292

hymn composed for, 69

infallibility doctrine of, 341–42

Italian background of, 57, 70

Italian nationalism as viewed by, xx, xxi, 3, 23, 25–26, 43–44, 59–62, 67, 68–70, 77–78, 79, 81, 83–84, 94, 105, 106, 108, 112, 131, 140, 154, 165–66, 297–98, 339–40, 361n–62n, 368n–70n, 394n

keys of Rome given to, 254, 255, 260, 265

lay ministers of, 33–34, 49, 51–54, 59, 74–77, 79, 80–81, 86, 87–88, 90, 101, 104, 108–9, 119, 131–32, 133, 174, 228, 262–63, 274, 283–84, 291, 292, 366n

liberal support for, 29, 37–38, 46, 53–54, 59, 74–77, 85, 99–100, 105, 112, 131, 133, 138, 139–40, 142, 175, 185–86, 231–32, 243, 262–67, 275–76, 277, 280–82, 288, 293–98, 331, 340, 420n

lifestyle of, 30–31, 125–26

manifesto issued by, 175–76

meals taken by, 30–31

modernization and reform supported by, xx, xxi, xxiii, xxiv, xxvi, xxvii–xxviii, 12, 19–20, 23, 24–29, 32–34, 47–48, 63, 70, 73, 75, 89, 90, 93, 130–31, 147, 173–74, 175, 185, 200–202, 210–11, 215, 255, 265–66, 275–76, 280–81, 292–94, 295, 296–98, 328, 411n, 416n–17n

motu proprio ("letter in his own hand") of, 91–92, 273, 302, 418n

name taken by, 17–18

Neapolitan support for, 24–25, 154, 155, 167, 169, 174, 281, 297, 301–2

New Year's Day address of, 55, 56–57, 143, 144, 315, 365n

ordination of, xx, 15

personal belongings of, 117, 135, 141

personality of, xx, xxviii, 31, 36, 47, 50–54, 62–63, 70, 73, 77–79, 83–84, 90–91, 93, 99, 126, 138, 141,

147, 151, 169–70, 201, 254–55,
268–69, 281–82, 293–94, 295, 302,
329, 331, 357n, 373n, 419n
personal name of (Giovanni Maria
Mastai Ferretti), xx, 3, 30, 70, 143,
357n
physical appearance of, 18
political sense of, 17, 48, 51, 52–54,
62–63, 78, 126, 147, 345–46, 380n,
411n
as pope-king, 3–4, 8–9, 71, 77, 86,
111, 114, 147, 155, 255–56, 297–98,
346–47
popular support for, xxvii–xxviii, 3,
19–23, 27–30, 34, 39–40, 52–53,
55, 59–63, 65, 68, 79–80, 83, 112,
118–19, 131, 142–43, 157, 173–74,
241, 301, 304–5
Portici residence of, 290–302, 304,
307, 309–10, 314–15, 317, 318, 321,
322–24, 327–28, 424n
portraits of, iv, 19, 44, 61
post-return proclamation of, 265,
292–94
post-surrender proclamation of,
263–64, 273
press coverage of, 10, 31–32, 53, 84,
85–86, 88, 121–22, 139, 264, 267,
296, 323–24, 326, 344, 388n,
412n–15n, 417n, 422n–23n, 425n
as "prisoner of the Vatican," 319–20,
344–45
Quanta cura encyclical (1864) of,
340, 428n
Qui pluribus encyclical (1846) of,
28–29, 298, 358n, 418n
reactionary policies of, xix, xx,
28–29, 62–63, 77–79, 84, 109, 125,
130–32, 138–39, 142, 157, 185–86,
200–202, 210–11, 228–30, 241–42,
255–56, 258–59, 263–67, 273,
275–76, 281–82, 292–97, 302–4,

309–13, 331–35, 340, 341–42,
414n–17n
relics of, 344
republican ideals as viewed by,
43–44, 77–78, 131, 140
reputation of, 15, 17–18, 52–54
resentment felt by, 62–63, 138, 141,
142, 157, 266–67, 296–97, 341–42
return and restoration of (1849), xix,
xxv, 127, 133, 135, 138–39, 141,
142–47, 155, 168, 175, 178–79, 185,
194, 209–10, 214–15, 239, 257,
258–59, 263, 265, 277, 286, 290–91,
296–97, 301, 304–5, 309–11,
314–15, 316, 318, 319–20, 322–35,
416n, 423n, 425n–26n
revolt against, 79–80, 91–92, 100,
111–12, 131, 136, 143–44, 156–57,
169–70, 176, 178–79, 185–86,
192–96, 209–10, 241–42, 255, 259,
262, 267, 273, 296–97, 301, 304–5,
335
Rossi's assassination and, 102–5,
104, 110, 111, 131, 152, 162, 260,
274, 276–77, 292, 294, 337,
375n–76n
secretary of states appointed by, xix,
23–24, 25, 31, 32, 37–39, 48, 58, 64,
88–89, 91, 95–96, 99–100, 106,
109, 111, 126, 150–51, 216–17, 268,
293–94, 299, 304, 345–46, 360n,
364n, 371n, 379n, 411n, 418n, 426n
seminary education of, xx, 71
sense of humor of, xxviii, 16, 47
servants of, xxix
sovereignty of, 51–52, 77–78, 80–81,
86, 90, 99–100, 111–12, 115–16,
122, 131, 138–39, 140, 296–97, 333,
339–40, 346–47
Spanish support for, 10, 12, 110, 113,
115, 117–18, 145–46, 154, 167, 174,
281, 388n

Pius IX, Pope (*cont.*):
  spiritual authority of, 3–4, 71, 77, 92,
    126, 131–32, 148–49, 154, 160,
    165–66, 230–31, 252, 255–56,
    326–27, 341–42, 345
  steamship travel of, 291
  temporal authority of, xxvii–xxviii,
    3–4, 32–33, 35, 43, 51–52, 64–65,
    77–78, 87–88, 90, 99–100, 108–9,
    111–12, 128, 131–32, 138–39, 140,
    148–49, 154, 158–59, 160, 165–66,
    171–74, 199, 200–201, 209–10,
    228–31, 255–56, 263–64, 265, 273,
    283, 285–88, 292–94, 295, 297–98,
    304–5, 326–27, 339–40, 346–47,
    394n
  theological doctrines of, 28–29, 134,
    144, 170, 277, 283, 295, 298,
    311–12, 340, 341–42
  U.S. relations with, 92–93, 144,
    160–61, 363n
  vacillation of, 77–79, 83–84, 90–91,
    126, 138, 201, 268–69, 281–82,
    293–94, 295, 302
  Vatican Council (1864) convened by,
    341–42, 345
  in Velletri, 324–25
Pius XI, Pope, 345
Place de la Bastille, 89
police, 7, 9, 55–56, 80, 93, 96, 102, 158,
    267, 274, 275, 283–84, 289, 296,
    300–302, 305–6, 309, 315, 320–21,
    325, 342, 345, 407n, 420n–21n,
    424n, 425n, 427n
political prisoners, 19–23, 34, 152
Polk, James K., 92–93
pope (papacy):
  absolutist rule of, 170, 229–31, 333,
    394n
  armed guard of, 55–56, 125–26, 142,
    147, 186, 187–88
  attendants of, 27

  in Avignon, 113, 380n
  as bishop of Rome, 27, 92
  cardinal advisers to, xx, 21–25, 30,
    31, 32, 37–38, 47, 51–52, 63, 64, 74,
    75–76, 85, 88–89, 101, 108–9, 125,
    130–31, 134, 138–39, 145, 150–51,
    155, 173–74, 185–86, 241, 255, 261,
    264, 266–68, 273, 283–86, 288,
    294, 295, 309–14, 322–23, 326,
    373n–74n, 385n–86n, 402n, 411n,
    415n, 424n, 426n
  chaplains for, 184, 279
  coat of arms of, 73, 143, 315
  conclaves for, 3–20, 23, 69, 357n
  coronation of, 20
  divine right of, 14, 28, 36, 64–65,
    110, 132, 311–12, 333, 335
  elections of, 13–18
  encyclicals issued by, 28–29, 134,
    298, 311–13, 339, 340, 343–44
  flag (banner) of, 60, 79, 180, 200,
    205, 210, 228, 238, 242, 257, 261,
    339, 368n, 370n, 409n
  as head of Catholic Church, 28–29,
    34, 35, 65, 84, 77–78, 80, 92, 110,
    112, 117, 126, 127–28, 132, 144, 157,
    159, 165–66, 169–70, 231, 234,
    236–37, 261, 263–64, 269, 293–94,
    299, 304–5, 311–12, 362n, 402n,
    417n
  infallibility of, 341–42
  as king, 3–4, 8–9, 71, 77, 86, 111, 114,
    147, 155, 255–56, 297–98, 346–47
  kissing foot of, 51
  legates of, 23, 267–68
  legionnaires of, 102–5, 106, 108,
    109
  nuncios of, xx, 10, 13–14, 64, 73, 76,
    89, 90, 118, 127, 145, 148, 150, 157,
    159, 169, 173, 229, 268, 284, 293,
    315, 316, 355, 377n, 378n, 382n,
    391n, 415n

palaces of, 135, 156–57, 159; *see also* Quirinal Palace

press coverage of, 10, 31–32, 53, 84, 85–86, 88, 121–22, 139, 264, 267, 296, 323–24, 326, 344, 388*n*, 412*n*–15*n*, 417*n*, 422*n*–23*n*, 425*n*

as "prisoner of the Vatican," 319–20, 344–45

ring of, 31

as ruler of Papal States, xxvii–xxviii, 3–4, 32–33, 35, 43, 51–52, 64–65, 77–78, 87–88, 90, 99–100, 108–9, 111–12, 128, 131–32, 138–39, 140, 148–49, 154, 158–59, 160, 165–66, 171–74, 199, 200–201, 209–10, 228–31, 255–56, 263–64, 265, 273, 283, 285–88, 292–94, 295, 297–98, 304–5, 326–27, 339–40, 346–47, 394*n*

as Supreme Pontiff, 9, 36, 78, 80–81, 97, 115–16, 126, 144, 154, 165–66, 340, 384*n*, 386*n*

Swiss Guards of, xxvii, 14–15, 20, 27, 107, 108, 359*n*, 362*n*, 377*n*

vestments of, 143

as Vicar of Christ, 36, 43, 56, 65, 107, 110, 112, 115–16, 170, 384*n*

popolani ("little people"), xxi, 39–41, 89, 198–99, 251–52, 257–58, 306, 321

Popular Club, 52, 103–4, 106, 133, 136–37, 187, 260

popular vote (suffrage), 66, 84–85, 140–41, 157, 181, 252, 386*n*

Po River, 42, 155–56

Porta Angelica, 192

Porta Cavalleggieri, 190, 191–92

Porta Pertusa, 191

Porta Pia, 343

Porta San Pancrazio, 190, 192, 194, 218, 227, 238, 405*n*–6*n*

Porta San Paolo, 80

Portici, 291, 292, 297, 304, 315, 317, 321, 323, 327–28

Portugal, 10, 127, 380*n*

poverty, 4–8, 29–30, 41–42, 74–75, 97–98

prelates, xix, 7, 49, 51, 76, 82, 89, 152, 229, 266–67, 342, 366*n*, 420*n*

press, freedom of the, 23, 63, 65, 186, 230, 340, 341, 347

press coverage, 10, 31–32, 53, 84, 85–86, 88, 121–22, 139, 264, 267, 296, 323–24, 326, 344, 388*n*, 412*n*–15*n*, 417*n*, 422*n*–23*n*, 425*n*

Presse, 412*n*–13*n*

priests, xx, 15, 49, 148–49, 158–59, 169–70, 259, 261, 284, 291, 296, 312–13, 321, 344, 404*n*

printing presses, 31–32, 43

"prisoner of the Vatican," 319–20, 344–45

prisoners of war, 200

prisons, 19–23, 34, 149, 152, 156–57, 195, 275, 283–84, 296, 312–13, 328–29, 333, 337, 343

private property, 53–54, 141, 156–57, 159, 169, 170, 293

"Proclamation of the People," 59–60

proclamations, 57–60, 75, 81, 91, 106, 118–19, 140–41, 143–44, 154–55, 188–89, 191, 194, 248–49, 263–64, 271, 288–89, 291–92, 320–21, 325, 328, 401*n*, 416*n*

prostitutes, xxi, 149, 196, 312–13, 422*n*–23*n*

Protestants, 93, 94, 120, 126, 299, 301, 363*n*, 399*n*, 400*n*

Prussia, 10, 342

public charities, 31, 39–40, 159

Quanta cura encyclical (1864), 340, 428*n*

quarantines, 309–10

Qui pluribus encyclical (1846), 28–29,
    298, 358*n*, 418*n*
Quirinal Palace, xxvii–xxx, 14, 15, 18,
    19, 27, 33, 40, 46, 51, 55–56, 60–62,
    65, 81, 91–92, 102, 106–11, 114,
    117, 142, 149, 156, 159, 273, 275,
    325–26, 344, 357*n*, 363*n*
Quirinal Square, xxviii, 60–62, 65,
    106–8, 142

Radetzky, Joseph, 66, 72, 163, 179,
    243, 396*n*
railroads, 4, 10, 20, 27, 119
Ravenna, 278
Rayneval, Alphonse de, xxv–xxvi,
    121, 130, 168, 172–73, 185–86, 187,
    200–201, 204–5, 210–11, 212,
    216–17, 221, 228, 231, 255, 258, 259,
    265–67, 268, 280–81, 282–83, 284,
    286, 287, 288–90, 291, 292,
    295–96, 297, 298, 302, 304, 307–8,
    309, 314, 316, 318, 322, 323, 330,
    334, 379*n*, 381*n*, 382*n*, 383*n*, 388*n*,
    389*n*, 391*n*, 393*n*, 394*n*, 396*n*,
    397*n*, 398*n*, 399*n*, 402*n*, 405*n*,
    407*n*–8*n*, 410*n*, 411*n*, 412*n*, 413*n*,
    414*n*, 415*n*–17*n*, 418*n*, 419*n*, 420*n*,
    421*n*, 423*n*, 424*n*, 425*n*, 426*n*,
    427*n*
red triumvirate (cardinals
    commission), 273–74, 282–85,
    289, 290, 423*n*
refugees, xxi, xxii, 89, 218, 233,
    259–60, 277–80, 291, 293, 409*n*,
    425*n*
Reichsadler (Austrian imperial crest),
    66–67, 73
relics, 344
religion, freedom of, 3–4, 33, 340,
    341, 346–47
republicanism, xxiii, 136–41, 152–54,
    156, 158–70, 178–80, 214–16,

    219–20, 223, 230–31, 234, 235–39,
    245, 247–52, 260, 265–67, 274, 275,
    291, 293, 332, 334, 338, 366*n*, 387*n*,
    392*n*, 395*n*, 400*n*, 401*n*, 407*n*,
    411*n*, 419*n*, 423*n*
Restoration (1814), 71
revolutions of 1848, xxi, xxii, xxiv,
    xxvi, 3–4, 9, 16, 42, 55, 63–66,
    82–83, 90, 91, 99–100, 101, 102–5,
    126, 130, 202, 210, 212, 223, 246,
    275, 302, 344
Rhineland, xxiii, 66
Rieti, 375*n*
Rignano, duke of, 104–5
rioni (neighborhoods), 39, 152
Ripari, Pietro, 275, 412*n*
Risorgimento, 43
"Roba vecchia?" (street cry), 41
Roman Club, 52, 69
Roman Curia, 17, 109, 255, 319
romanesco (Roman dialect), 39, 199*n*
Roman Republic (ancient), 194*n*
Romans, Epistle to the, 311
Rome:
    amnesty in, 267, 288, 292, 293–94,
        295
    anti-clerical sentiment in, 70–71,
        143, 148–49, 156–59, 196, 221, 226,
        255, 259, 261, 274, 284, 296,
        300–302, 321, 328, 344–45
    anti-French sentiment in, 259,
        264–65, 274, 302–4
    anti-papal sentiment in, 273–74, 275,
        277, 289, 301–2, 309–13, 315,
        319–28, 334–35, 344–45
    aqueducts of, 236
    aristocratic families of, 60, 110, 192,
        233, 252, 310, 321
    armed resistance in, 156, 162,
        163–90, 248–50, 253–54
    arrests and imprisonment in, 275,
        279–80, *279*, 283–84, 286, 309–10,

312–13, 314, 320, 328–31, 333, 337–38, 340, 413*n*, 426*n*

Austrian forces as threat to, 159–60, 163, 164–65, 166, 168, 170, 171–73, 175, 177, 178, 179, 180–81, 194, 196, 198, 201, 203–4, 208, 210, 213, 214–16, 219, 226, 228, 229, 234, 237, 238, 242, 243, 249, 257, 259, 261, 267, 274, 303, 317, 387*n*

barricades in, 210, 227, 237, 239–40, 247–48, 291

board of censors in, 300–301

business activities in, 41, 42, 63, 291

cannons used against, 141, 190–92, 200, 202, 227, 232–33, *232*, 236–38, *239*, 242–48, 274, 326, 403*n*

as capital of Papal States, 3–4, 66–67, 70, 158, 166, 167–68, 221, 261, 407*n*

cardinal vicar's tribunal in, 274, 276, 300–301, 326, 333

Carnival celebrations in, 98, 149, 320–21

cast of characters for, xix–xxx

casualties in, 218–19, 232–33, 246, 296, 312–13

cease-fire for, 209

children in, 232–33, 243

cholera epidemic in, 243, 309, 409*n*–10*n*, 420*n*

churches of, 6, 66, 87, 141, 143, 148, 156, 191, 205, 210, 326; *see also specific churches*

church property in, 141, 156–57, 158, 159, 169, 170, 173

city council of, 45–46, 56, 135, 250, 261, 262–63, 266, 267–79, 273, 283–84, 289, 295, 315, 322–23, 329, 414*n*

Civil Guard of, xxvii, xxviii, xxix, 16, 38, 44, 55–56, 60–61, 65, 80, 91–92, 97–98, 102, 104–6, 108, 109, 111, 114, 142, 152, 154, 359*n*, 360*n*, 368*n*

clerical rule in, 6–8, 17, 25, 27, 32–33, 59–60, 62, 71, 75, 78, 85, 126, 139, 156–59, 160, 180, 188, 194, 196, 197, 201, 213, 221, 223, 226, 264, 266–68, 274, 290, 295, 321, 386*n*, 420*n*

clubs in, 52, 69, 79, 81, 89, 92, 103–4, 106, 133, 136–37, 139, 186, 187, 253, 260

Constituent Assembly of, xxi, xxii, 106, 119, 139, 140, 142, 143, 147, 148, 151–55, 156, 159, 162–63, 169, 170, 180–81, 184, 188, 189, 196, 214, 223, 225, 226, 232, 234, 237, 241, 244, 247–50, 252, 253, 254, 277, 284, 291, 293, 300, 306, 384*n*–85*n*, 387*n*–88*n*, 390*n*, 397*n*, 401*n*, 407*n*, 415*n*, 421*n*

constitution of, 252, 295, 303, 323, 388*n*, 399*n*–400*n*

contraband in, 291

curfew imposed in, 257–58

currency of, 274

death penalty in, 252, 330–31, 337–38, 340, 426*n*

demonstrations in, 21–23, 25, 27–28, 30, 32, 34–35, 37–38, 40, 55, 59–63, 65, 66–67, 70–71, 79–81, 87, 98, 106–7, 136–37, 143, 173–74, 210, 237–39, 242, 252–53, 322–23, 344–45, 409*n*

dialect of (*romanesco*), 39, 199*n*

economic conditions in, 41, 42, 63, 142, 283, 291

elections in, 157, 158, 161–62, 195, 214

Rome (*cont.*):

as Eternal City, 4, 6, 16, 87, 122, 126,
    131, 138, 181, 193, 209, 221, 243,
    265, 333, 339, 340, 344
exiles from, xxi, xxii, 152, 233,
    259–60
flooding of, 29–30, 39–40, 41, 58, 74
foreign intervention in, 138, 159–60,
    213–15, 218–19, 227–28
foreign residents of, 5–6, 51, 178,
    187, 195, 259–60, 369n
fortifications of, 120, 156, 190,
    196–97, 205–6, 214–15, 218, 220,
    227, 228, 232–33 232, 234, 235–36,
    238, 239, 243–44, 246, 341–42
four-power conference on, 167–68,
    173–75, 208, 210, 282–83, 391n
French attack against, 189, 190–243,
    397n, 400n, 403n, 405n–6n, 408n,
    409n
French conquest and subjugation of,
    190–97, 205–6, 235–55, 256
French military headquarters in, 255,
    264–65, 274–75, 288, 291
French military intervention against,
    xxiii, xxvi, 155, 164, 166, 168,
    169–72, 175–239, 232, 239, 254,
    290, 295, 307
French occupation of, xxv, xxvi,
    174–77, 213, 249, 252, 254, 257,
    274–77, 284, 302–4, 305, 309–10,
    314, 317–18, 324, 325, 327, 328, 335,
    338, 340, 341, 342, 420n
gates of, 190, 195, 207, 209–10, 233,
    236, 254, 255, 260, 265, 325–26
governing commission for, xix, 133,
    156, 382n
hospitals of, 159, 246, 296,
    312–13
interim (provisional) government
    for, 148–49, 156, 158, 180–81,
    195–98, 205, 207, 209, 243

Jewish ghetto of, 29–30, 41–42,
    74–75, 97–98, 265, 299, 301,
    305–6, 315–19, 332–33, 338, 369n,
    374n, 407n, 420n–21n, 427n
keys to, 254, 255, 260, 265
leadership of, xxi, xxiii–xxiv, 39–41,
    160–67
leaflets distributed in, 143–44
local government for, 261, 262–63,
    267, 273–74
malaria in, 93, 200, 214, 265, 330,
    398n
map (1849) of, *xvi–xvii*
markets of, 6, 41
middle class of, 89
monuments and ruins of, 5, 227,
    242–44, 333–34
Neapolitan troops as threat to, 178,
    179, 180–81, 194, 195, 196,
    198–200, 202, 207, 208, 210, 212,
    216, 220, 225, 227–28, 237, 317,
    390n, 396n
negotiated settlement for, 228–30
newspapers of, 73, 143–44, 216–17,
    289, 306, 321, 329, 368n
police of, 7, 9, 55–56, 80, 93, 96, 102,
    158, 267, 274, 275, 283–84, 289,
    296, 300–302, 305–6, 309, 315,
    320–21, 325, 342, 345, 407n,
    420n–21n, 424n, 425n, 427n
pope as bishop of, 27, 92
popolani ("little people") of, xxi,
    39–41, 89, 198–99, 251–52, 257–58,
    306, 321
prices in, 63
prisons in, 195, 275, 283–84, 296,
    312–13, 328–29, 333, 337, 343
proclamations in, 57–60, 75, 81, 91,
    106, 118–19, 140–41, 143–44,
    154–55, 188–89, 191, 194, 248–49,
    263–64, 271, 288–89, 291–92,
    320–21, 325, 328, 401n, 416n

refugees from, xxi, xxii, 233, 259–60, 277–80, 291, 293, 409*n*, 425*n*

republican government of, xxiii, 136–41, 152–54, 156, 158–70, 178–80, 214–16, 219–20, 223, 230–31, 234, 235–39, 245, 247–52, 260, 265–67, 274, 275, 291, 293, 332, 334, 338, 387*n*, 392*n*, 395*n*, 400*n*, 401*n*, 407*n*, 411*n*, 419*n*, 423*n*

republican military defense of, 178–88, 207, 210, 214–20, 225–40, 247–49, 254–55, 404*n*

revolt in (1848), xxiii–xxiv, 23, 90–93, 131, 135, 142–57, 160–67, 195–96, 207, 209–10, 250, 319–21, 328, 387*n*, 390*n*, 415*n*, 426*n*

rioni (neighborhoods) of, 39, 152

schools and universities of, 156, 300–301, 319, 333

Spanish forces as threat to, 168–69, 200, 202, 213, 216, *217*, 220, 228, 237, 259, 317, 422*n*

surrender of, 205, 235–47, 248–55, 257

theaters of, 291

Trastevere neighborhood of, 5, 42, 232–33, 247–48, 262, 320

triumvirate of, xxii, 163–67, *165*, 178, 179, 180, 184–85, 191, 195, 198, 200, 207–8, 210, 216–17, 219, 220, 247, 401*n*, 414*n*–15*n*

veterans of, 253–54, 259–60

violence in, 106–7, 131–32, 156, 158, 162, 163–76, 248–50, 253–54

walls of, 90, 156, 158, 180, 188–89, 248–49, 253, 263, 273, 293, 320, 325

weather conditions in, 29–30, 39–40, 41, 58, 65, 74, 149, 207, 257–58

women in, 193–94, 217–18, 237, 243, 262, 312–13, 325, 403*n*, 419*n*, 422*n*–23*n*, 425*n*–26*n*

Roncalli, Nicola, 243, 262, 356*n*, 358*n*, 359*n*, 360*n*, 361*n*, 364*n*, 373*n*, 375*n*, 376*n*, 377*n*, 379*n*, 383*n*, 384*n*, 386*n*, 387*n*, 389*n*, 391*n*, 393*n*, 395*n*, 398*n*, 401*n*, 403*n*, 404*n*, 405*n*, 407*n*, 410*n*, 419*n*, 421*n*, 423*n*, 426*n*

Roothaan, Jan, 70

Roselli, Pietro, 208

Rosmini, Antonio, xx, 94, *95*, 96–97, 108, 132, 138, 148, 150, 229–30, 402*n*

Rossi, Pellegrino, xxi, xxvi, 18–20, 22, 24, *25*, 37, 38, 48, 51, 59, 94–111, *104*, 110, 131, 132, 134, 152, 162, 260, 263, 274, 292–94, 309, 337, 356*n*, 357*n*–58*n*, 363*n*, 364*n*, 365*n*, 366*n*, 368*n*, 371*n*, 373*n*–76*n*, 386*n*, 387*n*, 394*n*, 398*n*, 427*n*

Rostolan, Louis de, xxvi, 257, 282, 287, 288, 289, 291–92, 299, 307, 415*n*–16*n*, 417*n*, 418*n*–21*n*

Rothschild, Charles, 318

Rothschild, James, 315–16, 319

Rothschild, Salomon, 316

Rothschild family, 299, 314, 315–19, 332–33, 338, 423*n*, 424*n*, 427*n*

Rovereto, xx

ruins, 5, 227, 242–44, 333–34

Rusconi, Carlo, 387*n*, 388*n*, 390*n*, 394*n*, 401*n*–2*n*, 403*n*, 404*n*, 406*n*, 407*n*

Russian Empire, xxv, 216

Sacchetti, Giralomo, 135

sacraments, 113, 158, 191

see also specific sacraments

Sacred College of Cardinals, xix, 13, 15, 47, 64, 77, 151, 295, 314, 329, 402n, 416n, 420n

Saffi, Aurelio, 164, *165*, 198–99

St. John Lateran Basilica, 27, 91–92, 251, 326

St. Peter's Basilica, 20, 51, 154, 157, 169–70, 191, 238, 245, 274, 326, 334, 341–42, 343, 369n, 404n, 412n

St. Petersburg, xxv

St. Peter's Square, 187–88, 190, 250–51, 261, 343, 407n

St. Peter's Throne, 36, 77, 138, 292

saints, 121–22

Sts. Marcellino e Pietro Church, 114

Sala, Giuseppe, 426n

salt, 27

San Lorenzo Basilica, 344

San Lorenzo in Lucina Church, 250

San Marino, 278

sans culottes protests, 56

San Silvestro Church, 14–18

San Silvestro Convent, 184–85

Santa Maria in Ara Coeli Basilica, 151–52

Santa Maria in Cosmedin Church, 331

Santa Maria Maggiore Basilica, 362n

Sant'Angelo in Pescheria Church, 427

Sant'Egidio Convent, 232–33, 403n

Santo Spirito Church, 419n

Sardinia, Kingdom of, xxii, 11, 31, 32, 36, 59, 66, 67, 69–70, 72, 74, 84, 87, 92, 94, 96–97, 108, 109, 110, 111, 127, 138, 141, 144, 155, 163, 166, 167, 215, 226, 294, 297, 339, 342, 360n, 361n, 369n–70n, 373n, 375n, 381n–82n, 383n, 385n, 388n–89n, 390n, 405n, 409n

Savelli, Domenico, 55–56, 283–84, 300–301, 414n, 419n

Savoyard Kingdom, xxi, 96, 127, 155, 339, 371n

schools, 156, 300–301, 319, 333

Schwarzenberg, Felix, xxiii, 59, 145–46, *146*, 159–60, 169, 179, 202, 208–9, 215, 242, 268, 332, 385n, 387n, 388n, 389n, 390n, 391n, 392n, 393n, 396n, 397n, 398n, 399n, 402n, 405n, 411n, 412n, 414n, 416n, 417n, 420n, 421n, 422n, 426n

Schwarzenberg, Friedrich, 385n

"secret consistory," 77

secularization, 287–88

sedia gestatoria (papal throne), 20

Senator of Rome, 98

Senigallia, xx, 15

Senior, Nassau William, 334, 415n

"separation of church and state" principle, 3–4, 33, 340, 341, 346–47

Sicily, xxii, 12, 43, 57–58, 66, 71, 77–78, 85, 110, 119, 121, 136, 144, 152, 167, 168, 173, 207, 213, 339, 342

Sistine Chapel, 15, 333–34, 391n

slavery, 75, 312, 340

socialism, 63, 392n

Soglia, Giovanni, 89, 100, 110, 111, 126, 372n, 373n, 377n

South America, xxi, 137, 152, 181, 183

sovereignty, 51–52, 77–78, 80–81, 86, 90, 99–100, 111–12, 115–16, 122, 131, 138–39, 140, 296–97, 333, 339–40, 346–47

Spain, xxiv, xxv, xxx, 12, 110, 113, 118, 145, 150, 154, 155, 167, 168, 169, 174, 200, 229, 237, 281, 283, 317, 387n, 388n

Spanish ambassador, xxx, 110, 113, 115, 116, 168–69, 283, 377n

Spaur, Karl von, 114, 116, 117, 118, 130, 355n, 378n, 379n

speech, freedom of, 65, 252, 340, 341, 347

Spoleto, xx, 16–17, 18, 19, 20, 330

steamships, 128, 179, 291, 377, 424*n*

Sterbini, Pietro, 133, *134*, 140–41, 148, 156, 188, 260, 376*n*

Story, William Wetmore, 5, 187, 369*n*

suffrage (popular vote), 66, 84–85, 140–41, 157, 181, 252, 386*n*

Swiss Guards, xxvi, xxvii, 14–15, 20, 24, 26, 27, 107, 108, 260, 275, 309, 359*n*, 362*n*

Switzerland, xxiv, 26, 95, 260, 275, 309

Syllabus of Errors, 340

taxation, 7, 99, 283, 293, 295

Te Deum, 154

telegrams, 128, 190, 196–97, 206, 220–21

Ténare, 114, 117, 128, 130

theocracy, xx, xxvi, 9–10, 12, 34, 64–65, 112, 145, 153, 171, 230, 262, 277, 283, 295, 303–4, 310, 311–12, 327

theology, 28–29, 82, 134, 144, 156–57, 170, 277, 283, 295, 298, 311–12, 340, 341–42

Tiber River, 5, 29, 30, 42, 143, 188, 200, 205, 228, 232, 242, 245, 305, 326, 328, 331, 344–45

Times (London), 10, 121–22, 139, 203, 264, 267, 275, 326, 328, 380*n*, 388*n*, 400*n*, 408*n*, 414*n*–15*n*, 425*n*

Tocqueville, Alexis de, xxiv, xxv, xxvi, 223–25, *224*, 230–31, 238, 239, 242–43, 244, 254, 255, 257, 258–59, 262, 265, 268–69, 275–76, 277, 280, 282, 283, 285, 288, 294, 296–97, 299, 303, 306–8, 310,

380*n*–81*n*, 385*n*, 401*n*, 402*n*, 403*n*, 404*n*, 405*n*, 406*n*, 407*n*, 408*n*, 409*n*, 410*n*, 411*n*, 412*n*–19*n*, 420*n*, 421*n*

"To Pius IX" (Whittier), ix

Tosti, Antonio, 261

Tosti, Luigi, 141

Toulon, 395*n*, 419*n*

town councils, 293

Trastevere, 5, 42, 232–33, 247–48, 262, 320

Trevi Fountain, 188

tricolor (national) flag, 58, 65, 103, 141, 142, 151, 154, 170, 180, 210, 245, 252, 253, 254, 259

triumvirate, xxii, 163–67, *165*, 178, 179, 180, 181, 184–85, 191, 195, 198, 200, 207–8, 213, 216–17, 219, 220, 247, 248, 397*n*, 401*n*, 414*n*–15*n*

tuberculosis, 329

Turin, 23, 32, 35, 41, 59, 64, 94, 96, 111, 120, 313, 361*n*, 381*n*, 385*n*

Tuscany, Grand Duchy of, 8, 10, 11, 12, 46, 59, 66, 73, 101, 159, 175, 179, 260, 297, 325, 341, 360*n*, 390*n*, 396*n*, 409*n*

typography, 31–32

Umbria, 219

universities, xx, xxvi, 156, 300–301, 319, 333

U.S. chargé d'affaires, 93, 149, 152, 187, 193, 213–14, 217–18, 236–37, 243, 250, 260, 331–32, 334–35, 342–43, 363*n*, 409*n*

Valence, 15, 113

Vannicelli, Luigi, 267–68, 425*n*

vassalage, 98

Vatican City, 345

Vatican Council (1864), 341–42, 345

Vatican Council (1962), 345, 347

Vaucluse, 380n

Vaure, Father, 226, 401n

Velletri, 198–99, 208, 227–28, 265, 324–25, 327, 396n, 425n

Venetian Republic, 65–66, 96–97

Veneto, xxii, 8, 11, 12, 65–66, 67, 82, 86, 87, 91, 99

Venice, 4, 11, 15, 65–66, 83, 91, 96–97, 141, 147, 170, 213, 277, 278, 290, 339, 370n, 371n, 416n

Verdi, Giuseppe, 149

Verona, 66

vestments, 143

vetos, 10, 12, 13

Via Aurelia, 187

Via Condotti, 212

vice gerents, 152, 156

Vicenza, 87

Victor Emmanuel I, King of Sardinia, 385

Victor Emmanuel II, King of Italy, 163, 339, 342, 343, 344

Victoria, Queen of England, 363n

"Victorious Cross, The" (Bassi), 413n

Vienna, xxii, xxiii, 4, 10, 20, 63–64, 66, 73, 76, 82, 84–85, 90, 98–99, 145, 150, 154, 159–60, 165, 166, 169, 175, 202, 204, 241, 268, 293, 316, 317, 332, 335, 365n, 371n, 373n, 385n, 388n, 391n, 396n, 399n, 402n, 403n, 411n, 414n, 416n, 422n, 425n

Villa Corsini, 238

Villa Pamfili, 227

Villa Spada, 246

Virgin Mary (Madonna), 7–8, 134, 221, 238, 377n

visas, 260

"Viva il Papa!," xxviii, 22, 31, 43, 44–45, 46, 47, 58, 64, 65, 75, 80, 83, 85, 179, 262, 366n

"Viva l'Italia!," 43, 44–45, 75, 256, 252, 338, 419n

voting rights (suffrage), 66, 84–85, 140–41, 157, 181, 252, 386n

weather conditions, 29–30, 39–40, 41, 58, 65, 74, 149, 207, 257–58

Whittier, John Greenleaf, ix

Wimpfen, Franz von, 216, 396n

women, 193–94, 217–18, 237, 243, 262, 312–13, 325, 403n, 419n, 422n–23n, 425n–26n

Württemberg, counsel of, 193

Young Italy, xxi, 26

ʒelanti (zealots), 14, 15

Zucchi, Carlo, 100–101, 104–5, 147, 375n, 382n, 385n–86n

ABOUT THE AUTHOR

———

DAVID I. KERTZER, winner of a 2015 Pulitzer Prize for his book *The Pope and Mussolini,* is the Paul Dupee, Jr. University Professor of Social Science at Brown University, where he served as provost from 2006 to 2011. Among his many books are *The Kidnapping of Edgardo Mortara,* a finalist for the National Book Award in Nonfiction, published in seventeen languages, and *The Popes Against the Jews,* a finalist for the Mark Lynton History Prize. Cofounder of the *Journal of Modern Italian Studies,* he has been elected to membership in the American Academy of Arts and Sciences and serves on the board of trustees of the American Academy in Rome. He and his wife, Susan, live in Providence, Rhode Island, and Harpswell, Maine.

davidkertzer.com

Twitter: @davidkertzer

A B O U T   T H E   T Y P E

———

This book was set in Fournier, a typeface named for Pierre-Simon Fournier (1712–68), the youngest son of a French printing family. He started out engraving woodblocks and large capitals, then moved on to fonts of type. In 1736 he began his own foundry and made several important contributions in the field of type design; he is said to have cut 147 alphabets of his own creation. Fournier is probably best remembered as the designer of St. Augustine Ordinaire, a face that served as the model for the Monotype Corporation's Fournier, which was released in 1925.